Frommer's

Washington State

4th Edition

by Karl Samson

Here's what the critics say about Frommer's:

"Amazingly easy to use. Very portable, very complete."
—*Booklist*

"Detailed, accurate, and easy-to-read information for all price ranges."
—*Glamour Magazine*

"Hotel information is close to encyclopedic."
—*Des Moines Sunday Register*

"Frommer's Guides have a way of giving you a real feel for a place."
—*Knight Ridder Newspapers*

WILEY
Wiley Publishing, Inc.

About the Author

Karl Samson lives in Oregon, where he spends his time juggling his obsessions with traveling, gardening, outdoor sports, and wine. Each winter, to dry out his webbed feet, he flees the soggy Northwest to update the *Frommer's Arizona* guide. However, he always looks forward to his return to the land of good espresso. Karl is also the author of *Frommer's Seattle.*

Published by:

Wiley Publishing, Inc.

111 River St.
Hoboken, NJ 07030-5774

ISBN 0-7645-4471-3

Editor: William Fox
Production Editor: Bethany André
Cartographer: Roberta Stockwell
Photo Editor: Richard Fox
Production by Wiley Indianapolis Composition Services

Front cover photo: Rocky Mountain goats in Olympic National Park
Back cover photo: Sea rocks off Second Beach

For information on our other products and services or to obtain technical support, please contact our Customer Care Department within the U.S. at 800/762-2974, outside the U.S. at 317/572-3993 or fax 317/572-4002.

Wiley also publishes its books in a variety of electronic formats. Some content that appears in print may not be available in electronic formats.

Manufactured in the United States of America

5 4 3 2 1

Contents

5   The San Juan Islands, Whidbey Island & the Emerald Coast   147

6   South Puget Sound & West Sound   190

7   The Olympic Peninsula   215

8   Southwest Washington   251

9   The Cascades   271

10 Eastern Washington 326

List of Maps

An Invitation to the Reader

In researching this book, we discovered many wonderful places—hotels, restaurants, shops, and more. We're sure you'll find others. Please tell us about them, so we can share the information with your fellow travelers in upcoming editions. If you were disappointed with a recommendation, we'd love to know that, too. Please write to:

Frommer's Washington State, 4th Edition
Wiley Publishing, Inc. • 111 River St. • Hoboken, NJ 07030-5774

An Additional Note

Please be advised that travel information is subject to change at any time—and this is especially true of prices. We therefore suggest that you write or call ahead for confirmation when making your travel plans. The authors, editors, and publisher cannot be held responsible for the experiences of readers while traveling. Your safety is important to us, however, so we encourage you to stay alert and be aware of your surroundings. Keep a close eye on cameras, purses, and wallets, all favorite targets of thieves and pickpockets.

Frommer's Star Ratings, Icons & Abbreviations

Every hotel, restaurant, and attraction listing in this guide has been ranked for quality, value, service, amenities, and special features using a **star-rating system.** In country, state, and regional guides, we also rate towns and regions to help you narrow down your choices and budget your time accordingly. Hotels and restaurants are rated on a scale of zero (recommended) to three stars (exceptional). Attractions, shopping, nightlife, towns, and regions are rated according to the following scale: zero stars (recommended), one star (highly recommended), two stars (very highly recommended), and three stars (must-see).

In addition to the star-rating system, we also use **seven feature icons** that point you to the great deals, in-the-know advice, and unique experiences that separate travelers from tourists. Throughout the book, look for:

Finds	Special finds—those places only insiders know about
Fun Fact	Fun facts—details that make travelers more informed and their trips more fun
Kids	Best bets for kids, and advice for the whole family
Moments	Special moments—those experiences that memories are made of
Overrated	Places or experiences not worth your time or money
Tips	Insider tips—great ways to save time and money
Value	Great values—where to get the best deals

The following **abbreviations** are used for credit cards:

AE	American Express	DISC	Discover	V	Visa
DC	Diners Club	MC	MasterCard		

Frommers.com

Now that you have the guidebook to a great trip, visit our website at **www.frommers.com** for travel information on more than 3,000 destinations. With features updated regularly, we give you instant access to the most current trip-planning information available. At Frommers.com, you'll also find the best prices on airfares, accommodations, and car rentals—and you can even book travel online through our travel booking partners. At Frommers.com, you'll also find the following:

- Online updates to our most popular guidebooks
- Vacation sweepstakes and contest giveaways
- Newsletter highlighting the hottest travel trends
- Online travel message boards with featured travel discussions

What's New in Washington

The world of travel is always changing. New hotels and museums open. Restaurants and nightclubs close. Establishments move. Washington is no exception, so, in this book, we've tried to keep tabs on what's new and noteworthy throughout the state. The following are some of the highlights.

SEATTLE Orientation If you're flying in to **Sea-Tac International Airport** (www.seatac.org/seatac), expect to encounter construction. The central terminal is in the midst of a major expansion that is expected to be completed sometime in 2005. Concourse A is being completely rebuilt and is scheduled to reopen in mid-2004. So leave lots of time for getting around the airport. Of course, you were already planning on extra time in the airport due to security measures, right? Oh, yes, and if you're looking for a shuttle van or taxi, be sure to head to the third floor of the parking garage. If you're looking for a Metro bus, you'll find them outside the baggage claim area.

Where to Stay The big news on the Seattle hotel scene is the opening of the new **Seattle Marriott Waterfront,** 2100 Alaskan Way (© **800/228-9290** or 206/443-5000; www.marriott. com), a luxury hotel right across the street from where cruise ships bound for Alaska dock.

Dining With the slow economic times, 25 of Seattle's high-end restaurants have been joining together for a month in the spring and again in the fall to offer three-course fixed-price dinners for $25. This "25 for $25"

program has been very popular, but unfortunately is not offered during the busy summer months. However, if you happen to be in town during the spring or fall, check local papers for advertisements for this program.

In the International District, don't miss the atmospheric **Panama Hotel Tea & Coffee House,** 607 S. Main St. (© **206/515-4000**), which is filled with historic photos and offers a fascinating glimpse into the neighborhood's past.

Seeing the Sights The Seattle Aquarium, Pier 59, 1483 Alaskan Way (© **206/386-4300;** www.seattle aquarium.org), has added a new exhibit called "Life of a Drifter," which focuses on jellyfish. The pulsing, diaphanous moon jellies are fascinating to watch. There are also new tanks for the aquarium's giant octopus and its hideous wolf eels.

Fans of contemporary art won't want to miss the new James Turrell Skyspace at the **Henry Art Gallery,** University of Washington, 15th Avenue NE and NE 41st Street (© **206/543-2280;** www. henryart.org). The little sky-viewing room is a tranquil and mesmerizing space. At night, colored lights illuminate the glass outer skin of the Skyspace.

The **Seattle Seahawks** (© **888/ NFL-HAWK** or 206/682-2800; www. seahawks.com) football team has now moved into the new Seahawks Stadium adjacent to Safeco Field. The roof of this behemoth doesn't roll back (as the roof of adjacent Safeco Field does), but then, who ever heard of calling off a football game on account of rain?

Nightlife   Opera fans, take note. The **Seattle Opera** (© **800/426-1619** or 206/389-7676; www.seattle opera.org), world renowned for its stagings of Wagner's *The Ring of the Nibelungen,* has a new state-of-the-art home. Seattle Center's new Marion Oliver McCaw Hall opened in the summer of 2003, replacing the aging Seattle Opera House.

Down Pike Place Market's Post Alley, you'll find **The Tasting Room,** 1924 Post Alley (© **206/770-WINE;** www.winesofwashington.com), a cozy wine bar with the feel of a wine cellar. This wine bar is cooperatively operated by several small Washington state wineries.

THE SAN JUAN ISLANDS, WHID-BEY ISLAND & THE EMERALD COAST   Whidbey Island   In Langley, you'll find creative meals and good views at **The Edgecliff,** 510 Cascade Ave. (© **360/221-8899**). In Coupeville, you'll find the best meals in town are at a tiny hole-in-the-wall called **The Oystercatcher,** 901 Grace St. (© **360/678-0683**), which is located a block off the waterfront.

Anacortes   Even if you're just passing through town on the way to or from the San Juan Islands, you may want to leave time in your schedule for a meal at **Adrift,** 510 Commercial Ave. (© **360/588-0653**), a casual new restaurant that serves some of the best food in Anacortes.

The San Juan Islands   Fares on the **Washington State Ferries** (© **800/84-FERRY** or 888/808-7977 in Washington, or 206/464-6400; www. wsdot.wa.gov/ferries) route to the San Juan Islands continue to skyrocket. At press time, it will now cost you (and your car) as much as $40 to travel from the mainland to Friday Harbor on San Juan Island.

For economical meals in Friday Harbor, check out **The Market Chef,** 225 A St. (© **360/378-4546**), a new combination espresso bar and gourmet takeout restaurant that also bakes outrageously good chocolate chip cookies. Although it's hard to find, **Backdoor Kitchen & Catering,** 400b A St. (© **360/378-9540**), another new and inexpensive restaurant, is well worth searching out. It has a patio dining area that is part of a plant nursery.

On Orcas Island, **Rosario Resort & Spa,** 1400 Rosario Rd., Eastsound (© **800/562-8820** or 360/376-2222; www.rosarioresort.com), is planning a major renovation in time for the 2004 summer season. This resort was already the finest full-service resort in the islands, and the renovation should make it even better.

Not far away, **The Inn at Ship Bay,** 326 Olga Rd., Eastsound (© **877/276-7296** or 360/376-5886; www.inn atshipbay.com), has a new chef who formerly worked at Rosario Resort & Spa.

Bellingham   The wonderful little **American Museum of Radio,** 1312 Bay St. (© **360/738-3886;** www. americanradiomuseum.org), continues to expand.

SOUTH PUGET SOUND & WEST SOUND   Tacoma   Move over, Seattle: Tacoma is on its way to becoming the cultural capital of the Puget Sound region. With the recent openings of the new **Museum of Glass,** 1801 Dock St. (© **800/4-MUSEUM** or 253/396-1768; www.museumof glass.org), and the new home of the **Tacoma Art Museum,** 1701 Pacific Ave. (© **253/272-4258;** www.tacoma artmuseum.org), Tacoma has become the best museum town in the state. Within 3 blocks, you can visit both of the above museums as well as the **Washington State History Museum,** 1911 Pacific Ave. (© **888/238-4373** or 253/272-3500; www.wshs.org/ wshm). And right outside this latter museum, you can hop aboard one of Tacoma's new light-rail cars. Although the light-rail line isn't very long (from the Tacoma Dome to the downtown theater district), it's convenient for visitors. Best of all, it's free.

While in town, you might also want to visit the **W.W. Seymour Botanical Conservatory,** Wright Park, 316 South G St. (© **253/591-5330**), which, at press time, was getting ready to reopen after a thorough renovation.

Tacoma also has a new waterfront hotel. The **Silver Cloud Inn Tacoma,** 2317 N. Ruston Way (© **866/820-8448;** www.silvercloud.com), is not just on the waterfront, it's built on a pier over the water.

THE OLYMPIC PENINSULA Sequim   Lavender lovers should be sure to schedule an Olympic Peninsula vacation to coincide with the July flowering of the lavender fields in Sequim. Lavender farms continue to proliferate in the area. For good economical accommodations in the area, check out **BJ's Garden Gate,** 397 Monterra Dr., Port Angeles (© **800/880-1332;** www.bjgarden.com); **Juan de Fuca Cottages,** 182 Marine Dr., Sequim (© **866/683-4433;** www.juandefuca.com), and **Sunset Marine Resort,** 40 Buzzard Ridge Rd., Sequim (© **360/681-4166;** www.sunsetmarineresort.com).

Olympic National Park West   Way out on the western shores of the Olympic Peninsula, in the town of La Push, you'll find some of the best accommodations on the coast at the **La Push Ocean Park Resort,** 330 Ocean Dr. (© **800/487-1267;** www.ocean-park.org). There's also good food at the **River's Edge Restaurant,** 41 Main St., La Push. (© **360/374-5777**). Both of these businesses are on the Quileute Indian Reservation.

SOUTHWEST WASHINGTON The Long Beach Peninsula   To the Long Beach Peninsula's list of great restaurants, add **The Depot Restaurant,** 38th Street and L Place, Seaview (© **360/642-7880**), which is situated in a former railroad depot and serves very creative food.

THE CASCADES Lake Chelan For many years, apples were one of the mainstays of the Lake Chelan economy. However, with apple prices down for several years now, local farmers have been looking for new ways to make money. Several have hit on wine-making as a potential new business, so, if you're in the area, be sure to do some wine tasting at some (or all) of these new wineries: **Chelan Wine Company,** 105 Spader Rd., Chelan (© **866/455-WINE**); **Lake Chelan Winery,** 3519 Wash. 150, Chelan (© **509/687-9463**); **Wapato Point Cellars,** 200 Quetilquasoon Rd., Manson (© **509/687-4000;** www.wapatopointcellars.com); or **Tsillan Cellars,** 3875 U.S. 97A, Chelan (© **877/682-8463** or 509/682-9463; www.tsillancellars.com).

To go along with this newfound wine-country appeal, the town of Chelan also has a new gourmet dining establishment. **Capers,** 127 E. Johnson St. (© **509/682-1611**), serves the best food in town.

The Wenatchee Valley   The Wenatchee Valley apple and pear growers have also been giving winemaking a try. New wineries between Leavenworth and Wenatchee include **Eagle Creek Winery & Cottage,** 10037 Eagle Creek Rd. (© **509/548-7668;** www.eaglecreekwinery.com); **Icicle Ridge Winery,** 8977 North Rd., Peshastin (© **509/548-7851;** www.icicleridgewinery.com); **Wedge Mountain Winery,** 9534 Saunders Rd. (© **509/548-7068;** www.wedgemountainwinery.com); and **La Toscana Winery & Bed & Breakfast,** 9020 Foster Rd., Cashmere (© **509/548-5448;** http://communities.msn.com/latoscana).

The Columbia Gorge When you're ready to get up to your neck in hot water, check out the new **Bonneville Hot Springs Resort,** 1252 E. Cascade Dr., North Bonneville (© **866/459-1678;** www.bonnevilleresort.com), a classically elegant hotel deep in the woods of the Columbia Gorge.

EASTERN WASHINGTON Yakima & the Wine Country Some new and noteworthy wineries in this book include **Chandler Reach,** 9506 W. Chandler Rd., Benton City (© **509/588-8800;** www.chandler reach.com); **Hedges Cellars at Red Mountain,** 53511 N. Sunset Rd., Benton City (© **509/588-3155;** www. hedgescellars.com); **Maison de Padgett Winery,** 2231 Roza Dr., Zillah (© **509/829-6412**); **Paradisos del Sol,** 3230 Highland Dr. (© **509/ 829-9000;** www.paradisosdelsol.com); **Snoqualmie Vineyards,** 660 Frontier Rd., Prosser (© **509/786-2104;** www. snoqualmie.com); **Wineglass Cellars,** 260 N. Bonair Rd., Zillah (© **509/ 829-3011;** www.wineglasscellars.com); and **Windy Point Vineyards,** 420 Windy Point Dr., Wapato (© **509/ 877-4446**).

If you're in the Yakima Valley wine tasting, be sure to have a meal at the new **Barrel House,** 22 N. First St. (© **509/453-3769;** www.barrelhouse. net), which serves lots of local wines by the glass.

Walla Walla The Walla Walla wine country continues to boom at a phenomenal rate, with new wineries opening up monthly. Among the new wineries (or wineries with new tasting rooms) highlighted in this book are **Amavi Cellars,** 635 N. 13th Ave. (© **509/525-3541;** www.amavicellars. com); **Pepper Bridge Winery,** 1704 J.B. George Rd. (© **509/525-6502;** www.pepperbridge.com); and **Rulo Winery,** 2525 Pranger Rd. (© **509/ 525-7856;** www.rulowinery.com).

At lunch or dinner, you can't miss with a meal at the new **Creek Town Cafe,** 1129 S. Second St. (© **509/522-4777**), near downtown Walla Walla.

Spokane The big news in Spokane is the reopening of **The Davenport Hotel,** 10 S. Post St. (© **800/899-1482;** www.thedavenporthotel.com), a luxurious historical hotel that has the most elaborate and palatial lobby of any hotel in the state. Definitely not to be missed.

Just a block or so away from the Davenport is a very atmospheric little basement restaurant called the **Catacombs Pub,** 110 S. Monroe St. (© **509/838-4610**), which has the feel of a German rathskeller.

If you like good wine, and good port in particular, be sure to drive north of Spokane to **Townshend Cellar,** 16112 Greenbluff Rd. (© **509/238-1400;** www.townshendcellar.com), which produces a wide range of ports, including one made from huckleberries.

1

The Best of Washington

Despite what you may have heard to the contrary, there is more to Washington state than lattes, rain, and Microsoft. Washington is actually such a diverse state that it could have served as a model for the song "America the Beautiful." Out in the eastern high desert country, there are beautiful spacious skies as big as Montana's (part of the Rocky Mountains even reaches into Washington). In the Cascades, there are mountains that turn majestically purple at sunset. In the Palouse country of the southeastern corner of the state, amber waves of grain stripe the steep hillsides. In the Yakima, Wenatchee, and Chelan valleys, the fruited plains produce the world's most familiar apples (and some pretty good wine, too). Out on the Pacific Coast, there are beaches white with foam, and with an inland sea across the Olympic Peninsula from the Pacific, the sun in Washington shines from sea to shining sea. From its mountains to its valleys, Washington is indeed beautiful country.

But the diversity of this state goes far beyond mere song lyrics. There's an island archipelago as beautiful as the coast of Maine (though without the harsh winters). There are beaches as long and sandy as those of North Carolina's Outer Banks (though the waters are too cold for swimming). There are granite mountains as rugged as the Sierra Nevada (though not as crowded with hikers). There are desert canyons like those of the Southwest (though not nearly as hot). There are vineyard-covered hillsides like those of the Napa Valley (though without the crowds). There's even a bayfront city with dauntingly steep streets (no cable cars, though).

With such a complex and diverse landscape to be explored, planning a trip can become a daunting task. Where should we go? Where should we stay? Where should we eat? Planning a trip to Washington involves making a lot of these sorts of decisions, and, especially if you only have a week for your entire trip, you probably want to be sure you get the most from your trip. To help you get a better a grip on the state's highlights, its not-to-be-missed attractions and activities, we've put together this list of some of the best the state has to offer. Keep in mind that most are written up in more detail elsewhere in this book, but this chapter will give you an overview and get you started.

1 The Best Natural Attractions

- **The San Juan Islands:** Forested mountains rise up from the cold waters north of Puget Sound to form the archipelago known as the San Juan Islands. Here, bald eagles wheel overhead while orca whales dive for salmon below. All this natural beauty is a powerful magnet and, despite the hordes of tourists in the summer, the San Juans remain the state's best summer vacation spot. See "The San Juan Islands" in chapter 5.

- **Olympic National Park:** This park contains the only rainforests in the contiguous United States,

Washington

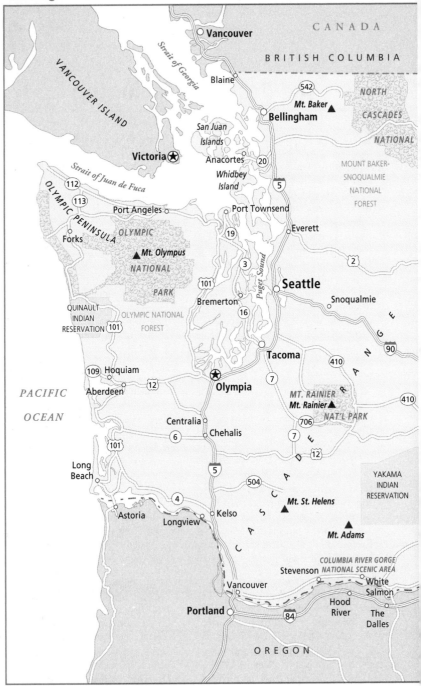

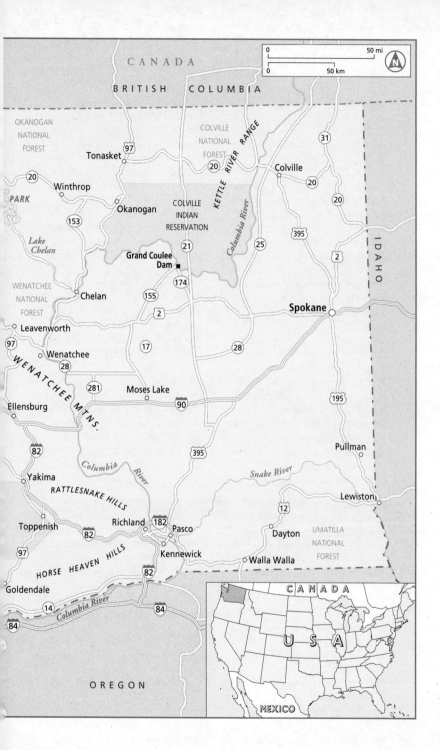

and they comprise a fascinating ecosystem—living plants stake out almost every square inch of space, from towering Sitka spruce trees to mosses and lush ferns. The park also preserves miles of pristine, fog-shrouded beaches and beautiful alpine and subalpine scenery dotted with lush meadows. See chapter 7.

- **The North Cascades National Park Complex:** Actually comprised of one national park and two national recreation areas, this remote and rugged region is among the least explored in the state. Most visitors view the park from the North Cascades Scenic Highway, from which there are stupendous views on clear days, but which is closed by snow for nearly half the year. See "Mount Baker & the North Cascades Scenic Highway" in chapter 9.
- **Mount Rainier National Park:** With its glaciers and easily accessible alpine meadows, Mount Rainier is Washington's favorite mountain. Sunrise and Paradise are the two best vantage points for viewing the massive bulk of Mount Rainier, and in these two areas of the park, you'll also find some of the best hiking trails. See "Mount Rainier National Park & Environs" in chapter 9.
- **Mount St. Helens National Volcanic Monument:** Mount St. Helens is slowly recovering from the 1980 volcanic blast that turned one of the Cascades' most beautiful peaks into a scarred landscape of fallen trees and fields of ash. Several visitor centers relate the events of the eruption and what has been happening on the mountain since. See "Mount St. Helens National Volcanic Monument" in chapter 9.
- **Columbia Gorge National Scenic Area:** Carved by ice-age floods that were as much as 1,200 feet deep, the Columbia Gorge is a unique feature of the Northwest landscape. Waterfalls by the dozen cascade from the basalt cliffs on the Oregon side of the Gorge, but the best wide-angle views are from the Washington side, where you'll also find one of the largest monoliths in the world. See "The Columbia Gorge & the Mount Adams Area" in chapter 9.

2 The Best Outdoor Activities

- **Sea Kayaking in the San Juan Islands:** Emerald islands, clear water, orca whales, bald eagles, and remote campsites that can only be reached by boat lure sea kayakers to the San Juan Islands. You can paddle the islands on your own (if you're experienced) or go out with a guide for a few hours or a few days. See "The San Juan Islands" in chapter 5.
- **Hiking the Olympic Coast:** Within the contiguous United States, there are very few miles of wilderness coastline left. Among the longest, and most spectacular, are those of Olympic National Park along the west side of the Olympic Peninsula. Whether you just want to do a good daylong hike, or spend several days backpacking along the beach, you've got several options along this coast. See chapter 7.
- **Cross-Country Skiing in the Methow Valley:** This valley on the east side of Washington's North Cascades has more than 100 miles of immaculately groomed trails, making it one of the premier cross-country ski destinations in the country. Skiers can ski from

one lodge to the next down the valley, or use one of the luxurious lodges as a base for doing day skis. See "Winthrop & the Methow Valley" in chapter 9.

- **Hiking on Mount Rainier:** Fed by huge amounts of melting snow each summer, the meadows of wildflowers on the flanks of Mount Rainier burst into bloom each year in July. Through these colorful hillsides meander miles of hiking trails that are among the most memorable in the state. Sure you'll encounter crowds, but the wildflower displays, with Mount Rainier for a backdrop, far outweigh the inconvenience of dealing with hordes of other hikers. See "Mount Rainier National Park & Environs" in chapter 9.

- **Climbing Mount St. Helens:** Though it isn't the highest peak in the Washington Cascades, Mount St. Helens is certainly the most interesting mountain to climb (you'll need a permit, and numbers of climbers are limited). You don't need any technical climbing skills for this one, just plenty of stamina and a tolerance for hiking in dusty conditions (if the snow has melted off, you'll be hiking in volcanic ash). See "Mount St. Helens National Volcanic Monument" in chapter 9.

- **Windsurfing at Hood River:** Winds that blow through the Columbia Gorge whip up white-capped standing waves and have turned this area into the windsurfing capital of the United States, attracting boardsailors from around the world. See "The Columbia Gorge & the Mount Adams Area" in chapter 9.

3 The Best Beaches

- **Alki Beach** (Seattle): Located in West Seattle, this is the closest Washington comes to a Southern California–style beach scene. There's a sandy beach and a paved path crowded with in-line skaters, walkers, and cyclists. Across the street from the sand, you'll find lots of cheap restaurants and places to buy sunglasses. See chapter 4.

- **Obstruction Pass State Park** (Orcas Island): Set at the end of a half-mile-long trail through the woods, this tiny cove is barely big enough for a dozen sea kayakers to beach their boats, but therein lies this beach's charm. This is the quintessential little San Juan Islands cove beach, and you don't have to have a boat to get to it. See "The San Juan Islands" in chapter 5.

- **Deception Pass State Park Beaches** (Whidbey Island): There's a reason this is the most popular state park in Washington—the many miles of beach, spread out on two sides of Deception Pass, are among the prettiest in the Puget Sound area. See "Whidbey Island" in chapter 5.

- **Dungeness Spit** (Dungeness): With 6 miles of windswept sand stretching out to a lighthouse in the Strait of Juan de Fuca, Dungeness is a hikers' beach, and the reward for hiking several miles out this narrow strip of sand is the chance to see some of the area's resident harbor seals. See "Sequim & Dungeness Valley" in chapter 7.

- **Rialto Beach** (Olympic National Park outside Forks): Located on the north side of the Quillayute River, this beach is the southern terminus of a 29-mile-long stretch of wilderness beach. However, most visitors simply walk a mile up the beach to Hole in the Wall, a huge monolith through which the ocean's waves have bored a tunnel. See "Olympic National Park West" in chapter 7.

- **Second Beach & Third Beach** (Olympic National Park outside Forks): It's difficult to pick the best beach in the national park, since they are almost all ruggedly beautiful, but these two beaches

just outside the community of La Push are our personal favorites. Here you can listen to the calls of the eagles and gulls and contemplate the sheer vastness of the Pacific. See "Olympic National Park West" in chapter 7.

4 The Best Hikes

- **Trails Out of Hurricane Ridge:** Hurricane Ridge is the most easily accessible alpine region of Olympic National Park, and from here, and nearby Obstruction Peak, there are several possible hikes that will give you a glimpse of a superb part of the Olympic wilderness. See "Olympic National Park North & the Northern Olympic Peninsula" in chapter 7.

- **Hall of Mosses Trail/Hoh River Trail** (Hoh River Valley): Whether you're only up for a short walk in the woods or want to do a multi-day backpacking trip, this is the best place to experience the Olympic Peninsula's famed rainforest. Just don't forget your rain gear. See "Olympic National Park West" in chapter 7.

- **The Maple Pass Loop Trail:** Along the North Cascades Scenic Highway, you simply won't find a more rewarding hike than this one. The trail climbs nearly 2,000 feet from Rainy Pass to a ridge with an astounding view of seemingly all the mountains in Washington. See

"Mount Baker & the North Cascades Scenic Highway" in chapter 9.

- **Trails Out of Sunrise:** The Sunrise area, on the northeast flanks of Washington's Mount Rainier, offers fabulous unobstructed views of both the mountain and Emmons Glacier, the largest glacier in the contiguous 48 states. From Sunrise more than a dozen trails of different lengths head off to viewpoints and lakes. Take your pick. See "Mount Rainier National Park & Environs" in chapter 9.

- **The Beacon Rock Trail** (Columbia Gorge West of Stevenson): Although this hike is less than 2 miles long, it makes up for its short length with its steep pitch. In fact, much of the trail is on metal stairs bolted to the sheer cliff face of Beacon Rock, a massive monolith that rivals the Rock of Gibraltar in size. The view from the top is superb. See "The Columbia Gorge & the Mount Adams Area" in chapter 9.

5 The Best Scenic Drives

- **Chuckanut Drive:** This road winds south from Bellingham through the Chuckanut Mountains, which rise straight up from the waters of Chuckanut and Samish bays. Across the water lie the San Juan Islands, and the sunsets are spectacular. Larrabee State Park provides an opportunity to

get out of your car and walk down to a pretty little beach. See "Bellingham & Environs" in chapter 5.

- **The North Cascades Scenic Highway:** Passing through the most rugged and spectacular mountains in the Northwest, this highway was not opened until

1972 because of the difficulty of building any sort of road through Washington's glacier-carved North Cascades. Even now it is closed for half of every year due to heavy snows and avalanches. See "Mount Baker & the North Cascades Scenic Highway" in chapter 9.

- **The Columbia River Scenic Highway:** Wash. 14 parallels the Columbia River from Vancouver, Washington, eastward through the Columbia Gorge, and along its length provides some of the most awe-inspiring vistas in the Northwest. Visible across the river in Oregon are not only the basalt cliffs of the Gorge but also the snow-clad summit of Mount Hood. See "The Columbia Gorge & the Mount Adams Area" in chapter 9.

- **The Yakima River Canyon:** Wash. 821, which connects Ellensburg with Yakima, is a little-known gem of a road. This route follows the Yakima River through a deep canyon bounded by rolling sagebrush hills and is a memorable alternative to I-82, which also connects Ellensburg and Yakima. See chapter 10.

- **The Palouse:** This wheat-farming region in southeastern Washington is a convoluted landscape of steep hills and narrow valleys, and a meandering drive through the region is a trip into another time. Small towns and boldly striped hillsides make this the most fascinating farm country in the state. See "The Palouse: A Slice of Small-Town Rural Washington" in chapter 10.

- **Soap Lake to the Grand Coulee Dam:** Although today the landscape of central Washington is that of a desert, vast floodwaters once poured across this landscape. Today a drive up the Grand Coulee provides a glimpse into one of the most fascinating events in Northwest geologic history. Canyons, mineral lakes, caves, and a huge dry waterfall provide the roadside distractions. See "The Grand Coulee Dam Area" in chapter 10.

6 The Best B&Bs & Inns

- **The Gaslight Inn** (Seattle; ✆ 206/325-3654): Beautifully decorated with lots of original Stickley furniture, this inn consists of two houses in the Capitol Hill neighborhood. One house is done in a more contemporary style if you don't happen to be a fan of Arts and Crafts style. There's also a swimming pool. See p. 81.

- **Spring Bay Inn** (Orcas Island; ✆ 360/376-5531): This secluded waterfront inn is a luxurious island retreat, and a stay here includes not only bed-and-breakfast, but brunch and a daily sea-kayak excursion as well. In-room fireplaces and a hot tub right on the beach add a touch of romance. See p. 171.

- **Willcox House** (The Kitsap Peninsula; ✆ 800/725-9477 or 360/830-4492): This 1930s Art Deco mansion, set on the shore of Hood Canal, is straight out of an old Hollywood movie (and indeed many movie stars did stay here back in the '30s and '40s). Because it is located in such a secluded spot, the inn also serves dinner. See p. 197.

- **Chinaberry Hill** (Tacoma; ✆ 253/272-1282): Located in Tacoma's Stadium Historic District, this grand Victorian is as impressive as any of the historic B&Bs in Port Townsend. The inn is steeped in classic Northwest elegance and abounds in beautiful woodwork. See p. 207.

- **The Villa Bed & Breakfast** (Tacoma; ✆ **888/572-1157** or 253/572-1157): Regardless of the fact that this inn would be more appropriate to Santa Barbara, the Italianate villa in Tacoma's Stadium Historic District is a real gem. Large rooms have whirlpool or soaking tubs and most have gas fireplaces. See p. 208.
- **Thornewood Castle Inn** (Lakewood; ✆ **253/584-4393**): Few B&Bs in America can truly claim to be castles, but Thornewood, built in 1909, certainly can. With 28 bedrooms and 22 bathrooms, this sprawling mansion is as close as you'll come in this country to a European manor home. See p. 208.
- **Ann Starrett Mansion** (Port Townsend; ✆ **800/321-0644** or 360/385-3205): This is the premier Victorian B&B in the Northwest. The outrageously ornate Queen Anne–style mansion is packed to the rafters with antiques, and staying here is a bit like spending the night in a museum. See p. 222.
- **Hoquiam's Castle** (Hoquiam; **877/542-2785** or 360/533-2005):

Built in 1897 by a local timber baron, this stately Victorian inn is an amazing assemblage of turrets and gables, balconies and bay windows. Although the town of Hoquiam isn't exactly a major tourist destination, this inn is reason enough to spend a weekend in the area. See p. 258.

- **Abendblume Inn** (Leavenworth; ✆ **800/669-7634** or 509/548-4059): Of all the many alpine chalet accommodations in Leavenworth, this is the most luxurious. The attention to detail shown in the construction of this chalet makes the inn an especially enjoyable place to spend a romantic weekend. See p. 299.
- **Run of the River Bed & Breakfast** (Leavenworth; ✆ **800/288-6491** or 509/548-7171): Set amid beautiful rock gardens on a side channel of the Wenatchee River, this rustic yet contemporary log inn is as tranquil a place to stay as you'll find in the region. The innkeepers are extremely helpful and eager to share their love of the area with guests. See p. 299.

7 The Best Mountain Lodges/Resorts/Retreats

- **Lake Crescent Lodge** (Olympic National Park west of Port Angeles; ✆ **360/928-3211**): Set on the shore of Lake Crescent, a landlocked fjord in Olympic National Park, this lodge is the best base for exploring the north side of the park. The lodge has simple rooms in the old main lodge building and larger though less memorable rooms in various newer buildings around the property. See p. 240.
- **Lake Quinault Lodge** (Lake Quinault; ✆ **800/562-6672** or 360/288-2900): This gracefully aging lodge on the shore of Lake Quinault has the most character of any of the lodges scattered around

the perimeter of Olympic National Park. It's something of a cross between a mountain lodge and a classic lake resort. See p. 248.

- **The Heathman Lodge** (Vancouver; ✆ **888/475-3100** or 360/254-3100): The only thing wrong with this modern mountain lodge is that it's located in suburban Vancouver, Washington, rather than in the mountains. Nevertheless, with its log, stone, and cedar-shingle construction, it manages to conjure up the Northwest's historic mountain lodges. See p. 270.
- **Sun Mountain Lodge** (Winthrop; ✆ **800/572-0493** or 509/996-2211): Perched atop a mountain

and overlooking the remote Methow Valley, this is Washington's premier mountain resort. Luxurious and rustic at the same time, the lodge is a base for cross-country skiing in winter and hiking and mountain biking in summer. See p. 282.

- **Freestone Inn** (Mazama; $\textcircled{C}$ **800/ 639-3809** or 509/996-3906): This impressive log lodge beside a small trout lake at the west end of the Winthrop Valley is not as extensive a place as nearby Sun Mountain Lodge, but the guest rooms here are among the most luxurious in the state. See p. 283.

- **Mountain Home Lodge** (Leavenworth; $\textcircled{C}$ **800/414-2378** or 509/ 548-7077): Set in the middle of a large pasture high on the slopes above the town of Leavenworth, this lodge enjoys a breathtaking view of the Stuart Range, and in winter is only accessible by snow coach (complimentary transport provided by the lodge). See p. 298.

- **Sleeping Lady** (Leavenworth; $\textcircled{C}$ **800/574-2123** or 509/548-6344): Although primarily a conference resort, this place on the outskirts of Bavarian Leavenworth is far too pleasant to be reserved for those in town for business. With the feel of an upscale summer camp, the lodge is tucked amid granite boulders and ponderosa pines. See p. 298.

- **Salish Lodge and Spa** (Snoqualmie Falls; $\textcircled{C}$ **800/272-5474** or 425/888-2556): Perched on the brink of Snoqualmie Falls near the town of North Bend, this elegant country lodge is a favorite weekend getaway for Seattleites who come to be pampered at the spa and to enjoy the nearby farm country, mountain trails, and ski slopes. See p. 304.

- **Paradise Inn** (Mount Rainier National Park; $\textcircled{C}$ **360/569-2275**): Perched high on the slopes of Washington's Mount Rainier, this classic mountain lodge was built in 1917, and was completely renovated a few years ago. Because the lodge is only open May through October, it books up early in the year and stays packed throughout the summer. You just can't beat the location. See p. 311.

- **Bonneville Hot Springs Resort** ($\textcircled{C}$ **866/459-1678** or 509/427-7767): Tucked amid the trees not far from Bonneville Dam, this newly opened hot springs resort has a traditional elegance. Although there are no views to speak of, the spa and warm-springs-fed pools more than make up for the lack of vista. See p. 323.

- **Dolce Skamania Lodge** (Stevenson; $\textcircled{C}$ **800/221-7117** or 509/427-7700): Set amid the grandeur of the Columbia Gorge, this modern mountain resort makes the ideal base for exploring the Gorge. The resort's golf course has a very distracting view of the Oregon side of the Columbia Gorge. See p. 323.

8 The Best Island & Beach Resorts & Lodges

- **Woodmark Hotel on Lake Washington** (Kirkland; $\textcircled{C}$ **800/822-3700** or 425/822-3700): Set on spacious grounds on the eastern shore of Lake Washington, this luxurious hotel is the Seattle area's finest waterfront hotel and has a very resort-like feel. See p. 84.

- **Friday Harbor House** (Friday Harbor; $\textcircled{C}$ **866/722-7356** or 360/ 378-8455): Okay, so this one isn't right on the water. Still, they're the most luxurious accommodations on San Juan Island, and the guest rooms have views of the water and distant island peaks. See p. 164.

- **Rosario Resort & Spa** (Orcas Island; ✆ **800/562-8820** or 360/376-2222): With an elegant historic mansion as its focal point and enough activities and amenities to keep you busy for a week's vacation, this is the premier resort in the San Juan Islands. See p. 171.
- **La Conner Channel Lodge** (La Conner; ✆ **888/466-4113** or 360/466-1500): Set on the shore of the Swinomish Channel, this inn is steeped in Northwest styling. River rocks and weathered wood siding lend an air of age to the exterior, which is brightened by lovely perennial gardens. In the guest rooms, balconies, fireplaces, fir accents, and slate floors yield an unexpected sophistication. See p. 181.
- **The Inn at Langley** (Whidbey Island; ✆ **360/221-3033**): The setting alone, overlooking Saratoga Passage, would be enough to rank this place firmly among the best small inns in the region. However, Japanese-influenced styling, soaking tubs with water views, and fireplaces all add up to uncommon luxuries at this romantic retreat. See p. 152.
- **Resort Semiahmoo** (Blaine; ✆ **800/770-7992** or 360/318-2000): Located on a spit of land looking across the water to Canada, this is Washington's premier golf and beach resort. It's on a long stretch of beach, which makes this a great place to get away from it all whether you want to play golf or tennis or just walk on the beach. See p. 187.
- **The Captain Whidbey Inn** (Whidbey Island; ✆ **800/366-4097** or 360/678-4097): This unusual inn was built in 1907 of local madrona-tree logs, which give it a thoroughly unique appearance. The island's seafaring history is evoked throughout the inn, and the seat in front of the lobby's beach-stone fireplace is a wonderful spot to while away a gray afternoon. See p. 152.
- **The Resort at Ludlow Bay** (Port Ludlow; ✆ **877/805-0868** or 360/437-2222): Located a few miles south of Port Townsend, this small, luxury inn offers all the best aspects of the San Juan Islands without the hassles of the ferries. An adjacent golf course adds to the appeal. See p. 224.
- **Kalaloch Lodge** (Forks; ✆ **866/525-2562** or 360/962-2271): Comprised primarily of bluff-top cabins overlooking a wild and windswept beach, this is Olympic National Park's only oceanfront lodge. As such it is extremely popular. See p. 248.
- **Ocean Crest Resort** (Moclips; ✆ **800/684-8439** or 360/276-4465): Perched high on a forested bluff above the crashing waves of the Pacific Ocean, this casual resort enjoys the most spectacular setting of any lodging on the Washington coast. There's also a good restaurant on the premises. See p. 257.

9 The Best Off-the-Beaten-Path Restaurants

- **The Herbfarm** (Woodinville; ✆ **425/485-5300**): This restaurant, located northeast of Seattle adjacent to several wineries, was once little more than a roadside farm stand specializing in herbs, but over the years has become the most highly acclaimed (and most expensive) restaurant in the state. See p. 97.
- **The Chef's Kitchen Restaurant at the Inn at Langley** (Langley; ✆ **360/221-3033**): This quintessentially Northwestern inn on Whidbey Island is one of the state's most luxurious accommodations.

Open on weekends only, the restaurant serves some of the best multicourse gourmet dinners in Washington. Make reservations early. See p. 152.

- **Olga's** (Orcas Island; © 360/376-5862): Although this delightfully eclectic little restaurant is only open for breakfast and lunch, the food served at these two meals is as creative as you'll find at any gourmet restaurant in the state. See p. 173.

- **Molly Ward Gardens** (Poulsbo; © 360/779-4471): Housed in an old barn in a small rural valley outside the Scandinavian theme town of Poulsbo, this restaurant sums up Northwest lifestyles with its country gardens, eclectic decor, and creative cuisine. See p. 198.

- **The Ajax Cafe** (Port Hadlock; © 360/385-3450): With excellent food, live old-time music on the weekends, and silly hats hanging from the ceiling (and frequently worn by dinner guests), the Ajax Cafe is a hidden gem of a restaurant south of Port Townsend. Housed in an old wooden waterfront building, the restaurant is a favorite of people with something to celebrate. See p. 226.

- **The Ark Restaurant & Bakery** (Nahcotta; © 360/665-4133): Oyster lovers take note, this restaurant on the Long Beach Peninsula is just down the road from Oysterville and is adjacent to oyster farms and an oyster packing plant, so you know the shellfish here is as fresh as it gets. See p. 226.

- **The Depot Restaurant** (Seaview; © 360/642-7880): Small, out of the way, casual and inexpensive, yet with excellent food—this is just the sort of restaurant you dream of finding on vacation. The Depot was indeed once a railroad depot, and today, the cooking here is right on track. See p. 266.

- **Sun Mountain Lodge** (Winthrop; © 800/572-0493 or 509/996-4707): If you get vertigo easily, you may want to forego meals at this precipitously perched dining room overlooking the Methow Valley. However, if you relish creative cooking accompanied by dizzying mountain views, this restaurant should not be missed. See p. 284.

- **Whitehouse-Crawford Restaurant** (Walla Walla; © 509/525-2222): Located in downtown Walla Walla, which is at the heart of Washington's fastest-growing wine region, this restaurant is housed in a former mill building and shares space with a winery. The scene and the menu have a decidedly Seattle feel. See p. 347.

- **Patit Creek Restaurant** (Dayton; © 509/382-2625): The small town of Dayton seems an unlikely place for one of the state's best restaurants, but the reliable French-inspired fare served at this unpretentious place draws diners from miles around. See p. 349.

10 The Best Wineries (Open to the Public)

- **Fair Winds Winery** (Port Townsend; © 360/385-6899): This out-of-the-way winery is a surprising little gem. The winery produces a wide range of excellent wines, including a port and Aligoté, a French varietal that is rarely produced in the U.S. See p. 222.

- **Chandler Reach** (Yakima Valley; © 509/588-8800): With its underground tasting room, this is one of the more memorable wineries in the Yakima Valley, but it's the outstanding syrahs and bordeaux blends that make this winery unforgettable. See p. 335.

- **Maison de Padgett Winery** (Yakima Valley; ✆ **509/829-6412**): Distinctive wines in distinctive bottles with distinctive labels. That about sums up this winery. Come with an open mind (and an open check book). See p. 333.
- **Paradisos del Sol** (Yakima Valley; ✆ **509/829-9000**): Winemaker Paul Vandenberg, who has also made wines for Portteus Vineyards (another of our favorite wineries), produces some wonderfully complex and atypical, barrel-aged white wines. See p. 333.
- **Portteus Vineyards** (Yakima Valley; ✆ **509/829-6970**): Intensely flavored, full-bodied red wines are the specialty at this winery about midway down the Yakima Valley. Prices are moderate and their red table wine is a great value. See p. 333.
- **Kestrel Vintners** (Yakima Valley; ✆ **888/343-CORK** or 509/786-2675): Winemaker Ray Sandidge is one of Washington's top winemakers and here produces many outstanding red wines. Just don't expect to find any deals. See p. 335.
- **Wineglass Cellars** (Yakima Valley; ✆ **509/829-3011**): This small, unassuming, family-run winery produces some of the most awesome red wines in the state. This is perhaps the most underrated and little known winery in the Yakima Valley. See p. 334.
- **Amavi Cellars** (Walla Walla; ✆ **509/525-3541**): This is one of the newer wineries in Walla Walla and is a sister winery to the celebrated Pepper Bridge Winery. The syrah here can be among the finest in the region. See p. 343.
- **Rulo Winery** (Walla Walla; ✆ **509/525-7856**): A small, family-owned winery, Rulo crafts complex, full-bodied syrah, creamy chardonnay, and aromatic viognier. Reasonable prices and high quality make this winery truly memorable. See p. 345.
- **Woodward Canyon Winery** (Walla Walla; ✆ **509/525-4129**): This winery produces some of Washington's premier red wines, yet, surprisingly, they offer great wines at under $20 (as well as plenty of more expensive bottlings). See p. 344.
- **Townshend Cellar** (Spokane; ✆ **509/238-140**): Quite a few Washington wineries are now making port, but none makes them as good as this little, out-of-the-way winery north of Spokane. The huckleberry port is pure ambrosia. See chapter 10.

11 The Best Family Attractions & Activities

- **Seattle Center** (Seattle): As the site of the Space Needle, Seattle Center is one of the city's required stops. However, families will also find here a children's museum, a children's theater, an interactive science museum, amusement park rides, and an arcade area. See p. 106.
- **Museum of Flight:** Okay, so airplanes may not be quite as fascinating to kids as fire engines and trains, but there are so many cool airplanes and things to do at this museum that kids usually don't want to leave when you're ready to go. See p. 111.
- **Whale-Watching Tours in the San Juan Islands:** Sure you can see orca whales perform at marine parks, but in the San Juan Islands during the summer, you can see genuinely free Willies, and lots of them. During whale-watching tours minke whales, harbor seals, and bald eagles may be spotted also. See "The San Juan Islands" in chapter 5.

- **Fort Worden State Park** (Port Townsend): With a beach, old gun batteries, a science center that has tide pool touch tanks, and miles of hiking trails, this park is a one-stop entertainment center for kids. See p. 221.
- **Point Defiance Park** (Tacoma): This gigantic city park at the north end of Tacoma packs in more fun stuff for kids than a family could ever hope to do in a day. There's a zoo, a replica of a historic trading fort, and an old-time logging camp. See p. 204.
- **Long Beach:** With minigolf, horseback riding, miles of wide beaches, and perfect winds for kite flying, this beach community on the southern Washington coast is the state's best family beach. See "The Long Beach Peninsula" in chapter 8.

12 The Best Small Towns

- **La Conner:** Surrounded by tulip fields and filled with art galleries and interesting shops, this former fishing and farming town gets jammed on weekends, but if you stop by on a weekday or in the off season, you can easily be seduced by its vintage charm. See "La Conner & the Skagit Valley" in chapter 5.
- **Langley:** Located near the south end of Whidbey Island, this former fishing village is now something of an upscale arts community. There are art galleries, antiques and fashion shops, and several good restaurants. All this right on the shore of Saratoga Passage. Some buildings even rise straight out of the water. See "Whidbey Island" in chapter 5.
- **Port Townsend:** Late in the 19th century, this town on the Olympic Peninsula was poised to become the region's most important city, but when the railroad passed it by, it slipped into obscurity. Today Port Townsend is obscure no more. With block after block of Victorian homes and a waterfront setting, it has become a favorite weekend destination for Seattle-ites. See "Port Townsend: A Restored Victorian Seaport" in chapter 7.
- **Leavenworth:** Lederhosen? Dirndls? Polka parties? Sounds like someplace to steer clear of, but actually, the Bavarian theme town of Leavenworth works. Maybe there are too many cuckoo clocks and nutcrackers for sale, but those mountains on the edge of town are the genuine article. See "The Wenatchee Valley and Bavarian Leavenworth" in chapter 9.
- **Winthrop:** If you saw an 1890s photo of Winthrop and then visited this remote community in north central Washington, you might think the town had been caught in a time warp. It just doesn't look much different than it did back then. See "Winthrop & the Methow Valley" in chapter 9.

2

Planning Your Trip to Washington

Planning your trip before you leave home can make all the difference between enjoying your vacation and wishing you'd stayed home. In fact, for many people, planning a trip is half the fun of going. If you're one of those people, then this chapter should prove useful. When should I go? What is this trip going to cost me? Can I catch a festival during my visit? Where should I head to pursue my favorite sport? These are just some of the questions we'll answer for you in this chapter. Additionally, you can contact information sources listed below to find out more about Washington and to take a look at photos (whether in brochures or on the Web) that are certain to get you excited about your upcoming trip.

1 The Regions in Brief

The state of Washington covers 68,139 square miles—roughly the same area as all of New England. Within this large area can be found surprising geographical diversity, including an inland sea dotted with hundreds of islands, temperate rainforests where rainfall is measured in feet, an arid land of sagebrush and junipers, several distinct mountain ranges, volcanoes both dormant and extinct, the West's most important river, and, of course, hundreds of thousands of acres of coniferous forests (hence the state's nickname—the Evergreen State).

Puget Sound Puget Sound, a convoluted maze of waterways, is a vast inland sea that stretches for more than 80 miles, from north of Seattle south to Olympia. Created when glaciers receded at the end of the last ice age, Puget Sound is characterized by deep waterways surrounded by hilly, forested terrain. Because the Sound's protected waters make such good harbors and are so full of fish and shellfish, this area has been the most densely populated region of the state since long before the first Europeans sailed into these waters. Today, the eastern shore of the Sound has become the largest metropolitan area in the state—one huge Pugetopolis that includes Seattle, Tacoma, Olympia, and dozens of smaller cities and bedroom communities. The western and southernmost reaches of the Sound are much less developed. These rural areas are popular weekend escapes for Seattleites and Tacomans but are much less familiar to visitors from out of state, who, though they might appreciate the Sound and Rainier vistas, tend to overlook this region because of its lack of major attractions.

The San Juan Islands Lying just to the north of Puget Sound, the San Juan Islands are a lush, mountainous archipelago, home to orca whales, harbor seals, and bald eagles. Of the 175 or so named San Juan Islands, only four are accessible by public ferry, and of these only three—San Juan, Orcas, and Lopez—have accommodations (however, the 4th, Shaw, does have a campground). The mild climate, watery vistas, and quiet, rural character of these islands have made the San Juans Washington's favorite summer-vacation destination. As such the islands are packed to overflowing throughout the summer and it can be impossible to get a hotel reservation at the last minute. A summer trip to the San Juans definitely requires plenty of advance planning. It also requires a great deal of patience, as waits for ferries can stretch into hours. To avoid the crowds, consider visiting in spring or fall, when the weather is often just as good as in the summer. Because the San Juans lie within the rain shadow of the Olympic Mountains, they get far less rain than Seattle (and therein lies much of their appeal for Seattleites).

The Olympic Peninsula Aside from a thin necklace of private land around its perimeter, this huge peninsula, wedged between Puget Sound and the Pacific Ocean, is almost entirely public land. At the heart of the peninsula is Olympic National Park, which encompasses almost the entirety of the Olympic Mountains. Surrounding the park is Olympic National Forest, which is distinguishable from the park by its many clear-cuts. Due primarily to the immensity of the forests and the size of the trees here, the forests of the Olympic Peninsula have, over the past 100 years, seen some of the most intensive logging in the nation. The gigantic size of the trees here is due to the astounding amount of rain that falls on parts of the peninsula. The western slopes of the Olympic Mountains contain some of the only temperate rainforests in the contiguous United States, and in these forests, the annual rainfall often exceeds 150 inches. Rugged remote beaches separated by rocky headlands characterize the Pacific shore of the peninsula, while along the north coast, there are several large towns, including the historic Victorian seaport of Port Townsend. Just remember when planning a vacation out here that you're likely to get rained on even in the summer; be prepared to get wet.

Southwest Washington The southwest corner of the state is, for the most part, a sparsely populated region of huge tree farms. However, along the southern coast, there are long sandy beaches and numerous beach resorts and towns, which, though popular with Portlanders and the residents of Puget Sound, lack a distinctly Northwest character. Inland, up the Columbia River, lies the city of Vancouver (not to be confused with Vancouver, B.C.), which though rich in regional history, has been overshadowed by Portland, Oregon, directly across the Columbia River.

The Cascade Range Dividing the state roughly into eastern and western regions, the Washington Cascades are actually two very distinct mountain ranges. The North Cascades are jagged, glaciated granite peaks, while the central and southern Washington Cascades are primarily volcanic in origin. Mount St. Helens, which erupted with awe-inspiring force in 1980, is the only one of these volcanoes to be active in recent years, but even Mount Rainier, the highest mountain in the state, is merely dormant and is expected to erupt again sometime in the next few hundred years (probably with devastating effect considering the large population that now resides at the foot of the mountain). Within this mountain range are North Cascades National Park, Mount Rainier National Park, Mount St. Helens National Volcanic Monument, the third deepest lake in the country (Lake Chelan), half a dozen ski areas, and a couple of interesting little theme towns. If you're thinking about a summer vacation in these mountains, keep in mind that the snow at higher elevations (where you'll find the beautiful wildflower meadows) often doesn't melt off until well into July.

Eastern Washington While to the west of the Cascade Range all is gray skies and green forests, to the east the sun shines 300 days a year, and less than 10 inches of rain falls in an average year. Although this sun-drenched and sparsely populated shrub steppe is highly valued by waterlogged residents of western Washington, it is, with the exception of its wine country, of little interest to out-of-state visitors. Irrigation waters from the Columbia River have allowed the region to become an agricultural powerhouse. From the Yakima Valley to the Walla Walla area, large areas of wine-grape vineyards have helped make Washington the second-largest producer of wine in the country. Also, in the Yakima, Wenatchee, and Chelan valleys, apple orchards produce the bulk of the nation's apple crop. Out in the southeast corner of the state lie the rolling Palouse Hills, where rich soils sustain the most productive wheat fields in the nation. Spokane, close to the Idaho state line, is the region's largest metropolitan area.

2 Visitor Information

For information on Washington, contact the **Washington State Tourism Office,** P.O. Box 42500, Olympia, WA 98504 (© **800/544-1800** or 360/725-5052; www.experiencewashington. com). For information on Seattle and vicinity, contact the **Seattle's Convention and Visitors Bureau,** 701 Pike St., Suite 800, Seattle, WA 98101 (© **206/461-5800;** www.seeseattle. org), which operates a visitor information center inside the Washington State Convention and Trade Center, 800 Convention Place, Galleria Level. If you're surfing the Net searching for information on the Seattle area, check out **www.ci.seattle.wa.us/html/visitor**, the city of Seattle's visitor information site. This site is basically a wide range of links to other sites.

Also keep in mind that most cities and towns in Washington have either a tourist office or a chamber of commerce that can provide you with information. When approaching cities and towns, watch for signs along the highway directing you to these information centers. See the individual chapters for specific addresses.

To get information on outdoor recreation in national parks and national forests of Washington, contact the **Outdoor Recreation Information Center,** Seattle REI Building, 222 Yale Ave. N., Seattle, WA 98109 (© **206/470-4060;** www.nps.gov/ ccso/oric.htm).

For information on Washington state parks, contact **Washington State Parks and Recreation Commission,** 7150 Cleanwater Lane (P.O. Box 42650), Olympia, WA 98504-2650 (© **360/ 902-8844;** www.parks.wa.gov).

For information on ferries, contact **Washington State Ferries,** 2911 Second Ave., Seattle, WA 98121-1012 (© **800/843-3779** or 888/808-7977 within Washington state, or 206/464-6400; www.wsdot.wa.gov/ferries).

3 Money

ATMs

The easiest and best way to get cash away from home is from an ATM (automated teller machine). The **Cirrus** (© **800/424-7787;** www.master card.com) and **PLUS** (© **800/843-7587;** www.visa.com) networks span the globe; look at the back of your bank card to see which network you're on, then call or check online for ATM locations at your destination. Be sure you know your personal identification number (PIN) before you leave home and be sure to find out your daily withdrawal limit before you depart. Many banks impose a fee every time a card is used at a different bank's ATM, and that fee can be higher for international transactions (up to $5 or more) than for domestic ones (where they're rarely more than $1.50). The bank from which you withdraw cash may charge its own fee also.

You can also get cash advances on your credit card at an ATM. Credit card companies try to protect themselves from theft by limiting the funds someone can withdraw outside their home country, so if you're traveling to Washington from abroad, call your credit card company before you leave home.

TRAVELER'S CHECKS

These days, traveler's checks are less necessary because most cities have 24-hour ATMs that allow you to withdraw small amounts of cash as needed. However, since you will likely be charged an ATM withdrawal fee if the bank is not your own, you might be better off with traveler's checks—provided that you don't mind showing identification every time you want to cash one.

You can get traveler's checks at almost any bank. **American Express** offers denominations of $20, $50, $100, $500, and (for cardholders only) $1,000. You'll pay a service charge ranging from 1% to 4%. You can also

get American Express traveler's checks over the phone by calling ✆ **800/221-7282;** Amex gold and platinum cardholders who use this number are exempt from the 1% fee. AAA members can obtain checks without a fee at most AAA offices.

Visa offers traveler's checks at Citibank locations nationwide, as well as at several other banks. The service charge ranges between 1.5% and 2%; checks come in denominations of $20, $50, $100, $500, and $1,000. Call ✆ **800/732-1322** for information. **MasterCard** also offers traveler's checks. Call ✆ **800/223-9920** for a location near you.

CREDIT CARDS

Credit cards are a safe way to carry money, they provide a convenient record of all your expenses, and they generally offer good exchange rates. You can also withdraw cash advances from your credit cards at banks or ATMs, provided you know your PIN. If you've forgotten yours, or didn't even know you had one, call the number on the back of your credit card and ask the bank to send it to you. It usually takes 5 to 7 business days, though some banks will provide the number over the phone if you tell them your mother's maiden name or some other personal information.

4 When to Go

If you're reading this section, there's probably one question on your mind: When can I visit and not get rained on? The answer, of course, is never. Although the Northwest's infamous rains fall primarily between October and early July, it can rain any month of the year, so be sure to bring rain gear of some sort with you. This is especially important if you plan on visiting the Olympic Peninsula, parts of which receive more than 150 inches of rain each year. In fact, if you visit

any part of the coast, expect grayer, wetter weather than in the Seattle area. From the coast to the Cascade Range, moist winds off the Pacific Ocean keep temperatures mild year-round, so you're also likely to need a sweater or light jacket at night even in August.

July and August are the most reliably rainless months of the year, and consequently, are the most popular time of the year to visit Washington. It is during these 2 months that the sun is seen most often and rain is almost unheard of (though not unknown). During these dry summer months Washington families flock to the San Juan Islands to, among other things, watch the region's famous orca whales feeding in the waters off San Juan Island. July and August are also the state's main festival months, and several of the big festivals in the Seattle area can make finding a hotel room on a festival weekend difficult. Seafair is the biggest of these festivals, with Labor Day weekend's Bumbershoot festival packing the city as well.

However, Labor Day weekend aside, September is really one of the best months to visit. Skies are often still cloudless, and the kids are back in school (so the crowds at popular destinations such as the San Juan Islands and Mount Rainier are really bad only on weekends). In the mountains, wildflowers are often still in bloom (though peak bloom in the Cascade Range and Olympic Mountains is July–Aug).

With the coming of the rains, Washingtonians begin spending far more time indoors and consequently, the performing arts in Seattle and other major cities begin their annual seasons. So, if you're keen on catching the Seattle Opera or some of Seattle's fringe theater, you'll need to plan a rainy season visit. This may not be as bad as it sounds considering the fact that hotels in Seattle offer substantial discounts during the dreary winter months. Keep in mind, though, that winters usually include one or two blasts of Arctic air that bring snow and freezing weather to the Seattle area.

Winter also brings the ski season and sometimes record-setting snowfalls such as that of the winter of 1998–99, which dumped close to 100 feet of snow on Mount Baker. While the snow in Washington can be heavy and rains often fall in the mountains in the middle of winter, there are several very popular ski areas in the Cascades, as well as some smaller ski areas in eastern Washington.

Note that the preceding discussion applies to the west side of the Cascades. East of the Cascades, the climate is very different and some regions, sometimes referred to as the high desert, are characterized by temperature extremes and a lack of rain. These areas can be very cold in the winter and can get moderate amounts of snow in the foothill regions. In summer the weather can be blazing hot, though nights are often cool enough to require a sweater or light jacket. The dry lands of eastern Washington are primarily agricultural regions, and it is here that most of the state's wine grapes are grown. In winter, most wineries that are open to the public cut their hours or close down completely.

Seattle's Average Temperature & Days of Rain

	Jan	Feb	Mar	Apr	May	June	July	Aug	Sept	Oct	Nov	Dec
Temp. (°F)	46	50	53	58	65	69	75	74	69	60	52	47
Temp. (°C)	8	10	11	15	18	21	24	23	21	16	11	8
Rain (days)	19	16	17	14	10	9	5	7	9	14	18	20

WASHINGTON CALENDAR OF EVENTS

For additional information on events in Washington State, check the calendar section on the Washington State Tourism Office website at www.experiencewashington.com.

February

Northwest Flower & Garden Show (℃ 800/229-6311 or 206/789-5333; www.gardenshow.com), Washington State Convention and

Trade Center. This massive show for avid gardeners has astonishing floral displays. Mid-February.

Red Wine and Chocolate (© 800/258-7270; www.yakimavalleywine.com), Yakima Valley. Sample Yakima Valley reds, accompanied by tastings of decadent chocolate desserts. Presidents' Weekend.

April

Skagit Valley Tulip Festival (© 360/428-5959; www.tulipfestival.org), Skagit Valley. View a rainbow of blooming tulip fields. The month of April.

Spring Barrel Tasting (© 800/258-7270; www.yakimavalleywine.com), Yakima Valley. Straight-from-the-barrel wine tasting and spring-release wines at Yakima Valley wineries. Last full weekend in April.

Washington State Apple Blossom Festival (© 509/662-3616; www.appleblossom.org), Wenatchee. Many different events, including a parade and activities for families. End of April to early May.

May

Opening Day of Boating Season (© 206/325-1000; www.seattleyachtclub.org), Lake Union and Lake Washington. A parade of boats and much fanfare take place as Seattle boaters bring out everything from kayaks to yachts. First Saturday in May.

Irrigation Festival (© 360/683-6197; www.irrigationfestival.com), Sequim. More than 100 years old, this is the oldest continuous festival in Washington, with a grand parade, dancing, and arts and crafts. Early May.

Viking Fest (© 360/779-FEST; http://vikingfest.org), Poulsbo. Norwegian heritage on display in picturesque Poulsbo, with a parade and entertainment. Mid-May.

Spokane Lilac Festival (© 509/535-4554; www.lilacfestival.org), Spokane. A 60-year tradition celebrating the blooming of the lilacs. Don't miss the lilac gardens at Manito Park. Mid-May.

Northwest Folklife Festival (© 206/684-7300; www.nwfolklife.org), Seattle. This is the largest folk festival in the country, with dozens of national and regional folk musicians performing on numerous stages. In addition, you'll find crafts vendors from all over the Northwest, lots of good food, and dancing. The festival is held at the Seattle Center, and admission is by suggested $5 donation. Memorial Day weekend.

June

Mural-in-a-Day (© 509/865-6516), Toppenish. The small town of Toppenish has covered its blank walls with murals, and each June one more is added in a day of intense painting. Early June.

July

Fourth of Jul-Ivar's fireworks (© 206/587-6500; www.ivars.net), Myrtle Edwards Park, north end of Seattle waterfront. Fireworks over Elliott Bay. July 4.

Washington Mutual Family Fourth at Lake Union (© 206/281-7788; www.onereel.org), Lake Union. Seattle's other main Fourth of July fireworks display. July 4.

Walla Walla Sweet Onion Festival (© 509/525-1031; www.sweetonions.org), Walla Walla. Onion-themed entertainment and food booths featuring the delicious local onion. Mid-July.

Bellevue Art Museum Fair (© 425/519-0770; www.bellevueart.org), Bellevue Square shopping mall, Bellevue. This is the largest arts and fine crafts fair in the Northwest. Last weekend in July.

Seafair (© 206/728-0123; www. seafair.com), Seattle. This is the biggest Seattle event of the year, with daily festivities—parades, hydroplane boat races, an air show with the navy's Blue Angels, a Torchlight Parade, ethnic festivals, sporting events, and open house on naval ships. Events take place all over Seattle. Early July to early August.

Pilchuck Open House, Stanwood. The Pilchuck Glass School, founded by internationally renowned glass artist Dale Chihuly, is located in the foothills of the Cascade Mountains 50 miles north of Seattle. The school opens its doors once a year for visitors and reservations are necessary (© 206/621-8422, ext. 50). Late July.

August

Chief Seattle Days (© 360/598-3311), at Suquamish tribal headquarters. Celebration of Northwest Native American culture across Puget Sound from Seattle. Third weekend in August.

Washington State International Kite Festival (© 800/451-2542; www.kitefestival.com), Long Beach. World-class kite flying competition. Third week in August.

Makah Days (© 360/645-2201; www.makah.com), Neah Bay. Canoe races, Native American arts, and salmon bake presented by the Makah tribe in the Northwest corner of the Olympic Peninsula. End of August.

September

Bumbershoot, the Seattle Arts Festival (© 206/281-7788; www. bumbershoot.org). Seattle's second-most popular festival derives its peculiar name from a British term for an umbrella—an obvious reference to the rainy weather. Lots of rock music and other events pack Seattle's youthful set into Seattle

Center and other venues. You'll find plenty of arts and crafts on display too. Labor Day weekend.

Ellensburg Rodeo (© 800/637-2444 or 509/962-7831; www. ellensburgrodeo.com), Ellensburg. The state's biggest rodeo, with a carnival and both country music and rock bands. Labor Day weekend.

Wooden Boat Festival (© 360/385-3628; www.woodenboat.org), Port Townsend. Historic boats on display, demonstrations. Early September.

Western Washington Fair (© 253/841-5045; www.thefair. com), Puyallup. One of the 10 largest fairs in the nation. Third week in September.

October

Salmon Days Festival (© 425/392-0661), Issaquah. This festival celebrates the annual return of salmon that spawn within the city limits. First full weekend in October.

Kinetic Sculpture Race (© 888/365-6978; www.ptguide.com), Port Townsend. The two rules of this race are (1) the vehicle must be people-powered; and (2) the wackier the contraption the better. First Sunday in October.

Oktoberfest (© 509/548-5807; www.leavenworth.org), Leavenworth. A traditional Oktoberfest in this Bavarian town comes complete with kegs of beer shipped in from Munich and traditional German dancing. First and second weekend in October.

Cranberrian Fair (© 800/451-2542 or 360/642-3446), Ilwaco, Long Beach Peninsula. Cranberry bog tours, cranberry products, arts and crafts. Mid-October.

November

Thanksgiving in the Wine Country (© 800/258-7270; www.yakima valleywine.com), Yakima Valley.

Foods and the wines that complement them are offered for tasting by Yakima-area wineries. Thanksgiving weekend.

Zoolights (© 253/591-5337; www.pdza.org), Tacoma. The Point Defiance Zoo is decorated with thousands of sparkling lights, creating colorful fantasy scenes. Day after Thanksgiving to December 31.

December

Christmas Lighting (© 509/548-5807; www.leavenworth.org), Leavenworth. This Bavarian village was practically made for Christmas, and looks most photogenic when surrounded by snow and decorated with twinkling lights. Sleigh rides, roasted chestnuts, and all the traditional Bavarian trimmings. First three weekends of December.

Tree Lighting and Santa's Visit (© 888/365-6978; www.ptguide.com), Port Townsend. Santa arrives in this historic Victorian town by boat. First Saturday night in December.

Seattle Christmas Ships (© 800/642-7816 or 206/623-1445; www.argosycruises.com), various locations. Boats decked out with imaginative Christmas lights parade past various waterfront locations. **Argosy Cruises** offers tours; see "Organized Tours" in chapter 4 for more details. Throughout December.

AT&T New Year's at the Needle, Seattle Center. The Space Needle ushers in the new year by bursting into light when midnight strikes. Call © 206/443-2100 for information. December 31.

5 Travel Insurance, Health & Safety

Check your existing insurance policies and credit card coverage before you buy travel insurance. You may already be covered for lost luggage, canceled tickets, or medical expenses. The cost of travel insurance varies widely, depending on the cost and length of your trip, your age, health, and the type of trip you're taking.

TRIP-CANCELLATION INSURANCE Trip-cancellation insurance helps you get your money back if you have to back out of a trip, if you have to go home early, or if your travel supplier goes bankrupt. Allowed reasons for cancellation can range from sickness to natural disasters to the State Department declaring your destination unsafe for travel. In this unstable world, trip-cancellation insurance is a good buy if you're getting tickets well in advance. Insurance policy details vary, so read the fine print—and especially make sure that your airline or cruise line is on the list of carriers covered in case of bankruptcy. For information, contact one of the following insurers: **Access**

America (© 866/807-3982; www.accessamerica.com); **Travel Guard International** (© 800/826-4919; www.travelguard.com); **Travel Insured International** (© 800/243-3174; www.travelinsured.com); and **Travelex Insurance Services** (© 888/457-4602; www.travelex-insurance.com).

MEDICAL INSURANCE Most health-insurance policies cover you if you get sick away from home—but check, particularly if you're insured by an HMO. If you require additional medical insurance, try **MEDEX International** (© 800/527-0218 or 410/453-6300; www.medexassist.com) or **Travel Assistance International** (© 800/821-2828; www.travelassistance.com; for general information on services, call the company's Worldwide Assistance Services, Inc., at © 800/777-8710).

LOST-LUGGAGE INSURANCE On domestic flights, checked baggage is covered up to $2,500 per ticketed passenger. On international flights (including U.S. portions of international trips), baggage is limited to approximately $9.10 per pound, up to approximately $640 per checked bag. If you plan to check items more valuable than the standard liability, see if your valuables are covered by your homeowner's policy, get baggage insurance as part of your comprehensive travel-insurance package, or buy Travel Guard's "BagTrak" product (see above for Travel Guard's number). Don't buy insurance at the airport, as it's usually overpriced. Be sure to take any valuables or irreplaceable items with you in your carry-on luggage, as many valuables (including books, money, and electronics) aren't covered by airline policies.

If your luggage is lost, immediately file a lost-luggage claim at the airport, detailing the luggage contents. For most airlines, you must report delayed, damaged, or lost baggage within 4 hours of arrival. The airlines are required to deliver luggage, once found, directly to your house or destination free of charge.

WHAT TO DO IF YOU GET SICK AWAY FROM HOME   If you worry about getting sick away from home, consider purchasing **medical travel insurance** and carry your ID card in your purse or wallet. In most cases, your existing health plan will provide the coverage you need. See the section on insurance earlier in this chapter for more information.

If you suffer from a chronic illness, consult your doctor before your departure. For conditions like epilepsy, diabetes, or heart problems, wear a **Medic Alert Identification Tag** (© 888/ 633-4298 or 209/668-3333; www. medicalert.org), which will immediately alert doctors to your condition and give them access to your records through a 24-hour hot line.

Pack **prescription medications** in your carry-on luggage, and carry prescription medications in their original containers. Also bring along copies of your prescriptions in case you lose your pills or run out.

And don't forget **sunglasses** and an extra pair of **contact lenses** or **prescription glasses.**

6 The Active Vacation Planner

The abundance of outdoor recreational activities is one of the reasons people choose to live in Washington. With both mountains and beaches within an hour's drive of the major metropolitan areas, there are numerous choices for the active vacationer.

ACTIVITIES A TO Z
BICYCLING/MOUNTAIN BIKING
The San Juan Islands, with their winding country roads and Puget Sound vistas, are the most popular bicycling locales in the state. Of the four main San Juan Islands (San Juan, Orcas, Lopez, and Shaw), Lopez has the easiest and Orcas the most challenging terrain for bikers. Here you can pedal for as many or as few days as you like, stopping at parks, inns, and quaint villages.

Other popular road-biking spots include Bainbridge and Vashon islands, with their easy access to Seattle; the Olympic Peninsula, with its scenic vistas and campgrounds; and the Long Beach Peninsula, with its miles of flat roads. Seattle, Tacoma, Spokane, and Yakima also all have many miles of easy bicycle trails that are either in parks or connect parks. The longest of these are in Seattle and Spokane.

The region's national forests provide miles of logging roads and single-track trails for mountain biking. However, the state's premier mountain-biking destination is the Methow Valley, where miles of cross-country ski trails are opened to bicycles in the summer.

To get a bicycling map of Washington, contact the **Bicycle Hot Line,** Washington State Department of Transportation, at © **360/705-7277.**

If you're interested in participating in an organized bicycle tour, there are a couple of companies you might want to contact. **Backroads,** 801 Cedar St., Berkeley, CA 94710-1800 (© **800/462-2848** or 510/527-1555; www.backroads.com), offers road bike trips in the San Juan Islands. Tour prices range from $1,198 to $2,198. **Bicycle Adventures,** P.O. Box 11219, Olympia, WA 98508 (© **800/443-6060** or 360/786-0989; www.bicycle adventures.com) offers biking trips in the San Juan Islands and Victoria, B.C., on the Olympic Peninsula, and to the volcanoes of Washington. Tour prices range from $954 to $2,488.

BIRD-WATCHING With a wide variety of habitats, Washington offers many excellent bird-watching spots. Each winter in January, bald eagles flock to the Skagit River, north of Seattle, to feast on salmon. Birders can observe from shore or on a guided raft trip. Outside the town of Hoquiam, migratory shorebirds make annual stops at the Gray's Harbor Wildlife Refuge in the Bowerman Basin area. One of Washington's best birding excursions is a ride through the San Juan Islands on one of the state-run ferries. From these floating observation platforms, birders can spot bald eagles and numerous pelagic birds.

CAMPING Public and private campgrounds abound all across Washington, with those in Mount Rainier National Park and Olympic National Park being the most popular. North Cascades National Park has campgrounds as well. At Olympic and North Cascades national parks, camping is on a first-come, first-served basis, while at two campgrounds within Mount Rainier National Park, reservations are taken. To get information on outdoor recreation in Washington's

national parks and forests, contact the **Outdoor Recreation Information Center,** Seattle REI Building, 222 Yale Ave. N., Seattle, WA 98109 (© **206/470-4060;** www.nps.gov/ccso/oric. htm). The Forest Service's regional Web page (**www.fs.fed.us/r6**) is another good source of information.

Washington also has more than 80 state parks with campgrounds. Moran State Park on Orcas Island and Deception Pass State Park have two of the most enjoyable campgrounds. For information on Washington state parks, contact **Washington State Parks and Recreation Commission,** 7150 Cleanwater Lane (P.O. Box 42650), Olympia, WA 98504-2650 (© **360/902-8844;** www.parks.wa.gov).

For state campsite reservations, contact **Washington State Parks Reservations** (© **888/226-7688;** www.parks. wa.gov). To make campsite reservations at national forest campgrounds, contact the **National Recreation Reservation Service** (© **877/444-6777** or 518/885-3639; www.reserve usa.com). For reservations at Mount Rainier, the only national park in Washington that offers campsite reservations, contact the **National Park Reservation Service** (© **800/365-2267** or 301/722-1257; http:// reservations.nps.gov).

One economical way to tour the Northwest is with a recreational vehicle. They can be rented for a weekend, a week, or longer. RVs can be rented in Washington from **Western Motorcoach Rentals,** 19303 Hwy. 99, Lynnwood, WA 98036 (© **800/800-1181** or 425/775-1181; www.western rv.com).

CANOEING/KAYAKING Whitewater kayakers in Washington head for such rivers as the Wenatchee around Leavenworth, the Methow near Winthrop, the Skagit and Skykomish rivers north of Seattle, and the White Salmon River near Trout Lake. On the Olympic Peninsula, the

Queets, Hoh, and Elwha rivers are the main kayaking rivers. One of the most popular canoeing lakes in Washington is Lake Ozette in Olympic National Park.

FISHING For information on freshwater fishing in Washington, contact the **Department of Wildlife,** Natural Resources Building, 1111 Washington St. SE, Olympia, WA 98501 (℃ **360/902-2200;** www.wa. gov/wdfw); mailing address: 600 Capitol Way N., Olympia, WA 98501-1091.

GOLFING Although the rainy weather in western Washington puts a bit of a damper on golfing, the mild temperatures mean that it's possible to play year-round. The state has only a handful of resorts with golf courses, but most larger cities have public courses. A couple of the state's most celebrated courses are in eastern Washington near the city of Wenatchee.

HIKING & BACKPACKING Washington has an abundance of hiking trails, including a section of the Pacific Crest Trail, which runs along the spine of the Cascades from Canada to the Oregon state line (and onward through California to Mexico). In the Olympic National Park, you'll find hikes along the beach, through valleys in rainforests, and through alpine meadows; at Mount Rainier National Park, you can hike through forests and the state's most beautiful meadows (hikes from Sunrise and Paradise are the most spectacular); and in North Cascades National Park, there are hiking trails through the state's most rugged scenery. The Alpine Lakes region outside Leavenworth is breathtakingly beautiful, but so popular that advance-reservation permits are required. Another popular hike is to the top of Mount St. Helens. Lesser known are the hiking trails on Mount Adams in Washington's southern Cascades. In the Columbia Gorge,

the hike up Dog Mountain is strenuous but rewarding. For general information on hiking in the Northwest and for information on the Northwest Forest Pass, which is required at most national forest trail heads in Washington, contact **Nature of the Northwest,** 800 NE Oregon St., Suite 177, Portland, OR 97232 (℃ **503/872-2750;** www.naturenw.org).

If you'd like to hike the wild country of Washington state with a knowledgeable guide, you've got a couple of good options. The **Olympic Park Institute,** 111 Barnes Point Rd., Port Angeles, WA 98363 (℃ **360/928-3720;** www.yni.org/opi), offers a variety of hiking and backpacking trips, as does the **North Cascades Institute,** 810 State Rte. 20, Sedro-Woolley, WA 98284-1239 (℃ **360/856-5700,** ext. 209; www.ncascades.org).

SEA KAYAKING Sea kayaks differ from river kayaks in that they are much longer, more stable, and able to carry gear as well as a paddler or two. There are few places in the country that offer better sea kayaking than the waters of Puget Sound and around the San Juan Islands, and therefore this sport is especially popular in the Seattle area. The protected waters of Puget Sound offer numerous spots for a paddle of anywhere from a few hours to a few days. There's even a water trail called the **Cascadia Marine Trail** that links camping spots throughout the Sound. For more information about this trail, contact the Washington Water Trails Association (℃ **206/545-9161;** www.wwta.org).

The San Juan Islands are by far the most popular sea-kayaking spot in the region, and several tiny islands, accessible only by boat, are designated state campsites. In the Seattle area, Lake Union and Lake Washington are both popular kayaking spots. Willapa Bay, on the Washington coast, is another popular paddling spot.

If you'd like to explore Puget Sound or Seattle's Lake Union in a sea kayak, contact the **Northwest Outdoor Center,** 2100 Westlake Ave. N., Suite 1, Seattle, WA 98109 (© **800/683-0637** or 206/281-9694; www.nwoc.com). This center rents kayaks and also offers various classes and guided trips. Day trips are $70, 3-day trips are $295, and 5-day classes are $625.

In the San Juan Islands, **San Juan Kayak Expeditions** (© **360/378-4436;** www.sanjuankayak.com) offers multi-day kayak trips, charging $380 for a 3-day trip and $480 for a 4-day trip. **Orcas Outdoors** (© **360/376-4611;** www.orcasoutdoors.com) offers 3-day trips for $350. **Crystal Seas Kayaking** (© **877/SEAS-877** or 360/378-4223; www.crystalseas.com) runs kayak camping trips ranging from 2 days ($279) to 6 days ($839), and inn-to-inn trips ranging from 2 days ($569) to 6 days ($1,999). **Sea Quest Expeditions/Zoetic Research** (© **888/589-4253** or 360/378-5767; www.sea-quest-kayak.com), is a non-profit organization that sponsors educational sea-kayaking trips through the San Juans. Three-day trips are $359 and 5-day trips are $599.

SKIING & SNOWBOARDING

Washington has about half a dozen major ski areas and about the same number of lesser areas. The major ski areas are all located in the Cascade Range. These include Mount Baker, a snowboarding mecca near Bellingham; Mission Ridge, which is located near Wenatchee and is known for its powder snow; Stevens Pass, which is near the Bavarian-theme town of Leavenworth; the Summit at Snoqualmie, which is located less than an hour from Seattle; Crystal Mountain near the northeast corner of Mount Rainier National Park; and White Pass, which is southeast of Mount Rainier National Park. For information on all of these ski areas, see chapter 9. Smaller and more remote ski areas include Mount Spokane and 49 Degrees North, both north of Spokane; and Ski Bluewood, near Walla Walla (see chapter 10 for information on these three ski areas). Tiny locals-only ski areas with only a handful of runs include Hurricane Ridge, in Olympic National Park (see chapter 7); Loup Loup, near Winthrop (see chapter 9); and Echo Valley, near Lake Chelan (see chapter 9). Heli-skiing is also available in the Methow Valley (see chapter 9).

Many downhill ski areas also offer groomed cross-country ski trails. The most popular cross-country areas in Washington include the Methow Valley (one of the largest trail systems in the country), Leavenworth, the Summit at Snoqualmie, White Pass, Stevens Pass, and near Mount St. Helens and Mount Adams.

WHALE-WATCHING

Orca whales, commonly called killer whales, are a symbol of the Northwest and are often seen in Puget Sound and around the San Juan Islands, especially during the summer. Dozens of companies offer whale-watching trips from the San Juans. You can also spot orcas from San Juan Island's Lime Kiln State Park. For information on orca-watching opportunities, see chapter 5. Out on the Washington coast, migrating gray whales can be seen March through May. In the town of Westport, there are both viewing areas and companies operating whale-watching excursions. For more information, see chapter 8.

WHITE-WATER RAFTING

Plenty of rain and lots of mountains combine to produce dozens of good white-water rafting rivers, depending on the time of year and water levels. In the Washington Cascades, some of the popular rafting rivers include the Wenatchee outside Leavenworth, the Methow near Winthrop, the Skagit and Skykomish rivers north of Seattle, and the White Salmon River near Trout Lake. On the Olympic Peninsula, the Queets, Hoh, and Elwha rivers are the main rafting rivers. See the respective chapters for information on rafting companies operating on these rivers. Rates generally range from about $50 to $75 for a half day to around $90 for a full day of rafting.

Many companies offer trips on several different rivers. Among these companies are Alpine Adventures Wild & Scenic River Tours (© **800/ RAFT-FUN** or 206/323-1220; www. alpineadventures.com), DownStream River Runners (© **800/234-4644** or 360/805-9899; www.riverpeople. com), North Cascades River Expeditions (© **800/634-8433;** www.river expeditions.com), Osprey Rafting Company (© **800/743-6269;** www. shoottherapids.com), River Riders (© **800/448-RAFT;** www.riverrider. com), and Wildwater River Tours (© **800/522-WILD** or 253/939-2151; www.wildwater-river.com).

SAILBOARDING   The Columbia River Gorge is one of the most renowned windsurfing spots in the world. Here, high winds and a strong current come together to produce radical sailing conditions. As the winds whip up the waves, skilled sailors rocket across the water and launch themselves skyward to perform aerial acrobatics. On calmer days and in spots where the wind isn't blowing so hard, there are also opportunities for novices to learn the basics. Summer is the best sailing season, and the town of Hood River, Oregon, just across the Columbia River from Bingen, Washington, is the center of the boarding scene with plenty of windsurfing schools and rental companies. Windsurfing is also popular on Lake Union in Seattle and Vancouver Lake in Vancouver, Washington.

7 Educational & Volunteer Vacations

On the Olympic Peninsula, the **Olympic Park Institute,** 111 Barnes Point Rd., Port Angeles, WA 98363 (© **360/928-3720;** www.yni.org/ opi), offers a wide array of summer field seminars ranging from painting classes to bird-watching trips to multiday backpacking trips.

The **North Cascades Institute,** 810 State Rte. 20, Sedro-Woolley, WA 98284 (© **360/856-5700,** ext. 209; www.ncascades.org), is a nonprofit organization that offers field seminars focusing on natural and cultural history in the North Cascades.

The Nature Conservancy is a nonprofit organization dedicated to the global preservation of natural diversity, and to this end it operates educational field trips and work parties to its own nature preserves and those of other agencies. For information about field trips in Washington, contact **The Nature Conservancy,** 217 Pine St.,

Suite 1100, Seattle, WA 98101 (© **206/343-4344;** http://nature.org).

If you enjoy the wilderness and want to get more involved in preserving it, consider a Sierra Club Service Trip. These trips are for the purpose of building, restoring, and maintaining hiking trails in wilderness areas. It's a lot of work, but it's also a lot of fun. For more information on Service Trips, contact **Sierra Club Outdoor Activities Department,** 85 Second St., Second Floor, San Francisco, CA 94105 (© **415/977-5500;** www.sierra club.org). Alternatively, you can call your local chapter of the Sierra Club or Washington's Cascade Chapter (© **206/523-2147;** http://cascade. sierraclub.org).

Earth Watch Institute, 3 Clock Tower Place, Suite 100 (Box 75), Maynard, MA 01754 (© **800/776-0188** or 978/461-0081; www.earthwatch. org), sends volunteers on scientific research projects. Contact them for a catalog listing trips and costs. Projects have included studies of glaciers in North Cascades National Park and programs on chimpanzee communication.

8 Specialized Travel Resources

TRAVELERS WITH DISABILITIES

When making airline reservations, always mention your disability. Airline policies differ regarding wheelchairs and Seeing Eye dogs. Most hotels now offer wheelchair-accessible accommodations, and some of the larger and more expensive hotels also offer TDD telephones and other amenities for the hearing and sight impaired.

The public transit systems found in most Northwest cities either have regular vehicles that are accessible for riders with disabilities or offer special transportation services for people with disabilities.

If you plan to visit Mount Rainier or Olympic National Park, you can avail yourself of the **Golden Access Passport.** This lifetime pass is issued free to any U.S. citizen or permanent resident who has been medically certified as disabled or blind (you will need to show proof of disability). The pass permits free entry into national parks and monuments and can be obtained through the visitor center at either Mount Rainier or Olympic National Park.

Many travel agencies offer customized tours and itineraries for travelers with disabilities. **Flying Wheels Travel** (© 507/451-5005; www. flyingwheelstravel.com) offers escorted tours and cruises that emphasize sports and private tours in minivans with lifts. **Accessible Journeys** (© 800/846-4537 or 610/521-0339; www. disabilitytravel.com) caters specifically to slow walkers and wheelchair travelers and their families and friends. **Wilderness Inquiry** (© 800/728-0719 or 612/676-9400; www. wildernessinquiry.org) offers trips to the San Juan Islands for persons of all abilities.

Organizations that offer assistance to travelers with disabilities include the **MossRehab Hospital** www.moss resourcenet.org), which provides a library of accessible-travel resources online; the Society for Accessible Travel and Hospitality (© 212/447-7284; www.sath.org; annual membership fees: $45 adults, $30 seniors and students), which offers a wealth of travel resources for all types of disabilities and informed recommendations on destinations, access guides, travel agents, tour operators, vehicle rentals, and companion services; and the **American Foundation for the Blind** (© 800/232-5463; www.afb.org), which provides information on traveling with Seeing Eye dogs.

GAY & LESBIAN TRAVELERS

Seattle is one of the most gay-friendly cities in the country, with a large gay and lesbian community centered around the Capitol Hill neighborhood. In Capitol Hill you'll find numerous bars, nightclubs, stores, and bed-and-breakfast inns catering to the gay community. Broadway Avenue, Capitol Hill's main drag, is also the site of the annual Gay Pride March, held each year in late June.

The *Seattle Gay News* (© 206/324-4297; www.sgn.org) is the community's newspaper, available at bookstores and gay bars and nightclubs.

Beyond the Closet, 518 E. Pike St. (© 206/322-4609), and Bailey Coy Books, 414 Broadway Ave. E. (© 206/323-8842), are the gay community's two main bookstores and are good sources of information on what's going on within the community.

The Lesbian Resource Center, 2214 S. Jackson St. (© **206/322-3953;** www. lrc.net), is a community resource center that provides housing and job information, therapy, and business referrals.

The Gaslight Inn is a gay-friendly bed-and-breakfast in the Capitol Hill area; see "Where to Stay " in chapter 4 for a full review. For information on gay and lesbian bars and nightclubs, see "After Dark" in chapter 4.

SENIOR TRAVEL

Don't be shy about asking for discounts, but always carry some kind of identification, such as a driver's license, that shows your date of birth, especially if you've kept your youthful glow. In Seattle, most attractions, some theaters and concert halls, tour companies, and the Washington State Ferries all offer senior discounts. These can add up to substantial savings, but you have to remember to ask.

Discounts abound for seniors, beginning with the 10%-off-your-airfare deal that most airlines offer to anyone age 62 or older. In addition, a number of airlines have clubs you can join and coupon books you can buy that may or may not increase your savings beyond that base 10% discount, depending on how often you travel, where you're going, and how long you're going to stay. Always ask an airline whether it has a club for seniors or sells coupon books, either of which often qualifies "mature" travelers for discounted tickets.

Many hotels offer senior discounts. **Choice Hotels** (Clarion Hotels, Quality Inns, Comfort Inns, and Sleep Inns), for example, give 20% to 30% off their published rates to anyone over 60 depending on availability, provided you book your room through their nationwide toll-free reservations numbers (not directly with the hotels or through a travel agent).

Members of **AARP,** 601 E St. NW, Washington, DC 20049 (© **800/ 424-3410** or 202/434-2277; www. aarp.org), get discounts on many lodgings, airfares, car rentals, and attractions throughout Washington. Anyone over 50 can join.

If you plan to visit either Mount Rainier National Park or Olympic National Park while in the Seattle area, you can save on park admissions by getting a **Golden Age Passport,** available for $10 to U.S. citizens and permanent residents age 62 and older. This federal government pass allows lifetime entrance privileges. You can apply in person for this passport at a national park or other location where it's honored, as long as you can show reasonable proof of age. For more information, check out www.nps.gov/ fees_passes.htm or call © **888/GO-PARKS.**

Many reliable agencies and organizations target the 50-plus market. **Elderhostel** (© **877/426-8056;** www.elder hostel.org) arranges study programs for those ages 55 and over (and a spouse or companion of any age) in the U.S. and in more than 80 countries around the world. Most courses last 5 to 7 days in the U.S. (2–4 weeks abroad), and many include airfare, accommodations in university dormitories or modest inns, meals, and tuition.

FAMILY TRAVEL

If you have enough trouble getting your kids out of the house in the morning, dragging them thousands of miles away may seem like an insurmountable challenge. But family travel can be immensely rewarding, giving you new ways of seeing the world through smaller pairs of eyes.

Families traveling in Washington should be sure to take note of family admission fees at many museums and other attractions. These admission prices are often less than what it would cost for individual tickets for the whole family. At hotels and motels, children usually stay free if they share their parents' room and no extra bed is required, and sometimes they also get to eat for free in the hotel dining room. Be sure to ask.

Frommer's Family Vacations in the National Parks (Wiley Publishing, Inc.) has tips for enjoying your trip to Olympic National Park.

Note: If you plan to travel on to Canada during your Seattle vacation, be sure to bring your children's birth certificates with you.

9 Planning Your Trip Online

SURFING FOR AIRFARES

The "big three" online travel agencies, Expedia.com, Travelocity.com, and Orbitz.com, sell most of the air tickets bought on the Internet. (Canadian travelers should try expedia.ca and Travelocity.ca; U.K. residents can go for expedia.co.uk and opodo.co.uk.) Each has different business deals with the airlines and may offer different fares on the same flights, so it's wise to shop around. Expedia and Travelocity will also send you e-mail notification when a cheap fare becomes available to your favorite destination.

Also remember to check **airline websites,** especially those for low-fare carriers such as Southwest. Even with major airlines, you can often shave a few bucks from a fare by booking directly through the airline. Most airlines now offer **online-only fares** that even their phone agents know nothing about. For the websites of airlines that fly to and from your destination, go to "Getting There," below.

Great **last-minute deals** are available through free weekly e-mail services provided directly by the airlines. Most of these are announced on Tuesday or Wednesday and must be purchased online. Most are only valid for travel that weekend, but some (such as Southwest's) can be booked weeks or months in advance. Sign up for weekly e-mail alerts at airline websites or check mega-sites that compile comprehensive lists of last-minute specials, such as **Smarter Living** (smarterliving.com).

Frommers.com: The Complete Travel Resource

For an excellent travel-planning resource, we highly recommend Frommers.com (www.frommers.com). We're a little biased, of course, but we guarantee that you'll find the travel tips, reviews, monthly vacation giveaways, and online-booking capabilities indispensable. Among the special features are our popular **Message Boards,** where Frommer's readers post queries and share advice (sometimes we authors even show up to answer questions); **Frommers.com Newsletter,** for the latest travel bargains and insider travel secrets; and **Frommer's Destinations Section,** where you'll get expert travel tips, hotel and dining recommendations, and advice on the sights to see for more than 3,000 destinations around the globe. When your research is done, the **Online Reservations System** (www.frommers.com/book_a_trip) takes you to Frommer's preferred online partners for booking your vacation at affordable prices.

SURFING FOR HOTELS

Of the "big three" sites, **Expedia** may be the best choice, thanks to its long list of special deals. **Travelocity** runs a close second. Hotel specialist sites **hotels.com** and **hoteldiscounts.com** are also reliable. An excellent free program, **TravelAxe** (www.travelaxe.net), can help you search multiple hotel sites at once.

10 The 21st-Century Traveler

INTERNET ACCESS AWAY FROM HOME

Travelers have any number of ways to check their e-mail and access the Internet on the road. Of course, using your own laptop—or even a PDA (personal digital assistant) or electronic organizer with a modem—gives you the most flexibility. But even if you don't have a computer, you can still access your e-mail and even your office computer from cybercafes.

WITHOUT YOUR OWN COMPUTER

It's hard nowadays to find a city that *doesn't* have a few cybercafes. Although there's no definitive directory for cybercafes—these are independent businesses, after all—three places to look are **www.cybercaptive.com, www. netcafeguide.com**, and **www.cyber cafe.com**.

Aside from formal cybercafes, most **public libraries** across the country offer Internet access free or for a small charge. **Hotels** that cater to business travelers often have **in-room dataports** and **business centers,** but the charges can be exorbitant. Also, most **youth hostels** nowadays have at least one computer where you can access the Internet.

To retrieve your e-mail, ask your **Internet Service Provider (ISP)** if it has a web-based interface tied to your existing e-mail account. If your ISP doesn't have such an interface, you can use the free **mail2web** service (www. mail2web.com) to view your home e-mail. For more flexibility, you may want to open a free, web-based e-mail account with **Yahoo! Mail** (mail. yahoo.com). (Microsoft's Hotmail is another popular option, but Hotmail has severe spam problems.) Your home ISP may be able to forward your e-mail to the web-based account automatically.

WITH YOUR OWN COMPUTER

Major **Internet Service Providers (ISP)** have local access numbers around the world, allowing you to go online by simply placing a local call. Check your ISP's website or call its toll-free number and ask how you can use your current account away from home.

Wherever you go, bring a **connection kit** of the right power and phone adapters, a spare phone cord, and a spare Ethernet network cable.

Most business-class hotels throughout the world offer dataports for laptop modems, and a few thousand hotels in the U.S. and Europe now offer high-speed Internet access using an Ethernet network cable. You'll have to bring your own cables either way, so **call your hotel in advance** to find out what the options are.

Many business-class hotels in the U.S. also offer a form of computer-free web browsing through the room TV set. We've successfully checked Yahoo! Mail, but not Hotmail, on these systems.

If you have an 802.11b/**Wi-fi** card for your computer, several commercial companies have made wireless service available in airports, hotel lobbies, and coffee shops, primarily in the U.S. **T-Mobile Hotspot** (www.t-mobile. com/hotspot) serves up wireless connections at more than 1,000 Starbucks coffee shops nationwide. **Boingo** (www.boingo.com) and **Wayport**

Online Traveler's Toolbox

Veteran travelers usually carry some essential items to make their trips easier. Following is a selection of online tools to bookmark and use.

- **Mapquest** (www.mapquest.com): This best of the mapping sites lets you choose a specific address or destination, and in seconds, it will return a map and detailed directions.
- **http://seattle.citysearch.com**: CitySearch includes listings and reviews for dining, nightlife, shopping, and more by neighborhood and date (with a handy interactive calendar). In addition to places and events, you can also check the weather or get driving directions.
- **www.seeseattle.org**: Here at the official Seattle's Convention and Visitors Bureau website, you can check a calendar of events, learn more about attractions (from museums, to theaters, to shopping, to sports), and download coupons good for discounts at area attractions and on lodgings.
- **www.seattletimes.com**: A solid virtual version of Seattle's print stalwart, the *Seattle Times,* offers many of the paper's stories online. There's also an entertainment section with information on movies, theater, and concerts around town.
- **www.seattleweekly.com**: *Seattle Weekly* is Seattle's main arts-and-entertainment weekly and provides detailed information on what's happening in film, music, theater, and the arts. The weekly also features an extensive dining guide and database of restaurant reviews.
- **www.seatac.org/seatac**: At the Seattle–Tacoma International Airport's website, you'll find maps of individual terminals to help you find your way around. Parking and transportation news also comes in handy. Here you can also keep tabs on any construction projects underway at the airport. A large list of links will point you to everything from freeway traffic updates to local lodging.
- **www.wsdot.wa.gov/ferries**: This is the official website for Washington State Ferries, which are an essential part of any visit to Seattle. This site offers route destinations, schedule and fare information, and an online ferry reservation service for ferries to Sidney, British Columbia (near Victoria), as well as a section of things to do at various stops along the ferry routes.

(www.wayport.com) have set up networks in airports and high-class hotel lobbies. IPass providers (see above) also give you access to a few hundred wireless hotel lobby setups. Best of all, you don't need to be staying at the Four Seasons to use the hotel's network; just set yourself up on a nice couch in the lobby.

11 Getting There

BY PLANE
THE MAJOR AIRLINES
The **Seattle–Tacoma International Airport** (© **800/544-1965** or 206/431-4444; www.portseattle.org/seatac) is served by about 30 airlines. The major carriers include: **Air Canada** (© **800/247-2262;** www.aircanada.ca),

Alaska Airlines (✆ 800/426-0333; www.alaskaair.com), **America West** (✆ 800/235-9292; www.americawest. com), **American Airlines** (✆ 800/433-7300; www.aa.com), **Continental** (✆ 800/525-0280; www.continental. com), **Delta** (✆ 800/221-1212; www. delta.com), **Frontier** (✆ 800/432-1359; www.flyfrontier.com), **Horizon Air** (✆ 800/547-9308; www.horizon air.com), **JetBlue Airways** (✆ 800/ JETBLUE; www.jetblue.com), **North-west/KLM** (✆ 800/225-2525; www. nwa.com), **Southwest** (✆ 800/435-9792; www.southwest.com), **United** (✆ 800/241-6522; www.ual.com), and **US Airways** (✆ 800/428-4322; www. usairways.com).

For information on flights to the United States from other countries, see "Getting to the U.S." in chapter 3.

Seaplane service between Seattle and the San Juan Islands and Victoria, British Columbia, is offered by **Kenmore Air** (✆ **800/543-9595** or 425/486-1257; www.kenmoreair.com), which has its Seattle terminals at the south end of Lake Union and at the north end of Lake Washington.

There is also helicopter service to Seattle's Boeing Field from Victoria and Vancouver, British Columbia, on **Helijet Airways** (✆ **800/665-4354** or 250/382-6222; www.helijet.com). The flights take about 35 minutes from Victoria and 80 minutes from Vancouver (depending on the connection, as you must connect in Victoria for the flight to Seattle). Ballpark round-trip airfares are $238 to $278 between Victoria and Seattle and $440 to $506 between Vancouver and Seattle.

GETTING THROUGH THE AIRPORT

With the federalization of airport security, security procedures at U.S. airports are more stable and consistent than ever. Generally, you'll be fine if you arrive at the airport **1 hour** before a domestic flight and **2 hours** before

an international flight; if you show up late, tell an airline employee and he or she will probably whisk you to the front of the line.

Bring a **current, government-issued photo ID** such as a driver's license or passport. Keep your ID at the ready to show at check-in, the security checkpoint, and sometimes even the gate. (Children under 18 do not need photo IDs for domestic flights, but the adults checking in with them should have them.)

In 2003, the TSA phased out **gate check-in** at all U.S. airports. Passengers with E-tickets can still beat the ticket-counter lines by using **electronic kiosks** or even **online check-in.** Ask your airline which alternatives are available, and if you're using a kiosk, bring the credit card you used to book the ticket or your frequent-flier card. If you're checking bags or looking to snag an exit-row seat, you will be able to do so using most airlines' kiosks; again, call your airline for up-to-date information. **Curbside check-in** is also a good way to avoid lines, although a few airlines still ban curbside check-in; call before you go.

Security checkpoint lines are getting shorter than they were during 2001 and 2002, but some doozies remain. If you have trouble standing for long periods of time, tell an airline employee; the airline will provide a wheelchair. Speed up security by **not wearing metal objects** such as big belt buckles. If you've got metallic body parts, a note from your doctor can prevent a long chat with the security screeners. Keep in mind that only **ticketed passengers** are allowed past security, except for folks escorting children or passengers with disabilities.

Federalization has stabilized **what you can carry on** and **what you can't.** The general rule is that sharp things are out, nail clippers are okay, and food and beverages must be passed through the X-ray machine—but that security screeners can't make you drink from your coffee cup. Bring food in your carry-on rather than checking it, as explosive-detection machines used on checked luggage have been known to mistake food (especially chocolate, for some reason) for bombs. Travelers in the U.S. are allowed one carry-on bag, plus a "personal item" such as a purse, briefcase, or laptop bag. Carry-on hoarders can stuff all sorts of things into a laptop bag; as long as it has a laptop in it, it's still considered a personal item. The Transportation Security Administration (TSA) has issued a list of restricted items; check its website (www.tsa.gov/public/index.jsp) for details.

At press time, the TSA is also recommending that you **not lock your checked luggage** so screeners can search it by hand if necessary. The agency says to use plastic "zip ties" instead, which can be bought at hardware stores and can be easily cut off.

FLY FOR LESS: TIPS ON GETTING THE BEST AIRFARES

Passengers sharing the same airplane cabin rarely pay the same fare. Here are some ways to keep your airfare costs down.

- Passengers who can book their ticket **long in advance,** who can **stay over Saturday night,** or who **fly midweek** or **at less-trafficked hours** will pay a fraction of the full fare. If your schedule is flexible, say so, and ask if you can secure a cheaper fare by changing your flight plans.
- You can also save on airfares by keeping an eye out in local newspapers for **promotional specials** or **fare wars,** when airlines lower prices on their most popular routes. You rarely see fare wars offered for peak travel times, but if you can travel in the off-months, you may snag a bargain.

- **Consolidators,** also known as bucket shops, are great sources for international tickets, although they usually can't beat the Internet on fares within North America. Start by looking in Sunday newspaper travel sections. **Warning:** Bucket shop tickets are usually nonrefundable or rigged with stiff cancellation penalties, often as high as 50% to 75% of the ticket price, and some put you on charter airlines with questionable safety records. Several reliable consolidators are worldwide and available on the Net.
- For many more tips about air travel, including a rundown of the major frequent-flier credit cards, pick up a copy of *Frommer's Fly Safe, Fly Smart* (Wiley Publishing, Inc.).

BY CAR

Seattle is 1,190 miles from Los Angeles, 175 miles from Portland, 835 miles from Salt Lake City, 810 miles from San Francisco, 285 miles from Spokane, and 110 miles from Vancouver, British Columbia.

I-5 is the main north-south artery through Seattle, running south to Portland and north to the Canadian border. I-405 is Seattle's east-side bypass and accesses the cities of Bellevue, Redmond, and Kirkland on the east side of Lake Washington. I-90, which ends at I-5, connects Seattle to Spokane in the eastern part of Washington. Wash. 520 connects I-405 with Seattle just north of downtown and also ends at I-5. Wash. 99, the Alaskan Way Viaduct, is another major north-south highway through downtown Seattle; it passes through the waterfront section of the city.

One of the most important benefits of belonging to the **American Automobile Association (AAA)** (*©* **800/ 222-4357;** www.aaa.com) is that it supplies members with emergency road service and towing services if you have car trouble during your trip. You also get maps and detailed Trip-Tiks that give precise directions to a destination, including up-to-date information about areas of construction. In Seattle, AAA is located at 330 Sixth Ave. N. (© 206/448-5353).

See "Getting Around" in chapter 4 for details on driving, parking, and car rentals in Seattle.

BY TRAIN

Amtrak (© 800/872-7245; www. amtrak.com) service runs from Vancouver, B.C., to Seattle and from Portland and as far south as Eugene, Oregon, on the *Cascades* (a high-speed Talgo train). The train takes about 4 hours from Vancouver to Seattle and 3½ to 4 hours from Portland to Seattle. One-way fares from Vancouver to Seattle or from Portland to Seattle are usually between $25 and $30. There is also Amtrak service to Seattle from San Diego, Los Angeles, San Francisco, and Portland on the *Coast Starlight,* and from Spokane and points east on the *Empire Builder.* Amtrak also operates a bus between Vancouver and Seattle.

Like the airlines, Amtrak offers several discounted fares; although they're not all based on advance purchase, you have more discount options by reserving early. The discount fares can be used only on certain days and hours of the day; be sure to find out exactly what restrictions apply. Tickets for children ages 2 to 15 cost half the price of a regular coach fare when the children are accompanied by a fare-paying adult. Amtrak's website features a bargain fares service, "Rail Sale," which allows you to purchase tickets for one-way designated coach seats at great discounts. This program is only available on www.amtrak.com when you charge your tickets by credit card.

Also inquire about money-saving packages that include hotel accommodations, car rentals, tours, and so on with your train fare. Call © **800/321-8684** for details.

BY FERRY

If you are traveling between Victoria, British Columbia, and Seattle, several options are available from **Victoria Clipper,** Pier 69, 2701 Alaskan Way (© **800/888-2535,** 206/448-5000, or 250/382-8100 in Victoria; www. victoriaclipper.com). Throughout the year, a ferry taking either 2 or 3 hours makes the trip ($61–$127 round-trip for adults). The lower fare is for advance-purchase tickets. Some scheduled trips also stop in the San Juan Islands.

Bellingham, north of Seattle, is the port for Alaska ferries and cruise ships.

PACKAGE TOURS

Gray Line of Seattle (© **800/426-7505** or 206/626-5208; www.gray lineofseattle.com) offers 2- to 7-day bus and cruise tours that include Seattle, Mount Rainier, Vancouver, and Victoria. Prices range from about $135 for a 2-day trip to $785 for a 7-day trip.

If you prefer traveling on your own, but would like to have a custom itinerary planned for your trip to Washington or the Northwest, consider consulting **Pacific Northwest Journeys** (© **800/935-9730** or 206/935-9730; www.pnw journeys.com). This company can tailor a trip that suits your personal traveling style.

12 Getting Around

BY CAR

A car is by far the best way to see the state of Washington. There just isn't any other way to get to the more remote natural spectacles or to fully appreciate such regions as the Olympic Peninsula.

All the major car-rental agencies have offices in Seattle and at or near Seattle–Tacoma International Airport.

Washington Driving Distances

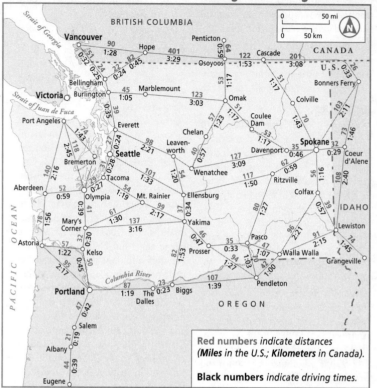

Red numbers *indicate distances* (**Miles** *in the U.S.;* **Kilometers** *in Canada).*

Black numbers *indicate driving times.*

Companies with a desk and cars inside the terminal include **Alamo** (℃ 800/327-9633 or 206/433-0182; www.go alamo.com), **Avis** (℃ 800/331-1212 or 206/433-5231; www.avis.com), **Budget** (℃ 800/527-0700 or 206/682-8989; www.budget.com), **Hertz** (℃ 800/654-3131 or 206/248-1300; www.hertz.com), and **National** (℃ 800/227-7368 or 206/433-5501; www.nationalcar.com). Companies with desks inside the terminal but cars parked off the airport premises include **Advantage** (℃ 800/777-5500 or 206/824-0161; www.arac.com), **Dollar** (℃ 800/800-4000 or 206/433-6777; www.dollar.com), **Enterprise** (℃ 800/736-8222 or 206/246-1953; www.enterprise.com), and

Thrifty (℃ 800/367-2277 or 206/625-1133; www.thrifty.com).

Gasoline Washington is a big state, so keep your gas tank as full as possible when traveling in the mountains or on the sparsely populated east side of the Cascades.

Maps Maps are available at most highway tourist information centers, at the tourist information offices listed earlier in this chapter, and at gas stations throughout the region. For a free map of Washington call the **Washington State Tourism Office** (℃ 800/544-1800).

Driving Rules A right turn on red is permitted after first coming to a complete stop. You may also turn left on a red light if you're in the far-left lane of a one-way street and are turning into another one-way street. Seat belts are required, as are car seats for children.

Breakdowns/Assistance In the event of a breakdown, stay with your car, lift the hood, turn on your emergency flashers, and wait for a police patrol car.

BY PLANE

Washington is a large state, and if you're trying to see every corner of it in a short time, you may want to consider flying. There are airports with regularly scheduled commercial flights at Bellingham, Whidbey Island, Port Angeles, Yakima, and Spokane. Fares vary but at press time, a one-way flight between Bellingham and Spokane (with a stop in Seattle) on Alaska Airlines was quoted at $193 with a 7-day advance purchase, and $225 with no advance purchase. Airlines operating short hops between many of these towns and cities include **Alaska Airlines** (© 800/426-0333; www. alaskaair.com), **Horizon Air** (© 800/ 547-9308; www.horizonair.com), and **Southwest** (© 800/435-9792; www. southwest.com).

Seaplane service between Seattle and the San Juan Islands and Victoria, British Columbia, is offered by **Kenmore Air** (© 800/543-9595 or 425/ 486-1257; www.kenmoreair.com), which has its Seattle terminals at the south end of Lake Union and at the north end of Lake Washington. **San Juan Airlines** (© 800/690-0086; www.sanjuanairlines.com) flies to the San Juans from Seattle's Boeing Field, while the affiliated **West Isle Air** (© 800/874-4434; www.westisle air.com) flies from Bellingham and Anacortes.

BY TRAIN

There is **Amtrak** service from Seattle to Spokane and points east, and service between Vancouver, B.C., Seattle, Portland, and points south, but otherwise the train isn't a viable way of getting around Washington state. If you do decide to take the train, booking early will save you money.

BY FERRY

Washington State Ferries (© 800/ 843-3779 or 888/808-7977 within Washington state, or 206/464-6400; www.wsdot.wa.gov/ferries) is the most extensive ferry system in the United States. Car ferries travel between downtown Seattle and both Bainbridge Island and Bremerton (on the Kitsap Peninsula) from Pier 52, Colman dock. Ferries also sail between Fauntleroy (in West Seattle) and both Vashon Island and the Kitsap Peninsula at Southworth; between Tahlequah at the south end of Vashon Island and Point Defiance in Tacoma; between Edmonds and Kingston (on the Kitsap Peninsula); between Mukilteo and Whidbey Island; between Whidbey Island at Keystone and Port Townsend; and between Anacortes and the San Juan Islands and Sidney, British Columbia (on Vancouver Island near Victoria). See specific destinations in chapters 4, 5, 6, and 7 for fare information.

There are also a number of smaller county or private ferries. The most important of these are the **Black Ball Transport** (© 360/457-4491, or 250/386-2202 in Victoria; www. cohoferry.com) and **Victoria Express** (© 800/633-1589 in Washington, or 360/452-8088; www.victoriaexpress. com) ferries that operate between Port Angeles and Victoria, British Columbia. Victoria Express runs only from Memorial Day weekend to the end of September. There's also passenger-ferry service between Seattle and San Juan Island and Orcas Island (summer only), and between Seattle and Victoria, British Columbia, on the **Victoria Clipper** ferries (© 800/888-2535 from outside Seattle and Victoria, 206/448-5000 or 250/382-8100 in Victoria; www.victoriaclipper.com).

13 Cruises

While Washington is not a big cruise-ship destination per se, there are several companies offering Alaska cruises that start in Washington and spend a little time cruising through the waters of Puget Sound and the San Juan Islands. There are also several smaller cruise lines that offer specialty cruises on small ships. Note that rates listed below are per person based on double occupancy.

In the big-ship category, there are several companies. There are 7-day, 6-night Alaska cruises offered by **Norwegian Cruise Lines** (✆ 800/327-7030; www.ncl.com). These cruises leave from Seattle and cost between about $1,800 and $2,800. **Holland America Line** (✆ 877/932-4259; www.hollandamerica.com) offers similar cruises starting around $1,000. Three- and 4-day cruises between Seattle and Vancouver, B.C. are also available and start around $400. **Princess Cruises** (✆ 800/421-1700; www.princess.com) also offers 7-day cruises aboard its *Star Princess.*

Cruises on smaller ships are offered by several other companies. **Lindblad Expeditions** (✆ 800/397-3348 or 212/765-7740; www.expeditions.com) offers a 7-day cruise through the San Juan Islands to Victoria. This cruise costs $2,330. **Cruise West** (✆ 800/580-0072; www.cruisewest.com) offers an 8-day cruise from Seattle to British Columbia and through the San Juan Islands. Fares range from about $1,649 to $3,399 per person. **Catalyst Cruises** (✆ 800/670-7678; www.cruise-nw.com) offers 7-day San Juan Island cruises on a 62-foot yacht. The fare is $1,750 per person based on double occupancy.

There are also a number of cruises up the Columbia River. Most of these play up the Lewis and Clark history and offer plenty of land excursions. If you prefer cruising aboard a small vessel, consider a trip with **Cruise West** (✆ 800/580-0072; www.cruisewest.com), which offers an 8-day cruise from Portland on the Columbia and Snake rivers. Fares range from $1,799 to $4,049 per person (with $200 discounts for 6-month advance bookings). A 7-day cruise with naturalists and historians on board is offered by **Lindblad Expeditions** (✆ 800/397-3348 or 212/765-7740; www.expeditions.com), which charges $2,390.

The *Queen of the West* and the *Empress of the North,* two modern paddle-wheel cruise ships operated by the **American West Steamboat Company,** 2101 Fourth Ave., Suite 1150, Seattle, WA 98121 (✆ 800/434-1232; www.columbiarivercruise.com), cruise the Columbia. Fares for the 7-night cruise range from $1,195 to $4,845 per person. The *Empress of the North* also cruises from Seattle to Alaska.

FAST FACTS: Washington

AAA If you're a member of the American Automobile Association and your car breaks down, call ✆ 800/AAA-HELP for 24-hour emergency road service.

American Express In Seattle, the Amex office is in the Plaza 600 building at 600 Stewart St. (✆ 206/441-8622). The office is open Monday through Friday from 8:30am to 5:30pm. For card member services, phone ✆ 800/528-4800. Call ✆ 800/AXP-TRIP or go to www.americanexpress.com for other locations or general information.

Car Rentals See "Getting Around," above.

Climate See "When to Go," earlier in this chapter.

Driving Rules See "Getting Around," above.

Drugstores Rite-Aid (www.riteaid.com for locations) and Walgreens (℃ 800/WALGREENS for locations) are two large pharmacy chains found in the Northwest.

Embassies & Consulates See "Fast Facts: For the International Traveler," in chapter 3.

Emergencies Call ℃ 911 for fire, police, and ambulance.

Information See "Visitor Information," earlier in this chapter, and individual city chapters for local information offices.

Liquor Laws The legal minimum drinking age in Washington state is 21. Aside from on-premise sales of cocktails in bars and restaurants, hard liquor can only be purchased in liquor stores. Beer and wine are available in convenience stores and grocery stores. Brewpubs tend to sell only beer and wine, but some also have licenses to sell hard liquor.

Maps See "Getting Around," above.

Police To reach the police, dial ℃ 911.

Taxes The state of Washington makes up for its lack of an income tax with its heavy sales tax, and counties add on their own as well. In Seattle you'll pay 8.8%. Hotel-room tax in the Seattle metro area ranges from 10% to 16%. On rental cars, you'll pay not only an 18.5% car-rental tax, but also, if you rent at the airport, an additional 10% to 11% airport concession fee, for a whopping total of around 30%! You eliminate 10% of this by renting your car somewhere other than the airport.

Time Zone Washington state is on Pacific Standard Time (PST) and observes daylight savings time from the first Sunday in April to the last Sunday in October, making it consistently 3 hours behind the U.S. East Coast.

Weather To check the weather report, call **206/442-2800,** ext. 2032. Check the *Seattle Times* or *Seattle Post-Intelligencer* newspapers for forecasts. If you want to know how to pack before you arrive, go to **www.wrh.noaa. gov/seattle, www.cnn.com/weather,** or **www.weather.com.**

3

For International Visitors

Although American trends have spread across Europe and other parts of the world to the extent that America may seem like familiar territory before your arrival, there are still many peculiarities and uniquely American situations that any foreign visitor will encounter.

1 Preparing for Your Trip

ENTRY REQUIREMENTS

Immigration law is a hot political issue in the United States these days, and the following requirements may have changed somewhat by the time you plan your trip. Check at any U.S. embassy or consulate for current information and requirements. You can also go to the **U.S. State Department** website at **www.travel.state.gov**.

VISAS The U.S. State Department has a **Visa Waiver Program** allowing citizens of certain countries to enter the United States without a visa for stays of up to 90 days. At press time, these countries included Andorra, Australia, Austria, Belgium, Brunei, Denmark, Finland, France, Germany, Iceland, Ireland, Italy, Japan, Liechtenstein, Luxembourg, Monaco, the Netherlands, New Zealand, Norway, Portugal, San Marino, Singapore, Slovenia, Spain, Sweden, Switzerland, the United Kingdom, and Uruguay. Citizens of these countries need only a valid machine-readable passport and a round-trip air or cruise ticket in their possession upon arrival. If they first enter the United States, they may also visit Mexico, Canada, Bermuda, and/or the Caribbean islands and return to the United States without a visa. Canadian citizens may enter the United States without a visa; they need only proof of residence.

Citizens of all other countries must have (1) a valid passport that expires at least 6 months later than the scheduled end of their visit to the United States, and (2) a tourist visa, which can be obtained without charge from any U.S. consulate.

To obtain a visa, the traveler must submit a completed application form (either in person or by mail) with a 1½-inch-square photo, and must demonstrate binding ties to a residence abroad. Usually you can get a visa at once or within 24 hours, but it may take longer during the summer rush from June to August. If you cannot go in person, contact the nearest U.S. embassy or consulate for directions on applying by mail. Your travel agent or airline office may also be able to supply you with visa applications and instructions. The U.S. consulate or embassy that issues your visa determines whether you will receive a multiple- or single-entry visa and any restrictions on the length of your stay.

British subjects can get up-to-date passport and visa information by calling the **U.S. Embassy Visa Information Line** (© 09055/444-556) or the **United Kingdom Passport Service** (© 0870/521-0410).

Irish citizens can obtain up-to-date visa information through the **Embassy of USA Dublin,** 42 Elgin Rd., Dublin

4, Ireland (℡ **3531/668-8777**), or by checking the "Consular Services" section of the website at www.us embassy.ie.

Australian citizens can obtain up-to-date visa information by contacting the **U.S. Embassy Canberra,** Moonah Place, Yarralumla, ACT 2600 (℡ **02/6214-5600**), or by checking the U.S. Diplomatic Mission's website at http://usembassy-australia.state.gov/consular.

Citizens of **New Zealand** can obtain up-to-date visa information by contacting the **U.S. Embassy New Zealand,** 29 Fitzherbert Terrace, Thorndon, Wellington (℡ **649/303-2724**), or get the information directly from the "Services to New Zealanders" section of the website at http://usembassy.org.nz.

MEDICAL REQUIREMENTS
Unless you're arriving from an area known to be suffering from an epidemic (particularly cholera or yellow fever), inoculations or vaccinations are not required for entry into the United States. If you have a medical condition that requires **syringe-administered medications,** carry a valid signed prescription from your physician—the Federal Aviation Administration (FAA) no longer allows airline passengers to pack syringes in their carry-on baggage without documented proof of medical need. If you have a disease that requires treatment with **narcotics,** you should also carry documented proof with you—smuggling narcotics aboard a plane is a serious offense that carries severe penalties in the U.S.

For **HIV-positive visitors,** requirements for entering the United States are somewhat vague and change frequently. According to the latest publication of *HIV and Immigrants: A Manual for AIDS Service Providers,* the Immigration and Naturalization Service (INS) doesn't require a medical exam for entry into the United States, but INS officials may stop individuals because they look sick or because they are carrying AIDS/HIV medicine.

For up-to-the-minute information, contact the Department of Health and Human Service's **AIDSinfo** (℡ **301/519-0459;** www.hivatis.org) or the **Gay Men's Health Crisis** (℡ **212/807-6655;** www.gmhc.org).

DRIVER'S LICENSES Foreign driver's licenses are usually recognized in the United States, although you may want to get an international driver's license if your home license is not written in English.

PASSPORT INFORMATION
Safeguard your passport in an inconspicuous, inaccessible place like a money belt. Make a copy of the critical pages, including the passport number, and store it in a safe place, separate from the passport itself. If you lose your passport, visit the nearest consulate of your native country as soon as possible for a replacement. Passport applications are downloadable from most of the websites listed below.

FOR RESIDENTS OF CANADA
You can pick up a passport application at one of 29 regional passport offices or at any Canada Post outlet. Canadian children who travel must have their own passport. However, if you hold a valid Canadian passport issued before December 11, 2001, that bears the name of your child, the passport remains valid for you and your child until it expires. Passports cost C$85 for those 16 years and older (valid 5 years), C$35 for children 3 to 15 (valid 5 years), and C$20 for children under 3 (valid for 3 years). Applications, which must be accompanied by two identical passport-size photographs and proof of Canadian citizenship, are available at travel agencies throughout Canada or from the central **Passport Office,** Department of Foreign Affairs and International Trade, Ottawa, ON K1A

0G3 (© **800/567-6868;** www.dfait-maeci.gc.ca/passport).

FOR RESIDENTS OF THE UNITED KINGDOM

To pick up an application for a standard 10-year passport (5-year passport for children under 16), visit the nearest Passport Office, major post office, or travel agency. You can also contact the **United Kingdom Passport Service** at © **0870/521-0410** or visit its website at www.passport.gov.uk. Passports are £33 for adults and £19 for children under 16, with an additional £30 fee if you apply in person at a Passport Office.

FOR RESIDENTS OF IRELAND

You can apply for a 10-year passport, costing €57, at the **Passport Office,** Setanta Centre, Molesworth Street, Dublin 2 (© **01/671-1633;** www.irl gov.ie/iveagh). Those under age 18 and over 65 must apply for a €12, 3-year passport. You can also apply at 1A South Mall, Cork (© **021/494-4700**) or over the counter at most main post offices.

FOR RESIDENTS OF AUSTRALIA

You can pick up an application from your local post office or any branch of Passports Australia, but you must schedule an interview at the passport office to present your application materials. Call the **Australian Passport Information Service** at © **131-232,** or visit the government website at www.passports.gov.au. Passports for adults are A$144 and for those under 18 are A$72.

FOR RESIDENTS OF NEW ZEALAND

You can pick up a passport application at any New Zealand Passports Office or download it from their website. Contact the **Passports Office** at © **0800/225-050** in New Zealand

or 04/474-8100, or log on to www. passports.govt.nz. Passports for adults are NZ$80 and for children under 16 NZ$40.

CUSTOMS
WHAT YOU CAN BRING IN

Every visitor over 21 years of age may bring in, free of duty, the following: (1) 1 liter of beer, wine, or hard liquor; (2) 200 cigarettes, 50 cigars (but not from Cuba; an additional 100 cigars may be brought in under your gift exemption), or 4.4 pounds of smoking tobacco; and (3) $100 worth of gifts. These exemptions are offered to travelers who spend at least 72 hours in the United States and who have not claimed them within the preceding 6 months. Meat (with the exception of some canned meat products) is prohibited, as are most fruits, vegetables, and plants (including seeds, tropical plants, and the like). Foreign tourists may bring in or take out up to $10,000 in U.S. or foreign currency with no formalities; larger sums must be declared to U.S. Customs on entering or leaving, which includes filing form Customs Form 4790. For specific information regarding U.S. Customs, call your nearest U.S. embassy or consulate, or contact the **U.S. Customs** office at © **202/927-1770** or www.customs.gov/xp/cgov/travel.

INSURANCE

Although it's not required of travelers, health insurance is highly recommended. Unlike many European countries, the United States does not usually offer free or low-cost medical care to its citizens or visitors. Doctors and hospitals are expensive, and in most cases require advance payment or proof of coverage before they render their services. Other policies can cover everything from the loss or theft of your baggage to trip cancellation to the guarantee of bail in case you're arrested. Good policies also cover the costs of an accident, repatriation, or death. See "Travel Insurance, Health & Safety" in chapter 2 for more information. In Europe, packages such as **Europ Assistance** are sold by automobile clubs and travel agencies at attractive rates. **Worldwide Assistance Services** (© 800/821-2828; www.worldwideassistance.com) is the agent for Europ Assistance in the United States.

Although lack of health insurance may prevent you from being admitted to a hospital in nonemergencies, don't worry about being left on a street corner to die: The American way is to fix you now and bill you later.

INSURANCE FOR BRITISH TRAVELERS Most big travel agents offer their own insurance and will probably try to sell you their package when you book a holiday. Think before you sign. **Britain's Consumers' Association** recommends that you insist on seeing the policy and reading the fine print before buying travel insurance. **The Association of British Insurers** (© 020/7600-3333; www.abi.org.uk) gives advice by phone and publishes *Holiday Insurance and Motoring Abroad,* a free guide to policy provisions and prices. You might also shop around for better deals: Try **Columbus Direct** (© 0845/330-8518; www.columbusdirect.net).

INSURANCE FOR CANADIAN TRAVELERS Canadians should check with their provincial health plan offices or call **Health Canada** (© 613/957-2991; www.hc-sc.gc.ca) to find out the extent of their coverage and what documentation and receipts they must take home in case they are treated in the United States.

MONEY
CURRENCY The U.S. monetary system is very simple: The most common **bills** are the $1 (colloquially, a

"buck"), $5, $10, and $20 denominations. There are also $2 bills (seldom encountered), $50 bills, and $100 bills (the last two are usually not welcome as payment for small purchases). All the paper money was recently redesigned, making the famous faces adorning them disproportionately large. The old-style bills are still legal tender.

There are seven denominations of coins: 1¢ (1 cent, or a penny); 5¢ (5 cents, or a nickel); 10¢ (10 cents, or a dime); 25¢ (25 cents, or a quarter); 50¢ (50 cents, or a half dollar); the new gold "Sacagawea" coin worth $1; and, prized by collectors, the rare, older silver dollar.

Note: The "foreign-exchange bureaus" so common in Europe are rare at smaller airports in the United States, and nonexistent outside major cities. It's best not to change foreign money (or traveler's checks denominated in a currency other than U.S. dollars) at a small-town bank, or even a branch in a big city; in fact, leave any currency other than U.S. dollars at home—it may prove a greater nuisance to you than it's worth.

TRAVELER'S CHECKS Though traveler's checks are widely accepted, make sure that they're denominated in U.S. dollars, as foreign-currency checks are often difficult to exchange. The three traveler's checks that are most widely recognized—and least likely to be denied—are **Visa, American Express,** and **Thomas Cook.** Be sure to record the numbers of the checks, and keep that information in a separate place in case they get lost or stolen. Most businesses are pretty good about taking traveler's checks, but you're better off cashing them in at a bank (in small amounts, of course) and paying in cash. *Remember:* You'll need identification, such as a driver's license or passport, to change a traveler's check.

CREDIT CARDS & ATMs   Credit cards are the most widely used form of payment in the United States. Among the most commonly accepted are **Visa** (www.visa.com), which is BarclayCard in Britain; **MasterCard** (www.master card.com), which is EuroCard in Europe, Access in Britain, and Chargex in Canada; **American Express** (www.americanexpress.com); **Diners Club** (www.dinersclub.com); and **Discover** (www.discovercard.com). You must have a credit or charge card to rent a car. There are, however, a handful of stores and restaurants, and even a few guest ranches and B&Bs, that do not take credit cards, so be sure to ask in advance. Most businesses display a sticker near their entrance to let you know which cards they accept. (***Note:*** Businesses may require a minimum purchase, usually around $10, to use a credit card.) Check the websites listed above to find an ATM or location where you can get a cash advance on your credit card.

It is strongly recommended that you bring at least one major credit card. Hotels, car-rental companies, and airlines usually require a credit card imprint as a deposit against expenses, and in an emergency a credit card can be priceless.

ATMs (automated teller machines) are easily found in U.S. cities. Some ATMs allow you to draw U.S. currency against your bank and credit cards. Check with your bank before leaving home, and remember that you need your personal identification number (PIN) to do so. Most accept Visa, MasterCard, and American Express, as well as ATM cards from other U.S. banks. Expect to be charged $1.00 or more per transaction, however. One way around these fees is to ask for cash back at grocery stores, which generally accept ATM cards and don't charge usage fees. Of course, you'll have to purchase something first.

SAFETY

GENERAL   SUGGESTIONS
Although tourist areas are generally safe, U.S. urban areas tend to be less safe than those in Europe or Japan. You should always stay alert. This is particularly true of large American cities. If you're in doubt about which neighborhoods are safe, don't hesitate to make inquiries with the hotel front desk staff or the local tourist office.

Avoid deserted areas, especially at night, and don't go into public parks after dark unless there's a concert or similar occasion that will attract a crowd.

Avoid carrying valuables with you on the street, and keep expensive cameras or electronic equipment bagged up or covered when not in use. Hold onto your pocketbook, and place your billfold in an inside pocket.

Always lock your room door—don't assume that once you're inside the hotel you are automatically safe and no longer need to be aware of your surroundings.

DRIVING SAFETY   Driving safety is important too, and carjacking is not unprecedented. Question your rental agency about personal safety and ask for a traveler-safety brochure when you pick up your car. Obtain written directions—or a map with the route clearly marked—from the agency

---

(*Tips* **In Case of Emergency**

Be sure to keep a copy of all your travel papers separate from your wallet or purse, and leave a copy with someone at home should you need it faxed in an emergency.

showing how to get to your destination. If possible, arrive and depart during daylight hours.

If you drive off a highway and end up in a dodgy-looking neighborhood, leave the area as quickly as possible. If you have an accident, even on the highway, stay in your car with the doors locked until you assess the situation or until the police arrive. If you're bumped from behind on the street or are involved in a minor accident with no injuries, and the situation appears to be suspicious, motion to the other driver to follow you. Go directly to the nearest police station, well-lit service station, or 24-hour store.

Park in well-lit and well-traveled areas whenever possible. Always keep your car doors locked, whether the vehicle is attended or unattended. Never leave any packages or valuables in sight. If someone attempts to rob you or steal your car, don't try to resist the thief/carjacker. Report the incident to the police department immediately by calling ⓒ **911.**

2 Getting to the United States

BY PLANE

For an extensive listing of airlines that fly into Seattle, see "Getting There" in chapter 2.

A number of U.S. airlines offer service from Europe to the United States. If they do not have direct flights from Europe to Seattle, they can book you straight through on a connecting flight.

You can make reservations by calling the following numbers in Great Britain: **American** (ⓒ 207/365-0777 in London, or 8457/789-789 outside London; www.aa.com), **British Airways** (ⓒ 0845/773-3377; www.british-airways.com), **Continental** (ⓒ 0800/776-464; www.continental.com), **Delta** (ⓒ 0800/414-767; www.delta.com), **Northwest/KLM** (ⓒ 08705/074-074; www.nwa.com), **United** (ⓒ 0845/8444-777; www.ual.com), and **US Airways** (ⓒ 0845/600-3300; www.usairways.com).

International carriers that fly from Europe to Los Angeles and San Francisco include **Aer Lingus** (ⓒ 0818/365-000 in Ireland; www.aerlingus.com) and **British Airways** (ⓒ 0845/773-3377; www.britishairways.com), which also flies direct to Seattle from London.

From New Zealand and Australia, there are flights to Los Angeles on **Qantas** (ⓒ 13 13 13 in Australia; www.qantas.com.au) and **Air New Zealand** (ⓒ 0800/737-000 in Auckland; www.airnewzealand.co.nz). From there, you can continue on to Seattle on a regional airline such as **Alaska Airlines** (ⓒ 800/426-0333; www.alaskaair.com) or **Southwest** (ⓒ 800/435-9792; www.southwest.com).

From Toronto, there are flights to Seattle on **Air Canada** (ⓒ 888/247-2262; www.aircanada.ca), **American Airlines** (ⓒ 800/433-7300; www.aa.com), **Northwest** (ⓒ 800/225-2525; www.nwa.com), and **United** (ⓒ 800/538-5561; www.ual.com).

From Vancouver, B.C., there are flights to Seattle on **Air Canada, Horizon Airlines** (ⓒ 800/547-9308; www.horizonair.com), **United Express,** and **Alaska Airlines** (ⓒ 800/426-0333; www.alaskaair.com).

Operated by the European Travel Network, **www.discount-tickets.com** is a great online source for regular and discounted airfares.

AIRLINE DISCOUNTS Travelers from overseas can take advantage of the APEX (Advance Purchase Excursion) fares offered by all major U.S. and European carriers. For more money-saving airline advice, see "Getting There" in chapter 2.

BY TRAIN

Amtrak (✆ **800/872-7245;** www. amtrak.com) offers service from Vancouver, B.C., to Seattle, a trip that takes about 4 hours. From Portland to Seattle takes about the same length of time. One-way fares from Vancouver to Seattle or from Portland to Seattle are usually around $25 or $30. Booking earlier will get you a less expensive ticket. Amtrak also operates a European-style (meaning fast and on time) train between Vancouver and Eugene, Oregon.

Like the airlines, Amtrak offers several discounted fares; although they're not all based on advance purchase, you have more discount options by reserving early.

BY FERRY

If you are traveling between Victoria, B.C., and Seattle, several options are available from **Victoria Clipper,** Pier 69, 2701 Alaskan Way (✆ **800/888-2535,** 206/448-5000, or 250/382-8100 in Victoria; www.victoriaclipper. com). Throughout the year, a ferry taking either 2 or 3 hours makes the trip ($61–$127 round-trip for adults).

IMMIGRATION & CUSTOMS CLEARANCE

The visitor arriving by air, no matter what the port of entry, should cultivate patience before setting foot on U.S. soil. Getting through Immigration Control might take as long as 2 hours on some days, especially summer weekends. Add the time it takes to clear Customs, and you'll see that you should make a very generous allowance for delay in planning connections between international and domestic flights—an average of 2 to 3 hours at least.

In contrast, travelers arriving by car, by ferry, or by rail from Canada will find border-crossing formalities somewhat more streamlined, though not nearly as easy as they were before the September 11, 2001, terrorist attacks. Air travelers from Canada, Bermuda, and some places in the Caribbean can sometimes go through Customs and Immigration at the point of departure, which is much quicker.

3 Getting Around the United States

For specific information on traveling to and around Seattle and Washington, see "Getting There" and "Getting Around" in chapter 2 and "Getting Around" in chapter 4, "Seattle."

BY PLANE   Some large airlines (for example, United and Delta) offer travelers on their transatlantic or transpacific flights special discount tickets under the name **Visit USA,** allowing mostly one-way travel from one U.S. destination to another at very low prices. These discount tickets are not on sale in the United States and must be purchased abroad in conjunction with your international ticket. This system is the best, easiest, and fastest way to see the United States at low cost. Get information well in advance from your travel agent or the office of the airline concerned, since the conditions attached to these discount tickets can be changed without advance notice.

BY CAR   The United States is a car culture through and through. Driving is the most convenient and comfortable way to travel here. The interstate highway system connects cities and towns all over the country, and in addition to these high-speed, limited-access roadways, there's an extensive network of federal, state, and local highways and roads. Driving will give you a lot of flexibility in making, and altering, your itinerary and in allowing you to see off-the-beaten-path destinations that cannot be reached easily by public transportation. You'll also have easy access to inexpensive motels at interstate highway off-ramps.

BY TRAIN   International visitors can buy a **USA Railpass,** good for 15 or 30 days of unlimited travel on **Amtrak** (© **800/USA-RAIL;** www.amtrak. com). These passes are available through many foreign travel agents. (With a foreign passport, you can also buy passes at staffed Amtrak offices in the United States, including locations in San Francisco, Los Angeles, Chicago, New York, Miami, Boston, and Washington, D.C.) Reservations are generally required and should be made for each part of your trip as early as possible. Amtrak also offers an **Air/Rail Travel Plan** that allows you to travel by both train and plane; for information, call © **877/937-7245.**

BY BUS   Although bus travel is often the most economical form of transit for short hops between U.S. cities, it can also be slow and uncomfortable— certainly not an option for everyone. **Greyhound/Trailways** (© **800/229- 9424** or 402/330-8552; www.grey hound.com), the sole nationwide bus line, offers an unlimited-travel **Ameripass/Discovery Pass** for 7 days at $199, 15 days at $299, 30 days at $389, and 60 days at $549. Passes must be purchased at a Greyhound terminal. Special rates are available for seniors and students.

FAST FACTS: **For the International Traveler**

Automobile Organizations Auto clubs can supply maps, suggested routes, guidebooks, accident and bail-bond insurance, and emergency road service. **AAA** is the major auto club in the United States. If you belong to an auto club in your home country, inquire about AAA reciprocity before you leave. You may be able to join AAA even if you're not a member of a reciprocal club; to inquire, call AAA at © **800/222-4357.** AAA is actually an organization of regional auto clubs; so look under "AAA Automobile Club" in the White Pages of the telephone directory. AAA's nationwide emergency road service telephone number is © **800/ AAA-HELP.**

Business Hours The following are general hours; specific establishments may vary. Banks are open Monday through Friday from 9am to 5pm (some also on Sat 9am–noon). Stores are open Monday through Saturday from 10am to 6pm and Sunday from noon to 5pm (malls usually stay open until 9pm Mon–Sat). Bars generally open around 11am, but are legally allowed to be open Monday through Saturday from 6am to 1am and Sunday from 10am to 1am.

Climate See "When to Go" in chapter 2.

Currency See "Money" under "Preparing for Your Trip," earlier in this chapter.

Currency Exchange You'll find currency-exchange services in most major international airports. There's a **Travelex Currency Exchange** kiosk (© **206/ 248-0401**) at Sea-Tac International Airport behind the Northwest Airlines ticketing counters. There's another Travelex office in downtown Seattle at Westlake Center shopping center, 400 Pine St. (© **206/682-4525**).

Drinking Laws The legal age for purchase and consumption of alcoholic beverages is 21; proof of age is required and often requested at bars, nightclubs, and restaurants, so it's always a good idea to bring ID when you go out.

Do not carry open containers of alcohol in your car or any public area that isn't zoned for alcohol consumption. The police can fine you on the spot. And nothing will ruin your trip faster than getting a citation for DUI ("driving under the influence"), so don't even think about driving while intoxicated.

See also the "Liquor Laws" entry in the "Fast Facts" at the end of chapter 2.

Electricity Like Canada, the United States uses 110 to 120 volts AC (60 cycles), compared to 220 to 240 volts AC (50 cycles) in most of Europe, Australia, and New Zealand. If your small appliances use 220 to 240 volts, you'll need a 110-volt transformer and a plug adapter with two flat parallel pins to operate them here. Downward converters that change 220 to 240 volts to 110 to 120 volts are difficult to find in the United States, so bring one with you.

Embassies & Consulates All embassies are located in Washington, D.C. Some consulates are located in major U.S. cities, and most nations have a mission to the United Nations in New York City. If your country isn't listed below, call directory information in Washington, D.C. (✆ 202/555-1212), for the number of your national embassy.

The embassy of **Australia** is at 1601 Massachusetts Ave. NW, Washington, DC 20036-2273 (✆ 202/797-3000; www.austemb.org). There is no consulate in Seattle; the nearest is at 625 Market St., Suite 200, San Francisco, CA 94105-3304 (✆ 415/536-1970).

The embassy of **Canada** is at 501 Pennsylvania Ave. NW, Washington, DC 20001 (✆ 202/682-1740; www.canadianembassy.org). There is a consulate in Seattle at 412 Plaza 600 Building, Sixth Avenue and Stewart Street, Seattle, WA 98101-1286 (✆ 206/443-1777).

The embassy of **Ireland** is at 2234 Massachusetts Ave. NW, Washington, DC 20008 (✆ 202/462-3939; www.irelandemb.org). There is no consulate in Seattle; the nearest is at 100 Pine St., 33rd Floor, San Francisco, CA 94111 (✆ 415/392-4214).

The embassy of **New Zealand** is at 37 Observatory Circle NW, Washington, DC 20008 (✆ 202/328-4800; www.nzemb.org). There is also a consulate near Seattle at 10649 N. Beach Rd., Bow, WA 98232 (✆ 360/766-8002).

The embassy of the **United Kingdom** is at 3100 Massachusetts Ave. NW, Washington, DC 20008 (✆ 202/588-7800; www.britainusa.com). There is a consulate in Seattle at 900 Fourth Ave., Suite 3001, Seattle, WA 98164 (✆ 206/622-9255).

Emergencies Dial ✆ 911 to report a fire, call the police, or get an ambulance. This is a free call (no coins are required at a public telephone).

If you encounter serious problems, contact **Traveler's Aid Society International** (✆ 202/546-1127; www.travelersaid.org) to help direct you to a local branch. This nationwide, nonprofit, social-service organization geared to helping travelers in difficult straits offers services that might include reuniting families separated while traveling, providing food and/or shelter to people stranded without cash, or even emotional counseling.

Gasoline (Petrol) Petrol is known as gasoline (or simply "gas") in the United States, and petrol stations are known as both gas stations and service stations. Gasoline costs less here than it does in Europe, and taxes are already included in the printed price. One U.S. gallon equals 3.8 liters or .85 Imperial gallons.

Holidays Banks, government offices, post offices, and many stores, restaurants, and museums are closed on the following legal national holidays: January 1 (New Year's Day), the third Monday in January (Martin Luther King Jr. Day), the third Monday in February (Presidents' Day, Washington's Birthday), the last Monday in May (Memorial Day), July 4 (Independence Day), the first Monday in September (Labor Day), the second Monday in October (Columbus Day), November 11 (Veterans' Day/Armistice Day), the fourth Thursday in November (Thanksgiving Day), and December 25 (Christmas Day). Also, the Tuesday following the first Monday in November is Election Day and is a federal government holiday in presidential-election years (held every 4 years).

Legal Aid If you are "pulled over" for a minor infraction (such as speeding), never attempt to pay the fine directly to a police officer; this could be construed as attempted bribery, a much more serious crime. Pay fines by mail, or directly into the hands of the clerk of the court. If accused of a more serious offense, say and do nothing before consulting a lawyer. Here the burden is on the state to prove a person's guilt beyond a reasonable doubt, and everyone has the right to remain silent, whether he or she is suspected of a crime or actually arrested. Once arrested, a person can make one telephone call to a party of his or her choice. Call your embassy or consulate.

Mail Mailboxes are blue with a red-and-white stripe and carry the inscription U.S. MAIL. Outside of major urban areas, such mailboxes can be difficult to locate. Look in front of supermarkets and at other large shopping centers. If your mail is addressed to a U.S. destination, don't forget to add the five-digit postal code (or ZIP code), after the two-letter abbreviation of the state to which the mail is addressed.

Domestic postage rates are 25¢ for a postcard and 35¢ for a letter. International mail rates vary. For example, a 1-ounce first-class letter to Europe or Asia costs 80¢ (60¢ to Canada and Mexico); a first-class postcard to Europe or Asia costs 70¢ (50¢ to Canada and Mexico).

Medical Emergencies To call an ambulance, dial ✆ 911 from any phone. No coins are needed.

Newspapers & Magazines National newspapers include the *New York Times, USA Today,* and the *Wall Street Journal.* National newsweeklies include *Newsweek, Time,* and *U.S. News & World Report.* For information on local publications, see the "Fast Facts" section of chapter 4.

Restrooms You won't find public toilets on the streets in most U.S. cities, but they can be found in hotel lobbies, bars, restaurants, museums, department stores, shopping malls, railway and bus stations, and service stations. Note, however, that restaurants and bars in resorts or heavily visited areas may reserve their restrooms for the use of their patrons. Some establishments display a notice that toilets are for the use of patrons only. You can ignore this sign or, better yet, avoid arguments by paying for a cup of coffee or a soft drink, which will qualify you as a patron.

Large hotels and fast-food restaurants are probably the best bet for good, clean facilities.

Safety See section 1 of this chapter.

Taxes The United States does not have a value-added tax (VAT) or other indirect tax at a national level. Every state, and each county and city in it, is allowed to levy its own local tax on purchases.

In Seattle, the sales tax rate is 8.8%. Also, you'll pay around 30% in taxes and concession fees when you rent a car at Seattle–Tacoma Airport. You'll save 10% to 11% by renting somewhere other than the airport. Hotel room taxes range from around 10% to 16%.

Telephone & Fax The telephone system in the United States is run by private corporations, so rates, especially for long-distance service and operator-assisted calls, can vary widely. Generally, hotel surcharges on long-distance and local calls are astronomical, so you're usually better off using a **public pay telephone.** Grocery stores, convenience stores, and gas stations almost always have them. Many supermarkets and convenience stores also sell **prepaid calling cards;** these cards can be the least expensive way to call home. Many public phones at airports now accept American Express, MasterCard, and Visa. **Local calls** made from public pay phones usually cost 35¢ or 50¢. Pay phones do not accept pennies, and few take anything larger than a quarter.

Most long-distance and international calls can be dialed directly from any phone. **For calls within the United States and to Canada,** dial 1 followed by the area code and the seven-digit number. **For other international calls,** dial 011 followed by the country code, city code, and telephone number of the person you are calling.

Calls to area codes **800, 888, 877,** and **866** are toll-free. However, calls to numbers in area codes **700** and **900** (chat lines, bulletin boards, "dating" services, and so on) can be very expensive—usually 95¢ to $3 or more per minute.

For **reversed-charge** or **collect calls,** and for **person-to-person calls,** dial 0 (zero, not the letter O) followed by the area code and number you want; an operator will then come on the line, and you should specify that you are calling collect, or person-to-person, or both. If your operator-assisted call is international, ask for the overseas operator.

For **local directory assistance** ("information"), dial 411; for long-distance information, dial 1, then the appropriate area code and 555-1212.

There are two kinds of telephone directories in the United States. The **White Pages** lists private households and business subscribers in alphabetical order. The inside front cover lists emergency numbers for police, fire, ambulance, and so on. The first few pages tell you how to make long-distance and international calls, complete with country codes and area codes. Government numbers are usually printed on blue paper within the White Pages. Printed on yellow paper, the **Yellow Pages** lists local services, businesses, industries, and such according to category. The Yellow Pages includes maps, postal ZIP codes, and public transportation routes.

Time The United States is divided into six time zones. From east to west, they are Eastern Standard Time (EST), Central Standard Time (CST), Mountain Standard Time (MST), Pacific Standard Time (PST), Alaska Standard

Time (AST), and Hawaii-Aleutian Standard Time (HST). Seattle is on Pacific Standard Time.

Tipping Tipping is so ingrained in the American way of life that the annual income tax of tip-earning service personnel is based on how much they *should* have received in light of their employers' gross revenues.

In hotels, tip **bellhops** at least $1 per bag ($2–$3 if you have a lot of luggage), and tip the **housecleaning** or **chamber staff** $1 to $2 per day (more if you've left a disaster area to clean up, or if you're traveling with kids and/or pets). Tip the **doorman** or **concierge** only if he or she has provided you with some specific service (for example, calling a cab for you or obtaining difficult-to-get theater tickets). Tip the **valet-parking attendant** $1 every time you get your car.

In restaurants, bars, and nightclubs, tip **service staff** and **bartenders** 15% to 20% of the check, tip **checkroom attendants** $1 per garment, and tip **valet-parking attendants** $1 per vehicle. Tip the **doorman** only if he has provided you with some specific service (such as calling a cab for you). Tipping is not expected in cafeterias and fast-food restaurants.

Tip **cab drivers** 15% of the fare.

As for other service personnel, tip **skycaps** (luggage carriers) at airports at least $1 per bag ($2–$3 if you have a lot of luggage) and tip **hairdressers** and **barbers** 15% to 20%.

4

Seattle

Imagine yourself sitting in a park on the Seattle waterfront, a double tall latte and an almond croissant close at hand. The snowy peaks of the Olympic Mountains shimmer on the far side of Puget Sound, and the ferryboats come and go across Elliott Bay. It's a summer day, and the sun is shining. (Hey, as long as we're dreaming, why not dream big?) It just doesn't get much better than this, unless of course you swap the latte for a microbrew and catch a 9:30pm summer sunset. No wonder people love this town so much.

Okay, so the waterfront is as touristy as San Francisco's Fisherman's Wharf, but what a view! Seattle is a city of views, and the must-see vista is, of course, the panorama from the top of the Space Needle. With the 21st century in full swing, this image of the "future" looks decidedly mid-20th-century, but still, it's hard to resist such an impressive elevator ride. And you can even take a monorail straight out of *The Jetsons* to get there (and pass right through the Frank Gehry–designed Experience Music Project en route).

EMP, as the Experience Music Project has come to be known, is one of Seattle's latest architectural oddities. Its swooping, multicolored, metal-skinned bulk rises at the foot of the Space Needle, proof that real 21st-century architecture looks nothing like the vision of the future people dreamed of when the Space Needle was built for the 1962 Seattle World's Fair. EMP is the brainchild of Microsoft cofounder Paul Allen, who built this rock 'n' roll cathedral to

house his vast collection of Northwest rock memorabilia.

Paul Allen's money has also been hard at work changing the architectural face of the south end of downtown Seattle, where, in March 2000, the Kingdome stadium came crashing down, imploded to make way for the new, state-of-the-art Seahawks Stadium, which is home to Allen's Seattle Seahawks NFL football team. Together with the Seattle Mariners' Safeco Field, the Seahawks Stadium has created a massive sports-arena district at the south end of downtown Seattle.

Paul Allen projects aside, Seattle has become one of the nation's most talked-about and popular cities, and life here has undergone dramatic changes in recent years. An influx of urban residents has brought a new vibrancy to the downtown area, and as the city has grown wealthier and more sophisticated, it has built itself not just a new football stadium and a retractable-roof baseball stadium (Safeco Field), but also chic condominiums, a new symphony hall, glittering new hotels, and countless upscale restaurants and shops. Still in the works are a controversial light-rail system and an extension of Seattle's monorail—although both transportation projects have repeatedly stalled and may end up being sidetracked completely.

It's clear that Seattle has not grown complacent. Sure, it's become a congested city, with traffic problems rivaling those of L.A. And yes, the weather really is lousy for most of the year. But Seattleites manage to overcome these minor inconveniences, in large part by spilling out into the streets and parks whenever the sun shines. To visit Seattle in the summer is to witness an exodus; follow the lead of the locals and head for the great outdoors. Should you brave a visit in the rainy season, don't despair: There are compensations for such misfortune, including a roof on Pike Place Market and an espresso bar on every block.

1 Orientation

ARRIVING
BY PLANE

Seattle–Tacoma International Airport (© 800/544-1965 or 206/431-4444; www.portseattle.org/seatac), most commonly referred to simply as Sea-Tac, is located about 14 miles south of Seattle.

Inside the arrivals terminal, you'll find a **Visitor Information Desk** (© 206/433-5218) in the baggage-claim area across from carousel no. 8. It is open daily from 9am to 5pm. Please note that this desk cannot make hotel reservations for you.

Also at the airport, you'll find a **Travelex** currency exchange desk (© 206/248-0401) and branches of all the major car-rental companies (for further details see "Getting Around," later in this chapter).

GETTING INTO THE CITY BY CAR   There are two main exits from the airport: From the loading/unloading area, take the first exit if you're staying near the airport. Take the second exit (Wash. 518) if you're headed to downtown Seattle. Driving east on Wash. 518 will connect you to I-5, where you'll then follow the signs for Seattle. Generally, allow 30 minutes for the drive between the airport and downtown—45 minutes to an hour during rush hour.

During rush hour, it's sometimes quicker to take Wash. 518 west to Wash. 509 north to Wash. 99 to Wash. 519 (which becomes the Alaskan Way Viaduct along the Seattle waterfront).

GETTING INTO THE CITY BY TAXI, SHUTTLE, OR BUS   A **taxi** into downtown Seattle will cost you about $32. There are usually plenty of taxis around, but if not, call **Yellow Cab** (© 206/622-6500) or **Farwest Taxi** (© 206/622-1717). The flag-drop charge is $1.80; after that, it's $1.80 per mile.

Gray Line Airport Express (© 800/426-7532 or 206/626-6088; www.gray lineofseattle.com) provides service between the airport and downtown Seattle daily from about 5am to 11pm and is your best bet for getting to downtown. These shuttle vans pick up from two booths outside the baggage claim area—one outside Door 24 and one outside Door 8. Shuttles operate every 20 minutes and stop at the following hotels: Madison Renaissance, Crowne Plaza, Four Seasons Olympic, Seattle Hilton, Sheraton Seattle, Westin, and Warwick. Fares are $8.50 one-way and $14 round-trip. Connector service to the above hotels is also provided from numerous other downtown hotels, as well as from the Amtrak station, the Washington State Ferries ferry terminal (Pier 52), and the Greyhound station. Connector service is free from some downtown hotels, but from other locations, it costs $2.50 one-way or $5 round-trip; call for details. The biggest drawback of this shuttle service is that you may have to stop at several hotels before getting dropped off, and it could take you 45 minutes to get from the airport to your hotel. However, if you're traveling by yourself or with one other person, this is your most economical choice other than the public bus.

Shuttle Express (© 206/622-1424 or 425/981-7000; www.shuttleexpress. com) provides 24-hour service between Sea-Tac and the Seattle, north Seattle, and Bellevue areas. The rate to downtown Seattle is $21 for one to three adults and $25 for four adults; children 12 and younger ride free when accompanied by a paying adult. You need to make a reservation to get to the airport, but to leave the airport, simply follow the red-and-black signs to the Ground Transportation Center on the third floor of the parking garage. If there are three or more of you traveling together, this is going to be your cheapest alternative for getting into town unless you take a public bus.

Metro Transit (© 800/542-7876 in Washington, or 206/553-3000; http:// transit.metrokc.gov) operates two buses between the airport and downtown. These buses leave from near Door 6 (close to baggage carousel 1) of the baggage claim area. It's a good idea to call for the current schedule when you arrive in town. Bus no. 194 operates (to Third Ave. and Union St. or the bus tunnel's Convention Place Station, depending on the time of day) every 30 minutes weekdays from 5:56am to 8:33pm, weekends from about 6:20am to about 7:20pm. Bus no. 174 operates (to Fourth Ave. and Union St.) about every 25 to 30 minutes from 4:47am to 2:43am (5:45am–2:47am Sat and 6:49am–2:46pm Sun). Bus trips take 40 to 50 minutes depending on conditions. The fare is $1.25 during off-peak hours and $2 during peak hours.

BY TRAIN OR BUS

Amtrak (© 800/872-7245 or 206/382-4125; www.amtrak.com) trains stop at King Street Station, which is located at 303 S. Jackson St., within a few blocks of the historic Pioneer Square neighborhood and adjacent to the south entrance of the downtown bus tunnel. Any bus running north through the tunnel will take you to within a few blocks of most downtown hotels. The Waterfront Streetcar also stops within a block of King Street Station and can take you to the The Edgewater hotel.

The **Greyhound bus station,** 811 Stewart St. (© 800/229-9424 or 206/ 628-5526; www.greyhound.com), is located a few blocks northeast of downtown Seattle not far from Lake Union and Seattle Center. Several budget-chain motels are located only a few blocks from the bus station. It's a bit farther to the Hostelling International–Seattle hostel, yet walkable if you don't have much luggage. Otherwise, you can grab a free ride on a Metro bus.

BY CAR

See section 11, "Getting There," at the end of chapter 2; and section 2, "Getting Around," below.

VISITOR INFORMATION

Visitor information on Seattle and the surrounding area is available by contacting **Seattle's Convention and Visitors Bureau Visitor Information Center,** Washington State Convention & Trade Center, 800 Convention Place, Galleria Level, at the corner of Eighth Avenue and Pike Street (© 206/461-5840; www. seeseattle.org). To find it, walk up Union Street until it goes into a tunnel under the Convention Center. You'll see the information center on your left. Alternatively, you can enter the building from Pike Street.

CITY LAYOUT

Although downtown Seattle is fairly compact and can easily be navigated on foot, finding your way by car can be frustrating. The Seattle area has been experiencing phenomenal growth for more than a decade, and this has created traffic-congestion problems. Here are some guidelines to help you find your way around.

MAIN ARTERIES & STREETS   Three interstate highways serve Seattle. Seattle's main artery is I-5, which runs through the middle of the city. Take the James Street exit west if you're heading for the Pioneer Square area, take the Seneca Street exit for Pike Place Market, or take the Olive Way exit for Capitol Hill. I-405 is the city's north-south bypass and travels up the east shore of Lake Washington through Bellevue and Kirkland (Seattle's high-tech corridor). I-90 comes in from the east, crossing one of the city's two floating bridges, and ends at the south end of downtown.

Downtown is roughly defined as extending from the stadium district just south of the Pioneer Square neighborhood on the south, to Denny Way on the north, and from Elliott Bay on the west to I-5 on the east. Within this area, most avenues are numbered, whereas streets have names. Exceptions to this rule are the first two roads parallel to the waterfront (Alaskan Way and Western Ave.) and avenues east of Ninth Avenue.

Many downtown streets and avenues are one-way. Spring, Pike, and Marion streets are all one-way eastbound, while Seneca, Pine, and Madison streets are all one-way westbound. Second and Fifth avenues are both one-way southbound, while Fourth and Sixth avenues are one-way northbound. First Avenue and Third Avenue are both two-way streets.

To get from downtown to Capitol Hill, take Pike Street or Olive Way. Madison Street, Yesler Way, or South Jackson Street will get you over to Lake Washington on the east side of Seattle. If you are heading north across town, Westlake Avenue will take you to the Fremont neighborhood, and Eastlake Avenue will take you to the University District. These two roads diverge at the south end of Lake Union. To get to the arboretum from downtown, take Madison Street.

FINDING AN ADDRESS   After you become familiar with the streets and neighborhoods of Seattle, there is really only one important thing to remember: Pay attention to the compass point of an address. Most downtown streets have no directional designation attached to them, but when you cross I-5 going east, most streets and avenues are designated "East." South of Yesler Way, which runs through Pioneer Square, streets are designated "South." West of Queen Anne Avenue, streets are designated "West." The University District is designated "NE" (Northeast), and the Ballard neighborhood, "NW" (Northwest). So if you're looking for an address on First Avenue South, head south of Yesler Way.

Another helpful hint is that odd-numbered addresses are likely to be on the west and south sides of streets, whereas even-numbered addresses will be on the east and north. Also, in the downtown area, address numbers increase by 100

Remembering Seattle's Streets

Locals use an irreverent little mnemonic device for remembering the names of Seattle's downtown streets, and since most visitors spend much of their time downtown, this phrase could be useful to you as well. It goes like this: "Jesus Christ made Seattle under protest." This stands for all the downtown east-west streets between Yesler Way and Olive Way/Stewart Street—Jefferson, James, Cherry, Columbia, Marion, Madison, Spring, Seneca, University, Union, Pike, Pine.

with each block as you move away from Yesler Way going north or south and as you go east from the waterfront.

STREET MAPS   If the streets of Seattle seem totally unfathomable to you, rest assured that even longtime residents sometimes have a hard time finding their way around. Don't be afraid to ask directions. You can obtain a free map of the city at the airport Visitor Information Desk or from the Seattle's Convention and Visitors Bureau Visitor Information Center (see above).

You can buy a decent map of Seattle in most convenience stores and gas stations around the area or, for a greater selection, stop in at **Metsker Maps,** 702 First Ave. (© **800/727-4430** or 206/623-8747; www.metskers.com).

If you're a member of AAA, you can get free maps of Seattle and Washington state, either at an AAA office near you or at the Seattle office, 330 Sixth Ave. N. (© **206/448-5353**).

THE NEIGHBORHOODS IN BRIEF

DOWNTOWN This is Seattle's main business district and can roughly be defined as the area from Pioneer Square in the south, to around Pike Place Market in the north, and from First Avenue to Eighth Avenue. It's characterized by steep streets, high-rise office buildings, luxury hotels, and a high density of retail shops (primarily national chains). This is also where you'll find the Seattle Art Museum and Benaroya Hall, which is home to the Seattle Symphony. Because hotels in this area are convenient to both Pioneer Square and Pike Place Market, this is a good neighborhood in which to stay. Unfortunately, the hotels here are the most expensive in the city.

FIRST HILL Because it is home to several large hospitals, this hilly neighborhood just east of downtown and across I-5 is known as Pill Hill by Seattleites. First Hill is home to the Frye Art Museum and a couple of good hotels.

THE WATERFRONT The Seattle waterfront, which stretches along Alaskan Way from roughly Washington Street in the south to Broad Street and Myrtle Edwards Park in the north, is the most touristy neighborhood in Seattle. In recent years, however, Seattleites have

been reclaiming the waterfront as a new residential area, and the north end of Alaskan Way is now lined with water-view condos. In addition to the many tacky gift shops, greasy fish-and-chips windows, and tour-boat docks, the waterfront also has the city's only waterfront hotel (The Edgewater), the Seattle Aquarium, and a few excellent seafood restaurants.

PIONEER SQUARE The Pioneer Square Historic District, known for its restored 1890s buildings, is centered around the corner of First Avenue and Yesler Way. The tree-lined streets and cobblestone plazas make this one of the prettiest downtown neighborhoods. Pioneer Square (which refers to the neighborhood, not a specific square) is full of antiques shops, art galleries, restaurants, bars, and nightclubs. Because of the number of bars in this neighborhood, late nights are not a good time to wander here—plus, the number of street people in this area is off-putting to many visitors.

THE INTERNATIONAL DISTRICT Known to locals as the I.D., this is the most distinctive of Seattle's neighborhoods and is home to a large Asian population. Here you'll find the Wing Luke Asian Museum, Hing Hay Park (a small park with an ornate pagoda), Uwajimaya (an Asian supermarket), and many other small shops and restaurants. The International District begins around Fifth Avenue South and South Jackson Street. This neighborhood is interesting for a stroll, but there really isn't a lot to do here.

BELLTOWN Located in the blocks north of **Pike Place Market** between Western and Fourth avenues, this area once held mostly warehouses, but over the past decade it has become gentrified. Today Belltown is ground zero for upscale Seattle restaurants. Keeping the restaurants in business are the residents of the neighborhood's many new high-rise condominiums. Belltown's many nightclubs attract crowds of the young, the hip, and the stylish—who, in turn, attract a lot of nighttime panhandlers.

QUEEN ANNE HILL Queen Anne is located just northwest of **Seattle Center** and offers great views of the city. This affluent neighborhood, one of the most prestigious in Seattle proper, is where you'll find some of Seattle's oldest homes. Today the neighborhood is divided into the Upper Queen Anne and Lower Queen Anne neighborhoods. Upper Queen Anne has a very peaceful neighborhood feel and abounds in moderately priced restaurants. Lower Queen Anne, adjacent to the theaters and Opera House at Seattle Center, is something of a theater district and has a more urban character.

CAPITOL HILL To the northeast of downtown, centered along Broadway near Volunteer Park, Capitol Hill is Seattle's main gay community and is also a popular youth-culture shopping district. Broadway sidewalks are always crowded, and it is nearly impossible to find a parking space in this neighborhood. Although there are lots of inexpensive restaurants in the area, few are really worth recommending. This is also the city's main hangout for runaways and street kids, many of whom have become involved in the city's infamous heroin scene. Despite the youthful orientation, Capitol Hill is also where you'll find many of the city's bed-and-breakfast inns. These inns are housed in some of the neighborhood's impressive old homes and mansions.

UNIVERSITY DISTRICT As the name implies, this neighborhood in the northeast section of the city surrounds the University of Washington. The "U" District, as it's known to locals, provides all the amenities of a college neighborhood: cheap ethnic restaurants, bars, pubs, espresso bars, and music stores. The neighborhood has several good hotels that offer substantial savings over comparable downtown Seattle hotels.

FREMONT Located north of the Lake Washington Ship Canal between Wallingford and Ballard, Fremont is home to Seattle's best-loved piece of public art—*Waiting for the Interurban*—as well as the famous Fremont Troll sculpture. This is Seattle's wackiest neighborhood and is filled with eclectic shops and ethnic restaurants. During the summer, there's a Sunday flea market, and outdoor movies are screened on Saturday nights. If you have time to visit only one neighborhood outside of downtown, make it Fremont.

BALLARD In northwest Seattle, bordering the Lake Washington Ship Canal and Puget Sound, you'll find Ballard, a former Scandinavian community that retains visible remnants of its past. Now known for its

Greater Seattle Orientation

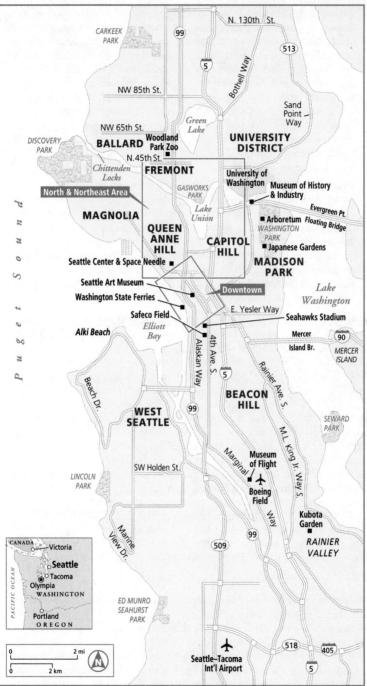

busy nightlife, Ballard is one of Seattle's up-and-coming neighborhoods and is undergoing a pronounced change in character. You'll find art galleries and a few interesting boutiques and shops along the tree-shaded streets of the neighborhood's old commercial center. It's definitely worth a stroll here to see what's happening. The neighborhood's Nordic Heritage Museum often has interesting art exhibits.

THE EASTSIDE Home to Bill Gates, Microsoft, countless high-tech spin-off companies, and seemingly endless suburbs, the Eastside lies across Lake Washington from Seattle proper and is comprised of the fast-growing cities of **Kirkland, Bellevue, Redmond, Bothell,** and a few other smaller communities. As

the presence of Bill Gates's media-hyped mansion attests, there are some pretty wealthy neighborhoods here; but wealth doesn't necessarily equal respect, and the Eastside is still much derided by Seattle citizens, who perceive it as an uncultured bedroom community.

WEST SEATTLE West Seattle, across the wasteland of the port facility from downtown Seattle, is not just the site of the ferry terminal for ferries to Vashon Island and the Kitsap Peninsula. It's also the site of Seattle's favorite beach (Alki), which is as close to a Southern California beach experience as you can get in the Northwest. Here too is the waterfront restaurant with the best view of Seattle: Salty's on Alki.

2 Getting Around

BY PUBLIC TRANSPORTATION

BY BUS   The best thing about Seattle's **Metro** bus system (© 800/542-7876 in Washington, or 206/553-3000; http://transit.metrokc.gov) is that as long as you stay within the downtown area, you can ride for free between 6am and 7pm. The Ride Free Area is between Alaskan Way (the waterfront) in the west, Sixth Avenue and I-5 in the east, Battery Street in the north, and South Jackson Street in the south. Within this area are Pioneer Square, the waterfront attractions, Pike Place Market, the Seattle Art Museum, and almost all of the city's major hotels. Two blocks from South Jackson Street is the Seahawks Stadium, 3 long blocks from South Jackson Street is Safeco Field (where the Mariners play), and 6 blocks from Battery Street is Seattle Center. Keeping this in mind, you can see a lot of Seattle without having to spend a dime on transportation.

The Ride Free Area also encompasses the Metro Tunnel, which allows buses to drive underneath downtown Seattle, thus avoiding traffic congestion. The tunnel extends from the International District in the south to the Convention Center in the north, with three stops in between. Commissioned artworks decorate each of the stations, making a trip through the tunnel more than just a way of getting from point A to point B. It's open Monday through Friday from 5am to 7pm and Saturday from 10am to 6pm (closed Sun and holidays). When the Bus Tunnel is closed, buses operate on surface streets. Because the tunnel is within the Ride Free Area, there is no charge for riding through it, unless you are traveling to or from outside of the Ride Free Area.

If you travel outside the Ride Free Area, fares range from $1.25 to $2, depending on the distance and time of day. (The higher fares are incurred during commuter hours.) Keep in mind when traveling out of the Ride Free Area that you pay when you get off the bus. When traveling into the Ride Free Area, you pay when you get on the bus. Exact change is required; dollar bills are accepted.

⟨Value⟩ Discount Passes

On Saturday, Sunday, and holidays, you can purchase an All Day Pass for $2.50; it's available on any Metro bus or the Waterfront Streetcar, and it's good for anywhere outside the Ride Free Area. For other days of the week, you can purchase a Visitor Pass for $5. These passes can be used on buses, the water taxi, and the Waterfront Streetcar. These latter passes are available at Metro Customer Service offices at the Westlake Tunnel Station on the mezzanine level or at King Street Center, 201 S. Jackson St. These passes can also be purchased at the Seattle's Convention and Visitors Bureau, Fifth Avenue and Pike Street, and at the Ticket/Ticket counters at Pike Place Market, First Avenue and Pike Street; in Capitol Hill's Broadway Market, 401 Broadway E., and in Bellevue at the Meydenbauer Center, NE Sixth Street and 112th Avenue. For more information contact **Metro (ⓒ 206/624-PASS;** http://transit.metrokc.gov).

BY WATERFRONT STREETCAR In addition to the bus system, **Metro** (ⓒ **800/542-7876** in Washington, or 206/553-3000; http://transit.metrokc.gov) also operates old-fashioned streetcars that follow a route along the waterfront from Pier 70 to Pioneer Square and then east to the corner of Fourth Avenue South and South Jackson Street, which is on the edge of the International District. These streetcars are more tourist attraction than commuter transportation and actually are much more useful to visitors than are most of the city's buses. Tourist sites along the streetcar route include Pioneer Square, the Seattle Aquarium, IMAX-Dome Film Experience, and Pike Place Market. In the summer, streetcars operate Monday through Friday from around 6:30am to 11:30pm, departing every 20 to 30 minutes; on Saturday, Sunday, and holidays they operate from around 9am to midnight (shorter hours in other months). One-way fare is $1.25 in off-peak hours and $1.50 in peak hours (50¢ for youth ages 5–17); exact change is required. If you plan to transfer to a Metro bus, you can get a transfer good for 90 minutes. Streetcars are wheelchair accessible.

BY MONORAIL If you are planning a visit to Seattle Center, there is no better way to get there from downtown than on the **Seattle Monorail** (ⓒ **206/905-2620;** www.seattlemonorail.com), which leaves from Westlake Center shopping mall (Fifth Ave. and Pine St.). The elevated trains cover the 1¼ miles in 2 minutes and pass right through the middle of the Experience Music Project as they arrive and depart from Seattle Center. The monorail operates Monday through Friday from 7:30am to 11pm, Saturday and Sunday from 9am to 11pm. Departures are every 10 minutes. The one-way fare is $1.50 for adults and 75¢ for seniors and children ages 5 to 12.

BY WATER TAXI As long as funding continues, a water taxi will operate between the downtown Seattle waterfront (Pier 54) and Seacrest Park in West Seattle, providing access to West Seattle's popular Alki Beach and adjacent paved path. For a schedule of service, check with the Metro (ⓒ **206/205-3866;** http://transit.metrokc.gov). The one-way fare is $2 (free for children under age 5). Also free with a valid bus transfer or all-day pass.

BY FERRY **Washington State Ferries** (ⓒ **800/84-FERRY** or 888/808-7977 within Washington state, or 206/464-6400; www.wsdot.wa.gov/ferries) is the most extensive ferry system in the United States, and while these ferries won't help you get around Seattle itself, they do offer scenic options for getting out of town (and cheap cruises, too). From downtown Seattle, car ferries sail to Bremerton (60-min. crossing) and Bainbridge Island (35-min. crossing). From West Seattle, car ferries go to Vashon Island (15-min. crossing) and Southworth (35-min. crossing), which is on the Kitsap Peninsula. One-way fares between Seattle and Bainbridge Island or Bremerton, or between Edmonds and Kingston via car ferry are $9.50 ($12 from mid-May to mid-Oct) for a car and driver, $5.40 for adult car passengers or walk-ons, $2.70 for seniors, and $4.40 for children ages 5 to 18. Car passengers and walk-ons only pay fares on westbound car ferries. One-way fares between Fauntleroy (West Seattle) and Vashon Island or between Southworth and Vashon Island are $12 ($16 from mid-May to mid-Oct) for a car and driver, $3.50 for car passengers or walk-ons, $1.70 for seniors, and $2.80 for children ages 5 to 18. At press time, passenger ferry service to Vashon Island and Bremerton was scheduled to be discontinued.

BY CAR

Before you venture into downtown Seattle in a car, keep in mind that traffic congestion is bad, parking is limited (and expensive), and streets are almost all one-way. You'll avoid a lot of frustration and aggravation by leaving your car in your hotel's parking garage or by not bringing a car into downtown at all.

Depending on what your plans are for your visit, you might not need a car at all. If you plan to spend your time in downtown Seattle, a car is a liability. The city center is well serviced by public transportation, with free public buses in the downtown area, the monorail from downtown to Seattle Center, and the Waterfront Streetcar connecting Pike Place Market and Pioneer Square by way of the waterfront. You can even take the ferries over to Bainbridge Island or Bremerton for an excursion out of the city. Most Seattle neighborhoods of interest to visitors are also well served by public buses. However, if your plans include any excursions out of the city, say to Mount Rainier or the Olympic Peninsula, you'll definitely need a car.

CAR RENTALS   Car-rental rates vary as widely and as wildly as airfares, so it pays to do some comparison-shopping. In Seattle, daily rates for a compact car might run anywhere from around $30 to $70, with weekly rates running between $150 and $350 (although the average is around $250). Rates are, of course, highest in the summer and lowest in the winter, but you'll almost always get lower rates the further ahead you reserve. Be sure to budget for the 18.5% car-rental tax (and, if you rent at the airport, an additional 10% to 12% airport concession fee and other charges will bring your cost up to a whopping total of around 30%!).

All the major car-rental agencies have offices in Seattle and at or near Seattle–Tacoma International Airport. Companies with a desk and cars inside the terminal include **Alamo** (© 800/327-9633 or 206/433-0182; www.goalamo.com), **Avis** (© 800/331-1212 or 206/433-5231; www.avis.com), **Budget** (© 800/527-0700 or 206/682-8989; www.budget.com), **Hertz** (© 800/654-3131 or 206/248-1300; www.hertz.com), and **National** (© 800/227-7368 or 206/433-5501; www.nationalcar.com). Companies with desks inside the terminal but cars parked off the airport premises include **Advantage** (© 800/777-5500 or 206/824-0161; www.arac.com), **Dollar** (© 800/800-4000 or 206/433-6777; www.dollar.com), **Enterprise** (© 800/736-8222 or 206/246-1953; www.enterprise.com), and **Thrifty** (© 800/367-2277 or 206/625-1133; www.thrifty.com).

PARKING   On-street parking in downtown Seattle is expensive, extremely limited, and, worst of all, rarely available near your destination. Most downtown parking lots (either above or below ground) charge from $12 to $20 per day, though many lots offer early-bird specials that allow you to park all day for around $8 if you park before a certain time in the morning (usually around 9am). With a purchase of $20 or more, many downtown merchants offer City-Park tokens that can be used for $1 off parking fees in many downtown lots (mostly in the main shopping district around Sixth and Pine). Look for the CityPark signs. In the Pioneer Square area, there is a similar program.

You'll also save money by parking near the Space Needle, where parking lots charge $3 to $6 per day. The parking lot at Fifth Avenue North and North Republican Street, on the east side of Seattle Center, charges only $5 for all-day parking if you show up with three or more people in your car. The Pike Place Market parking garage, accessed from Western Avenue under the sky bridge, offers free parking if you park for less than an hour (just enough time to run in and grab a quick bite). Also if you arrive at this lot before 9:30am, you can park all day for $6. Some market merchants validate parking permits, as do many market restaurants if you're dining after 5pm. In the International District, the Lower Queen Anne neighborhood, and a few streets south of Seattle Center, you'll find free 2-hour on-street parking.

Value   **Driving a Bargain in Seattle**

For the best deal on a rental car, make your reservation at least a week in advance. It also pays to call several times over a period of a few weeks just to check prices. You're likely to be quoted different rates every time you call, since rates fluctuate based on demand and availability. Remember the old Wall Street adage: Buy low!

Always ask about special weekend rates, promotional rates, or discounts for which you might be eligible (AAA, AARP, corporate, Entertainment Book). Also make sure you clarify whether there is a charge for mileage. And don't forget to mention that you're a frequent flier: You might be able to get miles for your car rental.

If you have your own car insurance, you may have collision coverage. If you do not hold your own policy, your credit card may provide collision coverage, allowing you to decline the collision-damage waiver, which can add a bundle to the cost of a rental. (Gold and platinum cards usually offer this perk, but check with your card issuer before relying on it. Note that while many cards provide collision coverage, they do not provide liability coverage.)

If there's any way you can arrange to pick up your car somewhere other than the airport, you can save the 10% to 11% airport concession fee.

It's always smart to decline the gasoline plans offered by rental agencies and simply plan on returning your rental car with a full tank of gas. The prices the rental companies charge you to fill your tank when you don't do it yourself are usually a rip-off.

DRIVING RULES A right turn at a red light is permitted after coming to a full stop. A left turn at a red light is permissible from a one-way street onto another one-way street.

If you park your car on a sloping street, be sure to turn your wheels to the curb—you may be ticketed if you don't. When parking on the street, be sure to check the time limit on your parking meter. Some allow only as little as 15 minutes of parking, while others are good for up to 4 hours. Also be sure to check whether or not you can park in a parking space during rush hour.

Stoplights in the Pioneer Square area are particularly hard to see, so be alert at all intersections.

BY TAXI

If you decide not to use the public-transit system, call **Yellow Cab** (𝒞 **206/622-6500**) or **Farwest Taxi** (𝒞 **206/622-1717**). Taxis can be difficult to hail on the street in Seattle, so it's best to call or wait at the taxi stands at major hotels. The flag-drop charge is $1.80; after that, it's $1.80 per mile. A maximum of four passengers can share a cab; the third and fourth passengers will each incur an extra charge of 50¢.

ON FOOT

Seattle is a surprisingly compact city. You can easily walk from Pioneer Square to Pike Place Market and take in most of downtown. Remember, though, that the city is also very hilly. When you head in from the waterfront, you will be climbing a very steep hill. If you get tired while strolling downtown, remember that between 6am and 7pm, you can always catch a bus for free as long as you plan to stay within the Ride Free Area. Cross the street only at corners and only with the lights in your favor. Jaywalking, especially in the downtown area, is a ticketable offense.

3 Where to Stay

Seattle is close on the heels of San Francisco as a West Coast summer-in-the-city destination, so its hotels stay pretty much booked solid for July and August. Not only do the hotels here stay full during the summer, if you aren't on an expense account, you may be faced with sticker shock when you see what Seattle's downtown hotels charge. However, if you're willing to head out a bit from downtown, you'll find prices a little easier to swallow.

Be sure to make reservations as far in advance as possible, especially if you plan a visit during Seafair or another major festival. See the "Washington Calendar of Events" on p. 22 for the dates of major festivals.

In the following listings, price categories are based on rates for a double room in high season (most hotels charge the same for a single or double room). Keep in mind that the rates listed do not include taxes, which add up to around 16% in Seattle.

Note: For comparison purposes, we list what hotels call "rack rates" or walk-in rates—but you should never have to pay these highly inflated prices. Various discounts and specials are often available, so make it a point to ask if any are being offered during your stay (and be sure to check the hotel's website for Internet specials). At inexpensive chain motels, discounted rates are almost always available for AAA members and seniors.

Room rates can be considerably lower from October through April (the rainy season), and downtown hotels often offer substantially reduced prices on weekends throughout the year (while budget hotels often charge more on weekends).

A few hotels include breakfast in their rates; others offer complimentary breakfast only on certain deluxe floors. Most Seattle hotels offer nonsmoking rooms, while most bed-and-breakfast inns are exclusively nonsmoking establishments. Most hotels, but few inns, also offer wheelchair-accessible rooms.

If you're having a hard time finding a room in your price range, consider using the services of **Pacific Northwest Journeys** (© **800/935-9730** or 206/935-9730; www.pnwjourneys.com). This company specializes in itinerary planning, but also offers a reservation service. The charge is $45 per reservation; however, you can usually make that up in savings on just a 2-night stay. If you're going to be in town for longer than that, you'll definitely save money. Last-minute reservations are often possible, too. A consultation service is also available for people who would like a little assistance with their itinerary.

Every year from November through March, more than two dozen Seattle hotels offer deep-cut discounts on their rooms through the **Seattle Hotel Hotline**'s (© **800/535-7071** or 206/461-5882) Seattle Super Saver Package. Room rates under this plan are generally 50% of what they would be in the summer months. Any time of year, you can call this hot line for help with making hotel reservations.

Seattle is a city of diverse neighborhoods, and in many of those neighborhoods, you'll discover fine B&Bs. Often less expensive than downtown hotels, these B&Bs provide an opportunity to see what life in Seattle is like for the locals. We've listed some of our favorites in the pages that follow, but to find out about other good B&Bs in Seattle, contact the **Seattle Bed & Breakfast Association** (© **800/348-5630** or 206/547-1020; www.seattlebandbs.com). Alternatively, you can contact **A Pacific Reservation Service** (© **800/684-2932** or 206/439-7677; www.seattlebedandbreakfast.com), which represents dozens of accommodations, mostly bed-and-breakfast homes, in the Seattle area. A wide range of rates is available.

DOWNTOWN & FIRST HILL

Downtown Seattle is the heart of the city's business community and home to numerous business hotels. Although these properties are among the most conveniently located Seattle hotels, they are also the most expensive choices and are designed primarily for business travelers on expense accounts, not vacationers. Many of these hotels do offer discounted weekend and winter rates, however. The area has plenty of good restaurants, but they tend to fall into one of two categories—cheap lunch spots and expense-account dinner places.

VERY EXPENSIVE

Alexis Hotel 🦆🦆   The Alexis is a sparkling gem in an enviable location halfway between Pike Place Market and Pioneer Square and only 3 blocks from the waterfront, the Seattle Art Museum, and Benaroya Hall. In the middle of the lobby is a massive Dale Chihuly chandelier, and throughout the hotel there's an extensive art collection. The pleasant mix of contemporary and antique furnishings, and cheerful and personalized service give the Alexis a very special atmosphere. In the guest rooms, classic styling with a European flavor prevails. Almost half of the rooms here are suites, including very comfortable fireplace suites with whirlpool baths. The spa suites are the real winners, offering whirlpool tubs in exceedingly luxurious bathrooms. The hotel has complimentary evening wine tastings.

1007 First Ave. (at Madison St.), Seattle, WA 98104. © **800/426-7033** or 206/624-4844. Fax 206/621-9009. www.alexishotel.com. 109 units. $299–$319 double; $419–$599 suite. Children under 18 stay free in parent's

Seattle Accommodations & Dining—Downtown Including First Hill

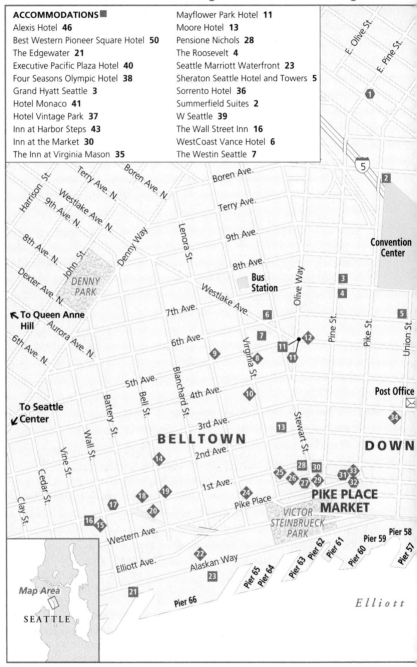

ACCOMMODATIONS

Alexis Hotel **46**
Best Western Pioneer Square Hotel **50**
The Edgewater **21**
Executive Pacific Plaza Hotel **40**
Four Seasons Olympic Hotel **38**
Grand Hyatt Seattle **3**
Hotel Monaco **41**
Hotel Vintage Park **37**
Inn at Harbor Steps **43**
Inn at the Market **30**
The Inn at Virginia Mason **35**

Mayflower Park Hotel **11**
Moore Hotel **13**
Pensione Nichols **28**
The Roosevelt **4**
Seattle Marriott Waterfront **23**
Sheraton Seattle Hotel and Towers **5**
Sorrento Hotel **36**
Summerfield Suites **2**
W Seattle **39**
The Wall Street Inn **16**
WestCoast Vance Hotel **6**
The Westin Seattle **7**

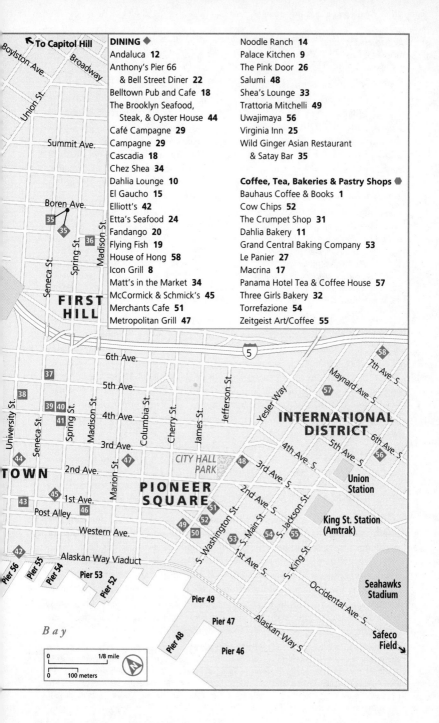

DINING ◆

Andaluca **12**
Anthony's Pier 66
    & Bell Street Diner **22**
Belltown Pub and Cafe **18**
The Brooklyn Seafood,
    Steak, & Oyster House **44**
Café Campagne **29**
Campagne **29**
Cascadia **18**
Chez Shea **34**
Dahlia Lounge **10**
El Gaucho **15**
Elliott's **42**
Etta's Seafood **24**
Fandango **20**
Flying Fish **19**
House of Hong **58**
Icon Grill **8**
Matt's in the Market **34**
McCormick & Schmick's **45**
Merchants Cafe **51**
Metropolitan Grill **47**

Noodle Ranch **14**
Palace Kitchen **9**
The Pink Door **26**
Salumi **48**
Shea's Lounge **33**
Trattoria Mitchelli **49**
Uwajimaya **56**
Virginia Inn **25**
Wild Ginger Asian Restaurant
    & Satay Bar **35**

Coffee, Tea, Bakeries & Pastry Shops ⬢

Bauhaus Coffee & Books **1**
Cow Chips **52**
The Crumpet Shop **31**
Dahlia Bakery **11**
Grand Central Baking Company **53**
Le Panier **27**
Macrina **17**
Panama Hotel Tea & Coffee House **57**
Three Girls Bakery **32**
Torrefazione **54**
Zeitgeist Art/Coffee **55**

To Capitol Hill
Boylston Ave.
Broadway
Union St.
Summit Ave.
Boren Ave.
Spring St.
Madison St.
Seneca St.
FIRST HILL

6th Ave.
5th Ave.
University St.
Seneca St.
Spring St.
Madison St.
4th Ave.
3rd Ave.
Columbia St.
Cherry St.
James St.
Jefferson St.
Yesler Way
Maynard Ave. S.
7th Ave. S.
INTERNATIONAL DISTRICT
4th Ave. S.
5th Ave. S.
6th Ave. S.
2nd Ave.
Marion St.
CITY HALL PARK
3rd Ave. S.
PIONEER SQUARE
2nd Ave. S.
S. Jackson St.
Union Station
1st Ave.
Post Alley
S. Washington St.
S. Main St.
King St. Station (Amtrak)
Western Ave.
1st Ave. S.
S. King St.
Alaskan Way Viaduct
Pier 53
Pier 52
Pier 55
Pier 54
Pier 56
Pier 49
Pier 47
Pier 48
Pier 46
Alaskan Way S.
Occidental Ave. S.
Seahawks Stadium
Safeco Field
Bay

TOWN

0   1/8 mile
0   100 meters

room. AE, DC, DISC, MC, V. Valet parking $26. Pets accepted. **Amenities:** Restaurant (New American); 2 lounges; exercise room and access to nearby health club; Aveda day spa; steam room; concierge; 24-hr. room service; massage; babysitting; laundry service; dry cleaning. *In room:* A/C, TV, fax, dataport, minibar, hair dryer, iron.

Four Seasons Olympic Hotel ★★★   If nothing but classically elegant surroundings will do, then head straight for the Four Seasons Olympic Hotel, an Italian Renaissance palace. Without a doubt, this hotel has the grandest lobby in Seattle. Gilt-and-crystal chandeliers hang from the arched ceiling, and ornate moldings grace the glowing hand-burnished oak walls and pillars. Although many of the guest rooms tend to be rather small (with either two twin beds or one king), all are very elegant. If you crave extra space, opt for one of the suites (however, be aware that the executive suites aren't much bigger than the hotel's deluxe rooms). For plush surroundings, excellent service, and great amenities, this hotel can't be beat. **The Georgian** is the most elegant restaurant in Seattle.

411 University St., Seattle, WA 98101. © **800/223-8772**, 800/821-8106 (in Washington state), 800/268-6282 (in Canada), or 206/621-1700. Fax 206/682-9633. www.fourseasons.com/seattle. 450 units. $325–$395 double; $415–$3,365 suite. Children 18 and under stay free in parent's room. AE, DC, DISC, MC, V. Valet parking $28. Pets accepted. **Amenities:** 2 restaurants (Continental/Northwest, seafood); 2 lounges; health club with indoor pool, exercise machines, Jacuzzi, and saunas; spa; children's programs; concierge; downtown courtesy car; business center; shopping arcade; 24-hr. room service; massage; babysitting; laundry service; dry cleaning; executive-level rooms. *In room:* A/C, TV, dataport, minibar, hair dryer, safe, free local calls.

Grand Hyatt Seattle ★★★   Luxury and technology merge at this downtown hotel, which is the most up-to-the-minute, business-savvy hotel in Seattle. A Willem de Kooning sculpture outside the hotel's front door and a spacious lobby full of regionally inspired glass art set the tone the moment you arrive. However, unless you spring for something pricier than the basic "deluxe guest room," you're going to be a bit cramped; the least expensive rooms here are definitely designed for solo travelers. The health club is well outfitted, but there's no swimming pool, which means that families might want to opt for the Four Seasons instead.

721 Pine St., Seattle, WA 98101. © **800/233-1234** or 206/774-1234. Fax 206/774-6120. www.grandseattle. hyatt.com. 425 units. $179–$340 double; $1,250–$3,000 suite. Children 18 and under stay free in parent's room. AE, DC, DISC, MC, V. Valet parking $28; self-parking $22. **Amenities:** Restaurant (New American); lounge; health club with Jacuzzi, sauna, and steam room; concierge; 24-hr. room service; massage; laundry service; dry cleaning. *In room:* A/C, TV, dataport, fridge, coffeemaker, hair dryer, iron, safe.

Hotel Monaco ★★   Housed in a building that was once a telephone-company switching center, the Monaco is one of downtown Seattle's hippest business hotels, attracting a young and affluent clientele. If you appreciate cutting-edge style, you'll go for the eclectic over-the-top retro-contemporary design here. In the guest rooms, you'll find wild color schemes, with bold striped wallpaper, stereos with CD players, and leopard-print terry-cloth robes. For a view of Mount Rainier, ask for room no. 1019, 1119, or 1219. Missing your pet at home? Call the front desk, and a staff member will send up a pet goldfish for the night. **Sazerac,** the hotel's restaurant, is as boldly designed as the rest of the hotel.

1101 Fourth Ave., Seattle, WA 98101. © **800/945-2240** or 206/621-1770. Fax 206/621-7779. www.monaco-seattle.com. 189 units. $299 double; $339–$928 suite. Rates include evening wine tasting. Children under 18 stay free in parent's room. AE, DC, DISC, MC, V. Valet parking $26. Pets accepted. **Amenities:** Restaurant (New American); lounge; exercise room and access to nearby health club; concierge; business center; 24-hr. room service; massage; babysitting; laundry service; dry cleaning. *In room:* A/C, TV, dataport, minibar, coffeemaker, hair dryer, iron.

Hotel Vintage Park ★★   Small, classically elegant, and exceedingly romantic, the Vintage Park is a must for both lovers and wine lovers. The guest rooms are named for Washington wineries and are perfect for romantic getaways, and each evening in the lobby, there is a complimentary wine tasting. Even the mini-bars are stocked with Washington wines. Rooms vary quite a bit here, but when you see the plush draperies framing the beds and the neo-Victorian furnishings in the deluxe rooms, you'll likely want to spend your days luxuriating amid the sumptuous surroundings. Deluxe rooms have the best views (including views of Mount Rainier), and although the bathrooms are small, they do have attractive granite counters. Standard rooms, though smaller and less luxuriously appointed, are still very comfortable, and surprisingly, the bathrooms are larger than those in the deluxe rooms.

1100 Fifth Ave., Seattle, WA 98101. © **800/624-4433** or 206/624-8000. Fax 206/623-0568. www.hotelvintage park.com. 126 units. $279–$309 double; $495 suite. Children under 18 stay free in parent's room. AE, DC, DISC, MC, V. Valet parking $26. Pets accepted. **Amenities:** Restaurant (Italian); lounge; access to nearby health club; concierge; 24-hr. room service; massage; babysitting; laundry service; dry cleaning. *In room:* A/C, TV, fax, data-port, minibar, hair dryer, iron.

Sorrento Hotel ★★★ With its wrought-iron gates, palm trees in the entrance courtyard, and plush seating in the octagonal lobby, the Sorrento, which first opened its doors in 1909, has a classic elegance and old-world atmos-phere. The guest rooms here, no two of which are alike, are among the finest in the city, and most are set up for business travelers. The hotel boasts command-ing views of downtown Seattle from its setting high on First Hill, yet downtown is only a few (steep) blocks away. Ask for a room on the west side of the hotel; you'll have a view of the city and Puget Sound. The hotel's dining room is a dark, clubby place, and in the lounge, you can get light meals and afternoon tea.

900 Madison St., Seattle, WA 99104-1297. © **800/426-1265** or 206/622-6400. Fax 206/343-6155. www.hotel sorrento.com. 76 units. $270–$295 double; $340–$2,500 suite. Children under 18 stay free in parent's room. AE, DC, DISC, MC, V. Valet parking $24. Pets accepted ($50). **Amenities:** Restaurant (Northwest/Mediterranean); lounge; exercise room and access to nearby health club; concierge; complimentary downtown shuttle; business center; salon; 24-hr. room service; massage; laundry service; dry cleaning. *In room:* A/C, TV, fax, dataport, mini-bar, coffeemaker, hair dryer, iron.

W Seattle ★★ The W hotel chain has won plenty of national attention and devoted fans for its oh-so-hip accommodations, and here in the land of espresso and high tech, the W is a natural. The lobby has the look and feel of a stage set, with dramatic lighting and sleek furniture, and in the evenings it's transformed into a trendy lounge scene. Not only are the rooms beautifully designed and filled with plush amenities, but they also tend to be larger than those at other W hotels. If you can spring for an additional $40 or $50 per night, the -09 or -02 "Cool Corner" rooms are worth requesting. Guest rooms are full of great perks such as Aveda bath products, goose-down comforters, and CD players (there's a CD library from which you can borrow disks).

1112 Fourth Ave., Seattle, WA 98101. © **877/W-HOTELS** or 206/264-6000. Fax 206/264-6100. www.whotels. com/seattle. 426 units. $199–$409 double; from $750 suite. Children under 18 stay free in parent's room. AE, DC, DISC, MC, V. Valet parking $25. Pets accepted. **Amenities:** Restaurant (Contemporary American); lounge; exercise room and access to nearby health club; concierge; business center; 24-hr. room service; in-room mas-sage; laundry service; dry cleaning. *In room:* A/C, TV, dataport, minibar, coffeemaker, hair dryer, iron, safe.

EXPENSIVE

Inn at Harbor Steps ★★ Situated on the lower floors of a modern apartment building across the street from the Seattle Art Museum, this inn offers an excel-lent location that's convenient to all of downtown Seattle's major attractions. The guest rooms, which overlook a courtyard garden, are so spacious that they feel like apartments, and styling leans decidedly toward the Martha Stewart aesthetic.

Every room has a gas fireplace, and the largest rooms have whirlpool tubs. The only real drawback here is the lack of views. Located in the same building as the hotel, the **Wolfgang Puck Cafe** features contemporary food and decor, plus water views.

1221 First Ave., Seattle, WA 98101. ℂ 888/728-8910 or 206/748-0973. Fax 206/748-0533. www.foursisters. com/inns/innatharborsteps.html. 28 units. $165–$230 double. Rates include full breakfast and afternoon tea and appetizers. Children 4 and under stay free in parent's room. AE, DC, MC, V. Parking $15. **Amenities:** Restaurant (New American); lounge; indoor pool; health club with Jacuzzi, sauna, basketball court; concierge; limited room service; massage; babysitting; laundry service; dry cleaning. *In room:* A/C, TV, dataport, minibar, coffeemaker, hair dryer, iron.

Sheraton Seattle Hotel and Towers ★★★
At 35 stories, this is one of the two largest hotels in Seattle. Because it's so large, it does a brisk convention business, and you'll almost always find the building buzzing with activity. But don't let the crowds put you off. There's a reason so many people want to stay here— the hotel does things right and captures much of the essence of Seattle in its many features. It has a 35th-floor exercise room and swimming pool with great views of the city. You also get good views from guest rooms on the higher floors. All the rooms have been renovated in the past 2 years and are fairly spacious. For even more space, book one of the king rooms, which are designed for business travelers.

1400 Sixth Ave., Seattle, WA 98101. ℂ 800/325-3535 or 206/621-9000. Fax 206/621-8441. www.sheraton. com/seattle. 840 units. $169–$385 double; $300–$5,000 suite. Children under 18 stay free in parent's room. AE, DC, DISC, MC, V. Valet parking $26; self-parking $24. **Amenities:** 3 restaurants (American, oyster bar, pizza); 2 lounges; indoor pool; health club; Jacuzzi; sauna; concierge; business center; 24-hr. room service; massage; babysitting; laundry service; dry cleaning; concierge-level rooms. *In room:* A/C, TV, dataport, minibar, coffeemaker, hair dryer, iron, safe.

The Westin Seattle ★★★
With its distinctive cylindrical towers, the 47-story Westin is the tallest hotel in Seattle, and consequently provides the best views of any hotel in the city. From rooms on the upper floors of the north tower's northwest side, you'll get breathtaking views of the Space Needle, Puget Sound, and the Olympic Mountains. Views from lower floors can be good, too, if you are higher than the buildings in the surrounding blocks. Couple those great views with the Westin's plush "heavenly beds," and you'll be sleeping on clouds both literally and figuratively. There are also two excellent restaurants. With great beds and great views, guest rooms here are some of the nicest in town.

1900 Fifth Ave., Seattle, WA 98101. ℂ 800/WESTIN-1 or 206/728-1000. Fax 206/728-2007. www.westin. com/seattle. 891 units. $169–$345 double; from $419 suite. Children under 18 stay free in parent's room. AE, DC, DISC, MC, V. Valet parking $24; self-parking $24. Small pets accepted ($50 deposit). **Amenities:** 3 restaurants (Euro-Asian, Japanese, American); lounge; large indoor pool; 2 exercise rooms; Jacuzzi; children's programs; concierge; business center; 24-hr. room service; laundry service; dry cleaning; concierge-level rooms. *In room:* A/C, TV, dataport, minibar, coffeemaker, hair dryer, iron.

MODERATE
Executive Pacific Plaza Hotel ★ (Value
There aren't too many reasonably priced choices left in downtown Seattle, but this hotel, built in 1928, offers moderately priced rooms and a prime location—halfway between Pike Place Market and Pioneer Square, and just about the same distance from the waterfront. Despite a tasteful renovation a few years ago, the rooms are still small (verging on tiny) and sometimes quite cramped. Consequently, this place is recommended mostly for solo travelers. Also, be aware that the hotel has no air-conditioning, and west-facing rooms can get warm in the summer. Bathrooms, although very small, have been completely upgraded.

400 Spring St., Seattle, WA 98104. © 800/426-1165 or 206/623-3900. Fax 206/623-2059. www.pacific plazahotel.com. 160 units. $89–$119 double. Rates include continental breakfast. Children under 14 stay free in parent's room. AE, DC, DISC, MC, V. Parking $16. **Amenities:** Concierge; laundry service; dry cleaning. *In room:* TV, dataport, coffeemaker, hair dryer.

The Inn at Virginia Mason 🤻

You may think we've sent you to a hospital rather than a hotel when you first arrive at this older hotel on Pill Hill—but don't have a heart attack. Although it is adjacent to the Virginia Mason Hospital, this is definitely a hotel. Regardless of the fact that most guests are here because of the hospital, the hotel is a good choice for vacationers as well. Rates are economical, the location is quiet, and you're close to downtown. There's a rooftop sun deck and a shady little courtyard just off the lobby. Although the carpets and furniture here are in need of replacement, the rooms are still serviceable. Because this is an old building, room sizes vary, but most have large closets, modern bathrooms, and wingback chairs. Deluxe rooms and suites can be quite large, and some have whirlpool baths and fireplaces.

1006 Spring St., Seattle, WA 98104. © 800/283-6453 or 206/583-6453. Fax 206/223-7545. 79 units. $115–$165 double; $175–$245 suite. AE, DC, DISC, MC, V. Parking $11. **Amenities:** Restaurant (American); access to nearby health club; limited room service; laundry service; dry cleaning. *In room:* TV, overhead heating/cooling systems.

Mayflower Park Hotel 🤻🤻

If your favorite recreational activities include shopping or sipping martinis, the Mayflower Park is for you. Built in 1927, this historic hotel is connected to the upscale Westlake Center shopping plaza and is within a block of both Nordstrom and Bon-Macys. Most rooms here are furnished with an eclectic blend of contemporary Italian and traditional European pieces. Some rooms still have small, old-fashioned bathrooms, but all have been recently renovated. The smallest guest rooms are cramped; if you crave space, ask for one of the larger corner rooms or a suite. Martini drinkers will want to spend time at the hotel's **Oliver's Lounge,** which serves the best martinis in Seattle and has free hors d'oeuvres in the evening. The hotel's **Andaluca** restaurant is a plush, contemporary spot serving a highly creative cuisine. See "Where to Dine," later in this chapter, for a full review.

405 Olive Way, Seattle, WA 98101. © 800/426-5100, 206/382-6990, or 206/623-8700. Fax 206/382-6997. www.mayflowerpark.com. 171 units. $119–$200 double; $139–$365 suite. Children 18 and under stay free in parent's room. AE, DC, DISC, MC, V. Valet parking $21. **Amenities:** Restaurant (Mediterranean/Northwest); lounge; exercise room and access to nearby health club; Jacuzzi; concierge; business center; shopping arcade; 24-hr. room service; laundry service; dry cleaning. *In room:* A/C, TV, dataport, coffeemaker, hair dryer, iron.

The Roosevelt, A Coast Hotel 🤻

With a small lobby decorated to resemble a library in an old mansion (complete with bookshelves around the fireplace and a grand piano off to one side), the Roosevelt is a vintage 1929 hotel with plenty of class. Be forewarned, though, that the rooms tend to be quite small, and rates can be high for what you get, unless you're visiting in the rainy season or can get some sort of discounted deal. The smallest rooms, known here as studios, have one double bed and a tiny bathroom with a shower only (no tub) and are very cramped. For more space, you'll have to opt for a queen or king room. Most units have small bathrooms with little counter space. The largest rooms verge on being suites and have double whirlpool tubs.

1531 Seventh Ave., Seattle, WA 98101. © 800/663-1144 or 206/621-1200. Fax 206/233-0335. www. coasthotels.com. 151 units. $139–$190 double. Children 18 and under stay free in parent's room. AE, DC, DISC, MC, V. Valet parking $18. **Amenities:** Restaurant (American); lounge; exercise room; concierge; limited room service; laundry service; dry cleaning. *In room:* A/C, TV, dataport, coffeemaker, hair dryer, iron.

Summerfield Suites by Wyndham ⭐ *Value* Located just a block uphill from the Washington State Convention and Trade Center, this hotel caters primarily to business travelers who need a bit of extra room for getting work done while in town. The hotel is about equidistant between the waterfront and the hip Capitol Hill shopping and nightlife district, which also makes it a good choice if you're just here for fun. The suites are well laid out and have full kitchens, so you can save on restaurant bills. Many rooms have good views that take in the Space Needle, but be aware that many rooms also get traffic noise. The pool, though tiny, is on a pleasant terrace in an attractively landscaped courtyard area.

1011 Pike St., Seattle, WA 98101. ✆ 800/833-4353 or 206/682-8282. Fax 206/682-5315. www.wyndham. com. 193 units. $99–$269 double. Rates include continental breakfast. Children 18 and under stay free in parent's room. AE, DC, DISC, MC, V. Valet parking $24. **Amenities:** Small outdoor pool; exercise room; Jacuzzi; concierge; downtown courtesy shuttle; coin-op laundry; dry cleaning. *In room:* A/C, TV, dataport, coffeemaker, hair dryer, iron.

THE WATERFRONT

The waterfront is Seattle's most touristy neighborhood, yet it also has the city's finest views and is home to several worthwhile attractions and activities. Although there are only two hotels here, it should be the top choice of anyone wanting to spend a Seattle vacation in the thick of things.

EXPENSIVE

The Edgewater ⭐⭐ *Value* Located on a pier at the north end of the waterfront, The Edgewater is Seattle's only hotel situated directly on the bay and is designed to resemble a deluxe fishing lodge. The views out the windows are among the best in the city, and sunsets are memorable. On a clear day you can see the Olympic Mountains across Puget Sound. Pull up a seat between the lobby's river-stone fireplace and the wall of glass that looks out on Elliott Bay, and you'll see why this is one of our favorite Seattle hotels. The mountain-lodge theme continues in the rooms, which feature rustic fireplaces and lodgepole-pine furniture. The least expensive rooms here overlook the city (and the parking lot), so it's worth it to spring for a water view. The rooms with balconies are a bit smaller than other rooms but are our top choice.

Pier 67, 2411 Alaskan Way, Seattle, WA 98121. ✆ 800/624-0670 or 206/728-7000. Fax 206/441-4119. www.edgewaterhotel.com. 234 units. $159–$399 double; $550–$2,500 suite. Children under 18 stay free in parent's room. AE, DC, DISC, MC, V. Valet parking $20. Pets accepted. **Amenities:** Restaurant (Pacific Rim/international); lounge; exercise room and access to nearby health club; courtesy bikes; concierge; business center; limited room service; laundry service; dry cleaning. *In room:* A/C, TV, dataport, coffeemaker, hair dryer, iron.

Seattle Marriott Waterfront ⭐⭐ Located across Alaskan Way from Elliott Bay, this is Seattle's newest luxury hotel, and although it does not have the superb views of the nearby Edgewater, it's your only other option if you want to stay on the waterfront. The hotel seems to do a brisk business putting up people about to head out on a cruise (some cruise ships dock right across the street). The best views here are from the large junior suites at the northwest corner of the hotel. Many standard rooms have only limited views because of the way the hotel is designed. However, at least the standard rooms have little balconies where you can stand and breathe in the salt air.

2100 Alaskan Way, Seattle, WA 98121. ✆ 800/228-9290 or 206/443-5000. Fax 206/256-1100. www.marriott. com. 358 units. $159–$251 double. AE, DC, DISC, MC, V. Valet parking $25. **Amenities:** 2 restaurants (seafood, American); 2 lounges; indoor/outdoor pool; exercise room; Jacuzzi; concierge; business center; 24-hr. room service; coin-op laundry; laundry service; dry cleaning. *In room:* A/C, TV, dataport, coffeemaker, hair dryer, iron, safe.

PIONEER SQUARE & THE INTERNATIONAL DISTRICT

The historic Pioneer Square area is Seattle's main nightlife district and can be a pretty rowdy place on a Saturday night. By day, however, the area's many art galleries and antiques stores attract a very different clientele. Still, even in the daylight, be prepared to encounter a lot of street people. Warnings aside, this is one of the prettiest corners of Seattle and the only downtown neighborhood with historic flavor. The International District lies but a few blocks away from Pioneer Square—again, a good place to explore by day but less appealing at night. There is only one recommendable hotel in the area.

EXPENSIVE

Best Western Pioneer Square Hotel 𝄞   This hotel is located right in the heart of the Pioneer Square historic district, Seattle's main nightlife neighborhood. As such, things get especially raucous on weekend nights, and this hotel is only recommended for urban dwellers accustomed to dealing with street people and noise. However, if you're in town to party (or to attend a Mariners or Seahawks game), there's no more convenient location in the city. This economical hotel is also convenient to the waterfront streetcars and the Washington State Ferries terminal. However, take care on the streets around here late at night. Guest rooms are, for the most part, fairly small (some are positively cramped) but are furnished in an attractive classic style.

77 Yesler Way, Seattle, WA 98104. ℂ 800/800-5514 or 206/340-1234. Fax 206/467-0707. www.pioneersquare. com. 75 units. July–Sept $149–$219 double; Oct–June $119–$199 double. Rates include continental breakfast. Children 12 and under stay free in parent's room. AE, DC, DISC, MC, V. Parking $15. **Amenities:** Access to nearby health club; concierge; business center; limited room service; babysitting; laundry service; dry cleaning. *In room:* A/C, TV, dataport, coffeemaker, hair dryer, iron, free local calls.

BELLTOWN & PIKE PLACE MARKET

Belltown, which extends north from Pike Place Market, has for several years been Seattle's fastest-growing urban neighborhood, sprouting dozens of restaurants and several good hotels. If your Seattle travel plans include lots of eating out at hip restaurants, then Belltown is the place to stay.

EXPENSIVE

Inn at the Market 𝄞𝄞   For romance, convenience, and the chance to immerse yourself in the Seattle aesthetic, it's hard to beat this small, European-style hotel in Pike Place Market. A rooftop deck overlooking the harbor provides a tranquil spot to soak up the sun on summer afternoons. To make the most of a stay here, be sure to ask for one of the water-view rooms, which have wide bay windows that overlook Puget Sound. Even if you don't get a water-view room, you'll still find spacious accommodations and large bathrooms. The decor is tastefully elegant, with the feel of an upscale European beach resort. **Campagne,** the hotel's formal main dining room, serves excellent southern French fare, while **Café Campagne** offers country-style French food amid casual surroundings (see "Where to Dine," later in this chapter, for full reviews of both restaurants). **Bacco,** open for breakfast and lunch, serves lighter meals.

86 Pine St., Seattle, WA 98101. ℂ 800/446-4484 or 206/443-3600. www.innatthemarket.com. 70 units. $195–$330 double; $499 suite. Children 18 and under stay free in parent's room. AE, DISC, MC, V. Parking $20. **Amenities:** 3 restaurants (country French; juice bar); access to nearby health club; concierge; courtesy downtown shuttle; limited room service; dry cleaning. *In room:* A/C, TV, dataport, minibar, coffeemaker, hair dryer, iron, safe.

MODERATE

Pensione Nichols   It's never easy finding an economical downtown-area lodging with character, but that's exactly what you'll discover at this European-style B&B,

located in the heart of Pike Place Market. It's a popular choice with younger travelers and families. The budget-priced units with shared bathroom are all on the third floor of the building, and though most of the eclectically furnished rooms don't have windows, they do have skylights. However, most guests spend their time in the comfortable lounging area, with huge windows overlooking Elliott Bay. If you want to splurge, the two suites are quite large and have private bathrooms and windows with water views. Be prepared to climb a lot of stairs.

1923 First Ave., Seattle, WA 98101. © **800/440-7125** or 206/441-7125. www.pensione-nichols.com. 12 units, 10 with shared bathroom. $110 double with shared bathroom; $195 suite with private bathroom. 2-night minimum on summer weekends. Rates include breakfast. AE, DISC, MC, V. Parking $10. Pets accepted. *In room:* A/C, no phone.

Vance Hotel 👉 *Value* Built in the 1920s by lumber baron Joseph Vance, this hotel has a very elegant little lobby with wood paneling, marble floors, Oriental carpets, and ornate plasterwork moldings. Accommodations vary in size and style, and some are absolutely tiny (bathrooms are also uniformly small); corner rooms compensate with lots of windows and decent views. Furniture is in keeping with the style of the lobby and for the most part is fairly upscale. If you're here on business, this hotel offers a convenient location, with the convention center only a couple of blocks away.

620 Stewart St., Seattle, WA 98101. © **877/956-8500** or 206/956-8500. Fax 206/443-5754. www.vancehotel. com. 165 units. $99–$149 double. AE, DC, DISC, MC, V. Parking $18. **Amenities:** Restaurant (nuevo Latino); lounge; access to nearby health club; concierge; limited room service; dry cleaning. *In room:* A/C, TV, dataport, coffeemaker, hair dryer, iron.

The Wall Street Inn 👉 *Value* Located in the heart of Belltown, upstairs from El Gaucho (Seattle's most stylish steak house), this B&B was once a sailors' union boardinghouse. Today, the rooms, though not fancy, are bright and modern, and a few still have kitchenettes. The inn has a comfortable living room with leather couches and a fireplace, and a small deck with a barbecue. Cookies, coffee, and tea are set out in the afternoon. Although Belltown is Seattle's most self-consciously hip neighborhood, this is a traditionally styled, comfortable, and conveniently located base from which to explore the city. Best of all, there are loads of great restaurants within a few blocks.

2507 First Ave., Seattle, WA 98121. © **800/624-1117** or 206/448-0125. Fax 206/448-2406. www.wallstreetinn. com. 20 units. $119–$179 double. Rates include deluxe continental breakfast. Children under 18 stay free in parent's room. AE, DISC, MC, V. Parking $6–$10. **Amenities:** Access to nearby health club; concierge; business center; massage; coin-op laundry. *In room:* TV, dataport, fridge, coffeemaker, hair dryer, iron, ceiling fans.

INEXPENSIVE

Moore Hotel If you've ever traveled through Europe on a tight budget, you'll know what to expect from this place. It's nothing fancy, and the rooms aren't in the best shape. However, you won't find many acceptable downtown-area hotels in this price range, so it's fine for young travelers who don't demand perfection from a cheap hotel. You certainly can't beat the location. Trendy restaurants, nightclubs, and Pike Place Market are all within a few blocks. The lobby, with its marble, tiles, and decorative moldings, is in much better shape than the rooms. There's a hip restaurant/lounge on the premises. Ask for a room with a view of the sound.

1926 Second Ave., Seattle, WA 98101. © **800/421-5508** or 206/448-4851. Fax 206/728-5668. www.moore hotel.com. 140 units, 45 with shared bathroom. $45 double with shared bathroom; $59–$74 double with private bathroom. MC, V. Parking $12. **Amenities:** Restaurant (American); lounge. *In room:* TV.

QUEEN ANNE & SEATTLE CENTER

The Queen Anne neighborhood is divided into an Upper Queen Anne and a Lower Queen Anne. The upper neighborhood is an upscale residential area with an attractive shopping district. The hotels listed here are in the lower neighborhood, which conveniently flanks Seattle Center. The neighborhood also offers lots of inexpensive restaurants for the budget-minded.

MODERATE

Comfort Suites Downtown/Seattle Center ★ *Kids*   Although it's none too easy to find this place (call and get specific directions for the approach you'll be taking), the bargain rates and spacious rooms make the Comfort Suites worth searching out. Since it's located only 3 blocks from Seattle Center, you could feasibly leave your car parked at the hotel for most of your stay and walk or use public transit to get around. If you've brought the family, the suites are a good deal, and the proximity to Seattle Center will help moms and dads keep the kids entertained. Ask for a room away from the busy highway that runs past the hotel.

601 Roy St., Seattle, WA 98109. ℂ **800/517-4000** or 206/282-2600. Fax 206/282-1112. www.comfortsuites. com. 158 units. $79–$159 double. Rates include continental breakfast. Children 18 and under stay free in parent's room. AE, DISC, MC, V. Free parking. **Amenities:** Exercise room; downtown courtesy shuttle; coin-op laundry. *In room:* A/C, TV, dataport, fridge, coffeemaker, hair dryer, iron, free local calls.

Inn at Queen Anne   Located in the Lower Queen Anne neighborhood close to Seattle Center and numerous restaurants and espresso bars, this inn is housed in a converted older apartment building. Though the rooms here aren't as nice as those at the nearby MarQueen, they're comfortable enough, albeit sometimes a bit cramped and not entirely modern. The convenient location and economical rates are the big pluses here. A pleasant garden surrounds the hotel.

505 First Ave. N., Seattle, WA 98109. ℂ **800/952-5043** or 206/282-7357. Fax 206/217-9719. www.innatqueen anne.com. 68 units. May–Sept $99–$109 double, $119–$159 suite; Oct–Apr $89 double, $109–$139 suite. Rates include continental breakfast. Children 12 and under stay free in parent's room. AE, DC, DISC, MC, V. Parking $10. **Amenities:** Coin-op laundry; laundry service; dry cleaning. *In room:* TV, kitchenette, fridge, ceiling fans, free local calls.

MarQueen Hotel ★ *Kids* *Finds*   Located in the up-and-coming Lower Queen Anne neighborhood, this hotel is in a renovated 1918 brick building that will appeal to travelers who enjoy staying in hotels with historic character. Seattle Center, with its many performance venues and museums, is only 3 blocks away, and from there you can take the monorail into downtown. Although the hotel is geared toward business travelers (with lots of high-tech amenities), it's a good choice for vacationers as well. Guest rooms are spacious, though a bit oddly laid out due to the hotel's previous incarnation as an apartment building. Many rooms have separate little seating areas and full kitchens, which makes this a good choice for families (especially considering the proximity to Seattle Center's kid-oriented attractions). Lots of dark wood trim and hardwood floors give rooms here a genuinely old-fashioned feel. There's an excellent espresso bar in the hotel building and numerous good restaurants nearby, and there are also occasional complimentary wine receptions in the hotel lobby.

600 Queen Anne Ave. N., Seattle, WA 98109. ℂ **888/445-3076** or 206/282-7407. Fax 206/283-1499. www. marqueen.com. 56 units. $130–$185 double; $195–$290 suite. Children under 12 stay free in parent's room. AE, DC, DISC, MC, V. Valet parking $15. **Amenities:** 2 restaurants (New American, espresso bar); access to nearby health club; limited room service; massage; laundry service; dry cleaning. *In room:* A/C, TV, dataport, kitchen, minibar, fridge, coffeemaker, hair dryer, iron, free local calls.

Seattle Accommodations & Dining—Capitol Hill, Lake Union, Queen Anne & North Seattle

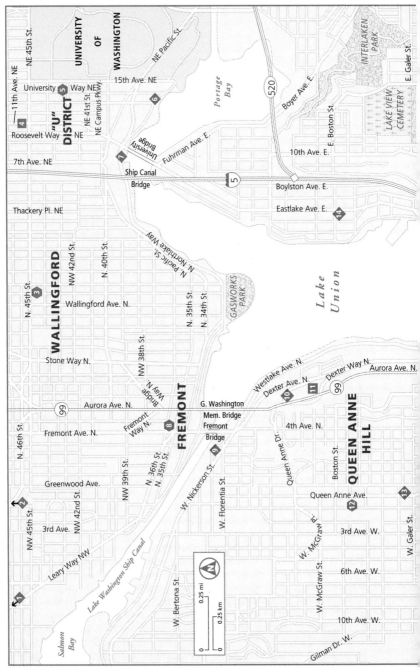

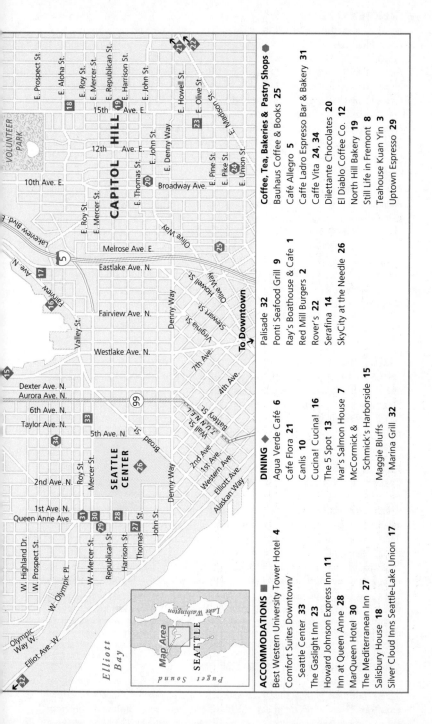

ACCOMMODATIONS ■

Best Western University Tower Hotel **4**
Comfort Suites Downtown/
  Seattle Center **33**
The Gaslight Inn **23**
Howard Johnson Express Inn **11**
Inn at Queen Anne **28**
MarQueen Hotel **30**
The Mediterranean Inn **27**
Salisbury House **18**
Silver Cloud Inns Seattle–Lake Union **17**

DINING ◆

Agua Verde Café **6**
Cafe Flora **21**
Canlis **10**
Cucina! Cucina! **16**
The 5 Spot **13**
Ivar's Salmon House **7**
McCormick &
  Schmick's Harborside **15**
Maggie Bluffs
  Marina Grill **32**

Palisade **32**
Ponti Seafood Grill **9**
Ray's Boathouse & Cafe **1**
Red Mill Burgers **2**
Rover's **22**
Serafina **14**
SkyCity at the Needle **26**

Coffee, Tea, Bakeries & Pastry Shops ●

Bauhaus Coffee & Books **25**
Café Allegro **5**
Caffe Ladro Espresso Bar & Bakery **31**
Caffe Vita **24, 34**
Dilettante Chocolates **20**
El Diablo Coffee Co. **12**
North Hill Bakery **19**
Still Life in Fremont **8**
Teahouse Kuan Yin **3**
Uptown Espresso **29**

INEXPENSIVE

Howard Johnson Express Inn ★ *(Value)*   Located on the eastern slopes of Queen Anne Hill, overlooking Lake Union and the distant Cascade Range, this older motel is just a short drive (or bus ride) from Seattle Center and is just across the Aurora Bridge from Fremont, which has lots of inexpensive restaurants. The best guest rooms, which can usually be had for around $80 to $85 in the summer, have balconies overlooking Lake Union. Right next door to the motel you'll find Canlis, one of Seattle's top restaurants (see "Where to Dine," below)—even if you can't afford to eat here, you can still have a drink at the bar and soak up the atmosphere.

2500 Aurora Ave. N., Seattle, WA 98109. ✆ **877/284-1900** or 206/284-1900. Fax 206/283-5298. www. howardjohnson.com. 94 units. $55–$99 double. Rates include continental breakfast. Children under 18 stay free in parent's room. AE, DC, DISC, MC, V. **Amenities:** Seasonal outdoor pool. *In room:* A/C, TV, coffeemaker.

The Mediterranean Inn ★   Don't be fooled by the name; this is not a bed-and-breakfast-type inn. But this modern apartment hotel in the Lower Queen Anne neighborhood is located just a couple of blocks from Seattle Center and is an ideal choice for longer stays in the city. Because the hotel is fairly new and because it was designed with travelers in mind, the rooms are much more comfortable than those at the nearby Inn at Queen Anne. Although all the rooms here are studio apartments, some have beds that roll back toward the wall to form a couch. We prefer the more standard rooms. A Starbucks is just off the lobby.

425 Queen Anne Ave. N., Seattle, WA 98109. ✆ **866/525-4700** or 206/428-4700. Fax 206/428-4699. www. mediterranean-inn.com. 180 units. $89–$109 double (from $450 weekly). AE, DC, DISC, MC, V. Parking $10. **Amenities:** Exercise room; business center; coin-op laundry. *In room:* A/C, TV, dataport, kitchenette, fridge, coffeemaker, hair dryer, iron.

LAKE UNION

Located less than a mile from downtown and lined with houseboats, marinas, and waterfront restaurants, Lake Union has a quintessentially Seattle character. Floatplanes use the lake as a runway, and you can rent a kayak, canoe, or rowboat from several places around the lake. If you are happiest when you're close to the water but want to avoid the crowds of the Seattle waterfront, this area is an excellent alternative.

EXPENSIVE

Silver Cloud Inns Seattle–Lake Union ★★ *(Kids) (Value)*   Located across the street from Lake Union, this moderately priced hotel offers good views (some of which take in the Space Needle). The rooms are big and filled with lots of amenities, which makes them convenient for long stays and family vacations. The two swimming pools (one indoors and one outdoors) should also appeal to kids. Although the hotel doesn't have a restaurant of its own, there are plenty of waterfront restaurants within walking distance. Floatplane tours also leave from right across the street. This is a good value for such a great location.

1150 Fairview Ave. N., Seattle, WA 98109. ✆ **800/330-5812** or 206/447-9500. Fax 206/812-4900. www.silver cloud.com. 184 units. June–Sept $129–$230 double; Oct–May $89–$179 double. Rates include continental breakfast. Children under 18 stay free in parent's room. AE, DC, DISC, MC, V. Free parking. **Amenities:** Indoor and outdoor pools; exercise room and access to nearby health club; 2 Jacuzzis; local courtesy shuttle; business center; laundry service; dry cleaning. *In room:* A/C, TV, dataport, fridge, coffeemaker, hair dryer, iron, free local calls.

CAPITOL HILL & EAST SEATTLE

Located a mile or so uphill and to the east of downtown Seattle, Capitol Hill is a neighborhood with a split personality. It's a hangout for the 20-something crowd and is the city's main gay neighborhood, yet it's also home to numerous large restored homes, many of which have been converted into bed-and-breakfast

Kids Family-Friendly Hotels

Comfort Suites Downtown/Seattle Center (p. 77) The suites make this a good family choice, and the location near the Seattle Center will make the kids happy.

MarQueen Hotel (p. 77) Located within a few blocks of Seattle Center and its many attractions, this converted apartment building provides a convenient location for families, and spacious suites with kitchenettes.

Seattle Marriott Sea-Tac Airport (p. 82) With a huge jungly atrium containing a swimming pool and whirlpool spas, kids can play Tarzan and never leave the hotel. A tiny game room has a few video game machines.

Silver Cloud Inns Seattle–Lake Union (p. 80) Located right across the street from Lake Union and with a good family restaurant (Cucina! Cucina!) a short walk away, this modern hotel is a good choice for families. It also has two swimming pools and big rooms.

inns. If you prefer B&Bs to corporate hotels, this is the best neighborhood in which to base yourself. Although Capitol Hill is a bit of a walk from downtown, the neighborhood has good public bus connections to the city center.

MODERATE

The Gaslight Inn ☆ Anyone enamored of Craftsman bungalows and the Arts and Crafts movement of the early 20th century should enjoy a stay in this 1906 home. Throughout the inn are numerous pieces of Stickley furniture, and everywhere you turn, oak trim frames doors and windows. The common rooms are decorated with a combination of Western and Northwestern flair, and throughout the inn's two houses are lots of art-glass pieces. In summer, guests can swim in the backyard pool. Guest rooms continue the design themes of the common areas with lots of oak furnishings and heavy, peeled-log beds in some rooms. An annex next door has a studio and suites with kitchens. The innkeepers here can provide a wealth of information about the surrounding Capitol Hill neighborhood, which is the center of Seattle's gay scene.

1727 15th Ave., Seattle, WA 98122. © 206/325-3654. Fax 206/328-4803. www.gaslight-inn.com. 15 units, 3 with shared bathroom. $78–$148 double; $128 studio; $148–$178 suite. Rates include continental breakfast. AE, MC, V. Off-street parking for suites. No children under 18 allowed. **Amenities:** Small outdoor pool; access to nearby health club; concierge. *In room:* TV, dataport, hair dryer, iron.

Salisbury House Located on tree-lined 16th Avenue East, this grand old house has a wide wraparound porch from which you can enjoy one of Seattle's prettiest residential streets. Inside there's plenty to admire as well. Two living rooms (one with a wood-burning fireplace) and a second-floor sun porch provide great spots for relaxing and meeting other guests. On sunny summer days, breakfast may even be served in the small formal garden in the backyard. Guest rooms all have queen-size beds with down comforters, and one has a fireplace and a whirlpool tub. One of the other rooms has an old claw-foot tub in the bathroom. Breakfasts here are deliciously filling and might include fresh fruit, juice, quiche, fresh-baked muffins or bread, and oatmeal pancakes. On top of all this, the Salisbury House also offers wireless Internet access!

750 16th Ave. E., Seattle, WA 98112. ℂ 206/328-8682. Fax 206/720-1019. www.salisburyhouse.com. 5 units. $95–$159 double. Rates include full breakfast. AE, MC, V. Children over 12 welcome. *In room:* Dataport, coffeemaker, hair dryer, iron, free local calls.

NORTH SEATTLE (THE UNIVERSITY DISTRICT)

Located 10 to 15 minutes north of downtown Seattle, the University District (more commonly known as the "U" District) appeals primarily to younger travelers, but it does offer less expensive accommodations than downtown and is still fairly convenient to Seattle's major attractions. Also nearby are the Burke Museum, Henry Art Gallery, Museum of History and Industry, Woodland Park Zoo, and, of course, the University of Washington. As you would expect in a university neighborhood, there are lots of cheap restaurants, making this an all-round good choice for anyone on a budget.

MODERATE

Best Western University Tower Hotel *Value*   Despite the location away from downtown, this is one of Seattle's handful of hip hotels, and the modern Art Deco decor will surround you in retro style. Best of all, it's considerably cheaper than comparable downtown hotels, and if you need to be near the university, this is definitely the top choice in the neighborhood. You'll even get views of downtown Seattle, distant mountains, and various lakes and waterways. Every room here is a large corner unit, which means plenty of space to spread out and plenty of views from the higher floors. Small bathrooms are the biggest drawback.

4507 Brooklyn Ave. NE, Seattle, WA 98105. ℂ 800/899-0251 or 206/634-2000. Fax 206/545-2103. www. universitytowerhotel.com. 155 units. June–Sept $129–$169 double; Oct–May $109–$139 double. Rates include continental breakfast. Children under 18 stay free in parent's room. AE, DC, DISC, MC, V. Free parking. **Amenities:** Restaurant (espresso bar); exercise room and access to nearby health club. *In room:* A/C, TV, dataport, coffeemaker, hair dryer, iron.

NEAR SEA-TAC AIRPORT

The airport is 20 to 30 minutes south of downtown Seattle, and other than convenience, there's nothing to recommend this area as a place to stay.

EXPENSIVE

Seattle Marriott Sea-Tac Airport *Kids*   With a steamy atrium garden in which you'll find plenty of tropical plants, a swimming pool, and two whirlpool tubs, this resort-like hotel is an excellent choice if you're visiting during the rainy season. There are even waterfalls and totem poles for that Northwest outdoorsy feeling; and best of all, it's always sunny and warm in here (which is more than you can say for the real Northwest outdoors). In the lobby, big saltwater aquariums further perpetuate the tropical feel and help you forget that this is really an airport hotel. With its stone pillars, rough-hewn beams, and deer-antler chandeliers, the hotel's restaurant conjures up a lodge feel. Guest rooms are comfortable though not memorable. Ask for one of the rooms with a view of Mount Rainier.

3201 S. 176th St., Seattle, WA 98188. ℂ 800/314-0925 or 206/241-2000. Fax 206/248-0789. www.marriott. com. 459 units. $134–$149 double ($84–$109 on weekends); $225–$450 suite. AE, DC, DISC, MC, V. Parking $12. Pets accepted. **Amenities:** Restaurant (American); lounge; indoor atrium pool; exercise room; Jacuzzi; sauna; concierge; car-rental desk; airport shuttle; business center; limited room service; massage; laundry service; dry cleaning; concierge-level rooms. *In room:* A/C, TV, dataport, coffeemaker, hair dryer, iron.

MODERATE

Red Lion Seattle Airport   Located almost directly across from the airport's main entrance, this hotel provides comfortable accommodations designed for business travelers. Guest rooms are generally quite large (if you need space, this is the place). The hotel backs onto a small lake, but only a few rooms have lake views.

18220 International Blvd., Seattle, WA 98188. ✆ **800/RED-LION** or 206/246-5535. Fax 206/246-9733. www. redlion.com/seatac. 146 units. $89–$135 double. Children under 18 stay free in parent's room. AE, DC, DISC, MC, V. Valet parking $14; free self-parking. Pets accepted. **Amenities:** Restaurant (American); lounge; outdoor pool; exercise room; Jacuzzi; sauna; courtesy airport shuttle; limited room service; laundry service; dry cleaning. *In room:* A/C, TV, dataport, coffeemaker, hair dryer, iron.

THE EASTSIDE

The Eastside (a reference to this area's location on the east side of Lake Washington) is Seattle's main high-tech suburb and is comprised of the cities of Bellevue, Kirkland, Issaquah, and Redmond. Should you be out this way on business, you may find that an Eastside hotel is more convenient than one in downtown Seattle. Surprisingly, two of the most luxurious hotels in the entire Seattle area are here on this side of Lake Washington. If it isn't rush hour, you can usually get from the Eastside to downtown in about 20 minutes via the famous floating I-90 and Wash. 520 bridges. During rush hour, however, it can take much longer.

VERY EXPENSIVE

Bellevue Club Hotel ★★★   In its gardens, architecture, and interior design, this hotel epitomizes contemporary Northwest style. Beautifully landscaped gardens surround the entrance, and works of contemporary art can be found throughout the public areas. The "club" in this hotel's name refers to a state-of-the-art health club that includes a full-service spa. Guest rooms are the most elegant anywhere in the Seattle area and are extremely plush. The high-ceiling garden rooms have a floor-to-ceiling wall of glass, massive draperies, and a private patio facing onto a beautiful garden. Luxurious European fabrics are everywhere, giving rooms a romantic feel. Bathrooms are resplendent in granite and glass, and most have whirlpool tubs. Because this is Microsoft country, the hotel offers both wireless Internet access and T-1 lines.

11200 SE Sixth St., Bellevue, WA 98004. ✆ **800/579-1110** or 425/454-4424. Fax 425/688-3101. www.bellevue club.com. 67 units. $255–$315 double ($130–$230 weekends); $575–$1,650 suite ($325–$895 weekends). AE, DC, DISC, MC, V. Parking $5. **Amenities:** 2 restaurants (Pacific Rim); lounge; espresso bar; 2 indoor pools and an outdoor pool; expansive health club with Jacuzzi, saunas, steam rooms, 11 tennis courts, racquetball courts, squash courts, and aerobics studios; children's programs; game room; concierge; business center; 24-hr. room service; massage; babysitting; laundry service; dry cleaning; executive-level rooms. *In room:* A/C, TV, dataport, minibar, hair dryer, iron, safe.

Willows Lodge ★★★ *Finds*   Located on the banks of the Sammamish River (actually little more than a shallow canal) about 30 minutes north of Seattle and adjacent to the much-celebrated Herbfarm Restaurant (see below), this lodge is a beautiful blend of rustic and contemporary. The abundance of polished woods (some salvaged from an old building in Portland) gives the lodge something of a Japanese aesthetic. It's all very soothing and tranquil, an ideal retreat from which to visit the nearby wineries. In the guest rooms, you'll find beds with lamb's-wool mattress pads, European linens, and down duvets; slate tables made from salvaged pool tables; and all kinds of high-tech amenities (including digital shower thermostats).

14580 NE 145th St., Woodinville, WA 98072. ✆ **877/424-3930** or 425/424-3900. Fax 425/424-2585. www. willowslodge.com. 86 units. $260–$320 double; $375–$750 suite. Rates include continental breakfast. Children under 18 stay free in parent's room. AE, DC, DISC, MC, V. Pets accepted ($200 refundable deposit). **Amenities:** 2 restaurants (Northwest); lounge; exercise room; full-service spa; Jacuzzi; sauna; bike rentals; 24-hr. room service; massage; laundry service; dry cleaning. *In room:* A/C, TV/DVD, dataport, fridge, coffeemaker, hair dryer, iron, safe, free local calls.

EXPENSIVE

Woodmark Hotel on Lake Washington ⭐⭐ Although Kirkland's Woodmark Hotel is 20 minutes from downtown Seattle (on a good day), it is the metro area's premier waterfront lodging. Surrounded by a luxury residential community, the Woodmark has the feel of a beach resort and looks out over the very same waters that Bill Gates views from his nearby Xanadu. There are plenty of lakeview rooms here, and you'll pay a premium for them. For less expensive lodging, try the creek-view rooms, which offer a pleasant view of an attractively landscaped little stream. Floor-to-ceiling windows that open are a nice feature on sunny summer days. The hotel's dining room is pricey, but several less-expensive restaurants are in the same complex of buildings. Complimentary late-night snacks and drinks are available.

1200 Carillon Point, Kirkland, WA 98033. © **800/822-3700** or 425/822-3700. Fax 425/822-3699. www.the woodmark.com. 100 units. $205–$275 double; $320–$1,800 suite. Children under 18 stay free in parent's room. AE, DC, DISC, MC, V. Valet parking $12; self-parking $10. Pets accepted ($100 deposit). **Amenities:** Restaurant (New American); lounge; exercise room; full-service spa; concierge; car-rental desk; business center; salon; 24-hr. room service; massage; laundry service; dry cleaning. *In room:* A/C, TV, dataport, minibar, coffeemaker, hair dryer, iron, safe.

INEXPENSIVE

Extended StayAmerica–Bellevue ⭐ Located just off I-405 near downtown Bellevue, this modern off-ramp motel caters primarily to long-term guests. To this end, the rooms are all large, have kitchenettes, and offer free local calls. If you're only staying for a few days, you'll have to pay around $85, but if you stay for a week, rates drop to around $60 per day. This is about the most expensive of the Seattle area's Extended StayAmerica hotels, so if you don't mind staying in a different less-upscale suburb, you can find even lower rates.

11400 Main St., Bellevue, WA 98004. © **800/EXT-STAY** or 425/453-8186. Fax 425/453-8178. www.extended stay.com. 148 units. $75–$99 double ($379–$470 weekly). Children under 12 stay free in parent's room. AE, DC, DISC, MC, V. Free parking. **Amenities:** Coin-op laundry. *In room:* A/C, TV, dataport, kitchenette, fridge, coffeemaker.

4 Where to Dine

With its abundant fresh seafood, Northwest berries, rain-fed mushrooms, and other market-fresh produce, Seattle has become something of a culinary capital. Although the dot-com crash winnowed out some of the city's higher-end restaurants, many of the top restaurants have lowered their prices considerably from their highs of a few years ago. Many of these restaurants now offer relatively inexpensive fixed-price dinners in order to keep their tables filled. This means great deals are to be had at restaurants that just a few years ago were prohibitively expensive.

Seattle is a city obsessed with fresh seafood, and a visitor would be remiss if he or she did not take advantage of the great fish and shellfish available here. Salmon, in myriad guises, is almost ubiquitous on Seattle menus, despite what you may have heard about dwindling salmon populations in Northwest rivers (much of the salmon served here is now caught in Canada or Alaska). There are also dozens of varieties of oysters available throughout the year. Dungeness crabs, another Northwest specialty, may not be as large as king crabs, but they're quite a bit heftier than the blue crabs of the eastern United States. You may also run across such unfamiliar shellfish as razor clams and geoducks (pronounced "gooey dux"). The former is shaped like a straight razor and can be chewy if not prepared properly, and the latter is a bivalve of prodigious proportions (as heavy as 12 lb.) that now is so highly prized in Asia that it rarely ever shows up on Seattle menus.

You'll find restaurants on the shores of virtually every body of water in the area, so be sure to plan some waterfront dining while you're in town. Views at these restaurants take in not only water, but also everything from marinas to Mount Rainier, the Space Needle to the Olympic Mountains.

DOWNTOWN & FIRST HILL
EXPENSIVE

The Brooklyn Seafood, Steak, & Oyster House ★★ SEAFOOD   This classic seafood restaurant looks as if it's been here since the great Seattle fire and is, in fact, housed in one of the city's oldest buildings. The specialty here is definitely oysters, with close to a dozen different types piled up at the oyster bar on any given night. If oysters on the half shell don't appeal to you, there are plenty of other tempting appetizers, ranging from cilantro-battered calamari to Dungeness crab cakes with wasabi aioli. For a classic Northwest dish, try the alder-planked king salmon (roasted on a slab of alder wood), or, for something a bit more unusual, try the grilled black tiger prawns with morel mushrooms and brandy cream sauce.

1212 Second Ave. ✆ 206/224-7000. Reservations recommended. Main courses $10–$15 at lunch, $16–$35 at dinner. AE, DC, DISC, MC, V. Mon–Thurs 11am–3pm and 5–10pm; Fri 11am–3pm and 5–10:30pm; Sat 4:30–10:30pm; Sun 4–10pm (oyster bar open later every night).

Metropolitan Grill ★★ STEAK   Fronted by massive granite columns that make it look more like a bank than a restaurant, the Metropolitan Grill is a very traditional steakhouse that attracts a well-heeled clientele, primarily men in suits. When you walk in the front door, you'll immediately encounter a case full of meat that ranges from filet mignon to triple-cut lamb chops (with the occasional giant lobster tail tossed in). Perfectly cooked 28-day-aged steaks are the primary attraction, and a baked potato and a pile of thick-cut onion rings complete the ultimate carnivore's dinner. Financial matters are a frequent topic of discussion here, and the bar even has a "Guess the Dow" contest. I hope you sold high, since it'll take some capital gains to finance a dinner for two here.

820 Second Ave. ✆ 206/624-3287. www.themetropolitangrill.com. Reservations recommended. Main courses $8–$31 at lunch, $22–$60 at dinner. AE, DISC, MC, V. Mon–Fri 11am–3pm and 5–10:30pm; Sat 4–11pm; Sun 4–10pm.

MODERATE

Andaluca ★★ NORTHWEST/MEDITERRANEAN   Located in the Mayflower Park Hotel, this sumptuous restaurant mixes the traditional and the contemporary like no other place in town. To step through its doors is to enter a world of vibrant artistry, in both decor and cuisine. Specialties include such dishes as traditional Spanish *zarzuela* (shellfish stew) and beef tenderloin crusted with *cabrales* (Spanish blue cheese) and served with grilled pears. The menu is divided into small and large plates, so you'll find something to satisfy your appetite regardless of its size. Don't miss the Dungeness crab tower, made with avocado, palm hearts, and gazpacho salsa—it's a work of art. Keep in mind that you can assemble a meal of small plates here and get away with a lighter bill.

In the Mayflower Park Hotel, 407 Olive Way. ✆ 206/382-6999. Reservations recommended. Main courses $18–$28, small plates $6–$9.25. AE, DC, DISC, MC, V. Mon–Thurs 6:30–11am, 11:30am–2:30pm, and 5–10pm; Fri 6:30–11am, 11:30am–2:30pm, and 5–11pm; Sat 7am–noon and 5–11pm; Sun 7am–noon and 5–9pm.

McCormick & Schmick's ★★ SEAFOOD   Force your way past the crowds of business suits at the bar and you'll find yourself in a classic fish house—complete with cafe curtains, polished brass, leaded glass, and wood paneling. Daily fresh sheets commonly list more than 30 seafood entrees and feature well-prepared seafood dishes such as grilled steelhead with artichokes and spinach, Dungeness crab and shrimp cakes with red-pepper aioli, and cedar-plank-roasted salmon with berry *beurre rouge* (red butter sauce). There are also usually a half-dozen or more different varieties of oysters available. In late afternoons and late evenings, bar appetizers are only $1.95. If the restaurant is crowded and you can't get a table, consider sitting at the counter and watching the cooks perform amazing feats with fire.

1103 First Ave. © **206/623-5500.** www.mccormickandschmicks.com. Reservations recommended. Main courses $7–$25. AE, DC, DISC, MC, V. Mon–Fri 11:30am–11pm; Sat 4:30–11pm; Sun 4:30–9pm (bar menu served later).

Wild Ginger Asian Restaurant & Satay Bar ★★ PAN-ASIAN   This Pan-Asian restaurant has long been a Seattle favorite and is now located across the street from Benaroya Hall. Pull up a comfortable stool around the large satay grill and watch the cooks grill little skewers of anything from chicken to scallops to pork to prawns to lamb. Each skewer is served with a small cube of sticky rice and pickled cucumber. Order three or four satay sticks and you have a meal. If you prefer to sit at a table and have a more traditional dinner, Wild Ginger can accommodate you. Try the Panang beef curry (rib-eye steak in pungent curry sauce of cardamom, coconut milk, Thai basil, and peanuts).

1401 Third Ave. © **206/623-4450.** Reservations recommended. Main courses $8.75–$30. AE, DC, DISC, MC, V. Mon–Sat 11:30am–11pm; Sun 4:30–11pm.

THE WATERFRONT
MODERATE

Anthony's Pier 66 & Bell Street Diner ★★ SEAFOOD   The Anthony's chain has several outposts around the Seattle area, but this complex is the most convenient and versatile. Anthony's not only has an upper-end, stylish seafood restaurant with good waterfront views, but it includes a moderately priced casual

---

Kids Family-Friendly Restaurants

Cucina! Cucina! (p. 95)   Every day's a party at this lively Italian restaurant on Lake Union, and kids always get special treatment (pictures to color, puzzles to do, pizza dough to shape and then let the kitchen cook). Birthdays are even better!

Ivar's Salmon House (p. 94)   This restaurant is built to resemble a Northwest Coast Native American longhouse and is filled with artifacts that kids will find fascinating. If they get restless, they can go out to the floating patio and watch the boats passing by.

Maggie Bluffs Marina Grill (p. 94)   Located at a marina overlooking Elliott Bay and downtown Seattle, this economical place has food the kids will enjoy and provides crayons to keep them occupied while they wait. Before or after a meal, you can take a free boat ride across the marina to an observation deck atop the breakwater.

restaurant and a walk-up counter. The bold contemporary styling and abundance of art glass set this place apart from most of the waterfront restaurants. The upscale crowd heads upstairs for Asian-inspired seafood dishes, and the more cost-conscious stay downstairs at the Bell Street Diner where meals are much easier on the wallet (though far less creative). For the higher prices, you get better views. In summer, the decks are the place to be.

2201 Alaskan Way. ⓒ 206/448-6688. www.anthonys.com. Reservations recommended. Pier 66 main courses $9–$24; Bell Street Diner main courses $7–$19. AE, DISC, MC, V. Pier 66 Mon–Thurs 5–9:30pm, Fri–Sat 5–10pm, Sun 5–9pm; Bell Street Diner Mon–Thurs 11:30am–10pm, Fri–Sat 11:30am–10:30pm, Sun 3–9pm.

Elliott's ⭐⭐ SEAFOOD   While most of its neighbors are content to coast along on tourist business, Elliott's actually aims to keep locals happy by serving some of the best seafood in Seattle. Maybe the quality of the food here is in inverse proportion to the view: Although the restaurant is right on the waterfront, the view isn't that great. If you're looking for superbly prepared fresh seafood, however, Elliott's is an excellent bet. The oyster bar can have as many as 20 varieties of oysters available, so this is definitely the place to get to know your Northwest oysters. Salmon and Dungeness crabs are usually prepared any of several different ways.

Pier 56, 1201 Alaskan Way. ⓒ 206/623-4340. Reservations recommended. Main courses $9–$39 at lunch, $16–$39 at dinner. AE, DISC, MC, V. Sun–Thurs 11am–10pm; Fri–Sat 11am–11pm.

PIONEER SQUARE & THE INTERNATIONAL DISTRICT

Also located in the International District is a large all-Asian food court at **Uwajimaya,** 600 Fifth Ave. S. (ⓒ **206/624-6248**), a huge Asian supermarket. The food court's stalls serve the foods of different Asian countries. It all smells great, and everything is inexpensive, which makes this a great place for a quick meal. With the bus tunnel entrance right across the street, Uwajimaya is easy to reach even from the north end of downtown.

MODERATE

Trattoria Mitchelli ⭐ ITALIAN/LATE-NIGHT   Located in the heart of Pioneer Square, Trattoria Mitchelli serves good, basic Italian food in a cozy spot with friendly, old-world atmosphere. A vintage wooden-topped lunch counter in a room with classic hexagonal tile floors is a popular after-work and late-night gathering spot, and the conversation is lively. You can't go wrong here with the fettuccine con pollo, pizza from the wood-fired oven, or the pasta of the week served with your choice of sauce. For a rich dessert, dig into a caramello, a creamy caramel with toasted walnuts and whipped cream. If you're a night owl, keep Mitchelli's in mind—full meals are served until 4am Friday and Saturday nights, catering to the starving hordes who pour out of the area's many bars after last call.

84 Yesler Way. ⓒ 206/623-3883. Reservations accepted only Sun–Thurs. Main courses $8–$15. AE, MC, V. Mon–Thurs 11:30am–11pm; Fri 11:30am–4am; Sat 8am–4am; Sun 8am–11pm.

INEXPENSIVE

House of Hong ⭐ 𝘝𝘢𝘭𝘶𝘦 CHINESE   If you're in the International District anytime between 10am and 5pm and want to sample the best dim sum in Seattle, head for the House of Hong. It's located at the uphill end of the neighborhood in a big yellow building. All the little dumplings, pot stickers, and stuffed wontons that comprise the standards of dim sum are done to perfection here—not too greasy, not too starchy, with plenty of meat in the fillings. Keep an eye out for the whole fried shrimp, crunchy on the outside and moist and meaty on the inside. There's lots of variety to the dim sum offerings, so pace yourself and keep an eye out for whatever looks particularly appetizing. The House of Hong also has free parking.

409 Eighth Ave. ℂ 206/622-7997. www.houseofhong.com. Reservations not necessary. Dim sum $2–$5; main courses $6.50–$27. AE, DC, DISC, MC, V. Mon–Fri 10am–midnight; Sat 9:30am–midnight; Sun 9:30am–10pm.

Merchants Cafe AMERICAN   Merchants Cafe is Seattle's oldest restaurant and looks every bit of its 100-plus years. A well-scuffed tile floor surrounds the bar, which came around the Horn in the 1800s, and an old safe and gold scales are left over from the days when Seattle was the first, or last, taste of civilization for Yukon prospectors. At one time the restaurant's basement was a card room, and the upper floors were a brothel. In fact, this may be the original Skid Row saloon (Yesler Way was the original Skid Road down which logs were skidded to a sawmill). Straight-forward sandwiches, salads, and soups are the mainstays of the menu.

109 Yesler Way. ℂ 206/624-1515. Main courses $6.50–$7. AE, DC, DISC, MC, V. Mon 11am–3pm; Tues–Sat 11am–8pm; Sun 10am–4pm.

Salumi ★ (Finds ITALIAN   For many folks, salami is a guilty pleasure. We all know it's got way too much fat, but it tastes too good to resist. Now, raise the bar on salami, and you have the artisan-cured meats of this closet-size eatery near Pioneer Square. The owner makes all his own salami (as well as traditional Italian-cured beef tongue). Order up a meat plate with a side of cheese and some roasted red bell peppers, pour yourself a glass of wine from the big bottle on the table, and you have a perfect lunchtime repast in the classic Italian style. Did I mention the great breads and tapenades? Wow! If you're down in the Pioneer Square area at lunch, don't miss this place.

309 Third Ave. S. ℂ 206/621-8772. Reservations not accepted. Main courses $6–$10. MC, V. Tues–Fri 11am–4pm.

BELLTOWN & PIKE PLACE MARKET
VERY EXPENSIVE

Cascadia ★★★ NORTHWEST   Chef Kerry Sear first made a name for himself in Seattle at the Georgian, the opulent restaurant at the Four Seasons Olympic Hotel. Here, at his own restaurant, he celebrates all foods Northwestern in an elegant, understated space in Belltown. For the full Cascadia experience, indulge in one of Sear's seven-course tasting menus. For the ultimate Northwest dinner, try the menu of dishes prepared exclusively with seasonal ingredients from around the Cascadia region, which stretches from British Columbia to Northern California. Because the menu changes with the seasons, you never know what you might find, but rest assured it will be memorable. There's also a seven-course vegetarian dinner. Just to make the meal prices more palatable, the wine list includes 30 wines for under $30. Want the dining experience but can't afford the prices? Try the bar, which has a menu of 10 dishes for under $10.

2328 First Ave. ℂ 206/448-8884. www.cascadiarestaurant.com. Reservations highly recommended. Main courses $20–$34; 3-course fixed-price dinner $25; 7-course fixed-price dinner $45–$75. AE, MC, V. Mon–Thurs 5–10pm; Fri–Sat 5–10:30pm.

El Gaucho ★★ LATE-NIGHT/STEAK   Conjuring up the ghosts of dinner clubs of the 1930s and 1940s, this high-end Belltown steakhouse looks like it could be a Fred Astaire film set. The pure theatrics make this place a must if you're in the mood to spend big bucks on a thick, juicy steak. Stage-set decor aside, the real stars of the show here are the 28-day dry-aged Angus beef steaks, definitely some of the best in town—but know that the perfect steak doesn't come cheap. All the classics are here, too, including Caesar salad tossed table-side, and chateaubriand carved before your eyes. Not a steak eater? How about venison chops, an ostrich filet, or Australian lobster tail? There's also a classy bar off to one side, a separate cigar lounge and, for after-dinner dancing, the affili-ated **Pampas Room** nightclub.

2505 First Ave. © 206/728-1337. www.elgaucho.com. Reservations recommended. Main courses $16–$90 (steaks $32–$42). AE, DC, MC, V. Mon–Sat 5pm–1am; Sun 5–11pm.

EXPENSIVE

Campagne ★★ COUNTRY FRENCH   With large windows that look out over the top of Pike Place Market to Elliott Bay, Campagne is an unpretentious, yet elegant, French restaurant. With such a prime location, it shouldn't be sur-prising that Campagne relies heavily on the wide variety of fresh ingredients that the market provides. Consequently, the menu changes with the seasons. How-ever, such classic dishes as foie gras terrine, beef tartare, and sautéed sweetbreads usually make appearances. Simple sauces and exotic ingredients are the rule here. Roasted baby beets might be drizzled with pistachio oil, while pan-roasted hal-ibut may come atop a pea-and-tarragon puree. There are always several interest-ing salads as well.

Inn at the Market, 86 Pine St. © 206/728-2800. www.campagnerestaurant.com. Reservations recom-mended. Main courses $23–$37; 3-course fixed-price dinner $45. AE, DC, MC, V. Daily 5–10pm.

Chez Shea ★★★ NORTHWEST   Quiet, dark, and intimate, Chez Shea is one of the finest restaurants in Seattle, and with only a dozen candlelit tables and views across Puget Sound to the Olympic Mountains, it's an ideal setting for romance. The menu changes with the season, and ingredients come primarily from the market below. On a recent spring evening, dinner started with arugula and red-grapefruit salad. This was then followed by a roasted asparagus soup. Among the five or so nightly entrees were pork tenderloin with pan-roasted asparagus; beef tenderloin with frizzled leeks and potato cakes and a cognac demi-glace; and salmon with sesame-rice noodles, lemon grass, and coconut milk broth. Though dessert is a la carte, you'll find it impossible to let it pass you by. The city may have equally fine restaurants, but none has quite the romantic atmosphere as Chez Shea.

Pike Place Market, Corner Market Building, 94 Pike St., Suitee 34. © 206/467-9990. www.chezshea.com. Reservations highly recommended. 4-course fixed-price dinner $43. AE, MC, V. Tues–Sun 5–10pm.

MODERATE

Café Campagne ★★ *Finds* FRENCH   This cozy little cafe is an offshoot of the popular Campagne, a much more formal French restaurant, and though it's in the heart of the Pike Place Market neighborhood, it's a world away from the market madness. We like to duck in here for lunch and escape the shuffling crowds. What a relief—so civilized, so very French. The dark and cozy place has a hidden feel to it, and most people leave feeling like they've discovered some secret hideaway. The menu changes with the seasons, but a daily rotisserie spe-cial such as stuffed quail or leg of lamb marinated with garlic and anchovy is always offered Tuesday through Saturday—highly recommended. The cafe dou-bles as a wine bar and has a good selection of reasonably priced wines by the glass or by the bottle.

1600 Post Alley. © 206/728-2233. Reservations accepted for dinner only. Main courses $15–$19; 3-course fixed-price menu $25. AE, DC, MC, V. Mon–Thurs 11am–10pm; Fri 11am–5pm and 5:30–11pm; Sat 8am–4pm and 5:30–11pm; Sun 8am–4pm and 5–10pm.

Great Brunch Choices

For brunch, there are some great options around the city. Try **Cafe Flora, Ivar's Salmon House, Palisade, Salty's on Alki Beach,** or **SkyCity at the Needle.** All these places have complete reviews in the appropriate neighborhood sections of this chapter.

Dahlia Lounge ✿✿ PAN-ASIAN/NORTHWEST   The neon chef holding a flapping fish may suggest that the Dahlia is little more than a roadside diner, but a glimpse at the stylish interior will likely have you thinking otherwise. One bite of any dish will convince you that this is one of Seattle's finest restaurants. Mouthwatering Dungeness crab cakes, a bow to Chef Tom Douglas's Delaware roots, are the house specialty and should not be missed. The menu, influenced by the far side of the Pacific Rim, changes regularly, with the lunch menu featuring some of the same offerings at lower prices. For dessert, it takes a Herculean effort to resist the crème caramel. It's way too easy to fill up on the restaurant's breads, which are baked in the adjacent Dahlia Bakery.

2001 Fourth Ave. ② 206/682-4142. www.tomdouglas.com. Reservations highly recommended. Main courses $9.50–$22 lunch, $18–$24 dinner. AE, DC, DISC, MC, V. Mon–Thurs 11:30am–2:30pm and 5:30–10pm; Fri 11:30am–2:30pm and 5:30–11pm; Sat 5:30–11pm; Sun 5–10pm.

Etta's Seafood ✿✿ SEAFOOD   Seattle chef Tom Douglas's strictly seafood (well, almost) restaurant, Etta's, is located smack in the middle of the Pike Place Market area and, of course, serves Douglas's signature crab cakes (crunchy on the outside, creamy on the inside), which are not to be missed (and if they're not on the menu, just ask). Don't ignore your side dishes, either; they can be exquisite and are usually enough to share around the table. In addition to the great seafood dishes, the menu always has a few other fine options, including several that date from Douglas's Café Sport days in the early 1980s. Stylish contemporary decor sets the mood, making this place as popular with locals as it is with tourists.

2020 Western Ave. ② 206/443-6000. www.tomdouglas.com. Reservations recommended. Main courses $9.50–$26. AE, DC, DISC, MC, V. Mon–Thurs 11:30am–9:30pm; Fri 11:30am–10:30pm; Sat 9am–10:30pm; Sun 9am–9pm.

Fandango ✿✿ LATIN AMERICAN   Fandango is another groundbreaking restaurant from celebrity chef Christine Keff, who also operates the ever-popular Flying Fish restaurant diagonally across the street. The focus here is on the sunny flavors of Latin America, and Fandango's menu is filled with combinations you aren't likely to have encountered this far north before. Fandango just might be the only place in the city where you can get a *huitlacoche* quesadilla (made with a corn fungus that's considered a delicacy in Mexico). Whether you order the *ceviche* (cold fish) of the day, the Brazilian seafood stew, or the suckling pig, you'll enjoy some real taste treats. If you're lucky, you just might find grilled bananas on the dessert menu. Be sure to have a *mojito* (minty rum cocktail) while you're here. The Sunday night family-style dinners ($25) are a good deal.

2313 First Ave. ② 206/441-1188. www.fandangoseattle.com. Reservations recommended. Main courses $16–$22. AE, DC, MC, V. Daily 5pm–1am (until 2am in the bar).

Flying Fish ✿✿ LATE-NIGHT/NORTHWEST/SEAFOOD   Chef Christine Keff has been on the Seattle restaurant scene for years now, and with Flying Fish, she hit on something the city really wanted. Not only does it offer the bold combinations of vibrant flavors demanded by the city's well-traveled palates, but the hip Belltown restaurant serves dinner until 1am every night, keeping late-night partiers from going hungry. Every dish here is a work of art, and with small plates, large plates, and platters for sharing, diners are encouraged to sample a wide variety of the kitchen's creations. The menu changes daily, but keep an eye out for the smoked rock shrimp spring rolls, which are positively sculptural. The festive desserts are almost a mini party on the plate. There's also a huge wine list.

2234 First Ave. ② 206/728-8595. www.flyingfishseattle.com. Reservations recommended. Main courses $15–$20. AE, DC, MC, V. Daily 5pm–1am.

Icon Grill ⚘ AMERICAN   With colorful art glass hanging from chandeliers, overflowing giant vases, and every inch of wall space covered with framed art-work, this place goes way overboard with its decor, but that's exactly what makes it so fun. Basically, it's an over-the-top rendition of a Victorian setting gone 21st century. The food is a mix of basic comfort food (including a molasses-glazed meatloaf that locals swear by) and more inventive dishes such as grilled pear salad, merlot-glazed lamb shank, and lamb tenderloin stuffed with prosciutto, arugula, and goat cheese. Unfortunately, the food can be unpredictable, so don't come here just for a culinary experience, but rather for a Seattle experience.

1933 Fifth Ave. ② 206/441-6330. Reservations recommended. Main courses $14–$33. AE, MC, V. Mon 11:30am–2pm and 5:30–9pm; Tues–Thurs 11:30am–2pm and 5:30–10pm; Fri 11:30am–2pm and 5:30–11pm; Sat 5:30–11pm; Sun 5–9pm.

Matt's in the Market ⚘⚘ *Finds* AMERICAN REGIONAL/INTERNA-TIONAL   Quite possibly the smallest gourmet restaurant in Seattle, Matt's is a tiny cubbyhole of a place in the Corner Market Building, directly across the street from the market information booth at First and Pike. The restaurant has only a handful of tables and a few stools at the counter, and the kitchen takes up almost half the restaurant, giving the cooks little more than the space of a walk-in closet in which to work their culinary magic. The menu changes regularly, with an emphasis on fresh ingredients from the market stalls only steps away, and there's a good selection of reasonably priced wines. The menu pulls in what-ever influences and styles happen to appeal to the chef at that moment, perhaps Moroccan, perhaps Southern. This is a real Pike Place Market experience. If you spot anything with smoked catfish on the menu, try it.

94 Pike St. ② 206/467-7909. Dinner reservations accepted for first seating and highly recommended. Main courses $9–$9.25 at lunch, $16–$18 at dinner. MC, V. Mon 11:30am–2:30pm; Tues–Sat 11:30am–2:30pm and 5:30–9:30pm.

Palace Kitchen ⚘⚘ AMERICAN REGIONAL/LATE-NIGHT/MEDITER-RANEAN   This is the most casual of chef Tom Douglas's three Seattle estab-lishments, with a bar that attracts nearly as many customers as the restaurant. The atmosphere is urban chic, with cement pillars, simple wood booths, and a few tables in the front window, which overlooks the monorail tracks. The menu is short and features a nightly selection of unusual cheeses and different prepara-tions from the apple-wood grill. To begin a meal, we like the creamy goat-cheese fondue. Entrees are usually simple and delicious and range from the Palace burger royale (a strong contender for best burger in Seattle) to Southern-influenced dishes such as pork loin with grits and greens. For dessert, the coconut cream pie is an absolute must.

2030 Fifth Ave. ② 206/448-2001. www.tomdouglas.com. Reservations only for parties of 6 or more. Main courses $11–$26. AE, DC, DISC, MC, V. Daily 5pm–1am.

The Pink Door ★ ITALIAN/LATE-NIGHT   Pike Place Market's better restaurants tend to be well hidden, and if we didn't tell you about this one, you'd probably never find it. There's no sign out front—only the pink door for which the restaurant is named (look for it between Stewart and Virginia sts.). On the other side of the door, stairs lead to a cellarlike space, which is almost always empty on summer days, when folks forsake it to dine on the deck with a view of Elliott Bay. What makes this place so popular is as much the fun atmosphere as the Italian food. You might encounter a tarot card reader or a magician, and most nights in the bar there's some sort of Fellini-esque cabaret performer (accordionists, trapeze artists, and the likes). Be sure to start your meal with the fragrant roasted garlic and ricotta-Gorgonzola spread. From there, you might move on to an Italian classic such as lasagna or something made with fresh seafood from Pike Place Market.

1919 Post Alley. (℃ 206/443-3241. Reservations recommended. Main courses $15–$20. AE, MC, V. Tues–Sat 11:30am–10pm; Sun 5–10pm.

Shea's Lounge ★★ NORTHWEST/INTERNATIONAL/LATE-NIGHT Convenient, casual, economical, romantic. What's not to like about this hidden jewel in Pike Place Market? This is the lounge for the ever-popular Chez Shea, and it's one of the most sophisticated little spaces in Seattle. Romantic lighting and a view of the bay make it a popular spot with couples, and whether you just want a cocktail and an appetizer or a full meal, you can get it here. The menu features gourmet pizzas, combination appetizer plates, a few soups and salads, and several nightly specials such as chicken stew with spicy chorizo sausage and chipotle pepper or risotto cakes with spinach and roasted fennel. You can even order dishes from the main restaurant's menu. The desserts are divinely decadent. This is a great spot for a light or late-night meal.

Pike Place Market, Corner Market Building, 94 Pike St., Suite 34. (℃ 206/467-9990. Reservations not accepted. Main courses $15–$28. AE, MC, V. Tues–Sun 4:30pm–midnight.

INEXPENSIVE

Noodle Ranch ★ *Finds* PAN-ASIAN   This Belltown hole-in-the-wall serves Pan-Asian cuisine for the hip-yet-financially-challenged crowd. It's a lively, boisterous scene, and the food is packed with intense, and often unfamiliar, flavors. Don't miss the fish grilled in grape leaves with its nice presentation and knockout dipping sauce. In fact, all of the dipping sauces here are delicious. The Mekong grill—rice noodles with a rice-wine vinegar and herb dressing topped with grilled pork, chicken, catfish, or tofu—is another dish not to be missed. You'll also find the likes of Laotian cucumber salad and Japanese-style eggplant. In fact, you'll find lots of vegetarian options. Although the place is frequently packed, you can usually get a seat without having to wait too long.

2228 Second Ave. (℃ 206/728-0463. Main courses $7–$12. AE, MC, V. Mon–Thurs 11am–10pm; Fri 11am–11pm; Sat noon–11pm.

QUEEN ANNE & SEATTLE CENTER
VERY EXPENSIVE

SkyCity at the Needle ★★ NORTHWEST   Both the restaurant and the prices are sky-high at this revolving restaurant, located just below the observation deck at the top of Seattle's famous Space Needle. However, because you don't have to pay extra for the elevator ride if you dine here, the high prices start to seem a little bit more in line with those at other Seattle splurge restaurants. Okay, so maybe you'd get better food somewhere else, and maybe you can dine with a view at other Seattle restaurants, but you won't get as spectacular a panorama anywhere but here. The menu works hard at offering some distinctly Northwestern flavor combinations but still has plenty of familiar fare for those diners who aren't into culinary adventures. Simply prepared steaks and seafood make up the bulk of the menu, with a couple of vegetarian options as well. We recommend coming here for lunch. The prices are considerably more reasonable, and the views, encompassing the city skyline, Mount Rainier, and the Olympic Mountains, are unsurpassed.

Space Needle, 400 Broad St. © 800/937-9582 or 206/905-2100. www.spaceneedle.com. Reservations highly recommended. Main courses $19–$29 at lunch, $28–$45 at dinner. Weekend brunch $37 adults, $16 children 5–12. AE, DC, DISC, MC, V. Mon–Thurs 11am–2:30pm and 5:30–9pm; Fri 11am–2:30pm and 5:30–10pm; Sat 11am–3pm and 5:30–10pm; Sun 11am–3pm and 5:30–9pm.

EXPENSIVE

Canlis ★★★ NORTHWEST   This is the perfect place to close a big deal or celebrate a very special occasion. A Seattle institution, Canlis has been in business since 1950, but a major remodeling a few years back gave the restaurant a stylish look that mixes contemporary decor with Asian antiques. The Northwest cuisine, with Asian and Continental influences, keeps both traditionalists and more adventurous diners content. Steaks from the copper grill are perennial favorites here, as are the spicy Peter Canlis prawns. To finish, why not go all the way and have the Grand Marnier soufflé? Canlis also has one of the best wine lists in Seattle.

2576 Aurora Ave. N. © 206/283-3313. www.canlis.com. Reservations highly recommended. Main courses $22–$57; chef's tasting menu $65 ($100 with wines). AE, DC, DISC, MC, V. Mon–Sat 5:30pm–midnight.

Palisade ★★★ NORTHWEST   With a panorama that sweeps from downtown to West Seattle and across the sound to the Olympic Mountains, Palisade has one of the best views of any Seattle waterfront restaurant. It also happens to have fine food and inventive interior design (incorporating a saltwater pond, complete with fish, sea anemones, and starfish, right in the middle of the dining room). The menu features both fish and meats prepared in a wood-fired oven and in a wood-fired rotisserie. The three-course sunset dinners, served before 6pm, cost $20 and are a great way to enjoy this restaurant on a budget. Palisade also has an excellent and very popular Sunday brunch. The restaurant is not easy to find, but it's more than worth the search. Call for directions.

Elliott Bay Marina, 2601 W. Marina Place. © 206/285-1000. Reservations recommended. Main courses $18–$46. AE, DC, DISC, MC, V. Mon–Fri 5–9pm; Sat 4–10pm; Sun 10am–2pm and 4:30–9pm.

INEXPENSIVE

The 5 Spot ★ AMERICAN REGIONAL/LATE-NIGHT   Every 3 months or so, this restaurant, one of Seattle's favorite diners, changes its menu to reflect a different regional U.S. cuisine. Maybe you'll find Brooklyn comfort food or Cuban-influenced Miami-style meals featured, but you can bet that whatever's on the menu will be filling and fun. The atmosphere here is pure kitsch—whenever the theme is "Florida," the restaurant is adorned with palm trees and flamingos and looks like the high school gym done up for prom night. This bustling diner is popular with all types, who appreciate the fact that you won't go broke eating here. To find The 5 Spot, look for the neon coffee pouring into the giant coffee cup sign at the top of Queen Anne Hill.

1502 Queen Anne Ave. N. © 206/285-SPOT. www.chowfoods.com. Reservations accepted only for parties of 6–10. Main courses $8.75–$18. MC, V. Mon–Fri 8:30am–midnight; Sat–Sun (and holidays) 8:30am–3pm and 5pm–midnight.

Maggie Bluffs Marina Grill ✿ *Kids* AMERICAN   It's never easy to find affordable waterfront dining in any city, and Seattle is no exception. However, if you're willing to drive a few miles from downtown Seattle, you can save quite a few bucks at this casual marina restaurant located at the foot of Magnolia Bluff (northwest of downtown Seattle). The menu is fairly simple, with burgers and fish and chips, but it includes a few dishes that display a bit more creativity. The restaurant overlooks a marina and, while the view is partially obstructed by a breakwater, you can still see Elliott Bay, West Seattle, downtown, and even the Space Needle. Crayons are on hand to keep the kids entertained. After a meal, walk out on Pier G and take a free shuttle boat a few yards through the marina to an observation deck atop the breakwater. The patio dining area is popular on sunny summer days.

Elliott Bay Marina, 2601 W. Marina Place. ✆ 206/283-8322. Reservations not accepted. Main courses $7–$11. AE, MC, V. Mon–Thurs 11:15am–9pm; Fri 11:15am–10pm; Sat 8am–10pm; Sun 8am–9pm.

LAKE UNION
MODERATE

Ivar's Salmon House ✿✿ *Kids* SEAFOOD   With a view of the Space Needle on the far side of Lake Union, flotillas of sea kayaks silently slipping by, sailboats racing across the lake, and powerboaters tying up at the dock out back, this restaurant on the north side of Lake Union is quintessential Seattle. Add to the scene an award-winning building designed to resemble a Northwest Coast Indian longhouse, and you have what just might be the very best place in town for a waterfront meal. Okay, so maybe, just maybe, you can find better food at a few other waterfront places, but none has the unequivocally Seattle atmosphere you'll find at Ivar's Salmon House. This place is a magnet for weekend boaters who abandon their own galley fare in favor of Ivar's clam chowder and famous alder-smoked salmon. Lots of artifacts, including long dugout canoes and historic photos of Native American chiefs, make Ivar's a hit with both kids and adults. Bear in mind that this restaurant's popularity means that service can be slow; just relax and enjoy the views.

401 NE Northlake Way. ✆ 206/632-0767. www.ivars.net. Reservations recommended. Main courses $7–$16 at lunch, $13–$28 at dinner. AE, DC, DISC, MC, V. Mon–Thurs 11am–9pm; Fri–Sat 11am–10pm; Sun 10am–2pm and 3:30–9pm.

McCormick & Schmick's Harborside ✿ SEAFOOD   With its waterfront setting and views of the marinas on the west side of Lake Union, this restaurant has the best location of any of Seattle's McCormick & Schmick's restaurants. The menu, which changes daily, includes seemingly endless choices of appetizers, sandwiches, salads, and creative entrees. Just be sure to order something with seafood, such as seared rare ahi with Cajun spices; Parmesan-crusted petrale sole; or salmon roasted on a cedar plank and served with a berry sauce. Sure, there are meat dishes on the menu, but why bother (unless you only came here for the excellent view)? Bar specials for $1.95 are available in the late afternoon and late evening, and there are always plenty of varieties of oysters on the half shell.

1200 Westlake Ave. N. ✆ 206/270-9052. www.mccormickandschmicks.com. Reservations recommended. Main courses $7–$25. AE, DC, DISC, MC, V. Sun–Thurs 11am–10pm; Fri–Sat 11am–11pm.

Serafina ✿✿ COUNTRY ITALIAN   Located a bit off the beaten tourist track, Serafina is one of our favorite Seattle dining spots. It has a nice touch of sophistication, but overall, it's a relaxed, neighborhood sort of place. The rustic, romantic atmosphere underscores the earthy, country-style dishes served here.

It's also hard to resist ordering at least one of the bruschetta appetizers, which come with any of three different toppings. Among the pasta offerings, you might find prawns with a sauce of orange zest, Campari, saffron, basil, and tomatoes all served over hand-cut fettuccine, or the ever-popular and delicious veal meatballs in a green olive-tomato sauce served over Italian penne pasta. Be sure not to miss the *melanzane alla Serafina* (thinly sliced eggplant rolled with ricotta cheese, basil, and Parmesan and baked in tomato sauce). There's live music (mostly jazz and Latin) Friday through Sunday nights.

2043 Eastlake Ave. E. ⓒ 206/323-0807. www.serafinaseattle.com. Reservations recommended. Main courses $9–$14 lunch, $14–$24 dinner. MC, V. Mon–Thurs 11:30am–2:30pm and 5:30–10pm; Fri 11:30am–2:30pm and 5:30–11pm; Sat 5:30–11pm; Sun 5:30–10pm.

INEXPENSIVE

Cucina! Cucina! ★ *Kids* ITALIAN   Although it's part of a local restaurant chain, Cucina! Cucina! is a good bet not only for its waterfront view and reliable pizzas and pasta, but for its lively party atmosphere. Located at the south end of Lake Union, this restaurant is also a favorite of Seattle families because of all the special attention kids are given here. But just because families are welcome doesn't mean this place isn't fun for grown-ups, too. In summer, the deck is the place to be.

Chandler's Cove, 901 Fairview Ave. N. ⓒ 206/447-2782. www.cucinacucina.com. Call ahead to place name on wait list. Main courses $8–$19. AE, DC, DISC, MC, V. Sun–Thurs 11:30am–10pm; Fri–Sat 11:30am–10:30pm.

CAPITOL HILL & EAST SEATTLE
VERY EXPENSIVE

Rover's ★★★ NORTHWEST   Tucked away in a quaint clapboard house behind a chic little shopping center in the Madison Valley neighborhood east of downtown, this is one of Seattle's most acclaimed restaurants. Thierry Rautureau, Rover's much-celebrated and award-winning chef, received classical French training before falling in love with the Northwest and all the wonderful ingredients it has to offer an imaginative chef. *Voilà!* Northwest cuisine with a French accent.

The delicacies on the frequently changing menu are enough to send the most jaded of gastronomes into fits of indecision. Luckily, you can simply opt for one of the fixed-price dinners and leave the decision making to a professional—the chef. Culinary creations include scrambled eggs with lime crème fraîche and caviar, baby white asparagus with prosciutto and Perigord truffle mousseline, spice-infused pinot noir sorbet, and venison with wild mushrooms and peppercorn sauce. *Vegetarians, take note:* You won't often find a vegetarian feast that can compare with the ones served here.

2808 E. Madison St. ⓒ 206/325-7442. www.rovers-seattle.com. Reservations required. 5-course menu degustation $80 (vegetarian) and $90; chef's 8-course grand menu $125. AE, DC, MC, V. Tues–Sat 5:30 to about 9:30pm.

INEXPENSIVE

Cafe Flora ★ VEGETARIAN   Big, bright, and airy, this Madison Valley cafe will dispel any ideas you might have about vegetarian food being boring. This is meatless gourmet cooking and draws on influences from around the world—it's a vegetarian's dream come true. One of the house specialties is a portobello Wellington made with mushroom-pecan pâté and sautéed leeks in a puff pastry. Keep an eye out for unusual pizzas (such as strawberries and brie or eggplant and pine nut), as well. On weekends, a casual brunch features interesting breakfast fare.

2901 E. Madison St. ℂ 206/325-9100. www.cafeflora.com. Reservations accepted only for parties of 8 or more. Main courses $9.25–$17. MC, V. Tues–Thurs 11:30am–9pm; Fri 11:30am–10pm; Sat 9am–2pm and 5–10pm; Sun 9am–2pm and 5–9pm.

NORTH SEATTLE (INCLUDING FREMONT, WALLINGFORD & THE UNIVERSITY DISTRICT)

MODERATE

Ray's Boathouse and Cafe ★★ SEAFOOD   When Seattleites want to impress visiting friends and relatives, this restaurant often ranks right up there with the Space Needle, the ferries, and Pike Place Market. The view across Puget Sound to the Olympic Mountains is superb. You can watch the boat traffic coming and going from the Lake Washington Ship Canal, and bald eagles can often be seen fishing just offshore. Then there's Ray's dual personality—upstairs is a lively (and loud) cafe and lounge, while downstairs is a much more formal, sedate scene. The downstairs menu is more creative but the upstairs menu is less expensive, but even upstairs you can order from the downstairs menu. The crab cakes are delicious and packed full of crab, and the black cod glazed with *sake kasu* (lees, or the residue left over after sake is fermented), a typically Northwestern/Pacific Rim preparation, is well worth trying. Whatever your mood, Ray's has got you covered. Be sure to take a peek in the crab tanks in front of the restaurant.

6049 Seaview Ave. NW. ℂ 206/789-3770. www.rays.com. Reservations recommended. Main courses $18–$45 (Boathouse), $9–$16 (Cafe). AE, DC, DISC, MC, V. Boathouse Mon–Thurs 5–9pm; Fri–Sat 5–10pm; Sun 5–9pm. Cafe daily 11:30am–10pm.

INEXPENSIVE

Agua Verde Café ★ (Finds) MEXICAN   Set on the shore of Portage Bay, which lies between Lake Union and Lake Washington, this casual Mexican restaurant is very popular with college students from the adjacent University of Washington. Consequently, there's often a line out the door as customers wait to give their orders at the counter. The menu is limited to tacos, Mexican-style sandwiches, empanadas, and quesadillas. It's hard to go wrong here, but I recommend the tacos, which come three to an order. Try the grilled halibut or yam tacos, both of which are topped with a delicious avocado sauce. Add a couple of sides—cranberry slaw, pineapple-jicama salsa, creamy chile potatoes—for a filling and inexpensive meal. They also serve pretty good margaritas here. In addition, the restaurant rents kayaks for $12 to $18 per hour.

1303 NE Boat St. ℂ 206/545-8570. Reservations not accepted. Main courses $2.50–$9. DC, MC, V. Mon–Sat 11am–4pm and 5–10pm.

Red Mill Burgers ★ AMERICAN   Located just a little north of the Woodland Park Zoo, this retro burger joint is tiny and always hoppin' because everyone knows they do one of the best burgers in Seattle. Try the verde burger, made with Anaheim peppers for just the right amount of fire. Don't miss the onion rings. And don't come dressed in your finest attire—burgers here are definitely multi-napkin affairs. There's a second Red Mill Burgers at 1613 W. Dravus St. (ℂ 206/284-6363), which is midway between downtown Seattle and the Ballard neighborhood.

312 N. 67th St. ℂ 206/783-6362. Burgers $2.90–$5.35. No credit cards. Tues–Sat 11am–9pm; Sun noon–8pm.

WEST SEATTLE

EXPENSIVE

Salty's on Alki Beach ★★ SEAFOOD   Although the prices here are almost as out of line as those at the Space Needle, and the service is unpredictable, this restaurant has *the* waterfront view in Seattle, and the food is usually pretty good. Because the restaurant is set on the northeast side of the Alki Peninsula, it faces downtown Seattle on the far side of Elliott Bay. Come at sunset for dinner and watch the setting sun sparkle off skyscraper windows as the lights of the city twinkle on. On sunny summer days, lunch on one of the two decks is a sublimely Seattle experience. Don't be discouraged by the ugly industrial/port area you drive through to get here; Salty's marks the start of Alki Beach, the closest Seattle comes to a Southern California beach scene. Just watch for the giant rusted salmon sculptures swimming amid rebar kelp beds and the remains of an old bridge. Hey, Seattle even recycles when it comes to art.

1936 Harbor Ave. SW. ⓒ **206/937-1600.** www.saltys.com. Reservations recommended. Main courses $10–$15 lunch, $20–$40 dinner. AE, DC, DISC, MC, V. Mon–Thurs 11am–2:30pm and 5–9pm; Fri 11am–2:30pm and 5–9:30pm; Sat 11am–3pm and 4–9:30pm; Sun 9am–2pm and 4–9pm.

THE EASTSIDE (INCLUDING BELLEVUE & KIRKLAND)
VERY EXPENSIVE
The Herbfarm Restaurant ★★★ NORTHWEST   The Herbfarm, the most highly acclaimed restaurant in the Northwest, is known across the nation for its extraordinarily lavish meals. The menu changes throughout the year, with themes to match the seasons. Wild gathered vegetables, Northwest seafood and meats, organic vegetables, wild mushrooms, and, of course, the generous use of fresh herbs from the Herbfarm gardens are the ingredients from which the restaurant's chef, Jerry Traunfeld, creates his culinary extravaganzas. Dinners are paired with complementary Northwest wines (and occasionally something particularly remarkable from Europe). Dinners here are so popular that reservations are taken only a couple of times each year, so you'll have to plan far in advance if you want to be sure of an Herbfarm experience. You can try calling on short notice, however; cancellations often open up tables.

14590 NE 145th St., Woodinville. ⓒ **425/485-5300.** www.theherbfarm.com. Reservations required. Fixed-price 9-course dinner $149–$189 per person with 5 or 6 matched wines ($50 per-person deposit required when reserving a table). AE, MC, V. Seatings Thurs–Sat at 7pm; Sun 4:30pm.

EXPENSIVE
Yarrow Bay Grill ★★ NORTHWEST   The combination of Northwest cuisine and a view across Lake Washington to Seattle has made this restaurant, in the upscale Carillon Point retail, office, and condo development, a favorite of Eastside diners (we've heard even Bill Gates eats here). The setting is decidedly nouveau riche and about as close as you get to a Southern California setting in the Northwest. The menu is not so long that you can't make a decision, but long enough to provide some serious options. The Thai-style crab-cake appetizers with a sweet mustard sauce are favorites of ours, as is the peanut-sesame dusted calamari. Entrees are usually equally divided between seafood and meats, with at least one vegetarian dish on the menu daily. Keep in mind that the menu changes daily. Nearly every table has a view, and there is a great deck for good weather.

1270 Carillon Point, Kirkland. ⓒ **425/889-9052.** www.ybgrill.com. Reservations recommended. Main courses $16–$34. AE, DC, DISC, MC, V. Daily 5:30–10pm.

MODERATE
Beach Cafe ★★ INTERNATIONAL   Affiliated with the Yarrow Bay Grill, which is located just upstairs, this casual waterfront cafe is the Eastside's best bet for an economical and creative meal with a view. In summer, the patio dining area just can't be beat. The menu circles the globe, bringing a very satisfying

mélange of flavors to its dishes. Because the menu changes daily, you never know what you might find when you drop by.

1270 Carillon Point, Kirkland. © 425/889-0303. www.ybbeachcafe.com. Reservations recommended. Main courses $13–$21. AE, DC, DISC, MC, V. Sun–Thurs 11am–10pm; Fri–Sat 11am–10:30pm.

COFFEE, TEA, BAKERIES & PASTRY SHOPS
CAFES, COFFEE BARS & TEA SHOPS

Unless you've been on Mars for the past decade, you're likely aware that Seattle has become the espresso capital of America. Seattleites are positively rabid about coffee, which isn't just a hot drink or a caffeine fix anymore, but rather a way of life. You'll never be more than about a block from your next cup. There are espresso carts on the sidewalks, drive-through espresso windows, espresso bars, gas station espresso counters, espresso milkshakes, espresso chocolates, even eggnog lattes at Christmas.

Starbucks, the ruling king of coffee, is seemingly everywhere you turn in Seattle. They sell some 36 types and blends of coffee beans. **SBC,** also known as Seattle's Best Coffee, and **Torrefazione,** two of Seattle's other favorite espresso-bar chains, were both bought up by Starbucks in 2003, so though the decor may be different, you can expect the same Starbucks coffee and service at these other two chains. Close on the heels of Starbucks and SBC in popularity and citywide coverage is the **Tully's** chain, which seems to have an espresso bar on every corner that doesn't already have a Starbucks or an SBC. Serious espresso junkies, however, swear by **Caffe Ladro** and **Caffé Vita.** If you see one of either of these chains, check it out and see what you think.

Coffee bars and cafes are as popular as bars and pubs as places to hang out and visit with friends. Among our favorite Seattle cafes are the following (organized by neighborhood):

Pioneer Square & the International District

The Pioneer Square location of **Torrefazione** 🛆🛆, 320 Occidental Ave. S. (© **206/624-5847**), with its hand-painted Italian crockery, has a very old-world feel. The foam on the lattes here is absolutely perfect. It has great pastries, too. Other Torrefaziones can be found at 622 Olive Way (© **206/624-1429**), 1310 Fourth Ave. (© **206/583-8970**), and in Fremont at 701 N. 34th St. (© **206/545-2721**).

Zeitgeist Art/Coffee 🛆, 171 S. Jackson St. (© **206/583-0497**), with its big windows and local artwork, is popular with the Pioneer Square art crowd.

In the International District, don't miss the atmospheric **Panama Hotel Tea & Coffee House** 🛆, 607 S. Main St. (© **206/515-4000**), which is filled with historic photos and offers a fascinating glimpse into the neighborhood's past.

Belltown & Pike Place Market

Seattle is legendary as a city of coffeeholics, and Starbucks is the main reason. This company has coffeehouses all over town (and all over the world), but the original **Starbucks,** 1912 Pike Place (© **206/448-8762**), is in Pike Place Market. In fact, this is the only chain store allowed in the market. Although you won't find any tables or chairs here, Starbucks fans shouldn't miss an opportunity to get their coffee at the source.

The Seattle Center & Queen Anne Areas

Caffe Ladro Espresso Bar & Bakery 🛆🛆, 2205 Queen Anne Ave. N. (© **206/282-5313**), in the heart of the pleasant Upper Queen Anne area, has the feel of a cozy neighborhood coffeehouse. There's another Caffe Ladro in the MarQueen

Hotel building in Lower Queen Anne at 600 Queen Anne Ave. N. (© **206/ 282-1549**). Other Caffe Ladros can be found downtown at 801 Pine St. (© **206/405-1950**) and at 108 Union St. (© **206/267-0600**); and in the Fremont neighborhood at 452 36th St. N. (© **206/675-0854**).

Uptown Espresso, 525 Queen Anne Ave. N. (© **206/285-3757**), with its crystal chandelier, gilt-framed classical painting, and opera music on the stereo, has a very theatrical, European feel. It has good baked goodies, too. There's another Uptown in Belltown at 2504 Fourth Ave.

Over the past few years, Caffe Vita has become known as one of Seattle's finest coffee roasters. In the Lower Queen Anne neighborhood, you can sample these superb coffees at their coffeehouse—**Caffe Vita,** 813 Fifth Ave. N. (© **206/ 285-9662**).

If you've tired of double tall raspberry mochas and are desperately seeking a new coffee experience, make a trip to Upper Queen Anne's **El Diablo Coffee Co.,** 1811 Queen Anne. Ave. N. (© **206/285-0693**), a Latin-style coffeehouse. The Cubano, made with two shots of espresso and caramelized sugar, and the *café con leche* (a Cubano with steamed milk) are both devilishly good drinks. *Viva la revolución!*

Capitol Hill & East Seattle

Bauhaus Coffee & Books ⟨★⟩, 301 E. Pine St. (© **206/625-1600**), on the downtown edge of Capitol Hill, is a great place to hang out and soak up the neighborhood atmosphere. There are always lots of interesting 30-something types hanging out reading or carrying on heated discussions.

Over the past few years, **Caffe Vita,** 1005 E. Pike St. (© **206/709-4440**), has developed a devoted following of espresso fanatics who swear by the perfectly roasted coffee beans and lovingly crafted lattes served here.

North Seattle

Café Allegro, 4214 University Way NE (© **206/633-3030**), located down an alley around the corner from University Way in the U District, is Seattle's oldest cafe and a favored hangout of University of Washington students. Keep looking; you'll find it.

Still Life in Fremont Coffeehouse ⟨★⟩, 709 N. 35th St. (© **206/547-9850**), in the eclectic Fremont neighborhood, harks back to hippie hangouts of old. It's big and always crowded, offering good vegetarian meals and great weekend breakfasts, too. There's also **Still Life on the Ave Cafe,** 1405 NE 50th St. (© **206/ 729-3542**), in the University District.

Teahouse Kuan Yin, 1911 N. 45th St. (© **206/632-2055**), in the Wallingford neighborhood, is one of Seattle's favorite coffee alternatives. This Asian-inspired tea shop not only serves an amazing variety of teas, but also sells all manner of tea paraphernalia.

BAKERIES & PASTRY SHOPS
Pioneer Square & the International District

Grand Central Baking Company ⟨★⟩, 214 First Ave. S. (© **206/622-3644**), in Pioneer Square's Grand Central Arcade, is responsible for awakening Seattle to the pleasures of rustic European-style breads. This bakery not only turns out great bread, but it also does good pastries and sandwiches.

Although the name is none too appealing, **Cow Chips,** 102A First Ave. S. (© **206/292-9808**), bakes the best chocolate chip cookies in the city, and the cookies come in different sizes depending on the size of your cookie craving.

Belltown & Pike Place Market

The Crumpet Shop ✿, 1503 First Ave. (© **206/682-1598**), in Pike Place Market, specializes in its British namesake pastries but also does scones. It's almost a requirement that you accompany your crumpet or scone with a pot of tea.

Le Panier, 1902 Pike Place (© **206/441-3669**), located in the heart of Pike Place Market, is a great place to get a croissant and a latte and watch the market action.

With a wall of glass cases full of baked goods and a window facing onto one of the busiest spots in Pike Place Market, **Three Girls Bakery,** 1514 Pike Place, Stall no. 1 (© **206/622-1045**), is a favorite place to grab a few pastries or other goodies to go. It also has a counter in back if you prefer to sit down.

Macrina ✿✿, 2408 First Ave. (© **206/448-4032**), a neighborhood bakery/cafe in Belltown, serves some of the best baked goodies in the city and is a cozy place for a quick, cheap breakfast or lunch. In the morning the smell of baking bread wafts down First Avenue and draws in many a passerby.

Tom Douglas's three Seattle restaurants—Dahlia Lounge, Palace Kitchen, and Etta's—are all immensely popular, and there was such a demand for the breads and pastries served at these restaurants that Douglas opened his own **Dahlia Bakery,** 2001 Fourth Ave. (© **206/441-4540**), where you can even get Douglas's fabled coconut cream pie to go.

Capitol Hill & East Seattle

Basically, **Dilettante Chocolates** ✿✿, 416 Broadway E. (© **206/329-6463**), is a chocolate restaurant that happens to be Seattle's leading proponent of cocoa as the next drink to take the country by storm. If you don't order something with chocolate here, you're missing the point.

If you've been on your feet at Volunteer Park for a while and need a snack, try the **North Hill Bakery,** 518 15th Ave. E. (© **206/325-9007**), just a few blocks east of the park. There's always a good selection of baked goods in the cases.

QUICK BITES

For variety, it's hard to beat the food court on the top floor of **Westlake Center** shopping mall, 400 Pine St. If you're downtown at lunch and just want a gourmet sandwich and pasta salad that you can grab out of a case, stop by **Briazz Cafe,** 1400 Fifth Ave. (© **206/343-3099**).

5 What to See & Do

I hope you've got a good pair of walking shoes and a lot of stamina (a double latte helps), because Seattle is a walking town. The city's two biggest attractions—the waterfront and Pike Place Market—are the sorts of places where you'll spend hours on your feet. When your feet are beat, you can relax on a tour boat and enjoy the views of the city from the waters of Puget Sound, or you can take a 2-minute rest on the monorail, which links downtown Seattle with Seattle Center, home of the Space Needle. If your energy level sags, don't worry; there's always an espresso bar nearby.

By the way, that monorail ride takes you right through the middle of Paul Allen's Experience Music Project, the Frank Gehry–designed rock music museum also located in Seattle Center. Paul Allen, who made his millions as one of the cofounders of Microsoft, has been busily changing the face of the south end of downtown over the past few years. He has renovated Union Station and developed the area adjacent to the new Seahawks Stadium, which was built for

Seattle Attractions

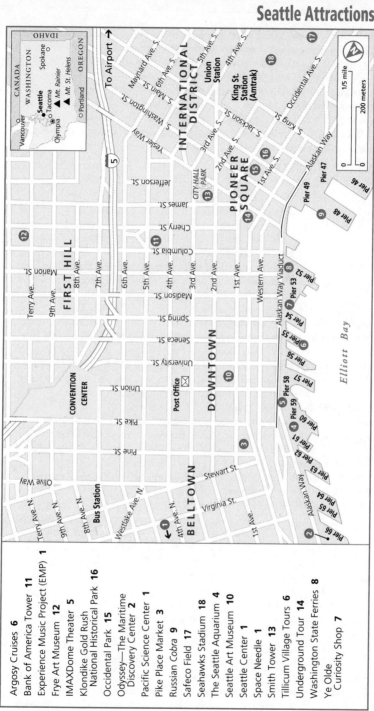

Argosy Cruises **6**
Bank of America Tower **11**
Experience Music Project (EMP) **1**
Frye Art Museum **12**
IMAXDome Theater **5**
Klondike Gold Rush
National Historical Park **16**
Occidental Park **15**
Odyssey—The Maritime
Discovery Center **2**
Pacific Science Center **1**
Pike Place Market **3**
Russian Cobra **9**
Safeco Field **17**
Seahawks Stadium **18**
The Seattle Aquarium **4**
Seattle Art Museum **10**
Seattle Center **1**
Space Needle **1**
Smith Tower **13**
Tillicum Village Tours **6**
Underground Tour **14**
Washington State Ferries **8**
Ye Olde
Curiosity Shop **7**

the Seattle Seahawks football team, whose owner is . . . you guessed it: Paul Allen. The new stadium is adjacent to the Seattle Mariners Safeco Field, which is one of the few stadiums in the country with a retractable roof.

Despite Seattle's many downtown diversions, however, the city's natural surroundings are still its primary attraction. You can easily cover all of Seattle's museums and major sights in 2 or 3 days, and with the help of the itineraries below, you should have a good idea of what not to miss. These itineraries will provide a good overview of the history, natural history, and cultural diversity that have made Seattle the city it is today.

ON THE WATERFRONT

The Seattle waterfront, which lies along Alaskan Way between Yesler Way in the south and Bay Street and Myrtle Edwards Park in the north, is the city's most popular attraction. Yes, it's very touristy, with tacky gift shops, saltwater taffy, T-shirts galore, and lots of overpriced restaurants, but it's also home to the Seattle Aquarium, the IMAXDome Theater, Odyssey–The Maritime Discovery Center, and Ye Olde Curiosity Shop (king of the tacky gift shops). Ferries to Bainbridge Island and Bremerton, as well as several different boat tours, also operate from the waterfront. This is also the best place to hire a horse-drawn carriage for a spin around downtown.

You'll find the Washington State Ferries terminal at **Pier 52,** which is at the south end of the waterfront near Pioneer Square. (A ferry ride makes for a cheap cruise.) At **Pier 55,** you'll find excursion boats offering harbor cruises and trips to Tillicum Village on Blake Island. At **Pier 56,** cruise boats leave for trips through the Chittenden (Ballard) Locks to Lake Union. See section 6, "Organized Tours," later in this chapter, for details. At Pier 57, you'll find both the Bay Pavilion, which has a vintage carousel and a video arcade to keep the kids busy, and **Pier 57 Parasail** (© **206/622-5757**), which will strap a parasail on your back, hook you to a long rope, and then tow you around Elliott Bay. The view from above the water is almost as good as the view from the Space Needle, and, because you take off and land from the back of the boat, you won't even get wet. Rides are $49 for one person and $89 for a tandem ride.

At **Pier 59,** you'll find the Seattle Aquarium (see below for details), the IMAXDome Theater (see below), and a small waterfront park. Continuing up the waterfront, you'll find **Pier 66,** the Bell Street Pier, which has a rooftop park. This is also the site of Odyssey–The Maritime Discovery Center (see below), which is dedicated to the history of shipping and fishing in Puget Sound, and Anthony's, one of the best seafood restaurants on the waterfront (see "Where to Dine," earlier in this chapter, for a full review). At **Pier 67,** you'll find The Edgewater hotel, a great place to take in the sunset over a drink or dinner (see "Where to Stay," earlier in this chapter, for details).

Next door, at **Pier 69,** you'll come to the dock for the ferries that ply the waters between Seattle and Victoria, British Columbia. Just north of this pier is grassy Myrtle Edwards Park, a nice finale to a very pleasant waterfront. This park has a popular bicycling and skating trail, and is the northern terminus for the Waterfront Streetcar, which can take you back to your starting point.

IMAXDome Theater ✪   The IMAXDome is a movie theater with a 180-degree screen that fills your peripheral vision and puts you right in the middle of the action. This huge wraparound theater is adjacent to the Seattle Aquarium, and for many years now has featured a film about the eruption of Mount St. Helens. Various other special features are screened throughout the year.

Pier 59, 1483 Alaskan Way. ✆ **206/622-1868** or 206/622-1869 for ticket reservations. www.seattleimaxdome. com. Admission $7 adults, $6 youth, free under 5 (IMAXDome–Aquarium combination tickets available). Screenings daily beginning at 10am. Closed Christmas. Bus: 10, 12, 15, or 18; then walk through Pike Place Market to the waterfront. Waterfront Streetcar: To Pike Place Market stop.

Odyssey–The Maritime Discovery Center   Sort of an interactive promotion for modern fishing and shipping, this facility at the north end of the Seattle waterfront is aimed primarily at kids and has more than 40 hands-on exhibits highlighting Seattle's modern working waterfront and its links to the sea. Exhibits include a kid-size fishing boat, a virtual kayak trip through Puget Sound, and a live radar center that allows you to track the movement of vessels in Elliott Bay. In another exhibit, you get to use a simulated crane to practice loading a scale model of a cargo ship.

Pier 66 (Bell St. Pier), 2205 Alaskan Way. ✆ **206/374-4000.** www.ody.org. Admission $7 adults, $5 seniors and students, $2 children ages 2–4, free for children under 2. Tues–Sat 10am–5pm; Sun noon–5pm. Closed day before Thanksgiving, Thanksgiving, Dec 24–25, Jan 1. Bus: 97 to Elliott Ave. Waterfront Streetcar: Bell St. Station.

Russian Cobra   This Cold War–era Russian submarine is berthed just south of Washington State Ferries' Colman Dock at the south end of the waterfront, and the long black submarine is an ominous sight on this touristy stretch of Seattle shoreline. This sub, code-named Cobra, was built in 1972 and was in service for 20 years. A visit includes an introductory video that provides a bit of background on Russian submarines. After watching the video, you board the sub for a self-guided tour of the sub's main deck. Although an audio recording explains different parts of the sub as you walk through, there is also usually a former U.S. Navy submariner on hand to answer general questions about submarines. For anyone who lived through the Cold War, it is thrilling just to be inside a sub that was once considered "the enemy."

Pier 48, 101 Alaskan Way. ✆ **206/223-1767.** Admission $10 adults, $8 seniors and children ages 5–14. Daily 9am–9pm (daily 9am–5pm fall through spring). Bus: 16. Waterfront Streetcar: To S. Main St. Station.

Seattle Aquarium ★★   Although it's not nearly as large and impressive as either the Monterey Bay Aquarium or the Oregon Coast Aquarium, the Seattle Aquarium is still quite enjoyable and presents well-designed exhibits dealing

---

⟨Value⟩ Saving Money on Sightseeing

If you're a see-it-all, do-it-all kind of person, you'll definitely want to buy a **CityPass** (✆ **888/330-5008** or 208/787-4300; www.citypass.com), which gets you into the Space Needle, Pacific Science Center, Seattle Aquarium, Woodland Park Zoo, and Museum of Flight, and also lets you take a boat tour of the harbor with Argosy Cruises at a savings of 50% if you visit all five attractions and do the harbor tour. The passes, good for 9 days from date of first use, cost $42 for adults and $29 for children ages 4 to 13. Purchase your CityPass at any of the participating attractions.

Before visiting any Seattle attractions, be sure to first stop by the **Seattle's Convention and Visitors Bureau Visitor Information Center,** Washington State Convention & Trade Center, 800 Convention Place, Galleria Level, at the corner of Eighth Avenue and Pike Street (✆ **206/461-5840;** www.seeseattle.org), where you can pick up a booklet full of two-for-one and other coupons.

with the water worlds of the Puget Sound region. The star attractions here are the playful river otters and the sea otters, as well as the giant octopus. There's also an underwater viewing dome, from which you get a fish's-eye view of life beneath the waves, and each September, you can watch salmon return up a fish ladder to spawn. Of course there are also plenty of small tanks that allow you to familiarize yourself with the many fish of the Northwest, a beautiful large coral-reef tank, and several smaller tanks that exhibit fish from distant waters. "Life on the Edge" focuses on tide-pool life along Washington's Pacific Ocean and Puget Sound shores, while "Life of a Drifter," the aquarium's newest exhibit, highlights jellyfish.

Pier 59, 1483 Alaskan Way. ⓒ 206/386-4300. www.seattleaquarium.org. Admission $11 adults, $7 ages 6–12, $5 ages 3–5 (joint Aquarium–IMAXDome tickets also available). Labor Day to Memorial Day daily 10am–5pm; Memorial Day to Labor Day daily 9:30am–7pm. Bus: 10, 12, 15, or 18; then walk through Pike Place Market to the waterfront. Waterfront Streetcar: To Pike Place Market stop.

PIKE PLACE MARKET TO PIONEER SQUARE

Pike Place Market and the Pioneer Square historic district lie at opposite ends of First Avenue; midway between the two is the Seattle Art Museum.

The **Pioneer Square** area, with its historic buildings, interesting shops, museum, and the **Underground Tour** (see the box titled "Good Times in Bad Taste," below), is well worth a morning or afternoon's exploration.

Klondike Gold Rush National Historical Park   It isn't in the Klondike (that's in Canada) and it isn't really a park (it's a single room in an old store), but this is a fascinating little museum. "At 3 o'clock this morning the steamship *Portland,* from St. Michaels for Seattle, passed up [Puget] Sound with more than a ton of gold on board and 68 passengers." When the *Seattle Post-Intelligencer* published that sentence on July 17, 1897, it started a stampede. Would-be miners heading for the Klondike gold fields in the 1890s made Seattle their outfitting center and helped turn it into a prosperous city. When they struck it rich up north, they headed back to Seattle, the first U.S. outpost of civilization, and unloaded their gold, making Seattle doubly rich. It seems only fitting that this museum should be here. Another unit of the park is in Skagway, Alaska.

117 S. Main St. ⓒ 206/553-7220. www.nps.gov/klse. Free admission. Daily 9am–5pm. Closed Thanksgiving, Christmas, and New Year's Day. Bus: 15, 16, 18, 21, or 22. Waterfront Streetcar: To Occidental Park stop.

Pike Place Market ★★★   Pike Place Market, originally a farmers' market, was founded in 1907 when housewives complained that middlemen were raising the price of produce. The market allowed shoppers to buy directly from producers, and thus save on grocery bills. By the 1960s, however, the market was no longer the popular spot it had been. World War II had deprived it of nearly half its farmers when Japanese Americans were moved to internment camps. The postwar flight to the suburbs almost spelled the end of the market, and the site was being eyed for a major redevelopment project. Fortunately, a grass-roots movement to save the 9-acre market culminated in its being declared a National Historic District.

Today the market is once again bustling, but the 100 or so farmers and fishmongers who set up shop on the premises are only a small part of the attraction. More than 150 local craftspeople and artists can be found here, selling their creations as street performers serenade milling crowds. There are also hundreds of small specialty shops throughout the market, plus dozens of restaurants, including some of the city's best. At the information booth almost directly below the large Pike Place Market sign, you can pick up a free map and guide to the market. Keep

Good Times in Bad Taste

If you love bad jokes and are fascinated by the bizarre (or maybe this describes your children), you won't want to miss the Underground Tour and a visit to Ye Olde Curiosity Shop. Together, these two attractions should reassure you that, espresso, traffic jams, and Microsoft aside, Seattle really does have a sense of humor.

If you have an appreciation for off-color humor and are curious about the seamier side of Seattle history, the **Underground Tour,** 608 First Ave. (© 206/682-4646; www.undergroundtour.com), will likely entertain and enlighten you. The tours lead down below street level in the Pioneer Square area, where you can still find the vestiges of Seattle businesses built before the great fire of 1889. Learn the lowdown dirt on early Seattle, a town where plumbing was problematic and a person could drown in a pothole. (Tours are held daily. The cost is $9 for adults, $7 for seniors and students ages 13–17 or with college ID, $5 for children ages 7–12; children under 7 are discouraged.)

Ye Olde Curiosity Shop, 1001 Alaskan Way, Pier 54 (© 206/682-5844), is a cross between a souvenir store and Ripley's Believe It or Not! It's weird! It's tacky! It's always packed! The collection of oddities was started in 1899 by Joe Standley, who developed a more-than-passing interest in strange curios. See Siamese-twin calves, a natural mummy, the Lord's Prayer on a grain of rice, a narwhal tusk, shrunken heads, a 67-pound snail, fleas in dresses—all the stuff that fascinated you as a kid.

an eye out for low-flying fish at the Pike Place Fish stall, and be sure to save some change for Rachel, the market's giant piggy bank, which has raised more than $100,000 over the years.

Victor Steinbrueck Park, at the north end of the market at the intersection of Pike Place, Virginia Street, and Western Avenue, is a popular lounging area for both the homeless and people just looking for a grassy place in which to sit in the sun. In the park, you'll find two 50-foot-tall totem poles.

For a glimpse behind the scenes at the market and to learn all about its history, you can take a 1-hour guided **Market Heritage Tour** (© 206/682-7453, ext. 653, for information and reservations). Tours are offered Wednesday through Sunday at 11am and 2pm. Tours depart from the market's Heritage Center, 1531 Western Ave. (take the Skybridge to the Market Garage and then take the elevator to the Western Ave. level). The Heritage Center is an open-air building filled with historical exhibits. Tours cost $7 for adults and $5 for seniors and children under age 18.

Between Pike and Pine sts. at First Ave. © 206/682-7453. www.pikeplacemarket.org. Mon–Sat 9am–6pm; Sun 11am–5pm; several restaurants keep late evening hours. Closed New Year's Day, Easter, Thanksgiving, Christmas. Bus: 10, 12, 15, or 18. Waterfront Streetcar: To Pike Place Market stop.

Seattle Art Museum ⊕⊕   You simply can't miss this downtown art museum. Just look for Jonathon Borofsky's *Hammering Man,* an animated three-story steel sculpture that pounds out a silent beat in front of the museum. Inside you'll find one of the nation's premier collections of Northwest Coast Indian art and artifacts and an equally large collection of African art. Exhibits cover European and American art ranging from ancient Mediterranean works to pieces from the medieval, Renaissance, and baroque periods. A large 18th-century collection and a smaller 19th-century exhibition lead up to a large 20th-century collection that includes a room devoted to Northwest contemporary art. (There's also a smattering of Asian art at this museum, but the city's major collection of Asian art is at the Seattle Asian Art Museum in Volunteer Park; see below for details.) Free guided tours of the different collections are offered.

100 University St. (✆ 206/654-3100. www.seattleartmuseum.org. Admission $7 adults, $5 seniors and students, free 12 and under (admission $10 for adults and $7 for seniors and students for some special exhibitions). Free first Thurs of each month (free for seniors first Fri of each month). Admission ticket also valid at Seattle Asian Art Museum if used within 1 week. Tues–Sun 10am–5pm (Thurs until 9pm). Also open on Martin Luther King Jr. Day, Presidents' Day, Memorial Day, July 4th, and Labor Day. Closed Columbus Day, Thanksgiving, Christmas, and New Year's Day. Bus: 10, 12, 15, 18, 39, 42, or any bus using the bus tunnel.

SEATTLE CENTER ATTRACTIONS

Built in 1962 for the World's Fair, Seattle Center is today not only the site of Seattle's famous Space Needle but also a cultural and entertainment park that doubles as the city's favorite festival grounds. Within Seattle Center's boundaries, you'll find the Experience Music Project (EMP), the Pacific Science Center, the Seattle Children's Museum, the Seattle Children's Theatre, Key Arena (home of the NBA's Seattle Supersonics), the Marion Oliver McCaw Hall, a children's amusement park, a fountain that's a favorite summertime hangout, the Intiman Theatre, and the Bagley Wright Theatre. See p. 115, "Especially for Kids," for further details on Seattle Center attractions that young travelers will enjoy.

Experience Music Project (EMP) ✶✶ The brainchild of Microsoft cofounder Paul Allen and designed by architect Frank Gehry, who is known for pushing the envelope of architectural design, this rock 'n' roll museum is a massive multicolored blob at the foot of the Space Needle. Originally planned as a memorial to Seattle native Jimi Hendrix, the museum grew to encompass not only Hendrix, but all of the Northwest rock scene (from "Louie Louie" to grunge) and the general history of American popular music.

One museum exhibit focuses on the history of guitars and includes some of the first electric guitars, which date from the early 1930s, but the most popular exhibits here (after the Jimi Hendrix room) are the interactive rooms. In one you can play guitar, drums, keyboards, or even DJ turntables. In another, you can experience what it's like to be onstage performing in front of adoring fans.

Regularly scheduled concerts are held in the museum's main hall, known as the Sky Church. To help you get the most out of your visit (and at almost $20 for a ticket, you certainly expect plenty), every visitor is issued a Museum Exhibit Guide (MEG), a hand-held electronic player filled with recorded audio clips explaining the various exhibits. Give yourself plenty of time to see this unusual museum.

325 Fifth Ave. N. (✆ 877/EMPLIVE or 206/EMPLIVE. www.emplive.com. Admission $20 adults, $16 seniors and children ages 13–17, $15 children ages 7–12, free for children 6 and under. Memorial Day to Labor Day Sun–Thurs 9am–6pm, Fri–Sat 9am–9pm; Labor Day to Memorial Day Sun–Thurs 10am–5pm, Fri–Sat 10am–9pm. Bus: 1, 2, 3, 4, 13, 15, 16, or 18. Monorail: From Westlake Center at Pine St. and Fourth Ave.

Pacific Science Center ✶✶ *Kids* Although its exhibits are aimed primarily at children, the Pacific Science Center is fun for all ages. The main goal of this sprawling complex at Seattle Center is to teach kids about science and to instill a desire to study it. To that end, there are life-size robotic dinosaurs, a butterfly house and insect village (with giant robotic insects), a Tech Zone where kids can play virtual-reality soccer or play tic-tac-toe with a robot, and dozens of other fun hands-on exhibits addressing the biological sciences, physics, and chemistry. The August Bubble Festival is always a big hit. There's a planetarium for learning about the skies (plus laser shows for the fun of it), and an IMAX theater. Be sure to check the schedule for special exhibits when you're in town.

200 Second Ave. N., Seattle Center. (C) 206/443-2001. www.pacsci.org. Admission $9 adults, $6.50 ages 3–13 and seniors, free for children under 3. IMAX $7.50–$8.50 adults, $6.50–$7.50 ages 3–13 and seniors, free for children under 3. Laser show $5–$7.50. Various discounted combination tickets available. Mid-June to Labor Day daily 10am–6pm; Labor Day to mid-June Mon–Fri 10am–5pm, Sat–Sun and holidays 10am–6pm. Closed Thanksgiving and Christmas. Bus: 1, 2, 3, 4, 13, 15, 16, or 18. Monorail: To Seattle Center.

The Space Needle ★★   From a distance it resembles a flying saucer on top of a tripod, and when it was built for the 1962 World's Fair, the 605-foot-tall Space Needle was meant to suggest future architectural trends. Today the Space Needle is the quintessential symbol of Seattle, and at 520 feet above ground level, the

Space Needle Alternatives

If you don't want to deal with the crowds at the Space Needle but still want an elevated downtown view, you have some alternatives. One is the big, black **Bank of America Tower** ((C) 206/386-5151) at the corner of Fifth Avenue and Columbia Street. At 943 feet, this is the tallest building in Seattle (twice as tall as the Space Needle), and has more stories (76, to be exact) than any other building west of the Mississippi. Up on the 73rd floor, you'll find an observation deck with views that dwarf those from the Space Needle. Admission is only $5 for adults and $3 for seniors and children. It's open Monday through Friday from 8:30am to 4:30pm.

Not far from the Bank of America Tower, you'll find the **Smith Tower**, 506 Second Ave. ((C) 206/622-4004; www.chineseroom.com/observation.html). Opened in 1914, this was Seattle's first skyscraper and, for 50 years, was the tallest building west of Chicago. Although Smith Tower has only 42 stories, it still offers excellent views from its 35th-floor observation deck, which surrounds the ornate Chinese Room, a banquet hall with a carved ceiling. A lavish lobby and original manual elevators all make this a fun and historic place to take in the Seattle skyline. April 16 to October 31, the observation deck is open daily from 11am to 6pm; November 1 to April 15, it's open Saturday and Sunday from 11am to 4pm. Admission is $6 for adults, $5 for seniors and students, and $4 for children ages 6 to 12.

If you've ever seen a photo of the Space Needle framed by Mount Rainier and the high-rises of downtown Seattle, it was probably taken from **Kerry Viewpoint** on Queen Anne Hill. If you want to take your own drop-dead photo of the Seattle skyline from this elevated perspective, head north from Seattle Center on Queen Anne Avenue North and turn left on West Highland Drive. When you reach the park, you'll immediately recognize the view.

Another great panorama is from the water tower in **Volunteer Park** on Capitol Hill at East Prospect Street and 14th Avenue East. See p. 114.

observation deck provides superb views of the city and its surroundings. Displays identify more than 60 sites and activities in the Seattle area, and high-powered telescopes let you zoom in on distant sights. You'll also find a pricey restaurant atop the tower (see the review of SkyCity on p. 92). If you don't mind standing in line and paying quite a bit for an elevator ride, make this your first stop in Seattle so that you can orient yourself. There are, however, cheaper alternatives if you just want a view of the city (see the box immediately above).

Seattle Center, Fourth Ave. N. at Broad St. ⓒ **800/937-9582** or 206/905-2100. www.spaceneedle.com. Admission $13 adults, $11 seniors, $10 youths ages 11–17, $5 ages 4–10, free under 4. No charge if dining in the SkyCity restaurant. Daily 9am–midnight. Valet parking $12 for 4 hr. Bus: 1, 2, 3, 4, 13, 15, 16, or 18. Monorail: From Westlake Center at Pine St. and Fourth Ave.

THE NEIGHBORHOODS
THE INTERNATIONAL DISTRICT

Seattle today boasts of its strategic location on the Pacific Rim, but its ties to Asia are nothing new. This is evident in the International District, Seattle's main Asian neighborhood, which is centered between Fifth Avenue South and 12th Avenue South (between S. Washington St. and S. Lane St.). Called the International District rather than Chinatown because so many Asian nationalities have made the area home, this neighborhood has been the center of the city's Asian communities for more than 100 years. You can learn about the district's history at the **Wing Luke Museum,** 407 Seventh Ave. S. (ⓒ **206/623-5124;** www.wingluke.org).

There are many restaurants, import stores, and food markets, and the huge **Uwajimaya** is all of these rolled up in one (see "Shopping," later in this chapter, for details).

At the corner of Maynard Avenue South and South King Street, you'll find **Hing Hay Park,** the site of an ornate and colorful pavilion given to the city by Taipei, Taiwan.

FIRST HILL (PILL HILL) & CAPITOL HILL

Seattle is justly proud of its parks, and **Volunteer Park,** on Capitol Hill (drive north on Broadway and watch for signs), is one of the most popular. Here you'll find not only acres of lawns, groves of trees, and huge old rhododendrons, but also an old water tower that provides one of the best panoramas in the city. A winding staircase leads to the top of the water tower, from which you get 360-degree views. On the observatory level there is also an interesting exhibit about the Olmsted Brothers and the system of parks they designed for Seattle. To find the water tower, park near the Seattle Asian Art Museum if you can, and walk back out of the parking lot to where the road splits. The view from directly in front of the museum isn't bad either.

Frye Art Museum ✦   Located on First Hill not far from downtown Seattle, this museum is primarily an exhibit space for the extensive personal art collection of Charles and Emma Frye, Seattle pioneers who began collecting art in the 1890s. The collection focuses on late-19th-century and early-20th-century representational art by European and American painters, with works by Andrew Wyeth, Thomas Hart Benton, Edward Hopper, Albert Bierstadt, and Pablo Picasso, as well as a large collection of engravings by Winslow Homer. In addition to galleries filled with works from the permanent collection, temporary exhibitions are held throughout the year.

704 Terry Ave. (at Cherry St.). ⓒ **206/622-9250.** www.fryeart.org. Free admission. Tues–Sat 10am–5pm (Thurs until 8pm); Sun noon–5pm. Closed July 4th, Thanksgiving, Christmas, and New Year's Day. Bus: 3, 4, or 12.

Seattle Asian Art Museum 🖈   Housed in a renovated Art Deco building, the Asian art collection has an emphasis on Chinese and Japanese art but also includes pieces from Korea, Southeast Asia, South Asia, and the Himalayas. Exhibits of Chinese terra-cotta funerary art, snuff bottles, and Japanese *netsukes* (belt decorations) are among the museum's most notable collections. One room is devoted to Japanese ceramics, while three rooms are devoted to Chinese ceramics. The central hall is devoted to the stone religious sculptures of South Asia (primarily India). There are frequent lectures and concerts.

1400 E. Prospect St., Volunteer Park (14th Ave. E. and E. Prospect St.). ☎ 206/654-3100. www.seattleart museum.org. Admission $3 adults, free 12 and under. Free to all on first Thurs and first Sat of each month (free for seniors on 1st Fri of each month). Admission ticket valid for $3 off admission to the Seattle Art Museum if used within 1 week. Wed–Sun 10am–5pm (Thurs until 9pm); Tues 10am–5pm between Memorial Day and Sept 1. Closed Labor Day, Thanksgiving, Christmas, and New Year's Day. Bus: 10.

Volunteer Park Conservatory 🖈   This stately old Victorian conservatory, built in 1912, houses a large collection of tropical and desert plants, including palm trees, orchids, and cacti. There are seasonal floral displays also.

1400 E. Galer St. ☎ 206/684-4743. Free admission. Labor Day to Memorial Day daily 10am–4pm; Memorial Day to Labor Day daily 10am–7pm. Bus: 10.

NORTH SEATTLE (INCLUDING THE U DISTRICT, FREMONT & MONTLAKE)

The **Fremont District,** which begins at the north end of the Fremont Bridge near the intersection of Fremont Avenue North and North 36th Street, is Seattle's funkiest and most unusual neighborhood. Even livelier, though not nearly as eclectic or artistic, the **University District** (known locally as the U District) has loads of cheap restaurants and the types of shops you would associate with a college-age clientele. But the main attractions for visitors are the two excellent museums on the university campus and the nearby Museum of History and Industry, which is just across the Montlake Bridge from the U District.

Burke Museum 🖈   Located in the northwest corner of the University of Washington campus, the Burke Museum features exhibits on the natural and cultural heritage of the Pacific Rim. Permanent exhibits include *Life & Times,* which covers 500 million years of Washington history (and prehistory) with lots of fossils, including a complete mastodon, on display. The second permanent exhibit, *Pacific Voices,* focuses on the many cultures of the Pacific Rim and their connections to Washington state. There is also a smaller temporary exhibit gallery. In front of the museum stand three modern totem poles carved in the style of the 1870s and 1880s.

17th Ave. NE and NE 45th St. ☎ 206/543-5590. www.burkemuseum.org. Admission $6.50 adults, $5 seniors, $3 ages 6–18, free for children under 6 (higher ticket prices in effect for special exhibits). For $1 more, you can get admission to the nearby Henry Art Gallery. Free the 1st Thurs of each month. Daily 10am–5pm (1st Thurs of each month until 8pm). Closed July 4, Thanksgiving, Christmas, and New Year's Day. Bus: 70.

Henry Art Gallery   The focus here is on contemporary art with retrospectives of individual artists, as well as exhibits focusing on specific themes or media. Photography and video are both well represented, and for the most part, the exhibits are the most avant-garde in the Seattle area. The museum's latest cutting-edge installation is a Skyspace by artist James Turrell, who uses light to create his artworks. The Skyspace is a small room with an oval opening in the ceiling to frame the sky. At night, the outside of the glass Skyspace is illuminated by an ever-changing light show. Located on the west side of the University of

Insider Tip

University of Washington campus parking is expensive on weekdays and Saturday mornings, so try to visit the Burke Museum or Henry Art Gallery on a Saturday afternoon or a Sunday, when parking is free.

Washington campus, this museum benefits from large, well-lit gallery spaces illuminated by pyramidal and cubic skylights that can be seen near the main museum entrance. There's also a cafe here and a small sculpture courtyard. Parking is often available at the Central Parking Garage at NE 41st Street and 15th Avenue NE. Expect the unexpected and prepare to be challenged in your concept of what constitutes art.

University of Washington, 15th Ave. NE and NE 41st St. ① 206/543-2280. www.henryart.org. Admission $8 adults, $6 seniors, free for students and children under 14. For $1 more, you can get admission to the nearby Burke Museum. Free Thurs 5–8pm. Tues–Sun 11am–5pm (Thurs until 8pm). Closed July 4, Thanksgiving, Christmas, and New Year's Day. Bus: 70.

Hiram M. Chittenden Locks ⭐   There is something oddly fascinating about locks. No, not the locks on doors, the locks that raise and lower boats. Locks don't provide panoramic views and they aren't nearly as dramatic as waterfalls, but for some strange reason, a lot of people are intrigued by the concept of two side-by-side bodies of water on two different levels. Consequently, the Hiram Chittenden Locks are among the most popular attractions in Seattle. These locks, operated by the Army Corps of Engineers, consist of a large lock and a small lock. The latter accommodates barges, large commercial fishing vessels, and the like, while the small lock stays busy shuttling small private boats (including sea kayaks) between the salt water of Puget Sound and the fresh water of the Lake Washington Ship Canal, which connects to both Lake Union and Lake Washington. It's a slow process locking boats back and forth, but none of the onlookers seem to mind, and people on shore and those on the boats often strike up conversations.

When the gates of the lock are closed, it's possible to continue to the far side of the ship canal to the fish ladders and fish-viewing windows that provide opportunities for salmon viewing during the summer months. The chance to see salmon in a fish ladder is as much of a draw as the locks themselves, and in the past the fish runs have also attracted hungry sea lions, which have become regular salmon-swallowing pests.

Also here at the locks, you can stroll the grounds of the Carl S. English, Jr. Ornamental Gardens, a city park filled with rare and unusual shrubs and trees. There are free tours of the grounds on Monday and Friday at 1 and 3pm and Saturday and Sunday at 11am and 1 and 3pm.

The locks are located a 10- to 15-minute drive north of downtown. To reach the locks, follow Elliott Avenue north along the waterfront from downtown Seattle; after crossing the Ballard Bridge, drive west on NW Market Street.

Hiram M. Chittenden Locks, 3015 NW 54th St. ① 206/783-7059. Free admission. Daily 7am–9pm; visitor center daily 10am–6pm. Closed Thanksgiving, Christmas Day, and New Year's Day. Bus: 17.

Museum of History and Industry (MOHAI) ⭐   If the Underground Tour's vivid description of life before the 1889 fire has you curious about what the city's more respectable citizens were doing back in those days, you can find out here, where re-created storefronts provide glimpses into their lives. Located at the north end of Washington Park Arboretum, this museum explores Seattle's history, with frequently changing exhibits on more obscure aspects of the city's past. While many of the displays will be of interest only to Seattle residents, anyone wishing to gain a better understanding of the history of the city and the Northwest may also enjoy the exhibits here. There's a Boeing mail plane from the 1920s, plus an exhibit on the 1889 fire that leveled the city. This museum also hosts touring exhibitions that address Northwest history. Although not actually in north Seattle, this museum is just across the Montlake Bridge from the University District.

McCurdy Park, 2700 24th Ave. E. © 206/324-1126. www.seattlehistory.org. Admission $7 adults, $5 seniors and ages 5–17, free for children under 5. Daily 10am–5pm. Closed Thanksgiving and Christmas. From I-5, take Wash. 520 east (exit 168B) to the Montlake exit, go straight through the stoplight to 24th Ave. E., and turn left. Bus: 43.

Woodland Park Zoo ★★ (Kids)   Located in north Seattle, this sprawling zoo has outstanding exhibits focusing on Alaska, tropical Asia, the African savanna, and the tropical rainforest. The brown bear enclosure, one of the zoo's best exhibits, is a very realistic reproduction of an Alaskan stream and hillside. In the savanna, zebras gambol and antelopes and giraffes graze contentedly near a reproduction of an African village. An elephant forest provides plenty of space for the zoo's pachyderms, and the gorilla and orangutan habitats are also very well done. There's even a large walk-through butterfly house ($1 additional fee) during the summer months. Don't miss the giant Komodo lizards from Indonesia. A farm animal area and petting zoo are big hits with the little ones.

601 N. 59th St. © 206/684-4800. www.zoo.org. Admission $10 adults, $9.25 seniors and college students, $7.50 people with disabilities and children ages 6–17, $5.25 ages 3–5, free for children 2 and under. Mar 15–Apr 30 and Sept 15–Oct 14 daily 9:30am–5pm; May 1–Sept 14 daily 9:30am–6pm; Oct 15–Mar 14 daily 9:30am–4pm. Parking $3.50. Bus: 5.

SOUTH SEATTLE

Museum of Flight (Kids)   Located right next door to busy Boeing Field, 15 minutes south of downtown Seattle, this museum will have aviation buffs walking on air. Within the six-story glass-and-steel repository are displayed some of history's most famous planes.

To start things off, there's a replica of the Wright brothers' first glider, and from there the collection of planes brings you to the present state of flight. Suspended in the Great Hall are more than 20 planes, including a 1935 DC-3, the first Air Force F-5 supersonic fighter, and the Gossamer Condor, a human-powered airplane; plus there are some 34 other planes on display. You'll also see one of the famous Blackbird spy planes, which were once the world's fastest jets (and you can even sit in the cockpit of one of these babies). A rare World War II Corsair fighter rescued from Lake Washington and restored to its original glory is also on display. Visitors get to board the original Air Force One presidential plane, used by Eisenhower, and can sit in the cockpit of an F/A-18 Hornet fighter. An exhibit on the U.S. space program features an Apollo command module. Of course, you'll also see plenty of Boeing planes, including a reproduction of Boeing's first plane, which was built in 1916. The museum also incorporates part of Boeing's old wooden factory building from its early years.

While any air-and-space museum lets you look at mothballed planes, not many have their own air-traffic control tower and let you watch aircraft taking off and landing at an active airfield. During the summer months, biplane rides are usually offered from in front of the museum.

The **Museum of Flight Restoration Center** (© 425/745-5150) is located north of Seattle at Paine Field, which is near the city of Everett. Here you'll see planes in various stages of restoration. This center is open Tuesday through

Thursday from 8am to 4pm and Saturday from 9am to 5pm. Call for directions. Paine Field is also where you'll find the Boeing Tour Center (see p. 120 for information on tours of the Boeing plant). Together these two make a fascinating half-day outing.

9404 E. Marginal Way S. © 206/764-5720. www.museumofflight.org. Admission $11 adults, $10 seniors, $6.50 ages 5–17, free for children under 5. Free 1st Thurs of each month 5–9pm. Daily 10am–5pm (until 9pm on 1st Thurs of each month). Closed Thanksgiving and Christmas. Take exit 158 off I-5. Bus: 174.

BEACHES, PARKS & PUBLIC GARDENS
BEACHES

Because the waters of **Puget Sound** stay chilly year-round, the salt-water beaches in the Seattle area are not really swimming beaches. They are primarily places to play in the sand, gaze across the water at the Olympic Mountains, and enjoy a picnic. Seattle is also bordered on the east by **Lake Washington**, a large lake with numerous parks and small beaches along its shores. Even though the waters never get truly warm, the lake is still popular for swimming. There is, however, one caveat. A parasite spread by geese and known as swimmer's itch is commonplace in the waters of Lake Washington. Consequently, you should always change out of your bathing suit and shower as soon after swimming as possible.

Alki Beach ✿, across Elliott Bay from downtown Seattle, is the city's most popular beach and is the nearest approximation you'll find in the Northwest to a Southern California beach scene. The paved path that runs along this 2½-mile-long beach is popular with skaters, walkers, and cyclists; and the road that parallels the beach is lined with shops, restaurants, and beachy houses and apartment buildings. But the views across Puget Sound to the Olympic Mountains confirm that this is indeed the Northwest. Despite the views, this beach lacks the greenery that makes some of the city's other beaches so much more appealing. A water taxi operates between the downtown Seattle waterfront and Alki Beach (see "Getting Around," earlier in this chapter, for details). By the way, Alki rhymes with *sky* not *key.*

For a more Northwestern beach experience (which usually includes a bit of hiking or walking), head to one of the area's many waterfront parks. **Lincoln Park,** 8011 Fauntleroy Ave. SW, south of Alki Beach in West Seattle, has bluffs and forests backing the beach. Northwest of downtown Seattle in the Magnolia area, you'll find **Discovery Park** ✿✿, 3801 W. Government Way (© **206/386-4236**), where miles of beaches are the primary destination of most park visitors. To reach Discovery Park, follow Elliott Avenue north along the waterfront from downtown Seattle, then take the Magnolia Bridge west toward the Magnolia neighborhood and follow Grayfield Street to Galer Street to Magnolia Boulevard.

North of the Ballard neighborhood, you'll find **Golden Gardens Park** ✿✿, 8498 Seaview Place NW (© **206/684-4075**), which, with its excellent views of the Olympic Mountains and its somewhat wild feeling, is our favorite Seattle beach park. Although the park isn't very large and is backed by railroad tracks, the views of the Olympic Mountains are magnificent, and on summer evenings people build fires on the beach. Wetlands, lawns, shade trees, and a short trail make this beach park ideal for a picnic. Although the water here is too cold for swimming, the sandy beach is a pleasant spot for a sunset stroll. To reach this park, drive north from the waterfront on Elliott Avenue, which becomes 15th Avenue West; after crossing the Ballard Bridge, turn left on Market Street and follow this road for about 2 miles (it will change names to become NW 54th St. and then Seaview Ave. NW).

Several parks along the shores of Lake Washington have small stretches of beach, many of which are actually popular with hardy swimmers. **Seward Park** ⋆, 5902 Lake Washington Blvd. S. (© **206/684-4075**), southeast of downtown Seattle, is a good place to hang out by the water and do a little swimming. To reach this park from downtown, take Madison Street east to Lake Washington Boulevard and turn right. Although this isn't the most direct route to Mount Baker Beach or Seward Park, it's the most scenic. Along the way, you'll pass plenty of other small parks.

PARKS

Seattle's many parks are part of what make this such a livable city. In the downtown area, **Myrtle Edwards Park** ⋆, 3130 Alaska Way W. (© **206/684-4075**), at the north end of the waterfront, is an ideal spot for a sunset stroll with views of Puget Sound and the Olympic Mountains. The park includes a 1¼-mile paved pathway.

Freeway Park, at Sixth Avenue and Seneca Street, is one of Seattle's most unusual parks. Built right on top of busy Interstate 5, this green space is more a series of urban plazas, with terraces, waterfalls, and cement planters creating walls of greenery. You'd never know that a roaring freeway lies beneath your feet. Unfortunately, although the park is convenient, the isolated nature of its many nooks and crannies often gives it a deserted and slightly threatening feel.

For serious communing with nature, however, nothing will do but **Discovery Park** ⋆⋆, 3801 W. Government Way (© **206/386-4236**). Occupying a high bluff and sandy point jutting into Puget Sound, this is Seattle's largest and wildest park. You can easily spend a day wandering the trails and beaches here. The park's visitor center is open Tuesday through Sunday from 8:30am to 5pm. Discovery Park is a 15-minute drive from downtown; to reach the park, follow the waterfront north from downtown Seattle toward the Magnolia neighborhood and watch for

Fish Gotta Swim

It's no secret that salmon in the Puget Sound region have dwindled to dangerously low numbers in recent years. But it's still possible to witness the annual return of salmon in various spots in the sound.

In the autumn, on the waterfront, you can see returning salmon at the **Seattle Aquarium,** which has its own fish ladder. But the very best place to see salmon is at **Hiram M. Chittenden Locks,** 3015 NW 54th St. (© **206/783-7059;** see listing above for hours of operation and directions to the locks). Between June and September (July and Aug are the peak months), you can view salmon through underwater observation windows as they leap up the locks' fish ladder. These locks, which are used primarily by small boats, connect Lake Union and Lake Washington with the waters of Puget Sound, and depending on the tides and lake levels, there is a difference of 6 to 26 feet on either side of the locks.

East of Seattle, in downtown Issaquah, salmon can be seen year-round at the **Issaquah Salmon Hatchery,** 125 Sunset Way (© **425/391-9094**). However, it is in October that adult salmon can be seen returning to the hatchery. Each year on the first weekend in October, the city of Issaquah holds a Salmon Days Festival to celebrate the return of the natives.

signs to the park. When you reach the park, follow signed trails down to the beach and out to the lighthouse at the point. Although the lighthouse is not open to the public, the views from the beach make this a good destination for an hour's walk. The beach and park's bluff-top meadows both make good picnic spots.

Up on Capitol Hill, at East Prospect Street and 14th Avenue East, you'll find **Volunteer Park** 🏛🏛, 1247 15th Ave. E. (© **206/684-4075**), which is surrounded by the elegant mansions of Capitol Hill. It's a popular spot for sunning and playing Frisbee, and it's home to the Seattle Asian Art Museum (p. 109), an amphitheater, a water tower with a superb view of the city, and a conservatory filled with tropical and desert plants (p. 109). With so much variety, you can easily spend a morning or afternoon exploring this park.

On the east side of Seattle, along the shore of Lake Washington, you'll find not only swimming beaches but also **Seward Park** 🏛, 5898 Lake Washington Blvd. (© **206/684-4075**). This large park's waterfront areas may be its biggest attraction, but it also has a dense forest with trails winding through it. Keep an eye out for the bald eagles that nest here. This park is south of the I-90 floating bridge off Lake Washington Boulevard South. From downtown Seattle, follow Madison Street northeast to a right onto Lake Washington Boulevard.

In north Seattle, you'll find several parks worth visiting. These include the unique **Gasworks Park** 🏛, 2101 N. Northlake Way, at Meridian Avenue North (© **206/684-4075**), at the north end of Lake Union. In the middle of its green lawns, this park holds the rusting hulk of an old industrial plant, and the park's small Kite Hill is the city's favorite kite-flying spot. North of here, on Green Lake Way North near the Woodland Park Zoo, you'll find **Green Lake Park** 🏛🏛, 7201 E. Green Lake Dr. N. (© **206/684-4075**), which is a center for exercise buffs who jog, bike, and skate around the park on a 2.8-mile paved path. It's also possible to swim in the lake (there are changing rooms and a beach with summer lifeguards) and picnic on the many grassy areas. For information on renting in-line skates or a bike for riding the path here, see p. 122 and p. 121 respectively.

PUBLIC GARDENS
See also the listings for Volunteer Park Conservatory on p. 109 and Hiram M. Chittenden Locks on p. 110.

Bellevue Botanical Gardens 🏛 Any avid gardener should be sure to make a trip across one of Seattle's two floating bridges to the city of Bellevue and the Bellevue Botanical Garden. Although this 36-acre garden only opened in 1992, it has matured very quickly to become one of the Northwest's most-talked-about perennial gardens. The summertime displays of flowers, in expansive mixed borders, are absolutely gorgeous. There are also a Japanese garden, a shade border, and a water-wise garden (designed to conserve water).

Wilburton Hill Park, 12001 Main St., Bellevue. © **425/452-2750**. www.bellevuebotanical.org. Free admission. Daily dawn to dusk; visitor center daily 9am–4pm. Take the NE Eighth St. east exit off I-405.

Japanese Garden Situated on 3½ acres of land, the Japanese Garden is a perfect little world unto itself, with babbling brooks, a lake rimmed with Japanese irises and filled with colorful *koi* (Japanese carp), and a cherry orchard (for spring color). A special Tea Garden encloses a Tea House, where, between April and October, on the third Saturday of each month at 1:30pm, you can attend a traditional tea ceremony. Unfortunately, noise from a nearby road can be distracting.

Washington Park Arboretum, 1075 Lake Washington Blvd. E. (north of E. Madison St.). © **206/684-4725**. Admission $3 adults, $2 seniors and ages 6–18, free for children under 6. Mar–Nov Tues–Sun 10am to dusk. Closed Dec–Feb. Bus: 11.

Kubota Garden ⟨★⟩   Located in south Seattle in a working-class neighborhood not far from the shores of Lake Washington, this 20-acre Japanese-style garden was the life's work of garden designer Fujitaro Kubota. Today the gardens are a city park, and the mature landscaping and hilly setting make this the most impressive and enjoyable Japanese garden in the Seattle area. Kubota began work on this garden in 1927, and over the years built a necklace of ponds, a traditional stroll garden, and a mountainside garden complete with waterfalls. A tall, arched moon bridge is a highlight. The self-taught Kubota went on to design gardens at Seattle University and at the Bloedel Reserve on Bainbridge Island. Free tours of the gardens are offered between April and October; call for details.

Renton Ave. S. and 55th Ave. S. ⓒ **206/684-4584.** www.kubota.org. Free admission. Daily dawn to dusk. To reach the gardens from downtown, drive I-5 south to exit 158 (Pacific Hwy. S./E. Marginal Way), turn left toward Martin Luther King Jr. Way and continue uphill on Ryan Way; turn left on 51st Ave. S., right on Renton Ave. S., and right on 55th Ave. S.

Washington Park Arboretum ⟨★⟩   Acres of trees and shrubs stretch from the far side of Capitol Hill all the way to the Montlake Cut (a canal connecting Lake Washington to Lake Union). Within the 230-acre arboretum are 5,000 varieties of plants and quiet trails that are pleasant throughout the year but that become most beautiful in spring, when the azaleas, cherry trees, rhododendrons, and dogwoods are all in flower. The north end of the arboretum, a marshland that is home to ducks and herons, is popular with bird-watchers as well as kayakers and canoeists (see p. 122 in "Outdoor Pursuits," later in this chapter, for places to rent a canoe or kayak). A boardwalk with views across Lake Washington meanders along the waterside in this area (though noise from the adjacent freeway detracts considerably from the experience).

2300 Arboretum Dr. E. ⓒ **206/543-8800.** http://depts.washington.edu/wpa/general.htm. Free admission. Daily 7am to dusk; Graham Visitors Center daily 10am–4pm. Enter on Lake Washington Blvd. off E. Madison St.; or take Wash. 520 off I-5 north of downtown, take the Montlake Blvd. exit, and go straight through the first intersection. Bus: 11, 43, or 48.

ESPECIALLY FOR KIDS

In addition to the listings below, kids will also enjoy many of the attractions described earlier in this chapter, including the **Pacific Science Center** (p. 106), the **Seattle Aquarium** (p. 103), the **IMAXDome Theater** (p. 102), **Odyssey** (p. 103), and the **Woodland Park Zoo** (p. 111).

Even the surliest teenagers will think you're pretty cool for taking them to the **Experience Music Project** (p. 106).

Adolescent and preadolescent boys seem to unfailingly love **Ye Olde Curiosity Shop** and the **Underground Tour** (see the "Good Times in Bad Taste" box on p. 105). Younger kids also love the **Museum of Flight** (p. 111).

When the kids need to burn off some energy, see "Beaches, Parks & Public Gardens," above, for descriptions of Seattle's best recreational areas; section 7, "Outdoor Pursuits," later in this chapter, will give you the lowdown on biking, in-line skating, and more. You can also take the kids to a sporting event; Seattle supports professional football, basketball, and baseball teams. See section 8, "Spectator Sports," later in this chapter.

You might also be able to catch a performance at the **Seattle Children's Theatre** (ⓒ **206/441-3322;** www.sct.org) in Seattle Center (see below); or at the **Northwest Puppet Center,** 9123 15th Ave. NE (ⓒ **206/523-2579;** www.nw puppet.org).

Children's Museum *Kids*   Seattle's Children's Museum is located in the basement of the Center House at Seattle Center, which is partly why Seattle Center is such a great place to spend a day with the kids. The museum includes plenty of hands-on cultural exhibits, a child-size neighborhood, a Discovery Bay for toddlers, a mountain wilderness area, a global village, and other special exhibits to keep the little ones busy learning and playing for hours.

305 Harrison St. at Center House in Seattle Center. © **206/441-1768.** www.thechildrensmuseum.org. Admission $6 children and adults, $5.50 seniors. Mon–Fri 10am–5pm; Sat–Sun 10am–6pm. Closed Thanksgiving, Christmas, and New Year's Day. Bus: 1, 2, 3, 4, 13, 15, 16, or 18. Monorail: From Westlake Center at the corner of Pine St. and Fourth Ave.

Seattle Center *Kids*   If you want to keep the kids entertained all day long, head to Seattle Center. This 74-acre cultural center and amusement park stands on the northern edge of downtown at the end of the monorail line. The most visible building at the center is the **Space Needle** (p. 107), which provides an outstanding panorama of the city from its observation deck. However, of much more interest to children is the **Fun Forest** (© **206/728-1585**), with its roller coaster, log flume, merry-go-round, Ferris wheel, arcade games, and minigolf. Seattle Center is also the site of the **Children's Museum** (see above) and **Seattle Children's Theatre** (© **206/441-3322;** www.sct.org). This is Seattle's main festival site, and in the summer months hardly a weekend goes by without some special event filling its grounds. On hot summer days, the **International Fountain** is a great place for kids to keep cool (bring a change of clothes).

305 Harrison St. © **206/684-7200.** www.seattlecenter.com. Free admission; pay per ride or game (various multiride tickets available). Fun Forest outdoor rides: mid-June to Labor Day Mon–Thurs noon–10 or 11pm; reduced days and hours other months (call for hours); indoor attractions open at 11am year-round. Bus: 1, 2, 3, 4, 13, 15, 16, 18, 24, or 33. Monorail: From Westlake Center at the corner of Pine St. and Fourth Ave.

6 Organized Tours

For information on the **Underground tour,** see the box titled "Good Times in Bad Taste" on p. 105.

WALKING TOURS

In addition to the walking tours mentioned here, there are walking tours of Pike Place Market offered by one of the market's organizations. See the Pike Place Market listing on p. 104 for details.

If you'd like to explore downtown Seattle with a knowledgeable guide, join one of the informative walking tours offered by **See Seattle Walking Tours** (© **425/226-7641;** www.see-seattle.com). The tours visit Pike Place Market, the waterfront, the Pioneer Square district, and the International District. Tours cost $20 and can last a half day or a full day, depending on how much stamina you have.

You can also learn a lot about Seattle history and wander through hidden corners of the city on 2-hour tours run by **Duse McLean/Seattle Walking Tour** (tel] **425/885-3173**). These tours start with a ride through the Bus Tunnel to the International District and then make their way back north to Pike Place Market, taking in historic buildings, public art, and scenic vistas. Tours are $15 per person and are offered year-round by reservation.

For an insider's glimpse of life in Seattle's International District, hook up with **Chinatown Discovery Tours** (© **425/885-3085;** www.seattlechamber. com/chinatowntour). On these walking tours, which last from 1½ to 3 hours, you'll learn the history of this colorful and historic neighborhood. "A Touch of

Chinatown" is a brief introduction to the neighborhood. The "Chinatown by Day" tour includes a six-course lunch. "Nibble Your Way Through Chinatown" provides a sampling of flavors from around the International District. The "Chinatown by Night" tour includes an eight-course banquet. Rates (for four or more on a tour) range from $15 to $40 per person (slightly higher for fewer than four people).

BUS TOURS

If you'd like an overview of Seattle's main tourist attractions, or if you're pressed for time during your visit, you can pack in a lot of sights on a tour with **Gray Line of Seattle** (© **800/426-7532** or 206/624-5077; www.graylineofseattle.com). Half-day tours are $29 for adults, $15 for children; full-day tours are $39 for adults, $20 for children. Many other tours, including tours to Mount Rainier National Park and to the Boeing plant in Everett, are also available.

Mid-May through mid-October, Gray Line also offers a **Trolley Tour** on a bus made up to look like an old trolley. The tour is really a day pass that allows you to use the trolley, which follows a set route that passes nearly all the major tourist attractions in downtown Seattle. The trolley stops at several places along the waterfront and at Seattle Center, Pike Place Market, the Seattle Art Museum, and Pioneer Square. Tickets are $17 for adults and $9 for children. Because buses in downtown are free and because both the Waterfront Streetcar and the monorail to Seattle Center cost no more than $1.25, the trolley is not a very good deal; but if you don't want to worry about finding the right bus stop, it's worth considering. A $36 family pass allows two adults and up to four children to use the trolley for 2 days. Gray Line also operates open-topped **double-decker bus tours** of the city. These tours operate from May 1 to September 30 and cost $21 for adults and $11 for children. Buses depart from Pier 55 and the Seattle Sheraton Hotel and Towers.

A second company, **Double Decker Tours of Seattle** (© **800/403-0024**), owned by Greyhound, operates seasonal double-decker buses on a fixed route around the city. There are seven stops where you can get on and off the bus. Basically, this is the same set-up as the Gray Line trolley tour. You buy your ticket ($15 adults, $6 seniors and children 12 and under, $34 family of four), and then you can get on and off the bus as often as you want throughout the day. Buses operate every 30 minutes between 8:30am and 8:30pm from late May to mid-September.

BOAT TOURS

In addition to the boat tours and cruises mentioned below, you can do your own low-budget cruise simply by hopping on one of the ferries operated by **Washington State Ferries** (© **800/84-FERRY** or 888/808-7977 within Washington state, or 206/464-6400; www.wsdot.wa.gov/ferries). Try the Bainbridge Island or Bremerton ferries out of Seattle for a 1½- to 2½-hour round-trip. For more information on these ferries, see section 12, "Getting Around," in chapter 2.

If you don't have enough vacation time scheduled to fit in an overnight trip to the San Juan Islands, it's still possible to get a feel for these picturesque islands by riding the San Juan Islands ferry from Anacortes to Friday Harbor. These ferries depart from Anacortes, 75 miles north of Seattle. If you get off in Friday Harbor, you can spend a few hours exploring this town before returning to Anacortes. It's also possible to take the first ferry of the day from Anacortes, ride all the way to Sidney, British Columbia, and then catch the next ferry back to Anacortes. However, if you're doing this trip in 1 day, you won't have any time to spend in

Seattle by Duck

Paul Revere would have had a hard time figuring out what to tell his fellow colonists if the British had arrived by Duck. A Duck, if you didn't know, is a World War II vintage amphibious vehicle that can arrive by land or by sea, and these odd-looking things are now used to provide tours of Seattle both on land and water. Duck tours take in the standard Seattle sights but then plunge right into Lake Union for a tour of the Portage Bay waterfront, with its many houseboats and great views. Ninety-minute tours leave from near the Space Needle and cost $22 for adults and $12 for kids. Contact **Seattle Duck Tours** ★ (© **800/817-1116** or 206/441-DUCK; www.seattleducktours. net). Tours leave from a parking lot across from the Space Needle. Because these tours encourage Seattle visitors to get a little daffy while they're in town, they are very popular; reservations are recommended.

Victoria. Alternatively, if you have more money to spend (and even less time), boat tours of the San Juan Islands depart from the Seattle waterfront. For information on ferries and boat excursions to the San Juan Islands, see chapter 5.

For a boat excursion that includes a salmon dinner and Northwest Coast Indian masked dances, consider coughing up the cash for the **Tillicum Village Tour** ★★, Pier 55 (© **800/426-1205** or 206/933-8600; www.tillicumvillage. com). Located at Blake Island State Park across Puget Sound from Seattle and only accessible by tour boat or private boat, Tillicum Village was built in conjunction with the 1962 Seattle World's Fair. The "village" is actually just a large restaurant and performance hall fashioned after a traditional Northwest Coast longhouse, but with totem poles standing vigil out front, the forest encircling the longhouse, and the waters of Puget Sound stretching out into the distance, Tillicum Village is a beautiful spot. After the dinner and dances, you can strike out on forest trails to explore the island (you can return on a later boat if you want to spend a couple of extra hours hiking). There are even beaches on which to relax. Tours cost $65 for adults, $59 for seniors, $25 for children ages 5 to 12, and are free for children under age 5. Tours are offered daily from May through early October, other months on weekends only. If you can opt for only one tour while in Seattle, this should be it—it's unique and truly Northwestern, the salmon dinner is pretty good, and the traditional masked dances are fascinating (although more for the craftsmanship of the masks than for the dancing itself).

Seattle is a city surrounded by water, and if you'd like to see it from various aquatic perspectives, you can head out with **Argosy Cruises** ★ (© **800/642-7816** or 206/623-4252; www.argosycruises.com). Offerings include a 1-hour harbor cruise (departs from Pier 55; $13–$16 adults and $6–$7 children ages 5–12), a 2-hour cruise through the Hiram Chittenden Locks to Lake Union (departs from Pier 56; $23–$29 adults and $9–$10 children ages 5–12), and two cruises around Lake Washington (a 2-hr. cruise departs from the AGC Marina at the south end of Lake Union, and a 1½-hr. cruise departs from downtown Kirkland on the east side of the lake; $20–$25 adults and $8–$9 children ages 5–12). The latter two cruises will take you past the fabled Xanadu built by Bill Gates on the shore of Lake Washington. However, of all these options, we recommend the cruise through the locks; it may be the most expensive outing, but you get good views and the chance to navigate the locks.

Want a meal with your cruise? Try one of Argosy Cruises' (see above) lunch or dinner cruises aboard the *Royal Argosy* (lunch cruises: $36 adults, $15 children ages 5–12, $34 seniors; dinner cruises: $69 adults, $25 children ages 5–12, $67 seniors). These cruises get our vote for best dinners afloat. Reservations are recommended for all cruises.

Looking for a quieter way to see Seattle from the water? From May 1 to October 15, **Emerald City Charters,** Pier 54 (ⓒ **206/624-3931;** www.sailingseattle.com), offers 1½- and 2½-hour sailboat cruises. The longer excursions are at sunset. Cruises are $23 to $38 for adults, $20 to $35 for seniors, and $18 to $30 for children under age 12. Tours operate May 1 to October 15.

VICTORIA EXCURSIONS

Among Seattle's most popular boat tours are day-long excursions to Victoria, British Columbia. These trips are offered by **Victoria Clipper** ★★, Pier 69, 2701 Alaskan Way (ⓒ **800/888-2535,** 206/448-5000, or 250/382-8100 in Victoria; www.victoriaclipper.com), and operate several times a day during the summer (once or twice a day in other months). The high-speed catamaran passenger ferry takes 2 to 3 hours to reach Victoria. If you leave on the earliest ferry, you can spend the better part of the day exploring Victoria and be back in Seattle for a late dinner. Round-trip fares range from $61 (7-day advance purchase) to $127 for adults, $61 (7-day advance purchase) to $117 for seniors, and $51 to $64 for children ages 1 to 11 (between Oct and mid-May, one child travels free with each adult paying for a 7-day advance-purchase round-trip fare). Some scheduled trips also stop in the San Juan Islands during the summer. Various tour packages are also available, including an add-on tour to Butchart Gardens. Overnight trips can also be arranged.

You can also fly to Victoria from Seattle in a floatplane operated by **Kenmore Air** (ⓒ **800/543-9595;** www.kenmoreair.com). Flights take only 45 minutes, which leaves plenty of time to explore Victoria and still make it back to Seattle in time for dinner. The round-trip fare is $184 to $216 per person and these fares sometimes include either a tour of Butchart Gardens, or a meal at the Empress Hotel. You can sometimes even get these flights for half price at **Ticket/Ticket** (ⓒ **206/324-2744**), which has locations in Pike Place Market (First Ave. and Pike St.; open Tues–Sun noon–6pm), on Capitol Hill at the Broadway Market (401 Broadway E.; open Tues–Sat noon–7pm and Sun noon–6pm), and in Bellevue at the Meydendbauer Center (NE Sixth St. and 112th Ave.; open Tues–Sun noon–6pm).

For more information on Victoria, pick up a copy of *Frommer's Vancouver & Victoria.*

SCENIC FLIGHTS

Seattle is one of the few cities in the United States where floatplanes are a regular sight in the skies and on the lakes. If you'd like to see what it's like to take off and land from the water, get in touch with **Seattle Seaplanes** ★, 1325 Fairview Ave. E. (ⓒ **800/637-5553** or 206/329-9638; www.seattleseaplanes.com), which takes off from the southeast corner of Lake Union, and offers 20-minute scenic flights over the city for $68.

Value Money-Saving Tip

The **Ticket/Ticket** booth under the big clock at Pike Place Market sometimes has boat tour tickets available at discounted prices. If your schedule is flexible, be sure to check here first.

Seattle Noir

If your tastes run to the macabre, you might be interested in the **Private Eye on Seattle** 🎯 tours (© 206/365-3739; www.privateeyetours.com). These somewhat bizarre van tours are led by a private eye named Jake who shares stories of interesting and unusual cases from the Emerald City. Tours are $22 per person. To balance things out, there's also a tour of some of Seattle's most distinctive churches ($25 per person) and a tour of some of the city's haunted locales ($25 per person).

If you'd rather pretend you're back in the days of *The English Patient,* you can go up in a vintage biplane with **Olde Thyme Aviation** 🎯 (© 206/730-1412; www.oldethymeaviation.com), which operates from Boeing Field. Flights are offered on sunny weekends. A 20-minute flight along the Seattle waterfront to the Space Needle costs $115 for two people; other flights range in price from $149 to $449 for two people.

A RAILWAY EXCURSION

If you're a fan of riding the rails, consider the **Spirit of Washington Dinner Train,** 625 S. Fourth St., Renton (© 800/876-7245 or 425/227-RAIL; www. spiritofwashingtondinnertrain.com). Running from Renton, at the south end of Lake Washington, to the Columbia Winery near Woodinville, at the north end of Lake Washington, this train rolls past views of the lake and Mount Rainier. Along the way, you're fed a filling lunch or dinner. At the turnaround point, you get to tour a winery and taste some wines. Dinner tours range from $60 to $75; lunch tours range from $50 to $65. The higher prices are for seatings in the dome car, which definitely offers finer views.

THE BOEING TOUR 🎯🎯

Until Bill Gates and Microsoft came to town, Boeing was the largest employer (by far) in the Seattle area. Although the company moved its corporate head-quarters out of Seattle a few years ago, Boeing is still a major presence in the city, and it still has something that Microsoft can never claim: the single largest building, by volume, in the world. This building, the company's Everett assembly plant, could easily hold 911 basketball courts, 74 football fields, 2,142 average-size homes, or all of Disneyland (with room left over for covered parking). Tours of the building let you see just how they put together the huge passenger jets that travelers take for granted.

The tours are quite fascinating and well worth the time it takes to get here from downtown Seattle. Guided 1-hour tours of the facility are held Monday through Friday throughout the year. The schedule varies with the time of year, so call ahead for details and directions to the plant. Tours cost $5 for adults and $3 for seniors and children under 16 who meet the height requirement (minimum of 50 in. tall). Tickets for same-day use are sold on a first-come, first-served basis beginning at 8am (8:30am Oct–May); in summer, tickets for any given day's tours usually sell out by noon. To check availability of same-day tickets, call the **Everett Tour Center,** Wash. 526, Everett, WA (© 425/342-8500; www.boeing.com/companyoffices/aboutus/tours), between 8:30am and 2pm. It is also possible to make reservations 24 hours or more in advance by calling © 800/464-1476 or 206/544-1264 between 9 and 11am or noon and 3pm

Booked aisle seat.

Reserved room with a view.

With a queen – no, make that a king-size bed.

With Travelocity, you can book your flights and hotels together, so you can get even better deals than if you booked them separately. You'll save time and money without compromising the quality of your trip. Choose your airline seat, search for alternate airports, pick your hotel room type, even choose the neighborhood you'd like to stay in.

Travelocity

**Visit www.travelocity.com
or call 1-888-TRAVELOCITY**

Monday through Friday. However, when making reservations, you'll pay $10 per person regardless of age. Everett is roughly 30 miles north of Seattle (a 30- to 45-min. drive) off I-5.

If you're in town without a car, you can book a tour to the plant through **Customized Tours and Charter Service** (© 800/770-8769 or 206/878-3965; www.customizedtours.net), which charges $40 and will pick you up at your Seattle hotel.

7 Outdoor Pursuits

See "Beaches, Parks & Public Gardens," earlier in this chapter, for a rundown of great places to play.

BIKING

Gregg's Green Lake Cycle, 7007 Woodlawn Ave. NE (© 206/523-1822), and the **Bicycle Center,** 4529 Sand Point Way NE (© 206/523-8300), both rent bikes by the hour, day, or week. Rates range from $5 to $7 per hour and $25 to $30 per day. These shops are both convenient to the **Burke-Gilman/Sammamish River Trail** ⊛⊛, a 27-mile paved pathway created mostly from an old railway bed. This path is immensely popular and is a great place for a family bike ride or to get in a long, vigorous ride without having to deal with traffic. The Burke-Gilman portion of this trail starts in the Ballard neighborhood of north Seattle, but the most convenient place to start a ride is at **Gasworks Park** on the north shore of Lake Union. From here you can ride north and east, by way of the University of Washington, to **Kenmore Logboom Park** at the north end of Lake Washington. Serious riders can then continue on from Kenmore Logboom Park on the Sammamish River portion of the trail, which leads to the north end of Lake Sammamish and Marymoor Park, which is the site of a velodrome (a bicycle racetrack). This latter half of the trail is our favorite portion of a ride along this trail. This section of the path follows the Sammamish River and passes through several pretty parks. Riding the entire trail out and back is a 54-mile round-trip popular with riders in training for races. Plenty of great picnicking spots can be found along both trails.

The West Seattle bike path along **Alki Beach** is another good place to ride and offers great views of the sound and the Olympics. If you'd like to pedal this pathway, you can rent single-speed bikes at **Alki Crab & Fish Co.,** 1660 Harbor Ave. SW (© 206/938-0975), which charges $10 for a 3-hour rental. Because this place has a limited number of bikes, it's a good idea to call ahead and make a reservation. You can then take the water taxi from the downtown waterfront to West Seattle. The water taxi dock is right at Alki Crab & Fish Co.

GOLF

While Seattle isn't a name that springs immediately to mind when folks think of golf, the sport is just as much a passion here as it is all across the country. Should you wish to get in a round of golf while you're in town, Seattle has three conveniently located municipal golf courses: **Jackson Park Golf Course,** 1000 NE 135th St. (© 206/363-4747); **Jefferson Park Golf Course,** 4101 Beacon Ave. S. (© 206/762-4513); and **West Seattle Golf Course,** 4470 35th Ave. SW (© 206/935-5187). This latter course has great views of the Seattle skyline. All three charge very reasonable greens fees of between $20 and $30. For information on the Web, check out **www.seattlegolf.com**.

HIKING

Within Seattle itself, there are several large nature parks laced with enough trails to allow for a few good long walks. Among these are **Seward Park,** 5898 Lake Washington Blvd., southeast of downtown; and **Lincoln Park,** 8011 Fauntleroy Ave. SW, south of Alki Beach in West Seattle. However, the city's largest natural park and Seattleites' favorite quick dose of nature is **Discovery Park,** 3801 W. Government Way (© **206/386-4236**), northwest of downtown at the western tip of the Magnolia neighborhood. This park covers more than 500 acres and has many miles of trails and beaches to hike—not to mention gorgeous views, forest paths, and meadows for lazing in after a long walk. To reach Discovery Park, follow Elliott Avenue north along the waterfront from downtown Seattle, then take the Magnolia Bridge west toward the Magnolia neighborhood and follow Grayfield Street to Galer Street to Magnolia Boulevard.

IN-LINE SKATING

The city has dozens of miles of paved paths that are perfect for skating. You can rent in-line skates at **Greg's Green Lake Cycle,** 7007 Woodlawn Ave. NE (© **206/523-1822**), for $7 to $10 per hour. The trail around **Green Lake** in north Seattle and the **Burke-Gilman/Sammamish River Trail** (see the description under "Biking," above) are both good places for skating and are convenient to Gregg's. Other favorite skating spots include the paved path in **Myrtle Edwards Park** just north of the Seattle waterfront, the paved path along **Lake Washington Boulevard** north of Seward Park, and the **Alki Beach** pathway in West Seattle.

JOGGING

The waterfront, from **Pioneer Square north to Myrtle Edwards Park,** where a paved path parallels the water, is a favorite downtown jogging route. The residential streets of **Capitol Hill,** when combined with roads and sidewalks through **Volunteer Park,** are another good choice. If you happen to be staying in the University District, you can access the 27-mile-long **Burke-Gilman/Sammamish River Trail** or run the ever-popular trail around **Green Lake.** Out in West Seattle, the **Alki Beach** pathway is also very popular and provides great views of the Olympics.

SEA KAYAKING, CANOEING, ROWING & SAILING

If you'd like to try your hand at **sea kayaking** 🌟🌟, try the **Northwest Outdoor Center** 🌟🌟, 2100 Westlake Ave. N. (© **800/683-0637** or 206/281-9694; www.nwoc.com), which is located on the west side of Lake Union. Here you can rent a sea kayak for between $10 and $15 per hour. You can also opt for guided tours lasting from a few hours to several days, and there are plenty of classes available for those who are interested.

   Moss Bay Rowing and Kayak Center, 1001 Fairview Ave. N. (© **206/682-2031;** www.mossbay.net), rents sea kayaks (as well as canoes, pedal boats, and sailboats) at the south end of Lake Union near Chandler's Cove. Rates range from $10 per hour for a single to $15 per hour for a double. Because this rental center is a little closer to downtown Seattle, it makes a better choice if you are here without a car.

   The **University of Washington Waterfront Activities Center,** on the university campus behind Husky Stadium (© **206/543-9433**), is open to the public and rents canoes and rowboats for $7.50 per hour. With the marshes of the Washington Park Arboretum directly across a narrow channel from the boat launch, this is an ideal place for beginner canoeists to rent a boat.

In this same general area, you can rent kayaks at the **Agua Verde Paddle Club,** 1303 NE Boat St. (© 206/545-8570, ext. 101; www.aguaverde.com), which is at the foot of Brooklyn Avenue on Portage Bay (the body of water between Lake Union and Lake Washington). Kayaks can be rented from March through October and go for $12 to $18 per hour. Best of all, this place is part of the Agua Verde Café, a great Mexican restaurant. Before or after a paddle, be sure to get an order of tacos. See "Dining," earlier in this chapter, for details.

At the **Green Lake Boat Rental,** 5900 W. Green Lake Way N. (© 206/527-0171), in north Seattle not far from the Woodland Park Zoo, you can rent canoes, paddleboats, and rowboats for a bit of leisurely time on the water. This park also has a paved path around it and is one of Seattle's most popular parks (a great place to join crowds of locals enjoying one of the city's nicest green spaces). Kayaks rent for $10 to $12 per hour; sailboats are $14 per hour; and canoes, rowboats, and paddleboats are $10 per hour.

8 Spectator Sports

With professional football, baseball, basketball, ice hockey, and women's basketball teams, as well as the various University of Washington Huskies teams, Seattle is definitely a city of sports fans. For those many fans, the sports landscape has been changing dramatically in recent years. In 1999, the state-of-the-art Safeco Field, with its retractable roof, was unveiled. In 2000, the venerable and much-disparaged Kingdome was demolished to make way for a new football stadium, which opened just in time to kick off the Seattle Seahawks' 2002 season.

Ticketmaster (© 206/628-0123; www.ticketmaster.com) sells tickets to almost all sporting events in the Seattle area. You'll find Ticketmaster outlets at area Fred Meyer stores and Tower Records. If they're sold out, try **Pacific Northwest Ticket Service** (© 800/281-0753; www.nwtickets.com).

BASEBALL

Of all of Seattle's major league sports teams, none are more popular than the American League's **Seattle Mariners** (© 800/MY-MARINERS or 206/346-4000; www.seattlemariners.org). The team has a devoted following, so you can expect tickets to be hard to find unless you buy yours well in advance.

The Mariners' retro-style **Safeco Field** ★★★ is indisputably one of the most gorgeous ballparks in the country. It's also one of only a handful of stadiums with a retractable roof (which can open or close in 10–20 min.), allowing the Mariners a real grass playing field without the worry of getting rained out.

Ticket prices range from $6 to $45. Though you may be able to get a single ticket on game day at the Safeco Field box office, it would be tough to get two seats together. Mariners' tickets are a hot commodity, so if you want to ensure that you get good seats, order in advance at Mariners Team Stores (see below), or through Ticketmaster (© 206/622-HITS; www.ticketmaster.com), which has outlets at Fred Meyer stores and Tower Records. Parking is next to impossible in the immediate vicinity of Safeco Field, so plan to leave your car behind.

If you'd like a behind-the-scenes look at the stadium, you can take a **1-hour tour** ($7 adults, $5 kids ages 3–12); tickets can be purchased at the Mariners Team Store at Safeco Field, other Mariners Team Stores around the city (there are locations at Fourth and Stewart sts. downtown and in Bellevue Sq.), or through Ticketmaster. Tour times vary, and tours are not offered on days when day games are scheduled.

BASKETBALL

The NBA's **Seattle SuperSonics** (℘ **800/4NBA-TIX** or 206/283-3865; www. supersonics.com) play in the Key Arena at Seattle Center, and though they always seem to trail behind the Portland Trailblazers, they generally put in a good showing every season. Tickets are $11 to $129 and are available at the arena box office and through Ticketmaster (℘ **206/628-0888**). Tickets can generally be had even on short notice, except for games against the Lakers and Blazers, which are always well attended.

The University of Washington Huskies women's basketball team has been pretty popular for years, and Seattle also has a pro women's basketball team. The Women's National Basketball Association's (WNBA) **Seattle Storm** (℘ **877/ WNBA-TIX** or 206/217-WNBA; www.storm.wnba.com) brings professional women's basketball to Seattle's Key Arena. Ticket prices range from $8 to $60 and are available at the arena box office and through Ticketmaster (℘ **206/628-0888**).

For information on the women's and men's Huskies basketball games, contact **University of Washington Sports** (℘ **206/543-2200;** www.gohuskies.com).

FOOTBALL

Although the NFL's **Seattle Seahawks** (℘ **888/NFL-HAWK** or 206/381-7816; www.seahawks.com) aren't the most highly regarded of Seattle's professional sports teams, they do have a new stadium. Seahawks Stadium stands on the site of the old Kingdome and is adjacent to the Seattle Mariners' Safeco Field. Tickets to games run $23 to $79 and are generally readily available, depending on how well the team is doing. However, games against Oakland, Denver, and a couple of other teams usually sell out as soon as tickets first go on sale in August. Tickets are sold through **Ticketmaster** (℘ **206/622-HAWK;** www.ticketmaster. com). Traffic and parking in the vicinity of Seahawks Stadium is a nightmare on game days, so take the bus if you can.

Tours of the new stadium are available daily at 12:30 and 2:30pm and cost $7 for adults and $5 for seniors and children 4 to 12 (free for children 3 and under). For reservations, contact **Seahawks Stadium** (℘ **206/381-7582;** www.seahawksstadium.com).

Not surprisingly, the **University of Washington Huskies** (℘ **206/543-2200;** www.gohuskies.com), who play in Husky Stadium on the university campus, have a loyal following. Big games (Nebraska or Washington State) sell out as soon as tickets go on sale in the summer. Other games can sell out in advance, but obstructed-view tickets are usually available on game day. Ticket prices range from $32 to $36 for reserved seats and from $16 to $18 for general admission.

9 Shopping

Nordstrom, Eddie Bauer, REI—these names are familiar to shoppers all across the country. They're also the names of stores that got their start here in Seattle, which has long been *the* place to shop in the Northwest. Throw in such regional favorites as Pendleton, Nike, and Filson, and you'll find that Seattle is a great place to shop, especially if you're in the market for recreational and outdoors gear and clothing.

As the Northwest's largest city, Seattle has also become home to all the national retail chains you would expect to find in a major metropolitan area. These chains have taken over many of the storefronts of downtown Seattle and have opened flashy stores. The names and merchandise should be familiar: Banana Republic, Levi Strauss, Ann Taylor, St. John, Louis Vuitton, Coach, Tiffany & Co., Old

Navy, FAO Schwarz, Barneys New York. These and many others now have stores in Seattle, so if you forgot to pick up that dress in Chicago or those running shoes in New York, have no fear—you can find them here.

Seattle does, however, have one last bastion of local merchandising, **Pike Place Market.** Whether shopping is your passion or an occasional indulgence, you shouldn't miss this historic market, which is one of Seattle's top tourist attractions. Once the city's main produce market (and quite a few produce stalls remain), this sprawling collection of buildings is today filled with hundreds of unusual shops. See also the listing for Pike Place Market on p. 104.

THE SHOPPING SCENE

Although Seattle is a city of neighborhoods, many of which have great little shops, the heart of the Seattle shopping scene is the corner of **Pine Street and Fifth Avenue.** Within 2 blocks of this intersection are two major department stores (Nordstrom and The Bon Marché) and two upscale urban shopping malls (Westlake Center and Pacific Place). There's even a sky bridge between Nordstrom and Pacific Place to make shopping that much easier. Fanning out east and south from this intersection are blocks of upscale stores that have begun to take on a very familiar look. Small local shops are rapidly being replaced by national and international boutiques and megastores. Here in this neighborhood you'll now find Ann Taylor, Barneys New York, NIKETOWN, Gap, MaxMara, Banana Republic, and FAO Schwarz. However, you'll still find a few local independents in the neighborhood as well.

The city's main tourist shopping district is the **Pike Place Market** neighborhood. Here you'll find dozens of T-shirt and souvenir shops, as well as import shops and stores appealing to teenagers and 20-somethings. Pike Place Market is a fascinating warren of cubbyholes that pass for shops. While produce isn't usually something you stock up on while on vacation, several market shops sell ethnic cooking supplies that are less perishable than a dozen oysters or a king salmon. You may not find anything here you really need, but it's fun to look (at least that's what millions of Seattle visitors each year seem to think).

Just west of Pike Place Market is the Seattle **waterfront,** where you'll find many more gift and souvenir shops.

South of downtown, in the historic **Pioneer Square area,** is the city's greatest concentration of art galleries, some of which specialize in Native American art. This neighborhood has several antiques stores but is also home to a dozen or more bars and attracts a lot of homeless people.

As the center of both the gay community and the city's youth culture, **Capitol Hill** has the most eclectic selection of shops in Seattle. Beads, imports, CDs, vintage clothing, politically correct merchandise, and gay-oriented goods fill the shops along Broadway. Capitol Hill's main shopping plaza is the Broadway Market, which has lots of small shops.

The **Fremont** neighborhood just north of Lake Union is filled with retro stores selling vintage clothing, mid-century furniture and collectibles, and curious crafts. As of this writing, however, the neighborhood is undergoing a fairly rapid gentrification that is forcing out many of the smaller and more unusual shops.

A couple of miles east of Fremont is the **Wallingford** neighborhood, which is anchored by an old school building that has been converted into a shopping arcade with interesting crafts, fashions, and gifts.

The **University District,** also in north Seattle, has everything necessary to support a student population and also goes upscale at the University Village shopping center.

SHOPPING A TO Z
ANTIQUES & COLLECTIBLES

If antiques are your passion, you won't want to miss the opportunity to spend a day browsing the many antiques stores in the historic farm town of **Snohomish,** located roughly 30 miles north of Seattle. The town has more than 400 antiques dealers and is without a doubt the antiques capital of the Northwest. There are also plenty of antiques stores right in Seattle. The following are some of our favorites.

The Crane Gallery Chinese, Japanese, and Korean antiquities are the focus of this shop in the Queen Anne neighborhood, which prides itself on selling only the best pieces. Imperial Chinese porcelains, bronze statues of Buddhist deities, rosewood furniture, Japanese ceramics, *netsukes* (small sculptures originally worn with kimonos), snuff bottles, and Chinese archaeological artifacts are just some of the quality antiques you'll find here. Some Southeast Asian and Indian objects are also available. 104 W. Roy St. ℭ 206/298-9425.

Honeychurch Antiques For high-quality Asian antiques, including Japanese wood-block prints, textiles, furniture, and ivory and woodcarvings, few Seattle antiques stores can approach Honeychurch Antiques. Regular special exhibits give this shop the feel of a tiny museum. The store's annex, called **Glenn Richards,** 964 Denny Way (ℭ **206/287-1877**), specializes in "entry-level" antiques. 1008 James St. ℭ 206/622-1225. www.honeychurch.com.

Jean Williams Antiques If your taste in antiques runs to 18th- and 19th-century French and English formal or country furniture, this Pioneer Square antiques dealer may have something to add to your collection. 115 S. Jackson St. ℭ 206/622-1110. www.jeanwilliamsantiques.com.

Laguna A Vintage American Pottery Shop Twentieth-century art pottery is the specialty of this shop in Pioneer Square. Pieces by such mid-century pottery factories as Fiesta, Roseville, Bauer, Weller, and Franciscan fill the shelves here. This is a great place to look for dinnerware and vintage tiles. 116 S. Washington St. ℭ 206/682-6162. www.lagunapottery.com.

ANTIQUES MALLS & FLEA MARKETS

Antiques at Pike Place Located in the Pike Place Market area, this antiques and collectibles mall is one of the finest in Seattle. There are more than 80 dealers, and much of what's available here is fairly small, which means you might be able to fit your find into a suitcase. 92 Stewart St. ℭ 206/441-9643.

Fremont Sunday Market Crafts, imports, antiques, collectibles, and fresh produce combine to make this Seattle's second favorite public market (after Pike Place Market). The market is open Sunday from 10am to 5pm year-round. N. 34th St. (1 block west of the Fremont Bridge). ℭ 206/781-6776.

Pioneer Square Antique Mall This underground antiques mall is in the heart of Pioneer Square right beside the ticket booth for the Underground Tour and contains more than 60 stalls selling all manner of antiques and collectibles. Look for glass, old jewelry, and small collectibles. 602 First Ave. ℭ 206/624-1164.

ART GALLERIES

The **Pioneer Square area** has for many years been Seattle's main art gallery district, and although it still has quite a few galleries, many have, in the past few years, moved to other parts of the metropolitan area, including the two wealthy Eastside suburbs of Bellevue and Kirkland. Still, there are enough galleries left around Pioneer Square that anyone interested in art should be sure to wander south of Yesler Way. Some galleries are closed on Mondays.

General Art Galleries

Carolyn Staley   This Pioneer Square area gallery specializes in Japanese prints and has a wide range of prints both old and new. The highlight, however, is the large collection of 19th- and 20th-century wood-block prints. 314 Occidental Ave. S. ⓒ 206/621-1888. www.carolynstaleyprints.com.

Davidson Galleries   Located in the heart of the Pioneer Square neighborhood, this gallery focuses on three different areas—contemporary paintings and sculptures (often by Northwest artists); contemporary prints by American and European artists; and antique prints, some of which date from the 1500s. 313 Occidental Ave. S. ⓒ 206/624-7684. www.davidsongalleries.com.

Greg Kucera Gallery   Established in 1983, this showroom in the Pioneer Square area serves as one of Seattle's most reliably cutting-edge galleries. The shows here tend to address political or social issues or movements within the art world. 212 Third Ave. S. ⓒ 206/624-0770. www.gregkucera.com.

Kimzey Miller Gallery   The evocative Northwest landscape paintings of Z. Z. Wei are always a highlight of a visit to this downtown gallery not far from the Seattle Art Museum. Keep an eye out for the sculptural glass-and-steel constructions of David Gignac. 1225 Second Ave. ⓒ 206/682-2339.

Lisa Harris Gallery   Landscapes and figurative works, by both expressionist and realist Northwest and West Coast artists, are specialties of this gallery, which is located on the second floor of a building in Pike Place Market. 1922 Pike Place. ⓒ 206/443-3315. www.lisaharrisgallery.com.

Art Glass

Foster/White Gallery   If you are enamored of art glass, as we are, be sure to stop by one, two, or all three of the Foster/White galleries in the Seattle area. These galleries represent Dale Chihuly and always have works by this master glass artist. Some of Chihuly's pieces even sell for less than $10,000! Foster/White also represents top-notch Northwest artists in the disciplines of painting, ceramics, and sculpture. 123 S. Jackson St. ⓒ 206/622-2833. www.foster white.com. Also at 1331 Fifth Ave. (ⓒ 206/583-0100) and in Kirkland at 107 Park Lane (ⓒ 425/822-2305).

Phoenix Rising Gallery   Artists from around the country are represented, and there is always some highly imaginative decorative work on display. The gallery sells ceramic pieces and wooden crafts as well. 2030 Western Ave. ⓒ 206/ 728-2332. www.phoenixrisinggallery.com.

Vetri   Vetri, which is affiliated with the prestigious William Traver Gallery, showcases innovative work primarily from emerging glass artists and local area studios, but includes works by artists from other countries. It's all high quality and riotously colorful. Prices are relatively affordable. 1404 First Ave. ⓒ 206/ 667-9608. www.vetriglass.com.

William Traver Gallery   In business for more than 25 years, this is one of the nation's top art-glass galleries and showcases the works of dozens of glass artists. Works shown here are on the cutting edge of glass art, so to speak, and will give you a good idea of the broad spectrum of work being created by contemporary glass artists. You'll find the gallery on the second floor. 110 Union St. ⓒ 206/587-6501. www.travergallery.com.

Native American Art

Flury and Company   This Pioneer Square gallery specializes in prints by famed Seattle photographer Edward S. Curtis, who is known for his portraits of Native Americans. The gallery also has an excellent selection of antique Native American art and artifacts. 322 First Ave. S. ℂ 206/587-0260. www.fluryco.com.

The Legacy Ltd.   In business since 1933, The Legacy Ltd. is Seattle's oldest and finest gallery of contemporary and historic Northwest Coast Indian and Alaskan Eskimo art and artifacts. You'll find a large selection of masks, boxes, bowls, baskets, ivory artifacts, jewelry, prints, and books for the serious collector. 1003 First Ave. ℂ 800/729-1562 or 206/624-6350. www.thelegacyltd.com.

Stonington Gallery   This is another of Seattle's top galleries specializing in contemporary Native American arts and crafts. Here you'll find a good selection of Northwest Coast Indian masks, totem poles, mixed-media pieces, prints, carvings, and Northwest Coast–style jewelry. 119 S. Jackson St. ℂ 206/405-4040. www.stoningtongallery.com.

BOOKS

In addition to the stores listed below, you'll find more than a half dozen locations of **Barnes & Noble** around the metro area, including one downtown at 600 Pine St. (ℂ **206/264-0156**). There's also a **Borders** at 1501 Fourth Ave. (ℂ **206/622-4599**).

Elliott Bay Book Company   With battered wooden floors, a maze of rooms full of books, and frequent readings and in-store appearances by authors, this Pioneer Square bookstore feels as if it has been around forever. It has an excellent selection of books on Seattle and the Northwest, so if you want to learn more about the region or are planning further excursions, stop by. There is also a good little cafe down in the basement. 101 S. Main St. ℂ 800/962-5311 or 206/624-6600. www.elliottbaybook.com.

Flora & Fauna   Gardeners, bird-watchers, and other naturephiles, take note. Down below street level in what passes for the active Seattle underground of the Pioneer Square area, you'll find a store filled with books that'll have you wishing you were in your garden or out in the woods identifying birds and flowers. 121 First Ave. S. ℂ 206/623-4727.

Seattle Mystery Bookshop   If books that keep you wondering whodunit are your passion, don't miss an opportunity to peruse the shelves of this specialty bookstore in the Pioneer Square area. You'll find all your favorite mystery authors, lots of signed copies, and regularly scheduled book signings. 117 Cherry St. ℂ 206/587-5737. www.seattlemystery.com.

COFFEE & TEA

All over the city, on almost every corner, you'll find espresso bars, cafes, and coffeehouses. And while you can get coffee back home, you might want to stock up on whichever local coffee turns out to be your favorite. If you're a latte junkie, you can even make a pilgrimage to the shop that started it all, the original Starbucks, listed below.

Starbucks   Seattle is well known as a city of coffeeholics, and Starbucks is the main reason. This company has coffeehouses all over town (and all over the world), but this is the original. Although you won't find any tables or chairs here, Starbucks fans shouldn't miss an opportunity to get their coffee at the source. 1912 Pike Place, Pike Place Market. ℂ 206/448-8762. www.starbucks.com.

Ten Ren Tea Co., Ltd. Ever wondered what $150-a-pound Chinese tea tastes like? At this International District tea shop, you can find out. Not only do they have dozens of different teas here, they also have tables where you can sit down and sample varieties and observe the traditional Chinese tea ceremony. 506 S. King St. ℂ 206/749-9855.

CRAFTS

The Northwest is a magnet for skilled craftspeople, and shops all around town sell a wide range of high-quality and imaginative crafts. At Pike Place Market, you can see what area craftspeople are creating and meet the artisans themselves.

Crackerjack Contemporary Crafts With colorful and imaginative crafts by more than 250 artists from around the country, this shop in the eclectic Wallingford Center shopping arcade (an old schoolhouse) is a great place to check for something interesting and unique to bring home from a trip to Seattle. You'll find lots of interesting jewelry here. Wallingford Center, 1815 N. 45th St., Suite 212. ℂ 206/547-4983.

Fireworks Fine Crafts Gallery Playful, outrageous, bizarre, beautiful—these are just some of the terms that can be used to describe the eclectic collection of Northwest crafts on sale at this Pioneer Square gallery. Cosmic clocks, wildly creative jewelry, and artistic picture frames are some of the fine and unusual items you'll find here. 210 First Ave. S. ℂ 206/682-8707. www.fireworksgallery.net. Also at Westlake Center, 400 Pine St. (ℂ 206/682-6462); Bellevue Sq., NE Eighth St. and Bellevue Way, Bellevue (ℂ 425/688-0933); and the University Village shopping plaza, 2629 NE University Village Mall (ℂ 206/527-2858).

Frank and Dunya Located in the middle of funky Fremont, this store epitomizes the Fremont aesthetic. The art, jewelry, and crafts here tend toward the colorful and the humorous, and just about everything is made by Northwest artists and artisans. 3418 Fremont Ave. N. ℂ 206/547-6760.

Northwest Fine Woodworking This store is a showcase for some of the most amazing woodworking you'll ever see. Be sure to stroll through while you're in the Pioneer Square area even if you aren't in the market for a one-of-a-kind piece of furniture. The warm hues of the exotic woods are soothing, and the designs are beautiful. Furniture, boxes, sculptures, vases, bowls, and much more are created by more than 35 Northwest artisans. 101 S. Jackson St. ℂ 206/625-0542. www.nwfinewoodworking.com. Also in Bellevue at 601 108th Ave. NE, Plaza 100 (ℂ 425/462-5382).

Twist This impressively large store is filled with items such as unusual artist-created jewelry, Adirondack chairs made from recycled water skis, twisted glass vases, candlesticks, and ceramics. All are slightly offbeat yet tasteful objets d'art. 1503 Fifth Ave. ℂ 206/315-8080. www.twistonline.com.

DEPARTMENT STORES

Bon-Macy's Seattle's "other" department store, established in 1890, is every bit as well stocked as the neighboring Nordstrom department store, and with such competition nearby, The Bon, as it's known, tries every bit as hard to keep its customers happy. Third Ave. and Pine St. ℂ 206/506-6000.

Nordstrom Known for personal service, Nordstrom stores have gained a reputation for being among the premier department stores in the United States. The company originated here in Seattle (opening its first store in 1901), and its customers are devotedly loyal. This is a state-of-the-art store, with all sorts of little boutiques, cafes, live piano music, and other features to make your shopping excursion an experience.

Best of all, whether it's your first visit or your 50th, the knowledgeable staff will help you in any way they can. Prices may be a bit higher than those at other department stores, but for your money you get the best service available. The store is packed with shoppers during the half-year sale in June and the anniversary sale in July. You'll also find Nordstrom at area shopping malls. 500 Pine St. *C* 206/628-2111. www.nordstrom.com.

DISCOUNT SHOPPING

Nordstrom Rack *(Value)*   This is the Nordstrom overflow shop where you'll find three floors of discontinued lines as well as overstock, all at greatly reduced prices. Women's fashions make up the bulk of the merchandise here, but there is also a floor full of men's clothes and shoes, plus plenty of kids' clothes. 1601 Second Ave. *C* 206/448-8522.

FASHION

In addition to the stores listed below, you'll find quite a few familiar names in downtown Seattle, including Ann Taylor, Banana Republic, Barneys New York, Eddie Bauer, Gap, and MaxMara.

Accessories

Byrnie Utz Hats   In the same location since 1934 and boasting the largest selection of hats in the Northwest, this cramped hat-wearer's heaven looks as if it hasn't changed in 50 years. There are Borsalino Panama hats, Kangol caps, and, of course, plenty of Stetsons. 310 Union St. *C* 206/623-0233.

Men's & Women's Clothing

Eddie Bauer   Eddie Bauer got his start here in Seattle back in 1922, and today the chain is one of the country's foremost purveyors of outdoor fashions—although these days, outdoor fashion is looking quite a bit more urban. 1330 Fifth Ave. *C* 206/622-2766. www.eddiebauer.com.

Northwest Pendleton   For Northwesterners, and for many other people across the nation, Pendleton is and always will be *the* name in classic wool fashions. This store features tartan plaids and Indian-pattern separates, accessories, shawls, and blankets. 1313 Fourth Ave. *C* 800/593-6773 or 206/682-4430. www.nwpendleton.com.

Women's Clothing

Alhambra   Alhambra stocks an eclectic collection of women's clothing and jewelry. There are purses from France, shoes from Italy, and fashions from Turkey and the U.S. These add up to an eclectic European look that's a little more refined than what you'll find at Baby and Co. 101 Pine St. *C* 206/621-9571. www.alhambranet.com.

Baby and Co.   Claiming stores in Seattle and on Mars, this up-to-the-minute store stocks fashions that can be trendy, outrageous, or out of this world. The designs are strictly French, so you aren't likely to find these fashions too many other places in the U.S. Whether you're into earth tones or bright colors, you'll likely find something you can't live without. 1936 First Ave. *C* 206/448-4077.

Passport Clothing Company   Soft and easygoing is the current style at this large store near Pike Place Market. Velvet, linen, cotton, rayon, and other natural fibers are the fabrics of choice here. 123 Pine St. *C* 206/628-9799.

Ragazzi's Flying Shuttle   Fashion becomes art and art becomes fashion at this chic boutique-cum-gallery on Pioneer Square. Hand-woven fabrics and hand-painted silks are the specialties here, but of course such sophisticated fashions require equally unique body decorations in the form of exquisite jewelry creations. Designers and artists from the Northwest and the rest of the nation find an outlet for their creativity at the Flying Shuttle. 607 First Ave. $\mathcal{C}$ 206/343-9762.

GIFTS/SOUVENIRS

Pike Place Market is the Grand Central Station of Seattle souvenirs, with stiff competition from Seattle Center and Pioneer Square.

Made in Washington   Whether it's salmon, wine, or Northwest crafts, you'll find a selection of Washington State products in this shop. This is an excellent place to pick up gifts for all those friends and family members who didn't get to come to Seattle with you. Pike Place Market (Post Alley at Pine St.). $\mathcal{C}$ 206/467-0788. www.madeinwashington.com. Also in downtown's Westlake Center mall (($\mathcal{C}$ 206/623-9753).

Portage Bay Goods   If you'd like to give a gift with a conscience, drop by this unusual store in the Fremont neighborhood. Almost everything here is made from recycled materials. We like the notebooks with covers made from computer boards, but there are lots of fun decorative home accessories as well. 706 N. 34th St. $\mathcal{C}$ 206/547-5221. www.portagebaygoods.com.

Ye Olde Curiosity Shop   If you can elbow your way into this waterfront institution, you'll find every inch of space, horizontal and vertical, covered with souvenirs and crafts, both tacky and tasteful (but mostly tacky). Surrounding this merchandise are the weird artifacts that have made this one of the most visited shops in Seattle. 1001 Alaskan Way, Pier 54. $\mathcal{C}$ 206/682-5844. www.yeoldecuriosityshop.com.

JEWELRY

Unique artist-crafted jewelry can be found at **Ragazzi's Flying Shuttle** (p. 130) and **Twist** (p. 129).

Fox's Gem Shop   Seattle's premier jeweler, Fox's has been around for more than 90 years, and always has plenty of a girl's best friends. Colorless or fancy colored diamonds available here are of the finest cut. 1341 Fifth Ave. $\mathcal{C}$ 206/623-2528. www.foxsgem.com.

MALLS/SHOPPING CENTERS

City Centre   This upscale downtown shopping center is the Seattle address of such familiar high-end retailers as Barneys New York, FAO Schwarz, and Ann Taylor. There are works of art by Dale Chihuly and other Northwest glass artists on display throughout City Centre, and also a very comfortable lounge where you can rest your feet and escape from the Seattle weather. 1420 Fifth Ave. $\mathcal{C}$ 206/624-8800. www.shopcitycentre.com.

Pacific Place   This downtown mall is located adjacent to Nordstrom and contains five levels of upscale shop-o-tainment, including Cartier, Tiffany & Co., bebe, J. Crew, MaxMara, five restaurants, and a multiplex movie theater. A huge skylight fills the interior space with much-appreciated natural light, and an adjoining garage ensures that you'll find a place to park (well, maybe). 600 Pine St. $\mathcal{C}$ 206/405-2655. www.pacificplaceseattle.com.

Westlake Center   Located in the heart of Seattle's main shopping district, this upscale, urban shopping mall has more than 80 specialty shops, including Godiva Chocolatier, Crabtree & Evelyn, Aveda, and Made in Washington. There is an extensive food court. The mall is also the southern terminus for the monorail to Seattle Center. 400 Pine St. $\mathcal{C}$ 206/467-3044. www.westlakecenter.com.

MARKETS

Pike Place Market   Pike Place Market is one of Seattle's most famous land-marks and tourist attractions. It shelters not only produce vendors, fishmongers, and butchers, but also artists, craftspeople, and performers. Hundreds of shops and dozens of restaurants (including some of Seattle's best) are tucked away in nooks and crannies on the numerous levels of the market. With so much to see and do, a trip to Pike Place Market can easily turn into an all-day affair. See also the sightseeing listing on p. 104. Pike St. and First Ave. © 206/682-7453. www.pikeplace market.org.

Uwajimaya   Typically, your local neighborhood supermarket has a section of Chinese cooking ingredients; it's probably about 10 feet long, with half that space taken up by various brands of soy sauce. Now imagine your local super-market with nothing but Asian foods, housewares, produce, and toys. That's Uwajimaya, Seattle's Asian supermarket in the heart of the International Dis-trict. A big food court here serves all kinds of Asian food. 600 Fifth Ave. S. © 206/624-6248. www.uwajimaya.com.

RECREATIONAL GEAR

Filson   This Seattle company has been outfitting people headed outdoors ever since the Alaskan gold rush at the end of the 1890s. You won't find any high-tech fabrics here, just good old-fashioned wool, and plenty of it. Filson's clothes are meant to last a lifetime (and have the prices to prove it), so if you demand only the best, even when it comes to outdoor gear, be sure to check out this Seat-tle institution. 1555 Fourth Ave. S. © 206/622-3147. www.filson.com.

REI   Recreational Equipment, Incorporated (REI), was founded here in Seat-tle back in 1938 and today is the nation's largest co-op selling outdoor gear. The company's impressive flagship store is located just off I-5 not far from Lake Union and is a cross between a high-tech warehouse and a mountain lodge. The store is massive and sells almost anything you could ever need for pursuing your favorite outdoor sport. The store also has a 65-foot climbing pinnacle, a rain room for testing rain gear, a mountain-bike trail for test-driving bikes, a footwear test trail, even a play area for kids. With all this under one roof, who needs to go outside? Up on the top floor is a cafe with an outstanding view of downtown. 222 Yale Ave. N. © 206/223-1944. www.rei.com.

SALMON

If you think that the fish at Pike Place Market look great but that you could never get it home on the plane, think again. Any of the seafood vendors in Pike Place Market will pack your fresh salmon or Dungeness crab in an airline-approved container that will keep it fresh for up to 48 hours. Alternatively, you can buy vacuum-packed smoked salmon that will keep for years without refrigeration.

Pike Place Fish   Located behind *Rachel,* Pike Place Market's life-size bronze pig, this fishmonger is just about the busiest spot in the market most days. What pulls in the crowds are the antics of the workers here. Order a big silvery salmon and you'll have employees shouting out your order and throwing the fish over the counter. Crowds are always gathered around the stall hoping to see some of the famous "flying fish." 86 Pike Place, Pike Place Market. © 800/542-7732 or 206/682-7181. www.pikeplacefish.com.

Totem Smokehouse   Northwest Coast Indians relied heavily on salmon for sustenance, and to preserve the fish they used alderwood smoke. The tradition is carried on today to produce smoked salmon, one of the Northwest's most delicious food products. This store, located at street level in Pike Place Market, sells vacuum-packed smoked salmon that will keep without refrigeration until the package is opened. 1906 Pike Place, Pike Place Market. © 800/972-5666 or 206/443-1710. www.totemsmokehouse.com.

TOYS

Archie McPhee   You may already be familiar with this temple of the absurd through its mail-order catalog. Now imagine wandering through aisles full of goofy gags. Give yourself plenty of time and take a friend. You'll find Archie's place in the Ballard neighborhood. 2428 NW Market St. © 206/297-0240. www. mcphee.com.

Magic Mouse   Adults and children alike have a hard time pulling themselves away from this, the wackiest toy store in downtown Seattle. It's conveniently located in Pioneer Square and has a good selection of European toys. 603 First Ave. © 206/682-8097.

10 After Dark

It's true that Seattleites spend much of their free time enjoying the city's natural surroundings, but that doesn't mean they overlook the more cultured evening pursuits. In fact, the winter weather that keeps people indoors, combined with a longtime desire to be the cultural mecca of the Northwest, have fueled a surprisingly active and diverse nightlife scene. The Seattle Opera is ranked one of the top opera companies in the country, and its stagings of Wagner's *Ring* series have achieved near-legendary status. The Seattle Symphony also receives frequent accolades. Likewise, the Seattle Repertory Theatre has won Tony awards for its productions, and a thriving fringe theater scene keeps the city's lovers of avant-garde theater contentedly discoursing in cafes about the latest hysterical or thought-provoking performances. Music lovers will also find a plethora of classical, jazz, and rock offerings.

Much of Seattle's evening entertainment scene is clustered in the Seattle Center Theater District and the Pioneer Square areas. The former hosts theater, opera, and classical music performances; the latter is a nightclub district. Other concentrations of nightclubs can be found in Belltown, where crowds of the young and the hip flock to the neighborhood's many nightclubs, and Capitol Hill, with its ultracool gay scene. Ballard, formerly a Scandinavian enclave in north Seattle, attracts a primarily middle-class, not-too-hip, not-too-old crowd, including lots of college students and techies. It's not the hipster Belltown scene, it's not the PBR-swilling blues scene of Pioneer Square, and it's not the sleek gay scene of Capitol Hill.

While winter is a time to enjoy the performing arts, summer brings an array of outdoor festivals. These take place during daylight hours as much as they do after dark, but you'll find information on all these festivals and performance series in this section.

To find out what's going on when you're in town, pick up a free copy of *Seattle Weekly* (www.seattleweekly.com), Seattle's arts-and-entertainment newspaper. You'll find it in bookstores, convenience stores, grocery stores, newsstands, and newspaper boxes around downtown and other neighborhoods. On Friday, the *Seattle Times* includes a section called "Ticket," a guide to the week's arts and entertainment offerings.

THE PERFORMING ARTS

While the Seattle Symphony performs in downtown's Benaroya Hall, the main venues for the performing arts in Seattle are primarily clustered in **Seattle Center,** the special events complex that was built for the 1962 Seattle World's Fair. Here, in the shadow of the Space Needle, you'll find the Marion Oliver McCaw Hall, Bagley Wright Theater, Intiman Playhouse, Seattle Children's Theatre, Seattle Center Coliseum, Memorial Stadium, and Experience Music Project's Sky Church performance hall.

OPERA & CLASSICAL MUSIC

The **Seattle Opera** (℗ **800/426-1619** or 206/389-7676; www.seattleopera.org) is considered one of the finest opera companies in the country and performs at Seattle Center's new Marion Oliver McCaw Hall. It is *the* Wagnerian opera company in the U.S. The stagings of Wagner's four-opera *The Ring of the Nibelungen* are breathtaking spectacles that draw crowds from around the country. However, the *Ring* cycle was staged in 2001 and won't be staged again until 2005. In addition to such classical operas as *Carmen* and *Parsifal,* the season usually includes a more contemporary production. Ticket prices range from $47 to $125.

The 90-musician **Seattle Symphony** (℗ **206/215-4747;** www.seattle symphony.org), which performs in the acoustically superb Benaroya Hall, offers an amazingly diverse musical season that runs from September to July. With several different musical series, there is a little something for every type of classical music fan. There are evenings of classical, light classical, and pops, plus afternoon concerts, children's concerts, guest artists, and more. Ticket prices range from $16 to $80.

THEATER
Mainstream Theaters

The **Seattle Repertory Theater** (℗ **877/900-9285** or 206/443-2222; www.seattlerep.org), which performs at the Bagley Wright and Leo K. theaters, Seattle Center, 155 Mercer St., is Seattle's top professional theater and stages the most consistently entertaining productions in the city. The Rep's season runs from September to June, with five plays performed in the main theater and four

---

Ticket, Please

Full-price advance-purchase tickets to the Seattle Symphony and to many performing-arts events are handled by Ticketmaster (℗ **206/292-ARTS;** www.ticketmaster.com).

For half-price, day-of-show tickets (and 1-day advance tickets for matinees) to a wide variety of performances all over the city, stop by **Ticket/Ticket** (℗ **206/324-2744**), which has three sales booths in the Seattle area: one in Pike Place Market, one on Capitol Hill, and one in Bellevue. The Pike Place Market location, in the Pike Place Market information booth, First Avenue and Pike Street, is open Tuesday through Sunday from noon to 6pm. The Capitol Hill booth is in the Broadway Market, 401 Broadway E., and is open Tuesday through Saturday from noon to 7pm and Sunday from noon to 6pm. The Bellevue booth is in the Meydenbauer Center, NE Sixth Street and 112th Avenue, and is open Tuesday through Sunday from noon to 6pm. Ticket/Ticket charges a small service fee, the amount of which depends on the ticket price.

in the more intimate Leo K. Theatre. Productions range from classics to world premieres. Ticket prices range from $15 to $46. When available, rush tickets are available half an hour before shows for $20.

With a season that runs from March to December, the **Intiman Theatre Company** (© 206/269-1900; www.intiman.org), which performs at the Intiman Playhouse, Seattle Center, 201 Mercer St., fills in the gap left by those months when the Seattle Rep's lights are dark. Ticket prices range from $35 to $42.

Performing in the historic Eagles Building theater adjacent to the Washington State Convention and Trade Center, **A Contemporary Theater (ACT),** 700 Union St. (© 206/292-7676; www.acttheatre.org), offers slightly more adventurous productions than the other major theater companies in Seattle, though it's not nearly as avant-garde as some of the smaller companies. ACT also puts on Seattle's annual staging of *A Christmas Carol.* The season runs from July to December. Ticket prices usually range from $30 to $45.

Fringe Theater

Not only does Seattle have a healthy mainstream performing-arts community, it has the sort of fringe theater life once only associated with such cities as New York, Los Angeles, London, and Edinburgh. The city's more avant-garde performance companies frequently grab their share of the limelight with daring, outrageous, and thought-provoking productions.

Seattle's interest in fringe theater finds its greatest expression each September, when the **Seattle Fringe Theater Festival** (© 206/342-9172; www.seattle fringe.org), a showcase for small, self-producing theater companies, takes over various venues. The festival includes more than 500 performances by theater groups from around the country.

Even if you don't happen to be in town for Seattle's annual fringe binge, check the listings in *Seattle Weekly* or the *Seattle Times'* Friday "Ticket" entertainment guide to see what's going on during your visit. The following venues are some of Seattle's more reliable places for way-off Broadway productions, performance art, and spoken-word performances:

- **Bathhouse Theater,** 7312 W. Greenlake Dr. N. (© 206/524-1300). Seattle Public Theater's performances at the old Green Lake bathhouse range from original musicals to updated versions of Shakespeare. The location right on the lake makes this a great place to catch some live theater.

- **Book-It Repertory Theater** (© 206/325-6500; www.book-it.org). This theater company specializes in adapting literary works for the stage, and also stages works by local playwrights. Performances are held at various venues around the city.

- **Empty Space Theatre,** 3509 Fremont Ave. N. (© 206/547-7500; www. emptyspace.org). One of Seattle's biggest little theaters, Empty Space stages mostly comedies and is popular with a young crowd.

- **Theater Schmeater,** 1500 Summit Ave. (© 206/324-5801; www. schmeater.org). Lots of weird and sometimes wonderful comedy, including ever-popular live late-night stagings of episodes from *The Twilight Zone.*

DANCE

Although it has a well-regarded ballet company and a theater dedicated to contemporary dance and performance art, Seattle is not nearly as devoted to dance as it is to theater and classical music. That said, hardly a week goes by without some sort of dance performance being staged somewhere in the city. Touring companies of all types, the University of Washington Dance Department faculty and student performances, the UW World Dance Series (see below for details), and the Northwest New Works Festival (see below) all bring plenty of creative movement to the stages of Seattle. When you're in town, check *Seattle Weekly* or the *Seattle Times* for a calendar of upcoming performances.

The **Pacific Northwest Ballet,** Seattle Center Opera House, 301 Mercer St. (© **206/441-2424;** www.pnb.org), is Seattle's premier dance company. During the season, which runs from September to June, the company presents a wide range of classics, new works, and (the company's specialty) pieces choreographed by George Balanchine (tickets $16–$125). This company's performance of *The Nutcracker,* with outstanding dancing and sets and costumes by children's book author Maurice Sendak, is the highlight of every season. The Pacific Northwest Ballet performs in the new Marion Oliver McCaw Hall at Seattle Center.

Much more adventurous choreography is the domain of **On the Boards,** Behnke Center for Contemporary Performance, 100 W. Roy St. (© **206/217-9888;** www.ontheboards.org), which, although it stages a wide variety of performance art, is best known as Seattle's premier modern-dance venue (tickets $18–$22). In addition to dance performances by Northwest artists, there are a variety of productions each year by internationally known performance artists.

MAJOR PERFORMANCE HALLS

With ticket prices for shows and concerts so high these days, it pays to be choosy about what you see, but sometimes *where* you see it is just as important. Benaroya Hall, the Seattle Symphony's downtown home, has such excellent acoustics that a performance here is worth attending just for the sake of hearing how a good symphony hall should sound. Seattle also has two restored historic theaters that are as much a part of a performance as what happens onstage.

Benaroya Hall (© **206/215-4747),** on Third Avenue between Union and University streets in downtown Seattle, is the home of the Seattle Symphony. This state-of-the-art performance hall houses two concert halls—the main hall and a smaller recital hall. The concert hall is home to the magnificent Watjen pipe organ. There's also a Starbucks, a cafe, a symphony store, and a pair of Dale Chihuly chandeliers. Amenities aside, the main hall's excellent acoustics are the big attraction.

The **5th Avenue Theatre,** 1308 Fifth Ave. (© **206/625-1900** for information, or 206/292-ARTS for tickets; www.5thavenuetheatre.org), which first opened its doors in 1926 as a vaudeville house, is a loose re-creation of the imperial throne room in Beijing's Forbidden City. In 1980, the theater underwent a complete renovation that restored this Seattle jewel to its original splendor, and today the astounding interior is as good a reason as any to see a show here. Don't miss an opportunity to attend a performance. Broadway shows are the theater's mainstay (tickets $15–$60).

The **Paramount Theatre,** 911 Pine St. (© **206/682-1414;** www.theparamount.com), one of Seattle's few historic theaters, has been restored to its original beauty and today shines with all the brilliance it did when it first opened. New lighting and sound systems have brought the theater up to contemporary standards. The theater stages everything from rock concerts to Broadway musicals. Tickets are available through Ticketmaster.

PERFORMING-ARTS SERIES

When Seattle's own resident performing-arts companies aren't taking to the dozens of stages around the city, various touring companies from around the world are. If you're a fan of Broadway shows, check the calendars at the Paramount Theatre and the 5th Avenue Theatre, both of which regularly serve as Seattle stops for touring shows.

The **UW World Series** (© 206/543-4880; www.uwworldseries.org), held at Meany Hall on the University of Washington campus, is actually several different series that include a chamber music series, a classical piano series, a dance series, and a world music and theater series. Together these four series keep the Meany Hall stage busy between October and May. Special events are also scheduled (tickets $26–$55).

Seattle loves the theater, and each September the city binges on the fringes with the **Seattle Fringe Theater Festival** (see "Fringe Theater," above). Avantgarde performances are also the specialty of the **Northwest New Works Festival** (© 206/217-9888; www.ontheboards.org), **On the Boards'** annual barrage of contemporary dance and performance art held each spring.

Another series worth checking out is the **Seattle Art Museum's "After Hours."** Every Thursday from 5:30 to 9pm, the museum hosts live music, frequently jazz, and sets up a bar in its main lobby. Shows are free with museum admission.

Summer is a time of outdoor festivals and performance series in Seattle, and should you be in town during the sunny months, you'll have a wide variety of alfresco performances from which to choose. The city's biggest summer music festivals are the **Northwest Folklife Festival** over Memorial Day weekend and **Bumbershoot** over Labor Day weekend. See the "Washington Calendar of Events" in chapter 2 for details.

AT&T Wireless Summer Nights at the Pier (© 206/281-7788 for information, or 206/628-0888 for tickets; www.summernights.org) presents a summer's worth of big-name acts at Pier 62/63 on the waterfront. Blues, jazz, rock, and folk acts generally pull in a 30-something to 50-something crowd (tickets $17–$75).

Here on the waterfront, at the Seattle Aquarium (© 206/386-4330; www.seattleaquarium.org), you can also catch some alfresco jazz at the **Sea Sounds** summer concert series. The concerts are held between June and early October (weather permitting) at the end of the Aquarium's pier (Pier 59). Tickets are $25 to $28.

At **Woodland Park Zoo** (© 206/615-0076; www.zoo.org), the Zoo Tunes concert series brings in more big-name performers from the world of jazz, easy listening, blues, and rock (tickets $14–$20). Bear in mind that tickets for these concerts usually sell out as soon as they go on sale at the end of May.

In Woodinville, on the east side of Lake Washington, Chateau Ste. Michele, 14111 NE 145th St., stages the area's most enjoyable outdoor summer concert series. The **Summer Festival On The Green** (© 425/415-3300 for information, or 206/628-0888 for tickets) is held at the winery's amphitheater, which is surrounded by beautiful estatelike grounds. Chateau Ste. Michele is Washington's largest winery, and plenty of wine is available. Once again the lineup is calculated to appeal to the 30- to 50-something crowd (Bonnie Raitt, Linda Ronstadt, Kenny Loggins, Cowboy Junkies, Gipsy Kings). Ticket prices mostly range from $40 to $99. See section 11 in this chapter for more on Woodinville and Chateau Ste. Michelle.

THE CLUB & MUSIC SCENE

If you have the urge to do a bit of clubbing and bar-hopping, there's no better place to start than **Pioneer Square**. Good times are guaranteed, whether you want to hear a live band, hang out in a good old-fashioned bar, or dance. Keep in mind that this neighborhood tends to attract a very rowdy crowd (lots of frat boys) and can be pretty rough late at night.

Belltown, north of Pike Place Market, is another good place to club-hop. Clubs here are far more trend-conscious than those in the Pioneer Square area. Club-goers tend to be style-conscious 20- and 30-somethings.

Seattle's other nightlife district is the former Scandinavian neighborhood of **Ballard,** where you'll find more than half a dozen nightlife establishments, including a brewpub, taverns, bars, and live-music clubs.

FOLK, ROCK & REGGAE
Pioneer Square

The Pioneer Square area is Seattle's main live music neighborhood, and the clubs have banded together to make things easy for music fans. The **"Joint Cover"** plan lets you pay one admission to get into seven different clubs. The charge is $5 Sunday through Thursday and $12 on Friday and Saturday ($10, 8–9pm Fri–Sat). Participating clubs currently include Larry's Blues Cafe, Doc Maynard's, the Central Saloon, the Bohemian Café, and the New Orleans. Most of these clubs are short on style and hit-or-miss when it comes to music (which makes the joint cover a great way to find out where the good music is on any given night).

The Central Saloon Established in 1892, the Central is the oldest saloon in Seattle. As a Seattle institution, it's a must-stop during a night out in Pioneer Square. You might catch sounds ranging from funk to reggae. 207 First Ave. S. ℭ **206/622-0209.** Joint cover $5–$12.

Fenix Underground This Fenix didn't rise from it's own ashes, it rose from the rubble of its earthquake-damaged former location. Once again this underground club, now located right on Occidental Park, is the most happening place in the neighborhood. 109 S. Washington St. ℭ **206/405-4323.** www.fenixunderground.com. Joint cover $5–$12.

Belltown & Environs

The Crocodile Cafe With its rambunctious decor, this Belltown establishment is a combination nightclub, bar, and restaurant. There's live rock Tuesday through Saturday nights, and the music calendar here is always eclectic, with everything from rock to folk to jazz. However, alternative rock dominates. 2200 Second Ave. ℭ **206/441-5611.** www.thecrocodile.com. Cover $5–$22.

EMP The Experience Music Project, Seattle's humongous lump o' color rock museum, isn't just some morgue for dead rockers. This place is a showcase for real live rockers, too. EMP's main hall, the **Sky Church,** plays host to everything from indie rockers to theater productions with live rock accompaniment. There's also the smaller **Liquid Lounge,** a club with no cover and a wide range of musical sensibilities. One night might be a reggae dance party while another night might feature hip-hop or an acoustic show. 325 Fifth Ave. N. ℭ **206/770-2702.** www. emplive.com. Cover: Liquid Lounge free; Sky Church $7–$32.

Showbox Located across the street from Pike Place Market, this club books a wide variety of local and name rock acts. Definitely *the* downtown rock venue for performers with a national following. 1426 First Ave. ℭ **206/628-3151.** www.showbox online.com. Cover $5–$30.

Capitol Hill

Baltic Room   This swanky Capitol Hill hangout for the beautiful people provides a wide range of entertainment, from happy-hour DJs between 5 and 9pm to live or DJ dance music ranging from Britpop to hip-hop and *bhangra* (a style derived from northern India) later in the evening. 1207 Pine St. © **206/625-4444.** www.balticroom.com. Cover $3–$10.

Century Ballroom   With a beautiful wooden dance floor and a genuine bandstand, this classic ballroom plays host to some of the best touring acts to come to town. This is also Seattle's top spot for swing and salsa dancing, each of which tops the bill a couple of nights per week. The crowd here is very diverse, with customers of all ages who come to check out a schedule that might include an evening of Hawaiian slack-key guitar music or an avant-garde electric violin performance. 915 E. Pine St. © **206/324-7263.** www.centuryballroom.com. Cover $5–$15.

Ballard

Ballard Firehouse   An eclectic assortment of musical styles finds its way onto the bandstand of this converted firehouse in Ballard. The crowd is young, and the music generally ranges from the latest local indie rockers to warmed-over heavy metal heavyweights. However, the emphasis these days is on reggae. 5429 Russell Ave. NW © **206/784-3516.** www.theballardfirehouse.com. No cover–$15.

Tractor Tavern   For an ever-eclectic schedule of music for people whose tastes go beyond the latest rap artist, the Tractor Tavern is the place to be. You can catch almost anything from Hawaiian slack-key guitar to rockabilly to singer-songwriters to banjo music to Celtic to folk to zydeco. Sound like your kind of place? 5213 Ballard Ave. NW. © **206/789-3599.** www.tractortavern.citysearch.com. Cover $5–$25.

JAZZ & BLUES

Dimitriou's Jazz Alley   Cool and sophisticated, this Belltown establishment is reminiscent of a New York jazz club and has been around for more than 20 years. Seattle's premier jazz venue, it books only the best performers, including many name acts. 2033 Sixth Ave. © **206/441-9729.** www.jazzalley.com. Cover $15.50–$30.

New Orleans   If you like your food and your jazz hot, check out the New Orleans in Pioneer Square. Throughout the week, there's Cajun, Dixieland, R&B, jazz, and blues. 114 First Ave. S. © **206/622-2563.** Joint cover $5–$12.

Tula's   This is the real thing: a jazz club that's a popular jazz musicians' after-hours hangout and a good place to catch up-and-coming musicians. American and Mediterranean food is served. 2214 Second Ave. © **206/443-4221.** www.tulas.com. Cover $5–$15.

CABARET

The Cabaret at Crepe de Paris   Throughout the year, this club stages a wide variety of entertaining programs of music, dance, and humor. Updated torch songs and numbers from classic musicals assure that the shows here will appeal to young and old alike. Reservations are required. Rainier Sq., 1333 Fifth Ave. © **206/ 623-4111.** $45 dinner and show; $18 show only.

The Pink Door   Better known as Pike Place Market's unmarked restaurant, the Pink Door has a hopping after-work bar scene that tends to attract a 30-something crowd. It also doubles as a cabaret featuring Seattle's most eclectic lineup of performers, including cross-dressing tango dancers, trapeze artists, and the like. Lots of fun and not to be missed. 1919 Post Alley © **206/443-3241.**

DANCE CLUBS

Bada Lounge   If Swedish modern, molded plastic, and techno are your scene, this place is for you. With its retro-futurist decor and wall of monitors projecting video wallpaper, this club/restaurant is as stylin' as they come here in Seattle. The white-on-white decor is calculated to make people in black look their very best. Early in the evening, this is a pan-Asian restaurant, and later on there's dancing to DJ-driven dance tracks. 2230 First Ave. ℂ **206/374-8717.**

Club Medusa   Located just a couple of blocks from Pike Place Market, this dance club affects a Roman/Greek ruins decor and, with its bouncer in a suit and tie, is a big hit with the young, fashion-conscious scene-makers from the Belltown clubs a few blocks away. This club is open Thursday through Saturday only. 2218 Western Ave. ℂ **206/448-8887.** Cover free to $15.

Contour   Located a few blocks up First Avenue from Pioneer Square, this modern dance club attracts a more diverse crowd than most Pioneer Square clubs. The music ranges from deep house to trance to drum-and-base, and the partying on Fridays and Saturdays goes on until 8am. Laser light shows, fire dancers—this joint is one wild party! 807 First Ave. ℂ **206/447-7704.** www.clubcontour.com. Cover $5–$10.

THE BAR & PUB SCENE
BARS
The Waterfront

Restaurant 67 Bar   If you get any closer to the water, you'll have wet feet. Located inside downtown Seattle's only waterfront hotel, this bar boasts what just might be the best bar view in the city. Watch the ferries come and go, or see the sun set over Puget Sound and the Olympics. In The Edgewater Hotel, Pier 67, 2411 Alaskan Way. ℂ **206/728-7000.**

Downtown

The Bookstore—a Bar   Located just off the lobby of the posh Alexis Hotel, this cozy little bar is—surprise—filled with books. There are plenty of interesting magazines on hand as well, so if you want to sip a single malt and smoke a cigar but don't want to deal with crowds and noise, this is a great option. Very classy. In the Alexis Hotel, 1007 First Ave. ℂ **206/382-1506.**

McCormick & Schmick's   The mahogany paneling and sparkling cut glass lend this restaurant bar a touch of class, but otherwise the place could have been the inspiration for *Cheers*. Very popular as an after-work watering hole of Seattle moneymakers, McCormick & Schmick's is best known for its excellent and inexpensive happy-hour snacks. 1103 First Ave. ℂ **206/623-5500.**

Oliver's   Maybe you've seen one too many places that claim to make the best martini and you're dubious. Here at Oliver's they've repeatedly put their martinis to the test and come out on top. The atmosphere is classy and the happy-hour appetizers are good, but in the end, only you can decide whether or not these martinis are the best in Seattle. In the Mayflower Park Hotel, 405 Olive Way. ℂ **206/623-8700.**

Belltown

Axis   This is where it all begins most nights for the black-clad crowds of ultra-hip Seattle scenesters who crowd the sidewalks and bars of Belltown on weekend nights. Get here early enough and maybe you'll even snag one of the coveted sidewalk tables. If you're too late, don't worry: The front walls roll up and there's still the second row. It's a serious singles scene with good food. 2214 First Ave. ℂ **206/441-9600.**

The Virginia Inn   Although the Virginia Inn is located in *tres chic* Belltown, this bar/restaurant has a decidedly old-Seattle feel, due in large part to the fact that this place has been around since 1903. Best of all, this is a nonsmoking bar and it serves French food! 1937 First Ave. ✆ 206/728-1937.

Pike Place Market

Alibi Room   If you've been on your feet all day in Pike Place Market and have had it with the crowds of people, duck down the alley under the market clock and slip through the door of this hideaway. The back-alley setting gives this place an atmospheric speakeasy feel. Popular with artists and other creative types. 85 Pike St. ✆ 206/623-3180.

The Tasting Room   Located in the Pike Place Market area, this cozy wine bar has the feel of a wine cellar and is cooperatively operated by several small Washington state wineries. You can taste the wines of Camaraderie Cellars, Harlequin Cellars, JM Cellars, Wilridge Winery, and Wineglass Cellars, or buy wine by the glass or bottle. Light snacks are also available. 1924 Post Alley. ✆ 206/770-WINE. www.winesofwashington.com.

Pioneer Square

FX McRory's   Located across the street from Seattle's new football stadium and not far from Safeco Field, this bar attracts well-heeled sports fans (with the occasional Mariners and Seahawks players thrown in for good measure). You'll also find Seattle's largest selection of bourbons here. There's also an oyster bar and good food. 419 Occidental Ave. S. ✆ 206/623-4800. www.fxmcrorys.com.

Marcus's   Seattle's only underground martini and cigar bar, Marcus's is hidden beneath a Taco del Mar just off First Avenue in Pioneer Square. You'll be drinking below street level with the ghosts of Seattle's past and the lounge lizards of today. There's DJ music several nights each week. This is a much mellower alternative to Pioneer Square's rowdy street-level bars. 88 Yesler Way. ✆ 206/624-3323.

BREWPUBS

Big Time Brewery and Alehouse   Big Time, Seattle's oldest brewpub, is located in the University District and is done up to look like a turn-of-the-20th-century tavern, complete with a 100-year-old back bar and a wooden refrigerator. The pub serves as many as 12 of its own brews at any given time, and some of these can be pretty unusual. 4133 University Way NE. ✆ 206/545-4509. www.bigtime brewery.com.

Elysian Brewing Company   Although the brewery at this Capitol Hill brewpub is one of the smallest in the city, the pub itself is quite large and has an industrial feel that says "local brewpub." The stout and strong ales are especially good, and the brewers' creativity here just can't be beat. Hands-down the best brewpub in Seattle. 1221 E. Pike St. ✆ 206/860-1920. www.elysianbrewing.com.

Hales Ales Brewery and Pub   Located about a mile west of the Fremont Bridge heading toward Ballard, this is a big, lively brewpub. 4301 Leary Way NW. ✆ 206/706-1544. www.halesales.com.

The Pike Pub and Brewery   Located in an open, central space inside Pike Place Market, this brewpub makes excellent stout and pale ale. There's live instrumental music a couple of nights a week and, with its comfortable couches, the Pike is a great place to get off your feet after a day of exploring the market. 1415 First Ave. ✆ 206/622-6044. www.pikebrewing.com.

Pyramid Ale House   Located south of Pioneer Square in a big old warehouse, this pub is part of the brewery that makes Thomas Kemper lagers and Pyramid ales. It's a favorite spot for dinner and drinks before or after baseball games at Safeco Field and football games at Seahawks Stadium. There's good pub food, too. 1201 First Ave. S. ℂ 206/682-3377. www.pyramidbrew.com.

IRISH PUBS

Fadó   This Irish pub is part of a national pub chain but has the feel of an independent. Lots of antiques, old signs, and a dark, cozy feel make it a very comfortable place for a pint. There's live Irish music several nights a week. 801 First Ave. ℂ 206/264-2700. www.fadoirishpub.com.

Kells   At one time the space now occupied by this pub was the embalming room of a mortuary. However, these days the scene is much more lively and has the feel of a casual Dublin pub. They pull a good pint of Guinness and feature live traditional Irish music 7 nights a week. Kells also serves traditional Irish meals. 1916 Post Alley, Pike Place Market. ℂ 206/728-1916. www.kellsirish.com. Cover Fri–Sat only, $5.

THE GAY & LESBIAN SCENE

Capitol Hill is Seattle's main gay neighborhood, with the greatest concentration of gay and lesbian bars and dance clubs. Look for the readily available *Seattle Gay News* (ℂ 206/324-4297; www.sgn.org), where you'll find ads for many of the city's gay bars and nightclubs.

BARS

C. C. Attle's   Located across the street from Thumpers, this bar is a Seattle landmark on the gay bar scene. It's well known for its cheap, strong cocktails, but it can be something of a regulars' scene. There are a couple of patios and three separate bars. 1501 E. Madison St. ℂ 206/726-0565.

R Place Bar and Grill   With three floors of entertainment, you hardly need to go anywhere else for a night on the town. There's a video bar on the ground floor, pool tables and video games on the second floor, and up on the top floor, a sports bar that turns into a dance club on weekends. 619 E. Pine St. ℂ 206/322-8828. www.rplaceseattle.com.

Thumpers   Perched high on Capitol Hill, Thumpers is a classy bar/restaurant done up in oak. It's been a favorite of Seattle's gay community for 20 years. The seats by the fireplace are perfect on a cold and rainy night, and for sunny days there are two decks with great views. There's live music several nights each week (maybe even a Judy & Liza show). 1500 E. Madison St. ℂ 206/328-3800.

Wildrose   This friendly restaurant/bar is a longtime favorite of the Capitol Hill lesbian community and claims to be the oldest lesbian bar on the West Coast. During the spring and summer, there is an outdoor seating area. 1021 E. Pike St. ℂ 206/324-9210. www.thewildrosebar.com.

DANCE CLUBS

Neighbours   This has been the favorite dance club of Capitol Hill's gay community for years, and, as at other clubs, different nights of the week feature different styles of music. You'll find this club's entrance down the alley. 1509 Broadway Ave. ℂ 206/324-5358. www.neighboursonline.com. Cover $1–$10.

Re-Bar   Each night there's a different theme, with the DJs spinning everything from world beat to funk and hip-hop. This club isn't exclusively gay, but it's still a favorite of Seattle's gay community. 1114 Howell St. ℂ 206/233-9873. No cover–$6.

AT THE MOVIES

The **Seattle Art Museum,** 100 University St. (© **206/654-3100;** www.seattle artmuseum.org), has Thursday-night screenings of classics and foreign films. If you're a movie buff, be sure to check out this series.

In Fremont, the **Fremont Saturday Nite Outdoor Movies** series (© **206/781-4230;** www.outdoorcinema.com), a summer event, shows modern classics, B movies (sometimes with live overdubbing by a local improv comedy company), and indie shorts. Films are screened in the parking lot at North 35th Street and Phinney Avenue North. The parking lot opens at 7:30pm, and there is a $5 suggested donation.

11 Easy Excursions: Seattle's Wine Country

SEATTLE'S WINE COUNTRY

The state of Washington is the fastest-growing wine region in the country and today produces more wine than any other state except California. Although the main wine country lies hundreds of miles to the east in central and eastern Washington, a small winery region is but a 30-minute drive north of Seattle outside the town of Woodinville. In the Woodinville area, five wineries are open to the public on a regular basis (several others are open only by appointment or not open to the public at all). Five wineries is just about the perfect number for an afternoon of wine tasting, and the proximity to Seattle makes this an excellent day's outing. Woodinville is also home to the Northwest's top restaurant and a gorgeous modern lodge that together with the wineries make this a great place for a romantic getaway.

To reach this miniature wine country, head north on I-5, take the NE 124th Street exit, and drive east to 132nd Avenue NE. Turn left here and continue north to NE 143rd Place/NE 145th Street. Turn right and drive down the hill. At the bottom of the hill, you will be facing the first of the area's wineries.

The **Columbia Winery,** 14030 NE 145th St., Woodinville (© **800/488-2347** or 425/488-2776; www.columbiawinery.com), has Washington's largest wine-tasting bar and produces a wide range of good wines (open daily 10am–7pm). This winery tends to be crowded on weekends, so try to arrive early.

Directly across NE 145th Street from the Columbia Winery, you'll find the largest and most famous of the wineries in the area, **Chateau Ste. Michelle** ✿, 14111 NE 145th St., Woodinville (© **800/267-6793** or 425/488-1133; www. ste-michelle.com). Open daily 10am to 5pm, this is by far the most beautiful winery in the Northwest, located in a grand mansion on a historic 1912 estate. It's also the largest winery in the state, and is known for its consistent quality. If you take a free tour of the winery, you can sample several of the winery's less expensive wines. For a $5 tasting fee, you can sample some older reserve wines. Because this winery is so big and produces so many different wines, you never know what you might find being poured in the tasting room. An amphitheater on the grounds stages big-name music performances throughout the summer.

If you drive north from Chateau Ste. Michelle, NE 145th Street becomes Woodinville-Redmond Road (Wash. 202) and you soon come to **Silver Lake Winery,** 15029 Woodinville-Redmond Rd. NE, Woodinville (© **425/485-2437;** www.silverlakewinery.com). This winery crafts good reds but can be hit-or-miss. It's open daily noon to 5pm. Next up the road heading north is a hidden gem, the small **Facelli Winery,** 16120 Woodinville-Redmond NE (© **425/488-1020;** www.facelliwinery.com), which is open Saturday and Sunday noon to 4pm and produces some excellent red wines. Continue a little farther to get to **DiStefano Winery,** 12280 Woodinville Dr. NE (© **425/487-1648;** www. distefanowinery.com), which is best known for its full-bodied red wines but also produces some memorable whites. The tasting room is open Saturday and Sunday from noon to 5pm.

FAST FACTS: Seattle

AAA The **American Automobile Association** (© 800/222-4357; www. aaa.com) has a local Seattle office at 330 Sixth Ave. N. (© 206/448-5353).

Airport See "Getting There" in chapter 2, and "Arriving" in section 1 of this chapter.

American Express In Seattle, the Amex office is in the Plaza 600 building at 600 Stewart St. (© 206/441-8622). The office is open Monday through Friday from 8:30am to 5:30pm. For card member services, phone © 800/528-4800. Call © 800/AXP-TRIP or go to **www.americanexpress.com** for other locations or general information.

Area Code The area code in Seattle is **206**; it's **425** for the Eastside (including Kirkland and Bellevue), and **253** for south King County (near the airport).

Business Hours The following are general hours; specific establishments may vary. Banks are open Monday through Friday from 9am to 5pm (some also on Sat 9am–noon). Stores are open Monday through Saturday from 10am to 6pm and Sunday from noon to 5pm (malls usually stay open until 9pm Mon–Sat). Bars generally open around 11am, but are legally allowed to be open Monday through Saturday from 6am to 1am and Sunday from 10am to 1am.

Car Rentals See section 2, "Getting Around," earlier in this chapter.

Climate See section 4, "When to Go," in chapter 2.

Dentist Contact the **Dental Referral Service** (© 800/577-7322).

Doctor To find a physician, check at your hotel for a referral, or contact **Swedish Medical Center** (© 800/SWEDISH; www.swedish.org).

Emergencies For police, fire, or medical emergencies, phone © **911.**

Hospitals Hospitals convenient to downtown include **Swedish Medical Center,** 747 Broadway (© 206/386-6000); and **Virginia Mason Hospital and Clinic,** 925 Seneca St. (© 206/583-6433 for emergencies, or 206/624-1144 for information).

Information See "Visitor Information" in section 1 of this chapter.

Internet Access First, ask at your hotel to see if it provides Internet access. If not, **Kinko's,** 735 Pike St. (© 206/467-1767) and other locations, is an alternative.

Liquor Laws The legal minimum drinking age in Washington state is 21. Aside from on-premise sales of cocktails in bars and restaurants, hard liquor can only be purchased in liquor stores. Beer and wine are available in convenience stores and grocery stores. Brewpubs tend to sell only beer and wine, but some also have licenses to sell hard liquor.

Lost or Stolen Credit Cards Be sure to tell all of your credit card companies the minute you discover your wallet has been lost or stolen and file a report at the nearest police precinct. Your credit card company or insurer may require a police report number or record of the loss. Most credit card companies have an emergency toll-free number to call if your card is lost or stolen; they may be able to wire you a cash advance immediately or deliver an emergency credit card in a day or two. Visa's U.S. emergency number is © **800/847-2911** or 410/581-9994. American Express cardholders and traveler's check holders should call © **800/221-7282.** MasterCard holders should call © **800/307-7309** or 636/722-7111. For other credit cards, call the toll-free number directory at © **800/555-1212.**

If you need emergency cash over the weekend when all banks and American Express offices are closed, you can have money wired to you via **Western Union** (© **800/325-6000**; www.westernunion.com).

Identity theft or fraud are potential complications of losing your wallet, especially if you've lost your driver's license along with your cash and credit cards. Notify the major credit-reporting bureaus immediately; placing a fraud alert on your records may protect you against liability for criminal activity. The three major U.S. credit-reporting agencies are **Equifax** (© **800/766-0008;** www.equifax.com), **Experian** (© **888/397-3742;** www.experian.com), and **TransUnion** (© **800/680-7289;** www.transunion.com). Finally, if you've lost all forms of photo ID call your airline and explain the situation; they might allow you to board the plane if you have a copy of your passport or birth certificate and a copy of the police report you've filed.

Newspapers & Magazines The *Seattle Post-Intelligencer* and *Seattle Times* are Seattle's two daily newspapers. *Seattle Weekly* is the city's free arts-and-entertainment weekly.

Pharmacies Conveniently located downtown pharmacies include **Rite Aid,** 319 Pike St. (© **206/223-0512**), and also at 2603 Third Ave. (© 206/441-8790). Alternatively, call Rite Aid (© **800/748-3243**) for the location nearest you. For 24-hour service, try **Bartell Drug Store,** 600 First Ave. N. (© **206/284-1353**) in the lower Queen Anne neighborhood.

Photographic Needs **Cameras West,** 1908 Fourth Ave. (© **206/622-0066**), is right downtown and offers 1-hour film processing. It's open Monday through Friday from 9:30am to 6pm, and on Saturday from 10am to 5pm.

Police For police emergencies, phone © **911.**

Restrooms There are public restrooms in Pike Place Market, Westlake Center, Pacific Place, Seattle Center, and the Washington State Convention & Trade Center. You'll also find restrooms in most hotel lobbies and coffee bars in downtown Seattle.

Safety Although Seattle is a relatively safe city, it has its share of crime. The most questionable neighborhood you're likely to visit is the Pioneer Square area, which is home to more than a dozen bars and nightclubs. By day, this area is quite safe (though it has a large contingent of street people), but late at night, when the bars are closing, stay aware of your surroundings and keep an eye out for suspicious characters and activities. Also take extra precautions with your wallet or purse when you're in the crush of people at Pike Place Market. Whenever possible, try to park your car in a garage, instead of on the street, at night. If you must park on the street, make sure there are no valuables in view and nothing that even looks like it might contain something of worth. We once had our car broken into because we left a shopping bag full of trash on the back seat.

Smoking Although many of the restaurants listed in this book are nonsmoking establishments, there are also many Seattle restaurants that do allow smoking. At most high-end restaurants, the smoking area is usually in the bar/lounge, and although many restaurants have separate bar menus, most will serve you off the regular menu even if you are eating in the bar. There are very few nonsmoking bars in Seattle.

Taxes In Seattle you'll pay an 8.8% sales tax, and in restaurants, you'll also pay an additional 0.5% food-and-beverage tax on top of the sales tax. The hotel-room tax in the Seattle metro area ranges from around 10% to 16%. On rental cars, you'll pay not only an 18.5% car-rental tax, but also, if you rent at the airport, an additional 10% to 11% airport concession fee, for a whopping total of around 30%!

Taxis See section 2, "Getting Around," earlier in this chapter.

Time Seattle is on Pacific Standard Time (PST), making it 3 hours behind the East Coast.

Transit Info For 24-hour information on Seattle's Metro bus system, call © **206/553-3000.** For information on the Washington State Ferries, call © **800/84-FERRY** or 888/808-7977 in Washington, or 206/464-6400.

Weather To check the weather report, call **206/442-2800,** ext. 2032. Check the *Seattle Times* or *Seattle Post-Intelligencer* newspapers for forecasts. If you want to know how to pack before you arrive, go to **www.wrh.noaa. gov/seattle, www.cnn.com/weather,** or **www.weather.com.**

The San Juan Islands, Whidbey Island & the Emerald Coast

Water, water everywhere, and quite a few islands, too. That about sums up the landscape of the north Puget Sound and San Juan Islands region. Here, within a vast inland sea, lie hundreds of islands both large and small, and the lure of these emerald isles is powerful. There may not be any turquoise waters, white-sand beaches, or palm trees swaying in the breeze, but an island is a getaway no matter where it is—and these islands are no exception. The fact that many of the region's islands bear Spanish names seems to further add to the romance of a trip to the San Juans.

When English explorer Capt. George Vancouver first sailed down the Strait of Juan de Fuca in 1792, he discovered a vast inland sea he named Puget Sound. To the north of this sound, within a convolution of twisting channels, narrow straits, and elongated bays, lay an archipelago of islands, and rising to the east in a magnificent backdrop stood a range of snowcapped peaks. Several of the archipelago's islands—San Juan, Lopez, Fidalgo, Guemes, Sucia, and Matia—had already been named by earlier Spanish explorers, but Vancouver's 2 months of exploring and charting the waters of the region left Northwest maps with many new names—Deception Pass, Whidbey Island, Bellingham Bay, Mount Baker.

From the mid–19th century to the mid–20th century, this region was primarily a fishing, farming, and logging region, but as early as the first decade of the 20th century, Washingtonians from the mainland had begun to discover the charms of island life. Today, the northern Puget Sound and San Juan Islands are Washington's favorite summer playgrounds and weekend getaways. Shimmering waters, mountain vistas, and tranquil islands are the ingredients of the tonic that revives the weary souls of vacationers from the densely populated and industrialized southern Puget Sound. Though it's only 30 miles from Seattle to Whidbey Island and 85 miles to the San Juans, the distance is multiplied by the serenity that descends as you cross the sound by ferry and leave the mainland behind.

However, this corner of the state isn't all about island life. On the mainland, the historic fishing village of La Conner has become the most charming little town in the state. Surrounding La Conner are the Skagit Valley bulb fields, which burst into bloom each spring with acres and acres of tulips and daffodils.

Farther north, the town of Bellingham serves as a base for exploring the Emerald Coast, one of the least visited stretches of coastline in the state (the San Juans seem to siphon off all the traffic). However, though there are few crowds here, the vistas (and the oysters) are as good as any you'll find in the islands. It is also on this coast that you'll find the state's premier waterfront golf resort.

1 Whidbey Island

30 miles N of Seattle, 40 miles S of Bellingham

While the San Juan Islands are beautiful, their beauty has become something of a liability—during the summer, they're just too crowded. If you don't relish the hours-long waits for ferries, you can still have an island experience here on Whidbey Island. At 45 miles in length, Whidbey is one of the largest islands in the continental United States; and, at only 30 miles from Seattle, it's also a popular weekend getaway for Seattleites who come here seeking tranquillity and relaxation. However, outside of Washington, Whidbey Island isn't nearly as well known as the San Juans. And that is exactly why it is less crowded in the summer.

Never more than a few miles wide, Whidbey offers views of the water at seemingly every turn of its winding country roads. Farms, forests, bluffs, and beaches provide the foregrounds to the aquatic vistas, and two historic villages, Langley and Coupeville, offer the same sort of quaint settings people expect from the San Juans. Old wooden commercial buildings have been restored and now house excellent restaurants, art galleries, and unique shops. Charming bed-and-breakfast inns (and one of the state's most luxurious small hotels) pamper visitors to the island and provide the romantic surroundings that are so much a part of the Whidbey experience.

But what, you wonder, is there to do on Whidbey Island? Next to nothing. And that is the island's main appeal. This is an island you visit in order to rest and rejuvenate. You don't have to do anything, just sit back and relax. However, there are a few options for burning off excess energy: wine tasting, shopping, garden touring, hiking in state parks and a national historic reserve, walking on beaches, sea kayaking. Sounds a lot like the San Juans, doesn't it?

Lest you get the impression that Whidbey Island is heaven on earth, let us make you aware of the Whidbey Island Naval Air Station, which, with its thundering jets, has considerably altered the idyllic atmosphere of the island's northern half. Oak Harbor, the island's largest community, is located just outside the base and is characterized by the sort of strip-mall sprawl that surrounds most military bases. For this reason, the vast majority of the island's B&Bs are located in central and south Whidbey. It's partly because of what has happened to Oak Harbor that Ebey's Landing National Historic Reserve was created. When people who had moved to the island because of its tranquil atmosphere saw the sprawl that was spreading around Oak Harbor, they acted quickly to preserve some of the island's rural beauty, the very essence of Whidbey Island.

ESSENTIALS

GETTING THERE From I-5, take Wash. 20 west at Burlington. The highway turns south before you reach Anacortes and crosses over the Deception Pass Bridge to reach the north end of Whidbey Island.

Washington State Ferries (✆ **800/84-FERRY** or 888/808-7977 in Washington, or 206/464-6400; www.wsdot.wa.gov/ferries) operates ferries between Mukilteo and Clinton at the south end of the island and from Port Townsend to Keystone near Coupeville. Fares are $5.75 to $7.25 for a car and driver and $3.20 for passengers between Mukilteo and Clinton and $7.50 to $9.50 for a car and driver and $2.10 for passengers between Port Townsend and Keystone. The **Airporter Shuttle** (✆ **866/235-5247** or 360/380-8800; www.airporter. com) offers daily service from Sea-Tac International Airport to Oak Harbor. The fare is $34 one-way and $60 round-trip.

Northwest Washington Coast

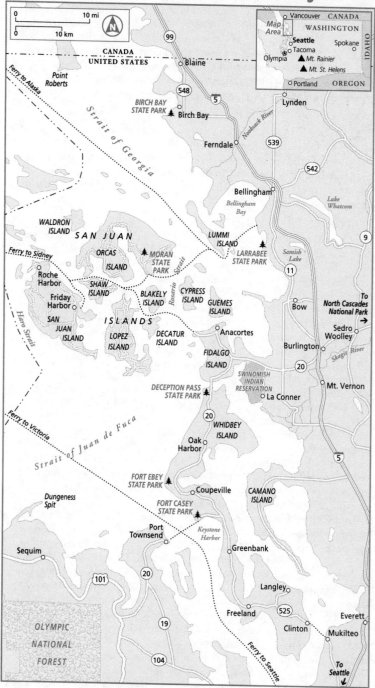

VISITOR INFORMATION   Contact **Island County Tourism,** P.O. Box 365, Coupeville, WA 98239-0365 (✆ **888/747-7777;** www.donothinghere.com); **Central Whidbey Chamber of Commerce,** 107 S. Main St., Coupeville, WA 98239-0152 (✆ **360/678-5434;** www.centralwhidbeychamber.com); or the **Langley South Whidbey Chamber of Commerce,** 208 Anthes St. (P.O. Box 403), Langley, WA 98260 (✆ **360/221-5676;** www.whidbey.com/langley).

GETTING AROUND   **Island Transit** (✆ **800/240-8747** or 360/678-7771; www.islandtransit.org) offers free public bus service on Whidbey Island.

FESTIVALS   On the first weekend of March, you can eat your fill of mussels at the **Penn Cove Mussel Festival,** and in mid-July, Langley celebrates the visual and performing arts with the **Choochokam** street festival. In early August, there's the **Coupeville Arts and Crafts Festival.** In late February, aspiring private detectives descend on Whidbey Island for the **Langley Mystery Weekend,** during which participants wander around trying to figure out who done it.

EXPLORING THE ISLAND

If you're coming from the south and take the ferry from Mukilteo, then the best place to start exploring Whidbey Island is in the historic fishing village of **Langley,** which is reached by taking Langley Road off Wash. 525. Before you ever reach town, you'll pass by the **Whidbey Island Vineyard & Winery,** 5237 S. Langley Rd. (✆ **360/221-2040;** www.whidbeyislandwinery.com), where you can taste a few wines before heading into town. Many of their white wines are made from grapes grown here on the island, while their reds are made from grapes grown in eastern Washington. The tasting room is open Wednesday through Sunday from noon to 5pm (in July and Aug, open Mon also).

Langley today is a compact little village with a mix of sophisticated shops, interesting art galleries, and good, moderately priced restaurants occupying restored wooden commercial buildings along the waterfront. **First Street Park,** right in downtown, provides access to a narrow, rocky beach and offers views of Saratoga Passage and the distant Cascades. A couple of blocks away, at the corner of Anthes Avenue and Second Street, you'll find the eclectic and artistic little **Langley Park,** which is a great place to sit and sip a latte. Across the street from this park, you'll find the **South Whidbey Historical Museum,** 312 Second St. (✆ **360/221-2101**), a small museum housing displays on local history. The museum is open Saturday and Sunday from 1 to 4pm (June–Aug, also open on Fri); admission is a $2 suggested donation.

Four miles northwest of **Freeland,** which is the narrowest point of the island, you'll find **South Whidbey State Park** (✆ **360/331-4559**), with 2 miles of shoreline, hiking trails through some old-growth forest, and a campground. Continuing north, you come to **Whidbey Island Greenbank Farm** (✆ **360/678-7700;** www.greenbankfarm.com), at Wash. 525 and Wonn Road in **Greenbank.** This former loganberry farm is now a community park. For many years the farm was known for its loganberry liqueur, and today, in the farm's tasting room, you can still sample both this liqueur and a loganberry wine, as well as other wines from around the region. In summer, you can even pick your own loganberries. In the farm's main building, you'll find both the tasting room and a small cafe known for its delicious loganberry pies. With its big red barns and rolling farmlands, Greenbank Farm is as picture perfect a farm as you will find anywhere in western Washington. A network of trails meanders around the farm property, making this a good place to stretch your legs. Not far away, you can sample more wines at **Greenbank Cellars,** 3112 Day Rd., Greenbank (✆ **360/678-3964;**

www.whidbey.com/wine). The winery is open April through October on Saturday and Sunday from 11am to 5pm. To reach the winery from Greenbank Farm, drive south on Wash. 525 and then take Bakken Road west to Day Road.

Also in Greenbank (just off Wash. 525) is **Meerkerk Rhododendron Gardens,** 3531 Meerkerk Lane (© **360/678-1912;** www.meerkerkgardens.org), which was originally a private garden but is now operated by the Seattle Rhododendron Society as a display and test garden. It's open daily from 9am to 4pm (peak bloom is Apr–May). Admission is $3.

Coupeville, located in central Whidbey Island just north of the turnoff for the ferry to Port Townsend, is another historic waterfront village. This town was founded in 1852 by Capt. Thomas Coupe, and the captain's 1853 home is among those in town that have been restored. The quiet charm of yesteryear is Coupeville's greatest appeal, and many of its old wooden commercial buildings now house antiques stores. At the north end of downtown, a gravel path leads up a bluff to the Coupeville Town Park, which is a good spot for a picnic. At the end of the Coupeville Wharf, you can see the skeleton of Rosie the gray whale, which hangs from the ceiling of the building at the end of the wharf.

In Coupeville you'll find the **Island County Historical Museum,** 908 NW Alexander St. (© **360/678-3310;** www.islandhistory.org), which is the best place to learn about the island's seafaring, farming, and military history. Between May and September, the museum is open Wednesday through Monday from 10am to 5pm; October through April, it's open Friday through Monday from 10am to 4pm. Admission is $3 for adults, and $2 for seniors and children under 18.

Much of the land around Coupeville is now part of the **Ebey's Landing National Historic Reserve.** The reserve, one of the first of its kind in the nation, was created "to preserve and protect a rural community which provides an unbroken historic record from the nineteenth century exploration and settlement of Puget Sound to the present time." There is no visitor center for the reserve, but there is an information kiosk near the dock in Coupeville, and the adjacent museum has copies of an informative brochure about the reserve as well as a brochure that outlines a driving and bicycling tour of the preserve.

Three miles south of Coupeville, adjacent to the Keystone ferry landing, is **Fort Casey State Park,** 1280 Engle Rd. (© **360/678-4519**), a former military base that was built in the 1890s to guard Puget Sound; it still has its gun batteries. In addition to the fort, the park includes beaches, hiking trails, a campground, and the 1897 **Admiralty Head lighthouse,** which is now an interpretive center that is open daily from 11am to 5pm in summer. Just south of Fort Casey State Park near the Keystone Ferry landing (Port Townsend ferries) is **Keystone State Park,** which is a designated underwater park for scuba divers. A few miles north of Fort Casey is the smaller **Fort Ebey State Park,** Libbey Road (© **360/678-4636**), another former military site built to protect the sound. Here there are excellent views of the Strait of Juan de Fuca, as well as a campground, hiking and mountain biking trails, and a lake for swimming and fishing.

Oak Harbor, at the north end of the island, was settled by Dutch immigrants, and here, at City Beach Park, which has a swimming lagoon, you'll find a large Dutch **windmill.** As the largest town on the island, Oak Harbor lacks the charm of Langley and Coupeville. At **Joseph Whidbey State Park,** west of Oak Harbor, there are great westerly views and a long sandy beach.

Deception Pass State Park (© **360/675-2417**), at the northern tip of the island, is the most popular state park in Washington. What draws the crowds are miles of beaches, quiet coves, freshwater lakes, dark forests, hiking trails, camping, and views of Deception Pass, the churning channel between Whidbey Island and Fidalgo Island. A high bridge connects these two large islands by way of a smaller island in the middle of Deception Pass, and overlooks at the bridge allow you to gaze down on the tidal waters that surge and swirl between the islands.

SPORTS & OUTDOOR ACTIVITIES

BOAT CHARTERS   Between May and September, the *Cutty Sark,* which operates out of the Captain Whidbey Inn, 2072 W. Captain Whidbey Inn Rd. (© **800/366-4097** or 360/678-4097; www.captainwhidbey.com), offers scheduled day-sail cruises for $30 per person. Multi-day excursions are also offered.

SEA KAYAKING   The easiest way to explore the waters off Whidbey Island is to rent a sea kayak at Coupeville's **Harbor Store on the Wharf** (© **360/678-3625**), which rents boats from the Coupeville Wharf. Single kayaks rent for $15 per hour, and double kayaks rent for $25 per hour.

WHERE TO STAY
IN LANGLEY

Boatyard Inn ★★   Located right on Langley's little marina and designed to look like an old cannery building, this three-story inn is clad in a combination of wood, cedar shingles, and corrugated metal. Guest rooms are huge and have full kitchens, water views, gas fireplaces, and small balconies. There are also four two-bedroom loft suites. Downtown Langley is a few hundred yards uphill from the inn, and there's a small adjacent beach as well as the marina. This is a good choice if you like to have lots of space or need a kitchen.

200 Wharf St. (P.O. Box 866), Langley, WA 98260. © 360/221-5120. Fax 360/221-5124. www.boatyardinn.com. 10 units. $165–$210 double (lower midweek rates in winter). AE, DC, DISC, MC, V. **Amenities:** Massage; babysitting. *In room:* TV/VCR, kitchenette, fridge, coffeemaker, hair dryer, iron.

The Inn at Langley ★★   This is one of the most luxurious and romantic inns in the Northwest. With its weathered cedar shingles, exposed beams, works of contemporary art, and colorful garden, the inn evokes all the best of life in the region, and the guest rooms have a Zen-like quality that soothes and relaxes. The inn's four floors jut out from a bluff overlooking Saratoga Passage, and with 180-degree views from every room, you'll have plenty of opportunities to spot orca whales and bald eagles. While the bedrooms and balconies are luxurious enough, it's the bathrooms that are the star attractions here. Each comes with an open shower and a double whirlpool tub that looks out over the water. Pull back an opaque sliding window and you also get a view of the room's fireplace. Every Friday and Saturday, the The Chef's Kitchen Restaurant serves a five-course fixed-price dinner focusing on creative Northwest flavors ($80 per person).

400 First St. (P.O. Box 835), Langley, WA 98260. © 360/221-3033. www.innatlangley.com. 26 units. $225–$250 double; $395 suite; $575 cottage. Rates include continental breakfast. 2-night minimum on weekends. AE, MC, V. Children over 12 accepted. **Amenities:** Restaurant (Northwest); access to nearby health club; spa; massage. *In room:* TV/VCR, dataport, fridge, coffeemaker, hair dryer.

WHERE TO DINE

The Chef's Kitchen Restaurant ★★ at the Inn at Langley serves the finest meals on the island. However, these five-course, fixed-price dinners are only available on Friday and Saturday evenings (and Sun evenings in summer) and cost a whopping $160 per couple (plus tax and tip). See "Where to Stay," above, for details on the inn. For baked goods and espresso, drop by the **Langley Village Bakery,** 221 Second St. (© **360/221-3525**).

Café Langley ★★ MEDITERRANEAN/NORTHWEST   Romantic and intimate, this restaurant seamlessly fuses Northwest and Middle Eastern flavors and aesthetics and has long been one of Langley's most popular restaurants. The cafe has been around for years and serves up familiar dishes such as spanakopita and shish kebabs, but also is known for its flank steak marinated in sherry and herbs. The prawns à la Greque are another good choice, as are the Penn Cove mussels. The latter are available as either an appetizer or an entree. Weekly specials add yet another dimension to the reliable menu. Much less lively than the nearby Star Bistro, Café Langley is a good bet for a romantic dinner.

113 First St. ✆ 360/221-3090. www.langley-wa.com/cl. Reservations recommended. Main courses $11–$18. AE, MC, V. Mon–Thurs 11:30am–2:30pm and 5–8:30pm; Fri 11:30am–2:30pm and 5–9pm; Sat 11:30am–3pm and 5–9pm; Sun 11:30am–3pm and 5–8:30pm (closed Tues in winter).

The Edgecliff ★ MEDITERRANEAN/NORTHWEST   Although the cliff on which this restaurant is built is more of a bluff, the views are still the best of any restaurant in Langley. The food is also quite good, and the setting, up the hill from the heart of the village, is quite tranquil. If you like oysters, then you'll love the way they're prepared here. They're done with an unusual sesame-seed crust and come accompanied by Thai peanut sauce. Also keep an eye out for the butternut squash ravioli with brown butter–brandy sauce, caramelized walnuts, roasted garlic, and fresh sage. Delicious! The restaurant has a small lounge in case you'd like to simply enjoy the setting over a cocktail or glass of wine.

510 Cascade Ave. ✆ 360/221-8899. Main courses $8–$11 lunch, $13–$27 dinner. MC, V. Mon–Thurs 11:30am–2:30pm and 5–9pm; Fri 11:30am–2:30pm and 5–10pm; Sat noon–3pm and 5–10pm; Sun noon–3pm and 5–9pm.

Star Bistro ★★ NORTHWEST/MEDITERRANEAN   Boisterous and boldly styled, this lively bistro is down a few doors from Café Langley and up a flight of stairs (on the second floor of one of Langley's old commercial buildings). Big black-and-white floor tiles and bold splashes of color give the bistro something of a party atmosphere. Creamy pasta dishes, flavorful salads, and fresh seafood are all reliable choices, and in addition there are nightly specials. Keep an eye out for the chicken with wild mushrooms and Whidbey's Port sauce. On sunny days everyone heads out to the rooftop patio.

201½ First St. ✆ 360/221-2627. www.star-bistro.com. Reservations recommended. Main courses $8–$17 lunch, $10–$22 dinner. AE, MC, V. Summer Sun–Thurs 11:30am–9pm, Fri–Sat 11:30am–10pm; fall–spring Tues–Thurs 11:30am–8pm, Fri–Sat 11:30am–9pm, Sun 11:30am–8pm.

IN COUPEVILLE

When its time for a latte and a muffin, search out **Great Times Waterfront Coffee House** ★, 12 NW Front St. (✆ **360/678-5358**), which is down a flight of stairs on the waterfront. With its battered wooden floors and great water views, this cozy place is the perfect place to hole up if the weather turns bad. For gourmet picnic fare, stop by **Bayleaf,** 901 Grace St. (✆ **360/678-6603**).

Christopher's ★ NORTHWEST   Located in a warehouse-style building in downtown Coupeville, Christopher's may not have any water views, but it does serves some of the best food in town. Chef/owner Andreas Wurzrainer is from Austria, and occasionally dishes from the home country show up on the menu. For the most part the menu sticks to familiar fare such as shrimp scampi and cioppino, though you'll also find dishes like barbecued salmon with raspberry barbecue sauce. It would be foolish to pass up the Penn Cove mussels, which are steamed with white wine, garlic, and herbs.

23 Front St. © **360/678-5480.** Reservations recommended. Main courses $7.25–$10 lunch, $13–$22 dinner. AE, DISC, MC, V. Mon–Fri 11:30am–2:30pm and 5–9pm; Sat–Sun noon–2:30pm and 5–9pm.

The Oystercatcher ★★ NORTHWEST   Located a block off the waterfront at the back of a small, modern building, this tiny restaurant is the best in town. Chef and owner Susan Vanderbeek has nearly 3 decades of experience at Northwest restaurants, and here looks over her handful of tables with great care. The menu changes every few weeks and usually only includes three appetizers and three or four entrees. With such a short menu, you can be sure every dish is perfectly done. On a recent fall menu, appetizers included oysters with a basil-lemon mayonnaise, as well as local mussels. Among the entrees were a curried chicken served with cranberry-fig chutney, and braised lamb shanks.

901 Grace St. © **360/678-0683.** Reservations highly recommended. Main courses $17–$19. MC, V. Wed–Sat 5–9pm.

2 Anacortes

75 miles N of Seattle, 39 miles S of Bellingham, 92 miles S of Vancouver, B.C.

For most people, Anacortes is little more than that town you drive through on the way to the San Juan Islands ferry terminal. Actually, Anacortes has much more to offer than a driver late for the ferry could ever know. The route to the ferry sticks to roads that are fine examples of commercial and suburban sprawl—strip malls, gas stations, aging motels, housing developments. However, if you have time to detour off the main road, you'll find a town that, while not nearly as quaint as those on the San Juans, does have some historic character and, perhaps best of all, plenty of good places to eat. The restored downtown business district, residential neighborhoods full of old Victorian homes, a large, forested waterfront park, and a mountain-top viewpoint are all worth a look. So, if you can, slow down and take a look at Anacortes before or after a trip to the San Juans.

Anacortes made its early fortunes on lumbering and fishing, and today commercial fishing, as well as boat building, are still important to the town's economy. This marine orientation has given the town its character, which can be seen in the many restored buildings along Commercial Avenue.

Anacortes also makes a good base for exploring the San Juans if you either can't get or can't afford a room on the islands. Using Anacortes as a base and leaving your car here on the mainland, you can travel as a passenger on the ferries and, by using public transit, mopeds, or bicycles, still manage to see plenty of the San Juan Islands. In any event, Anacortes is also on an island, Fidalgo Island, and has plenty of water views, the best of which are from Washington Park near the ferry terminal, from atop Mount Erie in the middle of the island, and from Deception Pass State Park at the south end of the island.

ESSENTIALS

GETTING THERE   From I-5 at Burlington, take Wash. 20 west to the Wash. 20 Spur. South of Anacortes, Wash. 20 connects to Whidbey Island by way of the Deception Pass Bridge.

See "Getting There," under "The San Juan Islands," below, for details on airport service to Anacortes from Seattle–Tacoma International Airport and for information on ferry connections to Anacortes from the islands and Vancouver Island, British Columbia.

The Name Game

Founded in the 1850s by Amos Bowman, Anacortes was named after Bowman's wife, Annie Curtis, but over the years the spelling and pronunciation were slowly corrupted to its current Spanish-sounding pronunciation (in keeping with such local Spanish names as San Juan, Lopez, and Guemes).

VISITOR INFORMATION   For information on Anacortes, contact the **Anacortes Chamber of Commerce,** 819 Commercial Ave., Anacortes, WA 98221 (© **360/293-3832;** www.anacortes.org).

EXPLORING ANACORTES

If you want to learn more about local history, stop by the **Anacortes Museum,** 1305 Eighth St. (© **360/293-1915;** www.anacorteshistorymuseum.org), housed in a former Carnegie Library. It's open Thursday through Monday from 1 to 5pm; admission is a suggested $2 donation. Across the street from the museum is **Causland Memorial Park,** the town's most unusual attraction. Built in 1919 to honor servicemen who died in World War I, the park contains rock walls that were constructed as giant mosaics. It's a piece of folk art that reflects a much simpler era. **Murals** are a mainstay of the Northwest's historic towns, and here in Anacortes they take the shape of more than 50 life-size cutouts of the town's forefathers. The murals, based on historic photos, were done by artist Bill Mitchell.

Any walking tour of downtown should be sure to include a visit to the historic *W. T. Preston* **Snagboat,** 703 R Ave. (© **360/293-1916**), a sternwheeler that was built in the 1890s to clear log jams on Puget Sound and now sits on dry land in a little park at the corner of Seventh Street and R Avenue. June through August, the sternwheeler is open daily from 11am to 5pm; April, May, and September, it's open on weekends only. Admission is $2 adults and $1 for seniors and children ages 6 to 16. Next door, at the corner of Seventh Street and R Avenue, is **The Depot Arts Center** (© **360/293-3663;** www.depotartscenter. com), a restored 1911 railway depot that now serves as an arts center, with a collection of art by regional artists.

For a glimpse of an old-fashioned hardware store, stop by **Marine Supply and Hardware Co.,** 202 Commercial St. (© **360/293-3014**), which is the oldest continuously operating marine supply store on the West Coast.

Nature lovers can head to **Washington Park,** just a short distance past the ferry terminal. The park contains not only a campground and several miles of hiking trails, but tranquil **Sunset Beach,** which looks out across Rosario Strait to the San Juan Islands. For even more spectacular views, head up to **Mount Erie Park** ★★ on the summit of 1,270-foot Mount Erie. From here, on a clear day you can see Mount Rainier, Mount Baker, and the Olympic Mountains. You'll find this park by heading south out of Anacortes on Commercial Avenue, turning right on 32nd Street and then left on H Avenue (which becomes Heart Lake Rd.), and then taking Erie Mountain Drive to the top of the mountain.

You don't have to go all the way to the San Juans if you want to do some whale-watching. Orca-viewing excursions are offered by **Island Adventures** (© **800/465-4604** or 360/293-2428; www.islandadventurecruises.com), which charges $45 to $69, and also by **Mystic Sea Charters** (© **800/308-9387;** www.mysticseacharters.com), which charges $55 to $65. This latter company also offers sightseeing and dinner cruises. It's also possible to do a little sea kayaking here in the Anacortes area. Sea-kayak rentals are available at **Eddyline Watersports Center,** 2403 Commercial Ave. (© **866/445-7506** or 360/ 299-2300; www.seakayakshop.com), which charges $30 to $45 for a half-day rental and $45 to $65 for a full-day rental. Guided kayak tours are also offered throughout the year.

WHERE TO STAY

Ship Harbor Inn ★ Located immediately adjacent to the ferry terminal for San Juan Islands ferries and overlooking a wetland that offers good bird-watching, this inn is a good choice if you weren't able to get a room on the islands or are planning on taking the early ferry all the way to Vancouver Island, Canada. This is also a good choice if you are planning to explore the islands by bicycle. Rooms are large and most have balconies and views of the water. If you plan to spend more than 1 night here, you might want to opt for one of the "cabin" rooms, which have full kitchens. There's also a Jacuzzi suite.

5316 Ferry Terminal Rd., Anacortes, WA 98221. © **800/852-8568** or 360/293-5177. Fax 360/299-2412. www. shipharborinn.com. 26 units. $80–$105 double. Rates include continental breakfast. AE, DC, DISC, MC, V. **Amenities:** Coin-op laundry. *In room:* TV, fridge, free local calls.

WHERE TO DINE

For good pastries and baked goodies, be sure to drop by **La Vie En Rose** ★, 418 Commercial Ave. (© **360/299-9546**), a great little French pastry shop that also serves interesting light meals. For healthy, light meals, fresh juices, and smoothies, try the **Star Bar Café,** 416½ Commercial Ave. (© **360/299-2120**). Before leaving town, you should also be sure to pick up some smoked salmon at **Seabear Smokehouse and Store** ★, 605 30th St. (© **800/645-FISH** or 360/ 293-4661; www.seabear.com), which offers tours of its smokehouse.

Adrift ★ INTERNATIONAL This restaurant could be a glimpse of things to come for downtown Anacortes. With its dark interior and urban vibe it is definitely an unexpected treat in this retirement community. The menu is highly eclectic and leans toward organic ingredients and Asian and Mediterranean influences. The white bean chicken chili is a real winner, but then most dishes here are. At lunch, try the smoked seafood plate. At dinner, try the crab cakes with spicy ginger-garlic sauce or the seared scallops with citrus butter. Feeling adventurous? Order a side of coconut-milk mashed sweet potatoes.

510 Commercial Ave. © 360/588-0653. Reservations recommended. Main courses $7–$14. AE, DC, DISC, MC, V. Tues–Sat 11am–9pm.

Gere-a-Deli ★ DELI Many places claim to be New York–style delis, but this is the only one in the Northwest that comes close to duplicating the genuine feel of a deli in Manhattan. Big and bustling, Gere-a-Deli is *the* place for lunch in Anacortes, and while the sandwiches may not be as good as those in the Big Apple, the urban feel, vintage signs, huge windows, and lively chatter of conversation all add up to a classic deli experience. Note that dinners are only served on Friday night.

502 Commercial Ave. © 360/293-7383. Reservations required for Fri dinner. Sandwiches $5–$7.75. AE, DISC, MC, V. Mon–Sat 7am–4pm; Fri 5–9pm.

Rockfish Grill and Anacortes Brewery ★ AMERICAN Although you can get good fish and chips, pizzas, and burgers in this brewpub, the menu also includes plenty of dishes that are unexpectedly imaginative. For a starter, try the tequila-lime shrimp cocktail or the double oyster "martini." Among the entrees, the wood-fired raviolis are a good bet. Wash it all down with one of the brewery's excellent beers.

320 Commercial Ave. ⓒ 360/588-1720. www.anacortesrockfish.com. Main courses $7–$18. AE, DISC, MC, V. Sun–Thurs 11:30am–10pm; Fri–Sat 11:30am–midnight.

3 The San Juan Islands

On a late afternoon on a clear summer day, the sun slants low, suffusing the scene with a golden light. The fresh salt breeze and the low rumble of the ferry's engine lulls you into a dream state. All around you, rising from a shimmering sea, are emerald-green islands that are the tops of glacier-carved mountains flooded at the end of the last ice age. A bald eagle swoops from its perch on a twisted madrona tree. Off the port bow, you spot several fat harbor seals lounging on a rocky islet. As the engine slows, you glide toward a narrow wooden dock with a simple sign above it that reads ORCAS ISLAND. With a sigh of contentment, you step out onto the San Juan Islands and into a slower pace of life.

There's something magical about traveling to the San Juans. Some people say it's the light, some say it's the sea air, some say it's the weather (temperatures are always moderate, and rainfall is roughly half what it is in Seattle). Whatever it is that so entrances, the San Juans have become the favorite getaway of urban Washingtonians, and if you make time to visit these idyllic islands, we think you, too, will fall under their spell.

There is, however, one caveat. The San Juans have been discovered. In summer, if you're driving a car, you may encounter waits of several hours to get on ferries. One solution is to leave your car on the mainland and come over either on foot or by bicycle. If you choose to come over on foot, you can rent a car, moped, or bike; take the San Juan island shuttle bus; or use taxis to get around. Then again, you can just stay in one place and relax.

Along with crowded ferries come hotels, inns, and campgrounds that can get booked up months in advance and restaurants that can't seat you unless you have a reservation. If it's summer, don't expect to find a place to stay if you come out here without a room reservation.

In other seasons, it's a different story. Spring and fall are often clear, and in spring, the islands' gardens and hedgerows of wild roses burst into bloom, making this one of the nicest times of year to visit. Perhaps best of all, in spring and fall room rates are much less than they are in the summer.

Depending on whom you listen to, there are between 175 and 786 islands in the San Juans. The lower number constitutes those islands large enough to have been named, while the larger number represents all the islands, rocks, and reefs that poke above the water on the lowest possible tide. Of all these islands, only four (San Juan, Orcas, Lopez, and Shaw) are serviced by the Washington State Ferries, and of these, only three (San Juan, Orcas, and Lopez) have anything in the way of tourist accommodations.

ESSENTIALS

VISITOR INFORMATION   For information on all the islands, contact the **San Juan Islands Visitor Information Service,** P.O. Box 65, Lopez Island, WA 98261 (ⓒ **888/468-3701** or 360/468-3663; www.travelsanjuans.com); the **San Juan Island Chamber of Commerce,** P.O. Box 98, Friday Harbor, WA 98250 (ⓒ **360/378-5240;** www.sanjuanisland.org); or the **Orcas Island Chamber of**

Commerce, P.O. Box 252, Eastsound, WA 98245 (© **360/376-2273;** www. orcasisland.org). For information on Lopez Island, contact the **Lopez Island Chamber of Commerce,** P.O. Box 102, Lopez, WA 98261 (© **360/468-4664;** www.lopezisland.com).

On the Internet, check out the following: www.sanjuanweb.com, www.orcasisle. com, www.thesanjuans.com.

GETTING THERE   Washington **State Ferries** (© **800/84-FERRY** or 888/ 808-7977 in Washington, or 206/464-6400; www.wsdot.wa.gov/ferries) operates ferries between Anacortes and four of the San Juan Islands (Lopez, Shaw, Orcas, and San Juan) and Sidney, British Columbia (on Vancouver Island near Victoria). The round-trip fare for a vehicle and driver from Anacortes to Lopez is $20 to $30, to Shaw or Orcas $24 to $35, to San Juan $27 to $40, and to Sidney $46 to $67. With the exception of trips to Sidney, B.C., fares are higher Wednesday through Saturday. Also, the higher fares listed here reflect a summer surcharge.

The round-trip fare for passengers from Anacortes to any of the islands ranges from $8 to $11 ($18 from Anacortes to Sidney). The fare for a vehicle and driver on all westbound inter-island ferries is $11 to $14, and walk-on passengers and passengers in cars ride free. Except for service from Sidney, fares are not collected on eastbound ferries, nor are walk-on passengers charged for inter-island ferry service. If you plan to explore the islands by car, you'll save some money by starting your tour on San Juan Island and making your way back east through the islands.

During the summer you may have to wait several hours to get on a ferry, so arrive early. If you plan to leave your car on the mainland, any time between late May and late September, you'll pay $7 to park it overnight at the Anacortes ferry terminal ($14 for 3 days, $25 for 1 week). There is also a free park-and-ride lot on the east side of Anacortes on South March Point Road (off Wash. 20). During the summer, a free shuttle operates from this parking lot to the ferry terminal.

There are also passenger-ferry services from several cities around the region. **Victoria Clipper** (© **800/888-2535** or 206/448-5000; www.victoriaclipper.com) operates excursion boats between Seattle and Friday Harbor on San Juan Island. There are also boats that go to Victoria. The round-trip fare to Friday Harbor is $53 to $63 depending on the time of year. Seven-day advance-purchase discounts of $10 are available on round-trip tickets. Children ages 1 to 11 are half price.

Between Port Townsend and Friday Harbor, passenger service is available from mid-April to early October from **P.S. Express** (© **360/385-5288;** www. pugetsoundexpress.com), which will also carry bicycles and sea kayaks. One-way fares are $35 for adults and $25 for children; round-trip fares are $53 for adults and $36 for children.

From Bellingham, there is passenger service to Friday Harbor (San Juan Island) on the **San Juan Island Commuter,** Bellingham Cruise Terminal, 335 Harris Ave. (© **888/734-8180** or 360/734-8180; www.islandcommuter.com). The round-trip adult fare to either island is $35. These passenger ferries operate between mid-May and mid-September.

If you're short on time, you can fly to the San Juans. **Kenmore Air** (© **800/ 543-9595** or 425/486-1257; www.kenmoreair.com), offers floatplane flights that take off from Lake Union (and also from the north end of Lake Washington). Round-trip fares to the San Juans are between $163 and $194 (lower for children). Flights go to Friday Harbor and Roche Harbor on San Juan Island, Rosario Resort, Deer Harbor, and Westsound on Orcas Island, and the Lopez

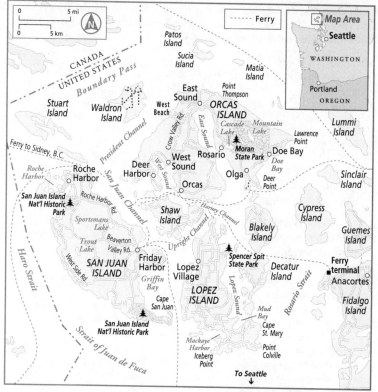

Islander Resort on Lopez Island. You can also get from Seattle to the San Juans on **San Juan Airlines** (© 800/690-0086; www.sanjuanairlines.com), which flies from Boeing Field and offers a free shuttle from Sea-Tac Airport.

West Isle Air (© 800/874-4434; www.westisleair.com) flies from Bellingham and Anacortes to San Juan, Orcas, Lopez, and several of the outer islands. Fares from Bellingham to Friday Harbor on San Juan Island are $45 one-way and $90 round-trip. Note that these airplanes are not floatplanes, but instead use island airports.

You can also get from Sea-Tac Airport to the San Juan Islands ferry terminal in Anacortes on the **Airporter Shuttle** (© 866/235-5247 or 360/380-8800; www.airporter.com), which charges $31 one-way and $56 round-trip.

GETTING AROUND   Car rentals are available on San Juan Island from **M&W Auto Sales,** 725 Spring St. (© 800/323-6037 or 360/378-2886; www. interisland.net/mandw), which charges between $30 and $70 per day. Cars can also be rented from **Susie's Mopeds** (© 800/532-0087 or 360/378-5244; www. susiesmopeds.com), which charges $96 per day.

For a cab, call **San Juan Taxi** (© 360/378-3550).

San Juan Transit (© 800/887-8387, or 360/378-8887 on San Juan; www.sanjuantransit.com) operates a shuttle bus during the summer. This shuttle can be boarded at the ferry terminal and operates frequently throughout the day, stopping at all the major attractions on the island, which makes this a great way to get around if you come out without a car. Day passes are $10 for adults,

$9 for seniors, and $5 for kids ages 5 to 12, with discounted 2-day rates available. One-way ($4 adults, $2 kids 5–12) and round-trip ($7 adults, $3 kids 5–12) tickets are available. Children ages 4 and under always ride free.

SAN JUAN ISLAND

San Juan Island is not the largest of these islands, but it is the most populous, and is home to the county seat, Friday Harbor, which is the biggest and most developed town in the islands. As the hub of island activity, San Juan Island is home to more whale-watching and sea-kayaking companies than any of the other islands. It also has charter boats, fishing boats, moped rentals, and lots of souvenir shops. This all adds up to crowds in the summer, so if you're looking for an idyllic island getaway, you might want to try Orcas or Lopez. See Orcas Island, p. 167.

However, what San Juan Island has going for it is lots of history, plus great views of the Olympic Mountains across the Strait of Juan de Fuca, and the only place in the islands where you can reliably see orca whales from shore.

EXPLORING FRIDAY HARBOR

Friday Harbor is the only real town on all of the islands, and as such it is home to numerous tourist-oriented shops, restaurants, motels, and B&Bs, as well as such island necessities as grocery and hardware stores. With its well-protected, large marina, it's also one of the most popular places in the islands for boaters to drop anchor.

If you arrived by car, you'll first want to find a parking space, which can be difficult in the summer. Once on foot, stroll around town admiring the simple wood-frame shop buildings built back at the turn of the 20th century. At that time, Friday Harbor was referred to as the southernmost port in Alaska and was a busy harbor. Schooners and steamships hauled the island's fruit, livestock, and lime (for cement) off to more populous markets. Today these pursuits have all died off, but reminders of the island's rural roots linger on, and these memories fuel the island's new breadwinner—tourism.

Whale-watching is one of the most popular summer activities in the San Juans. Before you head out, stop by the **Whale Museum** ✪, 62 First St. N. (© 800/ 946-7227 or 360/378-4710; www.whale-museum.org). Here you can see whale skeletons and models of whales and learn all about the area's pods of orcas (also known as killer whales). The museum is open daily from 10am to 5pm (shorter hours in winter); admission is $6 for adults, $5 for seniors, and $3 for children 5 to 18 and college students.

Here in Friday Harbor, you'll also find the headquarters of the **San Juan National Historic Park** ✪ (© 360/378-2240; www.nps.gov/sajh), at the corner of Spring and First streets. It's open daily from 8:30am to 5pm in summer (Mon–Fri 8:30am–4:30pm in winter). This park commemorates the San Juan Island Pig War, one of North America's most unusual and least remembered confrontations. Way back in 1859, San Juan Island nearly became the site of a battle between the British and the Americans. The two countries had not yet agreed upon the border between the United States and Canada when a British pig on San Juan Island decided to have dinner in an American garden. The owner of the garden didn't take too kindly to this and shot the pig. The Brits, rather than welcoming this succulent addition to their evening's repast, threatened redress. In less time than it takes to smoke a ham, both sides were calling in reinforcements. Luckily, this pigheadedness was defused and a more serious confrontation was avoided. While the park's headquarters is here in Friday Harbor, the main historic sites are English Camp, at the north end of the island, and American Camp, at the south end of the island. At both camps, you can visit historic buildings that are much as they might have looked in 1859.

If you're interested in island history, stop by the **San Juan Historical Museum,** 405 Price St. (© **360/378-3949;** www.sjmuseum.org), which is housed in an 1894 farmhouse and also includes several other historic buildings on its grounds. May to September the museum is open Thursday through Saturday from 10am to 4pm and Sunday from 1 to 4pm; October, March, and April the museum is open Saturday from 1 to 4pm. Open by appointment in other months. Admission is $2 for adults, $1 for children ages 6 to 18; free to children under 6.

Friday Harbor is also home to quite a few good art galleries and other interesting shops. At **Waterworks Gallery,** Argyle and Spring streets (© **360/378-3060;** www.waterworksgallery.com), you'll find fine art and contemporary crafts by local and regional artists. At **Arctic Raven Gallery,** 1 Front St. (© **360/378-3433**), you'll find contemporary Native American arts and crafts. At **The Garuda & I,** 60 First St. (© **360/378-3733**), you'll find fascinating imported items from throughout the world, with an emphasis on Asian imports.

If you need some wine for your vacation or want to take some home with you, be sure to stop by the tasting room at **Island Wine Company,** 2 Cannery Landing (© **360/378-3229;** www.sanjuancellars.com), which is the only place you can buy San Juan Cellars wines (made with grapes from eastern Washington). You'll find the wine shop on the immediate left as you leave the ferry.

SEEING THE REST OF THE ISLAND

Most of the island's main attractions can be seen on a long loop drive around the perimeter of the island. Start the drive by following Roche Harbor signs north out of Friday Harbor (take Spring St. to Second St. to Tucker Ave.). In about 3 miles, you'll come to **San Juan Vineyards** ⚶, 3136 Roche Harbor Rd. (© **360/378-9463;** www.sanjuanvineyards.com), which makes wines both from grapes grown off the island and from its own estate-grown Siegerrebe and Madeline Angevine grapes. The tasting room is housed in an old schoolhouse built in 1896 and is open daily 11am to 5pm in summer (spring and fall Wed–Sun 11am–5pm; by appointment in other months).

A little farther north, you come to **Roche Harbor Resort,** once the site of large limestone quarries that supplied lime to much of the West Coast. Today many of the quarries' old structures are still visible, giving this area a decaying industrial look, but amidst the abandoned machinery stands the historic Hotel de Haro, a simple whitewashed wooden building with verandas across its two floors. Stop and admire the old-fashioned marina and colorful gardens. The deck of the hotel's lounge is one of the best places on the island to linger over a drink. In an old pasture on the edge of the resort property, you'll find the **Westcott Bay Reserve** (© **360/370-5050;** www.wbay.org), a sculpture park that includes more than 85 works of art set in grassy fields and along the shores of a small pond. Back in the woods near the resort you'll find an unusual **mausoleum** that was erected by the founder of the quarries and the Hotel de Haro.

South of Roche Harbor, on West Valley Road, you'll find **English Camp.** Set amid shady trees and spacious lawns, the camp is the picture of British civility. There's even a formal garden surrounded by a white picket fence. You can look inside the reconstructed buildings and imagine the days when this was one of the most far-flung corners of the British Empire. If you're full of energy, hike up to the top of 650-foot **Mount Young** for a panorama of the island. An easier hike is out to the end of **Bel Point.**

South of English Camp, watch for the Bay Road turnoff. This connects to the Westside Road, which leads down the island's west coast. Along this road, you'll find **San Juan County Park,** a great spot for a picnic. A little farther south you'll come to **Lime Kiln State Park** ⚓⚓, the country's first whale-watching park and a great place to spot these gentle giants in summer. As Westside Road moves inland, a left onto Wold Road will bring you to **Pelindaba Lavender Farms,** 33 Hawthorne Lane (© **360/378-4248;** www.pelindaba.com). The farm has more than 5 acres of lavender plants, and although most of the flowers grown on these fields go into various products sold by the farm, there is a small field where visitors can cut their own lavender. The plants are at their peak bloom in July and August, and guided tours are offered May through October. The Gatehouse Store is packed full of an amazing variety of lavender products. Between May and October, the farm is open daily from 10am to 5pm. Other months, it is open Wednesday through Sunday from 10am to 5pm, with the exception of January when the farm is closed.

Near the south end of the island you'll find the windswept promontory on which stood the **American Camp** during the Pig War. Here you'll find a few reconstructed buildings, a beach, several miles of trails, and a visitor center (open daily 8am–5pm; in winter, Thurs–Sun 8:30am–4:30pm). Before the American Camp was built here, this was the site of a Hudson's Bay Company farm. The meadows sweeping down to the sea were once grazed by sheep and cattle, but today you'll see only rabbits browsing amid the high grasses and wildflowers. Some of the hiking trails here lead along the grassy bluffs and down to the beach. Our favorite area trails are the **Mt. Finlayson Trail,** which leads to the top of a grassy hill, and the **Lagoon Trail,** which leads through a dark forest of Douglas firs to a small log-choked Jackle's Lagoon, which is a good spot for bird-watching. Keep your eyes peeled for bald eagles.

Continuing past American Camp will bring you to Cattle Point, site of a lighthouse and the **Cattle Point Interpretive Area.** This latter locale was, in the 1920s, a Navy Radio Compass Station that helped ships navigate the nearby waters. Today, there are rock outcrops, two tiny beaches, great views of Lopez Island, interpretive signs, and a few picnic tables that make this one of the best picnic spots on the island. Cattle Point is also a good destination for a bike ride from Friday Harbor.

BOAT & BUS TOURS

If you come over to San Juan Island without a car and want to see as much of the island as possible in a short amount of time, consider taking a narrated bus tour through **San Juan Transit,** Cannery Landing building, Front and East streets (© **800/887-8387** or 360/378-8887; www.sanjuantransit.com), which has its office right at the ferry landing and charges $17 for adults, $16 for seniors, $10 for kids 8 to 17 with adult, free for children under 8 with adult.

SPORTS & OUTDOOR ACTIVITIES

BICYCLING Bicycling is a favorite sport of island visitors. Winding country roads are almost ideal for leisurely trips. If you didn't bring your own wheels, you can rent a bike in Friday Harbor from **Island Bicycles,** 380 Argyle St. (© **360/378-4941**), which charges $6 per hour (2-hr. minimum) and $30 per day. Here on San Juan Island you can also rent scooters and mopeds. They're available in Friday Harbor by the hour or by the day from **Island Scooter Rental,** 85 Front

St. (℡ **360/378-8811**), or from **Susie's Mopeds** (℡ **800/532-0087** or 360/378-5244; www.susiesmopeds.com), both located at the top of the ferry lanes. Expect to pay $20 to $25 per hour or $60 to $75 per day for a moped or scooter.

BOAT CHARTERS   If you and a few friends would just like to get out on the water for a leisurely cruise, there are always boats to be chartered in Friday Harbor. Check around the marina for notices. You can also try contacting **Cap'n Howard's Sailing Charters** (℡ **877/346-7245** or 360/378-3958; www.capn howard.com), which charges $70 per hour for up to six people ($200 minimum). If you're looking for a week-long bareboat charter, contact **Charters Northwest** (℡ **360/378-7196;** www.chartersnw.com).

FISHING   If you want to try catching some salmon, contact **Buffalo Works by Nash Brothers** (℡ **360/378-4612;** www.rockisland.com/~captnjer) or **Trophy Charters/Captain Monty** (℡ **360/378-2110;** www.globaltelesis.com/ trophy), both of which also offer bottom-fishing trips.

SCUBA DIVING   Believe it or not, scuba diving is also popular in the San Juans. Though the water stays frigid year-round, it's also exceedingly clear. If you're a diver and want to rent equipment or go on a guided dive, or if you want to take a diving class while you're here, contact **Island Dive & Watersports**, 2A Spring St. Landing, Friday Harbor (℡ **800/303-8386** or 360/378-2772; www. divesanjuan.com). A two-tank dive will cost you $75.

SEA KAYAKING ★★   Two- to five-hour sea-kayak tours ($39–$69) are offered by **San Juan Safaris** (℡ **800/450-6858** or 360/378-1323; www.san juansafaris.com) at Roche Harbor Resort, **Leisure Kayak Adventures** (℡ **800/ 836-1402** or 360/378-5992; www.leisurekayak.com), and **Crystal Seas Kayaking** (℡ **877/SEAS-877** or 360/378-4223; www.crystalseas.com).

Three- and four-day trips are offered by **San Juan Kayak Expeditions** (℡ **360/ 378-4436;** www.sanjuankayak.com), which charges $340 and $440, respectively, for its outings.

WHALE-WATCHING ★★   When it's time to spot some whales, you have two choices. You can take a whale-watching cruise or head over to **Lime Kiln State Park** ★★, where a short trail leads down to a rocky coastline from which orca whales, minke whales, Dall's porpoises, and sea lions can sometimes be seen. The best months to see orcas are June to September, but it's possible to see them year-round.

Three-hour whale-watching trips from Roche Harbor Resort, on the north side of the island, are offered by **San Juan Safaris** (℡ **800/450-6858** or 360/ 378-1323; www.sanjuansafaris.com), which charges $49 for adults and $39 for children 4 through 12. This company also operates boats out of Friday Harbor. Whale-watching cruises lasting from 4 to 6 hours are offered in the summer by **San Juan Excursions** (℡ **800/80-WHALE** or 360/378-6636; www.watch whales.com), which operates out of Friday Harbor. Cruises are $49 for adults and $39 for children age 4 to 12. You can have a more personalized experience with **Maya's Whale Watch Charters** (℡ **360/378-7996;** www.mayaswhale watch.biz), which goes out on a small boat that carries only six paying passengers (and that is also the fastest whale-watching boat in the San Juans). This is one of the only whale-watching companies that goes out year-round. A 3-hour tour with this company also costs $49.

WHERE TO STAY

In addition to the hotels, B&Bs, and inns listed here, there are also lots of vacation rentals available on San Juan Island through **Windermere San Juan Island,** 520 Spring St. (P.O. Box 488), Friday Harbor, WA 98250 (© **800/262-3596** or 360/378-3600; www.windermeresji.com). Rates range from $800 to $4,000 per week.

Expensive

Friday Harbor House ★★   With its contemporary yet distinctly Northwest architecture, this luxurious little boutique hotel brings urban sophistication to Friday Harbor. From the hotel's bluff-top location you can see excellent views of the ferry landing, the adjacent marina, and, in the distance, Orcas Island. Guest rooms have fireplaces and double whirlpool tubs, which make this place a great choice for a romantic getaway. As you relax in your tub, you can gaze out at both the view and your own crackling fire. Most rooms have decks or balconies.

All About Orcas

Although once known as killer whales and much maligned as the wolves of the deep, orcas whales, which are members of the porpoise family, are actually highly intelligent, family-oriented animals. Orcas can be found in every ocean, but one of their highest concentrations is in the waters stretching north from Puget Sound along the coast of British Columbia. Consequently, this has become one of the most studied and most publicized populations of orcas in the world.

These whales, which can grow to 30 feet long and weigh almost 9,000 pounds, are the largest member of the porpoise family. In the wild, they can live for up to 80 years, with female orcas commonly living 20 to 30 years longer than males. Orcas are among the most family-oriented animals on earth, and related whales will often live together for their entire lives, sometimes with three generations present at the same time. Family groups frequently band together with other closely related groups into extended families known as pods. A community of orcas consists of several pods, and in this region the community numbers around 100 individuals. There are three distinct populations of orcas living in the waters off Vancouver Island, British Columbia. They are referred to as the northern and southern resident communities and the transient community. It's the southern resident community that whale-watchers in the San Juan Islands are most likely to encounter.

As predators, orcas do live up to the name "killer whale," and have been known to attack other whales much larger than themselves. Some orcas off the coast of Argentina even swim up onto the shore, beaching themselves to attack resting sea lions, then thrashing and twisting their way back into the water. However, not all orcas feed on other marine mammals. Of the three communities in this area, only the transients feed on mammals. The two resident communities feed primarily on salmon, which are abundant in these waters, especially off the west side of San Juan Island during the summer.

These are some of the best rooms in the San Juan Islands, and if you enjoy contemporary styling, you'll love this place. The dining room is one of the best on the island and serves Northwest cuisine.

130 West St. (P.O. Box 1385), Friday Harbor, WA 98250. © 866/722-7356 or 360/378-8455. Fax 360/378-8453. www.fridayharborhouse.com. 20 units. Mid-June to Sept $210–$280 double, $310 suite; Oct to mid-June $150–$200 double, $260 suite. Rates include continental breakfast. AE, DISC, MC, V. **Amenities:** Restaurant (Northwest); lounge; massage. *In room:* TV/VCR, minibar, fridge, coffeemaker, hair dryer, iron.

Lakedale Resort ★★ (Kids)

Although best known as the island's favorite private campground, Lakedale Resort also has six very attractive modern cabins and a 10-room lodge that is a luxurious rendition of a classic log mountain lodge. The cabins are attractively and individually decorated and have porches that overlook the forest, and all have two bedrooms, two bathrooms, a full kitchen, and a gas fireplace. There's a hot tub in a gazebo, and guests have access to the resort's 82 acres, which include trails and several lakes that are good for swimming, canoeing (boat rentals are also available), and trout fishing. Think of this as a sort of summer camp for the entire family. Lots of fun and very woodsy. Guests staying in the lodge get a continental breakfast.

4313 Roche Harbor Rd., Friday Harbor, WA 98250. © 800/617-2267 or 360/378-2350. Fax 360/378-0944. www.lakedale.com. 16 units. $120–$195 lodge double; $160–$265 cabin. 2- to 3-night minimum. MC, V. Children over 13 welcome in lodge; children under 4 stay free in parent's cabin. **Amenities:** Jacuzzi; canoe rentals. *In room:* No phone in cabins.

Roche Harbor Village ★★ (Kids)

Located at the north end of the island, Roche Harbor Village is steeped in island history, with the historic Hotel de Haro, established in 1886, serving as the resort's centerpiece. A brick driveway and manicured gardens provide the foreground for the white two-story hotel, which overlooks the marina and has porches running the length of both floors. Although the rooms in the Hotel de Haro are quite basic (all but four have shared bathrooms) and have not been updated in years, the building has loads of atmosphere. The best accommodations here, however, are the four new luxury McMillin suites in a restored home adjacent to the historic hotel. These suites are among the finest rooms on the island. The modern condominiums are good bets for families. The resort's dining room has a view of the marina, and the deck makes a great spot for a sunset cocktail. In addition to amenities listed below, there are whale-watching cruises, sea kayak tours, a marina, and a general store.

248 Reuben Memorial Dr. (P.O. Box 4001), Roche Harbor, WA 98250. © 800/451-8910 or 360/378-2155. Fax 360/378-6809. www.rocheharbor.com. Historic hotel: 20 units, 16 with shared bathroom. Modern accommodations: 25 condos, 9 cottages, 4 suites. Mid-May to Sept $79–$99 double with shared bathroom, $139–$299 suite, $129–$299 condo, $155–$229 cottage. Lower rates Oct to mid-May. AE, MC, V. **Amenities:** 3 restaurants (Continental/Northwest, American); lounge; outdoor pool; 2 tennis courts; bike and moped rentals; coin-op laundry. *In room:* Hair dryer, iron.

Moderate

Friday's Historic Inn ★

Located right in downtown Friday Harbor only 2 blocks from the ferry landing, this small hotel is conveniently located and offers a few affordable rooms (and even the more expensive rooms are relatively good deals considering the generally high room rates on the island). The less expensive guest rooms are small and simply furnished, with the occasional antique and unusual driftwood headboards in some rooms. A few of the rooms have kitchenettes and eight have double whirlpool tubs. The best rooms are the new ground-floor rooms, including a two-bedroom suite that's a good choice for families. Most rooms have a TV and VCR, and many also have in-room Jacuzzi tubs, kitchenettes, or fireplaces.

35 First St. (P.O. Box 2023), Friday Harbor, WA 98250. (C) **800/352-2632** or 360/378-5848. www.friday-harbor. com. 18 units, 4 with shared bathroom. $99–$129 double with shared bathroom; $149–$299 double with private bathroom. Rates include continental breakfast. MC, V. **Amenities:** Massage. *In room:* No phone.

Olympic Lights Bed and Breakfast ★★   Located at San Juan's dry southwestern tip, the Olympic Lights is a Victorian farmhouse surrounded by windswept meadows, and if it weren't for the sight of Puget Sound out the window, you could easily mistake the setting for the prairies of the Midwest. There are colorful gardens, an old barn, even some hens to lay the eggs for your breakfast. The ocean breezes, nearby beach, and friendliness of innkeepers Christian and Lea Andrade lend a special feel to this American classic. Our favorite room here is the Ra Room, which is named for the Egyptian sun god and features a big bay window. The view out the windows is enough to settle the most stressed-out soul.

146 Starlight Way, Friday Harbor, WA 98250. (C) **888/211-6195** or 360/378-3186. Fax 360/378-2097. www. olympiclights.com. 4 units. May–Oct $125–$135 double; Nov–Apr $95 double. Rates include full breakfast. No credit cards. *In room:* No phone.

Campgrounds

Lakedale Campground ★★, 4313 Roche Harbor Rd., Friday Harbor, WA 98250 ((C) **800/617-2267** or 360/378-2350; www.lakedale.com), is 4 miles north of Friday Harbor. With over 80 acres, several lakes, and campsites for tents as well as RVs, this private campground makes an ideal spot for a family vacation. Rates vary by season and number in party; check out the website for the latest camping fees.

Our favorite campground on the island is **San Juan County Park** ★★, 380 Westside Rd. N. ((C) **360/378-8420** for information, or 360/378-1842 for reservations), which has unbeatable views and is set on the site of an old waterfront farm. Campsites are $23 to $32 per night, and reservations can be made up to 90 days in advance.

WHERE TO DINE

In addition to the restaurants listed below, Friday Harbor has several other places where you can get a quick, simple meal. About a block from the top of the ferry lanes is **The Market Chef**, 225 A St. ((C) 360/378-4546), a combination espresso bar and gourmet take-out restaurant that also bakes outrageously good chocolate chip cookies. Just around the corner, you'll find **Felicitations**, 120 Nichols St. ((C) **360/378-1198**), which is the best bakery on the island. Although it's hard to find, **Backdoor Kitchen & Catering**, 400b A St. ((C) **360/378-9540**), is worth searching out for its eclectic menu. At the **Garden Path Café**, 135 Second St. ((C) **360/378-6255**), you'll find a good selection of deli salads, soups, and baked goods.

If you're up near the north end of the island and suddenly find yourself hungry for lunch or a light dinner, try the **Lime Kiln Cafe** ((C) **360/378-2155**) on the dock at Roche Harbor Resort. This lively little cafe serves filling breakfasts and good chowder and fish and chips. Big windows let you gaze out at the boats in the marina.

Duck Soup Inn ★★ NORTHWEST/INTERNATIONAL   This restaurant 4½ miles north of Friday Harbor sums up the San Juans experience. Duck Soup is rustic and casual, set in a tranquil rural setting beside a small pond, and yet it serves superb multi-course dinners. Inside this quintessentially Northwestern building you'll find lots of exposed wood and a fieldstone fireplace. The menu changes frequently, depending on the availability of fresh produce, but it is always very creative. The chef has a penchant for the flavors of Asia and the Mediterranean. You might find sea scallops seared with Indian spices or Parmesan-and-herb-crusted quail. Of course, you're also likely to find duck, perhaps served in sour cherry–juniper sauce, and even soup made with duck broth!

50 Duck Soup Lane. ☎ 360/378-4878. www.ducksoupinn.com. Reservations highly recommended. Main courses $14–$29. MC, V. Summer Tues–Sun 5:30–8:30 or 9pm; spring and fall Fri–Sat 5:30–8:30 or 9pm. Closed Nov to early Apr.

Friday Harbor House Dining Room ★★ NORTHWEST   Located in the luxurious Friday Harbor House boutique hotel, this is the most sophisticated restaurant on San Juan Island. Striking contemporary decor sets the tone, but doesn't distract diners from the harbor views out the glass walls. The menu is short and relies heavily on local ingredients, including island-grown greens and Westcott Bay oysters (perhaps prepared with chanterelle mushrooms and Parmesan cheese). The chef draws on diverse inspirations for the dishes served here, which are always attractively presented and carefully prepared. A recent menu included succulent grilled prawns with a red-curry cocktail sauce and perfectly cooked wild salmon with a caper-herb sauce.

130 West St. ☎ 360/378-8455. Reservations highly recommended. Main courses $17–$27. AE, DISC, MC, V. Daily 5:30–9pm.

The Place Bar & Grill ★★ NORTHWEST/INTERNATIONAL   Located on the waterfront to the right as you get off the ferry and housed in a small wooden building that was once part of a U.S. Coast Guard station, this aptly named establishment is San Juan Island's finest waterfront restaurant. With lots of local art on the wall, The Place aims to attract the upscale Seattle market and is right on target. The menu changes regularly, with an emphasis on seafood preparations such as Asian-style crab cakes and Pacific Rim bouillabaisse.

1 Spring St. ☎ 360/378-8707. Reservations highly recommended. Main courses $19–$29. MC, V. Daily 4:30–9:30 or 10pm (Tues–Sat in winter).

Vinny's ★★ ITALIAN   From the name you might guess that this place is some dark dive serving New York–style pizza. Not exactly. Located across the street from the Friday Harbor House and claiming the same good views of the marina, Vinny's is San Juan Island's premier Italian restaurant. This is the sort of place you discover on the first night of your visit and decide to eat at every night until you leave. Local oysters and mussels are highlights of the appetizer menu, although the calamari with pine nuts, tomatoes, raisins, lemon, and vinaigrette should not be missed. This is seafood country, for sure, but the charbroiled steaks are a big hit (try one with Gorgonzola-Parmesan butter), and the menu features plenty of well-prepared standards such as lasagna and *penne alla puttanesca*—roughly translated: pasta like a prostitute would make it. In other words, spicy.

165 West St. ☎ 360/378-1934. Reservations recommended. Main courses $14–$34. AE, DISC, MC, V. Daily 5–10pm (in winter until 9pm Sun–Thurs).

ORCAS ISLAND

Orcas Island, the largest of the San Juans, is also the most beautiful of the islands. If you have time to visit only one island, make it Orcas. The island, which covers 58 square miles, is a particular favorite of nature lovers who come to enjoy the views of green rolling pastures, the hiking trails of Moran State Park, the forested mountains (at 2,409 ft. tall, Mount Constitution is the highest point in the islands), and fjord-like bays (East Sound, West Sound, and Deer Harbor).

EXPLORING THE ISLAND

Eastsound is the largest town on the island and has several interesting shops and good restaurants. Shops here worth checking out include **Darvill's Rare Print Shop,** Horseshoe Highway (© 360/376-2351), which sells antique prints and maps, and the adjacent **Darvill's Book Store** (© 360/376-2135), which specializes in Northwest fiction, history, and guidebooks. Just outside Eastsound, on Horseshoe Highway, you'll find **Howe Art** (© 360/376-2945; www.howeart.net), a studio and gallery run by sculptor Anthony Howe, who fashions fascinating hanging kinetic sculptures from stainless steel. The studio is open Tuesday through Sunday from 10am to 5pm. Other smaller villages include Deer Harbor, West Sound, and Olga.

To learn a little about the history of Orcas Island, drop by the **Orcas Island Historical Museum,** 181 N. Beach Rd., Eastsound (© 360/376-4849; www.orcasisland.org/~history). Between late May and September, the museum is open Tuesday through Sunday from 1 to 4pm (Fri until 7pm). Admission is $1. At the **Lambiel Home Museum** (© 360/376-4544), on Horseshoe Highway southeast of Eastsound, you can view a private collection of artwork by 169 artists from around the San Juan Islands. The museum is open daily by appointment. Admission is $10 and tours take about 2 hours.

Around the island you'll find several interesting pottery shops. A few miles west of Eastsound off Enchanted Forest Road is **Orcas Island Pottery,** 366 Old Pottery Rd. (© 360/376-2813; www.orcasislandpottery.com), the oldest pottery studio in the Northwest. Between Eastsound and Orcas on Horseshoe Highway is **Crow Valley Pottery,** 2274 Orcas Rd. (© 360/376-4260; www.crowvalley.com), in an 1866 log cabin. On the east side of the island in the community of Olga, you'll find **Orcas Island Artworks,** Horseshoe Highway (© 360/376-4408), which is full of beautiful work by island artists.

SPORTS & OUTDOOR ACTIVITIES

Moran State Park 🎯🎯 (© 360/376-2326; www.parks.wa.gov), which covers approximately 5,252 acres of the island, is the largest park in the San Juans and the main destination of most visitors to Orcas Island. If the weather is clear, you'll find great views from the summit of Mount Constitution, which rises 2,409 feet above Puget Sound. There are also five lakes and 33 miles of hiking trails. Fishing, hiking, boating, mountain biking, and camping are all popular park activities. The park is off Horseshoe Highway, approximately 13 miles from the ferry landing, and there is a $5 parking fee within the park.

BICYCLING   Although Orcas is considered the most challenging of the San Juan Islands for bicycling, plenty of cyclists still pedal the island's roads. One of the best places to rent bikes here is from **Dolphin Bay Bicycles** (© 360/376-4157; www.rockisland.com/~dolphin), which is located just to the right as you get off the ferry. From here you can explore Orcas Island or take a free ferry to Lopez Island or Shaw Island. Bikes rent for $30 per day, $70 for 3 days, and $100 for a week. Guided bike rides are also sometimes available. In Eastsound, you can rent bikes from **Wildlife Cycles,** North Beach Road, Eastsound (© 360/376-4708; www.wildlifecycles.com). Bikes rent for $30 to $40 per day. If you're exploring the island by mountain bike, you may want to take the unpaved Dolphin Bay Road to Eastsound; otherwise, take the Crow Valley Road.

BIPLANE RIDES   For a very fun overview of Orcas Island, try a scenic biplane ride in a restored 1929 Travelair. Thirty-minute flights with **Magic Air**

Tours (℡ **800/376-1929** or 360/376-2733; www.magicair.com) cost $200 for two people ($175 for one person).

BOAT TOURS, RENTALS & CHARTERS   Want to explore some of the outer islands or try a bit of mountain biking on a seldom visited island? Contact **North Shore Charters** (℡ **360/376-4855;** www.sanjuancruises.net), which offers a shuttle service ($55–$75 per person for two people) to some of the smaller islands. This company does a mountain-biking tour to Sucia Island ($95 per person for two people).

Big Wave Sea Adventures Company (℡ **800/732-4095** or 360/376-7078; www.bigwaveonline.com) operates exciting high-speed boat rides all the way around Orcas Island and out to some of the state marine park islands north of Orcas. Along the route, you'll likely see harbor seals, porpoises, bald eagles, and other wildlife (though usually not whales). Trips stop on Patos Island where you can hike the island trails. The basic 3-hour tour costs $100 per person.

If you're interested in heading out on the water aboard a 1940s sloop, contact Captain Ward Fay at **Classic Day Sails** (℡ **360/376-5581;** www.classicdaysails.com). Captain Fay charges $50 per person for a 3-hour cruise (with a two-person minimum and a maximum of six). At the **Rosario Resort Activities Center** (℡ **360/376-2222**), you can arrange a 3-hour sail ($65 per person) aboard the *Morning Star,* a 56-foot, two-masted sailboat.

At Rosario you can also rent a bareboat or skippered sailboat from **Orcas Sailing** (℡ **360/376-2113;** www.orcassailing.com), which charges $120 to $145 for a half-day bareboat rental and $220 to $260 for a 4-hour skippered charter. You can also rent small sailboats and powerboats at **Orcas Boat Rentals,** Deer Harbor Marina, Deer Harbor Road (℡ **360/376-7616;** www.orcasboats.com), which charges between $175 and $225 for an 8-hour rental.

GOLF   Golfers can head to the nine-hole **Orcas Island Country Golf Club,** 2171 Orcas Rd. (℡ **360/376-4400**) near Eastsound. Nine holes cost $22 and 18 holes cost $30. Golf carts are an additional $15 to $20.

HIKING   With 33 miles of hiking trails, Moran State Park offers hikes ranging from short, easy strolls alongside lakes, to strenuous, all-day hikes. South of the community of Olga, on the east arm of the island, you'll also find a half-mile trail through **Obstruction Pass Park** ★★. This trail leads to a quiet little cove that has a few walk-in/paddle-in campsites. The park is at the end of Obstruction Pass Road. You can learn all about the natural history and plant life of the islands on guided hikes offered by **Gnats Nature Hikes** (℡ **360/376-6629;** www.orcasislandhikes.com). Half-day hikes ($30) head out on the trails of Moran State Park, or take you by boat to another island to do your hiking ($65).

SCUBA DIVING   Sure the waters are cold, but they're usually quite clear and there's lots to see. If you're interested in diving the waters off Orcas Island, make arrangements through **Island Dive & Water Sports** (℡ **800/303-8386** or 360/378-2772; www.divesanjuan.com), which operates out of Rosario Resort. A two-tank boat dive is $75.

SEA KAYAKING ★★   The best way to see the Orcas Island coast is by sea kayak. Located at the Orcas Island ferry landing, **Orcas Outdoors** (℡ **360/376-4611;** www.orcasoutdoors.com) offers guided sea-kayak tours lasting from 1 hour ($25) to overnight ($220). Three-hour guided tours ($49) are offered by **Shearwater Adventures** (℡ **360/376-4699;** www.shearwaterkayaks.com). Two-hour paddles ($25) are offered by **Spring Bay Inn** (℡ **360/376-5531;**

www.springbayinn.com), which is located on the east side of the island near the village of Olga. These trips are in an area where bald eagles nest in the summer.

WHALE-WATCHING ⭐⭐   If you want to see some of the orca whales for which the San Juans are famous, you can take a whale-watching excursion with **Deer Harbor Charters** (© 800/544-5758 or 360/376-5989; www.deerharbor charters.com), which operates out of both Deer Harbor and Rosario Resort and charges $47 for adults and $32 for children; or with **Orcas Island Eclipse Charters** (© 800/376-6566; www.orcasislandwhales.com), which operates out of the Orcas Island ferry dock and charges $47 for adults and $30 for children.

WHERE TO STAY
Expensive
The Inn at Ship Bay ⭐⭐   Set on a high bluff just outside the village of Eastsound, this inn boasts a tranquil setting and rooms that are both luxurious and very comfortable. Pillow-top king beds and gas fireplaces make it easy to spend way too much of your visit just cozying up in the rooms here. And, if you sit back in the Adirondack chairs on your balcony and gaze out over the water, you may never leave. Although guest rooms are in modern buildings that have been designed to look old, the centerpiece of the inn is an 1869 home that now serves as the inn's restaurant.

326 Olga Rd. (P.O. Box 1374), Eastsound, WA 98245-1374. © 877/276-7296 or 360/376-5886. Fax 360/376-4675. www.innatshipbay.com. 11 units. Summer $150–$195 double, $250–$295 suite; fall–spring lower rates. AE, DISC, MC, V. **Amenities:** Restaurant (Northwest). *In room:* TV, dataport, fridge, coffeemaker.

The Inn on Orcas Island ⭐⭐   Looking as if it were transplanted directly from Cape Cod or Martha's Vineyard, this inn blends traditional styling with contemporary lines to create a classically inspired beauty. Situated on a meadow overlooking a marsh just off Deer Harbor, the inn has rooms in the main house plus a cottage and a carriage house that has its own kitchen. Rooms can best be described as Martha Stewart meets Eddie Bauer—a blend of feminine and masculine styling. There are rooms with balconies and suites with jetted tubs, and all the accommodations have water views. A sun room in the main house is a wonderful place to while away the morning.

114 Channel Rd. (P.O. Box 309), Deer Harbor, WA 98243. © 888/886-1661 or 360/376-5227. Fax 360/376-5228. www.theinnonorcasisland.com. 5 units. May–Oct $145 double, $175–$245 suite, cottage, or carriage house; Nov–Apr $125 double, $145–$225 suite, cottage, or carriage house. Rates include full breakfast. 2-night minimum May–Oct, all weekends, and holidays. AE, MC, V. Children under 18 not accepted. **Amenities:** Bikes. *In room:* Dataport, fridge.

The Resort at Deer Harbor ⭐⭐   Set on an open hillside above the spectacular Deer Harbor inlet, this casual resort looks across the water to a forested cliff and offers the best views on the island. Add to this a few small islands at the mouth of the inlet and a marina with sailboats bobbing at anchor, and you have the quintessential island setting. Each of the 26 cottages has a hot tub on its porch; of these, 11 are particularly luxurious accommodations that have fireplaces, separate seating areas, and double whirlpool tubs in the bathrooms. The **Starfish Grill,** the resort's casual and moderately priced bistro, is one of the best restaurants in the San Juans.

P.O. Box 200, Deer Harbor, WA 98243. © 888/376-4480 or 360/376-4420. Fax 360/376-5523. www.deerharbor.com. 26 units. July–Sept $189–$399 suite or cottage; Oct–June $129–$299 suite or cottage. Rates include continental breakfast. AE, DISC, MC, V. **Amenities:** Restaurant (International); outdoor pool; Jacuzzi; massage. *In room:* A/C, TV, fridge, coffeemaker, hair dryer, iron.

Rosario Resort & Spa ★★★ *(Kids)* Rosario is the most luxurious accommodations on Orcas Island and is the only place in the San Juans that can actually claim to be a resort. Although the resort has a wide variety of modern accommodations, the centerpiece remains the 1904 Moran Mansion, an imposing white stucco building on the shore of Cascade Bay. This mansion houses the resort's main dining room, lounge, spa, and library. The larger and more luxurious rooms (with fireplaces and good views) are across the marina and up a steep hill from this main building. However, for the ultimate in luxury, stay in the Round House, a suite in an unusual round building set on a rocky knoll near the marina.

1400 Rosario Rd., Eastsound, WA 98245. ✆ **800/562-8820** or 360/376-2222. Fax 360/376-2289. www. rosarioresort.com. 116 units. June to mid-Oct $229–$399 double, $369–$650 suite; mid-Oct to May $129–$299 double, $269–$550 suite. AE, DC, DISC, MC, V. **Amenities:** 3 restaurants (American, seafood); lounge; poolside bar; 1 indoor and 2 outdoor pools; tennis court; exercise room; full-service spa; Jacuzzi; sauna; watersports equipment rentals; concierge; car-rental desk; limited room service; massage; babysitting; coin-op laundry. *In room:* TV, coffeemaker, hair dryer, iron, free local calls.

Spring Bay Inn ★★ Just by virtue of being one of the only waterfront B&Bs in the San Juans, this inn would deserve a recommendation. However, innkeepers Sandy Playa and Carl Burger, both retired park rangers, make a stay here both fun and educational, and the setting and inn are great for a romantic getaway. You can soak in the hot tub on the beach and watch the sunset, spot bald eagles from just outside the inn's front door, hike on the nature trails, and best of all, go for a guided sea-kayak tour each morning. All of the guest rooms have a woodstove, two have views from their tubs, and two have balconies. There's even wireless Internet connectivity.

P.O. Box 97, Olga, WA 98279. ✆ **360/376-5531.** Fax 360/376-2193. www.springbayinn.com. 5 units. $220–$260 double. 2-night minimum. Rates include continental breakfast, brunch, and daily kayak tour. DISC, MC, V. **Amenities:** Jacuzzi; watersports equipment; concierge; activities desk. *In room:* Dataport, fridge, hair dryer, free local calls.

Turtleback Farm Inn ★★ Nowhere on Orcas will you find a more idyllic setting than this bright-green restored farmhouse overlooking 80 acres of farmland at the foot of Turtleback Mountain. Simply furnished with antiques, the guest rooms range from cozy to spacious, and each has its own special view. Our favorite room in the main house is the Meadow View Room, which has a private deck and a claw-foot tub. The four rooms in the Orchard House are among the biggest and most luxurious on the island (gas fireplaces, claw-foot tubs, balconies, wood floors, refrigerators). Days here start with a big farm breakfast served at valley-view tables that are set with bone china, silver, and linen, or, if you are staying in the Orchard House, with a breakfast delivered to your room. Finish your day with a nip of sherry by the fire. Although there is one small room that is moderately priced, most rooms here fall in the expensive category.

1981 Crow Valley Rd., Eastsound, WA 98245. ✆ **800/376-4914** or 360/376-4914. Fax 360/376-5329. www. turtlebackinn.com. 11 units. Main house: May 1–Oct 15 $90–$175 double; Orchard House: June 15–Sept 15 $225 double. Lower rates other months. Rates include full breakfast. 2-night minimum stay June 15–Sept 15, weekends and holidays. DISC, MC, V. **Amenities:** Access to nearby health club; concierge; massage. *In room:* Hair dryer, iron.

Moderate

Cascade Harbor Inn ★ Formerly a part of Rosario Resort, this hotel enjoys similar Eastsound views and is adjacent to both the Rosario marina and Moran State Park. Guest rooms range from standard motel rooms to studios with Murphy beds to spacious suites with kitchens. All the rooms have water views, though in some cases the view is somewhat hidden by trees. The lodge sits on a steep hillside above the water, and a path leads down to the Rosario marina.

1800 Rosario Rd., Eastsound, WA 98245. ✆ 800/201-2120 or 360/376-6350. Fax 360/376-6354. www.cascade harborinn.com. 48 units. Summer $129–$399 double; spring and fall $90–$279 double; winter $65–$199 double. Children 9 and under stay free in parent's room ($10 for children 10–17). Rates include continental breakfast (summer only). AE, DISC, MC, V. **Amenities:** Concierge. *In room:* TV, coffeemaker, free local calls.

The Kingfish Inn ✦ *Finds* Housed in the old West Sound general store, this inn is about as quaint as they come. Downstairs, the old general store has been converted into a cozy little cafe, while upstairs, there are three rooms with views over West Sound. These views are among the best on the island. The fourth room is just off the cafe's deck. However, the upstairs rooms are much more attractively furnished, with a sort of Tuscan feel, and you should try to get one of them. These rooms have rustic armoires and beautiful beds with fluffy duvets. One of the rooms has a woodstove and one has a picture-perfect porch. Bathrooms, however, are very basic and have showers only.

Deer Harbor and Crow Valley roads, Westsound (mailing address 4362 Crow Valley Rd., Eastsound, WA 98245). ✆ 360/376-4440. www.kingfishinn.com. 4 units. $90–$140 double. Rates include breakfast. MC, V. **Amenities:** Restaurant (American); access to nearby health club; bike rentals; sea-kayak rentals; massage. *In room:* TV/VCR, hair dryer, iron.

Orcas Hotel ✦ Located right at the Orcas ferry landing, this B&B is a good choice for anyone coming over without a car. On the other hand, the proximity of the ferry precludes the tranquil setting available at other island B&Bs. Nonetheless, the Orcas is an attractive old Victorian hotel and has been welcoming guests since 1904. The guest rooms, done in a simple country style, vary in size, but all are carpeted and furnished with antiques. A couple of the rooms have whirlpool tubs with stained-glass windows above them. On the first floor of this three-story building you'll find a lounge, bakery/cafe, and a good restaurant, which together can meet all your dining needs should you be using this hotel as a base for a car-free vacation here on Orcas.

P.O. Box 155, Orcas, WA 98280. ✆ 888/672-2792 or 360/376-4300. Fax 360/376-4399. www.orcashotel.com. 12 units, 8 with private bathroom. $79–$109 double with shared bathroom; $99–$159 double with half bathroom; $105–$198 double with private bathroom. Rates include continental breakfast. AE, MC, V. **Amenities:** 2 restaurants; lounge; concierge. *In room:* No phone.

Campgrounds

With 151 sites, **Moran State Park** ✦✦ (✆ 360/376-2326) is the most popular camping spot on the island. Reservations are accepted (and highly recommended) May 15 through September 15 and can be made up to 9 months in advance through **Washington State Parks Reservations** (✆ 888/226-7688; www.parks.wa.gov). Additional campsites are available at the **Doe Bay Village Resort & Retreat** ✦ (✆ 360/376-2291; www.doebay.com), a sort of Deadhead beach resort. If you enjoy roughing it, there are hike-in or paddle-in sites at **Obstruction Pass State Park** ✦ at the south end of the east arm of the island (near Olga). Keep in mind that there is no water available at this isolated and beautifully situated park.

WHERE TO DINE

For baked goods, imported cheeses, and other gourmet foodstuffs, stop by **Rose's,** 382 Prune Alley (✆ 360/376-4292), which is in Eastsound Square. For great cookies, don't miss **Teezer's Cookies** (✆ 360/376-2913) at the corner of North Beach Road and A Street. In West Sound, at the corner of Deer Harbor Road and Crow Valley Road, the **West Sound Cafe** (✆ 360/376-4440), housed in a former general store and with a great view of the water, serves good breakfasts, lunches, and light meals.

Bilbo's Festivo ⭐ MEXICAN   If you catch the scent of a mesquite fire as you wander the streets of Eastsound, it isn't your imagination. At this casual restaurant housed in an old bungalow in the heart of Eastsound, the Southwest comes to the Northwest. The garden outside is purely Northwestern but the stucco, tile work, and low wall around the patio dining area all say New Mexico. The menu, though it has plenty of Mexican standards, is most noteworthy for its more unusual regional dishes such as mesquite-grilled chicken in an herb-and-orange juice marinade or mesquite-grilled flank steak marinated in lime juice. Summers see the crowds lining up to get into the restaurant's patio where the barbecue grill stays fired up with mesquite. The margaritas here are the best on the island.

N. Beach Rd., Eastsound. ☎ 360/376-4728. Reservations recommended. Main courses $8–$18. MC, V. Apr–Sept Mon–Thurs 4–9pm, Fri–Sun 11:30am–3pm and 5–9pm; Oct–Mar daily 4–9pm.

Cafe Olga ⭐ (Finds) INTERNATIONAL   Housed in an old strawberry-packing plant that dates from the days when these islands were known for their fruit, Cafe Olga is a good spot for reasonably priced breakfasts and lunches. Everything here is homemade, using fresh local produce whenever possible. The blackberry pie is a special treat, especially when accompanied by Lopez Island Creamery ice cream. This building also houses Orcas Island Artworks, a gallery representing more than 65 Orcas Island artists.

Horseshoe Hwy., Olga. ☎ 360/376-5098. Main courses $7–$15. MC, V. Daily 10am–6pm (until 5pm Nov–Dec). Closed Jan–Feb.

Christina's ⭐⭐ NORTHWEST   Located on the second floor of an old waterfront building in Eastsound, Christina's has a beautiful view down the sound, just right for sunsets. If the weather is pleasant, the deck is *the* place on the island for sunset dinner. The menu here is short, changes regularly, and features innovative cuisine prepared with an emphasis on local ingredients. For the most part, Christina's showcases its creativity in its appetizers rather than in its entrees, so whether you crave the unusual or the familiar, you'll likely be satisfied here. The desserts can be heavenly.

Porter Building, 310 Main St., Eastsound. ☎ 360/376-4904. www.christinas.net. Reservations highly recommended. Main courses $26–$34. DISC, MC, V. Summer daily 4–9pm; fall–spring Thurs–Mon 4–9pm. Closed 3 weeks in Nov.

The Inn at Ship Bay ⭐⭐ NORTHWEST   About midway between Eastsound and the turnoff for the Rosario Resort, you'll spot the Inn at Ship Bay, an old white house that sits in a field high above the water. (Should you arrive after dark and be tempted to walk over to the water, be aware that the restaurant's front yard ends in a sheer cliff.) Inside, you'll find plenty of windows to let you gaze out to sea. Chef Geddes Martin worked at nearby Rosario Resort for many years and now brings his skills to his own kitchen. You can't miss with the local oysters on the half shell, and the clam chowder is excellent. If the mussels in shallot-saffron broth are on the menu, don't miss them. There are always plenty of other great seafood dishes on the menu as well.

326 Olga Rd., Eastsound. ☎ 877/276-7296 or 360/376-5886. www.innatshipbay.com. Reservations recommended. Main courses $18–$24. AE, DISC, MC, V. Tues–Sat 5:30–9pm.

Olga's ⭐⭐ (Finds) ECLECTIC   Until a few years ago, the building that now houses Olga's was a little general store. However, it has now been transformed into an unforgettable breakfast and lunch spot serving unexpectedly creative and delicious dishes. This is the sort of place you at first think is too expensive and then later realize was absolutely your favorite restaurant in the islands. The menu changes regularly, but look for tiger-prawn pasta, halibut chowder, a fried-oyster Caesar salad, and a Monte Cristo sandwich made with fresh-baked brioche. If you're full, looking at the dessert menu is tantamount to self-flagellation. There's also a very eclectic gift shop on the premises.

Olga Road, Olga. 🕐 360/376-5862. www.olgasonorcas.com. Main courses $10–$16. MC, V. Daily 9am–5pm.

The Sunflower Café ⭐⭐ NORTHWEST   Located in the village of Eastsound, this casual and eclectic restaurant serves some of the most creative cuisine on the island, and whether you come for lunch, dinner, or even Sunday brunch, you'll likely leave pleasantly surprised by your meal here. Sure you can start your meal with a good cup of oyster stew, but you might also encounter African peanut soup or steamed clams in cilantro-lime broth. At lunch try the mahimahi tacos or the grilled halibut sandwich. At dinner, the pumpkin-seed and cumin-dusted halibut is a winner.

A St. and Prune Alley, Eastsound. 🕐 360/376-2335. Reservations recommended. Main courses $9–$12 lunch, $18–$20 dinner. MC, V. Mon–Fri 11:30am–2:30pm and 5:30–8:30pm; Sat–Sun 8:30am–2:30pm and 5:30–8:30pm.

LOPEZ ISLAND

Of the three islands with accommodations, Lopez is the least developed. Although it is less spectacular than Orcas or San Juan, it is flatter, which makes it popular with bicyclists who often prefer easy grades to stunning panoramas. Lopez maintains more of its agricultural roots than either of the two previously mentioned islands, and likewise has fewer activities for tourists. If you just want to get away from it all and hole up with a good book for a few days, Lopez may be the place for you.

EXPLORING THE ISLAND

Lopez Village is the closest this island has to a town, and here you'll find almost all of the island's restaurants and shops. Here in the village, you'll also find the **Lopez Island Historical Museum** (🕐 360/468-2049), where you can learn about the island's history and pick up a map of historic buildings. In July and August the museum is open Wednesday through Sunday from noon to 4pm. In May, June, and September, it's open Friday through Sunday from noon to 4pm.

   Lopez Island Vineyards ⭐, 724B Fisherman Bay Rd. (🕐 **360/468-3644;** www.lopezislandvineyards.com), located between the ferry landing and Lopez Village, was until recently the only winery that actually made wine from fruit grown here in the San Juans. Both their Siegerrebe and Madeleine Angevine are from local grapes, as are their organic fruit wines. They also make wines from grapes grown in the Yakima Valley. In summer, the winery tasting room is open Wednesday through Saturday from noon to 5pm; spring and fall, it's open on Friday and Saturday from noon to 5pm.

SPORTS & OUTDOOR ACTIVITIES

Eight county parks, one state park, and various Bureau of Land Management and San Juan County Land Bank properties provide plenty of access to the woods and water on Lopez Island. The first park off the ferry is **Odlin County Park** (🕐 360/468-2496), which has a long beach, picnic tables, and a campground. Athletic fields make this more of a community sports center than a natural area, so this should be a last resort camping choice. For a more natural setting within a short easy hike, check out **Upright Channel Park,** which is on

Doing the Lopez Wave

Want to feel like a Lopez Island native? As you drive the island, give passing cars a quick wave of the hand. Among the friendly residents of this island, the drivers' greeting is so commonplace that it has come to be known as the Lopez Wave.

Military Road (about a mile north of Lopez Village in the northwest corner of the island). This secluded park has a short beach and is often totally deserted. A little farther south and over on the east side of the island, you'll find **Spencer Spit State Park** ✴ (© **360/468-2251**), which also has a campground. Here, the forest meets the sea on a rocky beach that looks across a narrow channel to Frost Island. You can hike the trails through the forest or explore the beach. South of Lopez Village on Bay Shore Road, you'll find the small **Otis Perkins Park,** which is between Fisherman Bay and the open water and has one of the longest beaches on the island.

Down at the south end of the island, you'll find the tiny **Shark Reef Sanctuary** ✴✴, where a short trail leads through the forest to a rocky stretch of coast that is among the prettiest on all the ferry-accessible islands. Small islands offshore create strong currents that swirl past the rocks here. Seals and occasionally whales can be seen just offshore. This is a great spot for a picnic.

BIKING ✴✴   Because of its size, lack of traffic, numerous parks, and relatively flat terrain, Lopez is a favorite of cyclists. You can rent bikes for $5 to $20 an hour or $25 to $65 a day from **Lopez Bicycle Works & Kayaks,** 2847 Fisherman Bay Rd. (© **360/468-2847;** www.lopezbicycleworks.com), at the marina on Fisherman Bay Road.

SEA KAYAKING ✴✴   If you want to explore the island's coastline by kayak, contact **Lopez Island Sea Kayaks** (© **360/468-2847;** www.lopezkayaks.com), which is located at the marina on Fisherman Bay Road and is open May through October. Tours cost $75 for a full-day trip with lunch included. Single kayaks can also be rented here for $12 to $25 per hour, or $25 to $50 per half day. Double kayaks rent for $20 to $35 per hour and $40 to $60 per half day.

WHERE TO STAY

Edenwild Inn ✴✴   Located right in Lopez Village, this modern Victorian B&B is a good choice if you've come here to bike or want to use your car as little as possible. Within a block of the inn are all the island's best restaurants. Most of the guest rooms here are quite large, and most have views of the water. All the rooms have interesting antique furnishings, and several have fireplaces. In summer, colorful gardens surround the inn, and guests can breakfast on a large brick patio. The front veranda, overlooking Fisherman Bay, is a great place to relax in the afternoon.

132 Lopez Rd. (P.O. Box 271), Lopez Island, WA 98261. © **800/606-0662** or 360/468-3238. www.edenwild inn.com. 8 units. $110–$170 double. Lower rates Oct–Mar. Rates include full breakfast. AE, MC, V. *In room:* No phone.

Lopez Farm Cottages and Tent Camping ✴✴ *Value*   Set on 30 acres of pastures, old orchards, and forest between the ferry landing and Lopez Village, these modern cottages are tucked into a grove of cedar trees on the edge of a large lawn (in the middle of which stand several huge boulders). From the outside, the board-and-batten cottages look like old farm buildings, but inside you'll find a combination of Eddie Bauer and Scandinavian design. There are kitchenettes, plush beds with lots of pillows, and, in the bathrooms of four of the cottages, showers with double shower heads. If showering together isn't romantic enough for you, there's a hot tub tucked down a garden path. Also on the property is a deluxe tents-only campground.

555 Fisherman Bay Rd., Lopez Island, WA 98261. © 800/440-3556. www.lopezfarmcottages.com. 5 units. $99–$175 double. Tent sites (available May–Oct) $33 double. Cottage rates include continental breakfast. MC, V. **Amenities:** Jacuzzi. *In room:* Kitchenette, fridge, coffeemaker.

Lopez Islander Resort ★ *Kids*   Located about a mile south of Lopez Village, the Lopez Islander may not look too impressive from the outside, but it's a very comfortable lodging. All the rooms have great views of Fisherman Bay, and most rooms have balconies. The more expensive rooms have coffeemakers, wet bars, microwaves, and refrigerators. In addition to amenities listed below, the Islander has a full-service marina with kayak rentals.

Fisherman Bay Rd. (P.O. Box 459), Lopez Island, WA 98261. © 800/736-3434 or 360/468-2233. Fax 360/468-3382. www.lopezislander.com. 31 units. July–Sept $90–$143 double, $200–$260 suite. Lower rates Oct–June. Children under 18 stay free in parent's room. AE, DISC, MC, V. **Amenities:** Restaurant (American); lounge; outdoor pool; tennis court; exercise room; Jacuzzi; bike rentals; coin-op laundry. *In room:* TV, fridge, coffeemaker, hair dryer, iron.

MacKaye Harbor Inn ★   This former sea captain's home was originally built in 1904 and was the first home on the island to have electric lights. Since that time this old house has gone through many incarnations, and is today a very comfortable B&B with a mix of classic country styling and plenty of modern creature comforts. Located down at the south end of the island, the big white farmhouse is set on a pretty little stretch of flat beach. There's a tea cottage out in the garden, and massages, as well as afternoon tea, can be taken in this sunny little building. With kayaks for rent and the calm water of MacKaye Harbor right across the road, this is a good place to give sea kayaking a try. There are also bikes available for guests and the innkeepers can direct you to good hikes in the area. The inn also rents two beautiful Cape Cod–style apartments in an adjacent carriage house.

949 MacKaye Harbor Rd., Lopez Island, WA 98261. © 888/314-6140 or 360/468-2253. Fax 360/468-2393. www.mackayeharborinn.com. 7 units, 2 with shared bathroom. $89–$195 double. 2-night minimum weekends and holidays. Rates include breakfast. MC, V. Pets accepted in carriage house ($200–$500 deposit). **Amenities:** Access to nearby health club; bikes; sea-kayak rentals/instruction. *In room:* Hair dryer.

Campgrounds

Spencer Spit State Park (© 360/468-2251) is the island's largest and best campground. This park has 37 campsites set amid tall fir trees. Campsites are $10 to $22 per night, and reservations can be made by contacting **Washington State Parks** (© 888/226-7688; www.parks.wa.gov/reserve.asp). There are also campsites at **Odlin County Park** (© 360/468-2496 for information, or 360/378-1842 for reservations, which are taken noon–4pm Mon–Fri), which is just south of the ferry landing and has 30 campsites along the water. Athletic fields make this more of a community sports center than a natural area. Campsites are $11 to $19 per night. Tent campsites are also available at the privately owned **Lopez Farm Cottages and Tent Camping** ★★, 555 Fisherman Bay Rd. (© 800/440-3556; www.lopezfarmcottages.com), which has 10 walk-in campsites about 2½ miles south of the ferry landing. These campsites have a very private feel, and both showers and a covered cooking area are provided. This campground is open May through October. Campsites are $33 per night for one or two people, and campers must be 14 or older.

WHERE TO DINE

When it's time for espresso, head to Lopez Village and drop by **Isabel's Espresso** (© **360/468-4114**), a locals' hangout in the Village House Building on the corner of Lopez Road North, Lopez Road South, and Old Post Road. Across the street, you'll find divinely decadent pastries and other baked goods at **Holly B's Bakery** (© **360/468-2133**). For fresh-squeezed juices and healthy light meals, try **Vortex Juice Bar & Good Food,** Lopez Road South (© **360/468-4740**), which is located in Lopez Village in the Old Homestead. Turn up Village Road North and you'll find **Vita's Wildly Delicious** (© **360/468-4268**), which is housed in a colorfully painted Victorian house and sells wines and delicious gourmet takeout food. A little farther along this same street is the **Lopez Island Old-Fashioned Soda Fountain,** 157 Village Rd. (© **360/468-4511**), which is located in the Lopez Island Pharmacy. During the summer, there's a Saturday farmers market across the street from these latter two businesses.

Bay Café ⭐⭐ NORTHWEST/INTERNATIONAL   Housed in an eclectically decorated old waterfront commercial building with a deck that overlooks Fisherman Bay, the Bay Café serves some of the best food in the state. This is the sort of place where diners animatedly discuss what that other flavor is in the molé sauce on the pork tenderloin and where people walk through the door and exclaim, "I want whatever it is that smells so good!" The menu, though short, spans the globe and changes frequently. Come with a hearty appetite; meals include soup and salad, and the desserts are absolutely to die for and often come decorated with colorful flower petals. Accompany your meal with a bottle of wine from Lopez Island Vineyards for the quintessential Lopez dinner.

Village Center, Lopez Village. © **360/468-3700.** Reservations highly recommended. Main courses $18–$26. AE, DISC, MC, V. Daily 5–8:30pm (hours may vary in winter).

Bucky's ⭐ AMERICAN   With a laid-back island feeling and an outside waterfront deck, this tiny place is where the locals hang out. The food, though simple, is consistently good—nothing fancy, just delicious. The black-and-blue burger with blue cheese and Cajun spices definitely gets our vote for best burger in the islands. If you feel more like seafood, there are fish tacos and fish and chips.

Lopez Village Plaza. © **360/468-2595.** Reservations taken for parties of 5 or more only. Main courses $6–$16. MC, V. Apr–Sept daily 11:30am–8:30pm. Closed Oct–Mar.

SHAW ISLAND

Shaw Island is the least developed of the four San Juan Islands served by regular ferries. Most San Juan visitors know Shaw Island only as the island where the nuns run the ferry dock. In addition to having a convent, the island is home to a few hundred tranquillity-loving residents who like the solitude of the island and want to keep it undeveloped. If you enjoy leisurely drives (or bike rides) in the country, Shaw Island makes a good day trip from any of the other three islands. However, there are no hotels, B&Bs, or restaurants, only a general store at the ferry landing and one small county park down at the south end of the island. The park, **Shaw Island County Park** (© **360/378-1842**), does, however, have a small campground (that takes summer reservations) and is popular with sea kayakers. Reservations can be made up to 90 days in advance.

THE OTHER SAN JUAN ISLANDS: SEA-KAYAK TRIPS & CHARTER BOAT CRUISES

If you want to explore some of the other 168 islands that are not served by the ferries, you'll need a boat. Sailboats, powerboats, and sea kayaks are all popular vessels for exploring these other San Juans, and during the summer months, the waters are full of vessels of all shapes and sizes. Although many of the islands are private property, a few are, or have on them, state parks with campsites. If you want to find out about these marine parks, contact the **Washington State Parks Information Center** (© 360/902-8844; www.parks.wa.gov). Those without their own boat can still visit some of these islands either on a multi-day kayak tour, on a boat excursion, or on a charter boat cruise.

See "The Active Vacation Planner" in chapter 2, "Planning Your Trip to Washington," for information on companies offering multi-day sea-kayak tours in the San Juan Islands.

Charter boats, both motorboats and sailboats, can also be hired for multi-day cruises around the San Juan Islands. This is the easiest (though not the cheapest) way to see some of these outer islands. Anchoring in secluded coves, exploring marine parks, scanning the skies for bald eagles, spying on orcas, porpoises, and sea lions—these are the activities that make a charter cruise through the San Juans such a memorable experience.

During the summer, **Viking Cruises** (© 888/207-2333 or 360/466-2639; www.vikingcruises.com) operates 3-day/2-night San Juan cruises that overnight at Rosario Resort on Orcas Island. Rates are $483 to $527 per person, and though the trips are usually booked by groups, individuals can often find space on these cruises. Cruises of from 5 to 8 days are offered by **Fantasy Cruises** (© 800/234-3861 or 360/378-1874; www.sanjuanislandcruises.com). These cruises, aboard a 125-foot cruise ship that carries only 34 passengers, stop not only in the San Juans, but at other picturesque area ports including La Conner and Port Townsend. Boats can also be chartered through **Anacortes Yacht Charters** (© 800/233-3004; www.ayc.com), which has both powerboats and sailboats in its fleet.

Know Before You Go

If you're considering adding Victoria or Vancouver, British Columbia, to your travel plans, be sure you have the necessary documents to make the trip across the border and back. U.S. citizens born in the United States need to carry proof of U.S. citizenship (a birth certificate or passport), although often a picture ID such as a driver's license is all that is asked for at the border. Play it safe and carry a birth certificate or passport. If you are not a citizen of the U.S. or Canada, you need to carry your passport and valid visa (if you needed a visa to enter the country). For naturalized U.S. citizens (those not born in the U.S.), a passport or certificate of naturalization is required. Children traveling with both parents must have a birth certificate or passport. Children traveling with only one parent should have both a birth certificate/passport and either a custody document or death certificate for the absent parent. A notarized letter of consent to travel signed by both parents or guardians is advised for children traveling without their parents or guardians.

4 La Conner & the Skagit Valley

70 miles N of Seattle, 10 miles E of Anacortes, 32 miles S of Bellingham

In a competition for quaintest town in Washington, La Conner would leave the other contenders wallowing in the winter mud. This town, a former fishing village, has a waterfront street lined with restored wooden commercial buildings, back streets of Victorian homes, and acres of tulip and daffodil fields stretching out from the town limits. Add to this three museums, numerous plant nurseries and gardening-related stores, art galleries, luxurious inns, and good restaurants, and you have a town almost too good to be true.

La Conner does, however, have a couple of shortcomings. In the springtime, when the tulips blossom, the town and surrounding country roads are so jammed with cars that it can make a Seattle rush-hour commute seem pleasant. The other drawback is that La Conner is so close to the San Juans that it is hard to justify spending more than a day here when the islands are calling. If, however, you have some free time in your schedule, this town should not be missed.

La Conner dates from a time when Puget Sound towns were connected by water and not by road, and consequently, the town clings to the shore of Swinomish Channel. The town reached a commercial peak around 1900 (when steamers made the run to Seattle) and continued as an important grain- and log-shipping port until the Great Depression. La Conner never recovered from the hard times of the 1930s, and when the highways bypassed the town it became a neglected backwater. The wooden false-fronted buildings built during the town's heyday were spared the waves of progress that swept over the Northwest during the latter half of the 20th century, and today these quaint old buildings give the town its charm.

Beginning in the 1940s, La Conner's picturesque setting attracted several artists and writers. By the 1970s, La Conner had become known as an artists' community, and tourism began to revive the economy. The town's artistic legacy eventually led to the building here of the Museum of Northwest Art, which is dedicated to the region's many contemporary artists.

Adding still more color to this vibrant little town are the commercial flower farms of the surrounding Skagit Valley. In the spring, tulips and daffodils carpet the surrounding farmlands with great swaths of red, yellow, and white. These flowers are grown to supply the fall bulb planting needs of gardeners across the country, and heartbreaking as it sounds, the flowers are cut off in their prime to channel more energy into the bulbs.

One more thing, although the name sounds as if it's a combination of Spanish and Irish, La Conner is actually named for Louisa A. (LA) Conner, who helped found the town in the 1870s.

ESSENTIALS

GETTING THERE   From I-5, take U.S. 20 west toward Anacortes. La Conner is south of U.S. 20 on La Conner–Whitney Road. Alternatively, take exit 221 off I-5 and head west on Fir Island Road to a left onto Chilberg Road, which leads into La Conner.

The **Airporter Shuttle** (© 866/235-5247 or 360/380-8800; www.airporter. com) operates between Sea-Tac Airport and the Anacortes ferry terminal, stopping at the Farmhouse Inn, which is at the junction of Wash. 20 and La Conner–Whitney Road, north of La Conner ($30 one-way, $53 round-trip).

VISITOR INFORMATION   Contact the **La Conner Chamber of Commerce,** 413 Morris St. (P.O. Box 1610), La Conner, WA 98257 (© **888/642-9284** or 360/466-4778; www.laconnerchamber.com).

FESTIVALS   For a few short weeks each year, from late March to mid-April, the countryside around La Conner is awash with color as hundreds of acres of Skagit Valley tulip and daffodil fields burst into bloom in a floral display that rivals that of the Netherlands. These flowers are grown for their bulbs, which each fall are shipped to gardeners all over the world. The **Skagit Valley Tulip Festival** (© **360/428-5959;** www.tulipfestival.org), held each year during bloom time, is La Conner's biggest annual festival and includes dozens of events. Contact the festival office or stop by the La Conner Chamber of Commerce (see above), for a scenic tour map of the flower fields. On festival weekends area roads are clogged with cars, so you should consider opting to ride the Tulip Transit buses that loop through the flower fields. Contact the festival office to find out about these buses.

Whether you're here in tulip time or not, you might want to stop by some of the area's farms, gardens, and nurseries. **Roozengaarde Flowers & Bulbs,** 15867 Beaver Marsh Rd. (© **800/732-3266** or 360/424-8531; www.tulips.com), is the largest grower of tulips, daffodils, and irises in the country and has a gift shop. At **Christianson's Nursery & Greenhouse,** 15806 Best Rd. (© **360/466-3821**), you'll find more than 600 varieties of roses and lots of other plants as well. Nearby you can tour the beautiful English country gardens of **La Conner Flats,** 15920 Best Rd. (© **360/466-3190**), where high tea is served by reservation. Both of these nurseries are northeast of town off McLean Road (the main road to Mount Vernon). At the visitor center in La Conner, you can pick up the **Skagit Valley Farm Trails** map, which will help you find other area farms.

EXPLORING LA CONNER & ITS ENVIRONS

The **Museum of Northwest Art** ★★, 121 S. First St. (© **360/466-4446;** www. museumofnwart.org), occupies a large contemporary building in downtown La Conner. The museum, which mounts a variety of exhibits throughout the year, features works by Northwest artists, including Morris Graves, Mark Tobey, and Guy Anderson, all of whom once worked in La Conner. This museum would be right at home in downtown Seattle, so it comes as a very pleasant surprise to find it in this tiny town. It's open daily from 10am to 5pm; admission is $4 for adults and $2 for students and children 12 and over, free for children under 12. You can also see art around the streets of downtown La Conner where more than a dozen sculptures (all for sale) are set up each year in the spring.

High atop a hill in the center of town, you can learn about the history of this area at the **Skagit County Historical Museum,** 501 S. Fourth St. (© **360/466-3365;** www.skagitcounty.net/museum). It's open Tuesday through Sunday from 11am to 5pm; admission is $4 for adults, $3 for seniors and children ages 6 to 12, free for children 5 and under. A few blocks away, you'll find the **La Conner Quilt Museum,** 703 S. Second St. (© **360/466-4288;** www.laconnerquilts. com), which is housed in the historic Gaches Mansion. On the first floor of this museum, you'll find rooms furnished with antiques, while on the second floor there are quilt displays. The museum is open Wednesday through Saturday from 11am to 4pm and Sunday from noon to 4pm; admission is $4. Two blocks down the street from the Gaches Mansion is the much more humble **Magnus Anderson Cabin,** built in 1869 by the area's first white settler. Beside the cabin is the **La Conner Town Hall,** which is housed in a triangular bank building that was built in 1886. Across the street from these two buildings is **Totem Pole Park,** which in addition to having a totem pole, has a dugout canoe carved by local Swinomish artisans, whose reservation is just across the Swinomish Channel.

There is excellent bird-watching around the Skagit Valley, especially during the winter months when migratory waterfowl, including trumpeter swans and snow geese, and various raptors, including peregrine falcons and bald eagles, flock to the area's marshes, bays, and farm fields. Eight miles north of La Conner at the **Padilla Bay National Estuarine Research Reserve and Breazeale Interpretive Center,** 10441 Bayview-Edison Rd. (© 360/428-1558; www.padillabay.gov), you can bird-watch along 3 miles of trails through fields and along a dike. Interpretive exhibits explain the importance of estuaries and allow visitors to explore life in Padilla Bay and its salt marshes. The reserve is open daily; the interpretive center, Wednesday through Sunday from 10am to 5pm. Admission is free. The Skagit Wildlife Area, south of La Conner and west of Conway, is another good winter birding area.

Shopping is the most popular pastime in La Conner, and as you wander up and down First Street, stop in at **The Wood Merchant,** 709 S. First St. (© **360/ 466-4741**), which features handcrafted wooden furniture and accent pieces; and **Earthenworks Gallery,** 713 S. First St. (© **360/466-4422;** www.earthenworks gallery.com), which has fine crafts in ceramic, glass, wood, and other media. Other interesting shops include **Two Moons,** 620 S. First St. (© **360/466-1920;** www.twomoonsgallery.com), a gallery featuring regional art and fine crafts; and **Caravan Gallery,** 619 S. First St. (© **360/466-4808**), which sells fascinating crafts and jewelry from around the world.

After a hard day of touring the tulip fields, wouldn't a massage feel great? You can make an appointment at **Watergrass Day Spa,** 117 Maple Ave. (© **877/ 883-8899;** www.watergrassdayspa.com).

If you are heading north to Bellingham, consider driving the scenic Chuckanut Drive, which begins about 15 miles north of La Conner. For details on this beautiful stretch of road, see "Chuckanut Drive" in "Bellingham & Environs," below.

WHERE TO STAY

La Conner Channel Lodge ★★ Luxurious accommodations, Northwest styling, and views of Swinomish Channel from all but seven of the rooms make this a truly memorable lodge. A flagstone entry and woodsy garden, cedar-shake siding, and a river-rock fireplace in the lobby set the tone for the rest of the lodge, and the lobby, with its small library alcove, has the sort of nautical feel you'd expect to find in a home built by a ship's captain 100 years ago. Most guest rooms are large and all have small balconies and gas fireplaces. Fir accents and a combination of slate flooring and carpeting give the rooms a natural richness.

205 N. First St., La Conner, WA 98257. © 888/466-4113 or 360/466-1500. Fax 360/466-1525. www.laconner lodging.com. 40 units. Apr and July–Sept $130–$285 double; Oct–Mar and May–June $130–$140 double. Rates include continental breakfast. AE, DC, DISC, MC, V. *In room:* TV, fridge, coffeemaker, hair dryer, iron.

La Conner Country Inn ★★ Under the same management as the La Conner Channel Lodge, the Country Inn is a much more casual, folksy sort of place. Although it's also in downtown La Conner, it's set back a block from the water and lacks much in the way of views. However, if you can do without the water views, you'll save a bundle on your room bill. The board-and-batten exterior of the inn gives the impression that this is a mountain lodge, though the interior is more modern country inn than classic mountain lodge. In the cozy lobby there's a huge stone fireplace, and every guest room also has its own fireplace. The second-floor rooms have high, beamed ceilings, for that rustic country-inn feel. Although the rooms are fairly large, the furnishings are quite basic. Room no. 28 has the feel of a separate cottage and is worth requesting.

107 S. Second St., La Conner, WA 98257. (℄ 888/466-4113 or 360/466-3101. Fax 360/466-5902. www.laconner lodging.com. 28 units. Apr and July–Sept $99–$130 double; Oct–Mar and May–June $92–$102 double. Rates include continental breakfast. AE, DC, DISC, MC, V. Pets accepted ($25). **Amenities:** Restaurant (International); pub. *In room:* TV, coffeemaker.

White Swan Guest House 🌟   If you're here for the tulip blossoms or if you're a gardener, make this your first choice. Located out in the country, this yellow Victorian farmhouse is set beneath ancient poplar trees and is surrounded by stunning perennial gardens. Of the guest rooms in the main house, we like the one with the turret, though all are comfortable enough. For more space and privacy, opt for the rustic little cottage set on the far side of the gardens. Peter Goldfarb, the owner, bakes up some of the best chocolate chip cookies around.

15872 Moore Rd., Mount Vernon, WA 98273. www.thewhiteswan.com. (℄ 360/445-6805. 4 units, including 1 (cottage) with private bathroom. $75–$85 double; $140–$175 cottage. Rates include continental breakfast. MC, V. *In room:* No phone.

The Wild Iris 🌟🌟   The Wild Iris is a modern Victorian inn on the edge of town, and most second-floor rooms have views of distant Mount Baker (these rooms are definitely worth asking for). The inn was designed for romantic weekends, and many of the rooms have double whirlpool tubs. In some the whirlpool tub is in the room, while in others it's on the balcony. Friday and Saturday, dinner is also available ($18–$26 for entrees) in the inn's small dining room, which serves up some of the best meals in town. This is a good bet for a romantic getaway.

121 Maple Ave. (P.O. Box 696), La Conner, WA 98257. (℄ 800/477-1400 or 360/466-1400. www.wildiris.com. 19 units. $109 double; $129–$189 suite. Rates include full breakfast. AE, MC, V. **Amenities:** Restaurant (Northwest); concierge. *In room:* TV, dataport.

WHERE TO DINE

Kerstin's 🌟🌟 NORTHWEST   Located in a tall, narrow building across the street from the water, this contemporary restaurant and wine bar is your best bet in the area for a romantic dinner. Kerstin's also serves the most creative menu in town. While it looks from the street as though this restaurant only has a couple of tables, you'll find a larger dining room on the second floor. The local Samish Bay oysters, baked on the half shell, should not be missed. You'll also find plenty of other well-prepared local seafood, including wild salmon (perhaps with a lime-butter sauce). Lamb shanks, prepared various ways, also show up regularly on the menu.

505 S. First St. (℄ 360/466-9111. Reservations recommended. Main courses $9–$12 lunch, $18–$32 dinner. AE, MC, V. Daily noon–9pm.

La Conner Brewing Company 🌟 *(Finds)* PIZZAS/PUB FARE   If you eschew tourist haunts when it comes time to dine, then you might want to check out the menu at this stylish modern pub. A favorite of the locals, the pub lacks water views but more than makes up for this with its excellent beers and creative pub fare. While pizzas are the main beer accompaniment here, there are also interesting panini, quesadillas (including one with smoked salmon), and good Caesar salads.

117 S. First St. (℄ 360/466-1415. www.laconnerbrewing.com. Main courses $7.50–$11. MC, V. Sun–Thurs 11:30am–8 or 8:30pm; Fri–Sat 11:30am–9pm.

Nell Thorn Restaurant & Pub ★★ INTERNATIONAL   Some of La Conner's finest meals are to be had at this cozy little restaurant attached to the La
Conner Country Inn. The emphasis is on fresh, local, and organic, and the menu
in the main dining room is limited. You might start with a warm scallop salad or
local oysters dusted with lavender-scented herbes de Provence. For a main course,
the beach bowl, which is packed with local fish and shellfish, is delicious. If you're
in the mood for a more casual meal, dine in the tiny downstairs pub, where you
can get soups, salads, and sandwiches. The abundance of wood and the cramped
quarters of the pub give it the feel of a room on an old sailing ship.

La Conner Country Inn, 205 E. Washington Ave. ✆ 360/466-4261. Reservations recommended. Main
courses $11–$22. AE, MC, V. Mon–Thurs 4–10pm; Fri 4–11pm; Sat 11:30am–11pm; Sun 11:30am–10pm.

5 Bellingham & Environs

90 miles N of Seattle, 60 miles S of Vancouver

Perhaps best known outside of Washington state as the southern terminus for ferries heading north to Alaska, Bellingham is a vibrant little city that boasts excellent views of the San Juan Islands. Still an active shipping port, Bellingham has, at
Squalicum Harbor, a large commercial and private boat marina, a hotel and commercial complex, and a park that together provide residents and visitors with a
chance to enjoy the bay. South of downtown Bellingham, near the Alaska ferry terminal, is the historic community of Fairhaven. Fairhaven's old brick commercial
buildings and interesting shops are a highlight of a visit to Bellingham.

Bellingham is in Whatcom County, which extends from the coast to the top
of 10,778-foot Mount Baker and beyond; it is still primarily a rural area. Near
the coast, farming predominates, and the nearby farm towns of Ferndale and
Lynden are worth visiting for a glimpse of local history and a chance to explore
the countryside. At Mount Baker there is a popular downhill skiing and snowboarding area in winter, while in summer hiking trails lead through meadows
and forests. South of the city, the mountains and saltwater come together along
one of Washington's most scenic stretches of coastline. Winding along this coastline is Chuckanut Drive, which provides glimpses of rugged shores, expansive
waters, and the San Juan Islands.

ESSENTIALS

GETTING THERE   I-5 connects Bellingham with Seattle to the south and
Vancouver to the north. Wash. 542, the North Cascades Scenic Highway, connects Bellingham with eastern Washington by way of Winthrop.

Bellingham International Airport (✆ 460/671-5674; www.portofbellingham.
com/airport), 5 miles northwest of downtown Bellingham, is served by Horizon
Airlines. The **Airporter Shuttle** (✆ 866/235-5247 or 360/380-8800; www.
airporter.com) runs between Sea-Tac Airport and Bellingham ($32 one-way, $55
round-trip).

Both **Amtrak** trains and **Greyhound** buses stop in Bellingham at the
Fairhaven Station, which is adjacent to the Bellingham Cruise Terminal on Harris Avenue in the Fairhaven district.

VISITOR INFORMATION   Contact the **Bellingham/Whatcom County
Convention & Visitors Bureau,** 904 Potter St., Bellingham, WA 98226 (✆ 800/
487-2032 or 360/671-3990; www.bellingham.org), which is located just east of
I-5 at exit 253. On the Internet, check out http://whatcom.kulshan.com, which is
filled with great information on the area.

GETTING AROUND   Rental cars are available at Bellingham International Airport from Avis, Budget, and Hertz. If you need a taxi, contact **Yellow Cab** (✆ **360/734-8294**). Public bus service around the Bellingham area is provided by the **Whatcom Transportation Authority** (✆ **360/676-7433;** www.ride wta.com).

WHAT TO SEE & DO
MUSEUMS
If your interest is art, you shouldn't miss the **Western Washington University Outdoor Sculpture Collection,** off the Bill McDonald Parkway south of downtown. With more than 20 large sculptures, including one by Isamu Noguchi, this is the largest collection of monumental sculptures on the West Coast. You can pick up a map and guide to the collection at Bellingham/Whatcom County Convention & Visitors Bureau, at the university's visitor center, or at **Western Gallery** (✆ **360/650-3900;** www.westerngallery.wwu.edu), which is also on the campus and features exhibits of contemporary art. When the university is in session, the gallery is open Monday, Tuesday, Thursday, and Friday from 10am to 4pm, Wednesday from 10am to 8pm, and Saturday from noon to 4pm.

American Museum of Radio ★★   These days MP3s, CDs, and DVDs are so much a part of everyday life that it is easy to forget that sound recording is barely 100 years old. At this not-to-be-missed museum in downtown Bellingham, you can examine more than 800 antique radios (mostly pre-1930s wooden table-top models) and lots of other unusual instruments of early electrical technology. Among the displays is a mock-up of the radio room from the *Titanic,* and if you're lucky, curators Jonathon Winter or John Jenkins might demonstrate the Tesla coil, which can generate enough electricity to light up a fluorescent light several feet away. There's even an original Theremin, which was sort of a forerunner to modern electronic synthesizers.

1312 Bay St. ✆ **360/738-3886.** www.americanradiomuseum.org. Free admission. Wed–Sat 11am–4pm.

Whatcom Museum of History and Art ★★   This museum is housed in the former city hall building, which was built in 1892 and is one of Washington's finest examples of Victorian municipal architecture. Inside you'll find reconstructions of old stores from early-20th-century Bellingham, and a variety of exhibits on area history. You'll also find a large collection of Native American baskets, and exhibits focusing on Northwest artists. Up on the museum's third floor you'll find old toys, tools, and fashions. A building across the street houses the gift shop and a gallery that often is used for unusual art installations. A block away, in the city's old fire hall, you'll find a photo archive and more historical exhibits.

121 Prospect St. ✆ **360/676-6981.** www.whatcommuseum.org. Admission by donation. Tues–Sun noon–5pm.

FAIRHAVEN HISTORIC DISTRICT
Though downtown Bellingham has a fair number of restaurants and a few galleries, the **Fairhaven Historic District** is the most interesting neighborhood in town (and is also the site of the Bellingham Cruise Terminal, the southern terminus for ferries to Alaska). Fairhaven was once a separate town, and many of its brick buildings, built between 1880 and 1900, have now been restored and house interesting shops, art galleries, and several good restaurants. Around the neighborhood, you'll find more than two dozen historical markers, many of which commemorate the seamier side of life in Fairhaven in the 1890s.

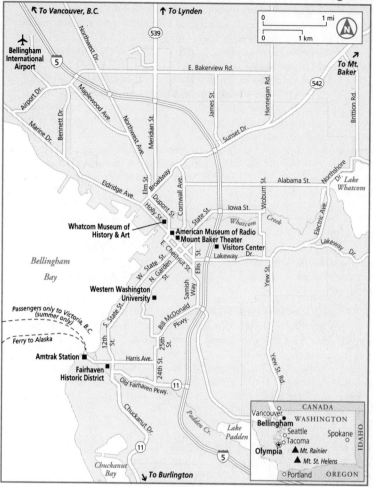

Today, **Village Books,** 1210 11th St. (© **360/671-2626;** www.villagebooks. com), serves as the cultural anchor for the neighborhood and has readings and book signings. Here in Fairhaven, you'll also find several cafes and bakeries and even an old double-decker British bus that serves fish and chips.

CHUCKANUT DRIVE

Chuckanut Drive (Wash. 11), which begins on the southern edge of the Fairhaven Historic District and heads south for almost a dozen miles to the Samish farmlands, is one of the most scenic stretches of road in northwestern Washington. The road clings to the shoreline of Chuckanut and Samish bays as it winds south through the Chuckanut Mountains, which rise straight out of the water. Though most of the way is through dense woods, there are several pull-offs where you can gaze out to the San Juan Islands or up and down the rugged coastline. There are also numerous trail heads that allow you to head down to the shore or up into the Chuckanut Mountains, which are home to an extensive network of hiking and mountain-biking trails. Chuckanut Drive is particularly popular at sunset, and there are several good restaurants at the southern end of the drive (see "Where to Dine," below).

At the northern end of the drive, be sure to stop in at the **Chuckanut Bay Gallery and Garden Shop,** 700 Chuckanut Dr. (© **360/734-4885**), which is full of interesting artworks by Northwest artists and craftspeople. Continuing south, watch for the **North Chuckanut Mountain Trail Head,** which provides access to **Teddy Bear Cove** 🐾🐾, where you'll find a pair of tiny beaches separated by a small, rocky promontory. It's about a 2-mile round-trip hike to the cove. Although part of the trail is quite steep, part of the route follows the **Interurban Trail** 🐾, a 6-mile-long hiking and mountain-biking trail that follows the route of an old trolley line and extends from Fairhaven Parkway and 20th Street in Fairhaven to **Larrabee State Park** 🐾🐾 (© **360/676-2093** or 360/902-8844). This latter park is the most popular stop along Chuckanut Drive and can be quite crowded in summer. The pretty little beach and access to miles of hiking trails make this a required stop along the scenic drive. Admission is $5.

To explore Chuckanut Bay from a sea kayak, contact **Moondance Sea Kayak Adventures** (© **360/738-7664**; www.moondancekayak.com), which offers half-day ($40 per person) and full-day ($70 per person) excursions that start at Larrabee State Park.

HISTORIC EXCURSION TRAIN

If you're a fan of riding the rails, check the schedule of the **Lake Whatcom Railway** (© **360/595-2218**; www.lakewhatcomrailway.com), which operates a historic excursion train from the town of Wickersham southeast of Bellingham. There are Saturday and Tuesday trips from early July to early September, as well as runs in October and December. Along the route, you'll get occasional glimpses of Mount Baker. The trips last 1½ hours and the fare is $10 for adults and $5 for children under age 18.

WHERE TO STAY

The Chrysalis Inn & Spa at the Pier 🐾🐾 *(Finds)*   The Chrysalis is the most luxurious hotel in Bellingham, and, with its contemporary lodge styling, perfectly captures the essence of the Northwest today. In the lobby, big walls of glass focus the attention on the waters of Bellingham Bay, but the slate floors, burnished wood beams, and fireplace all give the views some stiff competition. Guest rooms all have water views and are designed both for romantic getaways and for business travel. Double tubs, gas fireplaces, and window seats (complete with pillow and comforter) make these rooms the ideal place to hide away on a rainy Northwest weekend. To make a getaway even better, there is a full-service spa and a boldly styled wine bar serving good Mediterranean meals. About the only drawback to this inn is the presence of a railroad track between the inn and the water. However, excellent insulation keeps the train noises to a minimum and earplugs are provided free of charge.

804 10th St., Bellingham, WA 98225. © **888/808-0005** or 360/756-1005. www.thechrysalisinn.com. 43 units. Mid-May to Sept $179–$189 double, $245–$265 suite; Oct to mid-May $155–$169 double, $199–$239 suite. Rates include full breakfast. AE, DISC, MC, V. **Amenities:** Restaurant (Mediterranean); lounge; full-service spa; concierge; limited room service; massage; laundry service; dry cleaning. *In room:* A/C, TV/VCR, dataport, fridge, coffeemaker, hair dryer, iron.

Fairhaven Village Inn 🐾🐾   Although this hotel in the heart of Fairhaven was only recently constructed, it was designed to resemble an old hotel and blends in quite well with the adjacent historic buildings. There's even a cashier's cage for a front desk. Guest rooms are, however, quite modern and are tastefully traditional in their decor and furnishings. While the balcony rooms, which also have fireplaces, are the most luxurious rooms, they really aren't worth the additional cost since they only look out on adjacent rooftops (with the bay in the distance). The location, amid Fairhaven's shops and restaurants—only a few blocks from the Alaska ferry terminal—makes this one of Bellingham's best hotel choices.

1200 Tenth St., Bellingham, WA 98225. (C) 877/733-1100 or 360/733-1311. Fax 360/756-2797. www.nw countryinns.com. 22 units. Summer $139–$159 double, $279 suite; other months $109–$159 double, $239 suite. Rates include continental breakfast. Children 12 and under stay free in parent's room. AE, DC, DISC, MC, V. Pets accepted ($20). *In room:* A/C, TV, dataport, coffeemaker, hair dryer, iron.

Hotel Bellwether on Bellingham Bay ★★ This hotel is the centerpiece of Squalicum Harbor, which also includes several restaurants, shops, a marina, and grassy Zuanich Park. The marina setting served as the design theme for this hotel, which has a distinct yacht-club feel. Dark wood paneling abounds, and a traditional styling predominates. Guest rooms are large and have soaking tubs (for one person), fireplaces, and balconies. The hotel's most unusual room is a three-story "lighthouse" suite that was designed to resemble a lighthouse and has a viewing deck on its third floor. This hotel lacks much in the way of Northwest character and seems designed to appeal to an older and more conservative crowd than the nearby Chrysalis.

1 Bellwether Way, Bellingham, WA 98225. (C) 877/411-1200 or 360/392-3100. Fax 360/392-3101. www. hotelbellwether.com. 66 units. $129–$234 double; $174–$699 suite. Rates include continental breakfast. AE, DC, DISC, MC, V. Pets accepted ($65 nonrefundable deposit). **Amenities:** Restaurant (Northwest); lounge; putting green; exercise room; bike rentals; concierge; business center; limited room service; massage; laundry service; dry cleaning. *In room:* A/C, TV, dataport, minibar, coffeemaker, hair dryer, iron, safe.

NEARBY ACCOMMODATIONS

Resort Semiahmoo ★★★ Located on 1,100 acres at the end of a long sandy spit that reaches almost to Canada, Resort Semiahmoo is, despite the remote location, Washington's premier golf resort and health spa. Gables and gray shingles give the resort a timeless look, and throughout the classically styled interior of the main lodge are numerous lounges overlooking the water. Artwork abounds, with Native American and nautical themes prevailing. Not all guest rooms have views, but those that do have beds facing out to sea. The main dining room overlooks the water and offers excellent Northwest-style meals and an extensive wine list. There's also an oyster bar and lounge in an old salmon-packing plant. In addition to amenities listed below, the resort has a marina and paved bike and running paths. It's very popular with Canadians.

9565 Semiahmoo Pkwy., Blaine, WA 98230-9326. (C) 800/770-7992 or 360/318-2000. www.semiahmoo.com. 198 units. May–Sept $169–$259 double, $289–$399 suite; Oct–Apr $99–$199 double, $239–$319 suite (all rates plus $3 resort fee). Children 17 and under stay free in parent's room. AE, DC, DISC, MC, V. Pets accepted ($50 nonrefundable deposit). **Amenities:** 3 restaurants (Northwest, American); lounge; indoor and outdoor pool; 2 18-hole golf courses; 4 tennis courts; health club and exercise room; full-service spa; Jacuzzi; sauna; bike rentals; children's programs; game room; concierge; limited room service; massage; babysitting; laundry service; dry cleaning. *In room:* A/C, TV, dataport, fridge, coffeemaker, hair dryer, iron.

WHERE TO DINE
IN TOWN

For great coffee, stop in at **Tony's Coffee House,** 1101 Harris Ave. (C) **360/ 738-4710**), which has been a favorite Fairhaven hangout for many years. At downtown's **La Vie en Rose,** 111 W. Holly St. (C) **360/715-1839**), you can start your day with a French pastry. For regional microbrews, imported beers, and pub fare, try the very atmospheric and traditional **Archer Ale House,** 1212 Tenth St. (© **360/647-7002**), in a basement in Fairhaven; or, for locally brewed beers, try **Boundary Bay Brewery & Bistro,** 1107 Railroad Ave. (© **360/ 647-5593**), in downtown Bellingham.

Anthony's 🐾🐾 SEAFOOD   Just about every waterfront city from Bellingham to Olympia now boasts an outpost of Seattle's popular Anthony's seafood restaurant chain, and for good reason. These places just seem to do things right. This impressive lodgelike waterfront building has big walls of glass overlooking a marina, an open kitchen with an eating bar, a lounge, and a bi-level dining room that assures everyone a water view. Whether you're in the mood for fish and chips or swordfish with orange-tequila glaze, there is always plenty of variety on the menu. However, you can be sure there will be plenty of salmon (the alder-planked preparation is a Northwest classic). Monday through Friday, four-course sunset dinners ($15) are served from 4:30 to 6pm.

25 Bellwether Way. © **360/647-5588.** www.anthonys.com. Reservations recommended. Main courses $8–$13 lunch, $14–$30 dinner. AE, DISC, MC, V. Sun–Thurs 11:30am–9:30pm; Fri–Sat 11:30am–10:30pm.

Colophon Café & Deli 🐾 SOUPS/SANDWICHES   Northwesterners spend a lot of time in bookstores hiding from the rain, so, of necessity, bookstores often provide sustenance. Here at the Colophon, you can chill out with some ice cream in summer, warm up with an espresso in winter, or make a filling meal of the star attractions here—homemade soups. You'll always find African peanut soup on the menu, as well as big sandwiches, quiches, and salads. However, for a generation of Bellingham readers, the Colophon's desserts, and in particular its chocolate-chunk cake, have been the quintessential accompaniment to a good book.

In Village Books, 1208 11th St. © **360/647-0092.** www.colophoncafe.com. Main courses $5.50–$11. MC, V. Mon–Sat 9am–10pm; Sun 10am–8pm (summer, Sun 10am–10pm).

D'Anna's Café Italiano 🐾 ITALIAN   This casual little hole-in-the-wall in downtown Bellingham specializes in fresh house-made ravioli and has become so famous in the region that it is now turning out the tasty little pasta pillows for restaurants in Seattle. The standard ravioli fillings include cheese, spinach, or chard and meat. There are also seasonal fillings such as butternut squash or roasted red pepper. Your meal comes with a salad and a couple of slices of Sicilian bread, which is basically a thick-crust pizza. You can even accompany your meal with a glass of wine from nearby Mount Baker Vineyards. The menu is about the same at lunch and dinner, although portions and prices are a little higher in the evening. By the way, all the other pastas are also made in house.

1319 N. State St. © **360/714-0188.** Main courses $6–$11 lunch, $9–$18 dinner. AE, DISC, MC, V. Mon–Thurs 11:30am–2:30pm and 4:30–9pm; Fri 11:30am–2:30pm and 4:30–10pm; Sat 4:30–10pm; Sun 4:30–9pm.

Pacific Café 🐾🐾 NORTHWEST   Located in the Mount Baker Theater building, this romantic little cafe is, of course, the perfect spot for dinner before the show, but it's also a good choice for a flavorful lunch or dinner even if you aren't on your way to a performance. The menu is always eclectic and usually reflects current trends in flavor combinations, but you can be sure you'll find plenty of Asian and Mediterranean influences. The Thai chicken Panang coconut curry is a good bet if you like Thai food, as are the garlic-Parmesan prawns. Also keep an eye out for the passion fruit sorbet. Lunches are among the most creative in the city, and many of the same dishes served at dinner are also served at lunch. There's also an excellent wine list.

100 N. Commercial St. ℂ 360/647-0800. Reservations recommended. Main courses $9–$12 lunch, $15–$24 dinner. AE, MC, V. Mon–Thurs 11:30am–2pm and 5:30–8:30pm; Fri 11:30am–2pm and 5:30–9pm; Sat 5:30–9pm.

ON CHUCKANUT DRIVE

The Oyster Bar ★★ NORTHWEST   Located near the southern end of Chuckanut Drive, this restaurant is the most upscale and formal of the handful of restaurants along the scenic drive. Of course, as the name implies, fresh local oysters are one of the specialties here, but the restaurant also serves up a wide range of imaginative dishes, the likes of which you aren't likely to find on any other area menus: wild boar with wild mushroom gravy, salmon with champagne-raspberry-and-pistachio sauce, abalone with hazelnut-lime butter. There are also great views of Samish Bay and the distant San Juan Islands. Desserts here often feature local fruits and berries, and there is an excellent wine cellar.

2578 Chuckanut Dr. ℂ 360/766-6185. www.theoysterbaronchuckanutdrive.com. Reservations highly recommended. Main courses $7–$13 lunch, $15–$50 dinner. AE, MC, V. Daily 11:30am–10pm.

Rhododendron Café ★★ *Finds* NORTHWEST/INTERNATIONAL Located at the southern end of Chuckanut Drive amid the Samish farmlands, this place looks from the outside like any other farm-country roadside diner. However, take one look at the menu, and you'll find that the farmers in this area are a lucky group. The menu melds creative Northwest cookery with influences from around the world, and each month there are specials from a different part of the world. You might find Vietnamese, Guatemalan, Turkish, or Caribbean food on the menu when you stop by, and these adventurous specials are always worth trying. The regular menu includes lots of local produce, fresh herbs from the restaurant's garden, and oysters from nearby Samish Bay. The casual atmosphere and creative meals are a surprising and very welcome mix.

5521 Chuckanut Dr., Bow. ℂ 360/766-6667. www.rhodycafe.com. Main courses $7–$11 lunch, $12–$17 dinner. AE, DISC, MC, V. Wed–Fri 11:30am–9pm; Sat–Sun 9am–9pm. Closed Thanksgiving–Jan 1.

BELLINGHAM NIGHTLIFE

The **Mount Baker Theatre,** 104 N. Commercial St. (ℂ **360/733-5793;** www.mountbakertheatre.com), is downtown Bellingham's other major landmark and is the city's premier performing-arts venue. The theater's 110-foot-tall lighthouse tower is visible from all over the city, and though the exterior decor is quite subdued, inside you'll find an extravagant lobby designed to resemble a Spanish galleon.

6

South Puget Sound & West Sound

With more arms than an octopus, the southern reaches of Puget Sound are a region of convoluted waterways, inlets, bays, and harbors. Tucked among the coves, peninsulas, and islands that separate all this salt water are some of Washington's most charming little towns. Past glacial activity gave this region the look of Scandinavian fjords, and it was that very similarity that more than a century ago attracted Scandinavian fishermen who founded what are today two of the region's most picturesque towns: Poulsbo and Gig Harbor. However, this region is also home to a couple of the state's largest cities—Tacoma and Olympia. While there aren't many major attractions in the area, there is an abundance of natural beauty (with plenty of parks to explore) and, in Tacoma, several interesting museums and attractions as well.

The people who choose to live in this region, as well as those who visit, tend to do so for the water. Forest-ringed waterways, old fishing villages turned yacht havens, idyllic rural settings, the romance of living on an island—these are the aspects of life that attract people to this area. However, down in the southern reaches of the Sound a very different aesthetic rules. Here are found Tacoma and Olympia. The former, once derided as an industrial wasteland, is in the middle of a renaissance that has turned it into a very livable city. The latter, as the capital of the state and home of a particularly liberal, liberal-arts university, has a mellow, laid-back air and, when the state legislature and the university shut down, becomes one of the quietest cities in the Northwest.

While green forests and blue waters are this region's dominant characteristics, life here is ruled by ferries and bridges, and visitors are advised to keep this in mind as they explore the region. While distances here are not great, missed ferries and traffic back-ups at the Tacoma Narrows bridge can add significantly to travel time. Leave plenty of room in your travel schedule for unforeseen delays.

However, it is these transportation problems that provide much of the region with its slower pace of life, and that slower pace in turn presents opportunities for Seattleites and others to make quick escapes to the country by simply crossing to the west side of Puget Sound, where island time prevails and the views of the Olympic Mountains are just that much better.

1 Bainbridge Island

10 miles W of Seattle (by ferry), 35 miles NE of Bremerton, 46 miles SE of Port Townsend

Bainbridge Island, popular for its miles of waterfront, sound-and-mountain views, and rural feel, is for the most part an affluent bedroom community

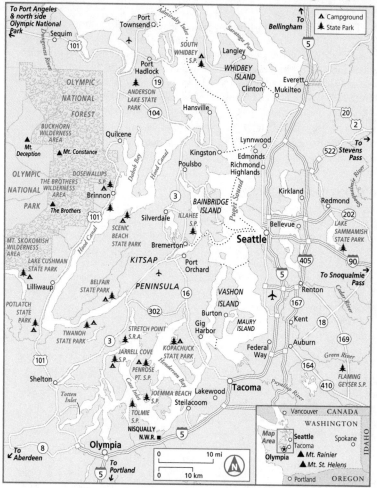

To Port Angeles & north side Olympic National Park

Sequim — 101

Port Townsend

Admiralty Inlet

Saratoga Passage

To Bellingham — 5

△ Campground
♣ State Park

Dungeness River

OLYMPIC
NATIONAL
FOREST

Port Hadlock

ANDERSON LAKE STATE PARK — 19

SOUTH WHIDBEY S.P.

Langley

WHIDBEY ISLAND

Everett
Mukilteo
Clinton

Hansville — 104

BUCKHORN WILDERNESS AREA

Quilcene

Mt. Deception ▲ Mt. Constance

OLYMPIC
NATIONAL — DOSEWALLIPS S.P.
PARK — THE BROTHERS WILDERNESS AREA
Brinnon

The Brothers — 101

Lynnwood

Kingston
Poulsbo

Edmonds
Richmond Highlands

To Stevens Pass — 522

Snoqualmie River

20
2

MT. SKOKOMISH WILDERNESS AREA

LAKE CUSHMAN STATE PARK

Silverdale — 3

ILLAHEE S.P.

BAINBRIDGE ISLAND

Kirkland

Redmond — 202

SCENIC BEACH STATE PARK

Bremerton

KITSAP

Puget Sound

Bellevue

LAKE SAMMAMISH STATE PARK

Seattle

405 — 90

Lilliwaup

BELFAIR STATE PARK

PENINSULA — 16

Port Orchard

VASHON ISLAND

Renton

To Snoqualmie Pass

5

Cedar River

POTLATCH STATE PARK

TWANOH STATE PARK — 3

302

STRETCH POINT S.R.A.

Burton
Gig Harbor

MAURY ISLAND

167

Kent — 18

169

JARRELL COVE S.P.

KOPACHUCK STATE PARK

Federal Way

Auburn

Green River

Shelton — 101

PENROSE PT. S.P.

Henderson Bay

164

410 — FLAMING GEYSER S.P.

Totten Inlet

Case Inlet

JOEMMA BEACH S.P.

Lakewood
Steilacoom

Tacoma

Puyallup River

TOLMIE S.P.

To Aberdeen — 8

NISQUALLY N.W.R.

Olympia

5

To Portland — 5

0   10 mi
0   10 km

N

Vancouver   CANADA

WASHINGTON

Map Area

Seattle
Tacoma

Olympia

Spokane

IDAHO

▲ Mt. Rainier
▲ Mt. St. Helens

Portland   OREGON

for Seattle. However, with its bustling little downtown area (reminiscent of tony towns in the San Francisco Bay area), excellent restaurants and B&Bs, many parks, and good bicycling and sea kayaking, it is also a great spot for a quick getaway.

Roughly 10 miles long and 3½ miles wide, Bainbridge Island had long been the home of the Suquamish Indians when the island was first charted by Capt. George Vancouver in 1792. Within less than a century after Vancouver's visit, the island had become the site of the world's largest lumber mill (though this is now long gone). The island's early settlement centered around the ferry docks of what was known as the mosquito fleet, though eventually, when car ferries began using the community of Winslow (now known as downtown Bainbridge Island), that community became the island's business center. The island was not linked to the mainland by bridge until the Agate Pass Bridge was opened in 1950.

ESSENTIALS

GETTING THERE   **Washington State Ferries** (© **800/84-FERRY** or 888/
808-7977 within Washington, or 206/464-6400; www.wsdot.wa.gov/ferries)
operates a ferry service between Seattle's Pier 52 Colman Dock ferry terminal
and Bainbridge Island. The trip takes 35 minutes and costs $9.50 ($12 mid-May
to mid-Oct) for a car and driver one-way, $5.40 for adult car passengers or walk-
ons, $2.70 for seniors, and $4.40 for children ages 5 to 18; free for children
4 and under. Car passengers and walk-ons only pay fares on westbound ferries.

VISITOR INFORMATION   For more information on Bainbridge Island,
contact the **Bainbridge Island Chamber of Commerce,** 590 Winslow Way E.,
Bainbridge Island, WA 98110 (© **206/842-3700;** www.bainbridgechamber.
com).

EXPLORING BAINBRIDGE ISLAND

Just up the hill from the Bainbridge Island ferry terminal is the island's main
shopping district, where you'll find interesting shops and restaurants. If you'd like
to sample some local wines, drop in at the **Bainbridge Island Vineyards and
Winery,** 682 Wash. 305 (© **206/842-9463;** www.wineryloop.com), which is
located half a mile up the hill from the ferry landing and specializes in European-
style white wines made from estate-grown grapes. These wines are quite good and
are only available here and at a few select restaurants. The winery is open
Wednesday through Sunday from noon to 5pm.

There are two state parks on Bainbridge Island. Down at the south end of the
island, you'll find **Fort Ward State Park** (© **206/842-4041**) on the quiet shore
of Rich Passage. The park offers picnicking and good bird-watching. Up at the
northern tip of the island, you'll find **Fay Bainbridge State Park** (© **206/
842-3931**), which offers camping and great views across the sound to the Seattle skyline. This park will give you a good idea of why people are willing to pay
a premium to live on this island. Admission to either park is $5.

Garden enthusiasts will want to call ahead and make a reservation to visit the
Bloedel Reserve ✪, 7571 NE Dolphin Dr. (© **206/842-7631**), which is 6 miles
north of the ferry terminal off Wash. 305 (turn right on Agate Point Rd.). The
expansive and elegant grounds are the ideal place for a quiet stroll amid plants
from around the world. Admission is $6 for adults and $4 for seniors and children ages 5 to 12. The gardens are open Wednesday through Sunday from 10am
to 4pm (last reservations are for 2pm). Also well worth a visit is **Bainbridge
Gardens,** 9415 Miller Rd. NE (© **206/842-5888;** www.bainbridgegardens.
com), which is on the west side of the island. These gardens, which today are
primarily a plant nursery for garden-crazed Bainbridge Islanders, are also the site
of gardens started in 1908 by Zenhichi Harui when he emigrated from Japan.
The gardens were abandoned in the 1940s when Harui and his family were
forced to leave the island. Today little remains of the original gardens, but the
grounds are still quite beautiful.

Between mid-June and Labor Day weekend, if you'd like to do a little paddling in a sea kayak or canoe, turn left as you get off the ferry and head to Waterfront Park, where you'll find **Bainbridge Island Boat Rentals** (© **206/842-
9229**), which rents sea kayaks ($20–$30 for 2 hr.) and canoes ($25 for 2 hr.).

With its water views and winding country roads, Bainbridge is a favorite of
bicyclists. You can rent from **B. I. Cycle Shop,** 162 Bjune Dr. SE (© **206/842-
6413;** www.b-i-cycle.com), which is located a block off Winslow Way near the
corner of Madison Avenue (in downtown Bainbridge Island/Winslow just a few

blocks from the ferry) and charges $5 per hour (2-hr. minimum) or $25 a day for mountain bikes. They can give you a map of the island and outline a good ride for you.

WHERE TO STAY

Island Country Inn ⭐   Located right in downtown Bainbridge Island, this is the only motel-style lodging on the island, and with its convenient location and its outdoor swimming pool and Jacuzzi, it makes a good choice for anyone coming to the island in summer. Guest rooms are just a cut above your usual motel room. If you're planning a longer stay, the suites, which have kitchens, might be what you need.

920 Hildebrand Way NE, Bainbridge Island, WA 98110. © 800/842-8429 or 206/842-6861. www.nw countryinns.com/Bainbridge.html. 46 units. $109–$119 double; $139–$159 suite. Rates include continental breakfast. Children 12 and under stay free in parent's room. AE, DISC, MC, V. Pets accepted ($20). **Amenities:** Small outdoor pool; Jacuzzi. *In room:* A/C, TV, dataport, coffeemaker, hair dryer, iron.

Waterfall Gardens ⭐   This unusual B&B is located in the middle of the island on 5 acres of gardens and natural landscaping. A salmon and trout stream flows through the property and has been slowly brought back to a natural state by the inn's owners. Accommodations are in two buildings, one of which is designed to resemble an old farmhouse and has 15-foot ceilings and a full kitchen. However, for most people, the smaller Waterfall and Weeping Cedars rooms should be more than adequate. Both of these rooms are quite large and the Waterfall Room has a double whirlpool tub. Note that breakfast is not included in the rates here, so you might want to bring along some breakfast fare so that you don't have to leave this beautiful place too early. Also, be sure to play a round of "bobo" golf while you're here. It's played with a golf club and a tennis ball.

7269 Bergman Rd., Bainbridge Island, WA 98110. © 206/842-1434. www.waterfall-gardens.com. 4 units. $95–$165 double. No credit cards. *In room:* TV, fridge, coffeemaker.

WHERE TO DINE

If you're heading out to one of the island's state parks and need some rustic bread for a picnic, stop by **Blackbird Bakery,** 210 Winslow Way E. (© **206/780-1322**), where you can also get good cookies and pastries. When you need a steaming cup of espresso to warm and wake you, head to the **Pegasus Coffee House & Gallery,** 131 Parfitt Way SW (© **206/842-6725;** www.pegasus coffeehouse.com), which is located near the marina in Winslow. Soups, salads, sandwiches, and pastries are also available. If you'd prefer a pint of ale in a cozy waterfront pub, drop in at the **Harbour Public House,** 231 Parfitt Way SW (© **206/842-0969;** www.harbourpub.com), which overlooks a marina about a block away from Pegasus Coffee. This place also serves good pub food including burgers, fish and chips, and other seafood. To find either of these latter two establishments, follow Winslow Way east through "downtown" Bainbridge Island and turn left onto Madison Avenue.

The Four Swallows ⭐⭐ ITALIAN/NORTHWEST   Located less than a block off Winslow Way in downtown Bainbridge Island, this casual and unpretentious restaurant is housed in a restored farmhouse that was built in 1889. Out front, under the shade trees, is a big deck for summer alfresco dining, and inside, rustic "primitive" antiques and old, high-backed wooden booths set the tone. The menu changes daily, but any month of the year the antipasti for two, which showcases a wide range of seasonal specialties, makes a good starter. If you like seafood, keep an eye out for the delicious *brodetto,* a fish stew similar to bouillabaisse. Pizzas and pastas make up a good portion of the menu, and there are always plenty of fresh seafood dishes.

481 Madison Ave. ⓒ **206/842-3397.** Reservations recommended. Main dishes $12–$29. AE, MC, V. Tues–Sat 5:30–9pm (longer hours in summer).

Winslow Way Cafe 🐾🐾 MEDITERRANEAN/NORTHWEST   Although pasta and pizzas dominate the menu here and prices are reasonable, this contemporary place oozes Seattle attitude. Sure, the restaurant is housed in the funkiest building in downtown Bainbridge Island (it looks as though it could be on a beach in the Caribbean), but inside all is indirect lighting and contemporary styling. The big bar to one side fairly screams "Have a martini!" The pizzas are just the sort of designer pies you would expect in such a setting and are generally excellent, but it is often hard to ignore the creative seafood dishes on the daily fresh sheet.

122 Winslow Way E. ⓒ **206/842-0517.** Reservations recommended. Main dishes $7.25–$18. MC, V. Mon–Wed 4:30–9pm; Thurs 11am–3:30pm and 4:30–9pm; Fri–Sat 11am–3:30pm and 4:30–10:30pm; Sun 10am–3:30pm and 4:30–9pm.

2 Poulsbo & the Kitsap Peninsula

Poulsbo: 15 miles NW of Bainbridge Island ferry dock, 35 miles S of Port Townsend, 45 miles N of Tacoma

Roughly 45 miles long and confusingly convoluted, the Kitsap Peninsula looks something like an arrowhead wedged between Seattle and the Olympic Peninsula. Tucked amid the folds of its many glacial hills and its fjordlike waterways is an eclectic assortment of small towns, each with a very different character.

For thousands of years this region was home to several Native American tribes, including the Suquamish, who once had a 900-foot-long longhouse on the shores of Agate Pass between the Kitsap Peninsula and Bainbridge Island. Chief Sealth (pronounced *see*-alth), for whom Seattle is named, was a member of the Suquamish tribe and today his grave can be visited near the town of Suquamish.

The region's earliest pioneer history is linked to the logging industry. It was at Port Gamble, on the north end of the peninsula, that Andrew Pope and William Talbot chose to build their sawmill, which went on to become the longest operating mill in the Northwest. Although the mill is now closed, Port Gamble remains a company town and still, for the most part, looks as if it hasn't changed in 100 years. However, it is currently undergoing development in the wake of the mill closing.

The state of Washington seems obsessed with theme towns; there's a Dutch town, a Wild West town, a Bavarian town, and here on the Kitsap Peninsula, a Scandinavian town. Though at first the town of Poulsbo seems merely a contrivance to sell tacky Scandinavian souvenirs, on closer inspection it proves to have much more character than that. The town's waterfront park, marinas, and picturesque setting on Liberty Bay leave no doubt that this town has great appeal for the boating crowd.

The deep, protected harbors of the Kitsap Peninsula have for more than a century seen the comings and goings of the U.S. Navy, which has naval yards here in the town of Bremerton. Today the Bremerton Naval Yards are also home to a large fleet of mothballed navy ships, and these have become the town's greatest tourist asset in recent years, with two museums and a Vietnam-era destroyer open to the public. Not far away there is also a Trident nuclear submarine base, which, however, is not open to the public.

Across Sinclair Inlet from Bremerton, and accessible via the last privately owned passenger ferry still operating on the Puget Sound, lies the small town of Port Orchard, which is filled with antiques malls.

ESSENTIALS

GETTING THERE   The Kitsap Peninsula lies between Puget Sound and the east side of the Olympic Peninsula and is bounded on its west side by Hood Canal (which is not a canal but rather a long fjordlike extension of Puget Sound). Wash. 16 connects the peninsula with I-5 at Tacoma, while Wash. 3 connects the peninsula with U.S. 101 west of Olympia and continues north to the Hood Canal Bridge, a floating bridge that serves as the Kitsap Peninsula's northern link to the Olympic Peninsula. Bainbridge Island is connected to the Kitsap Peninsula by the Agate Pass Bridge on Wash. 305.

Washington State Ferries (© 800/84-FERRY or 888/808-7977 in Washington, or 206/464-6400; www.wsdot.wa.gov/ferries) operates three ferries between the Kitsap Peninsula and the east side of Puget Sound: the Fauntleroy-Southworth ferry (a 35-min. crossing) from West Seattle, the Seattle-Bremerton ferry (a 60-min. crossing) from downtown Seattle, and the Edmonds-Kingston ferry (a 30-min. crossing) from north of Seattle. Fares range between $7 and $8.75 for a car and driver on the Seattle-Bremerton ferry and between $9.50 and $12 for a car and driver on the other two ferries. Passenger fare is $5.40. Car passengers and walk-ons only pay fares on westbound ferries.

VISITOR INFORMATION   For information on the Kitsap Peninsula, contact the **Kitsap Peninsula Visitor and Convention Bureau,** 32220 Rainier Ave. NE (P.O. Box 270), Port Gamble, WA 98364 (© 800/416-5615 or 360/297-8200; www.visitkitsap.com). For more information on Poulsbo, contact the **Greater Poulsbo Chamber of Commerce,** 19168-C Jensen Way NE (P.O. Box 1063), Poulsbo, WA 98370 (© 877/768-5726 or 360/779-4848; www.poulsbo.net).

FESTIVALS   In Poulsbo each May the **Viking Fest** celebrates traditional Scandinavian culture, as do the October **First Lutheran Church Annual Lutefisk Dinner** and the December **Yul Fest.**

EXPLORING THE KITSAP PENINSULA

Just across the Agate Pass Bridge from Bainbridge Island lies the Kitsap Peninsula and the Suquamish Indian Reservation. Take your first right after crossing the bridge from Bainbridge Island, and in the village of **Suquamish,** you'll see signs for the grave of Chief Sealth, for whom Seattle was named. Nearby (turn at the Texaco station on the edge of town) you'll also find **Old Man House State Park,** which preserves the site of a large Native American longhouse. The Old Man House itself is long gone, but you'll find an informative sign and a small park with picnic tables. From Suquamish, head back to Wash. 305, continue a little farther west and watch for signs to the **Suquamish Museum,** 15838 Sandy Hook Rd. (© 360/598-3311; www.suquamish.nsn.us/museum), on the Port Madison Indian Reservation. The museum houses a compelling history of Puget Sound's native people, with lots of historic photos and quotes from tribal elders about growing up in the area. May through September, the museum is open daily from 9am to 5pm; October through April, it's open Friday through Sunday from 11am to 4pm. Admission is $4 for adults, $3 for seniors, and $2.50

for children 12 and under. In this same general area, right on Wash. 305 at the west end of the Agate Pass Bridge, you'll also find the **Clearwater Casino,** 15374 Suquamish Way NW, Suquamish (✆ **800/375-6073** or 360/598-6889).

Continuing north on Wash. 305, you next come to the small town of **Poulsbo,** which overlooks fjordlike Liberty Bay. Settled in the late 1880s by Scandinavians, Poulsbo was primarily a fishing, logging, and farming town until the town decided to play up its Scandinavian heritage. Shops in the Scandinavian-inspired downtown sell all manner of Viking and Scandinavian souvenirs. Between downtown and the waterfront, you'll find Liberty Bay Park, and at the south end of Front Street, you'll find the **Poulsbo Marine Science Center,** 18743 Front St. NE (✆ **360/779-5549;** www.poulsbomsc.org), which houses interpretive displays on Puget Sound and is a great place to bring the kids. The center is open daily 11am to 5pm. Admission is $4 for adults, $3 for seniors and teenagers, and $2 for children ages 2 through 12.

If you're interested in seeing Poulsbo from the water, you can rent a sea kayak from **Olympic Outdoor Center,** 18971 Front St. (✆ **360/697-6095;** www.kayakproshop.com), which charges $12 to $17 per hour or $50 to $70 by the day.

If you have time and enjoy visiting historic towns, continue north from Poulsbo on Wash. 3 to **Port Gamble,** which looks like a New England village dropped down in the middle of the Northwest woods. This community was established in 1853 as a company town for the Pope and Talbot lumber mill. Along the town's shady streets are Victorian homes that were restored by Pope and Talbot. Stop by the Port Gamble Country Store, which now houses the **Port Gamble Historical Museum** (✆ **360/297-8074**), a collection of local memorabilia. Admission is $2.50 for adults and $1.50 for seniors and students (free for children 5 and under). From May 1 to October 31, the museum is open daily from 10:30am to 5pm; the rest of the year, it's open by appointment. The same location is home to the **Of Sea and Shore Museum** (✆ **360/297-2426**), which houses an exhibit of seashells from around the world. This museum is open daily from 9am to 5pm, and admission is free.

South of Port Gamble on Wash. 3, you can explore the Kitsap Peninsula's naval history. Between Poulsbo and Silverdale, you will be passing just east of the Bangor Navy Base, which is home port for a fleet of Trident nuclear submarines. The base is on Hood Canal. Near the town of Keyport, you can visit the **Naval Undersea Museum,** 610 Dowell St. (✆ **360/396-4148**), which is located 3 miles east of Wash. 3 on Wash. 308 near the town of Keyport. The museum examines all aspects of undersea exploration, with interactive exhibits, models, and displays that include a deep-sea exploration and research craft, a Japanese kamikaze torpedo, and a deep-sea rescue vehicle. The museum is open daily from 10am to 4pm (closed on Tues Oct–May), and admission is free.

⸤Finds⸥ Chocolate to Take the Chill Off

While in Port Gamble, don't miss **LaLa Land Chocolates** (✆ **360/297-4291**), which is across the street from the two museums. Although this shop makes a wide variety of truffles, its chili-chocolate truffles and its Mayan hot chocolate, made with habanero chili, are unforgettable. The shop also does a chocolate-inspired afternoon tea.

Continuing south, you come to **Bremerton,** which is home to the Puget Sound Naval Shipyard, where mothballed U.S. Navy ships have included the aircraft carriers USS *Nimitz* and USS *Midway* and the battleships USS *Missouri* and USS *New Jersey.* There are always plenty of navy ships to be seen here in the harbor.

One mothballed destroyer, the USS *Turner Joy,* is open to the public as a memorial to those who have served in the U.S. Navy and who have helped build the navy's ships. Operated by the **Bremerton Historic Ships Association** (© **360/792-2457**), the *Turner Joy* is docked about 150 yards east of the Washington State Ferries terminal. From May through September, the ship is open daily from 10am to 5pm; call for hours in other months. Admission is $7 for adults, $6 for seniors and military, and $5 for children ages 5 to 12.

Nearby is the **Bremerton Naval Museum,** 402 Pacific Ave. (© **360/479-7447**), which showcases naval history and the historic contributions of the Puget Sound Naval Shipyard. From Memorial Day to Labor Day, the museum is open Monday through Saturday from 10am to 4pm and Sunday from 1 to 4pm. Admission is by donation.

Connecting all of these waterfront attractions is the Bremerton Boardwalk, which provides a pleasant place to stroll along the waters of Sinclair Inlet. Also here in Bremerton, you'll find the **Kitsap County Historical Society Museum,** 280 Fourth St. (© **360/479-6226;** www.waynes.net/kchsm), which is housed in a 1940s-era streamline modern bank building. The interesting architecture of the building is reason enough for a visit, but there are also historical photos by Edward S. Curtis and his brother Asahel, who at one time resided here in Kitsap County. The museum is open Tuesday through Saturday from 9am to 5pm (until 8pm first Fri of each month). Admission is by suggested donation ($2 adults, $1 seniors and students).

One of the last remaining private mosquito-fleet ferries still operates between Bremerton and **Port Orchard.** If you park your car on the waterfront in Bremerton, you can step aboard the little passenger-only ferry and cross the bay to Port Orchard. In this little waterfront town, you'll find several antiques malls that can provide hours of interesting browsing.

WHERE TO STAY

Manor Farm Inn ★★   Although it's located only about an hour from Seattle, between Poulsbo and the Hood Canal Bridge, Manor Farm Inn (which is actually a working farm) feels a little like a New England country inn. Whether you want to hide away in the comfort of your room or hang out with the farm animals, you're likely to feel content at this retreat from urban stress. If you crave lots of space, you might want to opt for the Carriage Room, which has the original carriage house doors on display. For a large bathroom request The Loft, which is up a flight of stairs and has great views. Scones at your door in the morning are followed by a full breakfast in the dining room. In the afternoon, tea and cookies are available in the common drawing room.

26069 Big Valley Rd. NE, Poulsbo, WA 98370. © **360/779-4628.** Fax 360/779-4876. www.manor farminn.com. 6 units. $140–$170 double; Jan–Apr Sun–Thurs $125 double. Rates include full breakfast. AE, MC, V. *In room:* No phone.

Willcox House ★★   Set on the shore of Hood Canal and with a superb view of the Olympic Mountains, this 1930s Art Deco mansion is one of the state's finest inns. The inn was once a private estate and is surrounded by lush gardens of rhododendrons and azaleas that erupt into bloom each spring. Today guests get the feeling that they have stepped into a Merchant-Ivory drama. There's a library where you can curl up in a leather chair beside the fire, a billiards room (also with a fireplace), a home theater with big-screen TV and an eclectic assortment of videotapes, and, of course, an elegant great room. Guest rooms are similarly elegant. In the Constance Room, the inn's largest, you'll find a fireplace and an Art Deco bathroom. Stay in the Clark Gable Room, and you'll have your own private balcony. Dinners are also served at the inn (reservation only) with fixed-price meals ranging in price from $24 on weeknights to $36 on Saturday nights. Regional cuisine and an excellent wine list make this one of the finest restaurants on the Kitsap Peninsula.

2390 Tekiu Rd. NW, Seabeck, WA 98380. © **800/725-9477** or 360/830-4492. www.willcoxhouse.com. 5 units. $129–$199 double. Rates include full breakfast. DISC, MC, V. **Amenities:** Dining room (Northwest). *In room:* Hair dryer, no phone.

WHERE TO DINE

The most elegant meals on the Kitsap Peninsula are served at the Willcox House, a luxurious inn overlooking the Hood Canal. Although it is mostly guests of the inn who dine here, the fixed-price meals are also open to the public by reservation. See above for details.

IN POULSBO

If you have a sweet tooth, don't miss **Sluys Poulsbo Bakery,** 18924 Front St. NE (© **360/697-2253**), which bakes mounds of Scandinavian-inspired goodies (very sweet), as well as stick-to-your-ribs breads. When you need a cup of espresso, head to the **Poulsbohemian Coffeehouse,** 19003 Front St. (© **360/ 779-9199**), which has an excellent view of Liberty Bay from atop the bluff on the edge of downtown.

Molly Ward Gardens ★★ *Finds* NORTHWEST   What a surprise to open the door of this rambling old barn in a picturesque little valley and find that inside is a magical hobbit-like interior trimmed to the rafters with dried flowers and herbs. This is a husband-and-wife-operation. Sam, the chef, turns out such dishes as pork tenderloin with homemade rhubarb chutney, rack of lamb with zinfandel sauce, and spaghetti squash with Gorgonzola sauce. Fresh fish, lamb, and duck are sure to pop up on the menu, and vegetarian dishes are available. Lynn is the artist, and at Christmas the restaurant is decked out with splendiferous garlands and arrangements created with bounty from woods and field. In summer, there's outdoor seating among the flowers. Molly Ward Gardens is located quite near the Manor Farm Inn.

27462 Big Valley Rd. © 360/779-4471. www.mollywardgardens.com. Reservations recommended. Main courses $11–$15 lunch, $19–$37 dinner. AE, MC, V. Wed–Sat 11am–3pm and 6–9:30pm; Sun 10am–3pm and 6–9:30pm; Mon 6–9:30pm.

Sheila's Bay Café ★ *Finds* NORWEGIAN/AMERICAN   Although this place is nothing fancy, just a casual diner where fishermen feel comfortable in their rain gear, it is one of the few places in town that actually serves Scandinavian food. Although fish cakes and pickled herrings aren't likely to ever replace Thai food as our ethnic cuisine of choice, such dishes are worth a try if you're here in town to soak up the Scandinavian atmosphere. Breakfast here is great, and is served all day.

On the marina, Poulsbo. © 360/779-2997. Main dishes $5–$11. MC, V. Mon–Thurs 8am–2pm; Fri 7:30am–2pm; Sat–Sun 7:30am–3pm.

3 Gig Harbor

45 miles S of Seattle, 30 miles S of Bremerton, 45 miles N of Olympia

On the far side of the Tacoma Narrows Bridge from Tacoma is the quaint waterfront town of Gig Harbor. With its interesting little shops, art galleries, seafood restaurants, fleet of commercial fishing boats, and marinas full of private pleasure craft, this town is the quintessential Puget Sound fishing village. Framing this picture of Puget Sound's past is the snowcapped bulk of Mount Rainier, which lends this town a near storybook quality.

Long the site of a Native American village, Gig Harbor was not discovered by Euro-Americans until 1841, when sailors from an exploratory expedition who were charting the area from a gig (a small boat that had been launched from the expedition's main ship) rowed into the bay. Settlers arrived here in 1867 and soon Gig Harbor was a thriving fishing village of Scandinavians and Croatians.

ESSENTIALS

GETTING THERE   Gig Harbor lies just across the Tacoma Narrows Bridge from Tacoma off Wash. 16.

VISITOR INFORMATION   For more information on this area, contact the **Gig Harbor Peninsula Chamber of Commerce,** 3302 Harborview Dr., Gig Harbor, WA 98332 (© **888/553-5438** or 253/851-6865; www.gigharbor chamber.com).

EXPLORING GIG HARBOR

Gig Harbor is a boaters' town. Up and down the length of the town's waterfront there are marinas crowded with sailboats and powerboats, and shops along the waterfront cater primarily to the boating crowd. However, all the boats, and the backdrop of Mount Rainier, also make this a very pleasant town for a leisurely stroll. There are also a couple of options for casual visitors to get out on the water.

On the waterfront you'll find **Gig Harbor Rent-a-Boat,** 8829 N. Harborview Dr. (© **253/858-7341;** www.gigharborrentaboat.com), where you can rent a sailboat, powerboat, or sea kayak. Rates range from $12 an hour for a single sea kayak to $70 an hour for a 19-foot powerboat. If you are an experienced paddler, guided sea-kayak trips are available from **Gig Harbor Kayak Center,** 8809 N. Harborview Dr. (© **888/429-2548** or 253/851-7987; www.clearlight.com/kayak). A half-day paddle costs $40.

Most visitors to Gig Harbor come because of the boating opportunities, but landlubbers can stroll the town's main street, Harborview Drive, enjoy the view of the harbor, and stop to browse in dozens of interesting little shops and art galleries. Toward the south end of the waterfront, you'll find Jerisich Park, which has a public dock and is a good place for a picnic. At the north end, after you make the bend in the bay, you'll come to the Finholm area. Across from the water here stands the Finholm View Climb, a flight of 90 steps that lead up a steep hill. At the top of the hill, you'll find the quintessential Gig Harbor view of the bay and Mount Rainier.

If you're curious about the history of the area, visit the **Gig Harbor Peninsula Historical Society & Museum,** 4218 Harborview Dr. (© **253/858-6722;** www.gigharbormuseum.org), which is located on the bend of the bay just before Finholm. The museum is open Tuesday through Saturday from 10am to 4pm, and admission is $2 for adults and $1 for seniors and children.

Finds Bonsai by the Bay

Driving west from Gig Harbor on Wash. 16, just past the town of Port Orchard, you can't help but be curious about the odd collection of stunted trees and sculptures wedged between the highway and the waters of Sinclair Inlet. **Elandan Gardens,** milepost 28, Wash. 16, Gorst (© **360/373-8260;** www.elandangardens.com), is the result of one man's passion for bonsai. The bonsai collection includes trees that are more than 1,000 years old and that have been trained for decades. There are also Japanese-style gardens to wander. The garden is open Tuesday through Sunday from 10am to 5pm (closed in Jan); and admission is $5 for adults and $1 for children under 12.

Within a short drive of Gig Harbor, you'll also find three waterfront state parks—**Penrose Point, Joemma,** and **Kopachuck**—all of which have beaches and campgrounds. Of these, Penrose Point (© **253/884-2514**) is the prettiest. This park is situated on Mayo Cove and has 2 miles of shoreline. To reach this park from Gig Harbor, drive north on Wash. 16 to Purdy, take Wash. 302 west and then follow signs to Key Center and the park. From both Joemma (which is about 4 miles beyond Penrose Point) and Kopachuck (from Wash. 16 in Gig Harbor, follow signs for the park) there are good spots to watch sunsets, and there is a nice sandy beach at Kopachuck.

WHERE TO STAY

The Maritime Inn *⭐⭐*   Located across from the waterfront in downtown Gig Harbor, this small modern hotel manages to conjure up the image of old beach resort cottages with its classic, simple styling. All the guest rooms have gas fireplaces and are romantic without being frilly. Pine furnishings lend a further air of classicism to the rooms. While most rooms have some sort of view of the water, the views are better from those few rooms that are on the second floor.

3212 Harborview Dr., Gig Harbor, WA 98335. © 253/858-1818. Fax 253/858-1817. www.maritimeinn.com. 15 units. $69–$139 double. Rates include continental breakfast. AE, DC, DISC, MC, V. *In room:* A/C, TV, dataport, coffeemaker, hair dryer.

WHERE TO DINE

When it's time for coffee, head to **Le Bistro Coffee House,** 4120 Harborview Dr. (© **253/851-1033**), at the north end of downtown.

The Green Turtle *⭐⭐* PAN-ASIAN/INTERNATIONAL   With the hands-down best view in town (Mount Rainier can be seen looming beyond the mouth of the harbor on clear days), this elegant little restaurant is tucked away in an unlikely spot next door to a yacht sales office. Two walls of glass let everyone enjoy the views, and in summer there is a deck under a big old maple tree. The menu is almost entirely seafood, but you will find a few chicken, duck, and steak dishes listed. Preparations lean toward the far side of the Pacific, with such dishes as fish and shellfish in a spicy Thai peanut sauce, pan-seared peppercorn-crusted ahi with a roasted garlic and ginger glaze, and curried halibut with artichoke hearts and basil.

2905 Harborview Dr. © 253/851-3167. www.thegreenturtle.com. Reservations recommended. Main courses $6–$9 lunch, $16–$30 dinner. AE, DISC, MC, V. Tues–Thurs 11am–2:30pm and 4:30–9pm; Fri 11am–2:30pm and 4:30–10pm; Sat 4:30–10pm; Sun 4:30–9pm.

Tides Tavern ⚓ AMERICAN   This is basically just a tavern with an extensive menu, but because of its great location over the water at the east end of town, it's a good place for lunch or a casual dinner. The building that houses the tavern was originally constructed as a general store back in 1910, but has been the Tides Tavern since 1973. The menu is basic tavern fare—burgers, sandwiches, and pizzas— and if not entirely memorable, can be tasty. On Friday and Saturday nights there's live music. Because this is a tavern, you must be 21 or older to eat here.

2925 Harborview Dr. ⓒ 253/858-3982. www.tidestavern.com. Reservations recommended for large parties. Main courses $7.25–$14. MC, V. Sun–Thurs 11am–10pm; Fri–Sat 11am–midnight.

4 Tacoma

32 miles S of Seattle, 31 miles N of Olympia, 93 miles S of Port Townsend

Tacoma is a city that, in the words of Rodney Dangerfield, just don't get no respect. For years its industrial image made it the brunt of jokes, many of which centered around the aroma of Tacoma. I'd like to be able to tell you that the skies over Tacoma are always clear and that the air is fresh and clean, but that would be stretching the truth just a bit. However, it is definitely time to forget the old jokes and take a new look at this city in the midst of a profound transformation.

Things have changed quite a bit here since the days when the city's waterfront was lined with smoke-belching lumber and paper mills, and, with a newfound commitment to the arts, Tacoma now competes with Seattle as a city on the move. Tacoma has been making great strides toward reinventing itself, and the past few years have seen the opening of the Museum of Glass and the new Tacoma Art Museum. Connecting the Museum of Glass to the Washington State History Museum is the Chihuly Bridge of Glass, which spans I-705 in downtown Tacoma. Tacoma also beat Seattle to the punch when it comes to public transit. A new light-rail line now connects the Tacoma Dome with the downtown theater district and stops in the museum district as well. However, despite all these recent developments, Tacoma's downtown still becomes something of a ghost town after the office workers head home at the end of the day.

Tacoma is also in the process of reclaiming its shoreline, and today a waterfront park runs the length of Ruston Way just north of downtown. Walkers, joggers, cyclists, and in-line skaters all flock to the paved trail that runs through this park, and along the park's length there are several good waterfront restaurants. Despite Tacoma's ongoing makeover, little has changed at Point Defiance Park, a local favorite. With miles of trails, a world-class zoo and aquarium, numerous other attractions, and great bicycling and in-line skating, this is one of the premier parks in the Puget Sound region.

In between Point Defiance and downtown Tacoma lies one of the most impressive historic neighborhoods in the state. The streets of the Stadium Historic District are lined with beautiful mansions, most of which have been renovated and some of which are now B&Bs. These homes are a testament to the important role Tacoma played in Washington history. In 1883, Tacoma became the end of the line for the Northern Pacific Railroad, thus sealing the city's fate as the industrial center of the Puget Sound. It was largely due to the railroad that Tacoma became a center of industry in this region, a fate that the city today is trying to overcome.

To see the past and the future of Tacoma, drop by downtown's Fireman's Park. From this small park, you can look down on smoke-belching mills and commercial port facilities, but if you then turn around, you'll be facing a new, revitalized Tacoma where the arts are flourishing and historic buildings are being preserved and renovated.

ESSENTIALS

GETTING THERE Tacoma is on I-5 south of Seattle at the junction of Wash. 16, which is the main route north through the Kitsap Peninsula to Port Townsend and the Olympic Peninsula. Wash. 7 from the Mount Rainier area leads into downtown Tacoma from the south. Tacoma's city center is accessed by I-705, a short spur that leads from I-5 into the middle of downtown.

Seattle-Tacoma International Airport is located 22 miles north of Tacoma. **ShuttleExpress** (© **800/487-7433** or 425/981-7000; www.shuttleexpress.com) operates an airport shuttle service; the fare is $24 one-way to downtown Tacoma.

Amtrak has service to Tacoma. The station is at 1001 Puyallup Ave.

VISITOR INFORMATION For more information on this area, contact the **Tacoma Regional Visitor & Convention Bureau,** 1119 Pacific Ave., Fifth Floor, Tacoma, WA 98402 (© **800/272-2662** or 253/627-2836; www.travel tacoma.com), which has an information desk inside the gift shop at the Washington State History Museum, 1911 Pacific Ave.

GETTING AROUND See "Getting Around" in chapter 4 for information on renting cars at Sea-Tac International Airport. If you need a taxi, contact **Yellow Cab** (© **253/472-3303**). Public bus service is provided by **Pierce Transit** (© **800/562-8109** or 253/581-8000; www.piercetransit.org).

WHAT TO SEE & DO
MUSEUMS

Karpeles Manuscript Library Museum ⭐ Housed in an imposing building across the street from Wright Park, and one of eight such manuscript libraries across the country, this museum is dedicated to the preservation of original handwritten documents and letters. The founder of the libraries has amassed an astounding collection of original manuscripts ranging from original musical scores by Beethoven to ancient papyrus texts to the cover letter for the Declaration of Independence.

407 South G St. © 253/383-2575. Free admission. Tues–Sun 10am–4pm.

Museum of Glass ⭐⭐ Although it was Chihuly's work that inspired the construction of this museum here in Tacoma, the Museum of Glass travels far and wide to bring the very best of art glass to Tacoma. Art glass in all its myriad forms finds its way into the galleries of this high-style building on the Tacoma waterfront. Whether it is stained glass in the style of Tiffany, a traveling exhibit from a European museum, or the latest thought-provoking installation by a cutting-edge glass artist, you'll find it here. The museum highlight is the hot shop, a huge cone-shaped studio space where visitors can watch glass artists work at several kilns. Connecting the museum to the rest of the city is the 500-foot-long Chihuly Bridge of Glass, which spans the I-705 freeway. Adjacent to this museum, you'll find **Vetri International Glass,** 1821 E. Dock St. (© **253/383-3692;** www.vetriglass.com), which is an affiliate of the Northwest's premier art-glass gallery.

1801 Dock St. © 800/4-MUSEUM or 253/396-1768. www.museumofglass.org. Admission $10 adults, $8 seniors, $4 children 6–12, free for children under 6. Free 3rd Thurs of each month. Tues–Sat 10am–5pm (until 8pm on 3rd Thurs of each month); Sun noon–5pm. Closed Thanksgiving, Christmas, and New Year's Day.

Tacoma Art Museum ⭐⭐ In May of 2003, the Tacoma Art Museum moved into a spacious new home designed by noted architect Antoine Predock. This new building has given the museum lots of beautiful new galleries in which to display both its collections and traveling exhibitions. Although perhaps best

Tacoma

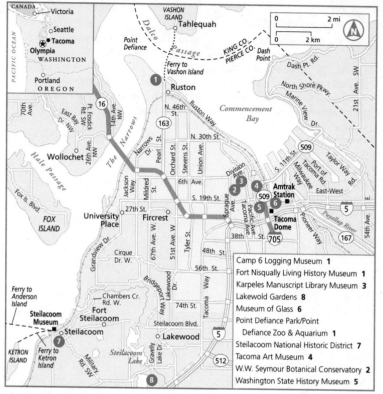

Camp 6 Logging Museum **1**
Fort Nisqually Living History Museum **1**
Karpeles Manuscript Library Museum **3**
Lakewold Gardens **8**
Museum of Glass **6**
Point Defiance Park/Point
  Defiance Zoo & Aquarium **1**
Steilacoom National Historic District **7**
Tacoma Art Museum **4**
W.W. Seymour Botanical Conservatory **2**
Washington State History Museum **5**

known for its large collection of art by native son Dale Chihuly, this museum also has respectable collections of European Impressionism, Japanese woodblock prints, and American graphic art. However, the new gallery spaces mean that the museum can also now bring in large traveling shows. The Northwest Biennial, held every other summer, is a juried exhibit of works by artists from Washington, Oregon, Idaho, and Montana.

1701 Pacific Ave. ☏ 253/272-4258. www.tacomaartmuseum.org. Admission $6.50 adults, $5.50 seniors and students, free for children under 6. Free 3rd Thurs of each month. Tues–Wed and Fri–Sat 10am–5pm; Thurs 10am–8pm; Sun noon–5pm. Closed Thanksgiving, Christmas, New Year's Day, and July 4.

Washington State History Museum ⭐⭐ *Kids*   A massive archive of Washington state history, this impressive museum is like no other history museum in the Northwest. The museum uses a full barrage of high-tech displays to make history both fun and interesting. From a covered wagon to a sprawling HO-scale (3.5mm: 1 ft.) model railroad layout, a Coast Salish longhouse to a Hooverville shack, the state's history comes alive through the use of life-size mannequins, recorded narration, and "overheard" conversations. With loads of interactive exhibits and several films screened daily, it's obvious that this museum is trying to appeal to the video-game generation, but older visitors will have fun, too.

1911 Pacific Ave. ☏ 888/238-4373 or 253/272-3500. www.wshs.org/wshm. Admission $7 adults, $6.50 seniors, $5 students 6–17, free for children 5 and under. Free for all Thurs 5–8pm. Mon–Wed and Fri–Sat 10am–5pm; Thurs 10am–8pm; Sun noon–5pm. Closed New Year's Day, Memorial Day, July 4, Labor Day, Thanksgiving, and Christmas.

Tips **Triple Tuesdays**

With the Museum of Glass, the Tacoma Art Museum, and the Washington State History Museum all within 3 blocks of one another, Tacoma is an even better museum town than Seattle. You can save a little on the cost of visiting these three museums by visiting on a Tuesday when you can get into all three museums for $17 ($14 for seniors and $12 for students and children). For adults, this is a savings of $6.50, or, put another way, you get to visit the art museum for free!

POINT DEFIANCE PARK

Point Defiance Park, on the north side of town at the end of Pearl Street, is Tacoma's center of activity and one of the largest urban parks in the country. In the park are several of the city's top attractions, including the Point Defiance Zoo & Aquarium, Fort Nisqually Historic Site, and the Camp 6 Logging Museum. Founded in 1888, this park preserved one of the region's most scenic points of land. Winding through the wooded park is **Five Mile Drive,** which connects all the park's main attractions as well as the picnic areas, and hiking and biking trails. Also in the park are a rose garden, a Japanese garden, a rhododendron garden, a dahlia test garden, and a native-plant garden. You can reach the park by following Ruston Way or Pearl Street north.

Camp 6 Logging Museum *Kids* This museum focuses on the days of steam power in Washington's logging history. Exhibits include plenty of steam equipment as well as old bunkhouses and a rail-car camp. The latter was a rolling logging camp with bunkhouses built on railroad cars. Although the indoor exhibits are closed November through January, outdoor exhibits can be viewed throughout the year. On weekends in spring and summer and again in December, Camp 6 offers rides on an old logging train.

5400 N. Pearl St. 253/752-0047. Free admission to museum; logging train rides $1. Feb to Memorial Day and Oct Wed–Sun (and holidays) 10am–4pm; Memorial Day to Sept 30 Wed–Fri 10am–5pm, Sat–Sun 10am–7pm. Closed Nov–Jan.

Fort Nisqually Living History Museum Fort Nisqually was a trading post founded in 1833 by the Hudson's Bay Company for the purpose of acquiring beaver pelts. However, it was established at a time when the fur trade was in decline and was soon moved to a new location and converted to a commercial farming business. This reconstruction, built in the 1930s, is based on the design of that second fort. Inside the stockade walls are two original buildings and several reconstructed buildings. Throughout the summer (and on weekends in other months), costumed interpreters are on hand. Numerous living-history events are staged throughout the year.

5400 N. Pearl St. 253/591-5339. www.fortnisqually.org. Admission Mar–Oct $3 adults, $2 seniors and students, $1 children 5–12, free for children under 5; Nov–Feb $2 adults, $1.50 seniors and students, $1 children 5–12, free for children under 5 (weekend after Labor Day to Mar, admission charged on weekends only). Memorial Day to Labor Day daily 11am–6pm; Labor Day to Mar Wed–Sun 11am–4pm; Apr to Memorial Day Wed–Sun 11am–5pm.

Point Defiance Zoo & Aquarium *Kids* As the name implies, this is both a zoo and an aquarium, and both facilities are outstanding. The focus here is on the wildlife of the Pacific Rim countries, and to that end you'll find animals from such far-flung locations as the Arctic tundra, Southeast Asia, and the Andes

Mountains. In the aquarium, the *Rocky Shores* exhibit features marine mammals, including beluga whales, and the *Jewels of the Sea* exhibit sheds a new light on jellyfish. Other exhibits include a northern Pacific aquarium, a tropical coral reef aquarium that's home to more than 40 sharks, an aquarium of deadly sea creatures, and a new seahorse exhibit. At the farm zoo, kids can pet various animals. The zoo's biggest event of the year is its annual Zoolights program, which each December turns the grounds into a fantasy of Christmas lights.

5400 N. Pearl St. ℭ 253/591-5337. www.pdza.org. Admission $7.75 adults, $7 seniors, $6 children 4–13, free for children under 4. Daily 9:30am to between 4–6pm (hours vary with season, call for details). Closed 3rd Fri in July, Thanksgiving, and Christmas.

TACOMA AREA PUBLIC GARDENS

Lakewold Gardens 🅐 Formerly a private estate, this 10-acre garden, designed by noted landscape architect Thomas Church, includes extensive collections of Japanese maples and rhododendrons. There are also rose, fern, and alpine gardens that include numerous rare and unusual plants.

12317 Gravelly Lake Dr. SW. ℭ 888/858-4106 or 253/584-4106. www.lakewold.org. Admission $5 adults, $3 seniors and students, free for children under 12. Apr–Sept Thurs–Mon 10am–4pm; Oct–Mar Fri–Sun 10am–3pm.

Pacific Rim Bonsai Collection 🅐🅐 Assembled by the Weyerhaeuser Company in 1989 to honor trade relations with Pacific Rim nations, this bonsai collection includes more than 50 miniature trees from Japan, China, Korea, Taiwan, and Canada. This is the most impressive public bonsai collection in the state. There are free guided tours of the collection on Sundays at noon.

33663 Weyerhaeuser Way S., Weyerhaeuser Corporate campus, Federal Way. ℭ 253/924-5206. www. weyerhaeuser.com/bonsai. Free admission. Mar–May Fri–Wed 10am–4pm; June–Feb Sat–Wed 11am–4pm.

Rhododendron Species Foundation and Botanical Garden 🅐🅐 Covering 22 acres, this garden has one of the most extensive collections of species of (wild) rhododendrons and azaleas in the world. More than 2,100 different varieties of plants put on an amazing floral display March through May. Also included in these gardens are collections of ferns, maples, heathers, and bamboos. For serious gardeners, this is one of the Northwest's garden musts.

2525 S. 336 St., Weyerhaeuser Corporate campus, Federal Way. ℭ 253/838-4646 or 253/661-9377. www.rhodygarden.org. Admission $3.50 adults, $2.50 seniors and students, free for children under 12. Mar–May Fri–Wed 10am–4pm; June–Feb Sat–Wed 11am–4pm.

W.W. Seymour Botanical Conservatory 🅐 Constructed in 1908, this elegant Victorian conservatory is one of only three of this kind on the West Coast and is listed on the National Register of Historic Places. More than 200 species of exotic plants (including plenty of orchids) are housed in the huge greenhouse,

---

Kids Wild Waves & an Enchanted Village

Recently acquired by the Six Flags theme-park company, **Wild Waves/ Enchanted Village**, 36201 Enchanted Parkway S., Federal Way (ℭ **253/ 661-8000;** www.sixflags.com), is a combination water park and amusement park that has been kicked up a notch with the addition of a large wooden roller coast. When temperatures heat up in July and August, the water slides here are the cool place to be. Bring your kids here on vacation, and they'll never forget their trip to Washington.

which is built of more than 4,000 panes of glass. The conservatory stands in Wright Park, which has more than 700 trees of 100 species and is a shady retreat from downtown's pavement. At press time, the conservatory was just getting ready to reopen after an extensive restoration.

Wright Park, 316 South G St. (℃) 253/591-5330. Free admission. Daily 10am–4:30pm. Closed Thanksgiving and Christmas.

OTHER TACOMA PARKS

Although Point Defiance Park is Tacoma's premier park, the **Ruston Way Parks** rank a close second. Once jammed with smoking, decaying industrial buildings and piers, the Tacoma waterfront was an industrial area of national infamy. However, since the city of Tacoma reclaimed the shore of Commencement Bay and turned it into parkland, it has become one of the most attractive waterfront parks on Puget Sound. With grassy areas, a sandy beach, a public fishing pier, and a paved pathway, the waterfront is popular with strollers, cyclists, and in-line skaters.

Downtown at the corner of A Street and South Ninth, you'll find **Fireman's Park,** which has one of the world's tallest totem poles (carved in 1903) as well as a view of the Port of Tacoma below. After gazing down on the port, if you want to have a closer look, stop by the **Port of Tacoma Observation Tower** off East 11th Street. Here you can watch as ships from around the world are loaded and unloaded. To reach the port tower, take the 11th Street bridge from downtown.

HISTORIC DISTRICTS & BUILDINGS

Tacoma has quite a few historic buildings, the most notable of which is **Union Station,** 1717 Pacific Ave. Built in the beaux arts style as the terminal for the first transcontinental railroad to reach the Northwest, the imposing building is now home to the federal courts and is adjacent to the Washington State History Museum. In the lobby of this building you'll find a large glass installation by Dale Chihuly.

Stadium High School, 111 North E St., is a French château–style structure that was built as a hotel and later converted to a high school. The school is the centerpiece of the historic **Stadium District,** which is at the north end of Broadway and has more than 100 Victorian homes. This is one of the prettiest residential neighborhoods in the entire state, and many of the old homes verge on being mansions. At the south end of the Stadium District is the **Old City Hall Historic District,** which is the city's main antiques neighborhood. Along Broadway just north of Ninth Street, you'll find a dozen or so large antiques stores and malls. At the visitor center in the Washington State History Museum, you can pick up brochures on the city's historic districts.

VISITING HISTORIC STEILACOOM 🐾

Founded in 1854 by a Maine sea captain, Steilacoom is Washington's oldest incorporated town. Once a bustling seaport, the quiet little community 10 miles south of Tacoma is today a National Historic District with 32 preserved historic buildings. To reach Steilacoom, take exit 125 off I-5 south between Tacoma and Olympia, drive to Lakewood and turn left on Steilacoom Boulevard.

The Steilacoom Museum, 112 Main St. (℃ **253/584-4133**), in the old town hall, houses exhibits on Steilacoom's pioneer history. The museum is open March through October, Wednesday through Sunday from 1 to 4pm; in February, November, and December, Friday through Sunday from 1 to 4pm (closed Jan). Suggested donation is $2. This museum is operated by the Steila-coom Historical Museum Association, which also maintains the nearby **Nathaniel Orr Pioneer Home and Orchard,** 1811 Rainier St., which was built between 1854 and 1857 and contains original furnishings. Between April and October, this house is open on Saturday and Sunday from 1 to 4pm. At the **Steilacoom Tribal Cultural Center and Museum,** 1515 Lafayette St. (© 253/ 584-6308), you'll find an old-fashioned museum with displays on the area's Steilacoom tribe. It's open Tuesday through Saturday from 10am to 4pm; admission is $2 for adults and $1 for seniors and students.

Steilacoom is also the site of the ferry landing for the small ferry that runs to **Anderson Island,** a quiet rural island that is popular with bicyclists. There are several parks on the island and enough scenic Puget Sound vistas to make the island a pleasant place for a leisurely afternoon drive.

WHERE TO STAY

Chinaberry Hill 🎇🎇 Located amid the stately old homes of the Stadium His-toric District, this grand Victorian home features luxurious guest rooms and commanding views of Commencement Bay. For sheer opulence, it's hard to beat the Pantages Suite, which features a beautifully dressed bed, harbor views, and a whirlpool tub tucked into an alcove under the eaves. The Carriage Suite, in the former carriage house, has a hot tub for two tucked into what was once a horse stall. Above this suite is a room in what was once the hayloft. Beautiful century-old trees shade the grounds. Classic Northwest elegance makes this one of the finest inns in the state.

302 Tacoma Ave. N., Tacoma, WA 98403. © 253/272-1282. Fax 253/272-1335. www.chinaberryhill.com. 5 units. $125–$195 double; $295 cottage. Rates include full breakfast. MC, V. Children 12 and over welcome in main house, all ages welcome in cottage. In room: TV/VCR, dataport.

Sheraton Tacoma Hotel 🎇🎇 This 26-story downtown high-rise is Tacoma's biggest, best, and only downtown business hotel, and because it is attached to the Tacoma Convention Center, it stays busy most of the year. Guest rooms are none too large, but are both comfortable and tastefully decorated. Be sure to ask for a room with a view of Mount Rainier (these are the even-numbered rooms). For more personal services such as evening turndown, morning newspaper, and a continental breakfast, opt for a room on one of the concierge floors. Up on the 26th floor you'll find an Italian restaurant with one of the best views in town.

1320 Broadway Plaza, Tacoma, WA 98402. © 800/325-3535 or 253/572-3200. Fax 253/591-4105. www. sheratontacoma.com. 319 units. $109–$139 double; $149–$350 suite. AE, DC, DISC, MC, V. Valet parking $15. Pets accepted. **Amenities:** 2 restaurants (Italian, American); lounge; exercise room and access to nearby health club; concierge; business center; limited room service; laundry service; dry cleaning; concierge level. In room: A/C, TV, dataport, minibar, coffeemaker, hair dryer, iron.

Silver Cloud Inn Tacoma 🎇🎇 Built out over the waters of Commencement Bay, on a pier on the Ruston Way waterfront, this hotel offers water views from every room. There's not a bad room in the hotel, but you should try to get a third-floor room in order to maximize your views. If you're in the mood for a splurge, the corner Jacuzzi suites are very romantic. The tub is in a corner with two walls of bay-view windows, and there are also gas fireplaces. Within 2 blocks of the hotel, you'll find the restaurants of Old Town Tacoma, and along the Rus-ton Way waterfront pathway, you'll find several good seafood restaurants. Don't miss the Belgian waffles at breakfast.

2317 N. Ruston Way, Tacoma, WA 98402. (✆ 866/820-8448 or 253/272-1300. www.silvercloud.com. 90 units. $129–$139 double; $169–$229 suite. Rates include full breakfast. AE, DC, DISC, MC, V. **Amenities:** Local courtesy shuttle; laundry service. *In room:* A/C, TV, dataport, fridge, coffeemaker, hair dryer, iron, free local calls.

Thornewood Castle Inn ★★★ *(Finds*   There may not be any real castles in the United States, but this imposing 30,000-square-foot manor house, located a few miles south of Tacoma, sure comes close. Built in 1909, Thornewood has 28 bedrooms and 22 bathrooms, and incorporated into its design are a 15th-century wood-paneled staircase and stained-glass windows dating from the 15th to 17th centuries. Guest rooms are, as you might expect, quite large, and if not quite as sumptuously appointed as the rest of the house, they are certainly grand in design. The mansion sits on the shore of American Lake, and the gardens were designed by the Olmsted Brothers. This is truly a one-of-a-kind inn. About the only drawback here is that nearby suburban homes dispel the fantasy that you are lord or lady of all you survey. If you aren't staying here, you can still arrange a tour of the castle for $25, and a tour and high tea can be arranged for $50.

8601 N. Thorne Lane SW, Lakewood, WA 98498. (✆ **253/584-4393.** Fax 253/584-4497. www.thornewood castle.com. 10 units. $175–$400 double. Rates include full breakfast. AE, DISC, MC, V. No children under 12. *In room:* TV/VCR, coffeemaker, no phone.

The Villa Bed & Breakfast ★★   From the red roof tiles to the covered portico to the naiad statue in the garden pond, this inn cries out authentic Italianate villa. The only odd thing about this 1920s mansion is that it is in Tacoma and not Santa Barbara. Lovingly restored and filled with antiques as well as unusual pieces of furniture handmade by innkeeper Greg Anglemyer, the inn feels for all the world like a villa in Italy. Designed for romantic getaways, all the rooms have either a whirlpool or antique soaking tub. All but one room also have gas fireplaces, and three of the rooms have their own private verandas. If you crave lots of space, opt for the Sorrento Suite, which has a gas fireplace, a private veranda, a four-poster bed, and views of the Olympic Mountains and Commencement Bay.

705 N. Fifth St., Tacoma, WA 98403. (✆ **888/572-1157** or 253/572-1157. www.villabb.com. 6 units. $125–$225 double. Rates include full breakfast. AE, MC, V. Children over 12 welcome. **Amenities:** Exercise room; Jacuzzi; concierge; business center. *In room:* TV, dataport, hair dryer.

WHERE TO DINE
IN TACOMA

Located inside the Museum of Glass, **Prizm,** 1801 E. Dock St. (✆ **253/383-2228**), is a great place to grab a quick lunch or a latte before heading off to another of the area's museums. If you're downtown and just have to have a cup of espresso, **Tully's,** 764 Broadway (✆ **253/627-5646**), is the place to go. This coffeehouse claims the narrow corner space of a flatiron-style building in downtown Tacoma's antiques neighborhood.

Anthony's at Point Defiance ★★   SEAFOOD   Located adjacent to the Vashon Island ferry landing on the edge of Point Defiance Park, this modern seafood restaurant, part of a very popular Seattle restaurant chain, has the best location of any of Tacoma's many waterfront restaurants. When the skies are clear, it's possible to see Mount Rainier rising beyond the adjacent marina (although the best views of the mountain are from the bar area), and then, of course, there are the comings and goings of the ferries. The prices are surprisingly reasonable considering both the location and the contemporary decor, and

Anthony's stays pretty busy as a result. You'll find everything from clam chowder and pan-fried oysters to alder-planked salmon and cioppino. For a light meal, try the fish tacos.

5910 N. Waterfront Dr. ℂ 253/752-9700. www.anthonys.com. Reservations accepted for 6 or more people (call-ahead wait list available for smaller parties). Main courses $5–$17. AE, MC, V. Mon–Thurs 11am–9:30pm; Fri–Sat 11am–10:30pm; Sun 10am–9:30pm.

Café Divino ⭐ *(Finds* ITALIAN   This little hole-in-the-wall wine bar and restaurant is located in the historic Old Town Tacoma neighborhood, which is north of present-day downtown Tacoma. The menu is short and the wines by the glass tend to be a bit pricey, but the food is good and the atmosphere is boisterously convivial. Some simple sandwiches (try the pesto chicken) and a few pasta dishes comprise the bulk of the menu, but most people end up assembling meals from the excellent salads and appetizers. Try the oven-roasted prawns and the smoked salmon quesadilla. Because this restaurant is only 2 blocks from the Ruston Way waterfront, you should try to get in a stroll before or after a meal.

2112 N. 30th St. ℂ 253/779-4226. Reservations recommended. Main courses $8–$12. AE, DISC, MC, V. Mon–Thurs 11am–10pm; Fri 11am–11pm; Sat noon–10pm.

Harmon Pub and Brewery ⭐ AMERICAN   Located in a renovated old commercial building across from the Washington State History Museum, this large pub is Tacoma's favorite downtown after-work hangout and business lunch spot. The menu is primarily burgers and pizza, but there are also usually more interesting specials, and, of course, plenty of good microbrews. The pub has adopted an outdoors theme, with the winter ski season seeing various skiing-oriented special events.

1938 Pacific Ave. ℂ 253/383-2739. www.harmonbrewing.com. Reservations not accepted. Main courses $7–$16. AE, DC, DISC, MC, V. Mon–Fri 11am–10pm; Sat noon–11pm; Sun noon–8pm.

The Lobster Shop South ⭐⭐ SEAFOOD   This is the most upscale and expensive of the Ruston Way seafood places and has long been the city's top special-occasion seafood restaurant. The view's the thing here, and in summer there is lots of outdoor seating on the deck. Starters include a respectable New England–style clam chowder and a good lobster bisque. But the appetizer not to miss is the hot Dungeness crab dip, made with crab, artichoke hearts, onions, and Parmesan. Dishes on the main menu tend toward simple preparations made with lots of butter, but the daily fresh sheet has more creative dishes. The crab cakes and the cioppino are always good bets, too. Sunday through Friday between 4:30pm and 5:30pm, there are $15 three-course dinners.

4013 Ruston Way. ℂ 253/759-2165. www.lobstershop.com. Reservations recommended. Main courses $8–$15 lunch, $17–$30 dinner. AE, DC, DISC, MC, V. Mon–Thurs 11:30am–2:30pm and 4:30–9:30pm; Fri 11:30am–2:30pm and 4:30–10pm; Sat 4:30–10pm; Sun 9:30am–1:30pm (brunch) and 4:30–9:30pm.

IN STEILACOOM

The Bair Restaurant ⭐ *(Finds* SODA FOUNTAIN/INTERNATIONAL Perhaps the best reason to visit Steilacoom is to have a milkshake or an ice cream soda at this historic 1906 soda fountain. The interior of this old wooden building is kept the way it might have looked back when it was a hardware store, making the place part museum, part soda fountain. However, people no longer drop in for nails or tools, but they do line up for ice-cream sundaes and the like. This is the oldest soda fountain we know of in the Northwest and is one of our favorites. Although dinner is served on Friday and Saturday nights in summer and afternoon tea on Monday through Saturday afternoons, the real reason to come here is for an old-fashioned soda fountain experience.

1617 Lafayette St. (C) **253/588-9668**. www.thebairrestaurant.com. Reservations recommended for dinner. Main courses $5–$12 breakfast and lunch, $16–$20 dinner. MC, V. Daily 8am–3pm. Memorial Day to Labor Day dinner served Fri–Sat 5:30–9pm.

TACOMA AFTER DARK

Opened in 1983, the **Tacoma Dome,** 2727 East D St. ((C) **253/272-3663;** www. tacomadome.org), which rises beside I-5 on the east side of the city, is Tacoma's most visible landmark and is the world's largest wood-domed arena. With seating for 28,000 people, it is the site of concerts, sporting events, and large exhibitions. Smaller productions take to the stages at the **Broadway Center for the Performing Arts,** 901 Broadway ((C) **253/591-5894;** www.broadwaycenter.org). This center consists of three theaters within a block of each other. The **Pantages,** a renovated vaudeville theater with a neoclassical terra-cotta facade, and the **Rialto Theatre,** a classic Italianate movie palace, were both built in 1918, while the **Theatre on the Square** was built in 1993. Together these three theaters present a wide variety of nationally recognized theater, music, and dance, including performances by the **Tacoma Philharmonic,** the **Tacoma Symphony Orchestra,** the **Tacoma Opera,** and the **Tacoma City Ballet.**

If you're just looking for someplace interesting to have a drink, check out **The Swiss,** 1904 S. Jefferson Ave. ((C) **253/572-2821;** www.theswisspub.com), which is located just uphill from the Washington State History Museum. The pub is at the top of a long flight of stairs that links the museum with the University of Washington Tacoma Campus. The pub not only has a great beer selection and decent food, but it also has a collection of Dale Chihuly glass sculptures. **The Spar,** 2121 N. 30th St. ((C) **253/627-0895**), is another local favorite that has been around forever and is housed in a historic building in Old Town Tacoma.

5 Olympia

60 miles S of Seattle, 100 miles N of Portland

Located at the southernmost end of Puget Sound, Olympia is the capital of Washington and a pleasant little city, though aside from the state capitol building and a few parks, it has little of interest to attract visitors. The city does, however, cling to the shores of Budd Inlet's twin bays and boasts a fairly lively downtown and an attractive waterfront. The city is further divided by Capitol Lake, above which, on a high bluff, stands the capitol building. Despite the political importance of being the state capital, Olympia still has the air of a small town. The downtown is compact and low-rise, and when the legislature isn't in session the city can be downright ghostly. Keeping things alive, however, are the students of Evergreen State College, a very progressive liberal-arts college.

The Olympia area has a long history, and it was near here, in what is now the city of Tumwater, that the first pioneers settled in 1844. A historic district and historical park along the Deschutes River in Tumwater preserve a bit of this history.

ESSENTIALS

GETTING THERE   Olympia is on I-5 at the junction with U.S. 101, which leads north around the Olympic Peninsula. Connecting the city to the central Washington coast and Aberdeen/Hoquiam is U.S. 12/Wash. 8.

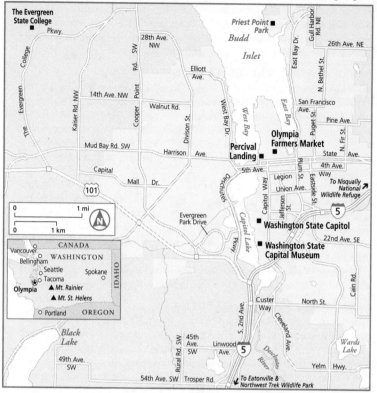

The nearest airport with scheduled service is Seattle-Tacoma International Airport, 54 miles north. **Capital Aeroporter** (℡ 800/962-3579 or 360/754-7113; www.capair.com) provides a shuttle between the airport and Olympia. The one-way fare is $28 and the round-trip fare is $45.

There is **Amtrak** (℡ 800/872-7245; www.Amtrak.com) rail service to Olympia; the station is at 6600 Yelm Hwy. SE.

VISITOR INFORMATION   Contact the **Olympia/Thurston County Visitor & Convention Bureau,** P.O. Box 7338, Olympia, WA 98507 (℡ 877/704-7500 or 360/704-7544; www.visitolympia.com), or the **State Capitol Visitor Information Center,** 14th Avenue and Capitol Way (P.O. Box 41020), Olympia, WA 98504-1020 (℡ 360/586-3460).

GETTING AROUND   If you need a taxi, contact **Red Top Taxi** (℡ 360/357-3700). Public bus service is provided by **Intercity Transit** (℡ 360/786-1881; www.intercitytransit.com), which operates downtown shuttle buses.

THE CAPITOL CAMPUS

Located at 14th Avenue and Capitol Way, the neoclassical **Washington State Capitol building,** constructed between 1911 and 1928, is set amid a large and attractively landscaped campus known for its flowering cherry trees and rose gardens. At 267 feet tall, this is the tallest domed masonry state capitol in the country and bears a surprising resemblance to the Capitol in that other Washington.

Around its campus you'll see sculptures, the Tivoli fountain, and a conservatory (Mon–Fri 8am–3pm). The capitol is open daily with tours offered hourly between 10am and 3pm. For more information on tours of the grounds, contact the **State Capitol Visitor Center** (② **360/586-8687**; www.ga.wa.gov/visitor).

OTHER AREA ATTRACTIONS

In downtown Olympia, you'll find the **Olympia Farmers Market,** 700 N. Capitol Way (② **360/352-9096**; www.farmers-market.org), on the waterfront adjacent to Percival Landing Park. This is the second-largest open-air produce market in the state; it also has numerous prepared-food vendors and features live music on the weekends. Between April and October, the market is open Thursday through Sunday from 10am to 3pm; from November to December it's open Saturday and Sunday only.

If you'd like to learn more about the area's history, especially that of the Native Americans who have called this region home for thousands of years, stop by the small **Washington State Capital Museum,** 211 W. 21st Ave. (② **360/753-2580**; www.wshs.org/wscm). However, it is the building itself, an Italian Renaissance mansion built in the 1920s for a former mayor of Olympia, that is the most interesting part of a visit to this museum. The museum is open Tuesday through Friday from 10am to 4pm and Saturday from noon to 4pm. Admission is $2 for adults, $1.75 for seniors, and $1 for children 6 to 18; free for children under 6.

PRESERVES, PARKS & GARDENS

Lying at the edge of downtown Olympia, **Capitol Lake** and its surrounding park lands are favorites of area joggers, canoeists, and anglers. There is an excellent view of the Capitol from the west side of the lake. Also in downtown is the 1½-mile-long **Percival Landing** boardwalk, which wanders along the shore of Budd Inlet past marinas, restaurants, public art, and interpretive panels. Between these two parks, you'll find Heritage Park and the Heritage Fountain, which has 47 choreographed water jets that are fun to watch. In summer, the fountain is a popular spot with local children who run through the fountains.

On the north side of Olympia along the East Bay of Budd Inlet, you'll find formal gardens, several miles of hiking trails, nice water views, and a beach at **Priest Point Park,** on East Bay Drive. The 3-mile round-trip Ellis Cove Trail provides beach access.

Just across I-5 from Olympia, you'll also find **Tumwater Falls Park,** along a rocky stretch of the Deschutes River. Here small waterfalls cascade over rocks and in the autumn, Chinook salmon can be seen as they return to the park's holding ponds. Within the park you'll find a couple of historic homes that are open to the public. The **Crosby House,** 703 Deschutes Way SW (② **360/943-9884**), was built by Bing Crosby's grandparents and is open for tours Thursday and Sunday from 1 to 4pm; admission is by $2 suggested donation. The adjacent **Henderson House,** 602 Deschutes Way SW (② **360/754-4163**), is open Thursday, Friday, and Sunday between 1 and 4pm; admission is by donation. Despite the waterfalls, salmon, and historic homes, the presence of the now-closed Miller Brewing Company's huge Tumwater Brewery (formerly the Olympia Brewery) looming overhead and the roaring traffic on I-5 a few feet away detract quite a bit from the aesthetics of the setting. Still, for the riverside trails and the chance to see salmon in the fall, this park is worth a visit.

Nisqually National Wildlife Refuge (② **360/753-9467**; http://nisqually. fws.gov), located 8 miles north of Olympia at exit 114 off I-5, preserves the delta

---

Finds Land of the Giant Gophers?

Some 13 miles south of Olympia, near the town of Littlerock, you'll find the **Mima Mounds Natural Area Preserve,** which is an area of hundreds of small hills, each around 7 feet high. No one is sure how the mounds were formed, but their curious topography has produced much speculation over the years. The preserve is open daily, and in spring the wildflower displays here are quite impressive. To reach the preserve, take the Little-rock exit off I-5 and drive west on Wash. 121 to Waddell Creek Road. Turn right and continue another 1½ miles.

---

of the Nisqually River, which is a resting and wintering ground for large numbers of migratory birds. There are 7 miles of trails through the refuge. The visitor center is open Wednesday through Sunday from 9am to 4pm. A $3 vehicle admission fee is charged.

TWO NEARBY WILDLIFE ATTRACTIONS

Northwest Trek Wildlife Park 🐾🐾 *Kids*   The animals of North America are the focus of Northwest Trek, a wildlife park that covers more than 600 acres near the town of Eatonville. Bison roam, elk bugle, and moose munch content-edly knee-deep in the park's lake. Visitors are driven around the grounds in a naturalist-guided tram, and at certain spots, you're allowed to get out and walk to various enclosures. Among the residents here are a grizzly bear, a wolf, cougars, lynx, and bobcats. There are also more than 5 miles of nature trails to wander after viewing the animals.

11610 Trek Dr. E., Eatonville. (C) 360/832-6117. www.nwtrek.org. Admission $8.75 adults, $8.25 seniors, $6 children 5–17, $4 children 3–4, free for children under 3. Mar–Oct daily; Nov–Feb Fri–Sun and selected holidays. Call for specific hours. Closed Thanksgiving and Christmas. To reach the park, take Wash. 510 south-east from I-5 (exit 111) to Yelm and continue west on Wash. 702.

Wolf Haven International 🐾 *Kids*   Dedicated to the preservation of wolves and the education of the general public on the subject of wolves, Wolf Haven is a sanctuary for more than 30 wolves. During tours of the facility, you'll get to meet many of these canines, including a small pack that allows visitors to observe wolf-pack behavior in action. Throughout the summer there are Satur-day night Howl-Ins that are particularly popular with families. Advance reserva-tions are required for Howl-Ins, which cost $10 for adults and $8 for children ages 3 to 12.

3111 Offut Lake Rd., Tenino. (C) 800/448-9653 or 360/264-4695. www.wolfhaven.org. Admission $6 adults, $5 seniors, $4 children 3–12, free for children under 3. May–Sept Wed–Mon 10am–5pm; Apr and Oct Wed–Mon 10am–4pm; Mar and Nov–Jan Sat–Sun 10am–4pm. Last tour starts 1 hr. before closing. Closed Feb.

WHERE TO STAY

Phoenix Inn Suites 🐾 *Value*   Located within 2 blocks of the water, the Perci-val Landing boardwalk, several restaurants, and the Olympia Farmers Market, this new downtown hotel is a great choice for vacationers who like to leave their car parked as much as possible. Although the hotel is geared toward business travelers, the great location, large guest rooms, and many amenities make this an especially good value. Although the rooms are more junior suites than the sort of two-room suites you might find at an Embassy Suites hotel, they are quite large and well designed.

(*Finds* **So, Who Needs Starbucks?**

When it's time for coffee, drop by **Batdorf & Bronson,** 513 S. Capitol Way (© **360/786-6717**), which is located right downtown. This espresso bar pours the best Americano (espresso topped off with hot water) in the state. Java junkies should also be sure to stop by the **Batdorf & Bronson Tasting Room,** 200 Market St. NE (© **360/753-4057**), which is located at the company roastery and usually has five different coffees available to taste (and buy by the cup or by the pound).

---

415 Capitol Way N., Olympia, WA 98501. © 877/570-0555 or 360/570-0555. Fax 360/570-1200. www. phoenixinnsuites.com. 102 units. $99–$169 double. Rates include continental breakfast. AE, DISC, MC, V. **Amenities:** Indoor pool; exercise room; Jacuzzi; business center; coin-op laundry. *In room:* A/C, TV, dataport, fridge, coffeemaker, hair dryer, iron, free local calls.

WHERE TO DINE

If tea is your drink of choice, don't miss the **Tea Lady,** 430 Washington St. SE (© **360/786-0350**), a shop that celebrates all things tea and always has several different hot teas available. If it's local microbrews you're after, drop by the **Fishbowl Brewpub,** 515 Jefferson St. SE (© **360/943-3650**), which is very popular as an after-work gathering spot.

Budd Bay Café ★★ SEAFOOD   Located in downtown Olympia, the Budd Bay Café is the city's favorite waterfront restaurant and its lavish Sunday seafood brunch is always popular. The views from both the dining room and large deck take in the waters of Budd Bay as well as the state capitol. Just outside, the Percival Landing Waterfront Park boardwalk stretches for 1½ miles, and is ideal for that after-dinner stroll. The menu includes such standards as seafood fettuccine, cedar-plank salmon, and pan-fried oysters, but you'll also find good steaks and prime rib. There are several good salads, including a delicious hot seafood salad.

Percival Landing, 525 N. Columbia St. © 360/357-6963. www.buddbaycafe.com. Reservations recommended. Main courses $8–$12 lunch, $10–$25 dinner. AE, DC, DISC, MC, V. Mon–Thurs 11am–9pm; Fri–Sat 11am–10pm; Sun 9:30am–9pm.

The Spar Cafe ★ AMERICAN   In business since 1935, this downtown diner is a Northwest classic. On the walls hang old black-and-white photos of period logging activities (the cafe's name refers to the spar trees that were used for rigging cables and pulleys), and along one wall is the original cigar counter, which is lined with glass-fronted humidor cabinets full of premium cigars. In back, through a swinging door, is a dark bar, but it's the cozy old booths out front that are the main attraction. Breakfasts here are some of the best in town (try the Fourth Avenue Mess). If it's genuine Olympia atmosphere you're looking for, this is the place.

114 E. Fourth Ave. © 360/357-6444. www.thesparcafe.com. Main courses $6.25–$15. AE, DISC, MC, V. Mon–Thurs 6am–9pm; Fri–Sat 6am–11pm; Sun 6am–8pm.

7

The Olympic Peninsula

The rugged and remote Olympic Peninsula, located in the extreme northwestern corner of Washington and home to Olympic National Park, was one of the last places in the continental United States to be explored. Its impenetrable, rain-soaked forests and steep, glacier-carved mountains effectively restricted settlement to the peninsula's more accessible coastal regions.

Though much of the Olympic Peninsula was designated a National Forest Preserve in 1897, and in 1909 became a national monument, it was not until 1938 that the heart of the peninsula—the jagged, snow-capped Olympic Mountains—became Olympic National Park. This region was originally preserved in order to protect the area's rapidly dwindling herds of Roosevelt elk, which are named for President Theodore Roosevelt (who was responsible for the area becoming a national monument). At the time the preserve was created, these elk herds were being decimated by commercial hunters.

Today, however, Olympic National Park, which is roughly the size of Rhode Island, is far more than an elk reserve. It is recognized as one of the world's most important wild ecosystems. The park is unique in the contiguous United States for its temperate rainforests, which are found in the west-facing valleys of the Hoh, Queets, Bogachiel, Clearwater, and Quinault rivers. In these valleys, rainfall can exceed 150 inches per year, trees (Sitka spruce, western red cedar, Douglas fir, and western hemlock) grow nearly 300 feet tall, and mosses enshroud the limbs of big-leaf maples.

Within a few short miles of the park's rainforests, the Olympic Mountains rise up to an alpine zone where no trees grow at all, and above these alpine meadows rises the 7,965-foot glacier-clad summit of Mount Olympus. Together, elevation and heavy snowfall (the rain of lower elevations is replaced by snow at higher elevations) combine to form 60 glaciers within the park. It is these glaciers that have carved the Olympic Mountains into the jagged peaks that mesmerize visitors and beckon to hikers and climbers. Rugged and spectacular sections of the coast have also been preserved as part of the national park, and the offshore waters are designated as the Olympic Coast National Marine Sanctuary.

With fewer than a dozen roads, none of which leads more than a few miles into the park, Olympic National Park is, for the most part, inaccessible to the casual visitor. Only two roads penetrate the high country, and only one of these is paved. Likewise, only two paved roads lead into the park's famed rainforests. Although a long stretch of beach within the national park is paralleled by U.S. 101, the park's most spectacular beaches can only be reached on foot.

While the park is inaccessible to cars, it is a wonderland for hikers and backpackers. Its rugged beaches, rainforest valleys, alpine meadows, and mountaintop glaciers offer an amazing variety of hiking and backpacking

The Olympic Peninsula

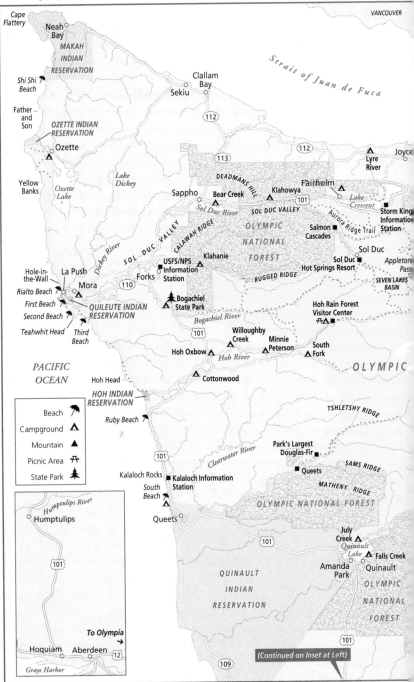

VANCOUVER

Cape Flattery
Neah Bay

MAKAH INDIAN RESERVATION

Shi Shi Beach

Father and Son

OZETTE INDIAN RESERVATION

Ozette

Yellow Banks

Ozette Lake

Lake Dickey

Clallam Bay
Sekiu

Strait of Juan de Fuca

112

113

112

Joyce
Lyre River

Fairholm

DEADMANS HILL

Sappho
Bear Creek
Klahowya

Sol Duc River

SOL DUC VALLEY

OLYMPIC

Lake Crescent

Storm King Information Station

101

Salmon Cascades

Aurora Ridge Trail

Sol Duc

Sol Duc River

SOL DUC VALLEY
CALAWAH RIDGE

NATIONAL

FOREST

Sol Duc Hot Springs Resort

Appleton Pass

Dickey River

Klahanie

USFS/NPS Information Station

RUGGED RIDGE

SEVEN LAKES BASIN

Hole-in-the-Wall
La Push
Mora

Rialto Beach
First Beach
Second Beach
Teawhit Head

110

Forks

Bogachiel State Park

Hoh Rain Forest Visitor Center

QUILEUTE INDIAN RESERVATION

Third Beach

Bogachiel River

101

Willoughby Creek

Minnie Peterson

South Fork

OLYMPIC

PACIFIC OCEAN

Hoh Head

Hoh Oxbow

Hoh River

Cottonwood

HOH INDIAN RESERVATION

Ruby Beach

TSHLETSHY RIDGE

Legend

Beach	🏖
Campground	⛺
Mountain	▲
Picnic Area	⛱
State Park	🌲

Clearwater River

Park's Largest Douglas-Fir

Queets

SAMS RIDGE

MATHENY RIDGE

OLYMPIC NATIONAL FOREST

Kalaloch Rocks
South Beach

Kalaloch Information Station

Humptulips River

Humptulips

101

July Creek
Falls Creek

Quinault Lake

Amanda Park

Quinault

QUINAULT INDIAN RESERVATION

OLYMPIC

NATIONAL

FOREST

Queets

101

101

To Olympia →

Hoquiam
Aberdeen

12

Grays Harbor

109

(Continued on Inset at Left)

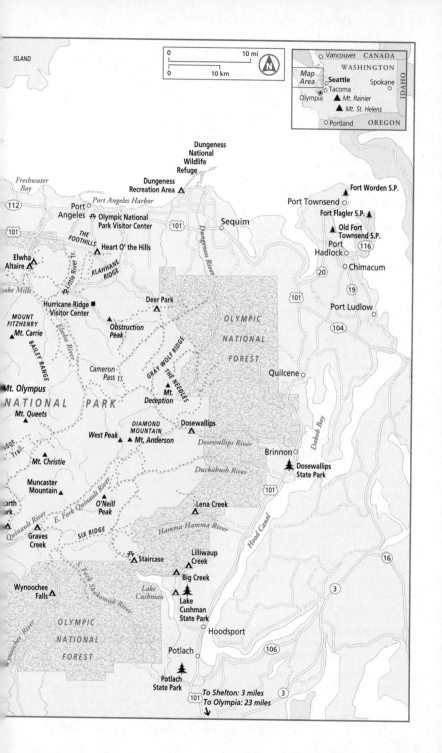

opportunities. For alpine hikes, there are the trail heads at Hurricane Ridge and Deer Park. To experience the rainforest in all its drippy glory, there are the trails of the Bogachiel, Hoh, Queets, and Quinault valleys. Of these rainforest trails, the Hoh Valley has the more accessible (and consequently more popular) trails, including the trail head for the multi-day hike to the summit of Mount Olympus. Favorite coastal hikes include the stretch of coast between La Push and Oil City and from Rialto Beach north to Lake Ozette and onward to Shi Shi Beach.

The restored Victorian seaport of Port Townsend in the northeast corner of the peninsula offers a striking contrast to the wildness of Olympic National Park. Here in Port Townsend, a restored historic commercial district on the waterfront is packed with interesting shops and good restaurants, while on the bluff above, the streets are lined with stately Victorian homes (many of which are now bed-and-breakfasts or inns). Together, the town's two historic neighborhoods have made Port Townsend one of the most popular destinations in Washington.

The rural community of Sequim (pronounced *skwim*) has also been developing quite a reputation in recent years for a very different reason. The Sequim area lies in the rain shadow of the Olympic Mountains and receives fewer than 20 inches of rain per year (less than half the average of Seattle). Sure, the skies here are still cloudy much of the year, but anyone who has lived very long in the Northwest begins to dream of someplace where it doesn't rain quite so much. In Sequim, these dreamers are building retirement homes as fast as they can. The dry climate has also proven to be an ideal environment for the growing of lavender, and fields of purple blossoms are sprouting all over the Sequim area.

Long before the first white settlers arrived, various Native American tribes called the Olympic Peninsula home. The Makah, Quinault, Hoh, Elwha, and Skokomish tribes all inhabited different regions of the peninsula, but all stayed close to the coast, where they could harvest the plentiful mollusks, fish, and whales. Today, there are numerous Indian reservations, both large and small, on the peninsula. On the Jamestown S'Klallam Reservation you'll find a casino, and on the Makah Reservation, a fascinating museum of culture and history.

While at first it might seem that the entire peninsula is a pristine wilderness, that just isn't the case. When the first white settlers arrived, they took one look at the 300-foot-tall trees that grew on the Olympic Peninsula and started sharpening their axes. The supply of trees seemed endless, but by the 1980s the end was in sight for the trees that had not been preserved within Olympic National Park. Today, U.S. 101, which loops around the east, north, and west side of the peninsula is lined with clear-cuts and second- and third-growth forests for much of its length, a fact that takes many first-time visitors by surprise.

1 Port Townsend: A Restored Victorian Seaport

60 miles NW of Seattle, 48 miles E of Port Angeles, 40 miles S of Anacortes

Named by English explorer Captain George Vancouver in 1792, Port Townsend did not attract its first settlers until 1851. However, by the 1880s the town had become an important shipping port and was expected to grow into one of the most important cities on the West Coast. Port Townsend felt that it was the logical end of the line for the transcontinental railroad that was pushing westward in the 1880s; and based on the certainty of a railroad connection, real estate speculation and development boomed. Merchants and investors erected mercantile palaces along Water Street and elaborate Victorian homes on the bluff above the wharf district. However, the railroad never arrived. Tacoma got the rails, and Port Townsend got the shaft.

With its importance as a shipping port usurped by Seattle and Tacoma, Port Townsend slipped into quiet obscurity. Progress passed it by and its elegant homes and commercial buildings were left to slowly fade away. However, in 1976 the waterfront district and bluff-top residential neighborhood were declared a National Historic District and the town began a slow revival. Today the streets of Port Townsend are once again crowded with people. The waterfront district is filled with boutiques, galleries, and other interesting shops, and many of the Victorian homes atop the bluff have become bed-and-breakfast inns.

ESSENTIALS

GETTING THERE   Port Townsend is on Wash. 20, off U.S. 101 in the northeast corner of the Olympic Peninsula. The Hood Canal Bridge, which connects the Kitsap Peninsula with the Olympic Peninsula and is on the route from Seattle to Port Townsend, sometimes closes due to high winds; if you want to be certain that it's open, call © **800/695-7623.**

Washington State Ferries (© **800/84-FERRY** or 888/808-7977 within Washington state, or 206/464-6400; www.wsdot.wa.gov/ferries) operates a ferry between Port Townsend and Keystone on Whidbey Island. The crossing takes 30 minutes and costs $7.50 to $9.50 for a vehicle and driver, and $2.10 for passengers (discounted fares for seniors and youths).

Between Port Townsend and Friday Harbor, passenger service is available from mid-April to early October from **P.S. Express** (© **360/385-5288;** www. pugetsoundexpress.com), which will also carry bicycles and sea kayaks. One-way fares are $35 for adults and $25 for children; round-trip fares are $53 for adults and $36 for children.

VISITOR INFORMATION   Contact the **Port Townsend Chamber of Commerce Visitors Information Center,** 2437 E. Sims Way, Port Townsend, WA 98368 (© **888/365-6978** or 360/385-2722; www.ptguide.com).

GETTING AROUND   Because parking spaces are hard to come by in downtown Port Townsend on weekends and anytime in the summer, **Jefferson Transit** (© **800/371-0497** or 360/385-4777; www.jeffersontransit.com), the local public bus service, operates a shuttle into downtown Port Townsend from a park-and-ride lot on the south side of town. Jefferson Transit also operates other buses around Port Townsend. Fares are 50¢ to $1.

FESTIVALS   As a tourist town, Port Townsend schedules quite a few festivals throughout the year. In early April, the town celebrates its Victorian heritage with the **Victorian Festival** (© **888/698-1116;** www.victorianfestival.org). The **Jazz Port Townsend** festival is held toward the end of July. The **Wooden Boat Festival,** the largest of its kind in the United States, is on the first weekend after Labor Day. During the **Kinetic Sculpture Race,** held the first Sunday in October, outrageous human-powered vehicles race on land, on water, and through a mud bog. To see inside some of the town's many restored homes, schedule a visit during the **Historic Homes Tour** on the third weekend in September.

The **Olympic Music Festival** (© **206/527-8839;** www.olympicmusicfestival. org), held nearby in an old barn near the town of Quilcene, is the area's most important music festival. This series of weekend concerts takes place between mid-June and mid-September.

EXPLORING THE TOWN

With its abundance of restored Victorian homes and commercial buildings, Port Townsend's most popular activity is simply walking or driving through the historic districts. The town is divided into the waterfront commercial district and the residential uptown area, which is atop a bluff that rises precipitously only 2 blocks from the water. Uptown Port Townsend developed in part so that proper Victorian ladies would not have to associate with the riffraff that frequented the waterfront. At the Port Townsend Visitor Information Center you can pick up a guide that lists the town's many historic homes and commercial buildings.

Water Street is the town's main commercial district. It is lined for several blocks with 100-year-old restored brick buildings, many of which have ornate facades. Within these buildings are dozens of interesting shops and boutiques, several restaurants, and a handful of hotels and inns. To learn a little more about the history of this part of town and to gain a different perspective, walk out on **Union Wharf,** at the foot of Taylor Street. Here you'll find interpretive plaques covering topics ranging from sea grass to waterfront history.

Before exploring the town, stop by the **Jefferson County Historical Society History Museum,** 540 Water St. (© **360/385-1003;** www.jchsmuseum.org), where you can learn about the history of the area. Among the collections here are regional Native American artifacts and antiques from the Victorian era. It's open Monday through Saturday from 11am to 4pm and Sunday 1 to 4pm (in July and Aug open daily until 6pm). Admission is $3 for adults and $1 for children under 12.

The town's noted Victorian homes are in uptown Port Townsend, atop the bluff that rises behind the waterfront's commercial buildings. Here you'll find stately homes, views, and the city's favorite park. To reach the uptown area, either drive up Washington Street (1 block over from Water St.) or walk up the stairs at the end of Taylor Street, which start behind the Haller Fountain.

At the top of the stairs are both an 1890 bell tower that once summoned volunteer firemen, and the **Rothschild House,** Taylor and Franklin streets (© **360/ 379-8076;** www.jchsmuseum.org). Built in 1868, this Greek Revival–style house is one of the oldest buildings in town and displays a sober architecture compared to other area homes. The gardens contain a wide variety of roses, peonies, and lilacs. It's open May through September, daily from 10am to 5pm. Admission is $3 for adults and $1 for children under 12.

However, the most fascinating uptown home open to the public is the **Ann Starrett Mansion,** 744 Clay St. (© **360/385-3205**), Port Townsend's most astoundingly ornate Queen Anne Victorian home. Currently operated as a bed-and-breakfast inn, this mansion is best known for its imposing turret, ceiling frescoes, and unusual spiral staircase. The house is open for guided tours daily from noon to 3pm. Tours cost $2.

Also here in the uptown neighborhood, at the corner of Garfield and Jackson streets, you'll find **Chetzemoka Park,** which was established in 1904 and is named for a local S'Klallam Indian chief. The park perches on a bluff overlooking Admiralty Inlet and has access to a pleasant little beach. However, it is the rose garden, arbor, and waterfall garden that attract most visitors.

Shopping is just about the most popular activity in Port Townsend's old town, and of the many stores in the historic district, several stand out. **Earthenworks Gallery,** 702 Water St. (© **360/385-0328**), showcases colorful ceramics, glass, jewelry, and other American-made crafts. **Ancestral Spirits Gallery,** 701 Water St. (© **360/385-0078**), is a large space with a great selection of Northwest Native American prints, masks, and carvings. Women enamored of Port Townsend's Victorian styling will want to visit the **Renaissance Rags,** 1012 Water St. (© **360/ 370-1661**), a dress shop specializing in modern Victorian fashions.

FORT WORDEN STATE PARK

Fort Worden State Park, once a military installation that guarded the mouth of Puget Sound, is north of the historic district and can be reached by turning onto Kearney Street at the south end of town, or onto Monroe Street at the north end of town, and following the signs. Built at the turn of the 20th century, the fort is now a 360-acre state park where a wide array of attractions and activities assure that it's busy for much of the year. Many of the fort's old wooden buildings have been restored and put to new uses.

At the **Fort Worden Commanding Officer's House** (© **360/344-4400;** www. olympus.net/ftworden), you can see what life was like for a Victorian-era officer and his family. The home has been fully restored and is filled with period antiques. In summer, it's open daily from 10am to 5pm, and in spring and fall, it's open weekends from noon to 4pm; admission is $2, free for children under 12.

Here at the park you can also learn about life below the waters of Puget Sound at the **Port Townsend Marine Science Center,** 532 Battery Way (© **360/385-5582;** www.ptmsc.org). The center has great tide-pool touch tanks filled with crabs, starfish, anemones, and other marine life. There's also a fascinating exhibit on the area's terrestrial natural history, complete with fossils from around the peninsula. Don't miss the exhibit on the glaciers that once covered this region. In summer, the center is open Wednesday through Monday from 11am to 5pm, and fall through spring, it's open Friday through Monday from noon to 4pm. Admission is $3 for adults and $2 for students and children.

For many people, however, the main reason to visit the park is to hang out on the beach or at one of the picnic areas. Scuba divers also frequent the park, which has an underwater park just offshore. In spring, the Rhododendron Garden puts on a colorful floral display. Throughout the year, there is a wide variety of concerts and other performances at the **Centrum** (© **800/733-3608** or 360/385-3102; www.centrum.org). Also within the park are campgrounds, a restaurant, and restored officers' quarters that can be rented as vacation homes.

Kids A Victory for Kids in a Victorian Town

There aren't a lot of children with an appreciation for Victorian architects, so parents visiting Port Townsend may find themselves at the mercy of whining young ones. Don't despair. You can all take a time out from touring mansions and head out to Fort Worden State Park. Here you'll find a fascinating marine science center where kids can grab starfish and poke anemones. There's also a long beach, and even though the water is cold, the kids might not mind. Then there are the trails through the woods and the very spooky old gun emplacements. Bring a flashlight and you can dig around in the dark corners of history.

PORT TOWNSEND FROM THE WATER (& AIR)

If you'd like to explore the town from the water, you've got several options. Three-hour sailboat tours ($65) are offered by **Brisa Charters** (© 877/41-BRISA or 360/385-2309; www.olympus.net/brisa_charters) and **Bryony Charters** (© 360/481-0605; www.sailbryony.com). This latter company only operates between April and October. Several times a year, **Port Townsend Marine Science Center** (© 360/385-5582; www.ptmsc.org) operates boat tours ($45) to nearby Protection Island, a wildlife refuge that is home to puffins, rhinoceros auklets, and other nesting sea birds. One trip a year is done on a 101-foot historic schooner. Late May through August, whale-watching cruises ($25 for adults, $15 for children ages 2–10) through the San Juan Islands are offered by **Puget Sound Express,** 431 Water St. (© 360/385-5288; www.pugetsound express.com), which also offers passenger ferry service to Friday Harbor.

If you'd like to try your hand at paddling a sea kayak around the area's waters, contact **Kayak Port Townsend,** 435 Water St. (© 800/853-2252 or 360/385-6240; www.kayakpt.com), which offers 2-hour ($30), half-day ($40), and full-day tours ($76), and also rents sea kayaks. At the nearby **Port Ludlow Marina** (© 360/437-0513), south of Port Townsend, you can rent sea kayaks ($10–$15 per hour) and motorboats ($20 per hour).

OTHER AREA ACTIVITIES

While in town, you might want to check out Port Townsend's two wineries, both located south of town. **Sorensen Cellars,** 274 S. Otto St. (© 360/379-6416; www.sorensencellars.com), is open March through September, Friday through Sunday from noon to 5pm (or by appointment). To find this winery, turn east off Wash. 20 onto Frederick Street and then south on Otto Street. **Fair Winds Winery,** 1984 Hastings Ave. W. (© 360/385-6899; www.fairwindswinery.com), is the only winery in the state producing Aligoté, a French-style white wine. Between April and October, the winery is open Friday through Monday from 11am to 5pm; October through March it is open Saturday and Sunday from noon to 5pm. To find the winery, drive south from Port Townsend on Wash. 20, turn west on Jacob Miller Road, and continue 2 miles to Hastings Avenue.

MARROWSTONE ISLAND

You'll find another old fort turned state park on nearby Marrowstone Island, which is reached by driving south 9 miles to Port Hadlock on Wash. 19 and then turning east on Wash. 116. From Port Hadlock it is another 11 miles to the northern tip of Marrowstone Island and **Fort Flagler State Park.** This large park has a campground, boat ramp, beaches, and hiking trails.

Between Port Hadlock and Marrowstone Island is Indian Island, most of which is an active military base. However, the waters off the island are popular with sea kayakers. At the south end of Indian Island is a small park popular with windsurfers.

WHERE TO STAY
IN PORT TOWNSEND
Moderate

Ann Starrett Mansion 🐠🐠   Built in 1889 for $6,000 as a wedding present for Ann Starrett, this Victorian jewel box is by far the most elegant and ornate bed-and-breakfast in Port Townsend (and the entire state for that matter). The rose and teal-green mansion is a museum of the Victorian era: A three-story turret towers over the front door, and every room is exquisitely furnished with period antiques. In fact, if you aren't staying here, you can still have a look during one of the afternoon house tours ($2). Breakfast is an extravaganza that can last all morning and will certainly make you consider skipping lunch. This B&B is all about being pampered amid Victorian elegance.

744 Clay St., Port Townsend, WA 98368. ℂ **800/321-0644** or 360/385-3205. Fax 360/385-2976. www. starrettmansion.com. 11 units. $105–$225 double. Rates include full breakfast. AE, DISC, MC, V. *In room:* No phone.

F. W. Hastings House/Old Consulate Inn ⭐⭐

Though not quite as elaborate as the Starrett Mansion, the Old Consulate Inn is another example of the Victorian excess so wonderfully appealing today. The attention to detail and quality craftsmanship both in the construction and the restoration of this elegant mansion are evident wherever you look. Despite its heritage, however, the Old Consulate avoids being a museum; it's a comfortable, yet elegant, place to stay. If you're here for a special occasion, consider splurging on one of the turret rooms. Of the other rooms, our favorite is the Parkside. For entertainment, you'll find a grand piano, a billiards table, and a VCR, as well as stunning views out most of the windows. A multi-course breakfast is meant to be lingered over, so don't make any early-morning appointments. Afternoon tea, evening cordials and dessert, and a hot tub add to the experience.

313 Walker St., Port Townsend, WA 98368. ℂ **800/300-6753** or 360/385-6753. Fax 360/385-2097. www.oldconsulateinn.com. 8 units. $99–$210 double. Rates include full breakfast. MC, V. Children 12 and older are welcome. **Amenities:** Jacuzzi. *In room:* Hair dryer, no phone.

James House ⭐⭐

With an eclectic blend of antique and new furnishings, this grand 1889 Victorian sits atop the bluff overlooking Admiralty Inlet. The entry hall features a parquet floor and a big staircase climbing straight up to the second floor. In the two parlors you'll find fireplaces that are the perfect gathering spot on a cool evening. The views from the upper front rooms are some of the best in town (ask for the Chintz Room, which has views and a deck, or the Master Suite). You can even see Mount Rainier on a clear day. If you don't like climbing stairs, opt for one of the ground-floor suites or the Gardener's Cottage. An additional private bungalow, done in a contemporary style, is adjacent to the James House, and has a water and mountain view.

1238 Washington St., Port Townsend, WA 98368. ℂ **800/385-1238** or 360/385-1238. Fax 360/379-5551. www.jameshouse.com. 12 units. May–Oct $125–$145 double, $150–$210 suite or cottage; Nov–Apr $110–$135 double, $135–$185 suite or cottage. Rates include full breakfast. AE, DISC, MC, V. **Amenities:** Massage. *In room:* Dataport, hair dryer.

Manresa Castle ⭐⭐ *Value*

Built in 1892 by a wealthy baker, this reproduction of a medieval castle later became a Jesuit retreat and school. Today traditional elegance pervades Manresa Castle, and of all the hotels and B&Bs in Port Townsend, this place offers the most historic elegance for the money. The guest rooms have a genuine, vintage appeal that manages to avoid the contrived feeling that so often sneaks into the room decor of B&Bs. The best deal in the hotel is the tower suite during the off season. For $135 a night you get a huge room with sweeping views from its circular seating area. An elegant lounge and dining room further add to the Grand Hotel feel of this unusual accommodations.

Seventh and Sheridan sts. (P.O. Box 564), Port Townsend, WA 98368. ℂ **800/732-1281** or 360/385-5750. Fax 360/385-5883. www.manresacastle.com. 40 units. May to mid-Oct $85–$100 double, $105–$175 suite; mid-Oct to Apr $75–$90 double, $95–$150 suite. Rates include continental breakfast. DISC, MC, V. **Amenities:** Restaurant (Continental/International); lounge. *In room:* TV.

Palace Hotel ⭐ Located in the heart of the historic district, the Palace Hotel occupies a building that once served as a bordello. Today Madame Marie's suite—a big corner room with a kitchenette—is the best room in the house. Most of the other rooms are named for former working girls. Miss Kitty's room is as nice as the Madame's and includes a cast-iron woodstove and the best views at the Palace. The Crow's Nest room is another interesting space, and features a sleeping loft, nautical theme, and woodstove. *Note:* The hotel is up a steep flight of stairs from the street, and some rooms are up on the third floor. The bathroom shared by three rooms has a big claw-foot tub, so you aren't doing too badly if you take one of these rooms.

1004 Water St., Port Townsend, WA 98368. ℂ 800/962-0741 or 360/385-0773. Fax 360/385-0780. www.palacehotelpt.com. 16 units, 3 with shared bathroom. $49–$69 double with shared bathroom; $99–$169 double or suite with private bathroom. Rates include continental breakfast. AE, DISC, MC, V. Pets accepted ($10 per day). *In room:* TV, coffeemaker.

Ravenscroft Inn ⭐⭐ Built in 1987 but designed in keeping with Port Townsend's historic homes, this inn offers rooms with distinctively different moods. The Mount Rainier Room, with its gorgeous views, fireplace, and whirlpool tub for two, is a perennial favorite; as is the Fireside Room, which has a fireplace, veranda, and four-poster bed. Two other rooms also open onto a veranda, and some rooms on the upper levels have good views of the mountains and water. Pretty gardens surround the house.

533 Quincy St., Port Townsend, WA 98368. ℂ 800/782-2691 or 360/385-2784. Fax 360/385-6724. www. ravenscroftinn.com. 8 units. $94–$199 double. Rates include full breakfast. AE, DISC, MC, V. Children over age 14 accepted. *In room:* No phone.

Inexpensive

The Belmont ⭐ Built in 1885, The Belmont is the oldest waterfront restaurant and saloon in town, and on the second floor, you'll find four very spacious, if not exactly luxurious, rooms. The two in back open right onto the water and offer one of the best views in town. Exposed brick walls provide character, and three of the rooms have loft sleeping areas. Expect some noise from the saloon downstairs. The Belmont also rents out three suites across the street, four cottages in nearby Port Hadlock, and a few vacation homes as well. Although these rooms are definitely not for the finicky, they've got loads of character.

925 Water St., Port Townsend, WA 98368. ℂ 360/385-3007. www.thebelmontpt.com. 4 units. $49–$89 double. AE, DC, DISC, MC, V. **Amenities:** Restaurant (Regional American). *In room:* Coffeemaker.

IN PORT LUDLOW

The Resort at Ludlow Bay ⭐⭐ Set on a tiny peninsula jutting into Ludlow Bay, this luxurious inn is one of the finest in the Northwest and has helped the Ludlow Bay resort community realize its dream of becoming one of *the* Puget Sound waterfront destinations. The setting rivals anything in the San Juan Islands, and the inn itself conjures up the image of a New England summer home at the shore. Designed for romantic getaways, the guest rooms are spacious and plush, with whirlpool tubs, fireplaces, and down-filled duvets on the beds. Best of all, every room has a water view and from some you can see Mount Baker or the Olympic Mountains. Breakfasts are served in a bright sun room with teak furnishings that evoke a nautical feel, and you can get casual meals in the inn's lounge. Additional amenities include paved walking paths through the adjacent resort and a croquet lawn.

One Heron Rd., Port Ludlow, WA 98365. ℂ **877/805-0868** or 360/437-2222. Fax 360/437-7410. www.
ludlowbayresort.com. 37 units. $139–$229 double; $189–$269 suite. Rates include continental breakfast.
AE, MC, V. **Amenities:** Lounge; 27-hole golf course; tennis courts; spa services; watersports rentals; bike
rentals; massage. *In room:* TV/VCR, dataport, fridge, coffeemaker, hair dryer, iron.

WHERE TO DINE
IN PORT TOWNSEND

One place on nearly everyone's itinerary during a visit to Port Townsend is **Elevated Ice Cream,** 627 Water St. (ℂ **360/385-1156**), which is open daily and
scoops up the best ice cream in town. For espresso, drop by **Tyler Street Coffee
House,** 215 Tyler St. (ℂ **360/379-4185**). For tea instead of coffee, check out
Wild Sage, 227 Adams St. (ℂ **360/379-1222**). For pastries, light meals, and
good coffee, try **Bread & Roses Bakery,** 230 Quincy St. (ℂ **360/385-1044**).

Expensive

Fins Coastal Cuisine ⋒ SEAFOOD   Located on the second-floor of a waterfront building, this restaurant is just far enough removed from the sidewalk
cruisers to have a sophisticated atmosphere. The food here is the most imaginative you'll find in downtown Port Townsend and can be as creative as pink
peppercorn–crusted sea bass with a vegetable spring roll. However, if you're
tastes lean to simpler fare, you can also get a great dry-aged New York steak with
either french fries or onion rings. However, this is seafood country, so you might
want to try the Portuguese fisherman's stew or the seared sea scallops instead.

1019 Water St. ℂ 360/379-FISH. www.finscoastalcuisine.com. Main courses $8–$14 lunch, $17–$28 dinner. AE, DISC, MC, V. Sun–Thurs 11:30am–3pm and 4:30–8pm; Fri–Sat 11:30am–3pm and 4:30–9pm.

Moderate

The Belmont ⋒ NORTHWEST   Housed in a building that dates back to
1885, this is the oldest waterfront restaurant and hotel in town. While the interior doesn't really conjure up the 1890s, the view out the back, especially from
the small deck, is great. The menu delves into interesting flavor combinations
and draws on a lot of influences (chicken with a pistachio and raspberry vinaigrette; grilled prawns with a citrus Grand Marnier sauce and cranberries; baby
back pork ribs baked in ale, brown sugar, and barbecue sauce).

925 Water St. ℂ 360/385-3007. Reservations recommended. Main courses $11–$22. AE, DC, DISC, MC, V.
Daily 11:30am–8:30 or 9pm (shorter hours in winter).

Lonny's Restaurant ⋒⋒ ITALIAN/NORTHWEST   Located across the
street from the Boat Haven marina south of downtown Port Townsend, this
romantic, low-key place is a welcome alternative to the touristy restaurants
downtown. The menu is fairly long and always features plenty of daily specials.
Be sure to start with the oyster stew, which is made with pancetta and fennel.
You'll find a wide variety of interesting pasta dishes from which to choose, but
the rigatoni Gorgonzola is our favorite. Traditional Spanish paella is another
tasty dish. Local oysters, mussels, and clams show up frequently on the fresh
sheet and are hard to resist. Interesting wines are usually available by the glass.

2330 Washington St. ℂ 360/385-0700. www.lonnys.com. Reservations recommended. Main courses $12–
$24. AE, DISC, MC, V. Daily 5–9pm (closed Tues Oct–June).

Sentosa ⋒ *(Finds* JAPANESE   This little side-street sushi place is a great escape
from the touristy restaurants along the Port Townsend waterfront. The cool vibe
makes this a popular spot with both weekending Seattle hipsters and urban

refugees who have taken shelter in Port Townsend. The menu is short, with lots of great sushi, including a blackened albacore roll, a roll made with salmon skin and daikon sprouts, and spicy scallop roll. The broiled black cod is a favorite, and they also do filling noodle bowls. Don't miss the ginger-cardamom ice cream.

218 Polk St. ℂ 360/385-2378. www.finscoastalcuisine.com. Reservations recommended. Main courses $9–$14; sushi $3.50–$12. DISC, MC, V. Daily 11:30am–2:30pm and 5–9pm.

Silverwater Café ★★ *Value* NORTHWEST   Works by local artists, lots of plants, and New Age music on the stereo set the tone for this casually chic restaurant. Though the menu focuses on Northwest dishes, it includes preparations from around the world. You can start your meal with an artichoke-and-Parmesan pâté and then move on to ahi tuna with lavender pepper, prawns with cilantro-ginger-lime butter, or smoked chicken with brandy and apples. The oysters in a blue-cheese sauce are a favorite of ours. If you're a vegetarian, you'll find a half-dozen options.

237 Taylor St. ℂ 360/385-6448. www.silverwatercafe.com. Reservations accepted only for 6 or more. Main courses $6–$9.50 lunch, $9–$18 dinner. MC, V. Mon–Fri 11:30am–2:30pm and 5–8:30pm; Sat 11:30am–2:30pm and 5–9:30pm; Sun 11:30am–8:30pm (shorter hours in winter).

Inexpensive

The Fountain Café ★ *Finds* ECLECTIC   Housed in a narrow clapboard building, this funky little place has long been a favorite of Port Townsend locals and counterculture types on a tight budget. Eclectic furnishings decorate the room and there are a few stools at the counter. The menu changes seasonally, but you can rest assured that the simple fare here will be utterly fresh and that the menu will include plenty of shellfish and pasta. The Greek pasta is a mainstay that's hard to beat. The wide range of flavors here assures that everyone will find something to his or her liking.

920 Washington St. ℂ 360/385-1364. Reservations accepted only for 6 or more. Main courses $7.25–$17. MC, V. Mon–Tues 11:30am–3pm and 5–9pm; Wed–Thurs 8am–3pm and 5–9pm; Fri–Sat 8am–3pm and 5–9:30pm; Sun 8am–3pm and 5–9pm.

Khu Larb Thai ★ THAI   Located half a block off busy Water Street, Khu Larb seems a world removed from Port Townsend's sometimes-overdone Victorian decor. Thai easy-listening music plays on the stereo, and the pungent fragrance of Thai spices wafts through the dining room. One taste of any dish on the menu and you'll be convinced that this is great Thai food. The *tom kha gai,* a sour-and-spicy soup with a coconut-milk base, is particularly memorable. The curry dishes made with mussels are also good bets.

225 Adams St. ℂ 360/385-5023. Reservations not accepted. Main courses $7.50–$9. AE, MC, V. Sun and Tues–Thurs 11am–8:30pm; Fri–Sat 11am–9:30pm.

IN PORT HADLOCK

If you're heading out to Marrowstone Island and want to have a picnic, be sure to stop at **The Village Baker,** 10644 Rhody Dr., Port Hadlock (ℂ **360/379-5310**), to get some organic artisan bread.

The Ajax Cafe ★★ *Value* INTERNATIONAL   With no two matching glasses and no two chairs the same, this long-time local favorite is as eclectic a place as you'll find—and a lot of fun, too. Located on the waterfront in Port Hadlock in an old wooden storefront, the restaurant is out of the way and funky, and that's exactly why it's so popular. Silly hats hang from the ceiling, the restroom walls are hung with loud ties, and patrons are encouraged to don silly garb while dining. To top it all off, there's live music on the weekends. The menu runs the gamut from a seafood pasta to ribs spiked with Jack Daniel's whiskey. However, it's the steaks that the locals rave about. If you like good times and good food, this is a "don't miss." The perpetual party atmosphere makes this is a great place for a celebration.

Lower Hadlock Rd., Port Hadlock. (℃ **360/385-3450**. www.ajaxcafe.com. Reservations recommended. Main courses $11–$15. MC, V. Tues–Sun 5–9pm. Closed Jan.

PORT TOWNSEND AFTER DARK
On weekend nights, you can catch live music at **Lanza's,** 1020 Lawrence St. (℃ **360/379-1900**), an Italian restaurant; and the **Public House,** 1038 Water St. (℃ **360/385-9708;** www.thepublichouse.com), which books an eclectic range of music and has the feel of a 19th-century tavern.

HIKING OLYMPIC PENINSULA EAST
South of Port Townsend, U.S. 101 follows the west shore of Hood Canal. Off this highway are several dead-end roads that lead to trail heads in Olympic National Forest. These trail heads are the starting points for many of the best day hikes on the Olympic Peninsula and lead into several different wilderness areas, as well as into Olympic National Park. Many of these hikes lead to the summits of mountains with astounding views across the Olympic Mountains and Puget Sound.

Two miles south of Quilcene, you'll find Penny Creek/Big Quilcene River Road, which leads to the trail heads for both **Marmot Pass** and **Mount Townsend**—two of the best day-hike destinations on the peninsula. Both of these trails are between 10- and 11-mile round-trip hikes. Up the Dosewallips River Road west of Brinnon, you'll find the trail head for the very popular 4-mile round-trip hike to **Lake Constance.** Up the Hamma Hamma River Road, just north of Eldon, you'll find the trail head for the hike to the beautiful **Lena Lakes** area. West of Hoodsport are the popular **Lake Cushman** and the trail heads for the 2-mile round-trip hike along the scenic **Staircase Trail,** the 4½-mile round-trip hike to the summit of **Mount Ellinor,** and the 16-mile round-trip hike to the **Flapjack Lakes,** which are a very popular overnight destination. For information contact **Quilcene Ranger Station,** 295142 U.S. 101 S. (P.O. Box 280), Quilcene, WA 98376 (℃ **360/765-2200;** www.fs.fed.us/r6/ olympic). Because floods frequently wash out trail bridges and sections of access road and trails, you should always check to see if a trail is open before heading out on a hike.

Moments Get High on the Olympic Peninsula
You don't have to drive all the way to Hurricane Ridge if you want an elevated perspective on the Olympic Peninsula. Just 5 miles south of the town of Quilcene, off U.S. 101, you can drive to the summit of 2,804-foot Mount Walker, which is the only peak on Puget Sound that has a road to its summit. The only drawback is that the 4-mile-long gravel road is steep and narrow, and is definitely not for the squeamish. At the summit, there are two viewpoints, from which you can see Mount Rainier, the Olympic Mountains, the Hood Canal Bridge, and sometimes Mount Baker and even the Seattle Space Needle.

---

2 Sequim & Dungeness Valley

17 miles E of Port Angeles, 31 miles W of Port Townsend

Located in the rain shadow of the Olympic Mountains, Sequim (remember, it's pronounced *skwim*) is the driest region of the state west of the Cascade Range and, consequently, sodden, moss-laden Northwesterners have taken to retiring here in droves. While the rains descend on the rest of the region, the fortunate few who call Sequim home bask in their own personal microclimate of sunshine and warmth.

The lack of rainfall and temperate climate here also make this an almost perfect place to grow lavender plants and today, parts of Sequim take on the look of Provence each summer when the lavender plants are in bloom. There are U-pick farms, shops selling all manner of lavender products, and, of course, an annual lavender festival.

Before this area became known for its lavender farms, it was famous for its hefty crustaceans. The nearby town of Dungeness is set at the foot of Dungeness Spit, which, at more than 6 miles in length, is the longest sand spit in the world. However, it is for lending its name to the Northwest's favorite crab that Dungeness is most famous. The Dungeness crab is as much a staple of Washington waters as the blue crab is in the Chesapeake Bay region.

ESSENTIALS

GETTING THERE The Sequim-Dungeness Valley lies to the north of U.S. 101 between Port Townsend and Port Angeles. **Jefferson Transit** (© **800/ 371-0497** or 360/385-4777; www.jeffersontransit.com) has service from Port Townsend to Sequim, and **Clallam Transit** (© **800/858-3747** or 360/452-4511; www.clallamtransit.com) operates west from Sequim and around the peninsula to Lake Crescent, Neah Bay, La Push, and Forks.

VISITOR INFORMATION For more information contact the **Sequim-Dungeness Valley Chamber of Commerce,** 1192 E. Washington St. (P.O. Box 907), Sequim, WA 98382-0907 (© **800/737-8462** or 360/683-6197; www. visitsun.com).

FESTIVALS The **Irrigation Festival** (© **800/737-8462** or 360/683-6197; www.irrigationfestival.com), the oldest continuous festival in Washington, has been going on for nearly 110 years and takes place in early May. In mid-July, when the lavender gardens are in full bloom, the town observes the season with its **Celebrate Lavender Festival** (© **800/500-8401;** www.lavenderfestival.com).

EXPLORING THE AREA

Just east of Sequim on U.S. 101, you'll find the **7 Cedars Casino,** 270756 U.S. 101 (© **800/4-LUCKY-7** or 360/683-7777), which is operated by the Jamestown S'Klallam Tribe and is designed to resemble a traditional longhouse, with several large totem poles out front. Nearby, you can visit the tribe's **Northwest Native Expressions,** 1033 Old Blyn Hwy. (© **360/681-4640**), where both quality and prices are high.

In downtown Sequim, you'll find the **Museum & Arts Center,** 175 W. Cedar St., Sequim (© **360/683-8110;** www.sequimmuseum.org), which houses a pair of mastodon tusks that were found near here in 1977. The mastodon had been killed by human hunters, a discovery that helped establish the presence of humans in this area 12,000 years ago. The museum also has an exhibit on the much more recent culture of the region's Native Americans. Open Tuesday through Saturday from 8am to 4pm; admission is free.

Fun Fact   K-E-L-K Radio

Sequim is home to a herd of around 100 Roosevelt elk who constantly wander back and forth across U.S. 101 to travel from the foothills to their grazing land. To reduce the number of automobile-elk collisions, several members of the herd have had radio collars put on them. When the elk with radio collars approach the highway, the signals emitted by the collars signal yellow "Elk Crossing" warning lights to begin flashing.

If you've got the kids with you, Sequim's **Olympic Game Farm** ⚐, 1423 Ward Rd. (℃ **800/778-4295** or 360/683-4295; www.olygamefarm.com), is a must. The animals here have appeared in more than 100 movies and TV shows. You'll get up close and personal with bison, Kodiak bears, zebras, wolves, elk, deer, and many other species. There are drive-through and walking tours as well as a petting farm. In summer the farm is open daily from 9am until 5pm (closing earlier in other months); admission is $9 to $15 for adults, $7 to $12 for seniors and children ages 6 to 12, and free for children 5 and under.

The biggest attraction is Dungeness Spit, which is protected as the **Dungeness National Wildlife Refuge** ⚐⚐ (℃ **360/457-8451**). Within the refuge there is a half-mile trail to a bluff-top overlook, but it is the spit, where you can hike for more than 5 miles to the historic New Dungeness Lighthouse, that is the favorite hiking area within the refuge. Along the way you're likely to see numerous species of birds as well as harbor seals. There's a fee of $3 per family to visit the spit. Near the base of the Dungeness Spit, you'll also find the **Dungeness Recreation Area** (℃ **360/683-5847**), which has a campground, picnic area, and trail leading out to the spit. If you're not up for a 10-mile round-trip hike to the lighthouse, you can paddle out on a tour with **Dungeness Kayaking Tours** (℃ **360/681-4190;** www.dungenesskayaking.com). A 4-hour tour to the lighthouse costs $90 per person. There are also 2-hour tours of Dungeness Bay for $45 and kayaks can be rented if you're an experienced paddler. Camping and water access are also available at **Sequim Bay State Park** (℃ **360/683-4235**), about 3 miles southeast of Sequim.

Sequim has also become known for its many lavender farms, which paint the landscape with their colorful blooms each summer. Sequim's climate is ideal for growing lavender, and you'll likely pass numerous large fields of this fragrant Mediterranean plant as you tour the area. If you want to get into a lavender field, you've got plenty of options. **Purple Haze Lavender,** 180 Bell Bottom Rd. (℃ **888/852-6560** or 360/683-1714; www.purplehazelavender.com), a U-pick farm that is located east of downtown Sequim off W. Sequim Bay Road, is one of our favorites. April through September, the farm is open daily from 10am to 5pm and has a gift shop in a small barn. The farm also has a year-round shop in downtown Sequim. North of here, don't miss **Graysmarsh Farm,** 6187 Woodcock Rd. (℃ **360/683-5563;** www.graysmarsh.com), which has both beautiful lavender fields and U-pick berry fields, where, in season, you can pick strawberries, raspberries, blueberries, and loganberries. Up near the Dungeness Spit, you'll find another great farm, **Jardin du Soleil Lavender,** 3932 Sequim-Dungeness Way (℃ **877/527-3461** or 360/582-1185; www.jardindusoleil.com). This organic lavender farm surrounds an old farmhouse that has Victorian gardens. June through September, the farm is open daily from 10am to 5pm;

October through December, April, and May, it's open Friday through Sunday from 10am to 4pm. In the same area, you can visit the **Olympic Lavender Farm,** 1432 Marine Dr. (© 360/683-4475; www.olympiclavender.com), which is open daily from noon to 5pm in July and August. Although **Cedarbrook Herb Farm,** 1345 Sequim Ave. S. (© 800/470-8423 or 360/683-7733; www. cedarbrookherbfarm.com), isn't specifically a lavender farm, it is well worth a visit. Here you can buy herb plants as well as herb vinegars, potpourris, dried flowers, lavender wands, garlic braids, and the like. You'll find this farm south of downtown Sequim at the top of a hill overlooking the town. It's open Monday through Saturday from 9am to 5pm and Sunday from 10am to 4pm. Off to the southwest of Sequim, you'll find **Lost Mountain Lavender,** 1541 Taylor Cutoff Rd. (© 360/681-2782; www.lostmountainlavender.com). This farm is open Thursday through Monday from 9am to 5pm in June, July, and August and on weekends in May, September, and October. To find your way around the area's lavender farms, stop by the Sequim-Dungeness Valley Chamber of Commerce visitor center (see above) or, on the Web, check out **www.lavendergrowers.org**.

If you're interested in tasting some locally produced wine, drive out to the **Lost Mountain Winery,** 3174 Lost Mountain Rd. (© 360/683-5229; www. lostmountain.com), which produces Italian-style wines with no added sulfites. To find the winery from U.S. 101, go south 3 miles on Taylor Cut Off Road and turn right on Lost Mountain Road. You can also stop at **Olympic Cellars,** 255410 U.S. 101 (© 360/452-0160; www.olympiccellars.com), which is housed in a large barn on the west side of Sequim.

The Sequim-Dungeness Valley is also one of the best areas in the state for **bicycle touring.** The roads are flat, there are great views, and you don't have to worry as much about getting rained on. Also, the **Olympic Discovery Trail,** a partly paved and partly gravel bike path, crosses much of the Sequim Dungeness Valley and links Sequim to Port Angeles.

If you'd like to do some bird-watching while you're in Sequim, drop by the **Dungeness River Audubon Center,** Railroad Bridge Park, Hendrickson Road (© 360/681-4076; www.dungenessrivercenter.org), which has guided bird walks on Wednesday mornings at 8:30am. The center is open Tuesday through Saturday from 10am to 4pm and from noon to 4pm on Sunday. The center is on the west side of Sequim (from U.S. 101, take River Rd. north to Priest Rd. to Hendrickson Rd.).

WHERE TO STAY

BJ's Garden Gate 🏚🏚   For the ultimate in luxury, book a room at this modern Victorian farmhouse on a bluff overlooking the Strait of Juan de Fuca. The inn is located on the west side of the Sequim Dungeness Valley and is surrounded by 3 acres of English gardens and the views stretch all the way to Victoria on the far side of the straits. All the rooms have double Jacuzzi tubs, fireplaces, and water views and are furnished with European antiques. There are also showers for two and fluffy down comforters to make the rooms both romantic and cozy. Innkeeper BJ Paton makes all her guests feel like royalty.

397 Monterra Dr., Port Angeles, WA 98362. © 800/880-1332 or 360/452-2322. www.bjgarden.com. 5 units. $125–$205 double. Rates include full breakfast. AE, MC, V. *In room:* TV/VCR, dataport.

Domaine Madeleine 🏚🏚   Located 7 miles east of Port Angeles, this contemporary B&B is set at the back of a small pasture and has a very secluded feel. Big windows take in the views, while inside you'll find lots of Asian antiques and other interesting touches. Combine this with the waterfront setting and you have a fabulous hideaway—you may not even bother exploring the park. All rooms have fireplaces and views of the Strait of Juan de Fuca and the mountains beyond. Some rooms have whirlpool tubs, and some have kitchens or air-conditioning. For added privacy, there is a separate cottage. The guest rooms are in several different buildings surrounded by colorful gardens.

146 Wildflower Lane, Port Angeles, WA 98362. © **888/811-8376** or 360/457-4174. www.domaine madeleine.com. 5 units. $145–$225 double. Rates include full breakfast. 2-night minimum mid-Apr to mid-Oct and holidays. AE, DISC, MC, V. **Amenities:** Access to nearby health club; massage. *In room:* TV/VCR, dataport, hair dryer, iron, free local calls.

Dungeness Bay Motel ★ Despite the name, this is more a collection of cottages than a motel in the traditional sense of the word. Set on a bluff overlooking the Strait of Juan de Fuca and located across the street from the waters of Dungeness Bay, this place boasts great views and economical accommodations. Some units actually have views of both the water and the Olympic Mountains. The large San Juan Suite has a fireplace and is our favorite here. The summer sunsets here simply cannot be beat.

140 Marine Dr., Sequim, WA 98382. © **888/683-3013** or 360/683-3013. www.dungenessbay.com. 6 units. $85–$125 double. DISC, MC, V. *In room:* TV, kitchen, fridge, coffeemaker.

Juan de Fuca Cottages ★ Located across the street from the water and surrounded by wide green lawns, these well-tended cottages have excellent views. While most face the water, the best views are actually from the one cottage that faces the Olympic Mountains to the south. This cabin has skylights and a long wall of windows. Other cottages also have skylights and all have whirlpool tubs and kitchenettes. The cottages also have their own little private beach. Although prices seem high for what you get, these cottages can all sleep at least four people.

182 Marine Dr., Sequim, WA 98382. © **866/683-4433** or 360/683-4433. www.juandefuca.com. 6 units. May to late Oct $140–$235 double; late Oct to Apr $90–$100 double. DISC, MC, V. *In room:* TV/VCR, kitchenette, fridge, coffeemaker, hair dryer, iron.

Sunset Marine Resort ★ *(Finds)* Located on the east shore of Sequim Bay, this collection of waterfront cabins is a secluded little retro hideaway. It's decorated in shabby-chic style by the owners, who also operate a little shabby-chic shop in downtown Sequim. Cabins include a renovated ranger station and a boathouse that sits on pilings over the water. Other cabins date from the 1930s and 1940s. Five of the cabins have full kitchens. You can spend your day paddling around the bay or digging littleneck clams from in front of the cabins. Because these cabins are so distinctive and relatively economical, they tend to book up months in advance.

40 Buzzard Ridge Rd., Sequim, WA 98382. © 360/681-4166. www.sunsetmarineresort.com. 6 units. June–Sept $105–$165 double; Oct–May $95–$145 double. 2-night minimum June–Aug and all weekends. DISC, MC, V. Pets accepted ($15). **Amenities:** Kayak and canoe rentals. *In room:* Coffeemaker.

WHERE TO DINE

If you're in need of a light lunch, don't miss **Jean's Deli** ★, 134 S. Second St. (© **360/683-6727**). **Petals Garden Café** ★, Cedarbrook Herb Farm, 1345 S. Sequim Ave. (© **360/683-4541**), at the top of a hill on the south side of the highway bypass around Sequim, is a great place for lunch if you are an avid gardener. This sandwich shop is located in a historic church building a block off Sequim's main street. For coffee, head for **Hurricane Coffee,** 104 W. Washington St. (© **360/681-6008**) or **The Buzz,** 128 N. Sequim Ave. (© **360/683-2503**), which is right across the street and serves coffee from our favorite Seattle roastery. Craving a decadent dessert? **Raindrop Desserts & Espresso,** 128 E. Washington St. (© **360/582-1143**).

Khu Larb Thai ✷ THAI   Located a block off Sequim's main drag, this is our favorite Sequim restaurant. Sure it doesn't exactly conjure up the Northwest with its spicy cuisine, but on a damp dreary day, a plate of spicy Thai food goes a long way toward warming a person. The *tom kha gai,* a sour-and-spicy soup with a coconut-milk base, should not be missed.

120 W. Bell St. © 360/681-8550. Main courses $7.50–$10. MC, V. Tues–Sun 11am–9pm.

The Original Oyster House ✷ SEAFOOD   Located on the shore of Discovery Bay east of Sequim, this restaurant is hidden from the highway, down a winding driveway through an associated condominium complex. The restaurant has a cozy little dining room with big windows that offer a pristine view of the bay and the hills on the opposite shore. In summer, the deck is the place to dine. Not surprisingly, the menu is heavy on oyster dishes. If you don't eat oysters, try the coconut-almond prawns, cioppino, and salmon. Monday through Friday, there are early-bird dinners between 4 and 6pm.

280417 U.S. 101. © 360/385-1785. Reservations recommended. Main dishes $13–$30. AE, DC, DISC, MC, V. Daily 4–8 or 9pm.

The 3 Crabs ✷ SEAFOOD   The 3 Crabs is an Olympic Peninsula institution, and folks drive from miles around to enjoy the fresh seafood and sunset views at this friendly waterfront restaurant overlooking the Strait of Juan de Fuca and the New Dungeness Lighthouse. For more than 40 years The 3 Crabs has been serving up Dungeness crabs in a wide variety of styles. You can order your crabs as a cocktail, a sandwich, cracked, and as crab Louie salad. Clams and oysters also come from the local waters and are equally good.

11 Three Crabs Rd., Dungeness. © 360/683-4264. Reservations recommended. Main courses $8–$20. DISC, MC, V. Daily 11:30am–9pm (until 7pm in winter).

3 Olympic National Park North & the Northern Olympic Peninsula

Port Angeles park entrance: 48 miles W of Port Townsend, 57 miles E of Forks

The northern portions of Olympic National Park are both the most accessible and most heavily visited. It is here, south of Port Angeles, that two roads lead into the national park's high country. Of the two areas reached by these roads, Hurricane Ridge is the more accessible. Deer Park, the other road-accessed high-country destination, is at the end of a harrowing gravel road and thus little visited. West of Port Angeles within the national park's lowlands lie two large lakes, Lake Crescent and Lake Ozette, that attract boaters and anglers. Also in this region are two hot springs—the developed Sol Duc Resort and the natural Olympic Hot Springs.

Outside the park boundaries, along the northern coast of the peninsula, are several campgrounds, a beautiful stretch of coastline that is popular with kayakers, and a couple of small sportfishing ports, Sekiu and Neah Bay, that are also popular with scuba divers. Neah Bay, which is on the Makah Indian Reservation, is also the site of one of the most interesting little museums in the state. The Makah Indian Reservation encompasses Cape Flattery, which is the northwesternmost point in the contiguous United States.

Port Angeles, primarily a lumber-shipping port, is the largest town on the north Olympic Peninsula and serves both as a base for people exploring the national park and as a port for ferries crossing the Strait of Juan de Fuca to Victoria, British Columbia. It is here that you will find the region's greatest concentration of lodgings and restaurants.

ESSENTIALS

GETTING THERE   U.S. 101 circles Olympic National Park, with main park entrances south of Port Angeles, at Lake Crescent, and at the Hoh River south of Forks.

Horizon Air (© **800/547-9308;** www.horizonair.com) flies between Seattle–Tacoma International Airport and Port Angeles. Rental cars are available in Port Angeles from **Budget Rent-A-Car** (© **800/345-8038** or 360/457-4246).

There is a **bus shuttle** to Port Angeles from Seattle and Sea-Tac Airport on **Olympic Bus Lines** (© **800/457-4492** or 360/417-0700; www.olympicbuslines. com). Reservations are recommended. **Jefferson Transit** (© **800/371-0497** or 360/385-4777; www.jeffersontransit.com) has service from Port Townsend to Sequim, where you can transfer to service on **Clallam Transit** (© **800/858-3747** or 360/452-4511; www.clallamtransit.com), which operates from Sequim around the peninsula to Lake Crescent, Neah Bay, La Push, and Forks.

Two **ferries,** one for foot passengers only and the other for vehicles and foot passengers, connect Port Angeles and Victoria, British Columbia. The ferry terminal for both ferries is at the corner of Laurel Street and Railroad Avenue. **Victoria Express** (© **800/633-1589** or 360/452-8088; www.victoriaexpress.com) is the faster of the two ferries (1 hr. between Victoria and Port Angeles) and carries foot passengers only. This ferry runs only between Memorial Day weekend and the end of September. One-way fares are $13 for adults, $7.50 for children 5 to 11, and free for children under 5. The **Black Ball Transport** (© **360/457-4491,** or 250/386-2202 in Victoria; www.cohoferry.com) ferry operates year-round except 2 weeks in late January or early February and carries vehicles as well as walk-on passengers. The crossing takes slightly more than 1½ hours. The one-way fares are $8.50 for adults, $4.25 for children 5 to 11; $33 for a car, van, camper, or motor home and driver.

VISITOR INFORMATION   For more information on the national park, contact the **Olympic National Park,** 600 E. Park Ave., Port Angeles, WA 98362-6798 (© **360/565-3131** or 360/565-3130; www.nps.gov/olym). For more information on Port Angeles and the rest of the northern Olympic Peninsula, contact the **North Olympic Peninsula Visitor and Convention Bureau,** 338 W. First St. (P.O. Box 670), Port Angeles, WA 98362 (© **800/942-4042** or 360/452-8552; www.olympicpeninsula.org); or the **Port Angeles Chamber of Commerce Visitors Center,** 121 E. Railroad Ave., Port Angeles, WA 98362 (© **877/456-8372** or 360/452-2363; www.portangeles.org).

(Tips Don't Leave Home Without It

You may not be planning on taking an international vacation, but spend any time in the Port Angeles area, and you'll be tempted to hop a ferry to Victoria, British Columbia. So, just in case, bring your passport with you on your Olympic vacation. You don't absolutely have to have a passport to cross into Canada and return to the U.S., but it makes things much easier.

FESTIVALS   Each year in late August, **Makah Days** are celebrated in Neah Bay (on the Makah Indian Reservation) with canoe races, Indian dancing, a salmon bake, and other events.

PARK ADMISSION   Park admission is $10 per vehicle and $5 per pedestrian or cyclist. Another option, if you plan to visit several national parks in a single year, is the National Parks Pass or the Golden Eagle Passport, an annual pass good at all national parks and recreation areas. The pass costs $50 (plus $15 for the Golden Eagle upgrade) and is available at all national park visitor centers. If you're over 62, you can get a Golden Age Passport for $10, and if you have a disability, you can get a free Golden Access Passport.

EXPLORING THE PARK'S NORTH SIDE

Port Angeles is the headquarters for the park, and it's here that you'll find the **Olympic National Park Visitor Center,** 3002 Mount Angeles Rd. (© **360/ 565-3130**). Mount Angeles Road is on the south edge of town and leads up to **Hurricane Ridge.** In addition to having lots of information, maps, and books about the park, the center has exhibits on the park's flora and fauna, old-growth forests, and whaling by local Native Americans. It's open daily from 8:30am to 5pm in summer (shorter hours fall–spring).

From the main visitor center, continue another 17 miles up Mount Angeles Road to Hurricane Ridge, which on clear days offers the most breathtaking views in the park. In summer the surrounding subalpine meadows are carpeted with wildflowers. Several hiking trails lead into the park from here, and several day hikes are possible (the 3-mile **Hurricane Hill Trail** and the 1-mile **Meadow Loop Trail** are the most scenic). At the **Hurricane Ridge Visitor Center** (© **360/565-3130**), you can learn about the area's fragile alpine environment. In winter, Hurricane Ridge is a popular cross-country skiing area and also has two rope tows and a Poma lift for downhill skiing. However, because the ski area is so small and the conditions so unpredictable, this ski area is used almost exclusively by local families. For more information, contact **Hurricane Ridge Public Development Authority** (© **360/457-4519**, or 360/565-3131 for road conditions; www.hurricaneridge.com). The Hurricane Ridge Visitor Center has exhibits on alpine plants and wildlife. In summer, you're likely to see deer grazing in the meadows and marmots, relatives of squirrels, lounging on rocks or nibbling on flowers.

A few miles east of Port Angeles, another road heads south into the park to an area called **Deer Park.** This narrow, winding gravel road is a real test of nerves and consequently is not nearly as popular a route as the road to Hurricane Ridge. However, the scenery once you reach the end of the road is just as breathtaking as that from Hurricane Ridge. As the name implies, deer are common in this area. To reach this area, turn south at the Deer Park movie theater.

West of Port Angeles a few miles, up the Elwha River, you'll find the short trail (actually an abandoned road) that leads to **Olympic Hot Springs** *. These natural hot pools are in a forest setting and are extremely popular and often crowded, especially on weekends. For more developed hot springs soaking, head to Sol Duc Resort, west of Lake Crescent.

Also west of Port Angeles, on U.S. 101, lies **Lake Crescent,** a glacier-carved lake surrounded by steep forested mountains that give the lake the feel of a fjord. This is one of the most beautiful lakes in the state and has long been a popular destination. Near the east end of the lake, you'll find the 1-mile trail to 90-foot-high **Marymere Falls** and the **Storm King Ranger Station** (© **360/928-3380**), which is usually open in the summer and at other seasons when a ranger is in the station. From the Marymere Falls Trail, you can hike the steep 2 miles up **Mount Storm King** to a viewpoint overlooking Lake Crescent (climbing above the viewpoint is not recommended). On the north side of the lake, the **Spruce Railroad Trail** parallels the shore of the lake, crosses a picturesque little bridge, and is one of the only trails in the park open to mountain bikes. As the name implies, this was once the route of the railroad built to haul spruce out of these forests during World War I. Spruce was the ideal wood for building biplanes because of its strength and light weight. By the time the railroad was completed, however, the war was over and the demand for spruce had dwindled.

There are several places on the lake where you can rent various types of small boats during the warmer months. At **Lake Crescent Lodge** 🎃🎃 you can rent rowboats, and at the **Fairholm General Store** (☎ **360/928-3020**), at the lake's west end, rowboats, canoes, and motorboats are available between April and October. The **Log Cabin Resort** on the north side of Lake Crescent rents rowboats, canoes, and pedal boats.

Continuing west from Lake Crescent, watch for the turnoff to **Sol Duc Hot Springs** (☎ **360/327-3583**). For 14 miles the road follows the Soleduck River, passing the Salmon Cascades along the way. Sol Duc Hot Springs were for centuries considered healing waters by local Indians, and after white settlers arrived in the area, the springs became a popular resort. In addition to the hot swimming pool and soaking tubs, you'll find cabins, a campground, a restaurant, and a snack bar. The springs are open daily from late March to late October; admission is $10 for adults. A 4.5-mile loop trail leads from the hot springs to **Sol Duc Falls,** which are among the most photographed falls in the park. Alternatively, you can drive to the end of the Sol Duc Road and make this an easy 1.5-mile hike. Along this same road, you can hike the half-mile **Ancient Groves Nature Trail.** Note that Sol Duc Road is one of the roads on which you'll have to pay an Olympic National Park admission fee.

EXPLORING THE PENINSULA'S NORTHWEST CORNER

Continuing west on U.S. 101 from the junction with the road to Sol Duc Hot Springs brings you to the crossroads of Sappho. Heading north at Sappho will bring you to Wash. 112, which is an alternative route from Port Angeles. It is about 40 miles from this road junction to the town of **Neah Bay** on the Makah Indian Reservation.

Between Clallam Bay and Neah Bay, the road runs right alongside the water and there are opportunities to spot sea birds and marine mammals, including gray, orca, humpback, and pilot whales. Between February and April, keep an eye out for the dozens of bald eagles that gather along this stretch of coast. In Clallam Bay, at the county day-use park, you can hunt for agates and explore tide pools. Near Slip Point Lighthouse, there are fossil beds that are exposed at low tides.

Neah Bay is a busy commercial and sportfishing port, and is also home to the impressive **Makah Cultural and Research Center** 🎃🎃, Bayview Avenue (☎ **360/645-2711;** www.makah.com/museum.htm), which displays artifacts from a Native American village that was inundated by a mudslide 500 years ago. This is the most perfectly preserved collection of Native American artifacts in the Northwest; part of the exhibit includes reproductions of canoes the Makah once used for hunting whales. There's also a longhouse that shows the traditional lifestyle of the Makah people. Between Memorial Day and September 15, the museum is open daily from 10am to 5pm, and between September 16 and Memorial Day, it's open Wednesday through Sunday from 10am to 5pm; admission is $5 for adults, $4 for students and seniors, free for children 5 and under.

The reservation land includes **Cape Flattery** ☆☆☆, which is the northwesternmost point of land in the contiguous United States. Just off the cape lies Tatoosh Island, site of one of the oldest lighthouses in Washington. Cape Flattery is one of the most dramatic stretches of Pacific coastline in the Northwest, and is a popular spot for hiking and ocean viewing. There is an excellent 1.5-mile round-trip trail, complete with boardwalks, stairs, and viewing platforms, that leads out to the cliffs overlooking Tatoosh Island. Keep an eye out for whales and sea otters. Bird-watchers will definitely want to visit Cape Flattery, which is on the Pacific Fly Way. More than 250 species of birds have been spotted here, and in the spring, raptors gather here before crossing the Strait of Juan de Fuca. For directions to the trail head, stop by the Makah Museum. At the museum, you'll also need to purchase a $7 Recreational Use Permit that will allow you to park at the Cape Flattery trail head. *Note:* Be aware that car break-ins are not uncommon here, so take your valuables with you.

A turnoff 16 miles east of Neah Bay leads south to **Ozette Lake** ☆☆, where there are boat ramps, a campground, and, stretching north and south, miles of beaches that are only accessible on foot. A 3.25-mile trail on a raised boardwalk leads from the Ozette Lake trail head to **Cape Alava** ☆☆, which is one of two places claiming to be the westernmost point in the contiguous United States (the other is Cape Blanco, on the Oregon coast). The large rocks just offshore here are known as haystack rocks or sea stacks and are common all along the rocky western coast of the Olympic Peninsula, which is characterized by a rugged coastline. Aside from five coastal Indian reservations, almost all this northern coastline is preserved as part of the national park.

GUIDED TOURS, EDUCATIONAL PROGRAMS & OUTDOOR ADVENTURES

GUIDED TOURS

For an interesting offshore tour to the Olympic Coast National Marine Sanctuary, contact **Puffin Adventures** (① 888/305-2437; www.puffinadventures.com). These boat tours, which operate between April and November, explore the waters off Cape Flattery and Tatoosh Island, where you can see as many as eight species of pelagic birds, including tufted puffins.

EDUCATIONAL PROGRAMS

The **Olympic Park Institute,** 111 Barnes Point Rd., Port Angeles, WA 98363 (① 360/928-3720; www.yni.org/opi), which is located in the Rosemary Inn on Lake Crescent, offers a wide array of summer field seminars ranging from painting classes to bird-watching trips to multi-day backpacking trips.

OUTDOOR ADVENTURES

BICYCLING   If you're interested in exploring the region on a bike, you can rent one at **Sound Bikes & Kayaks,** 120 E. Front St., Port Angeles (① 360/457-1240; www.soundbikeskayaks.com), which can recommend good rides in the area and also offers bicycle tours. Bikes are $9 per hour or $30 per day.

FISHING   The rivers of the Olympic Peninsula are well known for their fighting salmon, steelhead, and trout. In Lakes Crescent and Ozette you can fish for such elusive species as Beardslee and Crescenti trout. No fishing license is necessary to fish for trout on national park rivers and streams or in Lake Crescent or Lake Ozette. However, you will need a state punch card—available wherever fishing licenses are sold—to fish for salmon or steelhead. For more information on freshwater fishing in the park, contact Olympic National Park (✆ **360/565-3130**). Boat rentals are available on Lake Crescent at Fairholm General Store, the Log Cabin Resort, and Lake Crescent Lodge. Fly fishermen can pick up supplies and equipment at **Waters West Fly Fishing Outfitters,** 219 N. Oak St., Port Angeles (✆ **360/417-0937;** www.waterswest.com).

If you want to hire a guide to take you out on the rivers to where the big salmon and steelhead are biting, try **Diamond Back Guide Service** (✆ **360/452-9966;** www.northolympic.com/diamondback), which charges $225 per day for two people; or **Sol Duc River Lodge Guide Service** (✆ **866/868-0128** or 360/327-3709; www.solducriverfishing.com), which charges $380 per day for two people—but that rate includes your room, breakfast, and lunch.

If you're more interested in heading out on open water to do a bit of salmon or deep-sea fishing, numerous charter boats operate out of Sekiu and Neah Bay. In the Sekiu/Clallam Bay area, contact **Puffin Adventures** (✆ **888/305-2437;** www.puffinadventures.com). In Neah Bay, try **King Fisher Charters** (✆ **888/622-8216;** www.kingfisherenterprises.com). Expect to pay from $100 to $160 per person for a day of fishing.

HIKING & BACKPACKING   For several of the most popular backpacking destinations in Olympic National Park (the Ozette Coast Loop, Grand Valley, Royal Basin, Badger Valley, Flapjack Lakes, and Lake Constance), advance-reservation hiking permits are required or highly recommended between May 1 and September 30 and can be made up to 30 days in advance. Reservations can be made by contacting the **Wilderness Information Center,** 3002 Mount Angeles Rd., Port Angeles (✆ **360/565-3100**). Both a Wilderness Use Fee ($5 for a group of up to 12 people) and a nightly camping fee ($2 per person per night) are charged. Should you be doing the Ozette Coast Loop, you'll also have to pay a $1-per-day trail head parking fee. For most other overnight hikes you can pick up a permit at a ranger station or at the trail head. If in doubt, check with a park ranger before heading out to a trail head for a backpacking trip. Also keep in mind that some trails start at trail heads on national forest land; for these trails, you'll need a Northwest Forest Pass. Also, should you be planning to backpack along the coast, keep in mind that some headlands can only be rounded at low tide, and others cannot be rounded at all. These latter headlands have marked (though often steep, muddy, and difficult) trails over them. In some cases these "trails" consist of cable ladders or handhold ropes. Also be aware that you'll have to ford quite a few creeks and even a river depending on which section of the coast you plan to hike. Always carry a tide table.

Most of the best backpacking trips in Olympic National Park are long and aren't easily turned into loop trips. If you want to do a one-way backpacking trip, you can arrange a shuttle through **Windsox Trailhead Shuttle,** 406 W. E St., Forks (✆ **360/374-2002**).

LLAMA TREKKING   If you want to do an overnight trip into the backcountry of the national park but don't want to carry all the gear, consider letting a llama carry your stuff. **Kit's Llamas,** P.O. Box 116, Olalla, WA 98359 (✆ **253/857-5274;** www.northolympic.com/llamas), offers llama trekking in the Olympic Mountains. Prices, based on a group of six to eight adults, are $35 to $75 per person for day hikes, $75 to $180 per person per day for overnight and multi-day trips, with special rates for children. **Deli Llama,** 17045 Llama Lane, Bow,

WA 98232 (© **360/757-4212;** www.delillama.com), also does trips of from 4 to 7 days in Olympic National Park ($135–$175 per person per day).

MOUNTAINEERING & ROCK CLIMBING   More adventurous tours ranging in length from half a day to 5 days are offered by **Olympic Mountaineering,** 140 W. Front St., Port Angeles 98362 (© **360/452-0240;** www. olymtn.com). This company's most popular tour is its climb to the summit of Mount Olympus, the highest peak on the Olympic Peninsula. Prices range from $100 for a half day of rock climbing to $495 for a combination climb to the summit of Mount Olympus and a day of ice climbing.

SCUBA DIVING   The waters off the town of Sekiu are the Olympic Peninsula's favorite dive site. For advice, air, and dive charters, divers will want to stop in at **Curley's Resort & Dive Center** (© **800/542-9680** or 360/963-2281; www. curleysresort.com), on the main road through town.

SEA KAYAKING & CANOEING   Sea-kayaking trips on nearby Lake Aldwell, at Freshwater Bay, and at Dungeness National Wildlife Refuge, are offered by **Olympic Raft & Kayak** (© **888/452-1443** or 360/452-1443; www.raftand kayak.com), which charges between $42 and $99 per person. Sea-kayak rentals are available at **Sound Bikes & Kayaks,** 120 E. Front St., Port Angeles (© **360/ 457-1240;** www.soundbikeskayaks.com), which charges $12 per hour or $40 per day. For sea-kayaking trips on the Hoh and Quillayute rivers, out on the west side of the peninsula, contact **Rainforest Paddlers,** 4883 Upper Hoh Rd., Forks (© **866/457-8398** or 360/374-5254; www.rainforestpaddlers.com). Between June and September, this company does half-day kayak outings on the Hoh River ($44 per person) as well as early morning and sunset paddles on the Quillayute River estuary ($69 per adult for morning trips and $89 per adult for evening trips).

SKIING/SNOWBOARDING/SNOWSHOEING   Cross-country skiing, downhill skiing and snowboarding, and snowshoeing are all possible in the winter at **Hurricane Ridge.** Here you'll find a tiny ski area with two rope tows and a Poma lift for downhill skiing and snowboarding. There are also many miles of marked, though ungroomed, cross-country ski trails here. For more information, contact **Hurricane Ridge Public Development Authority** (© **360/457- 4519** or 360/565-3131 for road conditions; www.hurricaneridge.net).

There are also 90-minute ranger-led **snowshoe walks** here on Fridays, Saturdays, and Sundays from late December through March (conditions permitting). Snowshoes are provided, and a $2 donation is requested. Contact the park visitor center for details.

WHALE-WATCHING   **Puffin Adventures** (© **888/305-2437;** www.puffin adventures.com) offers whale-watching and wildlife cruises for $50 per person.

WHITE-WATER RAFTING   The steep mountains and plentiful rains of the Olympic Peninsula are the source of some great white-water rafting on the Elwha and Hoh rivers. Contact **Olympic Raft & Kayak** (© **888/452-1443** or 360/452-1443; www.raftandkayak.com). Rates start at $49 for a 2- to 2½-hour rafting trip.

EXPLORING AROUND PORT ANGELES

If you're curious about the general history of this area, you may want to check out exhibits presented by **Clallam County Historical Society,** Federal Building, 138 W. First St. (© **360/452-2662**). It's open Monday through Friday from 8:30am to 4pm and admission is free.

Moments **Lose Yourself in a Labyrinth**

At the Port Angeles Fine Arts Center, you can lose yourself in a labyrinth hidden in a little glade in the art center's sculpture-filled woods. Mind you, this is not a maze, and the objective isn't to get physically lost. A labyrinth is a convoluted pathway that is meant to be used as a path for walking meditations. So, go on, get lost.

The **Port Angeles Fine Arts Center** ✿, 1203 E. Lauridsen Blvd. (© **360/417-4590** or 360/457-3532; www.portangelesartscenter.com), is the town's only other museum and hosts changing exhibits of contemporary art. The museum also maintains an unusual sculpture park in the woods surrounding the center. Sculptures within the park are often barely discernible from natural objects and are fascinating. The gallery is open Thursday through Sunday from 11am to 5pm; admission is free.

If you'd like to get a close-up look at some of the peninsula's aquatic inhabitants, stop by the **Arthur D. Feiro Marine Life Center,** Port Angeles City Pier, 315 N. Lincoln St. (© **360/417-6254;** www.olypen.com/feirolab). In the center's tanks, you may spot a wolf eel or octopus, and there's a touch tank where you can pick up a starfish or sea cucumber. In summer the center is open Tuesday through Sunday from 10am to 5pm; October through Memorial Day, on Saturday and Sunday from noon to 4pm. Admission is $2.50 for adults, $1 for seniors and children 5 to 12, and free for children 4 and under.

If you'd like to taste some local wine, stop by **Black Diamond Winery,** 2976 Black Diamond Rd. (© **360/457-0748**), which produces both fruit and grape wines and is open February through December, Thursday through Sunday from 10am to 5pm and Monday 10am to 4pm (closed Thanksgiving and Christmas). You can also visit **Camaraderie Cellars,** 334 Benson Rd. (© **360/417-3564;** www.camaraderiecellars.com). The winery's tasting room is open May to October on Saturday and Sunday from 11am to 5pm. This winery gets its grapes from eastern Washington and makes a range of red and white wines.

WHERE TO STAY

Beyond Port Angeles, accommodations are few and far between, and those places worth recommending tend to be very popular. Try to have room reservations before heading west from Port Angeles.

IN PORT ANGELES

The Downtown Hotel This little hotel in downtown Port Angeles isn't too fancy, but it sure is comfortable and a real bargain. Also, if you're planning on taking the ferry to Victoria, it's very convenient. Located on the second and third floors of a building with shops on the ground floor, this place is a lot like European hotels. Some of the rooms have shared baths, but even these are quite large and attractively furnished. Guest rooms with private bathrooms are equally comfortable. Reproductions of old French advertising posters further lend a European flavor to this place. One room has a kitchenette.

101½ E. Front St., Port Angeles, WA 98362. © **866/688-8600** or 360/565-1125. www.portangeles downtownhotel.com. 17 units. $45–$55 double with shared bathroom; $65–$95 double with private bathroom. DISC, MC, V. *In room:* TV.

Red Lion Hotel Port Angeles ⊛ If you're on your way to or from Victoria, there's no more convenient hotel than the Red Lion. This is Port Angeles's only waterfront hotel, and is located only steps from the Victoria ferry terminal. Rooms are large, if without much character, and most have balconies and large bathrooms. However, you'll pay a premium for a room with a view of the Strait of Juan de Fuca.

221 N. Lincoln St., Port Angeles, WA 98362. ℂ **800/RED-LION** or 360/452-9215. Fax 360/452-4734. www. redlion.com. 187 units. June 15–Sept 30 $129–$159 double. Lower rates off season. AE, DISC, MC, V. Pets accepted. **Amenities:** Restaurant (steak and seafood) and lounge; outdoor pool; exercise room; Jacuzzi; bike rentals; business center; limited room service; coin-op laundry. In room: A/C, TV, dataport, coffeemaker, hair dryer, iron.

The Tudor Inn ⊛ Located in a quiet residential neighborhood not far from the waterfront, this 1910 Tudor home is surrounded by a large yard and pretty gardens and is our favorite Port Angeles B&B. On the ground floor you'll find a living room and library, where, in one, there's a gas fireplace and in the other, a wood-burning fireplace. Either is a great spot for warming yourself if the weather should turn cold and damp. Upstairs there are five rooms furnished with European antiques, including sleigh beds and four-posters. Several rooms have good views of the Olympic Mountains, and these are worth requesting.

1108 S. Oak St., Port Angeles, WA 98362. ℂ **866/286-2224** or 360/452-3138. www.tudorinn.com. 5 units. Mid-May to mid-Oct $95–$145 double; mid-Oct to mid-May $85–$135 double. Rates include full breakfast. AE, DISC, MC, V. Children over age 12 are welcome. In room: No phone.

WEST OF PORT ANGELES

Elwha Ranch Bed & Breakfast ⊛ Located adjacent to Olympic National Park, this cedar-log inn, on a 95-acre ranch high above the Elwha River valley, has a superb view up the valley into the park, and deer and elk are regular visitors. The two suites are in the main house, which has a casual Western ranch feel and plenty of windows to take in the views. If you're traveling with friends or family, opt for the two-bedroom suite. However, the nicest and most comfortable room here is a modern cabin outside the front door of the main house. Fresh pies are a specialty of innkeeper Margaret Mitchell. Be sure to get directions to the inn.

905 Herrick Rd., Port Angeles, WA 98363. ℂ **360/457-6540**. www.elwharanch.com. 3 units. Summer $120–$130 double; other months $90–$110 double. Rates include full breakfast. No credit cards. In room: TV/VCR, fridge, coffeemaker.

Lake Crescent Lodge ⊛⊛ This historic lodge is located 20 miles west of Port Angeles on the south shore of picturesque Lake Crescent and is the lodging of choice for national park visitors wishing to stay on the north side of the park. Wood paneling, hardwood floors, a stone fireplace, and a sun room make the lobby a popular spot for just sitting and relaxing (especially on rainy days). The guest rooms in this main lodge building are the oldest and have shared bathrooms. If you'd like more modern accommodations, there are a number of standard motel-style rooms, but these lack the character of the lodge rooms. If you have your family or some friends along, we recommend reserving a cottage. The Roosevelt cabins, which have fireplaces, are the most comfortable, but a couple of Singer cabins (nos. 20 and 21) have great views. All but the main lodge rooms have views of either the lake or the mountains, and the dining room has a good view across the lake. Early November through mid-April, the lodge is only open on weekends, and only the Roosevelt cabins are available. The dining room is not open in winter.

416 Lake Crescent Rd., Port Angeles, WA 98363. ℂ 360/928-3211. Fax 360/928-3253. www.lakecrescent lodge.com. 52 units, 4 with shared bathroom. $54–$83 double with shared central bathroom; $81–$148 double with private bathroom; $87–$184 cottage. Children under 12 stay free in parent's room. AE, DISC, MC, V. Pets accepted ($12). **Amenities:** Restaurant (Continental); lounge; watersports rentals. *In room:* No phone.

Log Cabin Resort ✦ *(Kids)*   This log-cabin resort on the north shore of Lake Crescent first opened in 1895 and still has buildings that date from the 1920s. It is this historic character that makes this such a relaxing place to stay, especially for families. The least expensive accommodations are rustic one-room log cabins in which you provide the bedding and share a bathroom a short walk away (basically this is camping without the tent). More comfortable are the 1928 cabins with private bathrooms, some of which also have kitchenettes (you provide the cooking and eating utensils). The lodge rooms and a chalet offer the greatest comfort and best views. The lodge dining room overlooks the lake and specializes in local seafood. The resort also has a general store and RV sites.

3183 E. Beach Rd., Port Angeles, WA 98363. ℂ 360/928-3325. Fax 360/928-2088. www.logcabinresort.net. 28 units. $58 cabin for 2 with no indoor plumbing; $86–$104 cabin for 2 with bathroom; $115 double; $141 chalet. Children 4 and under stay free in parent's room. DISC, MC, V. Closed Nov–Mar. Pets accepted ($6.05). **Amenities:** Restaurant (American); watersports rentals; coin-op laundry. *In room:* No phone.

Sol Duc Hot Springs Resort ✦   The Sol Duc Hot Springs have for decades been a popular family vacation spot, with campers, day-trippers, and resort guests spending their days soaking and playing in the hot-water swimming pool. The grounds of the resort are grassy and open, but the forest is kept just at arm's reach. The cabins are done in modern motel style and are comfortable if not spacious. There's a good restaurant here, as well as a poolside deli and grocery store. Three hot spring–fed swimming pools are the focal point, and are open to the public for a small fee.

Sol Duc Rd., U.S. 101 (P.O. Box 2169), Port Angeles, WA 98362-0283. ℂ 360/327-3583. Fax 360/327-3593. www.northolympic.com/solduc. 32 units. $112–$132 cabin for 2. Children under 4 stay free in parent's room. AE, DISC, MC, V. Closed Nov–Mar. **Amenities:** 2 restaurants (American, deli); outdoor pool; 3 hot spring–fed soaking pools; massage. *In room:* No phone.

CAMPGROUNDS

The six national park campgrounds on the northern edge of the park are some of the busiest in the park due to their proximity to U.S. 101. **Deer Park Campground** ✦✦ (14 campsites) is the easternmost of these campgrounds (take Deer Park Rd. from U.S. 101 east of Port Angeles) and the only high-elevation (5,400 ft.) campground in Olympic National Park. Deer Park is reached by a winding one-lane gravel road. The national park's **Heart O' the Hills Campground** (105 campsites), on Hurricane Ridge Road 5 miles south of the Olympic National Park Visitor Center, is the most convenient campground for exploring the Hurricane Ridge area. On Olympic Hot Springs Road up the Elwha River, you'll find **Elwha Campground** (40 campsites) and **Altaire Campground** (30 campsites).

West of Port Angeles along Wash. 112, there are three public campgrounds on the shore of the Strait of Juan de Fuca. **Salt Creek County Park** ✦ (90 campsites), 13 miles west of Port Angeles, is among the most scenic spots on this whole coast. About 20 miles west of Port Angeles is the Washington Department of Natural Resources' **Lyre River Park** (16 campsites).

The only campground on Lake Crescent is **Fairholm** (88 campsites) at the west end of the lake. The nearby **Sol Duc Campground** (82 campsites), set amid impressive stands of old-growth trees, is adjacent to the Sol Duc Hot Springs.

Heading west from Lake Crescent on U.S. 101, there are several campgrounds along the banks of the Sol Duc River.

The national park's remote **Ozette Campground** (15 campsites), on the north shore of Lake Ozette, is a good choice for people wanting to day-hike out to the beaches on either side of Cape Alava.

National park and other campgrounds in this area don't take reservations. However, for general information, contact **Olympic National Park** (© **360/565-3130**) or **Olympic National Forest, Forks Ranger Station,** 437 Tillicum Lane, Forks (© **360/374-6522;** www.fs.fed.us/r6/olympic).

WHERE TO DINE
IN PORT ANGELES

For sandwiches, pastries, and espresso, don't miss **Bonny's Bakery,** 215 S. Lincoln St. (© **360/457-3585**), which is housed in an old fire station.

Bella Italia ★ ITALIAN   Located in downtown Port Angeles, this restaurant is only a couple of blocks from the ferry terminal for ferries to and from Victoria, which makes it very convenient for many travelers. Dinners start with a basket of delicious bread accompanied by an olive oil, balsamic vinegar, garlic, and herb dipping sauce. Fresh local seafood makes it onto the menu in smoked salmon ravioli, smoked salmon fettuccine, and steamed mussels and clams. There are also some interesting individual pizzas and a good selection of wines, as well as a wine bar, an espresso bar, and plenty of excellent Italian desserts.

118 E. First St. © **360/457-5442.** www.bellaitaliapa.com. Main courses $8–$20. AE, DC, DISC, MC, V. Mon–Thurs 4–9pm; Fri–Sat 4–10pm; Sun 10am–2pm and 4–9pm.

C'est Si Bon ★★ FRENCH   Located 4 miles south of town just off U.S. 101, C'est Si Bon is painted a striking combination of turquoise, pink, and purple—which gives the restaurant a sort of happy elegance. Inside, the nontraditional paint job gives way to more classic decor: reproductions of European works of art, crystal chandeliers, and old musical instruments used as wall decorations. The restaurant serves deftly prepared Gallic standards such as French onion soup or escargot for starters. Follow that with *coquille Saint Jacques* or a Dungeness crab soufflé, finish with a rich and creamy *mousse au chocolat,* and *voilà!* you have the perfect French meal. Specials feature whatever is fresh.

23 Cedar Park Rd. © **360/452-8888.** www.northolympic.com/cestsibon. Reservations recommended. Main courses $21–$33. AE, DISC, MC, V. Tues–Sun 5–11pm.

Michael's Divine Dining ★ NORTHWEST/MEDITERRANEAN   Located in the basement of a building in downtown Port Angeles, Michael's is a great place for a meal whether you're in the mood for tapas and a cocktail, a designer pizza, or a big dish of paella. This latter dish is the house specialty and shouldn't be missed. For dessert, be sure to try the banana fritter and sugar-caramelized banana with chocolate sauce, and also keep an eye out for the lavender ice cream. On Saturday and Sunday, brunch is served.

117B E. First St. © **360/417-6929.** www.michaelsdining.com. Reservations recommended. Main courses $12–$29. AE, DISC, MC, V. Daily 11am–9pm.

Toga's International Cuisine ★ INTERNATIONAL/GERMAN   Located on the west side of Port Angeles, this restaurant is an unexpected treat and serves some very unusual dishes the likes of which are not to be found anywhere else in the state. Chef Toga Hertzog apprenticed in the Black Forest and has brought to his restaurant the traditional *Jagerstein* style of cooking in which diners cook their own meat or prawns on a hot rock. With 24 hours notice you can also have traditional Swiss cheese fondue or a lighter seafood fondue. To start your meal, you might try the crabmeat Rockefeller or the sampler of house-smoked salmon, scallops, oysters, and prawns. For dessert nothing hits the spot like the chocolate mousse.

122 W. Lauridsen Blvd. ℰ 360/452-1952. Reservations recommended. Main courses $18–$29. AE, DISC, MC, V. Tues–Sat 5–10pm.

WEST OF PORT ANGELES

Outside of Port Angeles, the restaurant choices become exceedingly slim. Your best choices are the dining rooms at **Lake Crescent Lodge** (open mid-Apr through early Nov) and the **Log Cabin Resort** (open Apr–Oct), both located on the shores of Lake Crescent. One other dining option on this lake is the **Fairholm General Store & Cafe,** 221121 U.S. 101 (ℰ 360/928-3020), which is at the lake's west end and is open between April and October. Although all you'll get here are burgers, sandwiches, and breakfasts, the cafe has a deck with a view of the lake. Continuing west, you'll find food at the dining room of **Sol Duc Hot Springs Resort** (open Apr–Oct).

Way out west, near Ozette Lake, you'll find **The Lost Resort,** Hoko-Ozette Road (ℰ **800/950-2899** or 360/963-2899), a general store with a deli, espresso, and a tavern serving lots of microbrews.

4 Olympic National Park West

Forks: 57 miles W of Port Angeles, 50 miles S of Neah Bay, 77 miles N of Lake Quinault

The western regions of Olympic National Park can be roughly divided into two distinct sections—the rugged coastal strip and the famous rainforest valleys. Of course, these are the rainiest areas within the park, and many a visitor has called short a vacation here due to the rain. Well, what do you expect? It is, after all, a rainforest. Come prepared to get wet.

The coastal strip can be divided into three segments. North of La Push, which is on the Quileute Indian Reservation, the 20 miles of shoreline from Rialto Beach to Cape Alava are accessible only on foot. The northern end of this stretch of coast is accessed from Lake Ozette off Wash. 112 in the northwest corner of the peninsula. South of La Push, the park's coastline stretches for 17 miles from Third Beach to the Hoh River mouth and is also accessible only on foot. The third segment of Olympic Park coastline begins at Ruby Beach just south of both the Hoh River mouth and Hoh Indian Reservation and stretches south to South Beach. This stretch of coastline is paralleled by U.S. 101.

Inland of these coastal areas, which are not contiguous with the rest of the park, lie the four rainforest valleys of the Bogachiel, Hoh, Queets, and Quinault rivers. Of these valleys, only the Hoh and Quinault are penetrated by roads, and it is in the Hoh Valley that the rainforests are the primary attraction.

Located just outside the northwest corner of the park, the timber town of Forks serves as the gateway to Olympic National Park's west side. This town was at the heart of the controversy over protecting the northern spotted owl, and is still struggling to recover from the employment bust after the logging boom of the 1980s.

ESSENTIALS

GETTING THERE   The town of Forks is the largest community in this northwest corner of the Olympic Peninsula and is on U.S. 101, which continues south along the west side of the peninsula to the town of Hoquiam.

Bus service from Sequim to Lake Crescent, Neah Bay, La Push, and Forks is operated by **Clallam Transit** (© 800/858-3747 or 360/452-4511; www.clallamtransit.com). Bus service between Forks and Lake Quinault is provided by **Jefferson Transit** (© 800/371-0497 or 360/385-4777; www.jeffersontransit.com). There is service to Quinault Lake from Olympia and Aberdeen on **Grays Harbor Transit** (© 800/562-9730 or 360/532-2770; www.ghtransit.com).

VISITOR INFORMATION   For more information on this western section of Olympic National Park, see "Visitor Information," above, in section 3 of this chapter. For more information on the Forks area, contact the **Forks Chamber of Commerce,** 1411 S. Forks Ave. (P.O. Box 1249), Forks, WA 98331 (© 800/44-FORKS or 360/374-2531; www.forkswa.com).

FESTIVALS   Each year in mid-July, **Quileute Days** are celebrated in La Push (on the Quileute Indian Reservation) with canoe races, traditional dancing, a salmon bake, and other events.

EXPLORING THE PARK'S WEST SIDE

If you want to learn more about the area's logging history, stop by the **Forks Timber Museum,** south of town on U.S. 101 (© 360/374-9663). The museum chronicles the history of logging in this region, but it also has displays on Native American culture and pioneer days. It's open from mid-April to October, daily from 10am to 4pm; admission is by donation.

Also in the Forks area, there are quite a few artists' studios and galleries. You can pick up an **Olympic West Arttrek** guide and map to these studios and galleries at the Forks Chamber of Commerce (see above for contact information).

West of Forks lie miles of pristine beaches and a narrow strip of forest (called the Olympic Coastal Strip) that are part of the national park but that are not connected to the inland, mountainous section. The first place where you can actually drive right to the Pacific Ocean is just west of Forks. At the end of a spur road you come to the Quileute Indian Reservation and the community of **La Push.** Right in town there's a beach at the mouth of the Quillayute River; however, before you reach La Push, you'll see signs for **Third Beach** 🌲🌲 and **Second Beach** 🌲🌲, which are two of the prettiest beaches on the peninsula. Third Beach is a 1½-mile walk and Second Beach is just over half a mile from the trail head. **Rialto Beach** 🌲🌲, just north of La Push, is another beautiful and rugged beach; it's reached from a turnoff east of La Push. From here you can walk north for 24 miles to Cape Alava, although this is also a very popular spot for day hikes. One mile up the beach is a spot called **Hole in the Wall,** where ceaseless wave action has bored a large tunnel through solid rock. On any of these beaches, keep an eye out for bald eagles, seals, and sea lions.

Roughly 8 miles south of Forks is the turnoff for the Hoh River valley. It's 17 miles up this side road to the **Hoh Visitor Center** (© 360/374-6925), campground, and trail heads. This valley receives an average of 140 inches of rain per year (and as much as 190 in.), making it the wettest region in the continental United States. At the visitor center you can learn all about the natural forces that cause this tremendous rainfall. To see the effect of so much rain on the landscape, walk the .75-mile **Hall of Mosses Trail,** where the trees, primarily Sitka spruce, western red cedar, and western hemlock, tower 200 feet tall. Here you'll see big-leaf maple trees with limbs draped in thick carpets of mosses. If you're up for a longer walk, try the **Spruce Nature Trail.** If you've come with a backpack, there's no better way to see the park and its habitats than by hiking the **Hoh River Trail,** which is 17 miles long and leads to Glacier Meadows and

Look Out: Banana Slugs Crossing

If you happen to be a gardener who lives where summers are humid, you probably curse slugs, which can do immense damage to a vegetable patch. Now, imagine that those slimy little slugs chomping on your tomatoes are not an inch long, but a foot in length! Sound like a late-night monster movie? Think again. And if you go into the woods today, be sure to watch your step.

The banana slug *(Ariolimax columbianus),* which can grow to be a foot long and live for up to 5 years, is the only slug native to the Pacific Northwest. Making its yellowish, elongated way through the region's lowland forests, these slugs dine on plants, mushrooms, and decaying vegetable matter. Though slugs may seem to wander aimlessly, they have two eyes on the ends of long stalks and two olfactory organs on short stalks. The eyes detect light and dark and help them find cool dark places where they can sleep away the day, while the olfactory organs are used to locate food. A slug eats by shredding organic matter with a tonguelike structure called a radula, which is covered with thousands of tiny teeth.

Aside from their repulsive appearance and annoying habit of devouring gardens, slugs get a bad rap for sliming anyone unlucky enough to grab one accidentally. Slug slime, if you take the time to study it (instead of just rubbing your fingers furiously to remove it), is amazing stuff. It's at once as slippery as soap and as sticky as glue, an unusual combination of properties that allows slugs to use their slime as a sort of instant highway on which to travel. Secreting the slime from their chin like so much drool, slugs coat the surface of whatever they're crawling on and then just slide along.

Slug slime may also serve as a defense mechanism. Lacking the protective shell of their close relatives the snails, slugs defend themselves by secreting copious amounts of slime, rendering them unpalatable to predators such as shrews, beetles, crows, and garter snakes.

Think slugs are sluggish? Think again. One of these babies can do 0.007 mph (3–4 in. per min.) on the straightaway as the muscles along its foot constrict in waves and move it forward.

It's hard to believe that something as soft and slow moving as a slug could ever be a threat to anything, but slugs are real scrappers. That same serrated tongue that shreds lettuce so efficiently can also be used as a weapon against other slugs. If you start checking slugs closely, you're likely to find a few with old battle scars on their backs.

We know that birds do it and bees do it, but how do slugs do it? With any slug they chance to meet, if the mood strikes. Slugs are hermaphroditic, and they can mate with any other slug of the same species. What this means is that each one of those slugs out in your garden is capable of laying eggs!

And how did banana slugs get their name? No one is quite sure whether it's because they so closely resemble bananas, right down to the brown spots, or because when stepped on, they have an effect similar to that of a banana peel. Either way, it's an appropriate name.

Blue Glacier on the flanks of Mount Olympus. A herd of elk calls the Hoh Valley home and can sometimes be seen along these trails.

On your way up the Hoh Valley, you might want to stop in at **Peak 6 Adventure Store,** 4883 Upper Hoh Rd. (© **360/374-5254**), an outfitter that sells not only any outdoors gear you might have forgotten, but also Native American baskets and art by local artists.

Continuing south on U.S. 101, but before crossing the Hoh River, you'll come to Oil City Road, a secondary road that heads west from the Hoh Oxbow campground. From the end of the road it's a hike of less than a mile to a rocky beach at the **mouth of the Hoh River.** You're likely to see sea lions or harbor seals feeding just offshore here, and to the north are several haystack rocks that are nesting sites for numerous sea birds. Primitive camping is permitted on this beach, and from here hikers can continue hiking for 17 miles north along a pristine wilderness of rugged headlands and secluded beaches.

South of the Hoh River off U.S. 101, you can drive to the **world's largest western red cedar.** Known as the Duncan cedar, this tree stands 178 feet tall and is almost 20 feet in diameter. You'll find the tree about 4 miles off the highway on Nolan Creek Road. Near milepost 170, watch for road N1000 on the east side of U.S. 101 and follow this road to a right fork onto N1100. Then turn right onto road N1112, and right again onto N112.

U.S. 101 finally reaches the coast at **Ruby Beach.** This beach gets its name from its pink sand, which is comprised of tiny grains of garnet. With its colorful sands, tide pools, sea stacks, and driftwood logs, Ruby Beach is the prettiest of the beaches along this stretch of coast. For another 17 miles or so south of Ruby Beach, the highway parallels the wave-swept coastline. Along this stretch of highway there are turnoffs for five beaches that have only numbers for names. Beach 6 is a good place to look for whales and sea lions and also to see the effects of erosion on this coast (the trail that used to lead down to the beach has been washed away). At low tide, the northern beaches offer lots of tide pools to be explored. Near the south end of this stretch of road, you'll find Kalaloch Lodge, which has a gas station, and the **Kalaloch Ranger Station** (© **360/962-2283**), which is usually open in the summer and at other seasons when a ranger is in the station.

Shortly beyond Kalaloch the highway turns inland again and passes through the community of **Queets** on the river of the same name. The Queets River valley is another rainy valley, and if you'd like to do a bit of hiking away from the crowds, head up the gravel road to the Queets campground, from which a hiking trail leads up the valley.

A long stretch of clear-cuts and tree farms, mostly on the Quinault Indian Reservation, will bring you to **Quinault Lake.** Surrounded by forested mountains, this deep lake is the site of the rustic Lake Quinault Lodge and offers boating and freshwater fishing opportunities, as well as more rainforests to explore on a couple of short trails (there is a total of about 10 miles of trails on the south side of the lake). On the north shore of the lake you'll find one of the peninsula's largest red cedar trees. This is a good area in which to spot Roosevelt elk.

For more information on guided tours and other outdoor recreational possibilities throughout the park's west side, see "Guided Tours, Educational Programs & Outdoor Adventures" in section 3, earlier in this chapter.

WHERE TO STAY
IN THE FORKS AREA
The town of Forks has several inexpensive motels and is a good place to look for cheap lodgings if you happen to be out this way without a reservation. These

include the **Forks Motel,** 351 S. Forks Ave. (*©* **800/544-3416** or 360/374-6243; www.forksmotel.com), which has a pool; and the **Pacific Inn Motel,** 352 S. Forks Ave. (*©* **800/235-7344** or 360/374-9400; www.pacificinnmotel.com).

La Push Ocean Park Resort ✦   Located right on the sands of First Beach on the Quileute Indian Reservation, this rustic resort has a very wide range of accommodations. There are utterly basic cabins that don't even have hot water, but there are also new deluxe oceanfront cabins that are the best rooms anywhere on this stretch of coast. These cabins have whirlpool tubs, walls of glass, lots of cedar accents, full kitchens, and carved wood furniture with Northwest Coast Native American designs. It is these latter cabins that make this place worth recommending. Other older units are passable at best and are most popular with surfers and fishermen.

330 Ocean Dr. (P.O. Box 67), La Push, WA 98350. *©* **800/487-1267** or 360/374-5267. www.ocean-park.org. 70 units. May–Sept $69–$78 double, $72–$180 1-bedroom cabin, $72–$220 2- and 3-bedroom cabins; lower rates other months. 2-night minimum summer weekends, 3-night minimum on holidays. AE, DISC, MC, V. Pets accepted ($10). *In room:* No phone.

Manitou Lodge ✦   This secluded B&B is set on 10 private acres and is only minutes from some of the most beautiful and remote beaches in the Northwest. The best room in the house is the Sacagawea, which has a fireplace and king-size bed. A separate cabin houses two of the rooms. Guests tend to gravitate to the comfortable living room, where a huge stone fireplace is the center of attention (fires help chase away the chill and damp of this rainy corner of the Olympic Peninsula). Breakfasts are hearty, although you can also opt for a discounted light breakfast. The innkeepers also operate both a coffeehouse and a gift shop/art gallery in downtown Forks. The gallery specializes in Native American crafts and local artwork.

813 Kilmer Rd. (P.O. Box 600), Forks, WA 98331. *©* **360/374-6295.** Fax 360/374-7495. www.manitou lodge.com. 7 units. May–Oct $105–$150 double; Nov–Apr $90–$130 double. Rates include full breakfast. AE, DC, MC, V. Take Wash. 110 west from north of Forks; turn right on Mora Rd. and then right on Kilmer Rd. Pets accepted ($10). Children over age 5 welcome. **Amenities:** Bikes. *In room:* Coffeemaker, hair dryer.

Miller Tree Inn ✦   Located just a few blocks east of downtown Forks, this large farmhouse B&B is surrounded by pastures and large old trees. With its classic styling, it feels very civilized compared to the wilds of the Olympic Peninsula and is a welcome sight at the end of the long drive out to Forks. Best of all, there are rooms with jetted tubs and fireplaces. One room also has a kitchenette (a definite bonus out in this neck of the woods). There's nothing fussy or pretentious about this place—just a comfortable, friendly inn that caters primarily to outdoors enthusiasts. At the end of a long day of hiking, the hot tub on the back deck is very welcome.

654 E. Division St., Forks, WA 98331. *©* **800/943-6563** or 360/374-6806. Fax 360/374-6807. www.millertree inn.com. 7 units. Late June to late Sept $95–$180 double; early Feb to mid-June and late Sept to early Nov $85–$135 double; early Nov to early Feb $75–$125 double. 2-night minimum on summer weekends. Rates include full breakfast. DISC, MC, V. Pets accepted ($10). **Amenities:** Jacuzzi. *In room:* No phone.

Olympic Suites Inn ✦   Located just off U.S. 101 at the north end of Forks and set back in the forest a bit, this modern motel is your best bet in the area if you don't want to stay at a B&B. The motel has the look and feel of an apartment complex, and most of the rooms are suites with full kitchens. The Calawah River and a boat ramp are just downhill from the motel, and some rooms have limited river views. Other rooms look into the forest.

800 Olympic Dr., Forks, WA 98331. © **800/262-3433** or 360/374-5400. www.olympicsuitesinn.com. 32 units. July–Aug $74 double, $79–$99 suite; Sept and mid-May to June $64 double, $69–$99 suite; Oct to mid-May $54 double, $54–$84 suite. Children under age 5 stay free in parent's room. AE, DISC, MC, V. Pets accepted ($5). **Amenities:** Coin-op laundry. *In room:* TV, refrigerator, coffeemaker.

ALONG THE PARK'S WEST SIDE, SOUTH OF FORKS

Kalaloch Lodge ★★   This is the national park's only oceanfront accommodations, and has a rustic, cedar-shingled lodge and a cluster of cabins perched on a grassy bluff above the thundering Pacific Ocean. Wide sand beaches stretch north and south from the lodge, and at the base of the bluff huge driftwood logs are scattered like so many twigs. The rooms in the old lodge are the least expensive, and the oceanview bluff cabins are the most in demand. The log cabins across the street from the bluff cabins don't have the knockout views. For modern comforts there are motel-like rooms in the Sea Crest House. A casual coffee shop serves breakfast and lunch while a slightly more formal dining room serves rather unmemorable meals. The lodge also has a general store and a gas station. Because the lodge is popular throughout the year, you should make reservations at least 4 months in advance.

157151 U.S. 101, Forks, WA 98331. © **866/525-2562** or 360/962-2271. Fax 360/962-3391. www.visit kalaloch.com. 64 units. Late May to mid-Oct $137–$142 double, $164–$248 suite, $178–$264 bluff cabin, $155–$176 log cabin. Lower rates Sun–Thurs other months. Children under 6 stay free in parent's room. AE, MC, V. Pets accepted in cabins ($13). **Amenities:** 2 restaurants (American). *In room:* No phone.

Lake Quinault Lodge ★★   Located on the shore of Lake Quinault in the southwest corner of the park, this imposing grande dame of the Olympic Peninsula wears an ageless tranquillity. Huge old firs and cedars shade the rustic lodge, and Adirondack chairs on the deck command a view of the lawn. The accommodations include small rooms in the main lodge, modern rooms with wicker furniture and small balconies, and rooms with fireplaces. The annex rooms are the least attractive, but they do have large bathtubs. The dining room has the most creative menu this side of the peninsula. The lodge offers lawn games and rainforest tours.

345 S. Shore Rd. (P.O. Box 7), Quinault, WA 98575. © **800/562-6672** or 360/288-2900. www.visitlake quinault.com. 92 units. Mid-June to late Sept and winter holidays $115–$180 double, $250 suite; late Sept to mid-June $68–$130 double, $195 suite. Children under 6 stay free in parent's room. AE, MC, V. Pets accepted in Boat House building ($10). **Amenities:** Restaurant (Northwest); lounge; indoor swimming pool; sauna; boat rentals; game room; tour desk; massage. *In room:* No phone.

Lake Quinault Resort ★★ *Finds*   Located on the north shore of Lake Quinault, this little resort is more of a luxury motel or casual inn than a resort, but whatever you want to call it, it's exceedingly comfortable. It is also located on the sunny side of the lake (as opposed to the shady side, which is where the ever-popular Lake Quinault Lodge is located). Consequently, at the end of a day hiking in the darkness of the rainforest, you can return here and enjoy the sunset over the lake. There's a long covered veranda and a narrow lawn for enjoying those sunsets. Guest rooms are spacious and modern, with a bit of modern country decor and Northwest style. Several of the rooms have kitchens.

314 N. Shore Rd., Amanda Park, WA 98526. © **800/650-2362** or 360/288-2362. Fax 360/288-2218. www. lakequinault.com. 9 units. Mid-June to early Oct $119–$149 double; early Oct to mid-June $55–$100 double. AE, DISC, MC, V. *In room:* TV, coffeemaker, hair dryer.

Rain Forest Resort Village ★ *Kids*   If you can't get a room at the Lake Quinault Lodge, this should be your second choice in the area. Although the cabins and motel rooms here are for the most part pretty basic, they are comfortable enough (and are actually as nice as some of the lodge rooms). All the cabins have fireplaces and some have either a kitchen or a Jacuzzi tub. Wide lawns slope down to the lake, and most rooms and cabins have water views. In summer, you can rent canoes for exploring the lake. A short trail leads from the resort to the world's largest spruce tree.

516 S. Shore Rd., Lake Quinault, WA 98575. ℂ 800/255-6936 or 360/288-2535. Fax 360/288-2957. www. rfrv.com. 28 units. Late June to Aug $90–$101 double, $132–$195 cabin. Lower rates other months. AE, DISC, MC, V. **Amenities:** Restaurant (American); lounge; boat rentals; coin-op laundry. *In room:* TV.

CAMPGROUNDS

If you want to say you've camped at the wettest campground in the contiguous United States, head for the national park's **Hoh Campground** ⚐ (88 campsites) in the Hoh River valley. Almost as wet is the national park's **Queets Campground** (20 campsites). This campground is 14 miles up the Queets Road from U.S. 101. On Quinault Lake there are three campgrounds. On the north shore is the walk-in **July Creek Campground** (29 campsites). On the south shore are two national forest campgrounds—**Willaby** (34 campsites) and **Falls Creek** (31 campsites). East of Lake Quinault, up the Quinault River valley, are two more national park rainforest campgrounds—**North Fork** (7 campsites) and **Graves Creek** (30 campsites)—that provide access to a couple of the park's long-distance hiking trails.

Campsites at **Bogachiel State Park** ⚐ (42 campsites), on the Bogachiel River 6 miles south of Forks on U.S. 101, are set under huge old spruce trees. On the banks of the Hoh River, the Washington Department of Natural Resources operates four primitive campgrounds for tent users. **Hoh Oxbow Campground** (7 campsites) is right on U.S. 101 and is the most convenient. Heading up river on the Hoh Rain Forest Road are **Willoughby Creek** (19 campsites) and **Minnie Peterson** (7 campsites). Down river on Oil City Road is **Cottonwood Campground** (7 campsites), which is a good place to camp if you want to explore the national park coast north of the Hoh River. An alternative here is to hike ½ mile to the beach and camp there.

Along the peninsula's west side, there are also several beach campgrounds. These include the national park's **Mora Campground** ⚐ (94 campsites) on the beautiful Rialto Beach at the mouth of the Quillayute River west of Forks. If you're prepared to hike in with your gear, you can also camp on Second Beach (half-mile hike) and Third Beach (1½-mile hike). South of the Hoh River, along the only stretch of U.S. 101 that is right on the beach, you'll find **Kalaloch Campground** (175 campsites), which is the national park's largest campground and the only one that takes reservations. Make reservations by contacting the **National Park Reservation Service** (ℂ **800/365-2267;** http://reservations.nps. gov). For general information on national park campgrounds, contact **Olympic National Park** (ℂ **360/565-3130**). For information on nearby national forest campgrounds, contact the **Olympic National Forest, Quinault Ranger Station,** 353 S. Shore Rd., Quinault (ℂ **360/288-2525;** www.fs.fed.us/r6/olympic).

WHERE TO DINE

In the town of Forks, you'll find several basic diners and family restaurants, but nothing really worth recommending. South of Forks, your best bets are the dining rooms at the **Kalaloch Lodge** and the **Lake Quinault Lodge.** If you happen to be hungry up the Hoh River, don't miss the juicy burgers at the **Hard Rain Cafe,** 5763 Upper Hoh Rd. (ℂ **360/374-9288**). When you've just got to have a bracing latte to chase away the chill and the damp, drop by the **Riverrun Coffeehouse,** 71 N. Forks Ave. (ℂ **360/374-7580**).

River's Edge Restaurant ✦ *Finds* AMERICAN   Operated by the Quileute Tribal Enterprises and located in a renovated and converted old boathouse, this restaurant offers both great water views and the best food in the area. Fresh seafood is the specialty, and with salmon-fishing boats unloading at the adjacent marina, you can bet the salmon will be as fresh as it gets. Although preparations are generally quite simple, you might get a little mango salsa with your baked salmon. Big breakfasts make this a good place to start your day.

41 Main St., La Push. ✆ **360/374-5777.** Main courses $10–$20. MC, V. Summer daily 6am–9pm; other months call for hours.

8

Southwest Washington

Southwest Washington, which for the purposes of this book is defined as the area west of I-5 and south of U.S. 12, is for the most part sparsely populated and heavily dependent on the timber industry for its economic base. This said, however, the region also contains the state's busiest beach resort areas—the Long Beach Peninsula and the Central Coast area—as well as the often-overlooked city of Vancouver, which shares a name with the far more famous Canadian city to the north. Although present-day Vancouver, Washington, is little more than a bedroom community for Portland, it abounds in pioneer history.

Aside from two last rocky headlands at the mouth of the Columbia River, the coastline of southwest Washington is a tame strip of sandy beaches and windswept dunes. Grays Harbor and Willapa Bay divide this stretch of coast into three distinct strips of sand: North Beach, South Beach, and the Long Beach Peninsula. These three strands have far more in common with one another than they do with the wild, rock-strewn beaches to the north. And although these beaches are far less spectacular than those to the north, the abundance of tourist accommodations along this stretch of coast makes these the favored beach vacation destinations of the state.

Summers along the coast tend to be short and often wet or foggy, and the coastal waters are too cold and rough for swimming (although surfing is fairly popular). Consequently, the traditional beach pursuits of swimming and sunning aren't high on vacation priority lists around these parts. Instead, these beaches have come to rely on other activities to attract visitors. All up and down this coast, digging for razor clams is a popular pastime, though open seasons are now short and as closely regulated as the salmon-fishing seasons. The towns of Westport, at the north end of the South Beach area, and Ilwaco, at the south end of the Long Beach Peninsula, have become the region's main charter-boat ports, with Westport charter boats also doing double duty as whale-watching excursion boats. South Beach and the Long Beach Peninsula are also among the few regions in the country where cranberries are grown commercially. Long Beach, a beach resort town for more than 100 years, bills itself as the kite-flying capital of America and boasts of having the longest drivable beach in the world. While vacationing families fuel the local economy, oysters still reign supreme in Willapa Bay, one of the cleanest estuaries in the country. However, an invasive, nonnative marsh grass called spartina has taken hold in this estuary and is slowly crowding out native salt marsh plants and turning this bay into unproductive mud flats.

While most of this region's development has taken place around fishing and shipping ports both along the coast and up the Columbia River, the heart of the region is the Willapa Hills. These forested hills are almost entirely privately owned, mostly by large lumber companies. Consequently the forests of the Willapa Hills are among the hardest working forests in the region. Much of the region's forests have already been cut twice since the first settlers arrived in the area.

However, despite the lack of publicly held or otherwise protected forests, this coast still has its pockets of wildness. The Willapa National Wildlife Refuge and the Long Beach Peninsula's Leadbetter Point together host a vast number of bird species each year. These areas, when combined with the Grays Harbor National Wildlife Refuge to the north, offer the best bird-watching in the entire Northwest. Sea kayakers also are attracted to Willapa Bay, where the paddle around Long Island is as rewarding as any in the Puget Sound or San Juan Islands.

1 The Central Coast: Ocean Shores to Willapa Bay

67 miles W of Olympia, 67 miles S of Lake Quinault, 92 miles N of Long Beach

Washington's central coast, consisting of the North and South Beach areas and the Grays Harbor towns of Aberdeen and Hoquiam, is something of an anomaly. Though far from being the most scenic stretch of Washington coast, it contains the state's most popular beach destination, Ocean Shores, a modern beach development that now consists of numerous oceanfront hotels and hundreds of vacation homes. Although not as scenic as the Olympic Peninsula coastline, this area is popular for its easy access to the cities of Puget Sound, and, because Ocean Shores is less than an hour east of Olympia, it is a popular weekend vacation spot.

The most scenic stretch of this coastline is the area known as North Beach, which consists of the beach north of the mouth of Grays Harbor. The farther north you go on this stretch of coast the more spectacular is the scenery, even rivaling the beauty of the Olympic Peninsula's shoreline in some places. The South Beach area, so named because it occupies the south side of Grays Harbor, is an 18-mile stretch of flat beach that is bordered on the south by Willapa Bay. At the north end of South Beach is the town of Westport, Washington's busiest sportfishing and whale-watching port. Across the mouth of Willapa Bay from the South Beach area lies the northern tip of the Long Beach Peninsula.

Separating North Beach and South Beach is the large bay known as Grays Harbor, on whose shores are the two lumber-mill towns of Aberdeen and Hoquiam. These towns were once some of the most prosperous in the state, as attested to by each town's stately Victorian mansions and imposing commercial buildings. Unfortunately, these towns have yet to benefit from the prosperity that has overtaken the Puget Sound region, and historic commercial buildings stand empty and abandoned. Still, there is history to be seen in these towns, though it is for the beaches, the fishing, and the clamming that most people visit this region.

ESSENTIALS

GETTING THERE   U.S. 12 and Wash. 8 together connect Aberdeen with Olympia to the east, while U.S. 101 connects Aberdeen with Forks and Port Angeles to the north and Long Beach and Astoria to the south. Ocean Shores and the North Beach area are 20 miles west of Aberdeen on Wash. 109. The South Beach area is 20 miles west of Aberdeen on Wash. 105.

VISITOR INFORMATION   For more information on this area, contact **Tourism Grays Harbor,** P.O. Box 225, Aberdeen, WA 98520 (© **800/621-9625;** www.graysharbortourism.com); **Ocean Shores Visitor Information**

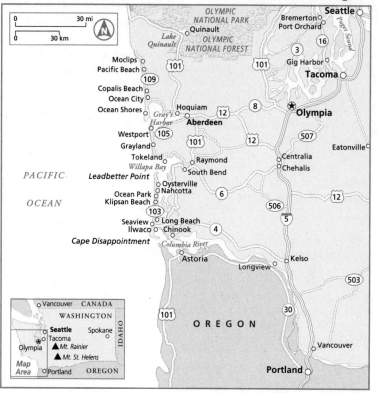

Southwest Washington

Center, 120 W. Chance-A-La-Mer (P.O. Box 382), Ocean Shores, WA 98569 (✆ **800/76-BEACH** or 360/289-2451; www.oceanshores.org); the **Washington Coast Chamber of Commerce,** 2602 State Rte. 109, Ocean City, WA 98569 (✆ **800/286-4552** or 360/289-4552; www.washingtoncoastchamber. org); the **Westport-Grayland Chamber of Commerce,** 2985 S. Montesano Ave. (P.O. Box 306), Westport, WA 98595 (✆ **800/345-6223** or 360/268-9422; www.westportgrayland-chamber.org); or the **Willapa Bay Organization** (✆ **360/942-9963;** www.visit.willapabay.org).

LEARNING ABOUT THE REGION'S HISTORY

Aberdeen and Hoquiam together comprise the largest urban area on the Washington coast and have long been dependent on the lumber industry, which once made this a very prosperous part of the state. If you're interested in the history of this region, stop by the **Polson Museum,** 1611 Riverside Ave., Hoquiam (✆ **360/533-5862**), which contains rooms full of antique furnishings and also houses various collections including dolls, vintage clothing, Native American artifacts, and logging memorabilia. It's open in summer, Wednesday through Sunday from 11am to 4pm; other months, on Saturday and Sunday from noon to 4pm. Admission is $2 for adults, $1 for students, and 50¢ for children under age 12. The **Aberdeen Museum of History,** 111 E. Third St., Aberdeen (✆ **360/533-1976**), has similar displays and is open Tuesday through Saturday from 10am to 5pm and Sunday from 11am to 5pm; admission is by donation.

Moments Pirates of the Caribbean North?

The wind in the rigging, the smell of the salt air. If you long for the life of a pirate or dream of being your own master and commander, then plan to visit Grays Harbor when the *Lady Washington* is here in her home port of Aberdeen. This tall ship, a replica of one of the ships Capt. Robert Gray sailed when he first explored the Northwest coast in 1788, was used in *Pirates of the Caribbean* as well as in *Star Trek Generations.* You'll find the *Lady Washington* docked beside the Wal-Mart in Aberdeen at **Aberdeen Landing,** 320 S. Newell St. (© **800/200-LADY** or 360/532-8611; www.ladywashington.org). Dockside tours cost $3 for adults, $2 for seniors and students, and $1 for children ages 12 and under. However, no aspiring pirate should settle for a mere tour when a sailing excursion can be had ($40 for adults and $20 for children 12 and under).

In the North Beach area, you can learn about both regional and natural history at the **Ocean Shores Interpretive Center,** 1033 Catala Ave., Ocean Shores (© **360/289-4617;** www.oceanshoresinterpretivecenter.com), which is at the corner of Catala and Discovery avenues. The interpretive center is open daily from 11am to 4pm between May 1 and Labor Day; in April and in September after Labor Day, it's open Thursday through Monday from 11am to 4pm.

If you aren't here during the whale-watching season, you can at least have a look at a couple of whale skeletons at the **Westport Maritime Museum,** 2201 Westhaven Dr., Westport (© **360/268-0078;** www.westportwa.com/museum). Housed in a 1939 Coast Guard station, the museum contains Coast Guard exhibits, displays on early pioneer life in the area, and, in a glass-enclosed building outside, the skeletons of a minke whale, a gray whale, and part of a blue whale. Between Memorial Day and Labor Day, the museum is open daily from 10am to 4pm (fall and spring, Thurs–Mon noon–4pm; winter, Sat–Sun and holidays noon–4pm), and admission is $3 for adults and $1 for children 5 to 14, free for children 4 and under. Nearby, you'll find the **Grays Harbor Light-house,** which was built in 1898 and is the tallest lighthouse in Washington. Tours of the lighthouse are operated by the Westport Maritime Museum and cost $3. The lighthouse is open the same hours as the museum. From the museum, you can walk the Maritime History Trail to reach the lighthouse.

FISHING, CLAMMING, WHALE-WATCHING & OTHER OUTDOOR ACTIVITIES

The stretch of coast known as North Beach begins in the vacation and retirement community of Ocean Shores and stretches north for 30 miles to Taholah, on the Quinault Indian Reservation. In the southern section of North Beach, in Ocean Shores, low windswept dunes covered with beach grass back the wide, sandy beach. Kite flying and horseback riding are among the favorite activities here. Horses can be rented at the north end of Ocean Shores from **Chenois Creek Horse Rental** (© **360/533-5591**), which is located on the beach at the end of Damon Road (beside the Best Western Lighthouse Suites Inn) and charges $20 for a 1-hour ride. Also in Ocean Shores are 23 miles of canals and interconnecting lakes that are fun to explore. Canoes can be rented at **Summer Sails** (© **360/289-2884**), which is located at Point Brown. If you're looking

for a game of golf, head to the **Ocean Shores Golf Course,** 500 Canal Dr. NE
(© **360/289-3357**).

North of Ocean City, high bluffs, haystack rocks, secluded beaches, and dark
forests create a more dramatic coastline. Along this stretch of coast there is **beach
access** at Ocean City, Griffiths-Priday, and Pacific Beach state parks. **Razor
clamming** is one of the most popular activities on the secluded beaches of this
area. To try your hand at clamming, you'll need a license, a shovel, and a tide
table. With all three in hand, head out to the beach at low tide and start looking for clam holes. When you spot one, dig fast. Good luck! Also, before heading out to the beach, find out if clamming season is open by calling the
Westport-Grayland Chamber of Commerce (© **800/345-6223**).

The 18 miles of coastline between Westport and Tokeland is called South
Beach or the Cranberry Coast, and along this stretch of beach, there are plenty
of places to access the sand and surf. Four state parks provide the best facilities
and easiest access. **Twin Harbors State Park** is 2 miles south of Westport and is
the largest of the four, with more than 3 miles of beach. **Grayland Beach State
Park** is just south of the town of Grayland and has less than a mile of beach.
Both of these parks have nature trails, picnic areas, and campgrounds. Just outside the marina area of Westport is **Westhaven State Park,** and just south of
town is **Westport Light State Park,** where you'll find the popular Dune Trail, a
paved 1-mile-long path that parallels the beach. These latter two parks are day-
use areas only.

In the South Beach area, charter fishing, clamming, and whale-watching are
the big attractions, and most of the activity centers on the marina at Westport.
Boats head out daily in summer in search of salmon, tuna, and bottom fish.
If you'd like to try your luck at reeling in a big one, try **Bran Lee Charters**
(© **800/562-0163** or 360/268-9177; www.branleecharters.com) or **Deep Sea
Charters** (© **800/562-0151** or 360/268-9300; www.oceansportfishing.com).
Rates range from about $60 to $110 for a day of fishing. In the fall, salmon fish-
ing is also popular right off the docks in the Westport Marina.

Each year between February and May, gray whales migrating to the calving
grounds off Baja California, Mexico, pass by the Washington coast. The whales
sometimes come so close to the mouth of Grays Harbor that they can be seen
from the observation tower at the marina in Westport. However, for a closer
look, you might want to head out on a **whale-watching** boat trip. Contact one
of the charter boat companies mentioned above if you're interested. Rates are
between $20 and $25 for adults and between $12 and $18 for children.

Crabbing is another favorite area activity. To give crabbing a try, you'll need
a crab ring (they can be bought for $20–$40 or rented for around $6 per day at
the Westport Marina) and some bacon or chicken necks for bait. Find a spot on
Westport's 1,000-foot-long pier, toss your trap over the side, and sit back and
wait for the crabs to come to you—it's that easy.

All along the South Beach area between Grayland and Tokeland, you'll see
cranberry bogs beside the highway. The cranberry harvest begins around Labor
Day and continues on through October. To harvest the tart berries, the bogs are
flooded, which causes the ripe berries to float on the surface of the water, where
they can be easily scooped up mechanically.

Each year in late April and early May, Bowerman Basin in **Grays Harbor
National Wildlife Refuge** (© **360/753-9467**; http://graysharbor.fws.gov)
becomes a staging ground for tens of thousands of Arctic-bound shorebirds.

This is one of the largest gatherings of such birds on the West Coast and is also one of the state's biggest annual events for bird-watchers. If you're a birder, you won't want to miss this impressive gathering. The wildlife refuge is adjacent to the Aberdeen/Hoquiam Airport on the west side of Hoquiam.

Between early May and September, the **Westport Ocean Shores Passenger Ferry,** Silver King Motel, 1070 Discovery Ave. SE, Ocean Shores (© **360/289-3386**), connects Ocean Shores with Westport Marina. The ferry operates daily between mid-June and Labor Day. From early May to mid-June and from Labor Day to late September, the ferry operates only on weekends. The crossing takes between 20 and 40 minutes, and the fare is $10 for a round-trip ticket. In Westport, the office is at 321 Dock St. (© **360/268-0047**).

DRIVING AROUND WILLAPA BAY

Though it's only about 5 miles across the mouth of Willapa Bay to the northern tip of the Long Beach Peninsula, it's about 85 miles around to the town of Long Beach by road. Along the way you skirt the shores of Willapa Bay. There aren't too many towns on this bay, which is why this is one of the least polluted estuaries in the country and is a great place to raise oysters. Punctuating the miles of unspoiled scenery are oyster docks and processing plants.

As you pass through the town of Raymond, keep an eye out for the 200 steel-plate sculptures that comprise the **Raymond Wildlife-Heritage Sculpture Corridor.** The majority of these sculptures are silhouettes that can be seen along U.S. 101 in the most unexpected places. Included are sculptures of Native Americans, modern sea kayakers, bicyclists, and dozens of wild animals. Also here in Raymond, you'll find the **Willapa Seaport Museum** ★, 310 Alder St. (© **360/942-4149**), a fascinating little museum dedicated to all things nautical. This is the best-designed little museum on the coast and is well worth a visit. The museum is open Wednesday through Sunday from noon to 4pm; admission is by donation.

Right next door to the Willapa Seaport Museum, you'll find the **Northwest Carriage Museum,** 314 Alder St. (© **360/942-4150;** www.nwcarriagemuseum. org), which is home to a large collection of immaculately restored antique carriages. On display are a wicker carriage, a hearse, and even a carriage that was used in *Gone With the Wind.* For the most part, these are luxury carriages that would have once been owned by the wealthy. Between October and March, the museum is open Wednesday through Saturday from 10am to 4pm and, between April and September, Sunday from noon to 4pm. Admission is $3 for adults, $1 for children ages 6 to 14, and free for children 5 and under.

Adjacent to these two museums is the **Public Market on the Willapa,** Fourth and Heath streets (© **360/942-4700**), which sells local produce, art, and crafts. The market is open mid-March to mid-December Wednesday to Saturday from 10am to 5pm. This market and the two museums are all located at Waterfront Park, which has some interesting interpretive displays and is on a 5-mile-long paved walking/biking trail.

By some accounts, one out of every six oysters consumed in the United States comes from Willapa Bay, and it is in the town of **South Bend** that oystering reaches its zenith. South Bend claims to be the oyster capital of the world and holds its annual **Oyster Stampede** festival each year on Memorial Day weekend. If you just have to have some oysters while you're in town, have a meal at The Boondocks (see below) or drop by **East Point Seafood,** U.S. 101, South Bend (© **888/317-8459** or 360/875-5419), which is at the north end of town.

South Bend's other claim to fame is its **county courthouse.** Though South Bend is the county seat today, back in 1893 it took a possibly rigged vote and armed force to wrest the title of county seat from Oysterville, across the bay on the Long Beach Peninsula. Construction of the new courthouse began 18 years later, and upon completion, the imposing structure was dubbed a "gilded palace of extravagance." The majestic courthouse, seeming quite out of place in such a quiet backwater, stands on a hill overlooking the town. The copper dome is lined inside with stained glass, and murals decorate the interior walls. It's definitely worth a look.

WHERE TO STAY
IN OCEAN SHORES & THE NORTH BEACH AREA

If you can't get a room at any of the hotels listed below, contact **Ocean Shores Reservations** (© 800/562-8612 or 360/289-2430; www.oceanshoresreservation. com), which handles reservations at many area hotels, motels, resorts, and condominiums.

Iron Springs Ocean Beach Resort ★ *Kids*   It's hard to imagine a more picture-perfect little cove than the one on which this rustic resort is set. Steep wooded hills surround the tiny cove, and at the mouth, a sandy beach begins. This is an isolated and little-developed stretch of coast, so even in summer you won't be bothered by crowds. The cottages here are scattered through the woods on a bluff overlooking the ocean and vary quite a bit in design, decor, and size. Although they definitely show their age, they're all relatively comfortable and have fireplaces and complete kitchens. There is also a playground here.

P.O. Box 207, Copalis Beach, WA 98535. © 360/276-4230. Fax 360/276-4365. www.ironspringsresort.com. 28 units. $78–$156 cottage or apt for 2; $96–$256 cottage or apt for 4. 3-night minimum stay in summer and on holidays. AE, DISC, MC, V. Pets accepted ($12). **Amenities:** Indoor pool. *In room:* Kitchen, fridge, coffeemaker.

Ocean Crest Resort ★★ *Kids*   You simply won't find a more spectacular location anywhere on the Washington coast. Perched high on a forested bluff and straddling a forested ravine, this hotel seems poised to go plummeting into the ocean below. The accommodations vary from small studios with no view to two-bedroom apartments with full kitchens and fireplaces. However, our vote for best rooms goes to the large third-floor ocean-view studios. These have cathedral ceilings, fireplaces, and balconies. The hotel's restaurant has one of the best views at the resort, and the adjacent lounge is a great spot for a sunset drink. In addition to other amenities, the resort also has a playground. A wooden staircase winds down through the ravine to the beach.

P.O. Box 7, Moclips, WA 98562. © 800/684-8439 or 360/276-4465. Fax 360/276-4149. www.oceancrest resort.com. 47 units. June to mid-Sept $58–$159 double; mid-Sept to Oct and Mar–May $44–$118 double; Nov–Feb $39–$105 double. AE, DISC, MC, V. Pets accepted ($15). **Amenities:** Restaurant (steak and seafood); lounge; indoor pool; health club; Jacuzzi; sauna; massage; coin-op laundry. *In room:* TV, coffeemaker.

Quinault Beach Resort and Casino ★★   By far the most luxurious resort anywhere on the Washington coast, this large casino resort is located a bit north of the rest of the Ocean Shores developments and thus feels a bit more secluded. With its modern Northwest lodge styling, it also has a far more contemporary feel than other area resorts. However, despite the attractive design and the miles of ocean beaches just outside, it is still the in-house casino that is this resort's main attraction. Don't worry, though—even if you aren't a fan of slot machines, you can actually stay here and almost not even notice the casino. All the rooms here have gas fireplaces and are designed so that the fireplace separates the bed from the seating area.

78 Wash. 115 (P.O. Box 2107), Ocean Shores, WA 98569. ℂ 888/461-2214 or 360/289-9466. Fax 360/289-5833. www.quinaultbchresort.com. 150 units. $99–$169 double; $250–$350 suite. AE, DISC, MC, V. **Amenities:** 2 restaurants (Northwest, American); 2 lounges; indoor pool; exercise room; full-service spa; Jacuzzi; limited room service; massage; casino. *In room:* A/C, TV, dataport, fridge, coffeemaker, hair dryer.

IN HOQUIAM

Hoquiam's Castle 🌟🌟 *Value*   This stately Victorian mansion, built in 1897 by a local timber baron, is an amazing assemblage of turrets and gables, balconies and bay windows. Rooms here have names inspired by the castlelike setting (King's, Queen's, Princess's, Knight's, Maid's), and all are furnished in luxurious Victorian style. There are antiques throughout the inn and the quality of construction of this 10,000-square-foot mansion is evident in the wood floors and paneling, crystal chandeliers, and stained-glass windows. Guests can enjoy the view of the city from the turret, play the piano in the parlor, and sip tea on the front porch or sherry in the second-floor lounge. The inn even has its own ballroom.

515 Chenault Ave., Hoquiam, WA 98550. ℂ 877/542-2785 or 360/533-2005. www.hoquiamscastle.com. 5 units. $95–$150 double. Rates include full breakfast. AE, DISC, MC, V. Children over age 12 welcome. *In room:* Hair dryer, iron.

IN THE SOUTH BEACH AREA

The Russell House 🌟   Located high on a hill at the east end of town, this restored Victorian home was built in 1891 by a local architect. Consequently, it abounds in interesting details, including some of the most amazing interior woodwork you'll find in any B&B in the state. The Emerald Suite is the inn's largest and best room and comes with a cute bathroom with a claw-foot tub and a tiny, enclosed sun porch. Wicker furniture and a four-poster bed complete the picture. The Rose Room, decorated with lace and shades of pink, has its private bathroom across the hall.

902 E. Water St. (P.O. Box F), South Bend, WA 98586. ℂ 888/484-6907 or 360/875-6487. www.willapabay. org/~srowan. 4 units. $75–$85 double. Rates include full breakfast. AE, MC, V. *In room:* No phone.

Tokeland Hotel 🌟 *Finds*   Located on the north shore of Willapa Bay, the Tokeland Hotel has been welcoming guests since 1889 and, with its remote setting and simple interior decor, feels like a genuine step back in time. Lawns surround the wood-frame inn, and beyond these lies the water. The first floor is taken up by a large open lobby and dining room, off which is a small library with a fireplace. Up on the second floor, rooms are arranged on either side of a long hall and have painted wood floors. Antique furnishings lend an air of authenticity to the inn. Shared bathrooms all have claw-foot tubs. The inn's moderately priced dining room is the most popular restaurant for miles around and is particularly noteworthy for its Sunday dinner, which includes a delicious cranberry pot roast (open daily 8am–8pm; winter hours vary).

100 Hotel Rd., Tokeland, WA 98590. ℂ 360/267-7006. Fax 360/267-7006. www.tokelandhotel.com. 18 units, all with shared bathroom. $49–$65 double. DISC, MC, V. Pets accepted. **Amenities:** Restaurant (American). *In room:* No phone.

CAMPGROUNDS

On Wash. 109 north of Ocean Shores are two state park campgrounds. **Pacific Beach State Park** (64 campsites) is a small, exposed, and crowded patch of sand with little to recommend it other than good razor clamming nearby. More appealing is **Ocean City State Park** ⚜ (178 campsites), which at least has trees for protection against the wind. This is a good choice if you plan to bicycle along this stretch of coast. To make a campsite reservation at either of these spots, contact **Washington State Parks** (② **888/226-7688;** www.parks.wa.gov/reserve. asp).

WHERE TO DINE
IN THE OCEAN SHORES & NORTH BEACH AREA
The best restaurants in this region are the dining rooms at the Ocean Crest Resort and the Quinault Beach Resort (see above for details).

IN ABERDEEN& HOQUIAM
Billy's Bar & Grill ⚜ AMERICAN   Named for an infamous local thug, Billy's evokes Aberdeen's rowdier days as a lawless, Wild West timber town. Although this is a perfectly respectable restaurant these days, there's a bar down the length of the room, a pressed-tin ceiling, and enough old paintings and prints to give this bar and grill just the right dance-hall atmosphere. The menu features everything from burgers (including yak-meat burgers) to fresh oysters to T-bone steaks.

322 E. Heron St., Aberdeen. ② **360/533-7144.** Main courses $5.25–$17. AE, MC, V. Mon–Thurs 8am–11pm; Fri–Sat 8am–midnight; Sun 8am–9pm.

Mallard's Bistro & Grill ⚜⚜ *Finds* CONTINENTAL   Located in downtown Aberdeen and owned by a Danish chef who cooked all over Europe before eventually locating here, this cozy little restaurant is one of the most unexpectedly enjoyable restaurants in the state. In a town filled with burger joints and cheap Chinese restaurants, Mallards dares to serve such creative fare as a delicious salmon with pinot noir sauce. The menu sticks mostly to traditional Continental fare, including coquille St. Jacques, and there are lots of good seafood preparations. The setting, with its many images of mallard ducks all around the dining room, is casual and homey. A good spot if you're in town bird-watching.

118 E. Wishkah St. ② **360/532-0731.** Reservations recommended. Main courses $14–$28. MC, V. Tues–Sat 5–8 or 8:30pm.

IN THE SOUTH BEACH AREA
Your best bet for a memorable meal in the South Beach area is the dining room at the historic Tokeland Hotel (see above for details).

Tokeland Hotel Dining Room ⚜ *Finds* AMERICAN   With its painted wood floors and wall of old wavy-glass windows looking out to the salt marsh, this restaurant has more historical feeling than just about any restaurant in the state. If you're anywhere on the central coast, you should be sure to have a meal here. Sunday suppers featuring cranberry pot roast are legendary, but any day of the week, you can get a sandwich made from the same tender pot roast. There are

---

⌒Fun Fact The Power of the Pacific

At the southern end of the South Beach area, just north of Tokeland, is a stretch of coastline known as Washaway Beach. This beach is so named because of the rapid rate at which it has eroded over the years. The old highway past this beach long ago began caving into the ocean, and the current highway has had to be protected with rocks to prevent it from disappearing into the breakers as well.

also plenty of good seafood dishes made with local fish and shellfish. Be sure to save room for some blackberry cobbler.

100 Hotel Rd., Tokeland. © **360/267-7006**. www.tokelandhotel.com. Main course $6–$17. DISC, MC, V. Mid-Mar to mid-Nov daily 8am–8pm; mid-Nov to mid-Mar Mon–Thurs 8am–2pm, Fri–Sun 8am–8pm.

IN SOUTH BEND

The Boondocks Restaurant ☆ AMERICAN   Long a locals' favorite, The Boondocks is right on the waterfront in downtown South Bend, a town that claims to be the oyster capital of the world. With a claim like that, there should be no question as to what to order. Whether it's a hangtown fry (oyster omelet) for breakfast, an oyster burger for lunch, or a pan-fried oyster platter for dinner, there are oyster options at every meal. At breakfast, you can even get a side of oysters with your hot cakes or waffles.

1015 W. Robert Bush Dr., South Bend. © **800/875-5158** or 360/875-5155. Main courses $6–$25. MC, V. Mon–Thurs 8am–9pm; Fri–Sat 8am–10pm; Sun 8am–8:30pm.

2 The Long Beach Peninsula

110 miles NW of Portland, 180 miles SW of Seattle, 80 miles W of Longview/Kelso

With 28 uninterrupted miles of sand, the Long Beach Peninsula, a long narrow strip of low forest and sand dunes, claims to be the world's longest beach open to vehicles. For more than a century, all those miles of sand have been attracting vacationers from the Portland area and parts of southwestern Washington, and today the Long Beach Peninsula is Washington's most developed stretch of beach. There are dozens of resorts, motels, rental cabins, vacation homes, and campgrounds up and down the peninsula.

Each of the peninsula's towns has its own distinct personality. In Seaview, there are restored Victorian homes. In Long Beach, go-cart tracks and family amusements hold sway. Klipsan Beach and Ocean Park are quiet retirement communities, while Nahcotta is still an active oystering port, albeit in a very attractive setting. Last is the tiny community of Oysterville, which is a National Historic District of restored homes and is hands-down the prettiest community on the peninsula.

While kite flying, horseback riding, and beachcombing are the most popular beach activities here, digging for razor clams ranks right up there, too. Razor clams (and the area's oysters) also show up on plenty of area restaurant menus. Bivalves aren't the only type of seafood that attracts folks to the south coast, either. In Ilwaco, south of Long Beach, there's a fleet of charter fishing boats that can take you out in search of salmon, tuna, or bottom fish.

Long Beach is one of the few beaches on the West Coast that allows vehicular traffic, so if you're of a mind to go for a drive on the beach, feel free. Just remember that the beach is a state highway and a 25-mph speed limit is enforced. There are beach-access roads up and down the peninsula, and once you're on the beach, be sure you stay above the clam beds (sand nearest to the low-tide area) and below the dry sand.

ESSENTIALS

GETTING THERE   The Long Beach Peninsula begins just off U.S. 101 in southwest Washington. U.S. 101 leads north to Aberdeen and south to Astoria, Oregon. Wash. 4 leads to Long Beach from Longview.

GETTING AROUND   Pacific Transit System (© **360/642-9418**) operates public buses that serve the area from Astoria in the south to Aberdeen in the north.

VISITOR INFORMATION   Contact the **Long Beach Peninsula Visitors Bureau,** P.O. Box 562, Long Beach, WA 98631 (✆ **800/451-2542** or 360/642-2400; www.funbeach.com), which operates a visitor center at the intersection of U.S. 101 and Pacific Avenue in Seaview.

FESTIVALS   Annual events on the Long Beach Peninsula include the **Northwest Garlic Festival** on the third weekend in June, the **Sand-Sations** sand-sculptures tournament in late July, the **International Kite Festival** in mid-August, the **Cranberrian Fair** in early October, and the **Water Music Festival** (chamber music) in late October.

SEEING THE SIGHTS

Fort Columbia State Park (✆ **360/642-3078**), a former military base that guarded the mouth of the Columbia River from 1896 until the end of World War II, is located 9 miles east of Ilwaco on Wash. 103 near the Astoria-Megler Bridge, which is a 4½-mile-long span that connects Washington with Oregon. The views from the park's wooded bluff are breathtaking, and there are some picnic tables from which you can enjoy the views. There are also 5 miles of hiking trails here. The park's 1903-vintage buildings have been restored and house an interpretive center with displays on the history of the fort. There are also exhibits on the local Chinook Indian tribe. From Memorial Day through September, an interpretive center is open daily from 10am to 5pm, and the old commanding officer's home is open daily from 11am to 4pm. There are also a couple of vacation rental homes here. For reservations, contact Washington State Parks (✆ **888/226-7688;** www.parks.wa.gov/reserve.asp).

To learn more about the history of the area, stop by the **Ilwaco Heritage Museum,** 115 SE Lake St., Ilwaco (✆ **360/642-3446**). This modern museum houses displays on the history of southwest Washington and has an excellent collection of Native American baskets and other artifacts. There's also an anxiety-inducing exhibit about Gerald D'Aboville, who, in 1991, made a solo journey by rowboat across the Pacific Ocean. A railroad exhibit includes a model railroad of Long Beach's Clamshell Railroad, as well as an actual passenger car that was used on this railroad. The museum is open Monday through Saturday from 9am to 5pm and Sunday from noon to 4pm (Oct–Apr Mon–Sat 10am–4pm). Admission is $3 for adults, $2.50 for seniors, $2 for youths 12 to 17, $1 for children 6 to 11, and free for children 6 and under.

Also in Ilwaco is the historic **Colbert House,** which is operated by the Washington State Parks and Recreation Commission. You'll find this restored home at the corner of Quaker and Spruce streets. It's open Friday through Sunday from noon to 4pm between Memorial Day and Labor Day.

Anchoring the south end of the peninsula is forested **Cape Disappointment State Park** ⚏⚏ (✆ **888/CAMPOUT** or 360/683-4985), which is located at the mouth of the Columbia River. The park is a former military installation used to guard the river mouth, and many of the bunkers and batteries are still visible. Also within the boundaries of the park are the North Head (open for tours in summer) and Cape Disappointment lighthouses. The former lighthouse suffers some of the highest winds on the West Coast, and has sustained winds as high as 160 mph. The latter lighthouse was built in 1856 and is the oldest lighthouse on the West Coast. The park is also home to the **Lewis and Clark Interpretive Center** ⚏⚏ (✆ **360/642-3029**), which chronicles the 1805–06 journey of the two explorers; it's open daily from 10am to 5pm and admission is by suggested $2 donation. Cape Disappointment, here in the park, was the end of the westward trail for Lewis and Clark. Also within the park are several picnic areas, hiking trails, a campground, and **Waikiki Beach,** the prettiest little beach between here and Moclips. This tiny cove backed by steep cliffs is named for several Hawaiian sailors who lost their lives near here. The park is open from dawn to dusk, and admission is free.

In the past 300 years more than 2,000 vessels and 700 lives have been lost in the treacherous waters at the mouth of the Columbia River. Consequently, the U.S. Coast Guard has its **National Motor Life Boat School** here. Lifeboat drills can sometimes be observed from observation platforms on the North Jetty. This jetty, completed in 1917, was built to improve the channel across the Columbia Bar. A side effect of the 2-mile-long jetty was the creation of a much wider beach to the north. This widening of the beach accounts for the town of Long Beach's current distance from the waves.

If you're a kite flyer, or even if you're not, you may want to stop by the **World Kite Museum & Hall of Fame** ✈, 112 N. Third St., Long Beach (ⓒ **360/642-4020;** www.worldkitemuseum.com), where you can see displays on kites of the world. Memorial Day to Labor Day, it's open daily from 11am to 5pm; September through May, it's open Friday through Monday from 11am to 5pm; admission is $3 for adults, $2 for seniors and children.

Up toward the north end of the peninsula, you'll find the historic village of **Oysterville** ✈✈, an old oystering community that is a National Historic District and is by far the quaintest little village on the peninsula. Old homes with spacious lawns cling to the edge of the marsh, creating a timeless scene. Oysterville had is heyday in the days of the California gold rush, when the village was shipping tons of oysters to San Francisco, where people were willing to pay as much as $50 a plate for fresh oysters. Today Oysterville is a sleepy little community of restored homes. In the town's white clapboard church, there are occasional music performances. Here in Oysterville, you'll also find **Oysterville Sea Farms** (ⓒ **800/272-6237** or 360/665-6585; www.oysterville.net), which has a seafood and cranberry-products shop on the waterfront at the north end of the village.

Willapa Bay, which is one of the cleanest estuaries on the West Coast, is still known for its **oysters.** Up and down the peninsula there are oyster farms and processing plants. If you're interested in learning more about the history of the area's oystering industry, drop by the **Willapa Bay Interpretive Center** (ⓒ **360/665-4547**) on the breakwater beside The Ark Restaurant in Nahcotta. The interpretive center is open Friday through Sunday from 10am to 3pm between Memorial Day and Labor Day, and admission is free.

The peninsula is also a major producer of cranberries, and if you take a drive down almost any side road north of Long Beach, you'll pass acres of **cranberry bogs.** If you're curious to learn how cranberries are grown, stop in at the **Pacific**

(Kids Believe It or Not!

Children and other fans of the bizarre won't want to miss **Marsh's Free Museum** ✈, 409 S. Pacific Ave., Long Beach (ⓒ **360/642-2188;** www.marshs freemuseum.com), a beachy gift shop filled with all manner of antique arcade games, oddities a la Ripley's Believe It or Not!, and, best of all, Jake the alligator man, who has been made famous by tabloids that rank this half-man, half-alligator creature right up there with aliens, Bigfoot, and the latest Elvis sighting.

Coast Cranberry Museum ☞, 2907 Pioneer Rd., Long Beach (© **360/642-5553**). The museum, which is on a demonstration cranberry farm, features exhibits on all the stages of cranberry growing both past and present. The museum is open April to December 15 daily from 10am to 5pm. Admission is free.

AREA ACTIVITIES: KITE FLYING, BIRD-WATCHING & CLAMMING

Active vacations are the norm here on the Long Beach Peninsula, and there are plenty of activities to keep you busy. However, one activity you won't be doing much of is swimming in the ocean. Although it gets warm enough in the summer to lie on the beach, the waters here never warm up very much. Add to this the unpredictable currents, riptides, undertows, and heavy surf and you have an ocean that's just not safe for swimming.

Instead of swimming, the beach's number-one activity is **kite flying.** Strong winds blow year-round across the Long Beach Peninsula, and with its 28 miles of beach, you won't have to worry about kite-eating trees. You'll find several kite shops in Long Beach. Another very popular Long Beach activity is beachcombing. The most sought-after treasures are hand-blown glass fishing floats used by Japanese fishermen.

Beach access is available up and down the peninsula, but the best beaches are at the peninsula's various state parks. The beaches of **Cape Disappointment State Park,** at the south end of the peninsula, are the most dramatic, while those at **Leadbetter Point State Park,** at the north end of the peninsula, are the most secluded. Just north of Ocean Park, there is beach access at the small **Pacific Pines State Park,** and south of Ocean Park, there is additional beach access at the west section of **Loomis Lake State Park.** This latter park is named for a popular fishing lake that is in the park's east section.

If you've ever dreamed of riding a horse down the beach, you can make your dream come true here in Long Beach. On South Tenth Street just in from the beach, you'll find both **Skipper's Equestrian Center** (© **360/642-3676**) and **Back Country Wilderness Outfitters** (© **360/642-2576**). A 1-hour ride will cost you $15.

Walking the dunes is a favorite Long Beach pastime. Between 17th Street South and 16th Street North, you'll find the 2-mile-long **Discovery Trail,** a paved path that parallels the beach. The trail winds through the grassy dunes that separate the town of Long Beach from the stretch of sand for which the town is named. For a half mile of its length, the Dunes Trail parallels an elevated boardwalk that provides views of the beach and ocean over the tops of the dunes. In celebration of the Lewis and Clark bicentennial, which will be celebrated in 2005, the Discovery Trail is slowly being extended from the town of Long Beach south to Ilwaco. At press time, however, only a few short sections of this new trail were completed. Along the stretch of trail in Long Beach, you'll find a whale skeleton, a basalt column, and a bronze statue of the gnarled tree on which Lewis and Clark carved their names. These monuments have been erected to commemorate Lewis and Clark's long-ago visit to this area.

If you'd just like to get away from the crowds and find a piece of isolated shoreline to call your own, head to Leadbetter Point at the peninsula's northern tip. Here you'll find both **Leadbetter Point State Park Natural Area** and a portion of the **Willapa National Wildlife Refuge** (© **360/484-3482**). This area is well known for its variety of birds. More than 100 species have been seen here, including the snowy plover, which nests at the point. Because the plovers nest on the sand, a portion of the point is closed to all visitors March through September. During these months you can still hike the trails, use the beach, and explore the marshes.

At Ilwaco, you'll find charter boats that will take you out fishing for salmon, halibut, sturgeon, or bottom fish. Try **Pacific Salmon Charters** (© **800/831-2695** or 360/642-3466; www.pacificsalmoncharters.com) or **Coho Charters** (© **800/339-2646** or 360/642-3333; www.cohocharters.com).

Long Island, located in the middle of Willapa Bay and accessible only by private boat, is part of the Willapa National Wildlife Refuge (© **360/484-3482**), which has its headquarters about 9 miles up U.S. 101 from Seaview. The island is known for its grove of huge old red cedars and is popular with sea kayakers. There are a few campsites and some hiking trails.

WHERE TO STAY

If you're heading down this way with the whole family and need an entire vacation home, contact **Pacific Realty Property Management,** 102 NE Bolstad St. (P.O. Box 97), Long Beach, WA 98631 (© **888/879-5479** or 360/642-4549; www.pacreal.com/rentals). Alternatively, you can contact the Long Beach Peninsula Visitors Bureau (see above), which maintains a list of most of the vacation homes in the area.

Among the most interesting accommodations options in the area are the two former **lighthouse-keepers' homes** at the North Head Lighthouse in Cape Disappointment State Park. These vacation homes can be rented through Cape Disappointment State Park (© **888/CAMPOUT** or 360/683-4985; www.parks. wa.gov/vacationhouses) and rent for $234 per night with a 2- to 3-night minimum depending on the season. The two houses are in a clearing in the woods about 100 yards from the old lighthouse, and hiking trails lead from the grounds down to the beach and through the park. There are also two more restored historic homes available at nearby Fort Columbia State Park. One rents for $146 per night and sleeps four people and the other rents for $350 per night and sleeps 12 people. Call the number above for reservations.

Boreas Bed & Breakfast Inn 🖈🖈   Although this inn is housed in a renovated 1920s beach house, you would never guess it from the contemporary styling both outside and within. The inn is only a few blocks from downtown Long Beach and is separated from the ocean by only the grassy dunes between you and the beach. The upstairs rooms have the best views, but, with their spaciousness and private decks, the two downstairs rooms are also very comfortable. One of these downstairs rooms was formerly a sun room and has two walls of windows. This room also has a whirlpool tub in the bathroom. On the grounds, there is an enclosed gazebo housing a whirlpool spa.

607 N. Ocean Blvd. (P.O. Box 1344), Long Beach, WA 98631. © **888/642-8069** or 360/642-8069. www.boreas inn.com. 5 units. $145–$155 double. Rates include full breakfast. AE, DISC, MC, V. **Amenities:** Access to nearby health club; Jacuzzi; concierge; massage. *In room:* Hair dryer.

The Inn at Ilwaco 🖈 *(Finds*   Built on a wooded hilltop on the outskirts of tiny Ilwaco at the south end of the Long Beach Peninsula, this inn is a former Presbyterian church. Though the church itself now serves primarily as a wedding facility and group rental spaces, an attached building, which once served as the Sunday school and minister's home, now houses the inn's guest rooms and a large and comfortable parlor. The setting includes plenty of nautical decor. Ilwaco makes a good base for exploring both the Long Beach Peninsula and Astoria.

120 Williams St. NE (P.O. Box 922), Ilwaco, WA 98624. © 888/244-2523 or 360/642-8686. Fax 360/642-8642. www.longbeachlodging.com. 9 units. $99–$149 double. Rates include full breakfast. MC, V. *In room:* No phone.

Moby Dick Hotel ★ *(Finds*

Though it looks a bit like a big yellow bunker from the outside, the Moby Dick is actually a comfortable bed-and-breakfast inn. Built as a hotel back in 1930 (the year before the train stopped running), the hotel quickly fell on hard times. Today it's a casual place, eclectically furnished in a 1930s style. The location, up at the north end of the peninsula, is removed from the beach strip of Seaview and Long Beach, and is convenient to Leadbetter Park and its wild dunes and beaches. You'll also be within walking distance of The Ark Restaurant (see below). Low rates, friendly atmosphere, and a tranquil setting make this a great choice. There is a sauna for taking off the chill, and dinners are available in the dining room. Breakfasts often included fresh oysters from the inn's oyster beds.

Sandridge Rd. and Bay Ave., Nahcotta, WA 98637. © 360/665-4543. Fax 360/665-6887. www.mobydick hotel.com. 8 units, 2 with private bathroom. $85–$100 double with shared bathroom; $110–$125 double with private bathroom. Rates include full breakfast. 2-night minimum on summer weekends, 3-night minimum on festival weekends. AE, DISC, MC, V. Pets accepted ($10). **Amenities:** Restaurant (Northwest); sauna. *In room:* No phone.

Shelburne Country Inn ★★

Despite its location in town, this inn's tone perfectly captures that of a country inn. Step though the front door and you enter rooms filled with a pale light that is filtered by walls of stained-glass windows salvaged from an English church. In the main lobby, dark fir-paneled walls, a big oak table, and a fire crackling on the hearth all extend a classic country welcome. Most guest rooms are on the second floor, but, on the ground floor, there are a couple of suites that overlook the gardens and have their own decks. All the guest rooms are filled with antiques and, even if sometimes a bit cramped, all feel very luxurious and old-fashioned. The inn's Shoalwater Restaurant is one of the state's finest restaurants (see below). The Shelburne also operates the China Beach Retreat (www.chinabeachretreat.com), which is on the waterfront in nearby Ilwaco (rooms are $179 double and the one suite is $199).

4415 Pacific Hwy. (P.O. Box 250), Seaview, WA 98644-0250. © 800/INN-1896 or 360/642-2442. Fax 360/642-8904. www.theshelburneinn.com. 15 units. $129–$159 double; $179 suite. Rates include full breakfast. AE, MC, V. **Amenities:** Restaurant (Northwest); lounge. *In room:* Hair dryer.

Sunset View Resort ★ *(Kids*

About midway up the peninsula, you'll find this attractive motel set back in the woods a bit, on the far side of a little bridge. Tall fir trees and attractive gardens surround the resort, and out back, dunes stretch for 100 yards to the beach. Although the furnishings are a bit dated, many of the rooms come equipped with kitchens, which makes this a good choice for families. Some rooms also have fireplaces and balconies (ask for a second-floor room; these have the best views). Although there isn't a pool here, you'll find plenty of other recreational amenities, including those listed below and a sauna, a whirlpool, volleyball and basketball courts, horseshoes, a playground, and a picnic area.

P.O. Box 399, Ocean Park, WA 98640. © 800/272-9199 or 360/665-4494. Fax 360/665-6528. www. washingtoncoast.net. 52 units. Mid-May to mid-Sept $70–$127 double; mid-Sept to mid-May, off-season discounts. AE, DISC, MC, V. Pets accepted ($15). **Amenities:** Tennis court; Jacuzzi; coin-op laundry. *In room:* TV.

CAMPGROUNDS

The only campground in this area worth recommending is **Cape Disappointment State Park** (227 campsites), which is at the southern end of the Long Beach Peninsula at the mouth of the Columbia River. This park has campsites on a small lake, as well as some at the foot of North Head. Some of the sites in the latter area are tucked in amid massive boulders. For reservations contact **Washington State Parks** (© 888/226-7688; www.parks.wa.gov/reserve.asp).

WHERE TO DINE

For smoked salmon and oysters, fresh fish and crab, and fresh clam chowder, stop in at **Ocean Park Crab & Seafood Market,** 254th Street and Pacific Highway, Ocean Park (© **360/665-3474**).

The Ark Restaurant & Bakery 🎯🎯 NORTHWEST   Located at the north end of the Long Beach Peninsula, the Ark is an oyster lover's paradise. Set at the foot of a working dock and surrounded by oyster canneries and huge piles of oyster shells, the restaurant has its own oyster beds, as well as its own herb and edible-flower garden. You can be sure that whatever you order here will be absolutely fresh, and that's exactly what has kept the Ark afloat for decades. Of course, oysters are the top dinner choice, and the Ark's oyster platter comes with 16 extra-small oysters. Even if you aren't an oyster fan, you'll find plenty of delicious dishes on the menu here, however, you had better like garlic, which is used liberally here. If you have a sweet tooth, be sure to save room for one of the Ark's excellent desserts.

3310 273rd St., Nahcotta. © 360/665-4133. www.arkrestaurant.com. Reservations highly recommended. Main courses $9–$11 lunch, $12–$28 dinner. AE, DISC, MC, V. Aug Tues–Sat 5–9:30pm, Sun 11am–2:30pm and 5–9:30pm; June–July and Sept–Oct Wed–Sat 5–9:30pm, Sun 11am–2:30pm and 5–9:30pm; mid-Mar to late May and Nov Thurs–Sat 5–9:30pm, Sun 11am–2:30pm and 5–9:30pm; Dec to mid-Mar Fri–Sat 5–9:30pm, Sun 11am–2:30pm and 5–9:30pm (call to confirm hours in Dec).

The Depot Restaurant 🎯🎯 *(Finds* ECLECTIC   This is the just the sort of restaurant you dream of finding on vacation. Small, out of the way, casual and inexpensive, yet with excellent food. Located in the old Seaview train depot, this restaurant abounds in vintage character, from its linoleum floors to its wooden counter to its old-fashioned hanging lights. The menu is short and varied, and includes Willapa Bay oysters (of course) and clam chowder made with local clams. However, the more elaborate preparations, such as scallops with porcini-mushroom risotto and truffle oil, are the real stars here. No matter what you order for an entree, you should be sure to start with the house salad, which is made with mixed greens, candied walnuts, blue cheese, and slices of pear.

38th St. and L Place, Seaview. © 360/642-7880. Reservations recommended. Main courses $10–$18. DISC, MC, V. Sun and Wed–Thurs 5–9pm; Fri–Sat 5–10pm (shorter hours in winter).

Sanctuary Restaurant 🎯🎯 *(Finds* NORTHWEST/SCANDINAVIAN   A 1906 church in the community of Chinook, between Long Beach and the Astoria-Megler Bridge, now serves as one of southwest Washington's most memorable dining experiences. The church has changed very little since its days as a house of worship, and people still pack the pews, which are used for bench seating at the tables (should you happen to get a table on the altar, you may wind up in the minister's throne-like chair). The menu includes such staples as pan-fried oysters, but the traditional (Swedish meatballs) and more imaginative Scandinavian dishes are the real attraction here. The fish specialties shouldn't be missed, nor should the *krumkaka* (crumb cake) dessert.

794 U.S. 101. 🕐 **360/777-8380.** www.sanctuaryrestaurant.com. Reservations recommended. Main courses $14–$21. AE, DISC, MC, V. Summer Wed–Sat 5–9pm, Sun 5–8pm; other months, call for hours.

The Shoalwater Restaurant/Heron and Beaver Pub ✸✸ NORTHWEST The Shoalwater is one of the best restaurants in Washington and should not be missed on a visit to this corner of the state. Stained-glass windows salvaged from an English church suffuse the elegant dining room with a soft light, while furnishings evoke Victorian times. The menu changes frequently, but you can be sure you'll find plenty of excellent oyster and clam dishes (made with local shellfish) at almost any time of year. Since this is cranberry country, you might want to start your meal with an appetizer of pâté with cranberry chutney and roasted-garlic crème fraîche. Here at the Shelburne Country Inn, you'll also find the casual Heron and Beaver Pub, which serves lighter fare at lower prices, and is open for both lunch and dinner.

4415 Pacific Way, in the Shelburne Inn, Seaview. 🕐 **360/642-4142.** www.shoalwater.com. Reservations highly recommended. Main courses $12–$24; pub entrees $6–$16. AE, DC, DISC, MC, V. Restaurant daily 5:30–9pm. Pub daily 11:30am–3pm and 5:30–9pm.

UP THE COLUMBIA RIVER

Between the Long Beach Peninsula and I-5 at Longview lies one of the state's most enjoyable and little known scenic drives. Wash. 4 passes through several small historic riverfront communities, and between Cathlamet and Longview it runs right alongside the Columbia River, often at the base of steep hillsides or basalt cliffs. The quiet backwaters along this stretch of the river seem little changed by the passing of time.

Heading east from Long Beach on U.S. 101, you first skirt the south end of Willapa Bay, which is the site of the Willapa National Wildlife Refuge. Each year in late April and early May, this area becomes a rest stop for thousands of birds heading north to summer breeding grounds in the Arctic. Roughly 20 miles east of the junction of U.S. 101 and Wash. 4, you'll come to the **Grays River covered bridge,** which was erected in 1905 and is one of only two covered bridges in Washington. The bridge is 2 miles off the highway.

Another 15 miles east, you'll come to the tiny community of **Skamokawa** (pronounced Skuh-*mah*-kuh-way), which is one of the only remaining Columbia River fishing villages dating from the early 20th century, when salmon canneries abounded along the Columbia River. Here you can visit the **River Life Interpretive Center** (🕐 **360/795-3007**), which is housed in Redmen Hall, a restored 1894 schoolhouse. The center is right on Wash. 4 and is open Thursday through Sunday from noon to 4pm. Just east of Skamokawa lies the **Julia Butler Hansen National Wildlife Refuge,** which protects the rare Columbia River white-tailed deer, and to the west is the **Lewis and Clark National Wildlife Refuge.** If you're interested in exploring the waterways of these refuges, contact the **Skamokawa Paddle Center,** 1391 W. State Rte. 4, Skamokawa, WA 98647 (🕐 **888/920-2777** or 360/795-8300; www.skamokawakayak.com), which offers a wide variety of 1- and 2-day trips. Prices range from $90 to $223 per person. Classes and canoe/kayak rentals are also available.

East of the refuge, you come to Cathlamet, which was settled in 1846 and is the largest town on this stretch of road. Here you can visit the **Wahkiakum Historical Society Museum,** 65 River St., Cathlamet (🕐 **360/795-3954**), learn about the early pioneer history of the region, and see old fishing exhibits. May through October, the museum is open Tuesday through Sunday from 11am to

---

Moments **Ship Ahoy!**

It's not unusual to come around a bend on Wash. 4 and be face to face with a freighter. In places, the shipping channel is no more than 100 yards from shore, and the sight of a rusty hulk of a ship rumbling through the trees just off the side of the road has caused more than a few unsuspecting motorists to hit the breaks and hit their brakes. Feel free to put on your starboard turn signal and pull over for a better look.

4pm; November through April, it's open Thursday through Sunday from 1 to 4pm. Admission is by donation. Cathlamet is connected by bridge to **Puget Island,** which was settled by Scandinavian fishermen in the late 1800s. Today the island is covered with farms and is a popular spot with bicyclists. The flat, uncrowded roads and river views make for an ideal day's bicycle tour. However, you'll have to bring your own bike as there are no bike rental shops on the island. The last ferry on the Columbia River connects the island to Oregon.

East of Cathlamet begins the most picturesque portion of this drive, with the cliffs of Little Cape Horn marking the start of this scenic stretch of road. Due to its strong winds, the Little Cape Horn area is popular with windsurfers.

WHERE TO STAY

Skamokawa Inn ⊛ *(Finds* Located in the tiny historic fishing village of Skamokawa, this inn caters primarily to people coming to town to go sea kayaking with the affiliated Skamokawa Paddle Center. The inn's rooms, which are in a restored historic building, are modern, comfortable, and cheerful. Two have their own small balconies and all have river views. If you have the family or some friends along, consider the apartment, which is in an adjacent house. The inn is located right on the water, with its own dock. On the ground floor, there's a general store that has a casual dining room as well as a store. Canoes, kayaks, and mountain bikes can all be rented here.

1391 W. State Rte. 4, Skamokawa, WA 98647. © **888/920-2777** or 360/795-8300. Fax 360/795-8304. www. skamokawakayak.com. 12 units. $85–$90 double; $135–$235 apt or suite. Rates include continental breakfast. MC, V. **Amenities:** Restaurant (American); watersports rentals; bike rentals. *In room:* TV.

3 Vancouver & Vicinity

6 miles N of downtown Portland, 120 miles SE of Long Beach, 40 miles S of Longview

Because Vancouver, Washington, is part of the Portland metropolitan area, and because it bears the same name as both a large island and a city in Canada, it is often overlooked by visitors to the Northwest. However, the city has several historic sites and other attractions that make it worth a stop. It was here, at Fort Vancouver, a Hudson's Bay Company (HBC) trading fort, that much of the Northwest's important early pioneer history unfolded.

ESSENTIALS

GETTING THERE Vancouver is located on I-5 just north across the Columbia River from Portland, Oregon. I-205 bypasses the city to the east, while Wash. 14 heads east up the Columbia Gorge.

With the Portland International Airport just across the river, Vancouver is also well connected to the rest of the world via numerous airlines. The city is also served by Amtrak trains.

VISITOR INFORMATION   For more information on this area, contact the **Southwest Washington Convention & Visitors Bureau,** 101 E. Eighth St., Vancouver, WA 98660 (© **877/600-0800** or 360/750-1553; www.southwest washington.com), which operates a visitor's center in the Slocum House, Esther Short Park, 605 Esther St.

VANCOUVER'S HISTORICAL ATTRACTIONS

The city of Vancouver, Washington, was one of the first settlements in the Northwest and consequently has a long pioneer and military history. After the British gave up Fort Vancouver, it became the site of the Vancouver Barracks U.S. military post, and stately homes were built for the officers of the post. The buildings of Officers' Row and their attractive, tree-shaded surroundings are now preserved as the **Vancouver National Historic Reserve** ★★. Within the reserve, which is located just east of I-5 (take the East Mill Plain Blvd. exit just north of the I-5 Interstate Bridge), you'll find not only Officers' Row, Fort Vancouver, and the Pearson Air Museum, but also the **Columbia River Waterfront Trail.** At the west end of this paved riverside trail, in a small park through a walkway under the railroad tracks, you'll find the **oldest apple tree** in the Northwest. It was planted in 1826.

Fort Vancouver National Historic Site ★★   It was here at Fort Vancouver, a trading post operated by the British Hudson's Bay Company, that much of the Northwest's important early pioneer history unfolded. The HBC came to the Northwest in search of furs and, for most of the first half of the 19th century, was the only authority in this remote region. Fur trappers, mountain men, missionaries, explorers, and settlers all made Fort Vancouver their first stop in the Oregon country, which at that time also encompassed present-day Washington. Today Fort Vancouver houses several reconstructed buildings that are furnished as they might have been in the middle of the 19th century. Throughout the year, there are a variety of living-history programs.

1501 E. Evergreen Blvd. © **800/832-3599** or 360/696-7655. www.nps.gov/fova. Admission (charged in summer only) $3. Year-round daily 9am–4pm. Closed Thanksgiving, Dec 24, 25, and 26, and Jan 1.

Pearson Air Museum ★   A very different piece of history is preserved at this small air museum on the far side of Fort Vancouver from Officers' Row. This airfield was established in 1905 and is the oldest operating airfield in the United States. Dozens of vintage aircraft, including several World War I–era biplanes are on display in a large hangar, and there is an exhibit on the Russian plane that made the first transpolar flight.

1115 E. Fifth St. © 360/694-7026. www.pearsonairmuseum.org. Admission $5 adults, $4 seniors, $3 children ages 13–18, $2 children ages 6–12, free for children under 6. Tues–Sun 10am–5pm.

EXPLORING OUTSIDE OF TOWN

In the town of Washougal, 16 miles east of Vancouver on Wash. 14, you can visit the **Pendleton Woolen Mills and Outlet Shop,** 2 17th St., Washougal (© **800/ 568-2480** or 360/835-1118; www.pendletonmillstore.com), and see how their famous wool blankets and classic wool fashions are made. The store is open Monday through Friday from 8am to 5pm, Saturday from 9am to 5pm, and Sunday from 1 to 5pm, with free mill tours offered Monday through Friday at 9, 10, and 11am, and 1:30pm.

Twenty-three miles north of Vancouver, in the town of Woodland, are the **Hulda Klager Lilac Gardens,** 115 S. Pekin Rd., Woodland (© **360/225-8996;** www.lilacgardens.com). Between late April and mid-May each year, these gardens burst into color and the fragrance of lilacs hangs in the air. The gardens are open daily from dawn to dusk. Admission is $2.

Ten miles east of Woodland off NE Cedar Creek Road, you'll find the **Cedar Creek Grist Mill,** Grist Mill Road (🕿 **360/225-5832;** www.cedarcreekgrist mill.com), the only remaining 19th-century grist mill in Washington. Built in 1876, the mill was restored over a 10-year period, and in 1989, once again became functional. When the mill is open, volunteers demonstrate how wheat is ground into flour. Hours of operation are Saturday from 1 to 4pm and Sunday from 2 to 4pm. Admission is by donation. Adjacent to the mill is one of Washington's only two historic covered bridges.

WHERE TO STAY

The Heathman Lodge ★★ *Value* Mountain lodge meets urban chic at this suburban Vancouver hotel adjacent to the Vancouver Mall. Located 20 minutes by car from downtown Portland, the hotel is well placed for exploring both the Columbia Gorge and Mount St. Helens. With its log, stone, and cedar-shingle construction, this hotel conjures up the Northwest's historic mountain lodges. As at Timberline Lodge on Oregon's Mount Hood, this hotel is filled with artwork and embellished with rugged Northwest-inspired craftwork, including totem poles, Eskimo kayak frames, and Pendleton blankets. Guest rooms feature a mix of rustic pine and peeled-hickory furniture as well as rawhide lampshades and Pendleton-inspired bedspreads.

7801 NE Greenwood Dr., Vancouver, WA 98662. 🕿 **888/475-3100** or 360/254-3100. Fax 360/254-6100. www.heathmanlodge.com. 143 units. $89–$139 double; from $159 suite. AE, DC, DISC, MC, V. Free parking. **Amenities:** Restaurant (Northwest); lounge; indoor pool; exercise room; Jacuzzi; sauna; concierge; business center; limited room service; guest laundry; laundry service; dry cleaning. *In room:* A/C, TV, dataport, fridge, microwave, coffeemaker, hair dryer, iron.

WHERE TO DINE

Hudson's, the dining room at The Heathman Lodge (see above for details), is one of the city's best restaurants and is open for three meals a day. When it's time for a pint of craft ale, the place to head in Vancouver is **McMenamins on the Columbia,** 1801 SE Columbia River Dr. (🕿 **360/699-1521;** www. mcmenamins.com), a brewpub with a view.

Beaches Restaurant & Bar ★ *Kids* INTERNATIONAL Sure it's a long way to the beach, but why let that stop you from having a good time? That seems to be the attitude of this waterfront restaurant. The gardens are full of sand and a party atmosphere prevails most of the time (there are early and late happy hours). The menu is long and includes everything from burgers to barbecue chicken pizza to a catfish burrito. With big walls of glass overlooking the Columbia, sunset dinners are very popular. Despite the large size, service is usually good. To reach the restaurant from I-5, take Wash. 14 east and then take exit 1.

1919 SE Columbia River Dr. 🕿 **360/699-1592.** Reservations recommended. Main courses $5–$23. AE, DISC, MC, V. Mon 11am–9pm; Tues–Fri 11am–10pm; Sat noon–10pm; Sun noon–9pm.

9

The Cascades

Cloaked in places by dark forests of old-growth trees and stripped bare by logging clear-cuts in others, the Washington Cascades are a patchwork quilt of narrow valleys, rolling foothills, snowcapped volcanic peaks, and rugged mountain ranges. Lakes of the deepest blue are cradled beneath emerald forests. Glaciers carve their way inexorably from peaks that experience some of the heaviest snowfalls in the nation. (It's possible to drive or hike a short distance to the edge of several of these glaciers and listen to their cracking and rumbling as gravity pulls at their centuries-old ice.) And the appropriately named Cascades send countless waterfalls cascading from the heights.

The I-5 corridor from the Canadian border south more than 150 miles to Olympia is the most densely populated region of Washington state, yet for the millions of people who live here, gazing upon mountain wilderness merely requires a look eastward on a clear day. Dominating the eastern skyline of the northern Puget Sound

region are volcanic Mount Baker and the North Cascades. In the southern regions of the sound, Mount Rainier, another dormant volcano, looms grandly on the horizon. It's the easy accessibility of these mountains that helps make the cities of Puget Sound so livable. With two national parks, a national volcanic monument, a half dozen major ski areas, one of the largest networks of cross-country ski trails in the country, hundreds of lakes (including the third-deepest lake in the United States), a Bavarian village, and a false-fronted Wild West frontier town, these mountains offer a diversity of recreational and sightseeing activities.

Whatever the season, in good weather and bad, active Washingtonians head for the hills whenever they get the chance. Summer and winter are, however, the most popular seasons in these mountains. In summer people come for the wildflowers and to go hiking, and in winter, they come for the skiing and snowboarding.

1 Mount Baker ✶✶ & the North Cascades Scenic Highway ✶✶✶

Diablo Lake: 66 miles E of Burlington (I-5), 65 miles W of Winthrop; Mount Baker Ski Area: 62 miles E of Bellingham

Wolves and grizzly bears still call this wilderness home, and names such as Mount Fury, Mount Terror, and Forbidden Peak are testament to the rugged and remote nature of this terrain. Much of the region is preserved within the two units of North Cascades National Park, one of the least visited national parks in the country. This lack of visitors is easy to understand when you realize there is but one gravel road within the boundaries of the park, and this road originates in the community of Stehekin on the north shore of Lake Chelan. Stehekin can only be reached by hiking trail, floatplane, or boat, which severely limits the number of vehicles that use this road. However, passing between the two units of the national park is the North Cascades Scenic Highway, which does provide access to viewpoints and trails that lead into the national park. While there is very little road access in this area, there are plenty of trails, and day hikers and backpackers can head off on hundreds of miles of trails through wilderness areas, national forest, national park, and national recreation areas.

Though numerous attempts were made over the years to build a road through the craggy, glacier-sculpted North Cascade mountains, it was not until 1972 that Wash. 20 finally connected the Skagit Valley communities on the west side of the North Cascades with Winthrop on the east side of the mountains. Today the road is known as the North Cascades Scenic Highway, and it's one of the most breathtakingly beautiful stretches of road anywhere in the United States. Unfortunately, because of heavy winter snows and avalanches, the road is only open from April to November (depending on the weather). The scenic highway begins east of Sedro-Woolley, and along its length you'll find more than a dozen campgrounds.

Lying just outside the northwestern corner of North Cascades National Park is 10,778-foot Mount Baker, which on a clear day dominates the skyline to the east of Bellingham and the San Juan Islands. This is the northernmost of Washington's Cascade Range volcanoes, and, as such, rises high above the surrounding North Cascade peaks, which are geologically unrelated to Mount Baker. Because it is open to the winter storms that sweep up the Strait of Juan de Fuca from the Pacific Ocean, Mount Baker usually receives more snow than any other Cascades peak, and in the winter of 1998–99, a world record 1,140 inches fell at the Mount Baker Ski Area.

While it is the North Cascades Scenic Highway, with its mountain vistas and excellent hiking, that attracts most people to this area, the slopes of Mount Baker are almost equally rewarding. In summer, hikers can explore alpine meadows, and in winter, skiers and snowboarders can sample some of the most legendary snows in the country.

ESSENTIALS

GETTING THERE   To reach Mount Baker ski area (and, in summer, Heather Meadows and Artist Point), head east from Bellingham on Wash. 542 (the Mount Baker Hwy.). The North Cascades Scenic Highway is Wash. 20, which leaves I-5 at Burlington.

VISITOR INFORMATION   For information on the Mount Baker area, contact the **Glacier Public Service Center,** Mount Baker Highway, Glacier (© **360/599-2714**). For information on the North Cascades National Park Complex, Mount Baker National Recreation Area, and Mount Baker–Snoqualmie National Forest, contact the jointly operated **Forest/Park Service Information Office,** 810 Wash. 20, Sedro-Woolley, WA 98284 (© **360/856-5700;** www.nps.gov/noca or www.fs.fed.us/r6/mbs).

VISITING THE MOUNT BAKER AREA

Wash. 542, known as the Mount Baker Highway, is a dead-end road that climbs to 5,140 feet in elevation at a ridge between 10,778-foot Mount Baker and 9,038-foot Mount Shuksan. The road ends at the aptly named **Artist Point** ★★★, an area of rugged beauty nearly unequaled in the state. Rising directly above Artist Point is flat-topped Table Mountain, up which there is a short but precipitous trail. Three miles before you reach Artist Point you'll come

The Washington Cascades

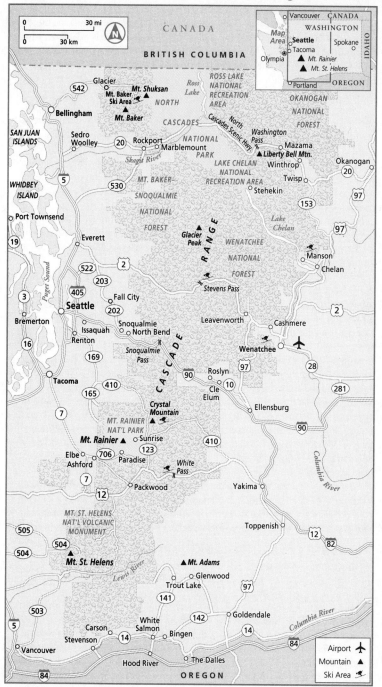

to **Heather Meadows** and Picture Lake, in which the reflection of Mount Shuksan can be seen when the waters are still. Each year in July and August the meadows of this area burst into bloom and attract crowds of weekend hikers who tramp the many miles of trails that radiate out from here. Between late July and early October, the **Heather Meadows Visitor Center,** milepost 56 on Mount Baker Highway (no phone), has trail maps for the area and information on this region's unusual geology.

Two of the most rewarding hikes in the Mount Baker area actually originate not in the Heather Meadows/Artist Point area but off side roads 1 mile east of the town of Glacier. These are the **Heliotrope Ridge Trail** (off Forest Service Rd. 39) and the **Skyline Divide Trail** (off Forest Service Rd. 37). Both of these trails climb up through meadows with excellent views of Mount Baker, and, from the Heliotrope Ridge Trail, there are also impressive glacier views. Also near Glacier, at milepost 41, is a short trail that leads to 100-foot Nooksack Falls.

In order to park at Heather Meadows, Artist Point, and other trail heads in the area, you'll need a Northwest Forest Pass. These permits cost $5 per day ($30 for an annual pass) and can be purchased at ranger stations and national forest visitor centers.

While Kodak-moment meadows of colorful wildflowers are a big attraction throughout the summer, Mount Baker is better known as one of the nation's top snowboarding areas. Each winter, Mount Baker receives an average of more than 500 inches of snow, and in the winter of 1998–99 set a world record with 1,140 inches of snow. All this snow, combined with lots of extreme terrain, produces awesome skiing and snowboarding conditions. Consequently, **Mount Baker Ski Area** (© **360/671-0211;** www.mtbakerskiarea.com), located at Heather Meadows, is well known throughout the region for always being the first ski area to open and the last to close each year. All-day lift tickets range from $29 to $37. Ski and snowboard rentals are available at the ski area, and snowboards can also be rented in the town of Glacier at **Mt. Baker Snowboard Shop,** 9996 Forest St. (© **360/599-2008).** Cross-country skiers will find a few miles of groomed trails at Mount Baker ski area, as well as many more miles at the **Salmon Ridge Sno-Park** farther down the mountain. Telemark skiers and backcountry snowboarders will find lots of great terrain adjacent to Mount Baker ski area.

En route to or from Mount Baker, you can sample local wines at **Mount Baker Vineyards,** 4298 Mt. Baker Hwy., Deming (© **360/592-2300**); and stock up on gourmet picnic foods at the unexpectedly hip **Everybody's Store,** 5465 Potter Rd., Van Zandt (© **866/832-4695** or 360/592-2297; www.everybodys.com).

THE NORTH CASCADES SCENIC HIGHWAY

Wash. 20, the North Cascades Scenic Highway, is a bit slow in sharing its beauties. Though it runs along the Skagit River on the west side of the Cascades, it is not until you get to the Ross Lake area that the scenery becomes truly grand. However, there are several distractions along the way before you reach the most scenic stretch of the highway.

North of Concrete, which was named for the cement it once produced, lie Lake Shannon and Baker Lake, the latter being a popular summer camping and boating destination. From the road leading to **Baker Lake,** you can also access the **Mount Baker National Recreation Area,** which lies on the south side of Mount Baker. Several trails here lead through beautiful alpine meadows. The Railroad Grade–Paul Scott Trail is absolutely breathtaking.

Natural History Seminars

Want to track radio-collared mountain caribou? Learn about Lummi Indian basketry? Delve into the mysteries of mycology? You can do any of these things if you sign up for the right class through the **North Cascades Institute.** Offering more than 80 natural history field seminars each year, the North Cascades Institute, 810 State Rte. 20, Sedro-Woolley, WA 98284-1239 (© **360/856-5700,** ext. 209; www.ncascades.org), is a non-profit educational organization that offers a wide range of courses each year. While these seminars—many of which involve camping out—focus on the North Cascades region, there are programs throughout the state.

Between Concrete and Marblemount, the highway parallels the Skagit River, and from December to February each year, hundreds of bald eagles descend on this stretch of the river to feed on dying salmon. Highway turnouts at the prime eagle-watching sites along this stretch of road provide opportunities to observe the eagles. To learn more about the eagles, stop by Rockport's **Eagle Interpretive Center,** Alfred Street (© 360/853-7283; www.skagiteagle.org), which is located 1 block south of Wash. 20 in the Rockport Fire Hall. The center is staffed Friday through Monday during eagle-watching season. This center can also provide information on the annual Upper Skagit Bald Eagle Festival, which takes place each year in late January or early February. The best way to do your eagle-watching is from a raft floating slowly down the river (no white water here). Companies offering **eagle-watching float trips** include **Chinook Expeditions** (© **800/241-3451;** www.chinookexpeditions.com) and **Alpine Adventures** (© **800/723-8386** or 206/323-1220; www.alpineadventures.com). An all-day trip costs about $75.

Right in the middle of the eagle-viewing area, you'll come to the town of Rockport. On its west side is **Rockport State Park,** where you can take a hike through a stand of old-growth Douglas firs, some of which are more than 300 years old. Three miles east of Rockport, keep an eye out for **Cascadian Farm Home Farm Roadside Stand,** 55749 Hwy. 20 (© **360/853-8173;** www.cfarm.com), which is open May through October and sells fresh organic berries during the summer months.

Hikers in search of mountain vistas and wildflower-filled meadows should hold out for **Rainy Pass** ✦✦ (and hope that the pass is not living up to its name). Here you'll find an easy paved trail to **Rainy Lake,** which can be combined with the strenuous, but astoundingly soul-satisfying, **Maple Pass Loop.** The view from Maple Pass is one of the finest in the Northwest. The Pacific Crest Trail also crosses the highway at Rainy Pass. If you head north along the Pacific Crest Trail, you will climb to Cutthroat Pass, with more superb views. A few miles farther east, you'll find the trail head for the short, but steep, hike to picturesque **Blue Lake.**

Roughly 20 miles before reaching the Wild West town of Winthrop, you come to the most breathtaking stretch of the North Cascades Scenic Highway. Here, at **Washington Pass** ✦✦✦ (5,447 ft. in elevation), the granite peak of Liberty Bell Mountain rises 2,200 feet above. Across the valley are the jagged Early Winter Spires, a full 200 feet taller than Liberty Bell Mountain. Below the pass the road has been blasted out of a steep cliff face in one huge switchback. The Washington Pass Overlook, with its short walking trail, provides an opportunity to enjoy these last awesome vistas of the North Cascades. With its in-your-face view of craggy peaks, this is the North Cascade Scenic Highway's big payoff and this sight alone makes the drive over the mountains worthwhile.

In Marblemount, the next town you come to, you'll find the **Wilderness Information Center** of the Ross Lake National Recreation Area (© **360/873-4500,** ext. 39), which provides backcountry permits and information.

In the town of Newhalem, a picturesque Seattle City Light company town at the foot of the Gorge Dam, you'll find the **North Cascades Visitor Center** (© **206/386-4495;** www.nps.gov/noca), the main visitor center for the North Cascades National Park Complex, which includes North Cascades National Park, Ross Lake National Recreation Area, and Lake Chelan National Recreation Area. The visitor center is filled with interesting exhibits on this remote national park. There are several short hikes in the area, and in the autumn, you can see spawning salmon at the base of the hydropower plant on the edge of town. Surrounding this powerhouse, there is an attractively landscaped garden that is reached by a swinging footbridge. Continuing east from Newhalem, the road passes through a deep, narrow gorge, where you can glimpse **Gorge Creek Falls** before reaching **Gorge Dam,** the first and smallest of the dams along this stretch of the Skagit River.

Beyond the Gorge Dam, you soon come to Diablo, another Seattle City Light company town, which stands at the base of Diablo Dam. Diablo is the starting point for one of the most fascinating excursions in this corner of the state—the 2-hour boat tour on the turquoise-colored waters of Diablo Lake. In places, steep cliffs rise directly from the waters of the lake and stunted conifers cling to the rock walls. At times this scenery looks as if it were lifted from a Chinese scroll painting. Tours are offered on Saturday and Sunday in June and September and Thursday through Monday in July and August. Tours cost $17 for adults, $15 for seniors, and $15 for children ages 6 to 12. For information, or to make a reservation (highly recommended), call **Skagit Tours/Seattle City Light** (© **206/684-3030;** www.skagittours.com).

Continuing on past Diablo, you cross the Thunder Arm of Diablo Lake and climb up to the spectacular **Diablo Lake Overlook** ✹✹. When the sun shines, the glacier-fed lake displays an astounding turquoise color due to the suspended particles of silt in the water. High above the lake you can see glaciated Colonial and Pyramid peaks.

At the **Ross Lake Overlook,** several miles farther east, the dammed waters of this huge reservoir come into view. The lake, and in fact this entire stretch of highway from east of Marblemount to east of Ross Lake, is designated the **Ross Lake National Recreation Area.** The lake itself extends 24 miles north, with its northern shore lying 1½ miles inside Canada. The only access to the lake from the United States is by trail or water, and with its many shoreline backcountry campsites and East Bank Trail it is a popular backpacker destination. Boaters in sea kayaks and canoes also frequent these remote waters. See "Where to Stay," below, for information on the Ross Lake Resort, which rents canoes and kayaks and offers both a water taxi service and a shuttle that will haul your kayak or canoe around Ross Dam. Trails lead down to the lake both at the dam (before the Ross Lake Overlook) and east of the overlook (access to the East Bank Trail).

WHERE TO STAY
IN THE MOUNT BAKER AREA

The best accommodations at the foot of Mount Baker are to be had through **Mt. Baker Lodging,** 7425 Mt. Baker Hwy. (P.O. Box 2002), Maple Falls, WA

98266-2002 (© **800/709-7669** or 360/599-2453; www.mtbakerlodging.com), which rents out more than 40 cabins, houses, and condos. Rates range from $99 to $265 per night.

The Inn at Mt. Baker ☆☆ Located high on a hill at the end of a steep, 3,000-foot-long gravel driveway (don't worry, the inn really is up there), this B&B is by far the best place to stay along the Mt. Baker Highway. A head-on, jaw-dropping view of Mount Baker is the inn's focal point and all five of the guest rooms have mountain views, as does the Jacuzzi out on the patio. The inn is a large modern home, and all the rooms are spacious and have superb beds and oversize soaking tubs. Perhaps the only drawback here is that the hill leading up to the inn was fairly recently clear cut. However, if not for the clear cut, there wouldn't be such a great view of Mount Baker.

8174 Mt. Baker Hwy. (P.O. Box 5150), Glacier, WA 98244. © **877/567-5526** or 360/599-1776. Fax 360/599-3000. www.theinnatmtbaker.com. 5 units. $120–$140 double. Rates include full breakfast. AE, DISC, MC, V. Children over 16 accepted. **Amenities:** Jacuzzi; massage. *In room:* No phone.

ALONG THE NORTH CASCADES SCENIC HIGHWAY

Ross Lake Resort ☆ *(Finds* Although this is primarily a fishing resort, the fact that all the rooms are in floating cabins makes it unusual enough that even non-anglers might enjoy a stay here. Most of the cabins are small and rustic, but there are two large cabins with vaulted ceilings and modern amenities. If you're looking to get away from it all, this is the place—there's not even a road to the resort. To reach the resort, you must first drive to Diablo Dam on Wash. 20, then take a ferry to the end of the lake where a truck carries you around Ross Dam to a boat landing where a speedboat from the lodge picks you up. Alternatively, you can hike in on a 2-mile trail from milepost 134 on Wash. 20. There's no grocery store or restaurant here, so be sure to bring enough food for your stay. What do you do once you get here? Rent a boat and go fishing, rent a kayak or canoe and go paddling, do some hiking, or simply sit and relax.

Rockport, WA 98283. © **206/386-4437.** www.rosslakeresort.com. 15 units. $69–$197 cabin for 2. Boat rental required on weekends. MC, V. **Amenities:** Watersports rentals. *In room:* Kitchen, fridge, coffeemaker.

Skagit River Resort/Clark's Cabins ☆ The first thing you notice when you arrive at this casual cabin resort is the rabbits. They're everywhere—hundreds of them in all shapes and sizes, contentedly munching the lawns or just sitting quietly. Although the bunnies are one of the main attractions here, it's the theme cabins that keep people coming back. Western, nautical, Victorian, Native American, Adirondack, and hacienda are among the choices of interior decor in these cabins. There are other cabins that are equally comfortable, but the theme cabins are what make this place just a bit different. These cabins are especially popular in winter when folks flock to the area to watch the bald eagles that congregate on the Skagit River. There is also a bed-and-breakfast lodge here.

58468 Clark Cabin Rd., Rockport, WA 98283. © **800/273-2606** or 360/873-2250. Fax 360/873-4077. www.northcascades.com. 38 units. $59–$129 double. Children under 6 stay free in parent's room. AE, DISC, MC, V. Pets accepted ($10). **Amenities:** Restaurant (American); coin-op laundry. *In room:* TV, coffeemaker.

CAMPGROUNDS
In the Mount Baker Area

There are several campgrounds in the forests along the banks of the Nooksack River along the Mount Baker Highway. **Silver Fir Campground** ☆ (20 campsites) 13 miles east of Glacier is the closest campground to the Heather Meadows area, and the **Douglas Fir Campground** ☆ (28 campsites) 2 miles east of

Glacier is the next best choice in the area. Reservations can be made at both of these campgrounds by calling the **National Recreation Reservation Service** (© 877/444-6777; www.reserveusa.com). The most developed campground in the area is at **Silver Lake County Park,** 9006 Silver Lake Rd. (© 360/599-2776), which is north of Maple Falls and has 88 campsites.

Along the North Cascades Scenic Highway

Heading over the North Cascades Highway from the west side, you'll find a very nice campground, with walk-in sites, at **Rockport State Park** ⚡ (58 campsites) just west of Rockport. This campground is set amid large old-growth trees and is on a first-come, first-served basis. Outside the town of Newhalem are **Goodell Creek** (21 campsites) and **Newhalem Creek** ⚡ (120 campsites), which is the site of the North Cascades Visitor Center. The next campground east is at **Colonial Creek** ⚡ (147 campsites) on the bank of Diablo Lake. This campground has some very nice sites right on the water.

East of Marblemount, there are a couple of small campgrounds on the Cascade River Road, which leads to the trail head for the popular hike to Cascade Pass. **Marble Creek** (23 campsites) is 8 miles east of Marblemount, and **Mineral Park** (8 campsites) is 15 miles east of Marblemount. Reservations at state park campgrounds can be made by calling **Washington State Parks Reservations** (© 888/226-7688; www.camis.com/wa). Some National Forest campgrounds also accept reservations. For more information call the **National Recreation Reservation Service** (© 877/444-6777; www.reserveusa.com).

WHERE TO DINE
IN THE MOUNT BAKER AREA

For microbrews and pizza, try the **North Fork,** 6186 Mt. Baker Hwy., Deming (© 360/599-BEER).

Milano's Market & Deli ⚡ *Value* ITALIAN   This casual deli and Italian eatery has long been a favorite of snowboarders and skiers coming down off the mountain after a day on the slopes. Fresh pasta dishes are the specialty here, and the menu usually includes four different types of ravioli (smoked salmon, mushroom, cheese, and meat). The desserts, including tiramisu, cappuccino chocolate torte, and polenta cake, are all big hits with the hungry downhill crowd.

9990 Mt. Baker Hwy., Glacier. © 360/599-2863. Main courses $10–$18. MC, V. Daily 10am–9pm (in winter, Sun–Thurs 10am–8 or 8:30pm).

ALONG THE NORTH CASCADES SCENIC HIGHWAY

In addition to the restaurant listed here, you can get decent, simple meals at the **Eatery Restaurant** at the Skagit River Resort, which is also in Marblemount.

Buffalo Run Restaurant ⚡ *Finds* AMERICAN   From the outside this looks like any other roadside diner, but once you see the menu, it's obvious this place is unique. The restaurant's owners have a buffalo ranch and feature buffalo meat on the menu. There are buffalo burgers, buffalo chili, and buffalo T-bones. You'll also find elk, venison, and ostrich on the menu. Of course there's a buffalo head (and skin) on the wall. You'll find the restaurant right in Marblemount.

60084 Hwy. 20 (milepost 106), Marblemount. © 360/873-2461. www.buffalorunrestaurant.com. Main courses $4.50–$40. AE, DISC, MC, V. Daily 9am–9pm.

2 Winthrop & the Methow Valley ✦✦

193 miles (summer) or 243 miles (winter) E of Seattle, 53 miles N of Chelan

Driving into Winthrop, you may think you've stumbled onto a movie set. A covered wooden sidewalk lines the town's main street, which includes a saloon and a blacksmith's shop. If it's a Saturday in summer, you might even see a staged shootout. But where are the cameras? No, this isn't a Hollywood set—it's the real Winthrop.

Well, not *exactly* the real Winthrop. Back in 1972, when the North Cascades Scenic Highway opened, Winthrop needed a way to stop a few of the cars that started crossing the mountains on the new highway. Someone suggested that they cash in on their Wild West heritage and put up some old-fashioned cowtown false fronts (based on old photos of the town). This rewriting of history worked and now Winthrop gets plenty of cars to stop. In fact it has become a destination in its own right, known for its cross-country skiing in winter and mountain biking, hiking, and horseback riding in summer.

Winthrop and the Methow River valley in which it is located really do have a Wild West history. Until 1883, there were no white settlers in this picturesque valley. The only inhabitants were Native Americans who annually migrated into the valley to harvest camas bulbs and fish for salmon. The Native Americans felt it was just too cold to live in the Methow Valley, but when the first white settlers showed up, they refused to listen to the Native Americans' weather reports and built their drafty log cabins anyway. Gold was discovered in the late 1800s and fueled a short-lived boom, but it was agriculture in the form of apples that kept the valley alive until the advent of tourism in the 1970s.

Why an Old West theme town? Possibly because Owen Wister, author of *The Virginian,* a Western novel that became a popular television series, was inspired to write his novel after coming to Winthrop to visit his former Harvard University roommate who ran a trading post here. You won't find any trading posts anymore, but you will find two of the finest mountain lodges in the state.

ESSENTIALS

GETTING THERE   In summer you can take Wash. 20, the North Cascades Scenic Highway, from I-5 at Burlington. However, in winter this road is closed and it's necessary to cross from north of Seattle on U.S. 2 to Wenatchee and then drive north on U.S. 97 to Wash. 153 at Pateros. If you're coming from north-central or eastern Washington, head east on Wash. 20 at Okanogan.

VISITOR INFORMATION   For more information on the Methow Valley, contact the **Winthrop Chamber of Commerce,** 202 Hwy. 20, Winthrop, WA 98862 (✆ **888/463-8469** or 509/996-2125; www.winthropwashington.com), which has its office on Winthrop's main intersection.

SPORTS & OUTDOOR ACTIVITIES

If you're here for the outdoors, then sooner or later you're going to need the **Mazama Store,** 50 Lost River Rd. (✆ **509/996-2855**), which is a general store for the multi-sport crowd. Not only are outdoor gear and clothing for sale, but there are gourmet groceries, Washington wines and microbrews, an espresso bar, and a deli.

FISHING   Fly-fishing is particularly popular in the Methow Valley, and the valley's fly-fishing headquarters is **Mazama Fly Shop & Troutfitters,** 50 Lost River Rd. (✆ **509/996-3674;** www.methow.com/mazamastore/trout.html), which rents all manner of gear, can give you tips on where the fish are biting, and also offers a guide service and classes.

HIKING   Hikers will find miles of trails, including the **Pacific Crest Trail,** within a few miles of Winthrop, although the best hiking trails are farther west off the North Cascades Scenic Highway. For information, contact the **Okanogan/ Wenatchee National Forest,** Methow Valley Ranger District, Visitor Information Center, 24 W. Chewuch Rd., Winthrop, WA 98862 (© **509/996-4000; www.fs.fed.us/r6/okanogan).**

If you want to head for the hills for a few days but don't want to carry a pack, consider a llama trek. These can be arranged through **Deli Llama Wilderness Adventures,** 17045 Llama Lane, Bow, WA 98232 (© **360/757-4212;** www. delillama.com); or **Pasayten Llama Packing,** P.O. Box 852, Twisp, WA 98856 (© **509/996-2326;** www.mtllama.com).

HORSEBACK RIDING   If you've come to Winthrop because you're a cowboy at heart, you'll probably be interested in doing some horseback riding. **Early Winters Outfitting** (© **800/737-8750** or 509/996-2659; www.earlywinters outfitting.com) in Mazama offers rides ranging from an hour ($20) to overnight ($160) or longer.

HOT-AIR BALLOONING   If you'd like to see the Methow Valley from the air, you can arrange a hot-air balloon flight through **Morning Glory Balloon Tours** (© **509/997-1700;** www.balloonwinthrop.com), which charges $175 per person for a 1-hour flight with a champagne picnic at the end of the flight.

MOUNTAIN BIKING   With its many miles of gravel and dirt roads and both national forest and **Methow Valley Sport Trails Association** (MVSTA) trails that are open to bikes in the snow-free months, the Methow Valley ranks as the best mountain-biking area in the entire state. Mountain-bike rentals and trail recommendations are available from **Winthrop Mountain Sports,** 257 Riverside Ave. (© **800/719-3826** or 509/996-2886; www.winthropmountainsports. com), which is located in downtown Winthrop and charges $20 to $30 per day for mountain-bike rentals.

ROCK CLIMBING   The best rock climbing in the state surrounds the Methow Valley, and if you'd like to hire a guide to lead you (or are interested in taking some climbing lessons), contact **North Cascades Mountain Guides,** 50 Lost River Rd., Mazama (© **509/996-3194;** www.ncmountainguides.com), which charges $130 to $210 per person per day for a day of guided climbing.

WHITE-WATER RAFTING   May through August is white-water rafting season on the Methow River. If you're interested, contact **Osprey River Adventures** (© **800/997-4116** or 509/997-4116; www.methow.com/osprey). Trips are about $70 per person.

WINTER SPORTS 🎿🎿🎿   With its sunshine and powdery winter snows, the Methow Valley is legendary in the Northwest for its cross-country skiing. The **Methow Valley Sport Trails Association** (© **509/996-3287** or, for trail conditions and pass information, 800/682-5787 or 509/996-3860; www.mvsta.com) maintains approximately 125 miles of groomed ski trails, which makes this the second-most extensive groomed trail system in the country. Trail passes are $16 for 1 day, $12 for a half day, or $36 for 3 days. Children ages 13 to 17 pay around half price, and children 12 and under ski free. Snowshoe passes are also available ($3 per day). The greatest concentration of trails for all skill levels are in the vicinity of Sun Mountain Lodge, while the trails around Mazama offer plenty of easy miles for distance skiing. The Rendezvous area trails are long and strenuous, but include huts that can be rented for overnight stays. For information on renting one of these huts, contact **Rendezvous Huts** (© **800/257-2452,** 800/422-3048, or 509/996-2148; www.methow.com/huts). Rental rates start at $25 per person.

You can pick up trail maps and rent equipment at **Sun Mountain Lodge** (© **509/996-4735**); **Winthrop Mountain Sports,** 257 Riverside Ave. (© **800/ 719-3826** or 509/996-2886; www.winthropmountainsports.com), in downtown Winthrop; **Mazama Country Inn** (© **509/996-2681**; www.mazamacountry inn.com); or **Jack's Hut at the Freestone Inn,** 17798 Wash. 20 (© **509/996-2752**). All of these either offer a variety of lessons or can point you in the right direction for instruction.

If you happen to be out here with downhill skis or maybe want to do a little telemark skiing, try the small ski hill at **Loup Loup Ski Bowl** (© **509/826-2720;** www.skitheloup.com), 20 minutes east of Twisp on Wash. 20. It's open Wednesday and Friday through Sunday, and daily lift passes are $25 to $30. Although this ski area is small, it does have a quad chairlift. Experienced downhill skiers in search of virgin powder can, if they can afford it, do some heliskiing with **North Cascade Heli-Skiing** (© **800/494-HELI** or 509/996-3272; www.heli-ski.com). A day of skiing that includes five runs and 10,000 vertical feet of slopes will cost $685 per person. However, most people coming here for heli-skiing opt for a 3-day package that includes room, board, and skiing for $2,270 to $2,410 per person (based on double occupancy). Overnight yurt tours are also available.

If you're interested in taking a backcountry skiing course, contact **North Cascades Mountain Guides** in Mazama (© **509/996-3194;** www.ncmountain guides.com), which offers 2-day courses for $265 per person.

OTHER AREA ATTRACTIONS

Though Winthrop is primarily a base for skiers, hikers, and mountain bikers, it also has a few interesting shops. If you're interested in the town's history, visit the **Shafer Historical Museum,** Castle Avenue (© **509/996-2712**), which consists of a collection of historic buildings from around the area. It's open Memorial Day to Labor Day, Thursday through Monday from 10am to 5pm. Admission is by donation. To find the museum, go up Bridge Street from the junction of Wash. 20 and Riverside Drive and turn right on Castle Avenue.

WHERE TO STAY

If you're interested in renting a cabin or vacation house, contact **Methow Valley Central Reservations** (© **800/422-3048** or 509/996-2148; www.methow reservations.com).

IN TWISP

Methow Valley Inn ⚐   If you're searching for a classic B&B experience in the Methow Valley, this is it. Built in 1912, this beautifully restored old home is just a block off Twisp's main street. The interior is bright and simple, with tasteful country decor. Breakfast is served in a large sun room, and, in addition, there is a comfy living room and a study where you can watch movies and munch popcorn. In summer, colorful gardens surround the inn.

234 Second St. (P.O. Box 668), Twisp, WA 98856. © **509/997-2253.** www.methowvalleyinn.com. 7 units, 4 with private bathroom. $89 double with shared bathroom, $99–$109 double with private bathroom. Rates include full breakfast. MC, V. Children 12 and over accepted. **Amenities:** Concierge; massage. *In room:* No phone.

IN WINTHROP

Hotel Rio Vista ✴ As with all the other buildings in downtown Winthrop, the Rio Vista looks as if it had been built for a Hollywood Western movie set. Behind the false front you'll find modern rooms with pine furnishings and an understated country decor. Step out onto your balcony and you'll have a view of the confluence of the Chewuch and Methow rivers and are likely to see deer and bald eagles and many other species of birds. A hot tub overlooks the river. The Rio Vista also rents out a loft cabin up the valley near Mazama.

285 Riverside Ave. (P.O. Box 815), Winthrop, WA 98862. ℂ 800/398-0911 or 509/996-3535. www.hotelrio vista.com. 29 units. $50–$130 double. MC, V. **Amenities:** Jacuzzi. *In room:* A/C, TV, dataport, fridge, coffeemaker.

River Run Inn ✴ Located only a few hundred yards from downtown Winthrop, this motel on the bank of the Methow River feels as if it is miles from town. The motel rooms all have balconies overlooking the river, with the mountains visible across the valley. Rustic peeled-log furniture made by a local craftsman gives the large motel rooms a Western feel. Aside from the riverside location, the best reason to stay here is the small indoor swimming pool and hot tub. The River Run Inn also rents out cabins and a large house.

27 Rader Rd., Winthrop, WA 98862. ℂ 800/757-2709 or 509/996-2173. www.riverrun-inn.com. 15 units. $70–$105 double; $130–$155 cabin; $340–$425 house. MC, V. Pets accepted ($10). **Amenities:** Indoor pool; Jacuzzi. *In room:* A/C, TV, coffeemaker.

Sun Mountain Lodge ✴✴✴ *(Kids* If you're looking for resort luxuries and proximity to hiking, cross-country skiing, and mountain-biking trails, Sun Mountain Lodge should be your first choice in the region. Perched on a mountaintop with grand views of the Methow Valley and the North Cascades, this luxurious lodge captures the spirit of the West in both its breathtaking setting and its rustic design. In the lobby, flagstone floors and stone fireplaces lend a classically Western style. Most guest rooms feature rustic Western furnishings and views of the mountains. The rooms in the Gardiner wing have balconies and slightly better views than those in the main lodge. If seclusion is what you're after, opt for one of the Patterson Lake cabins. The lodge's main dining room serves superb Northwest cuisine amid views that will take your breath away (see "Where to Dine," below, for details). The lounge has the same great view. In addition to amenities listed below, the resort also is right on the valley's ski-trail system and has a ski shop, ski and snowshoe rentals, a ski school, horseback and sleigh rides, an ice-skating pond, lawn games, and a playground.

604 Patterson Lake Rd. (P.O. Box 1000), Winthrop, WA 98862. ℂ 800/572-0493 or 509/996-2211. Fax 509/ 996-3133. www.sunmountainlodge.com. 115 units. Summer $170–$350 double, $325–$650 suite; $250–$650 cabin; winter $140–$280 double, $230–$480 suite, $190–$480 cabin. Lower rates spring and fall. Children 12 and under stay free in parent's room. AE, DC, MC, V. **Amenities:** 2 restaurants (Northwest, American); lounge; 2 outdoor pools; 4 tennis courts; exercise room; full-service spa; 2 Jacuzzis; watersports rentals; bike rentals; children's programs; concierge; activities desk; limited room service; massage; babysitting. *In room:* A/C, coffeemaker, hair dryer, iron.

WolfRidge Resort ✴ *(Kids* Set on 60 acres at the edge of a pasture on both the Methow River and the cross-country ski trails, this lodge, with its modern log buildings, is a great choice in winter or summer. The town houses and suites, which have full kitchens, are big enough for families, and the smaller rooms are fine for couples. The three new cabins are the most romantic and have jetted tubs. The pool, game room, and a playground together make this a good spot for a family vacation. However, the wide-open ranchlike feel and proximity to the ski trails also make this a good bet for active couples.

412-B Wolf Creek Rd., Winthrop, WA 98862. © **800/237-2388** or 509/996-2828. Fax 509/996-2804. www.
wolfridgeresort.com. 21 units. $79–$99 double; $138 suite; $189 town house; $194–$255 cabin. AE, MC, V.
Pets accepted ($10). **Amenities:** Outdoor pool; Jacuzzi; game room. *In room:* TV, fridge, coffeemaker.

IN MAZAMA

Freestone Inn ★★★   Located at the upper end of the Methow Valley outside
the community of Mazama, the Freestone Inn is second only to Sun Mountain
Lodge in its luxury and many amenities. The inn's main building, which sits on
the shore of a small lake and has a superb view of the mountains, is a huge log
lodge complete with massive stone fireplace and a cathedral ceiling. Guest rooms
are thoughtfully designed with gas fireplaces and double whirlpool tubs that
open to the bedroom so you can lie in the tub and still see the fireplace. All in
all these are some of the most memorable rooms in the state. For more privacy,
opt for one of the cabins. Families may want to rent one of the large lakeside
lodges. The restaurant is one of the finest in the valley (see "Where to Dine,"
below, for details). In addition to amenities listed below, the inn also has cross-
country ski rentals and lessons (ski trails are adjacent), sleigh rides, and a fly-
fishing and swimming lake (ice-skating in winter).

31 Early Winters Dr., Mazama, WA 98833. © **800/639-3809** or 509/996-3906. Fax 509/996-3907. www.
freestoneinn.com. 38 units. Summer $140–$215 double, $175–$270 suite, $135–$280 cabin, $275–$485
lodge; winter $120–$190 double, $155–$245 suite, $125–$260 cabin, $250–$435 lodge. Lower rates in
spring and fall. AE, DC, DISC, MC, V. **Amenities:** Restaurant (Northwest); lounge; outdoor pool; 2 Jacuzzis;
watersports rentals; bike rentals; children's programs; activities desk; massage. *In room:* A/C, TV, dataport,
fridge, coffeemaker, hair dryer, iron.

The Mazama Country Inn ★   Set on the flat valley floor but surrounded by
rugged towering peaks and tall pine trees, this modern mountain lodge is
secluded and peaceful and offers an escape from the crowds in Winthrop. If you're
out here to get some exercise, be it hiking, mountain biking, cross-country skiing, or horseback riding, the Mazama Country Inn makes an excellent base of
operations. After a hard day of having fun, you can come back and soak in the
hot tub and have dinner in the rustic dining room with its massive freestanding
fireplace and high ceiling. The guest rooms are medium-size and simply furnished, but modern and clean. The inn also rents out 10 cabins ranging in size
from one to five bedrooms, with a 2-night minimum. In addition to amenities
listed below, the inn also offers cross-country ski rentals and even has a squash
court.

15 Country Rd., Mazama, WA 98833. © **800/843-7951** or 509/996-2681. Fax 509/996-2646. www.mazama
countryinn.com. 18 units. Summer $80–$135 double, $140–$295 double cabin (2-night minimum); winter
$170–$240 double. Winter rates include all meals. MC, V. Pets accepted. **Amenities:** Restaurant (American);
tennis court; exercise room; Jacuzzi; sauna; bike rentals; massage; coin-op laundry. *In room:* Hair dryer.

CAMPGROUNDS

Lone Fir ★ (27 sites) is the first real campground below Washington Pass. Continuing eastward on Wash. 20, you come to **Klipchuck** (46 campsites) and
Early Winters (12 campsites) campgrounds. There are also several campgrounds
west of Early Winters on the Harts Pass Road. **Harts Pass** ★ (5 campsites) and
Meadows ★ (14 campsites), a little bit farther on this rough road, are both at
high elevations and provide access to the Pacific Crest Trail.

In the Winthrop area, **Pearrygin State Park** ★ (83 campsites) is a good
choice if you are in need of a hot shower. There are also more than half a dozen
Forest Service campgrounds north of here on the Chewuch River and Eightmile
Creek. Of these, **Falls Creek** (7 campsites), beside a 75-foot waterfall, and **Buck**

Lake (9 campsites) are two of the best. There are also several campgrounds up the Twisp River Road from Twisp. For reservations at **Pearrygin State Park,** contact **Washington State Parks Reservations** (© 888/226-7688; www.camis.com/wa). For information on all other campgrounds, contact the **Methow Valley Ranger District Visitor Information Center,** 24 W. Chewuch Rd., Winthrop, WA 98862 (© **509/996-4000;** www.fs.fed.us/r6/okanogan). For national forest campground reservations, contact the **National Recreation Reservation Service** (© 877/444-6777; www.reserveusa.com).

WHERE TO DINE
IN THE WINTHROP & TWISP AREAS

Down valley from Winthrop, in the town of Twisp, there are several options for quick meals. You'll find great baked goodies at **Cinnamon Twisp Bakery** 🛪, 116 N. Glover St. (© 509/997-5030). **Sage Cup Café** 🛪, 104 Glover St. (© **509/997-2342**), which is located inside the Confluence Gallery, serves good sandwiches. You should also look into the **Twisp River Pub,** Wash. 20 (© **888/ 220-3360** or 509/997-6822; www.methowbrewing.com), which is on the banks of the Methow River.

Duck Brand Cantina 🛪 MEXICAN/INTERNATIONAL   Located right in Winthrop in a funky old building up a flight of rickety stairs, the Duck Brand is a casual restaurant with a big, multi-level deck that's a great spot for a meal on a warm summer day. In cold or rainy weather you can grab a table in the small dining room and order a plate of fajitas or ribs and a microbrew to wash it all down. Breakfasts here are hearty, and the Duck Brand's muffins and cinnamon rolls make great trail-side snacks.

248 Riverside Ave. (Wash. 20). © 509/996-2192. www.methownet.com/duck. Reservations recommended in summer. Main courses $6.50–$20. AE, DC, MC, V. Summer daily 7am–10pm; winter daily 7am–9pm.

Sun Mountain Lodge 🛪🛪 NORTHWEST   Although most popular with guests at this mountaintop resort, the dining room here at Sun Mountain Lodge offers both the best meals and the best views in the Winthrop area. Consequently, whether you're staying here or not, your visit to the valley won't be complete without a meal here, preferably one when the sun is shining so you can enjoy the view. The menu changes regularly, but you might start with chicken-curry soup or a prosciutto tart with pine nuts, Parmesan, chard, and mushrooms. After this you could move on to elk loin, apple wood–smoked salmon, or rack of lamb done in a Greek marinade. Lunches, though much less expensive than dinners, are almost as creative, and you might find venison chili or a crab-cake salad on the menu.

604 Patterson Lake Rd. © 509/996-4707. Reservations recommended. Main courses $10–$16 lunch, $24–$34 dinner. AE, DC, MC, V. Mon–Thurs 7:30–11am, 11:30am–2pm, and 5:30–8:30pm; Fri–Sat 7:30–11am, 11:30am–2pm, and 5:30–9pm; Sun 7:30am–noon and 5:30–8:30pm.

Winthrop Brewing Company 🛪 (Finds) AMERICAN   Located in a tiny, wedge-shaped old schoolhouse in downtown Winthrop, this local watering hole is Winthrop's favorite gathering spot. The walls are covered with old rifles and business cards with lipstick prints. There's a deck out back overlooking the river and in summer, a beer garden. On Thursday and Friday nights there's usually some kind of live music going on. The beers are some of the best (and most unusual) in the state, and the menu is typical pub fare—pizza, burgers, fish and chips, steaks, sandwiches, chicken, fish, and ribs.

155 Riverside Ave. © 509/996-3183. Main courses $6–$18. DISC, MC, V. Daily noon–10pm .

IN MAZAMA

For gourmet groceries, decent deli food, and espresso drinks, drop by the **Mazama Store,** 50 Lost River Rd. (© **509/996-2855;** www.methow.com/mazamastore).

Freestone Inn Dining Room ★★ NORTHWEST The Freestone Inn is one of the two luxury lodges in the valley and its restaurant is, not surprisingly, one of the two best restaurants in the valley. Located pretty much in the lobby of the lodge, the dining room benefits from all the rustic styling that goes with the cathedral ceiling, while the menu is decidedly modern in focus. A recent menu included among the appetizers a skillet-roasted black tiger shrimp and Riesling-butter braised leeks. Main courses likewise include plenty of hearty, innovative dishes, such as pancetta-wrapped sea scallops, and pan-fried pecan-crusted rainbow trout.

31 Early Winters Dr. © **800/639-3809** or 509/996-3906. Reservations recommended. Main courses $17–$24. AE, DC, DISC, MC, V. Sun–Thurs 7–10:30am and 5:30–8pm; Fri–Sat 7–10:30am and 5:30–9pm (shorter hours in winter).

3 Lake Chelan ★

166 miles E of Seattle, 37 miles N of Wenatchee, 59 miles S of Winthrop

Formed when a glacier-carved valley flooded, Lake Chelan is 1,500 feet deep, 55 miles long, and less than 2 miles wide in most places. This land-locked fjord is the third-deepest lake in the United States (reaching 400 ft. below sea level) and is the longest natural lake in Washington. Only the southern 25 miles of the lake are accessible by road, yet at the northern end, the community of Stehekin (reachable only by boat, plane, or on foot) has managed to survive for more than 100 years despite not being connected to the outside world by road. Plenty of summer sunshine, clear water, and blue skies have made the lake one of the top destinations in eastern Washington, and today the town of Chelan has the feel of a beach town despite the rugged mountain views all around.

At the southern end of the lake, apple orchards cover the foothills, while at the northern end, forests and rugged slopes that are home to mountain goats and black bears come right down to the water's edge. While the southern end of the lake is the domain of ski boats and personal watercraft, the northern, remote end is as idyllic a locale as you could ever wish to find and feels as if it is completely cut off from the outside world.

ESSENTIALS

GETTING THERE Chelan is on U.S. 97, the main north-south highway in central Washington. From Seattle, take U.S. 2 to Wenatchee and then head north.

GETTING AROUND Although it is not very convenient for visitors, the Link bus system (© **509/662-1155**) services the Lake Chelan, Wenatchee, and Leavenworth areas.

VISITOR INFORMATION For more information on this area, contact the **Lake Chelan Chamber of Commerce,** 102 E. Johnson St. (P.O. Box 216), Chelan, WA 98816 (© **800/4-CHELAN** or 509/682-3503; www.lakechelan.com). For information on Stehekin on the Web, check out **http://stehekin choice.com**, which is the website of the community newspaper. This site has lots of information on things to do in Stehekin.

EXPLORING CHELAN & LOWER LAKE CHELAN

Downtown Chelan's **Riverwalk Park,** which stretches along both shores of the lake, has a 1-mile paved path and is a pleasant spot for a walk. The park is also home to the **Riverwalk Pavilion,** where outdoor concerts are held during the summer. Lake Chelan history is on display at the **Chelan Museum,** corner of Woodin and Emerson streets (© **509/682-5644**), open April through October daily from 10am to 4pm; other months, Friday and Saturday from 10am to 4pm. Admission is $2 for adults and $1 students and seniors.

Chelan has long been one of Washington's main apple-growing regions, but with low prices for apples in recent years, local farmers have been searching for other ways to make money. Many have now set up farm stands, while others have planted vineyards and are now making wine. In downtown Chelan, be sure to stop by **The Harvest Tree,** 109 E. Woodin Ave. (© **800/568-6062;** www. lakechelanapples.com), a shop dedicated almost exclusively to apples and apple products. At **Blueberry Hills Farms,** 1315 Washington St., Manson (© **509/ 687-BERY**), you can pick your own blueberries or sit down to a slice of pie. At the Chamber of Commerce visitor center (see contact information, above), you can pick up a copy of the "Agri-Tourism in the Lake Chelan Valley" brochure and head out on a fruit-finding mission.

Wineries on the north shore include **Chelan Wine Company,** 105 Spader Bay Rd. (© **866/455-WINE**), which produces a variety of wines under the Vin du Lac label. This winery's tasting room, which is in a little yellow house, is set amid vineyards and orchards and includes a deli case selling artisan cheeses from around the region. The tasting room is open daily 11am to 7pm. Continuing west from Chelan, you'll come to **Lake Chelan Winery,** 3519 Wash. 150 (© **509/687-9463**), which has its tasting room in an old apple-packing shed. The tasting room is open Wednesday through Sunday from 11am to 6pm. Out in Manson, you'll find **Wapato Point Cellars,** 200 Quetilquasoon Rd. (© **509/ 687-4000;** www.wapatopointcellars.com), which is located on the grounds of a condominium development. The tasting room is open daily from 11am to 7pm. On the south shore, you'll find **Tsillan Cellars,** 3875 U.S. 97A (© **877/682- 8463** or 509/682-9463), the area's most impressive winery. Built to resemble a Tuscan villa, the winery has a gorgeous view of the lake. Call for tasting room hours.

UP THE LAKE TO STEHEKIN ✹✹

If you have time for only one activity while in the Lake Chelan area, it should be an all-day boat ride up the lake to Stehekin, a community accessible only by boat, floatplane, or hiking trail, and located within the Lake Chelan National Recreation Area of the North Cascades National Park Complex. This remote community has been a vacation destination for more than 100 years and is set amid rugged, glacier-clad mountains at the far north end of Lake Chelan.

The **Lake Chelan Boat Company** (© **509/682-4584;** www.ladyofthelake. com), which has its dock 1 mile west of downtown Chelan on South Shore Road

---

Three Cherries in Apple Country

If you want to try recouping your vacation costs while you're in the area, stop by the **Mill Bay Casino,** Wash. 150 (© **800/648-2946**) in the town of Manson, which is on the north shore of the lake. The casino is operated by the Colville Confederated Tribes.

(U.S. 97A), operates three passenger ferries—*Lady of the Lake II, Lady Express,* and *Lady Cat*—between Chelan and Stehekin. The trip encompasses some of the most spectacular scenery in the Northwest as you travel from gentle rolling foothills to deep within the rugged North Cascades mountains. Wildlife, including deer, mountain goats, and even bears, are frequently seen from the boats.

The *Lady of the Lake II* takes 9½ hours for the round-trip (including a 90-min. layover) and charges $26 per person, while the *Lady Express* takes about 6 hours (including a 60-min. layover) and charges $45. The *Lady Cat,* the fastest of the three boats, makes the round-trip in only 4 hours (including a 90-min. layover) but costs $90. Children ages 2 to 11 pay half fare, and children under age 2 ride free. Unless you plan to stay overnight, you won't have more than 90 minutes to look around Stehekin unless you book a combination ticket that allows you to go up on one of the boats, spend 3¼ to 7¼ hours in Stehekin, and return on a boat other than the one you went up on. These combination tickets are only available in summer.

If you want to get to Stehekin in a hurry, you can make the trip by floatplane on **Chelan Airways** (© **509/682-5555;** www.chelanairways.com), which leaves from the dock next to the ferries. The fare is $120 round-trip. This company also offers flight-seeing trips for between $80 and $150.

A variety of day trips are also operated in conjunction with the two passenger ferries of the **Lake Chelan Boat Company** (© **509/682-4584;** www.lady ofthelake.com). Tours include the popular bus ride to 312-foot Rainbow Falls ($7 adults, $4 children 6–11, free for children under 6), and a narrated bus trip up the valley to High Bridge and then a picnic lunch ($20 adults, $10 children 6–11, $5 children under 6). Other hiking and biking tours are also available.

Although a road (paved for the first 4 miles) once led 23 miles up the Stehekin Valley to Cottonwood Campground, a flood in 1995 damaged much of the road toward the upper end of the valley and another flood in October 2003 did even more damage. Currently, the road is only open as far as High Bridge (10 miles up valley). Transportation up the Stehekin Valley Road is provided by two different buses. The National Park Service's shuttle operates between mid-May and mid-October and, depending on how far up the valley you go, costs between $6 and $12 ($3–$6 children 12 and under). Reservations for this bus should be made at least 2 days ahead of time (preferably much farther in advance) by calling the **Golden West Visitor Center** (© **360/856-5700,** ext. 340, then 14). Between late May and the end of September, another bus runs four times a day between Stehekin Landing and High Bridge. No reservations are required for this bus, and the cost is $6. If you just want to ride as far as the Stehekin Pastry Company, the fare is only $1.

A wide range of recreational activities can also be arranged in Stehekin through the **Courtney Log Office** (© **509/682-4677**), which is located 150 yards up the road from the boat landing. Horseback rides are offered through **Cascade Corrals** (© **509/682-7742**) at Stehekin Valley Ranch. A 2½-hour ride costs $38. White-water rafting trips on the Stehekin River are operated by Stehekin Valley Ranch and cost $45 per person. Mountain bikes can be rented for $20 per day from **Discovery Bikes** (no phone; http://stehekindiscoverybikes. com), which is located at the Courtney Log Office. Discovery Bikes also does a very fun Ranch Breakfast Tour that includes a hearty breakfast at Stehekin Valley Ranch and then a bike ride down the valley.

Along the length of the Stehekin Valley, there are many miles of excellent hiking trails ranging from easy strolls along the river to strenuous climbs high into the mountain wilderness that surrounds the valley. Many of the valley's trail heads can be accessed from the bus that runs up the valley, which makes this an excellent place for doing a variety of day hikes over several days. There are also many longer trails originating here in Stehekin, which makes this a popular starting point for backpacking trips. For information on hiking trails and to pick up permits for overnight backpacking trips, stop by the **Golden West Visitor Center,** which is operated by the National Park Service and is located near the boat landing. It's open daily between May and mid-October. Fly-fishing on the Stehekin River is also very popular and usually very productive. In winter there is good snowshoeing at Stehekin, and snowshoes can be rented from **North Cascades Stehekin Lodge** (© **509/682-4494**).

SPORTS & OUTDOOR ACTIVITIES

FISHING   Fishing is one of the top recreational activities at Lake Chelan, and in this deep lake's clear waters you'll find chinook and kokanee salmon, lake (mackinaw) trout, rainbow trout, smallmouth bass, and freshwater lingcod. Although there is bank fishing for stocked rainbows in the lower lake, most other fishing requires a boat. Up in Stehekin there is good fly-fishing for native cutthroat and rainbow trout. If you want to make sure you come home form Lake Chelan with some good fish stores, get in touch with Terry Allan of **Allan's Fishing Guide Service** (© **509/687-3084;** www.fishlakechelan.com). In 2001, Allan twice helped clients catch state record lake trout. Guided fishing trips cost $145 to $175 for a day of fishing.

GOLF   Right on the edge of town, golfers will find the municipal **Lake Chelan Golf Course,** 1501 Golf Course Dr. (© **800/246-5361** or 509/682-8026; www.lakechelangolf.com), where greens fees range from $30 to $34. However, anyone out this way with golf clubs is probably headed to **Desert Canyon Golf Resort,** 1201 Desert Canyon Blvd., Orondo (© **800/258-4173** or 509/784-1111; www.desertcanyon.com), which is located 17 miles south of Chelan and has been voted the best public course in Washington. Greens fees range from $45 to $89.

HIKING   Beyond the ends of the roads at the south end of Lake Chelan lie thousands of acres of unspoiled forests and many miles of hiking trails. Access to the trails is from trail heads at road ends or from flag stops along the route of the *Lady of the Lake II.* However, the best trails begin in the Stehekin area. For more information on hiking and biking opportunities, contact the **Chelan Ranger Station,** 428 W. Woodin Ave., Chelan, WA 98816-9724 (© **509/682-2576;** www.fs.fed.us/r6/wenatchee).

MOUNTAIN BIKING   During the snow-free months of the year, the extensive network of cross-country ski trails at Echo Ridge becomes a mountain-bikers' playground. The area has 18 miles of dirt roads and trails that are open to mountain bikes. The trail head for this trail system is just under 10 miles from downtown Chelan. Take the Manson Highway (Wash. 150) west to Boyd Road,

---

Fun Fact **Hang in There, Baby**

Chelan is one of the nation's top hang-gliding and paragliding spots. Strong winds and thermals allow flyers to sail for a hundred miles or more from the Chelan Sky Park atop Chelan Butte.

Fun Fact **Chelan Fish Stories**

Not all the big ones get away. In 2001, Lake Chelan twice set the state record for Mackinaw trout. On December 31, 2001, a 35.7-pound fish was reeled in. Four months earlier, a state record 33.65-pound fish was caught.

---

turn right and follow signs for Echo Valley Ski Area. From the ski area, continue on Forest Service Road 1821-100. Mountain bike rentals are available in Chelan from **Uncle Tim's Toys,** Lakeshore Marina Park, 619 W. Wash. 150 (© **509/670-8467;** www.uncletimstoys.com). A 4-hour rental runs $35.

WATERSPORTS   Opportunities for aquatic activities abound on Lake Chelan. Good places to swim include **Lakeside Park** on the South Shore Road, **Don Morse Memorial Park** on the edge of downtown Chelan, and **Manson Bay Park** in Manson. **Lake Chelan State Park** and **25-Mile Creek State Park,** both on South Shore Road, offer swimming, picnicking, and camping.

You can rent a personal watercraft (around $35 per hr. or $150 per day), powerboats ($75 per hr.), and canoes and paddleboats ($10 per hr.) from **Chelan Boat Rentals,** 1210 W. Woodin Ave. (© **509/682-4444**). Boats and personal watercraft are also available from **Shoreline Watercraft Rentals** (© **800/682-1561** or 509/682-1515) and **RSI Sports** (© **800/786-2637** or 509/669-4779).

If you've got the kids along, you'll find it impossible not to spend some time at **Slidewaters,** 102 Waterslide Dr. (© **509/682-5751;** www.slidewaters.com), which has 10 water slides, an inner-tube river ride, a 60-person hot tub, and a swimming pool. Admission is $14 for adults, $11 for children ages 3 to 7. You'll find this water park just outside town off the South Shore Road.

If you want to check out the water from above, call **Chelan Parasailing,** 158 Wapato Way (© **509/687-7245**), which charges around $40 for a parasail ride.

WINTER SPORTS   The Lake Chelan area offers both cross-country and downhill skiing opportunities at **Echo Valley Ski Area** (© **509/687-3167** or 509/682-4002), a small ski area 7 miles northwest of Chelan. With only one poma lift and three rope tows, this isn't much of a downhill area, but, there's also a tubing hill, which makes this place popular with families. A lift ticket is $18 for the day. Cross-country skiers, on the other hand, will find miles of groomed trails, many of which have great views, at Echo Ridge, which is a short distance past the downhill area. Trail passes are $5 per day. Ski, snowboard, and snowshoe rentals are available at Echo Valley from **Lakeland Ski** (© **509/687-3204**).

WHERE TO STAY
IN CHELAN

Best Western Lakeside Lodge (*Kids*)   With lake views from every room, indoor and outdoor pools, a whirlpool, and a public park with a beach adjacent to the property, this comfortable motel on the south shore of the lake is a good choice, especially for families. The guest accommodations range from standard motel rooms to spacious suites with full kitchens. Some of the rooms also have VCRs, and all have balconies or patios. If you're up for a splurge, request one of the large suites, preferably one on the top floor—these have high ceilings.

2312 W. Woodin Ave., Chelan, WA 98816. © 800/468-2781 or 509/682-4396. Fax 509/682-3278. www.bestwestern.com. 67 units. Mid-June to Aug $149–$189 double; $169–$239 suite; Sept to mid-Oct and early May to mid-June $99–$149 double, $119–$189 suite; mid-Oct to early May $79–$99 double, $99–$159 suite. AE, DC, DISC, MC, V. **Amenities:** Indoor and outdoor swimming pools; 2 Jacuzzis; coin-op laundry. *In room:* A/C, TV, fridge, coffeemaker.

Campbell's Resort on Lake Chelan ✦✦

The Campbell Hotel first opened in 1901 and has remained Chelan's most popular lodging ever since. Located on the banks of the lake right in downtown Chelan, Campbell's is now a small convention hotel with a 1,200-foot beach, acres of lawns, and boat docks. Over the past few years, Campbell's has updated most of its rooms, and though the main building's deluxe rooms (which feature furnishings and styling the equal of any Seattle luxury hotel) are still the best rooms, many of the other rooms are looking good these days, too. Fortunately, every room here has a lake view, and many, including several of the cottages, have a kitchen or kitchenette. The dining room is located in the original 1901 hotel, and offers the most elegant dining in town. There's a pub upstairs from the restaurant and, in summer, a beach bar.

104 W. Woodin Ave., Chelan, WA 98816. ✆ **800/553-8225** or 509/682-2561. Fax 509/682-2177. www.campbellsresort.com. 170 units. Mid-June to Aug $176–$260 double, $260–$380 suite, $212–$278 2-bedroom family unit. Lower rates off season. AE, MC, V. **Amenities:** 2 restaurants (American); lounge; 2 outdoor swimming pools; exercise room; day spa; 2 Jacuzzis; children's programs; business center; laundry service. *In room:* A/C, TV, dataport, coffeemaker, hair dryer.

IN STEHEKIN

If you're heading up to Stehekin and plan to do your own cooking during your stay, bring your own food. Only limited groceries are available here.

North Cascades Stehekin Lodge ✦

Located right at Stehekin Landing, the North Cascades Lodge is shaded by tall conifers and overlooks the lake. The variety of accommodations ranges from basic rooms with no lake view to spacious apartments. The studio apartments, which have kitchens, are the best deal and all have lake views. Between May and mid-October, the lodge's restaurant serves three meals a day; the rest of the year, three meals are served on weekends and lunch is available on weekdays. Snowshoe rentals are available in winter.

P.O. Box 457, Chelan, WA 98816. ✆ **509/682-4494.** Fax 509/682-5872. www.stehekin.com. 28 units. Memorial Day weekend and June 15–Oct 15 $94–$139 double; Oct 16–June 14, excluding Memorial Day weekend $69–$119 double. DISC, MC, V. **Amenities:** Restaurant (American); watersports rentals; bike rentals; activities desk; coin-op laundry. *In room:* No phone.

Silver Bay Inn & Resort ✦✦

Situated on the banks of both the lake and the Stehekin River, Silver Bay rents out two cabins and a house. The views are superb, and should you stay in the Lake View House, a spacious Northwest contemporary home on the banks of both the river and the lake, you'll find antiques, a big sun room, and a deck with a view of the river. This house also has a separate room with a river view (these are the least expensive accommodations here). Be sure to bring your own food to cook. Bicycles and canoes are available to guests free of charge, and allow guests to explore the lake and the Stehekin environs.

10 Silver Bay Rd. (Box 85), Stehekin, WA 98852. ✆ **509/687-3142.** www.silverbayinn.com. 4 units. $135–$245 double or cabin for 2. Lower rates off season. Minimum stay 2 nights (5 nights for cabins in summer). Children over 12 are welcome. MC, V. **Amenities:** Jacuzzi; watersports equipment; bikes. *In room:* Kitchen, no phone.

Stehekin Valley Ranch ✦ *(Kids*

If you're a camper at heart, then the tent cabins at the Stehekin Valley Ranch should be just fine. With canvas roofs, screen windows, and no electricity or plumbing, these "cabins" are little more than permanent tents. Bathroom facilities are in the nearby main building. For slightly more comfortable accommodations, opt for one of the permanent cabins. Activities available at additional cost include horseback riding, river rafting, and mountain biking. The ranch is accessible by ferry or floatplane to Stehekin Landing; from there you're taken 9 miles up the valley to the ranch in a Stehekin Valley Ranch shuttle bus.

P.O. Box 36, Stehekin, WA 98852. ✆ 800/536-0745 or 509/682-4677. www.courtneycountry.com. 12 units. Tent cabins $65–$75 per adult, $50–$60 per child 4–12, $5–$15 per child 1–3. Cabins $10 more per person than tents. Rates include all meals and transportation in lower valley. MC, V by phone only for reservations. **Amenities:** Restaurant (American); activities desk. *In room:* No phone.

CAMPGROUNDS

On Lake Chelan, there are two state park campgrounds at the southern end of the lake—**Lake Chelan State Park** (144 campsites) and **Twenty-Five Mile Creek State Park** (67 campsites)—both of which tend to be very crowded and noisy. At the north end of the lake, along the Stehekin Valley Road, there are 11 campgrounds, most of which are served by the shuttle bus from Stehekin. **Purple Point** ⚲ (7 campsites) is right in Stehekin and is the most convenient to the boat landing.

For reservations at the two state parks, contact **Washington State Parks Reservations** (✆ 888/226-7688; www.camis.com/wa). For information on campgrounds in the Stehekin Valley, contact the **Golden West Visitor Center** (✆ 360/856-5700, ext. 340, then 14; www.nps.gov/noca). For national forest campground reservations, contact the **National Recreation Reservation Service** (✆ 877/444-6777; www.reserveusa.com).

WHERE TO DINE
IN CHELAN

If you're looking for a good cup of coffee, try **Latte Da Coffee Stop Cafe,** 303 E. Wapato Ave. (✆ 509/682-4196), which is housed in an old house on the edge of downtown Chelan. For an espresso amid fun and funky decor, head to **Flying Saucers,** 116 Emerson St. (✆ 509/682-5129). For a touch of old-time Western hospitality, have a meal at **Banjo Creek Farms** (✆ 509/687-0708; www.banjocreekfarms.com), which does Western barbecues, complete with such appetizers as rattlesnake and Rocky Mountain oysters. Meals ($23 adults, $18 children 9–16, $10 children 4–8) include live music and a chance to wander around the barnyard. Reservations are required. Banjo Creek also offers a variety of other activities throughout the year.

Campbell House Restaurant ⚲ AMERICAN   Housed in the original 1901 Campbell Hotel, this is one of only two upscale restaurants in Chelan, and as such stays pretty busy in the summer months. While the menu is not overly creative, you'll find more imaginative offerings here than most places in town. The steaks and prime rib are your best bets here. If you prefer burgers to scallops flamed with brandy, then you'll be better off upstairs at the casual pub, which serves inexpensive steaks and other decent pub fare to go with its Northwest microbrews and single-malt Scotches.

104 W. Woodin Ave. ✆ 509/682-4250. Main courses $12–$28. AE, DISC, MC, V. Mon–Fri 6:45–11am, 11:30am–1:30pm, and 5–9pm; Sat 6:45–1pm and 5–9pm; Sun 6:45am–1pm and 5–8:30pm. Reduced hours in winter.

Capers ⚲ CONTINENTAL   Located in a very nondescript building in downtown Chelan, Capers may not boast a great location, but it does serve the best food in town. Crisp white linens may seem a bit out of place in this central Washington summer-vacation town, but sometimes a bit of formality adds a nice touch to an otherwise casual vacation. The menu includes a wide range of traditional favorites including vichyssoise, filet mignon with a red-wine-and-mushroom sauce, chateaubriand for two, and rock Cornish game hens. However, you'll also find some interesting, and very recommendable, game dishes such as pheasant-hazelnut-and-cognac sausage, rabbit and duck pâté, and loin of venison. However, just don't eat so much that you don't have room for the delicious pear poached in Pinot Noir.

127 E. Johnson St. ⓒ **509/682-1611.** Reservations recommended. Main courses $14–$29. AE, MC, V. June–Sept Sun–Thurs 5–9pm, Fri–Sat 5–10pm; Oct–May Thurs and Sun–Mon 5–8:30pm, Fri–Sat 5–9:30pm.

Deepwater Brewing & Public House ⭐ AMERICAN   Located just outside of Chelan on the road to the town of Manson, this big brewpub offers food that's definitely a step above that served at most pubs. On top of that, there are great views of the lake. In summer, the lake-view deck is the place to eat, but big windows let in plenty of views also. The menu includes lots of steaks, plenty of pasta dishes, and a handful of burgers (the fire burger is our favorite). There are usually six of their own brews on tap. Be sure to start your meal with the brandy-fired mushrooms.

225 Manson Hwy. ⓒ **509/682-2720.** www.deepwaterbrewing.com. Main courses $8–$24. DISC, MC, V. Daily 4–9pm.

IN STEHEKIN
The dining options in Stehekin are slim, and if you plan to stay in a cabin or camp out, be sure to bring all the food you'll need. Otherwise, simple meals are available at **North Cascades Stehekin Lodge** (ⓒ **509/682-4494**), which is located right at the ferry landing in Stehekin. Note that during the winter, the restaurant here is open for three meals a day only on weekends; weekdays, only lunch is available. When you just have to have something sweet, you're in luck; the **Stehekin Pastry Company** (ⓒ **509/682-4677**), which is located 2 miles up valley from the boat landing, serves pastries and ice cream, as well as pizza and espresso.

4 The Wenatchee Valley & Bavarian Leavenworth ⭐⭐
108 miles E of Everett, 22 miles W of Wenatchee, 58 miles SW of Chelan

You're out for a Sunday drive through the mountains, just enjoying the views, maybe doing a bit of hiking or cross-country skiing, when you come around a bend and find yourself in the Bavarian Alps. Folks in lederhosen and dirndls dance in the streets, a polka band plays the old oompah-pah, and all the buildings look like alpine chalets. Have you just entered the Twilight Zone? No, it's just Leavenworth, Washington's Bavarian village.

Many an unsuspecting traveler has had just this experience, but if you're reading this, you'll be prepared for the sight of a Bavarian village transported to the middle of the Washington Cascades. Whether you think it's the most romantic town in the state, a great place to go shopping, the perfect base for hiking and skiing, or just another example of *über*-kitsch, there's no denying that Leavenworth makes an impression.

ESSENTIALS
GETTING THERE   From I-5, take U.S. 2 from Everett, or, if you're coming from the south, take I-405 to Bothell and then head northeast to Monroe, where

you pick up U.S. 2 heading east. From U.S. 97, the main north-south route along the east side of the Cascades in the central part of the state, head west on U.S. 2. Wenatchee is at the junction of U.S. 2 and U.S. 97. Wash. 28 connects Wenatchee to the eastern part of the state.

Wenatchee's **Pangborn Memorial Airport** (© 509/884-2494; www.pangborn airport.com) is served by **Horizon Air** from Seattle. Amtrak trains stop in Wenatchee en route between Spokane and Seattle.

VISITOR INFORMATION   For more information on this area, contact the **Leavenworth Chamber of Commerce & Visitor Center,** P.O. Box 327, Leavenworth, WA 98826 (© **509/548-5807;** www.leavenworth.org), or, when you're in town, drop by the Visitor Center, 220 Ninth St., which is inside the Obertal Mall. For more information on the Wenatchee area, contact the **Wenatchee Valley Convention & Visitors Bureau,** 116 N. Wenatchee Ave., Wenatchee, WA 98801 (© **800/57-APPLE** or 509/663-3723; www.wenatchee valley.org).

GETTING AROUND   Car rentals are available in Wenatchee from Hertz and Budget. Although it is not very convenient for exploring this area, the Link bus system (© **509/662-1155;** www.linktransit.com) services the Leavenworth, Wenatchee, and Lake Chelan areas.

FESTIVALS   During the annual **Maifest** (mid-May) and **Washington State Autumn Leaf Festival** (late Sept), Leavenworth rolls out the barrel and takes to the streets and parks with polka bands, Bavarian dancing, and plenty of crafts vendors. In June, more music hits town with the **Leavenworth International Accordion Celebration.** In mid-September, the **Wenatchee River Salmon Festival** celebrates the annual return of salmon to the river, and in October there's **Oktoberfest.** In December, the whole town gets lit up in one of the most impressive **Christmas Lighting Festivals** in the Northwest. Nearby Wenatchee celebrates its apples each year with the **Washington State Apple Blossom Festival,** which includes more than a week of festivities in late April and early May.

EXPLORING LEAVENWORTH

Leavenworth's main attraction is the town itself. Back in the early 1960s, this was just another mountain town struggling to get by on a limited economy. Sure the valley was beautiful, but beauty wasn't enough to bring in the bucks. A few years after a motel with alpine architecture opened in town, Leavenworth decided to give itself a complete makeover. Today nearly every commercial building in town, from the gas station to the Safeway, looks as if it had been built by Bavarian gnomes. What may come as a surprise is that they did a good job! Stroll around town and you'll convince yourself that you've just had the world's cheapest trip to the Alps. People here even speak German.

Any time of year the town's most popular tourist activity seems to be shopping for genuine Bavarian souvenirs in the many gift shops—you'll find cuckoo clocks, Hummel figurines, imported lace, and nutcrackers. In fact, if nutcrackers are your passion, don't miss the **Leavenworth Nutcracker Museum,** 735 Front St. (© **800/892-3989** or 509/548-4573; www.nutcrackermuseum.com), which has more than 4,000 nutcrackers of all shapes and sizes. The museum is open May through October daily from 2 to 5pm and November through April on weekends only. Admission is $2.50 for adults and $1 for children ages 6 to 17. At press time, there were also plans to convert a beautiful historic Leavenworth home into the **Upper Valley Museum** and **Leavenworth Audubon Center,** 347

Division St. (© **509/548-0181** or 509/548-0728). If you're interested, call to see if the museum is up and running.

Classical music fans should be sure to see what's happening at the **Icicle Creek Music Center** ✮ (© **877/265-6026** or 509/548-6347; www.icicle.org), which is located at the Sleeping Lady resort and has programs throughout the year. There are also many musical performances and festivals in the small Front Street Park in downtown Leavenworth, where a large gazebo serves as a bandstand. If you're looking for something to do on a Friday night, drop by the **Community Coffeehouse,** Chumstick Grange Hall, 621 Front St. (© **509/548-1106;** www.leavenworthcoffeehouse.com), which has live acoustic music ranging from Celtic to contemporary to classical.

EXPLORING THE LOWER WENATCHEE VALLEY

As you drive east down the Wenatchee Valley from Leavenworth, you begin to see the valley's many apple and pear orchards. In summer and fall, you can taste the fruits of the valley at farm stands along U.S. 2. **Smallwood's Harvest** (© **509/548-4196;** www.smallwoodsharvest.com), and **Prey's Fruit Barn** (© **509/548-5771;** www.preysfruitbarn.com) are the biggest and best farm stands along this stretch of road. Because apple prices have been so low in recent years, some of the orchards have begun planting vineyards, and wineries have been proliferating in the area.

Eagle Creek Winery & Cottage, 10037 Eagle Creek Rd. (© **509/548-7668;** www.eaglecreekwinery.com), is one of the closest wineries to Leavenworth and is located off Chumstick Highway about 5 miles from town. May through October, the tasting room is open Saturday and Sunday from noon to 4pm; other months by appointment. Heading farther down the valley, you'll come to **Icicle Ridge Winery,** 8977 North Rd., Peshastin (© **509/548-7851;** www.icicleridgewinery.com), which has its tasting room in a log house in the middle of a pear orchard. May through October, the tasting room is open Thursday through Tuesday from 1 to 5pm; other months by appointment. Nearby, you'll find **Wedge Mountain Winery,** 9534 Saunders Rd. (© **509/548-7068;** www.wedgemountainwinery.com), which specializes in Bordeaux varietals. September and October, the tasting room is open daily from 10am to 6pm, other months it is open Saturday, Sunday, and holidays from 10am to 6pm. Although it is only open by appointment, **La Toscana Winery & Bed & Breakfast,** 9020 Foster Rd., Cashmere (© **509/548-5448;** http://communities. msn.com/latoscana), produces the best red wines in the valley. For more information on these and other area wineries, contact **Columbia Cascade Wine & Wineries** (© **509/782-0708;** www.columbiacascadewines.com).

CASHMERE: AN EARLY AMERICAN TOWN

Just west of Wenatchee you'll find the town of **Cashmere,** which has adopted an Early American theme. The town's main attraction is the **Aplets & Cotlets Candy Factory and Country Store,** 117 Mission Ave. (© **509/782-4088;** www.libertyorchards.com), where you can tour the kitchens that produce these unusual fruit-and-nut confections. Between April and December, the factory and store are open Monday through Friday from 8am to 5:30pm and Saturday and Sunday from 10am to 4pm; between January and March, they're open Monday through Friday from 8:30am to 4:30pm.

For a different sort of sweet treat, don't miss **Anjou Bakery,** 3898 Old Monitor Rd. (© **509/782-4360**), which is just off U.S. 2 in the middle of a pear

---

An Apple a Day

Apples are the single largest agricultural industry in Washington—in fact, more than 50% of the fresh apples sold in the United States come from Washington. The combination of warm, sunny days and abundant irrigation water from both the Columbia and Wenatchee rivers have made Wenatchee the center of this apple-growing region.

---

orchard on the outskirts of Cashmere. The ovens here produce great pastries and rustic breads.

Also worth a visit in Cashmere is the **Chelan County Historical Society Pioneer Village and Museum,** 600 Cotlets Way (© **509/782-3230**). Nearly 20 old log buildings have been assembled here and are filled with period antiques. Inside the main museum building you'll find exhibits on the early Native American cultures of the region, pioneer history, and natural history. The museum is open from March 1 to October 31, daily from 9:30am to 4:30pm. Admission is $4.50 for adults, $3.50 for students and seniors, and $2.50 for children ages 5 to 12.

WENATCHEE

More apple-industry displays are part of the focus of the **Wenatchee Valley Museum & Cultural Center,** 127 S. Mission St. (© **509/664-3340;** http://wenatcheevalleymuseum.com), but there are also interesting exhibits on local Native American cultures and the first transpacific flight. Model-railroading buffs will enjoy the HO-scale Great Northern Railway. The museum also hosts lectures, traveling exhibitions, and concerts, and at some concerts, the museum's 1919 Wurlitzer organ is played. The museum is open Tuesday through Saturday from 10am to 4pm. Admission is $3 for adults, $2 for seniors, and $1 for students.

Though it's only a dozen or so miles from the lush forests of the Cascades, Wenatchee is on the edge of central Washington's arid shrub-steppe region. To bring a bit of the mountains' greenery into this high desert, Herman Ohme and his family spent 60 years creating **Ohme Gardens** ★★, 3327 Ohme Rd. (© **509/ 662-5785;** www.ohmegardens.com), a lush alpine garden covering 9 cliff-top acres north of Wenatchee. The gardens wind along the top of a rocky outcropping that overlooks the Wenatchee Valley, Columbia River, and Cascade peaks. Rock gardens, meadows, fern grottoes, and waterfalls give the gardens a very naturalistic feel similar to that of a Japanese garden. The gardens are open from April 15 to October 15, daily from 9am to 6pm (until 7pm in summer). Admission is $6 for adults, $3 for children ages 7 to 17.

North of Wenatchee on the north side of the town of Entiat, watch for the **Columbia Breaks Fire Interpretive Center** (© **509/663-2062;** www.wildfire center.org), which has two old fire lookouts and the ½-mile Trail of Fire and Forest interpretive trail. This trail explains the role of fires in western forests.

OUTDOOR ACTIVITIES: FROM GOLF TO WHITE-WATER RAFTING

If your interests tend more toward hiking than to Hummel figurines, you'll still find plenty to do around Leavenworth. Leavenworth is on the valley floor at the confluence of the Wenatchee River and Icicle Creek, and rising all around are the steep, forested mountainsides of the Stuart Range and Entiat Mountains.

Spring through fall, there is rafting, hiking, mountain biking, and horseback riding, and, in winter, there is downhill and cross-country skiing and snowmobiling.

Twenty-five miles north of town you'll find **Lake Wenatchee,** a year-round recreation area with hiking and cross-country ski trails, horseback riding, canoe rentals, windsurfing, swimming, fishing, mountain biking, camping, and snowmobiling. **Lake Wenatchee State Park** (© **509/763-3101**) is the center of recreational activity here.

If you need to rent some gear, contact **Leavenworth Outfitters Outdoor Center,** 21312 Wash. 207 (© **800/347-7934** or 509/763-3733; www.leavenworth outfitters.com), which rents mountain bikes, cross-country skis, kayaks, and canoes.

FISHING   Icicle Creek, which runs through Leavenworth, has a short summer salmon season for fish headed upstream to the Leavenworth Fish Hatchery. Lake Wenatchee, at 5 miles in length, is the biggest lake in the area and holds kokanee, as well as Dolly Varden and rainbows. To fish for kokanee, you'll need a boat. Several of the rivers and streams in the Leavenworth area are open to fly-fishing only.

GOLF   Golfers can play 18 holes at the **Leavenworth Golf Club,** 9101 Icicle Rd. (© **509/548-7267;** www.leavenworthgolf.com), which charges $26 to $29 for a round of golf and is located on the outskirts of town, or north of Leavenworth near Lake Wenatchee at **Kahler Glen Golf Course,** 20700 Clubhouse Dr. (© **509/763-4025;** www.kahlerglen.com), which charges $24 to $36 for 18 holes. However, the new **Highlander Golf Club,** 2920 Eighth St., East Wenatchee (© **509/884-4653;** www.highlandergolfclub.com), with its Scottish links styling and awesome big-sky views, is the hottest course in the region these days. Greens fees range from $35 to $49 for 18 holes. If you want to practice your putting, check out the **Enzian Falls Championship Putting Course** (© **509/548-5269**), which is located across from the Enzian Motor Inn and is a beautiful bent-grass 18-hole putting course (not to be confused with your usual tacky miniature golf course).

HIKING   Right in town, you'll find a pleasant paved walking path in **Waterfront Park.** Out at the **fish hatchery** on Icicle Road, there is also a mile-long interpretive trail with information on the hatchery. In winter, both of these areas have cross-country ski trails. In Tumwater Canyon, the narrow gorge that serves as something of a gateway to Leavenworth as you approach from the west, there's an easy hiking trail along the banks of the Wenatchee River.

Just outside Leavenworth, in the **Alpine Lakes Wilderness** ✦✦✦, lies some of the most spectacular mountain scenery in the state, and the trails that lead into this wilderness are among the most popular. They're so popular, in fact, that backpackers must reserve camping permits months in advance to overnight in such heavily visited areas as the Enchantment Lakes basin. Most of the trails in the area are best suited for overnight trips because they climb steeply and steadily for many miles before reaching the more scenic areas. For information on hiking trails in Wenatchee National Forest, contact the **Leavenworth Ranger Station,** 600 Sherbourne St., Leavenworth, WA 98826 (© **509/548-6977;** www. fs.fed.us/r6/wenatchee). Reservations for backpacking permits are accepted starting March 1; to apply call the ranger station or visit their website. Permits go fast, so apply early.

HORSEBACK RIDING   If you'd like to go horseback riding, contact **Eagle Creek Ranch** (© **800/221-7433** or 509/548-7798; www.eaglecreek.ws), which offers everything from 1½-hour-long rides ($26) to day trips ($100) and wagon rides ($15 adults, $7.50 children); or **Icicle Outfitters & Guides** (© **800/497-3912** or 509/669-1518; www.icicleoutfitters.com), which offers a similar variety of rides and has stables both at Lake Wenatchee State Park and in Leavenworth on Icicle Road near the fish hatchery. A 1½-hour ride will cost you $37.

MOUNTAIN BIKING   From easy rides on meandering dirt roads to grueling climbs to mountaintops with spectacular views, the Leavenworth area has some of the best mountain-biking routes in the state. Mountain bikes can be rented at **Der Sportsmann,** 837 Front St. (© **509/548-5623**), and **Das Rad Haus,** 1207 Front St. (© **509/548-5615;** www.dasradhaus.com). This latter shop is only open April through October. Expect to pay $25 to $40 per day for a mountain bike. Ask at either of these shops for ride recommendations. You can also get a guide to area mountain biking from the Leavenworth Visitor Center.

ROCK CLIMBING   Two miles west of Cashmere on U.S. 2, you'll find **Peshastin Pinnacles State Park,** Washington's only state park created exclusively for rock climbing. The **Snow Creek Wall,** which is located about a mile up the trail to the Enchantment Lakes area, is another great climbing spot. The trail head is located about 4 miles up Icicle Creek Road. Over on the west side of Stevens Pass, the **Index Town Walls** outside the tiny community of Index are the area's other great climbing site. For climbing gear and advice, stop by **Leavenworth Mountain Sports,** 940 Wash. 2 (© **509/548-7874**).

WHITE-WATER RAFTING   The Wenatchee River flows right through Leavenworth and just downstream from town becomes one of the best white-water rafting rivers in the state. Rafting season runs from April to July. If you're interested, contact **Osprey Rafting Co.** (© **800/743-6269** or 509/548-6800; www.shoottherapids.com), or **River Riders** (© **800/448-RAFT** or 206/448-RAFT; www.riverrider.com). A half-day trip on the Wenatchee costs about $50 per person, and a full day $65 to $70.

WINTER SPORTS   Some of the best downhill skiing and snowboarding in the state is available 40 miles west of Leavenworth at **Stevens Pass** ★★ (© **206/812-4510** for general information, or 206/634-1645 for snow conditions; www.stevenspass.com). Adult all-day lift tickets are $44 and night skiing is $28. There are plenty of intermediate and advanced runs here, but not much in the way of beginner runs. Looking for steep, deep, untracked snow? Head out for some snowcat skiing with **Leavenworth Snowcat Skiing** (© **866/500-1514;** www.leavenworthsnowcat.com), which charges $210 to $225 for a day of skiing that might include 3-mile-long runs and up to 20,000 vertical feet of skiing each day.

Head down the valley from Leavenworth and then up into the hills outside Wenatchee, and you'll find **Mission Ridge** ski area ★★ (© **509/663-3200** for snow reports, or 509/663-6543; www.missionridge.com), which is known for its powder snow (a rarity in the Cascades) and its sunny weather. Lift ticket prices for adults are $37.

Cross-country skiers can find plenty of groomed trails in the area. **Stevens Pass Nordic Center** (© **360/812-4510;** www.stevenspass.com/crosscountry) has mostly intermediate and expert level trails. These trails are open Friday through Sunday and on holidays, and a trail pass costs $14 for adults. The **Leavenworth Winter Sports Club** (© **509/548-5477;** www.skileavenworth.com) maintains 15 miles of groomed trails (including 3 miles of lighted trails for night skiing) at several locations around Leavenworth. A trail pass runs $10 per day.

This ski club also operates the beginner-level **Leavenworth Ski Hill,** a mile outside of town. Although small, this little ski hill does have a ski jumping facility.

Skis can be rented at **Der Sportsmann,** 837 Front St. ((C) **800/548-4145** or 509/548-5623), which charges $14 to $22 per day for cross-country skis and $25 for snowboards. Snowshoes ($12 per day) can also be rented. Rental equipment is also available at **Leavenworth Mountain Sports,** 940 U.S. 2 ((C) **509/548-7864**).

If you'd rather experience the snow from a horse-drawn sleigh, you can do that, too. Sleigh rides are offered by **Red-Tail Canyon Farm,** 11780 Freund Canyon Rd., Leavenworth ((C) **800/678-4512** or 509/548-4512; www.redtail canyonfarm.com); and **Eagle Creek Ranch,** Eagle Creek Road ((C) **800/221-RIDE** or 509/548-7798; www.eaglecreek.ws). Rides cost roughly $15 adults, and $7.50 for children.

WHERE TO STAY

If you're interested in renting a house, cabin, or condo, contact **Bedfinders** ((C) **800/323-2920** or 509/548-4410; www.bedfinders.com), which can also help you find a hotel or B&B.

EXPENSIVE

Mountain Home Lodge ★★   Set 2½ miles up a very steep, narrow road that is only paved in its lower stretch, this mountain lodge is surrounded by a 20-acre meadow and has a spectacular view of the craggy Stuart Range. In winter, the road up here is not plowed and guests are brought to the lodge by Snowcat. At that time of year, 40 miles of cross-country ski trails are the main attraction (cross-country skis and snowshoes are available), but there are also guided snowmobile tours. In summer, hiking and mountain biking are the big draws. Guest rooms vary in size and each is individually decorated with themes that reflect the area's activities (Mountain Trout, The Harvest, The Ranch, The Mountain View). However, The Hide Away, atop the lodge, is the best room in the house (excluding the suite). If you're looking to get away from it all, this is the place! During the summer, when rates include only breakfast, gourmet lunches ($15) and dinners ($38) are available.

8201 Mountain Home Rd. (P.O. Box 687), Leavenworth, WA 98826. (C) **800/414-2378** or 509/548-7077. Fax 509/548-5008. www.mthome.com. 12 units. Summer $110–$160 double, $205 suite, $295 cabin; winter $270–$355 double, $375 suite, $455 cabin. Summer rates include full breakfast; winter rates include 3 meals daily. 2-night minimum weekends and winter; 3-night minimum holidays. DISC, MC, V. **Amenities:** Restaurant (American); outdoor pool; tennis court; Jacuzzi; bike rentals; concierge; room service; massage. *In room:* A/C, no phone.

Sleeping Lady ★★★   Although primarily a conference resort, Sleeping Lady (the name comes from a nearby mountain) is one of the best-designed mountain retreats in the state. Set on the outskirts of Leavenworth amid ponderosa pines and granite boulders, the small resort looks much like the summer camp it once was, with red-roofed cabins tucked amid the pines. Guest rooms are done in a rustic contemporary style, abound in natural wood, and have high ceilings with exposed beams. The grounds, including a meadow on the bank of Icicle Creek, are beautifully landscaped and a delight to wander. Meals here feature produce from the resort's large organic vegetable garden, and throughout the year, classical music performances and plays are staged. The boulder-lined swimming pool here is one of the most memorable pools in the state.

7375 Icicle Rd., Leavenworth, WA 98826. (C) **800/574-2123** or 509/548-6344. Fax 509/548-6312. www. sleepinglady.com. 59 units. $248–$260 double; $305 cabin. Rates include 3 meals. AE, DISC, MC, V. **Amenities:** 2 restaurants (Northwest, deli); lounge; outdoor pool; exercise room; Jacuzzi; sauna; bike rentals; business center; massage; coin-op laundry; dry cleaning. *In room:* Dataport, coffeemaker.

MODERATE

Abendblume Inn ★★ *Value*   This alpine chalet, complete with flower boxes overflowing with blossoms, is a luxurious and romantic B&B overlooking Leavenworth, the valley, and the surrounding mountains. An eye for detail is apparent throughout the inn, from the hand-carved front door to the wrought-iron stair railing. Although there are a couple of smaller rooms, the large rooms with balconies overlooking the valley are the rooms to book. In these you'll find fireplaces, VCRs, and wonderfully luxurious beds and linens, but it's the bathrooms that are the real attractions. Our favorite has a triangular tub for two, a pair of sinks, and heated marble floors. Nowhere in Leavenworth is there a more romantic room. Buffet breakfasts include enough variety to keep everyone happy. Guests also have use of both indoor and outdoor spas, and in winter, snowshoes are available.

12570 Ranger Rd. (P.O. Box 981), Leavenworth, WA 98826. © **800/669-7634** or 509/548-4059. Fax 509/ 548-4059. www.abendblume.com. 7 units. $108–$175 double. Rates include full breakfast. AE, DISC, MC, V. Children under 18 not accepted. **Amenities:** 2 Jacuzzis; bikes; concierge; massage. *In room:* A/C, TV/VCR, hair dryer, iron.

Blackbird Lodge ★   Located right in downtown Leavenworth overlooking the Icicle River, this hotel feels like a country inn despite the convenience of being within walking distance of all the town's shops and restaurants. Though the exterior is Bavarian chalet, this inn adopts something of a mountain-lodge decor in its lobby, which has a slate floor and dark, woodsy touches. This mountain-lodge styling alone sets the Blackbird apart from other moderately priced lodgings in town. The guest rooms are large, but otherwise are fairly standard motel-style rooms. However, the suites are both spacious and quite attractive; some have fireplaces or whirlpool tubs or both. The lodge also rents out an adjacent renovated cottage.

305 Eighth St., Leavenworth, WA 98826. © **800/446-0240** or 509/548-5800. www.blackbirdlodge.com. 21 units. $99–$119 double; $119–$189 suite. Lower midweek rates mid-Jan to mid-June. Rates include full breakfast. Children 12 and under stay free in parent's room. AE, DISC, MC, V. Pets accepted in cottage ($8). **Amenities:** Jacuzzi. *In room:* A/C, TV.

Enzian Inn ★   Located on the highway just outside downtown Leavenworth, the Enzian, which is something of an upgraded motel, offers both convenience and amenities. Of course, it has an alpine exterior (complete with half-timbering, steep roofs, and turrets), and inside you'll find an attractive lobby with a high ceiling and a stone fireplace. The guest rooms are decorated with reproduction antique furniture imported from Austria. If you feel like splurging, the tower suite is richly appointed with burgundy carpets, a heavy carved-wood canopy bed, and a double whirlpool tub in the sitting room. Other amenities include a racquetball court and complimentary use of cross-country ski equipment.

590 U.S. 2, Leavenworth, WA 98826. © **800/223-8511** or 509/548-5269. Fax 509/548-9319. www.enzian inn.com. 104 units. $95–$180 double; $190–$215 suite. Rates include full breakfast. Children 5 and under stay free in parent's room. AE, DISC, MC, V. **Amenities:** 2 pools (indoor/outdoor); 18-hole putting golf course; 2 Jacuzzis. *In room:* A/C, TV/VCR, dataport, coffeemaker, hair dryer, iron.

Run of the River Bed & Breakfast ★★   Tranquil, luxurious, rustic— you just won't find a more idyllic B&B anywhere in Washington. This contemporary log house is set on 2 acres outside of town on a bend of the river. As you drive past the alpine rock garden that lines the driveway, you can almost feel life's stresses fall away. With its abundance of bare wood, hand-hewn log furniture, and exposed stones, the inn has a timeless mountain-lodge feel. All the accommodations are large suites filled with special touches that make a stay here unforgettable. There are heated bathroom floors, balconies overlooking the river, binoculars for bird-watching, and porch swings for quiet moments. Walking sticks, day packs, and picnic hampers are always at the ready for your day's outing, and innkeeper Monty Turner is a wealth of tips on where to go and what to do in the area. Bicyclists will love all the old bikes used in the decor.

9308 E. Leavenworth Rd. (P.O. Box 285), Leavenworth, WA 98826. © **800/288-6491** or 509/548-7171. www.runoftheriver.com. 6 units. $205–$245 double. 2-night minimum May–Oct and Dec 1–20, and weekends throughout the year; 3-night minimum Dec 20–Jan 4 and 3-day weekends. DISC, MC, V. Children under 18 not accepted. **Amenities:** Complimentary bikes; massage. *In room:* TV/VCR, fridge.

INEXPENSIVE

Inexpensive rooms in Leavenworth are also available at The Edel House (see "Where to Dine," below).

Hotel Pension Anna *Finds*   Though the guest rooms in the Pension Anna's main building are attractively appointed with pine furniture, including a four-poster bed in the honeymoon suite, the annex building contains the inn's two most outstanding rooms. This annex is a renovated church built in 1913 (and later moved to this site), and the Old Chapel Suite is a grand space that includes part of the old choir loft (now a sleeping loft) and the old baptismal font. Ceilings 20 feet high give the room an expansive feel, and in the bedroom you'll find an ornately carved headboard framed by draperies that reach to the ceiling. Though considerably smaller, the Parish Nook Room has an ornate king-size bed, marble-top bedside stands, and the original arched windows. Only slightly more expensive than a regular room, the Parish Nook is the inn's best deal.

926 Commercial St., Leavenworth, WA 98826. © **800/509-ANNA** or 509/548-6273. Fax 509/548-4656. www.pensionanna.com. 16 units. $79–$139 double; $169–$239 suite. Rates include full breakfast. AE, DISC, MC, V. *In room:* A/C.

CAMPGROUNDS

Tumwater (84 campsites) is the biggest campground in the Leavenworth area, yet is always full on summer weekends. Up Icicle Road on the west side of Leavenworth, there are seven campgrounds.

The Lake Wenatchee area is one of the most popular summer camping destinations in the state and there are lots of choices in the area. If you want creature comforts such as hot showers stay at **Lake Wenatchee State Park** (197 campsites), which is at the south end of the lake. This campground has a sandy beach and a great view up the lake. Farther up the south shore of the lake, the Forest Service's **Glacier View Campground** (23 campsites) provides a similar lakeside atmosphere with walk-in campsites. Right outside the entrance to the state park, you'll find the **Nason Creek Campground** (73 campsites), which has some nice sites right on this large creek. Northwest of Lake Wenatchee, there are several campgrounds along both the White River and the Little Wenatchee River.

For reservations at Lake Wenatchee State Park, contact **Washington State Parks Reservations** (© **888/226-7688;** www.camis.com/wa). For information on all other campgrounds, contact the **Lake Wenatchee Ranger Station,** 22976 Wash. 207, Leavenworth, WA 98826 (© **509/763-3103;** www.fs.fed.us/r6/wenatchee); or the **Leavenworth Ranger Station,** 600 Sherbourne St., Leavenworth, WA 98826 (© **509/548-6977;** www.fs.fed.us/r6/wenatchee). For national forest campground reservations, contact the **National Recreation Reservation Service** (© **877/444-6777;** www.reserveusa.com).

WHERE TO DINE
IN LEAVENWORTH

For delectable baked goods, drop by the **Homefires Bakery,** 13013 Bayne Rd. (℗ **509/548-7362;** www.homefiresbakery.com), which is housed in an old log cabin off Icicle Road near the fish hatchery. If you're craving a good espresso, head to the Chevron station. That's right, Chevron, as in gas station. Here you'll find **Village Mercantile,** 920 U.S. 2 (℗ **509/548-7714**), which not only serves the best lattes in town but also is a great little gift shop.

Andreas Keller ★ *Kids* GERMAN   Down in a *keller* (cellar) opposite the gazebo on Front Street, you'll find one of Leavenworth's true German experiences. From the waitresses shouting across the restaurant in German to the accordionist who plays in the evening and on weekend afternoons, everything about this place is Bavarian. Take a seat and you'll be surrounded by *Gemütlichkeit*. Rotisseried chicken and wursts are the staples here, washed down with Bavarian beer. Be sure to get something with the wine kraut; it's delicious (so is the German potato salad). Casual and fun enough that even the kids will enjoy a meal here.

829 Front St. ℗ **509/548-6000.** www.andreaskellerrestaurant.com. Reservations recommended. Main courses $7–$10 lunch, $7–$18 dinner. MC, V. Sun–Thurs 11am–8:30pm; Fri 11am–9pm; Sat 11am–10pm (may close earlier in off season).

Cafe Mozart Restaurant ★★ GERMAN/CONTINENTAL   Located upstairs from the ever-popular Andreas Keller, this restaurant serves upscale German food, as well as French and American favorites, in a refined atmosphere. The cold-smoked Norwegian salmon and the Dungeness crab cakes make good non-German starters. Follow this up with Wiener schnitzel or Munich-style sauerbraten for a gourmet German meal. Of course, Mozart is played on the stereo, and on Friday and Saturday nights, there is live harp music.

829 Front St. ℗ **509/548-0600.** www.cafemozartrestaurant.com. Reservations recommended. Main courses $9–$14 lunch, $15–$35 dinner. AE, MC, V. Daily 11am–9pm.

The Edel House ★★ INTERNATIONAL   This restaurant, a simple little house above the Wenatchee River in the center of town, is Leavenworth's premier non-Bavarian restaurant with most of the menu offerings drawing on Asian and Mediterranean influences. There are always several pasta dishes, as well as such substantial entrees as venison medallions with morel mushroom sauce or roast duck with cherry confit. Sure, you'll also find a couple of Austrian or Bavarian dishes on the menu, but this is really the place to opt for something other than schnitzel and sauerkraut.

320 Ninth St. ℗ **509/548-4412.** www.edelhaus.com. Reservations recommended. Main courses $16–$28. MC, V. Daily 5–9pm.

IN WENATCHEE

The John Horan House ★★ AMERICAN   Though it's in a rather unlikely spot surrounded by industrial complexes, the Horan House, where the wealthy

---

⟨Tips **Leavenworth's Polka Spot**

If you happen to find yourself in Leavenworth on one of those rare weekends when there is no festival going on, you can still take in some polka music at **King Ludwig's Restaurant,** 921 Front St. (℗ **360/548-6625**), which features live Bavarian music on Friday and Saturday nights.

of Wenatchee dine, is well worth searching out. Secluded in its own little apple orchard, the 1899 Victorian farmhouse is a world apart. Sure, you can get Cajun seafood fettuccine and Greek pasta, but the real reason to come here is for the prime rib and the thick, juicy steaks. Be sure to start your meal with the Inga's salad, which is made with greens, mandarin oranges, spicy pecans, and a tahini dressing.

2 Horan Rd. (©) **509/663-0018.** www.johnhoranhouse.com. Reservations recommended. Main courses $16–$34. DISC, MC, V. Mon–Sat 5–9 or 10pm. Cross the Wenatchee River bridge from downtown, take the 1st right, the next right, and then, at the end of the road, turn right a 3rd time; at the end of this road, turn left onto the restaurant driveway.

McGlinn's Public House *⭐* AMERICAN   Located inside one of downtown Wenatchee's few historic buildings, this casual pub turns out good wood-oven pizzas, as well as burgers and a handful of more creative dishes. Although they don't brew their own beers here, they have lots of good regional microbrews. If you're really hungry, be sure to try the wood-fired jojos (potato wedges).

111 Orondo Ave. (©) **509/663-9073.** Main courses $5.75–$14. AE, MC, V. Mon–Thurs 11am–11pm; Fri 11am–midnight; Sat 8am–midnight; Sun 8am–9pm.

5 The Snoqualmie Pass Route *⭐⭐*

Snoqualmie Pass: 50 miles E of Seattle, 53 miles W of Ellensburg

While Seattle has become a sprawling city of congested highways and high housing prices, there is a reason so many put up with such drawbacks. Less than an hour east of the city lie mountains so vast and rugged that you could hike for a week without ever crossing a road. In winter, The Summit at Snoqualmie Pass ski area is so close to the city that people head up after work for a bit of night skiing.

Between the city and this wilderness lies the Snoqualmie Valley, the Seattle region's last bit of bucolic countryside. Here you'll find small towns, pastures full of spotted cows, U-pick farms, and even a few unexpected attractions, including an impressive waterfall and, in summer, a medieval fair. While driving the back roads of the Snoqualmie Valley, keep an eye out for historic markers that include old photos and details about the valley's past.

ESSENTIALS

GETTING THERE   Snoqualmie Pass is on I-90 between Seattle and Ellensburg.

VISITOR INFORMATION   For more information on the area, contact the **Snoqualmie Pass Visitor Center** (© **425/434-6111**), which is located just off I-90 at Snoqualmie Pass and is operated by the National Forest Service. Information is also available through the **Cle Elum/Roslyn Chamber of Commerce,** 401 W. First St., Cle Elum, WA 98922 (© **509/674-5958;** www.cleelumroslyn.org).

EXPLORING THE SNOQUALMIE VALLEY

Snoqualmie Falls *⭐⭐*, the valley's biggest attraction, plummet 270 feet into a pool of deep blue water. The falls are surrounded by a park owned by Puget Power, which operates a hydroelectric plant inside the rock wall behind the falls. The plant, built in 1898, was the world's first underground electricity-generating facility. Within the park you'll find two overlooks near the lip of the falls and a half-mile trail down to the base of the falls. The river below the falls is popular both for fishing and for white-water kayaking. These falls will be familiar to anyone who remembers the opening sequence of David Lynch's television show *Twin Peaks,* which was filmed in this area. To reach the falls, take I-90 east from

Seattle for about 40 minutes and get off at exit 27. If you're hungry for lunch, try the restaurant at **Salish Lodge,** the hotel at the top of the falls.

Snoqualmie Falls are located just outside the town of **Snoqualmie,** which is where you'll find the restored 1890 railroad depot that houses the **Northwest Railway Museum,** 38625 SE King St. (© **425/888-3030**). The museum, an absolute must for anyone with a child who is familiar with Thomas the Tank Engine, operates the **Snoqualmie Valley Railroad** on weekends April through October. The 65- to 75-minute railway excursions, using steam or diesel trains, run between here and the town of **North Bend.** Fares are $8 for adults, $7 for seniors, and $5 for children ages 3 to 12. Be sure to call ahead for a current schedule. The museum displays railroad memorabilia and has a large display of rolling stock. It's a big hit with kids—and it's free!

Between Fall City and the town of **Carnation,** you'll pass several U-pick farms, where you can pick your own berries during the summer or pumpkins in the fall.

The Snoqualmie Valley is also the site of **Camlann Medieval Village,** 10320 Kelly Rd. NE (© **425/788-8624;** www.camlann.org), which is located north of Carnation off Wash. 203. On weekends between mid-July and late August, this reproduction medieval village is home to knights and squires and assorted other costumed merrymakers. There are crafts stalls, food booths, and—the highlight each day—jousting matches. Medieval clothing is available for rent if you forgot to pack yours. Throughout the year, there is a wide variety of banquets and seasonal festivals, and the village's Bors Hede restaurant is open Tuesday through Sunday for traditional dinners. Fair admission is $9 for adults, $6 for seniors and children ages 12 and under. Admission to both the fair and a banquet is $39.

Thirty miles to the east of Snoqualmie Pass, you'll find the remote town of **Roslyn,** which was just a quietly decaying old coal-mining town until television turned it into Cicely, Alaska, for the hit TV show *Northern Exposure.* Although Cicely is but a fading memory now, visitors still wander up and down the town's 2-block-long main street soaking up the mining-town atmosphere. To learn more about the town's history, drop by the **Roslyn Museum,** 203 Pennsylvania Ave. (© **509/649-2776**). About the only other activity here is wandering through the town's 25 cemeteries, which are up the hill from the museum. These cemeteries contain the graves of miners who lived and died in Roslyn.

SPORTS & OUTDOOR ACTIVITIES

HIKING   Outside of North Bend rises **Mount Si,** one of the most frequently climbed mountains in the state. This mountain, carved by glaciers long ago, rises abruptly from the floor of the valley outside North Bend and presents a dramatic face to the valley. If you are the least bit athletic, it is hard to resist the temptation to hike to the summit, where awesome views are the payoff. Be forewarned, however, that it's a strenuous 8-mile round-trip hike, and you'll need to carry lots of water. To reach the trail head, drive east of downtown North Bend on North Bend Way, turn left on Mount Si Road, turn right after crossing the Snoqualmie River, and continue another 2 miles.

Farther east on I-90, at Snoqualmie Pass and before you reach the pass, there are several trail heads. Some trails lead to mountain summits, others to glacier-carved lakes, and still others past waterfalls deep in the forest. Due to their proximity to Seattle, these trails can be very crowded, and you'll need a Northwest Forest Pass in order to park at national forest trail heads. Passes are available at the ranger station in North Bend. A Northwest Forest Pass is not necessary for parking at the Mount Si trail head, which is on state land. For more information, contact the **North Bend Ranger District,** 42404 SE North Bend Way, North Bend, WA 98045 (© **425/888-1421;** www.fs.fed.us/r6/mbs).

HORSEBACK RIDING   If you're interested in spending a few hours or a few days in the saddle, contact **High Country Outfitters** (© **888/235-0111** or 509/ 674-4903; www.highcountry-outfitters.com), which charges about $90 for a day ride. Overnight and multi-day trips also available.

MOUNTAIN BIKING   Iron Horse State Park/John Wayne Pioneer Trail, a railroad right-of-way that has been converted to a gravel path stretching more than 110 miles, provides one of the most unusual mountain-biking routes in the Northwest. The trail passes under Snoqualmie Pass by way of the 2½-mile-long Snoqualmie Tunnel, which is usually open to bicycles from May through October. To ride the tunnel you'll need good lights, warm clothes, and rain gear (water constantly drips from the ceiling of the tunnel). To access the trail from the west side, take exit 38 off I-90. From the east side, take exit 62 off I-90.

SKIING   While much of the terrain is not very interesting and the snow can be frustratingly unreliable due to winter rains, **The Summit at Snoqualmie Pass** ★★ (© **425/434-7669,** or 206/236-1600 for snow conditions; www.summitat snoqualmie.com) is the closest ski area to Seattle and consequently sees a lot of business both on weekends and for after-work night skiing. There are 22 lifts and 65 ski runs here, and the past couple of years have seen more than $10 million worth of improvements. Rentals and lessons are available. Adult lift ticket prices range from $27 for night skiing to $42 for a weekend all-day pass. Call for hours of operation.

At Snoqualmie Pass, there are many miles of both groomed and ungroomed cross-country ski trails. **Summit Nordic Center** (© **425/434-7669** or 425/ 434-6708; www.summitatsnoqualmie.com/winter/nordic.html) offers rentals, instruction, and many miles of groomed trails, some of which are lighted for night skiing. Trail fees run $8 to $12.

There are also several sno-parks along I-90 at Snoqualmie Pass. Some of these have groomed trails while others have trails that are marked but not groomed. **Sno-Park permits** ($8–$9 for a 1-day pass; $20–$21 season pass) are required for parking at these areas and are available at ski shops. If you plan to ski on groomed trails, you'll have to pay an additional fee for your Sno-Park permit.

In winter, **Bee Line Tours** (© **800/959-8387** or 206/632-5162; www.beeline tours.com) provides bus service from Seattle area hotels to the Summit at Snoqualmie ski area. Round-trip fare is $35.

WHERE TO STAY
ON THE WEST SIDE

Salish Lodge and Spa ★★★   Set at the top of 270-foot Snoqualmie Falls and only 35 minutes east of Seattle on I-90, Salish Lodge is a popular weekend getaway spot for Seattle residents. With its country-lodge atmosphere, the Salish aims for casual comfort and hits the mark, though the emphasis is clearly on luxury. Guest rooms, which are designed for romantic weekend getaways, have fireplaces and whirlpool baths, feather beds, and down comforters. To make this an even more attractive getaway, there's a full-service spa. The lodge's country breakfast is a legendary feast that will likely keep you full right through to dinner. By the way, if you were a fan of the TV show *Twin Peaks,* you'll immediately recognize this hotel.

6501 Railroad Ave. SE (P.O. Box 1109), Snoqualmie, WA 98065. © **800/272-5474** or 425/888-2556. Fax 425/ 888-2533. www.salishlodge.com. 91 units. $229–$419 double; $599–$699 suite (all rates plus $15 resort fee). AE, DISC, MC, V. **Amenities:** 2 restaurants (Northwest, Mediterranean); lounge with view of the falls; exercise room; full-service spa with Jacuzzis and saunas; complimentary mountain bikes; activities desk; limited room service; massage; laundry service; dry cleaning. *In room:* A/C, TV, dataport, minibar, coffeemaker, hair dryer, iron.

ON THE EAST SIDE

Hidden Valley Guest Ranch ✿✿   If you're looking to get away from it all but don't have the time or inclination to head to the wilds of Montana, this 700-acre guest ranch is as good a substitute as you'll find in Washington. The setting, on a grassy ridge above Swauk Creek, is the absolute epitome of a mountain-ranch setting, and the cabins are suitably rustic yet have comfortably modern amenities. The Appletree Cabin is the best. Horseback riding ($35 for 1½ hr.) is the favorite activity here. The ranch is 15 minutes east of Cle Elum off Wash. 970, which connects to U.S. 97 (the route over Blewett Pass to Leavenworth and Wenatchee).

3942 Hidden Valley Rd., Cle Elum, WA 98922. ℂ **800/5-COWBOY** or 509/857-2322. Fax 509/857-2130. 13 units. $310 double. Rates include all meals. 2-night minimum in summer. Children 2 and under stay free in parent's room. MC, V. Closed Oct 16–May 14. **Amenities:** Restaurant (American); outdoor pool; tennis court; Jacuzzi; children's programs; game room; massage. *In room:* Coffeemaker.

Iron Horse Inn ✿   Railroad buffs won't want to miss an opportunity to stay at this restored Chicago, Milwaukee, St. Paul, and Pacific Railroad bunkhouse. The inn is filled with railroading memorabilia and each of the guest rooms is named for a railroad worker who once lived here. The rooms vary in size and are simply furnished with antiques. However, the most popular rooms here are the three cabooses on short lengths of track beside the inn. These are large enough to sleep four or five people.

526 Marie Ave. (P.O. Box 629), South Cle Elum, WA 98943. ℂ **800/22-TWAIN** or 509/674-5939. www.iron horseinnbb.com. 10 units, 6 with private bathroom. $80 double with shared bathroom; $95–$105 double with private bathroom; $135 suite or caboose. Rates include full breakfast. Children under 2 stay free in parent's room. MC, V. **Amenities:** Jacuzzi. *In room:* No phone.

CAMPGROUNDS

Along the I-90 corridor, there are only a couple of campground choices on the west side of Snoqualmie Pass. **Tinkham Campground** (47 campsites) at exit 42 off I-90 is the closest Forest Service campground to Seattle. It is set on the bank of the South Fork Snoqualmie River. **Denny Creek Campground** (33 campsites) is so close to the freeway that campers are lulled to sleep by the roaring of trucks.

   Kachess Campground (120 campsites), near the north end of Kachess Lake, is the biggest campground in the area. Powerboating and fishing are the most popular activities here, but there are also some nearby trail heads providing access to the Alpine Lakes Wilderness. The Cle Elum Lake area offers the I-90 corridor's greatest concentration of campgrounds including **Wish Poosh** (39 campsites), **Cle Elum River** (23 campsites), **Red Mountain** (10 campsites), and **Salmon la Sac** ✿ (99 campsites), which is this area's biggest and busiest campground.

   For information on campgrounds in this area, contact the **Snoqualmie Pass Visitor Center** (ℂ **425/434-6111**), which is located just off I-90 at the pass. For national forest campground reservations, contact the **National Recreation Reservation Service** (ℂ **877/444-6777;** www.reserveusa.com).

WHERE TO DINE
IN THE SNOQUALMIE VALLEY

The dining room at the **Salish Lodge** (see above) is by far the best restaurant on the west side of Snoqualmie Pass.

DINING & NIGHTLIFE IN ROSLYN

If you're heading to the hills and want to pack some great jerky, stop by **Carek's Market** ✪, 510 S. A St., Roslyn (© **509/649-2930**). Good pizzas can be had at **Village Pizza,** 105 Pennsylvania Ave., Roslyn (© **509/649-2992**). For nightlife or a simple meal, don't miss **The Brick Bar & Grill** ✪, 1 Pennsylvania Ave., Roslyn (© **509/649-2643**), which claims to be the oldest operating saloon in Washington and has a unique flowing-water spittoon under the bar. This place is an absolute classic. If it's good microbrews that you crave, wander up the street to the **Roslyn Brewery,** 208 Pennsylvania Ave. (© **509/649-2232**), which is a much more modern place.

6 Mount Rainier National Park ✫✫✫ & Environs

Paradise: 110 miles SE of Seattle, 70 miles SE of Tacoma, 150 miles NE of Portland, 85 miles NW of Yakima

At 14,410 feet high, Mount Rainier is the tallest mountain in Washington, and to the sun-starved residents of Seattle and south Puget Sound, the dormant volcano is a giant weather gauge. When the skies clear over Puget Sound, the phrase "The Mountain is out" is often heard around the region. And when the Mountain is out, all eyes turn to admire its broad slopes.

Those slopes remain snow-covered throughout the year due to the region's infamous moisture-laden air, which has made Mount Rainier one of the snowiest spots in the country. In 1972, the mountain set a record when 93½ feet of snow fell in 1 year (and that record held until Washington's Mount Baker received 95 ft. in the winter of 1998–99). Such record snowfalls have created numerous glaciers on the mountain's flanks, and one of these, the Carbon Glacier, is the lowest-elevation glacier in the continental United States.

Snow and glaciers notwithstanding, Rainier has a heart of fire. Steam vents at the mountain's summit are evidence that, though this volcanic peak has been dormant for more than 150 years, it could erupt again at any time. However, scientists believe that Rainier's volcanic activity occurs in 3,000-year cycles—and luckily we have another 500 years to go before there's another big eruption.

Known to Native Americans as Tahoma, Mount Rainier received its current name in 1792 when British explorer Capt. George Vancouver named the mountain for a friend (who never even visited the region). The first ascent to the mountain's summit was made in 1870 by Gen. Hazard Stevens and Philemon Van Trump, and it was 14 years later that James Longmire built the first hotel on the mountain's flanks. In 1899, Mount Rainier became the fifth national park.

ESSENTIALS

GETTING THERE   If you're coming from Seattle and your destination is Paradise (the park's most popular area), head for the southwest (Nisqually) park entrance. Take I-5 south to exit 127 and then head east on Wash. 512. Take the Wash. 7 exit and head south toward Elbe. At Elbe, continue east on Wash. 706.

If you're coming from Seattle and are heading for the northeast (White River) park entrance en route to Sunrise or Crystal Mountain, take I-90 to I-405 south. At Renton, take Wash. 169 south to Enumclaw, where you pick up Wash. 410 heading east.

Note that in winter only the road from the Nisqually entrance to Paradise is kept open.

From Portland, head north on I-5 to exit 68 and then take U.S. 12 east to the town of Morton. From Morton, head north on Wash. 7 to Elbe and then turn east on Wash. 706, which will bring you to the Nisqually (southwest) park entrance.

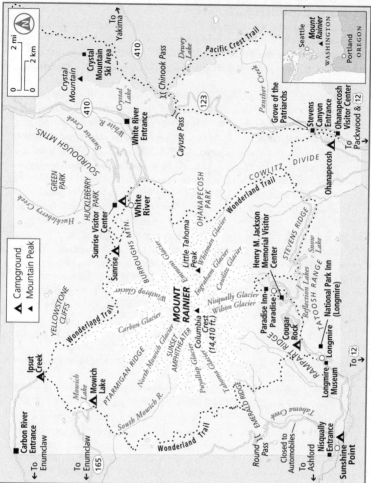

From May 1 to late September, **Grayline of Seattle** (*©* **800/426-7532** or 206/624-5077; www.graylineofseattle.com) operates one bus daily between Seattle and Mount Rainier; the round-trip fare is $54 for adults and $27 for children.

VISITOR INFORMATION For more park information, contact **Mount Rainier National Park,** Tahoma Woods, Star Route, Ashford, WA 98304 (*©* **360/569-2211;** www.nps.gov/mora).

PARK ADMISSION The park entrance fee is $10 per vehicle and $5 per person for pedestrians or cyclists. Another option, if you plan to visit several national parks in a single year, is the National Parks Pass or the Golden Eagle Passport, an annual pass good at all national parks and recreation areas. The pass costs $50 (plus $15 for the Golden Eagle upgrade) and is available at all national park visitor centers. If you're over 62, you can get a Golden Age Passport for $10, and if you have a disability, you can get a free Golden Access Passport.

SEEING THE HIGHLIGHTS

Just past the main southwest entrance (Nisqually), you'll come to **Longmire,** site of the National Park Inn, Longmire Museum (exhibits on the park's natural and human history; open daily year-round), a hiker-information center that issues backcountry permits, and a ski-touring center where you can rent cross-country skis in winter.

The road then climbs to **Paradise** (elevation 5,400 ft.), the aptly named mountainside aerie that affords a breathtaking close-up view of the mountain. Paradise is the park's most popular destination, so expect crowds. During July and August the meadows here are ablaze with wildflowers. The circular **Henry M. Jackson Memorial Visitor Center** (© 360/569-2211, ext. 2328) provides 360-degree panoramic views. The visitor center is open daily from early May to mid-October and on weekends and holidays from mid-October to early May. A 1¼-mile walk from the visitor center will bring you to a spot from which you can look down on the Nisqually Glacier. Many miles of other trails lead out from Paradise, looping through meadows and up onto snowfields above timberline. It's not unusual to find plenty of snow at Paradise as late as July.

In summer you can continue beyond Paradise to the **Ohanapecosh Visitor Center** (© 360/569-6046), which is open weekends from late May to mid-June and daily from mid-June to early October. Not far from this visitor center, you can walk through the **Grove of the Patriarchs** (see "Hiking & Backpacking," below, for details). Continuing around the mountain, you'll reach the turnoff for Sunrise.

Continuing counterclockwise around the mountain, you'll come to Cayuse Pass. A short detour from this pass will bring you to the picturesque **Chinook Pass** area, where there is a good 4½-mile day-hike loop trail that begins at Tipsoo Lake and circles Naches Peak.

Continuing around the mountain, you'll come to the turnoff for the park's **White River entrance.** This road leads to some of the park's best day hikes, and a spur road leads to the White River Campground. At 6,400 feet, **Sunrise** is the highest spot in the park accessible by car. A beautiful old log lodge serves as the **Sunrise Visitor Center** (© 360/663-2425), which is open daily from July through mid-September. From here you get a superb view of Mount Rainier, seemingly at arm's length, and **Emmons Glacier,** which is the largest glacier in the 48 contiguous states. From Sunrise, you can also see Mount Baker to the north and Mount Adams to the south. Some of the park's most scenic trails begin at Sunrise, providing lots of options for day hikes.

If you want to see a bit of dense forest or hike without crowds, head for the park's **Carbon River entrance** in the northwest corner. This is the least visited region of the park because it only offers views to those willing to hike several miles uphill. About 3 miles up the trail, you'll come face to face with the Carbon River Glacier, which is the lowest-elevation glacier in the contiguous 48 states. At its lower end this glacier plows through dense rainforest, an ominous and unforgettable sight. Continuing up this trail another 2 miles (following the glacier for much of the way) will bring you to beautiful wildflower meadows and close-up views of the northwest flank of Mount Rainier. The road into this area is in very bad shape. Currently high-clearance vehicles are recommended.

OUTDOOR ACTIVITIES IN & NEAR THE NATIONAL PARK

If, after a long day of taking advantage of the outdoor activities available in the park, you'd like to soak in a hot tub or get a massage, contact the little woodland spa called **Wellspring** (© 360/569-2514). You'll find Wellspring in Ashford not far from the Nisqually park entrance. An hour in the hot tub costs $10 per person, while an hour massage costs $60. Alternatively, you can soak in a hot tub and get a massage at nearby **Stormking** (℡ **360/569-2964;** www.stormking spa.com). Both of these places also have cabins available for overnight guests.

HIKING & BACKPACKING   Hikers have more than 240 miles of trails to explore within the park, though the vast majority of park visitors do their hiking at only two places—Paradise and Sunrise. However, despite the crowds, these two alpine areas do offer the most scenic day hiking opportunities.

At **Paradise** ★★, the 5-mile **Skyline Trail** ★★★ is the highest trail and climbs through beautiful meadows above the tree line. Unfortunately, the meadows here, which are among the park's most beautiful, have been heavily damaged by hikers' boots over the past century, and now there are signs everywhere telling hikers to stay on the trails. Along the route of this trail there are views of Mount Adams, Mount St. Helens, and the Nisqually Glacier. The **Lakes Trail,** of similar length, heads downhill to the Reflection Lakes, which have picture-perfect views of the mountain reflected in their waters. However, be forewarned that these lakes lie right alongside the road through the park, and are very popular with people who park by the roadside and get out of their cars for a brief stroll by the lakes.

At **Sunrise** ★★★ there are also numerous trails of varying lengths. Among these, the 5-mile **Burroughs Mountain Trail** and the 5.5-mile **Mount Fremont Trail** are both very rewarding—the latter even offers a chance to see mountain goats. The **Summerland Trail,** which starts 3 miles from the White River park entrance (the road to Sunrise), is another very popular day hike. This trail starts in forest and climbs 2,000 feet up into meadows with a great view of the mountain.

If you'd rather avoid most of the crowds, try the 2.5-mile round-trip trail to **Snow Lake,** which is set at the foot of Unicorn Peak. This trail involves only a few hundred feet of elevation gain. You'll find the trail head between Paradise and Ohanapecosh. For a longer day hike, try the 11-mile round-trip hike to **Indian Henry's Hunting Ground,** which involves more than 2,000 feet of elevation gain. This trail starts from the Kautz Creek turnout east of Longmire. In 1947, a huge mudflow swept down Kautz Creek and buried the road here under 30 feet of mud. Up in the northwest corner of the park, the 6-mile round-trip trail from Mowich Lake to **Spray Park** is another breathtaking route that starts in the forest and climbs a little more than 2,000 feet into beautiful alpine meadows.

The park's single most memorable low-elevation hike is the **Grove of the Patriarchs Trail** ★★. This 1.5-mile round-trip trail is fairly flat (good for kids) and leads through a forest of huge old trees to a grove of 1,000-year-old red cedars on an island in the Ohanapecosh River. The trail head for this hike is near the Stevens Canyon park entrance (southeast entrance).

Another interesting and easy low-elevation walk is the **Trail of the Shadows,** a .75-mile loop trail in Longmire. This trail, which circles a wet meadow, leads past bubbling mineral springs.

There are also naturalist-led programs and walks throughout the spring, summer, and fall, and on winter weekends there are guided snowshoe walks. Check the park newspaper for schedules.

The 95-mile-long **Wonderland Trail** ★★, which circles the mountain, is the quintessential Mount Rainier backpacking trip. This trail takes 10 days to 2 weeks to complete and offers spectacular scenery. However, there are also many shorter overnight hikes. Before heading out on any overnight backpacking trip, you'll need to pick up a permit at the Longmire Wilderness Information Center (© **360/569-4453;** fax 360/569-3131), the Paradise Ranger Station (© **360/569-2211,** ext. 2314), the White River Wilderness Information Center (© **360/663-2273,** ext. 222), or, seasonally, the Wilkeson Ranger Station (© **360/829-5127**) on the road to the Carbon River entrance to the park. For stays between May through September, reservations for backcountry campsites can be made beginning on April 1. Backcountry reservations cost $20 per party and can be made only by mail or fax.

HORSEBACK RIDING If you'd like to do some horseback riding, you've got a couple of choices in the area. In Elbe, you'll find **EZ Times Trail Rides,** 18703 Wash. 706 (© **360/569-2449**), which leads rides into the Elbe State Forest. During the summer, horseback riding is also available at **Crystal Mountain ski area** 🛷🛷 (© **360/663-2265**). East of White Pass on U.S. 12, you'll find **Indian Creek Corral** (© **509/672-2400**) near the shore of Rimrock Lake. Expect to pay $20 to $25 for a 1-hour ride and around $40 for a 2-hour ride.

MOUNTAIN BIKING Within the national park all trails are closed to mountain bikes, but cyclists are allowed to ride the West Side Road, a gravel road that has long been closed to cars due to mudslides that have repeatedly washed out one short stretch of the road. Off this road are several little-used hiking trails if you want to combine a ride with a hike.

MOUNTAINEERING Climbers know of Mount Rainier's reputation as a training ground for making attempts on higher peaks, such as Mount Everest. If you're interested in taking a mountain-climbing class, contact **Rainier Mountaineering,** P.O. Box Q, Ashford, WA 98304 (© **888/892-5462;** www.rmiguides.com), which operates inside Mount Rainier National Park and offers 1-day classes for $160, 3-day summit climbs for $770, and a 5-day mountaineering seminar for $1,150.

WHITE-WATER RAFTING The Tieton River, which flows down the eastern slopes of the Cascades to the east of the national park, is one of the state's most popular rafting rivers. However, the rafting season lasts for only about 3 weeks during the annual September drawdown of water from Rimrock Reservoir. Rafting companies offering trips on this river include **Alpine Adventures** (© **800/723-8386** or 206/323-1220; www.alpineadventures.com) and **River Riders** (© **800/448-RAFT** or 206/448-RAFT; www.riverrider.com). Expect to pay $60 to $80.

WINTER SPORTS In winter, there's good cross-country skiing at Paradise, and at Longmire, you'll find a ski touring and rental shop at the National Park Inn (© **360/569-2411**). Skis rent for around $15 per day. Daily between Christmas and New Year's and on winter weekends, there are 2-hour **guided snowshoe walks** at Paradise, with snowshoes provided ($1 suggested donation). Snowshoes ($12 per day) can also be rented in Longmire, should you want to explore on your own. Snowboarding is popular throughout the year, though there is no lift to get you up the slope, and it's about a 1½-hour climb to the best snowboarding area.

Outside the park, near the town of Packwood, you can ski cross-country from hut to hut on a 50-mile trail system. For more information, contact the **Mount Tahoma Trails Association,** P.O. Box 206, Ashford, WA 98304 (© **360/569-2451;** www.skimtta.com). Unfortunately, many of these trails are at such low elevations that snow cover is unreliable, and the official season for these trails does not begin until the end of December.

Just outside the northeast corner of the park, off Wash. 410, you'll find **Crystal Mountain Resort** (© **360/663-2265** for general information, or 888/SKI-6199 for snow conditions; www.skicrystal.com), which most Washingtonians agree is the state's best all-around ski area due to the variety of terrain. Lift ticket prices range from $20 for night skiing to $45 for a weekend all-day pass. Call for hours of operation. Experienced backcountry skiers will also find some challenging cross-country skiing here at Crystal Mountain.

You'll also find downhill and cross-country skiing less than 20 miles from the southeast corner of the park on U.S. 12 at the small **White Pass Ski Area** (✆ **509/672-3100;** www.skiwhitepass.com). Rental equipment is available. Lift rates range from $19 for an adult half-day midweek ticket to $38 for a full-day weekend ticket. Nordic track passes are $8.

OTHER ACTIVITIES & ATTRACTIONS OUTSIDE THE PARK
Between Memorial Day and the end of September (and also on Dec weekends), the **Mt. Rainier Scenic Railroad** (✆ **888/STEAM-11** or 360/569-2351; www.mrsr. com) operates vintage steam locomotives and both enclosed and open passenger cars along a 14-mile stretch of track between Elbe and Mineral Lake, just west of the park's Nisqually entrance. The trips last 1½ hours and cost $13 for adults, $12 for seniors, $8.50 for children 4 to 12, and are free for children under 3.

WHERE TO STAY
INSIDE THE PARK
National Park Inn   Located in Longmire, in the southwest corner of the park, this rustic lodge opened in 1920. The inn's front veranda has a view of the mountain, and it is here that guests often gather at sunset on clear days. There's also a lounge with a river-rock fireplace that's the perfect place to relax on a winter's night. Guest rooms vary in size and have rustic furnishings but are definitely not the most memorable part of a stay here. The inn's restaurant manages to have something for everyone, and there are a gift shop and cross-country ski/snowshoe rental shop adjacent to the inn. Because the setting here is not as spectacular as that of the Paradise Inn, this lodge is not nearly as popular, and consequently room reservations are easier to come by. In winter, the National Park Inn is popular with cross-country skiers and snowshoers.

Mount Rainier National Park, Ashford, WA 98304. ✆ **360/569-2275.** www.guestservices.com/rainier. 25 units, 7 with shared bathroom. $87 double with shared bathroom; $118–$159 double with private bathroom. Late Oct to late Apr, rates include breakfast. AE, DC, DISC, MC, V. Free parking. **Amenities:** Restaurant (American); lounge. *In room:* Coffeemaker, hair dryer, no phone.

Paradise Inn   Built in 1917 high on the flanks of Mount Rainier in an area aptly known as Paradise, this rustic lodge should be your first choice of accommodations in the park—but be sure to book early. Cedar-shake siding, huge exposed beams, cathedral ceilings, and a gigantic stone fireplace make this the quintessential mountain retreat. Offering breathtaking views of the mountain, the inn is also the starting point for miles of trails that in summer wander through flower-filled meadows. Guest rooms vary in size, but all have rustic hickory furniture. The Sunday brunch in the inn's large dining room is legendary. A snack bar and lounge are dining options.

Mount Rainier National Park, Ashford, WA 98304. ✆ **360/569-2275.** www.guestservices.com/rainier. 117 units, 33 with shared bathroom. $82 double with shared bathroom; $123–$169 double with private bathroom; $185 suite. AE, DC, DISC, MC, V. Closed early Oct to mid-May. Free parking. **Amenities:** 2 restaurants (American, snack bar); lounge. *In room:* No phone.

OUTSIDE THE SOUTHWEST (NISQUALLY) ENTRANCE
Alexander's Country Inn   Located just outside the park's Nisqually entrance, this large B&B first opened as an inn back in 1912. Today, as then, it

is one of the preferred places to stay in the area, offering not only comfortable rooms but some of the best food for many miles around. The first floor is taken up by the dining room, and on the second floor, you'll find a big lounge where you can sit by the fire on a cold night. By far the best room in the house is the tower suite, which is in a turret and has plenty of windows looking out on the woods (there's also a 2nd, smaller turret suite). After a hard day of playing on the mountain, there's no better place to relax than in the hot tub overlooking the inn's trout pond. The inn also rents two three-bedroom houses.

37515 SR 706 E., Ashford, WA 98304. ⓒ 800/654-7615 or 360/569-2300. Fax 360/569-2323. www.alexanders countryinn.com. 14 units. May–Oct $120 double, $150 suite, $210 house; Nov–Apr $99 double, $125 suite, $165 house. Rates include full breakfast. MC, V. **Amenities:** Restaurant (American); Jacuzzi. *In room:* No phone.

Stormking ⚑ *Finds* With three modern cabins, Stormking is a quiet getaway not far from the national park's main entrance. Two of the cabins are small and are best suited to couples, while the third is large enough for families and has a full kitchen. Our favorite cabin is set on the far side of a footbridge over a tiny pond and has a slate-floored entry hall, parquet floors, a woodstove, a stereo system with plenty of relaxing music, and a high ceiling. In the big bathroom, which has a flagstone floor and is filled with plants, you'll find a double shower amid the greenery. There's also a hot tub on the back deck; in fact, all three cabins have hot tubs.

37311 SR 706 E. (P.O. Box 126), Ashford, WA 98304. ⓒ 360/569-2964. www.stormkingspa.com. 3 units. $155–$175 cabin. 2-night minimum on weekends, holidays, and during the summer. MC, V. Pets accepted ($15). **Amenities:** Spa; Jacuzzi; massage. *In room:* No phone.

Wellspring ⚑⚑ *Value* This little retreat definitely isn't for everyone (although even Al Gore has stayed here), but it is certainly the most unique accommodations in the area. Private hot tubs and wood-fired saunas take the chill off even the coldest night, and massages are available to soothe aching muscles. Accommodations are an eclectic and fanciful mix. In the modern log cabins, which are tucked up against the edge of the forest, you'll find feather beds, woodstoves, and vaulted ceilings. In The Nest, there's a queen-size bed suspended from the ceiling by ropes and situated under a skylight. In the Three Bears Cottage, you'll find rustic log furniture and a full kitchen. In the Tatoosh Room, you'll find a large stone fireplace, a whirlpool tub, and a waterfall shower. The newest rooms are tent cabins (one has a tropical theme), and there's even a tiny tree house room! Hot tubs and saunas are an additional $5 to $10 per person per hour. Several spa treatments are also available.

54922 Kernahan Rd., Ashford, WA 98304. ⓒ 360/569-2514. 14 units. $79–$159 double. Rates for most rooms include continental breakfast. MC, V. **Amenities:** 2 Jacuzzis; 2 saunas; massage. *In room (except tent cabins):* Fridge, coffeemaker.

Whittaker's Bunkhouse ⚑ Though it definitely is nothing fancy, this lodge, a former mill-workers' bunkhouse built in 1912, is the lodging of choice for climbers headed to or from the summit of Mount Rainier. The Bunkhouse is owned by Lou Whittaker, one of Mount Rainier's most famous climbers (and owner of Rainier Mountaineering), and in the lodge's espresso shop, you'll find lots of climbing photos and certificates Whittaker received for climbing Mount Everest. The guest rooms are small and spartan, but they do have private bathrooms.

30205 SR 706 E. (P.O. Box 121), Ashford, WA 98304. ⓒ 360/569-2439. Fax 360/569-2436. www.welcome toashford.com. 20 units. $75 double; $30 dorm. AE, MC, V. **Amenities:** Espresso bar; Jacuzzi. *In room:* No phone.

OUTSIDE THE NORTHEAST (WHITE RIVER) ENTRANCE

Alta Crystal Resort at Mt. Rainier ⭐   This is the closest lodging to the northeast (White River) park entrance and the Sunrise area, and although this condominium resort with its wooded grounds is most popular in winter when skiers flock to Crystal Mountain's slopes (just minutes away), there's also plenty to do in summer. After spending the day hiking nearby trails, you can go for a swim or soak your body in a hot tub in the woods. Accommodations are in one-bedroom and loft chalets. The former sleep up to four people and the latter have bed space for up to six people. All of the condos have fireplaces.

68317 Wash. 410 E., Greenwater, WA 98022. ⓒ 800/277-6475 or 360/663-2500. Fax 360/663-2556. www. altacrystalresort.com. 24 units. $139–$249 chalet for 1–6 people. AE, MC, V. **Amenities:** Outdoor pool; Jacuzzi; bike rentals. *In room:* TV/VCR, dataport, kitchen, fridge, coffeemaker, hair dryer.

CAMPGROUNDS

There are six main campgrounds within Mount Rainier National Park, and because all the park's campgrounds stay full on summer weekends, you should be sure to either have a reservation (required for Ohanapecosh and Cougar Rock from late June to Labor Day) or arrive early in the day. Reservations can be made through the **National Park Reservation Service** (ⓒ **800/365-2267**; http:// reservations.nps.gov). Campsite fees range from $9 to $15 per campsite per night. No electrical or water hookups are available. Only the Sunshine Point Campground and, depending on snow level and road conditions, the Ipsut Creek Campground, stay open all year. The rest are open summer through early fall, with the White River Campground usually closing first.

Ohanapecosh (188 campsites), located in the southeast corner of the park, is the largest but is a long way from the alpine meadows that are what most visitors want to see. The closest campground to Paradise is **Cougar Rock** (173 campsites). **White River** ⭐ (112 campsites) is close to Sunrise, which is one of the most spectacular spots in the park. **Sunshine Point** (18 campsites) is near the Nisqually entrance. Up in the northwest corner of the park, there is **Ipsut Creek** (28 campsites), although due to frequent winter flood damage, the road to this campground isn't always open.

In addition to drive-in campgrounds and the many backcountry camps, there are two walk-in campgrounds that often have spaces available, even on weekends. **Mowich Lake** ⭐ (30 campsites) is in the northwest corner of the park not far from Ipsut Creek Campground, and the sites are only 50 yards from the parking lot. If you're prepared for a longer walk in, consider **Sunrise** ⭐ (8 campsites), which is officially a backcountry campsite but is only about a mile from the Sunrise parking lot (a backcountry camping permit is required).

When the park campgrounds are full, try **La Wis Wis** (90 campsites), a national forest campground on U.S. 12 and the Cowlitz River near the Ohanapecosh entrance. There are also numerous unremarkable National Forest Service campgrounds along U.S. 12 east of White Pass and along Wash. 410 east of the park.

For information on campgrounds in the national park, contact **Mount Rainier National Park,** Tahoma Woods, Star Route, Ashford, WA 98304-9751 (ⓒ **360/ 569-2211**; www.nps.gov/mora). For information on national forest campgrounds east of the park, contact the **Naches Ranger District,** 10237 U.S. 12, Naches, WA 98937 (ⓒ **509/653-2205**; www.fs.fed.us/r6/wenatchee); and for those west of the park, contact the **Cowlitz Valley Ranger District,** 10024 U.S. 12 (P.O. Box 670), Randle, WA 98377 (ⓒ **360/497-1100**; www.fs.fed.us/r6/gpnf). For national forest campground reservations, contact the **National Recreation Reservation Service** (© **877/444-6777** or 518/885-3639; www.reserveusa.com).

WHERE TO DINE

In the park there are dining rooms at Paradise Inn, open from mid-May to early October, and the National Park Inn, open year-round. As the only formal dining options within the park, these restaurants tend to stay busy. For quick meals, there are snack bars at the Henry M. Jackson Memorial Visitor Center, at Paradise Inn, and at Sunrise Lodge. In Ashford you'll find the **Copper Creek Restaurant,** 35707 SR 706 E., Ashford (© **360/569-2326**), which does good berry pies.

Alexander's AMERICAN   Alexander's, which is also a popular B&B, is the best place to dine outside the Nisqually entrance to the park. Fresh trout from the inn's pond is the dinner of choice here, but you'll also find steaks, pork chops, and pasta on the menu. Whatever you order, just be sure to save room for the wild blackberry pie.

37515 SR 706 E., Ashford. © **800/654-7615** or 360/569-2300. www.alexanderscountryinn.com. Reservations recommended. Main courses $11–$25. MC, V. Mid-May to Oct daily 8am–9pm; Nov to mid-May Fri 3–8pm, Sat 8am–8pm, Sun 8am–7pm.

7 Mount St. Helens National Volcanic Monument

Coldwater Ridge Visitor Center: 90 miles N of Portland, 168 miles S of Seattle

Named in 1792 by Capt. George Vancouver for his friend Baron St. Helens, Mount St. Helens was once considered the most perfect of the Cascade peaks, a snow-covered cone rising above lush forests. However, on May 18, 1980, all that changed when Mount St. Helens erupted with a violent explosion previously unknown in modern times.

The eruption blew out the side of the volcano and removed the top 1,300 feet of the peak, causing the largest landslide in recorded history. This blast is estimated to have traveled at up to 650 mph, with air temperatures of up to 800°F (425°C). The eruption also sent more than 540 million tons of ash nearly 16 miles into the atmosphere. This massive volume of ash rained down on an area of 22,000 square miles and could be measured as far away as Denver.

Today the volcano and 110,000 acres of both devastated and undisturbed forests have been preserved as Mount St. Helens National Volcanic Monument. Several visitor centers provide information on the eruption and the subsequent changes that have taken place here.

ESSENTIALS

GETTING THERE   Mount St. Helens National Volcanic Monument is accessed by three different routes. The one with all the major information centers is Wash. 504, the Spirit Lake Highway, which heads east from I-5 at Castle Rock. The southern section of the monument is reached via Wash. 503 from I-5 at Woodland. The east side of the monument is reached via U.S. 12 from I-5 at exit 68.

VISITOR INFORMATION   For more information on the national monument, contact **Mount St. Helens National Volcanic Monument,** 42218 NE Yale Bridge Rd., Amboy, WA 98601 (© **360/247-3900**; www.fs.fed.us/gpnf/mshnvm).

ADMISSION   Admission to one monument visitor center (or Ape Cave) is $3 ($1 for children 5–15) and to two or more visitor centers (and Ape Cave) is $6 ($2 for children 5–15). If you just want to park at one of the monument's trail

Mount St. Helens National Volcanic Monument

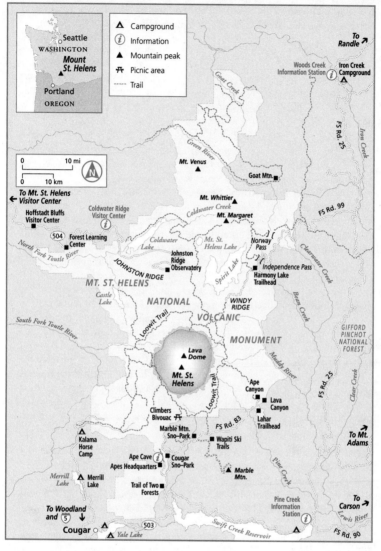

heads and go for a hike, all you need is a valid Northwest Forest Pass, which costs $5 per day. If it's winter, you'll need a Sno-Park Permit ($8–$9 per day).

EXPLORING THE NATIONAL MONUMENT
MOUNT ST. HELENS WEST

The best place to start an exploration of the monument is the **Mount St. Helens Visitor Center** (© 360/274-2100), which is located at Silver Lake, 5 miles east of Castle Rock on Wash. 504. The visitor center houses extensive exhibits on the eruption and its effects on the region. It's open daily from 9am to 6pm in summer (9am–5pm other months). Before reaching the center, you can stop and watch a 25-minute, 70mm film about the eruption at the **Mount St. Helens**

Cinedome Theater (© 877/ERUPTION or 360/274-9844), which is located at exit 49 off I-5 (tickets $6 adults, $5 seniors and children).

Continuing east from the visitor center, you'll come to the **Hoffstadt Bluffs Visitor Center** (© 360/274-7750; www.mt-st-helens.com) at milepost 27 (open daily 9am–8pm in summer; shorter hours other months), which has a snack bar and is the takeoff site for 25-minute helicopter flights over Mount St. Helens ($99 with a three-person minimum). A few miles farther, just past milepost 33, is the **Forest Learning Center** (© 360/414-3439), open mid-May through September daily 10am to 6pm (10am–5pm in early May and Oct). This is primarily a promotional center for the timber industry but, in a theater designed to resemble an ash-covered landscape, you can watch a short, fascinating video about the eruption. Outside either of these centers you can usually see numerous elk on the floor of the Toutle River valley far below.

The **Coldwater Ridge Visitor Center** (© 360/274-2114), which is at milepost 47 on Wash. 504, only 8 miles from the crater, is the second of the national monument's official visitor centers. This center features interpretive displays on the events leading up to the eruption and the subsequent slow regeneration of life around the volcano. You'll also find a picnic area, interpretive trail, restaurant, and boat launch at Coldwater Lake. The visitor center is open daily from 10am to 6pm.

Of the many visitor centers, none offers a more awe-inspiring view than that from the **Johnston Ridge Observatory** (© 360/274-2140), 10 miles past the Coldwater Ridge Visitor Center. Built into the mountainside and designed to blend into the landscape, this observatory houses the equipment that is still used to monitor activity within Mount St. Helens. The observatory is open between early May and October or November daily from 10am to 6pm. If you're up for a bit of hiking, the single best trail on this side of the monument is the Boundary Ridge Trail, which heads east from the Johnston Ridge Observatory, with a jaw-dropping view of the blast zone the entire way. This trail leads for many miles across the monument, so you can hike as much or as little as you want. There is a good turnaround point about a mile out from the observatory.

MOUNT ST. HELENS EAST

For a different perspective on the devastation wrought by Mount St. Helens's eruption, drive around to the mountain's east side and take the road up to Windy Ridge. Although it takes a couple of hours longer to get to this side of the mountain, you will be rewarded by equally amazing views, better hiking opportunities, and smaller crowds. To reach the east side of the mountain, take U.S. 12 east from exit 68 off I-5. In Randle, head south on Forest Road 25. The **Woods Creek Information Station,** on Forest Road 25 just before the junction with Route 26, has information on this part of the monument. South of Woods Creek, watch for Forest Road 99, the road to the **Windy Ridge Viewpoint.** This road crosses many miles of blown-down trees that were felled by a single blast, a reminder of the awesome power of nature. More than 2 decades after the eruption, life is slowly returning to the devastated forest. At the **Windy Ridge Viewpoint,** visitors get one of the best close-up views of the crater. A staircase of 439 stairs climbs 220 feet up the hill above the parking area for even better views. Below Windy Ridge lies Spirit Lake, once one of the most popular summer vacation spots in the Washington Cascades. Today the lake is desolate and lifeless. The 1-mile Harmony Trail leads down to the shore of Spirit Lake and is a very worthwhile hike. Just keep in mind that it is a 600-foot climb back up to the trail-head parking lot.

MOUNT ST. HELENS SOUTH

The south side of the monument was the least affected by the eruption, and consequently does not offer the dramatic scenes of devastation to be seen on the east and west sides of the monument. However, this area offers some good hiking and a couple of very interesting volcanic features. The first of these features you'll come to is the **Ape Cave,** a lava tube that was formed 1,900 years ago when lava poured from the volcano. When the lava finally stopped flowing, it left a 2-mile-long cave that is the longest continuous lava tube in the Western Hemisphere. At the Ape's Headquarters, you can join a regular ranger-led exploration of the cave or rent a lantern for exploring the cave on your own. This center is open daily from late June to early September.

Of the trails on this side of the monument, the **Lava Canyon Trail** is the most fascinating. It follows a canyon that was unearthed by a mudflow that swept down this side of the mountain after the eruption.

On Wash. 503, the road leading to the south side of the monument, you'll find, in the town of Ariel, the **Lelooska Foundation** ✸✸, 165 Merwin Village Rd. (© **360/225-9522;** www.lelooska.com). Something of a Native American cultural center, this combination museum and art gallery features Native American arts and crafts from around the country, though the emphasis is on the work of Northwest artists. This is one of the finest Native American galleries in the state. Additionally, one Saturday evening each month in the spring and fall, there are performances of traditional Northwest Coast Native American masked dances, which are accompanied by traditional storytelling. The performances are held in a reproduction of a traditional cedar longhouse. Tickets are $8.50 for adults and $7 for children 12 and under, and advance reservations are required.

CLIMBING THE MOUNTAIN

If you are an experienced hiker in good physical condition, you may want to consider climbing to the top of Mount St. Helens. However, be aware that it is an 8- to 10-hour, 10-mile hike and can require an ice ax. Permits are required year-round, and between April 1 and October 31 there is a fee of $15 per person for these permits. Because this is a very popular climb (summer weekends book up months in advance), it is advisable to make a reservation. Reservations are accepted beginning February 1 at the following address: **Climbing Coordinator,** Mount St. Helens NVM, 42218 NE Yale Bridge Rd., Amboy, WA 98601 (© **360/449-7861;** www.fs.fed.us/gpnf/mshnvm). Be sure to first get a copy of the permit application by contacting the national monument. If you don't have a reservation, you can try your luck by stopping by **Jack's Restaurant and Store** (© **360/231-4276**) on Wash. 503, 5 miles west of the town of Cougar. Each evening at 6pm, this store has a lottery of climbing permits for the next day; be sure to arrive 15 minutes early to get your name into the lottery. Between November 1 and March 31, when permits are free and reservations aren't necessary, you can expect lots of snow. The trail head is on the south side of the monument. A $5 Northwest Forest Pass (which can also be obtained at Jack's) is required for parking at the trail head.

A FEW UNIQUE WAYS TO SEE THE NATIONAL MONUMENT

If you'd like a bird's-eye view of the volcano, you can take a **helicopter flight** from the Hoffstadt Bluffs Visitor Center (© **360/274-7750**), for $99 per person. These rides are offered from mid-May through September and last about 25 minutes. Alternatively, you can go up in a small plane with **C&C Aviation** (© **503/760-6969;** www.ccavn.com), which flies out of the Evergreen Airport in Vancouver, Washington ($77 per person; two-person minimum). **Mount St. Helens Tours** (© 360/274-6542; www.ecoparkresort.com) offers van tours ($60 per person; three-person minimum) that are narrated by survivors of the big blast.

WHERE TO STAY

Blue Heron Inn Bed & Breakfast ★★   This modern inn on the road to the Coldwater and Johnston Ridge visitor centers is an excellent choice if you're searching for comfortable, modern accommodations in this area. Set on 5 acres of land across the highway from Silver Lake and Sequest State Park, the inn has an excellent view of Mount St. Helens. Lots of decks provide plenty of places for relaxing and soaking up the view, and during cooler weather, you can sit by the fire in the parlor. This inn is by far the best bet for accommodations in the area and is close to the Mount St. Helens Visitor Center.

2846 Spirit Lake Hwy., Castle Rock, WA 98611. © **800/959-4049** or 360/274-9595. www.blueheroninn.com. 7 units. $159–$205 double. Rates include full breakfast. MC, V. Children over age 5 welcome. *In room:* A/C, TV, hair dryer.

Mount St. Helens Adventures Tours Eco-Park and Tent & Breakfast ★ *Kids* This company's tented camp located inside the blast zone (though outside the monument) is by far the most unusual accommodation in the vicinity of Mount St. Helens. The large safari-style tents are set up on the shore of a small lake amid the devastation left by the blast. The camp is down a former logging road on private property and guests are transported there by van. The Eco-Park, on the other hand, is right on Wash. 504 and can be reached by personal vehicle. This lodging consists of modern cabins and yurts (circular tent cabins). Logger dinner shows—complete with flying wood chips—are also staged here at the Eco-Park during the summer and cost $18; horseback rides are also available.

14000 Spirit Lake Hwy. (P.O. Box 149), Toutle, WA 98649. © **360/274-6542** or 360/274-7007. www.ecopark resort.com. 5 tents at Tent & Breakfast, 6 cabins and 2 yurts at Eco-Park. Tent & Breakfast $285 double (rates include dinner, breakfast, and transportation); Eco-Park cabins $70–$95 double. MC, V. **Amenities:** Restaurant (American); activities desk. *In room:* No phone.

CAMPGROUNDS

West of the monument, **Sequest State Park** (88 campsites), set amid impressive old-growth trees on Wash. 504 about 5 miles off I-5, is the closest public campground to Coldwater Ridge. This campground is set on Silver Lake adjacent to the Mount St. Helens Visitor Center. For reservations, contact **Washington State Parks Reservations** (© **888/226-7688;** www.parks.wa.gov).

East of the monument, **Iron Creek** ★ (98 campsites), a Forest Service campground, is the closest to Windy Ridge. This campground is set amid old-growth trees on the bank of the Cispus River.

South of the monument, there are a couple of conveniently located campgrounds on Yale Lake—**Cougar** (45 campsites) and **Beaver Bay** (63 campsites)—and, at the east end of Swift Reservoir, **Swift** (93 campsites). For more tranquillity, try little **Merrill Lake** (7 campsites), which is operated by the Washington Department of Natural Resources. Although a bit out of the way for exploring the monument, the **Lower Falls Recreation Area** ★★ (42 campsites) on the Lewis River is a beautiful spot set beside the waterfalls for which it is named. For information on national forest campgrounds in the area, contact the **Cowlitz Valley Ranger District,** 10024 U.S. 12 (P.O. Box 670), Randle, WA 98377 (© **360/497-1100;** www.fs.fed.us/r6/gpnf). For national forest campground reservations, contact the

National Recreation Reservation Service (© 877/444-6777 or 518/885-3639; www.reserveusa.com).

WHERE TO DINE

There aren't a whole lot of dining options in the vicinity of the monument, but not to be missed are the berry cobblers served at the **19 Mile House,** 9440 Spirit Lake Hwy., Toutle (© **360/274-8779**), which is 19 miles up the Spirit Lake Highway (Wash. 504) and is open from April or May until October. They've got good burgers here, too. Other options include the **Mount St. Helens Restaurant** at the Hoffstadt Bluffs Visitor Center (Spirit Lake Hwy. milepost 27) and the restaurant at the Coldwater Ridge Visitor Center (Spirit Lake Hwy. milepost 43).

8 The Columbia Gorge & the Mount Adams Area

Stevenson: 45 miles E of Vancouver, 25 miles W of White Salmon

The Columbia Gorge, which begins a few miles east of Vancouver, Washington, and extends eastward for nearly 70 miles, cuts through the Cascade Range and connects the rain-soaked west-side forests with the sagebrush scrublands of eastern Washington. This change in climate is caused by moist air condensing into snow and rain as it passes over the crest of the Cascades. Most of the air's moisture falls on the western slopes, so that the eastern slopes and the land stretching for hundreds of miles beyond lie in what's called a rain shadow. Perhaps nowhere else on earth can you witness this rain-shadow effect so clearly. Between the two extremes lies a community of plants that's unique to the Columbia Gorge, and springtime in the gorge sees colorful displays of wildflowers, many of which occur naturally only here in the Columbia Gorge.

The Columbia River is older than the hills. It's older than the mountains, too. And it's this great age that accounts for the river's dramatic gorge through the Cascades. The mountains have actually risen up *around* the river. Although the river's geologic history dates back 40 million years or so, it was a series of recent events, geologically speaking, that gave the Columbia Gorge its very distinctive appearance. About 15,000 years ago, toward the end of the last Ice Age, in what is now Montana, huge glacial ice dams burst and sent floodwaters racing down the Columbia. As the floodwaters swept through the Columbia Gorge, they were as much as 1,200 feet high. Ice and rock carried by the floodwaters helped the river scour out the sides of the once gently sloping valley, leaving behind the steep-walled gorge that we know today. The waterfalls that elicit so many oohs and aahs are the most dramatic evidence of these great floods. In 1986, much of this area was designated the **Columbia Gorge National Scenic Area** to preserve its spectacular and unique natural beauty.

As early as 1915 a scenic highway was built through the gorge on the Oregon side. However, while the Oregon side of the Gorge has the spectacular waterfalls and scenic highway and tends to get all the publicity, it is actually from the Washington side, along **Wash. 14,** that you get the best views. From this highway the views take in both the southern wall of the Columbia Gorge and the snowcapped summit of Mount Hood. It is also on the Washington side of the Gorge, in Stevenson, that you'll find the informative Columbia Gorge Interpretive Center.

Roughly 45 miles north of the Columbia Gorge rises Mount Adams, which, at 12,276 feet in elevation, is the second-highest peak in Washington. However, because it is so inaccessible from Puget Sound and can't be seen from most of Portland (the nearest metropolitan area), it remains one of the least visited major peaks in the state. Though few get to this massive peak, those who do often make the strenuous, though non-technical, climb to the mountain's summit.

ESSENTIALS

GETTING THERE   Wash. 14 parallels the Columbia River from Vancouver through the Columbia Gorge and into eastern Washington. Mount Adams lies to the north of the Gorge and is accessed via Wash. 141 from White Salmon.

VISITOR INFORMATION   For more information on the Columbia Gorge, contact the **Columbia River Gorge National Scenic Area,** 902 Wasco Ave., Suite 200, Hood River, OR 97031 (*©* **541/386-2333;** www.fs.fed.us/r6/columbia). There's also a **Forest Service Information Center** in the lobby of **Skamania Lodge,** 1131 SW Skamania Lodge Dr. (*©* **509/427-2528**), in Stevenson, Washington. Information is also available from the **Skamania County Chamber of Commerce,** P.O. Box 1037, Stevenson, WA 98648 (*©* **800/989-9178** or 509/427-8911; www.skamania.org). For detailed information on the Oregon side of the Columbia Gorge, see *Frommer's Oregon* (Wiley Publishing, Inc.).

AN INTRODUCTION TO THE GORGE

Columbia Gorge Interpretive Center *★★*   Focusing on the Gorge's early Native American inhabitants and the development of the area by white settlers, this museum is your single best introduction to the Columbia Gorge. Exhibits contain historical photographs by Edward Curtis and others that illustrate the story of portage companies and paddle-wheelers that once operated along this stretch of the Columbia River. A 37-foot-high replica of a 19th-century fish wheel gives an understanding of how salmon runs have been threatened in the past and the present. Displays also frankly discuss other problems that the coming of civilization brought to this area. A slide program tells the history of the formation of the Gorge, and when the volcanoes erupt, the floor in the theater actually shakes from the intensity of the low-volume sound track. When it's not cloudy, the center has an awesome view of the south side of the Gorge.

990 SW Rock Creek Dr., Stevenson. *©* **800/991-2338** or 509/427-8211. www.columbiagorge.org. Admission $6 adults, $5 seniors and students, $4 children 6–12, free for children 5 and under. Daily 10am–5pm. Closed Thanksgiving, Christmas, and New Year's Day.

EXPLORING THE GORGE

Heading east from Vancouver, Wash. 14 passes through the industrial towns of Camas and Washougal before finally breaking free of the Portland/Vancouver metropolitan area. For much of the way, the highway stays close to the river, but at Cape Horn, an area where basalt cliffs rise straight out of the water, the highway climbs high above the river, providing one of the best views along this stretch of the highway. Several pull-offs let you stop and enjoy the views.

Roughly 35 miles east of Vancouver, you come to **Beacon Rock,** an 800-foot-tall monolith that has a 1-mile trail to its summit. The trail, which for much of the way consists of metal stairways and catwalks, was built between 1915 and 1918 by Henry Biddle, who saved Beacon Rock from being blasted into rubble for a jetty at the mouth of the Columbia River. Continuing east, you'll come to Stevenson, which is the site of the above-mentioned Columbia Gorge Interpretive Center.

In the town of North Bonneville, a few miles west of Stevenson, you can swim in the hot-springs-fed pool and soak in the tubs at **Bonneville Hot Springs Resort,** 1252 E. Cascade Dr. (*©* **866/459-1678** or 509/427-7767; www.bonnevilleresort.com), which charges $10 per day for the use of its pool and soaking tubs. Massages and other spa services are also available. East of Stevenson, in the town of Carson, you can also avail yourself of the therapeutic waters of the **Carson Hot Springs Resort** (© **800/607-3678** or 509/427-8292). This rustic "resort" has been in business since 1897 and looks every bit its age. However, it's just this old-fashioned appeal that keeps people coming back year after year. It's open daily from 8am to 7pm in summer and from 9am to 6pm other months, and charges $12 for a soak and post-soak wrap. An hour's massage is $55. If you're looking for natural hot springs, the folks here can give you directions to some that are nearby.

If you're up for a strenuous but rewarding hike, the 3-mile trail to the summit of 2,948-foot **Dog Mountain** provides ample views up and down the Gorge. In spring, the wildflower displays in the meadows on Dog Mountain's slopes are some of the finest in the Gorge. You'll find the trail head on Wash. 14, 12 miles east of the Bridge of the Gods, a bridge that now spans the river at a site where a huge landslide once blocked the Columbia, creating a natural "bridge" across the river.

For a less strenuous, though no less scenic hike, drive 5 miles east of Bingen and turn left onto Rowland Lake Road. In just over a mile, you'll come to the gravel roadside parking area for the **Catherine Creek** area. On the south side of the road, there is a 1.25-mile paved path that leads to several viewpoints. On the north side, there is an unpaved trail that leads up through the Catherine Creek canyon and connects to trails that climb up into the hills. *Warning:* Keep an eye out for poison oak.

THE MOUNT ADAMS AREA

While Mount Adams's summit is popular with mountain climbers, at lower elevations there are also excellent trails for hikers and backpackers. The favorite summer spot for a hike is **Bird Creek Meadows** on the Yakama Indian Reservation north of the town of Trout Lake. These meadows are ablaze with wildflowers in July. Eight miles west of Trout Lake, you can explore several **ice caves.** The caves were formed by lava flows centuries ago, and year-round cool temperatures allow ice to build up within the caves. For more information on hiking on Mount Adams, contact the **Gifford Pinchot National Forest,** Mt. Adams Ranger District, 2455 Wash. 141, Trout Lake, WA 98650 (© **509/395-3400;** www.fs.fed. us/r6/gpnf).

THE EAST END OF THE GORGE

Between The Dalles Dam and the town of Goldendale (north of Wash. 14 on U.S. 97), there are a few unusual attractions that are well worth a visit if you are exploring down at this eastern end of the Gorge. In addition to the attractions listed here, you'll also find three wineries. **Maryhill Winery,** 9774 Hwy. 14, Maryhill (© **877/627-9445;** www.maryhillwinery.com), has the best view of any winery in the Northwest and also produces some very good wines. **Cascade Cliffs Vineyard & Winery,** milepost 88.6, Hwy. 14, Wishram (© **509/767-1100;** www.cascade cliffs.com), is set at the foot of 400-foot-tall basalt cliffs and produces, among other wines, Nebbiolo and Barbera. **Marshal's Winery,** 150 Oak Creek Rd., Dallesport (© **509/767-4633**), which is located 2 miles up a gravel road, is a tiny family-run winery that produces some of Washington's smoothest cabernet sauvignons and merlots, as well as some unusual sweet wines.

Goldendale Observatory State Park ⚐ If you happen to be an amateur astronomer, you won't want to miss a visit to the Goldendale Observatory. The central 24½-inch reflector is one of the largest public telescopes in the country—large enough for scientific research—but instead, it's dedicated to sharing the stars with the general public. The observatory is out in this remote part of the state because this region's dry weather and distance from city lights almost guarantees that every night will be a good night for stargazing.

1602 Observatory Dr., Goldendale. © 509/773-3141. Admission by donation; parking $5. Apr–Sept Wed–Sun 2–5pm and 8pm–midnight; Oct–Mar open by appointment Sat 1–5pm and 7–9pm, Sun 1–5pm.

Horsethief Lake State Park ★ *Finds* Located between The Dalles Dam and Wishram on Wash. 14, Horsethief Lake is a popular fishing area and campground. However, long before the area was designated a state park, this was a gathering ground for Native Americans, who fished for salmon at nearby Celilo Falls. The park isn't far from the famous Celilo Falls, which were, before being inundated by the waters behind The Dalles Dam, the most prolific salmon-fishing spot in the Northwest. Each year for thousands of years Native Americans would gather here from all over the Northwest. These Native Americans drew petroglyphs on rocks that are now protected within this park. The most famous of these is Tsagaglalal ("she who watches"), a large face that gazes down on the Columbia River. Due to past vandalism, the only way to see this and other park petroglyphs is on ranger-led walks held on Friday and Saturday mornings at 10am. Reservations for these walks should be made at least 2 to 3 weeks in advance.

Wash. 14. © 509/767-1159. Free admission. Apr–Oct daily 6:30am–dusk. Closed Nov–Mar.

Maryhill Museum of Art/Stonehenge Monument ★★ *Finds* Between 1914 and 1926, atop a remote windswept bluff overlooking the Columbia River, eccentric entrepreneur Sam Hill built a grand mansion he called Maryhill. Though he never lived in the mansion, he did turn it into a museum that today is one of the finest, most eclectic, and least visited of the state's major museums. There is an acclaimed collection of sculptures and drawings by Auguste Rodin. An extensive collection of Native American artifacts includes the finest display of baskets in the state. Furniture, jewelry, and other items that once belonged to Hill's friend Queen Marie of Romania, are also on display, as are a collection of miniature French fashion mannequins from just after World War II. Note that the Rodins and fashion mannequins are sometimes loaned out to other museums. The lush grounds surrounding the museum have sculptures, picnic tables, and plenty of shade trees, making this an ideal spot for a picnic lunch (there's also a cafe inside the museum). A few miles east of Maryhill stands Hill's concrete reproduction of Stonehenge, which he had built as a memorial to local men who died in World War I.

35 Maryhill Museum Dr. (Wash. 14). © 509/773-3733. www.maryhillmuseum.org. Admission $7 adults, $6 seniors, $2 children 6–12. Mar 15–Nov 15 daily 9am–5pm. Closed Nov 16–Mar 14.

SPORTS & OUTDOOR ACTIVITIES

The Columbia Gorge is one of the nation's top windsurfing spots, and if you're here to ride the wind, or just want to watch others as they race back and forth across the river, head to the **fish hatchery,** west of the mouth of the White Salmon River, or **Swell City,** a park about 3 miles west of the Hood River Bridge. **Bob's Beach,** in downtown Stevenson, is another popular spot.

When there isn't enough wind for sailing, there's still the option to go **rafting** on the White Salmon River. Companies offering raft trips on this river include **Zoller's Outdoor Odysseys** (© **800/366-2004** or 509/493-2641; www.zooraft.com), **Wet**

Planet Rafting (© 800/306-1673 or 509/493-8989; www.wetplanetrafting.com), and **All Adventures Rafting** (© 877/641-RAFT or 509/493-3926; www.all adventures.net). The river-rafting season runs March through October, and a half-day trip will cost around $55 or $60 per person.

If you're interested in a bit of horseback riding, contact **Northwestern Lake Riding Stables** (© 509/493-4965; www.nwstables.com), which is at Northwestern Lake off Wash. 141 north of White Salmon. A 1-hour ride is $25.

WHERE TO STAY
IN STEVENSON

Bonneville Hot Springs Resort ★★   Although this new hot springs resort doesn't have any views to speak of, it is still one of your best bets for a memorable stay in the Columbia Gorge. With lots of stone and wood detail work used in the construction, this hideaway in the woods has the feel of a modern mountain lodge, although the furnishings are more classically European in styling. The focal point of the lobby is a huge river-rock fireplace. There's an 80-foot-long hot-springs-fed indoor pool, a full-service spa, and a big outdoor hot tub in a courtyard with an unusual stone wall down which water cascades. Guest rooms have balconies (ask for one overlooking the courtyard), beds with ornate wood headboards, and attractive bathrooms. Some of the rooms have their own mineral-water soaking tubs.

1252 E. Cascade Dr. (P.O. Box 356), North Bonneville, WA 98638. © 866/459-1678 or 509/427-7767. Fax 509/427-7733. www.bonnevilleresort.com. 78 units. $125–$175 double; $260–$320 suite. Children under 4 stay free in parent's room. AE, DISC, MC, V. **Amenities:** Restaurant (Continental); lounge; indoor pool; exercise room; full-service spa; 3 Jacuzzis; limited room service; massage. *In room:* A/C, TV, dataport, fridge, coffeemaker, hair dryer, iron.

Dolce Skamania Lodge ★★★   Boasting the most spectacular vistas of any hotel in the Gorge, Skamania Lodge is also the only golf resort around. However, it is also well situated whether you brought your sailboard, hiking boots, or mountain bike. The decor is classically rustic with lots of rock and natural wood, and throughout the hotel there are Northwest Indian artworks and artifacts on display. Huge windows in the lobby have superb views of the Gorge. Of course, the river-view guest rooms are more expensive than the forest-view rooms (which overlook more parking lot than forest), but these rooms are well worth the extra cost. There are also rooms with fireplaces available.

1131 Skamania Lodge Way, Stevenson, WA 98648. © 800/221-7117 or 509/427-7700. Fax 509/427-2547. www.dolce.com/skamania. 254 units. $119–$219 double; $239–$299 suite (lower rates in winter). Children under 17 stay free in parent's room. AE, DC, DISC, MC, V. **Amenities:** Restaurant (Northwest); lounge; indoor pool; 18-hole golf course; 2 tennis courts; exercise room; Jacuzzi; sauna; bike rentals; children's programs; activities desk; business center; limited room service; massage; babysitting; laundry service. *In room:* A/C, TV, dataport, minibar, coffeemaker, hair dryer, iron.

IN LYLE

Lyle Hotel ★ *Finds*   Located at the east end of the Gorge in the tiny town of Lyle, this old-fashioned hotel first opened for business in 1905. Today the rooms, though small and lacking private bathrooms, have a cozy, traditional feel, with quilts on the old wood or brass beds. Large windows let in lots of light. Best of all, there is an excellent restaurant on the ground floor, which makes this your best base for exploring the eastern end of the Gorge.

100 Seventh St. (P.O. Box 114), Lyle, WA 98635. © 509/365-5953. www.lylehotel.com. 10 units, all with shared bathrooms. $64 double. Rates include continental breakfast Mon–Sat. AE, MC, V. **Amenities:** Restaurant (International); lounge. *In room:* No phone.

IN GLENWOOD

Flying L Ranch ⟨⟩   With its meadows and ponderosa pines, this 160-acre ranch in a wide valley at the foot of Mount Adams is the ideal base for exploring this area. In summer, you can head up to the alpine meadows on the slopes of the mountain, and in winter, there are cross-country ski trails on the ranch and also nearby. While the two cabins, tucked under the pine trees, offer lots of room and privacy, the rooms in the old 1940s lodge have a classic ranch feel. Other rooms are in a separate guesthouse with a rooftop observation deck. The hot tub has a view of the mountain.

25 Flying L Lane, Glenwood, WA 98619. ℂ **888/682-3267** or 509/364-3488. Fax 509/364-3634. www. mt-adams.com. 14 units, 13 with private bathroom. $75 double with shared bathroom; $85–$110 double with private bathroom; $125–$150 cabin. 2-night minimum in cabins, 3-night minimum in cabins and rooms on holidays. Rates include full breakfast. AE, MC, V. **Amenities:** Jacuzzi; bikes. *In room:* No phone.

IN HOOD RIVER, OREGON

Columbia Gorge Hotel ⟨⟩⟨⟩   Just west of Hood River off I-84 and in business since shortly after 1915, this little oasis of luxury offers a genteel atmosphere that was once enjoyed by Rudolph Valentino and Clark Gable. With its yellow-stucco walls and red-tile roofs, this hotel would be at home in Beverly Hills, and the hotel gardens could hold their own in Victoria, British Columbia. The hotel is perched more than 200 feet above the river on a steep cliff, and it is difficult to take your eyes off the view. Unfortunately, the interior of the hotel has gone a little too long since it was last updated, and rooms are looking decidedly old-fashioned. Despite the canopy beds and brass beds, many of the rooms are rather cramped, as are the bathrooms, most of which have older fixtures. In addition to the hotel's famous breakfast, there is a complimentary champagne-and-caviar social hour each evening. On Sundays high tea is served.

4000 Westcliff Dr., Hood River, OR 97031. ℂ **800/345-1921** or 541/386-5566. Fax 541/386-9141. www. columbiagorgehotel.com. 40 units. $169–$259 double; $299–$379 suite. Rates include multi-course breakfast. AE, DC, DISC, MC, V. Pets accepted ($25). **Amenities:** Restaurant (Northwest/Continental); lounge; concierge; massage and spa treatments. *In room:* A/C, TV, dataport, hair dryer, iron, safe.

WHERE TO DINE

The dining rooms of **Bonneville Hot Springs Resort** in North Bonneville, **Dolce Skamania Lodge** in Stevenson, and the **Lyle Hotel** in Lyle are by far the best restaurants on the Washington side of the Gorge. See above for details.

IN HOOD RIVER, OREGON

Brian's Pourhouse ⟨⟩⟨⟩ ECLECTIC   Located in an old house a few blocks up the hill from downtown Hood River, this restaurant is a casual, fun place with very creative food. In summer, the big deck is the place to eat, and any time of year, the stylish little bar area is a cozy place for a cocktail or a local microbrew. For a starter, try the *unagi* (smoked eel) and avocado tempura roll, which is served with a mild wasabi cream sauce. You'll find other Asian influences on the menu in the form of coconut red curry and sesame-crusted ahi tuna with wasabi-potato rolls. However, there are also more straightforward dishes such as beef tenderloin with garlic mashed potatoes.

606 Oak St. ℂ 541/387-4344. www.brianspourhouse.com. Reservations not accepted. Main courses $6–$23. MC, V. Mon–Thurs 5–10pm; Fri 5–11pm; Sat 9am–2pm and 5–11pm; Sun 9am–2pm and 4–10pm.

Sixth Street Bistro ⟨⟩⟨⟩ AMERICAN/INTERNATIONAL   Just a block off Oak Street toward the river, the Sixth Street Bistro has an intimate little dining room and patio on the lower floor and a lounge with a balcony on the second floor. Each has its own entrance, but they share a menu. There are numerous international touches, such as chicken satay, coconut red curry, and hummus, and also juicy burgers. You'll find seasonal specials and vegetarian dishes as well.

509 Cascade Ave. © 541/386-5737. Reservations recommended. Main courses $7–$22. MC, V. Sun–Thurs 11:30am–9:30pm; Fri–Sat 11:30am–10pm.

Stonehedge Inn ★★ CONTINENTAL   Built as a summer vacation home in 1898, the Stonehedge Inn is in the woods west of downtown Hood River down a long gravel driveway off Cascade Drive. When you finally find the restaurant, you'll feel as though you've arrived at a remote Maine lodge. Inside the inn, there's a small lounge with a bar taken from an old tavern, and several dining rooms, all of which feel genuinely old-fashioned. Although the entree menu sticks to traditional Continental dishes such as steak Diane, rack of lamb, and chicken cordon bleu, you'll find some more creative offerings, such as grilled goat cheese with roasted garlic or seared ahi tuna, on the appetizer menu.

3405 Cascade Dr. © 541/386-3940. Reservations recommended. Main courses $12–$25. AE, DISC, MC, V. Daily 5–9 or 10pm.

10

Eastern Washington

For many people who live on the wet west side of the Cascades, life in Washington would be nearly impossible if it were not for the sunny east side of the mountains. Eastern Washington lies in the rain shadow of the Cascades, and many parts of the region receive less than 10 inches of rain per year. This lack of rain is also accompanied by plenty of sunshine—an average of 300 days per year. Statistics like these prove irresistible to folks from Puget Sound, who often head over to eastern Washington to dry out.

Though there's little rainfall, rivers such as the Columbia, which meanders through much of this region, have provided, with the assistance of dams such as the huge Grand Coulee Dam, sufficient irrigation water to make the region a major agricultural area. Apples, pears, cherries, wine grapes (and wine), wheat, and potatoes have become the staple crops of a land that once grew little more than sagebrush and bunchgrass. The Columbia River was also responsible thousands of years ago for creating the region's most fascinating geological wonders—a dry waterfall that was once four times larger than Niagara Falls and abandoned riverbeds known as coulees.

Down in the southeastern corner of the state, near the college and wheat-farming town of Walla Walla, the desert gives way to the Blue Mountains. It was near here that the region's first white settlers, Marcus and Narcissa Whitman, set up a mission in order to convert Native Americans to Christianity. They were later massacred by Cayuse Indians angered by the Whitmans' inability to cure a measles epidemic. In recent years, Walla Walla has become Washington's fastest-growing winery region. To the north of Walla Walla lie the Palouse Hills, a scenic region of rolling hills that are blanketed with the most productive wheat farms in the United States.

Though Yakima attracts sun-seekers from the western part of the state, it is Spokane, at the far eastern end of the state only a few miles from Idaho, that is the region's largest city. With its proximity to forests and mountains and its setting on the banks of the Spokane River, it appeals to those who value outdoor activities. The city's far easterly location, however, makes it seem less a part of the Northwest and more a part of the Rocky Mountain states.

1 Ellensburg: A Glimpse of the Wild West

110 miles SE of Seattle, 36 miles N of Yakima, 75 miles S of Wenatchee

Ellensburg, which lies on the edge of cattle- and sheep-ranching country just east of the last Cascade foothills, is a town with a split personality. On the one hand, it is a small college town, site of Central Washington University. However, it is also a classic cow town best known as the site of the Ellensburg Rodeo, one of the West's top rodeos. A downtown full of historic commercial buildings further adds to the character of this town, and proximity to the mountains and ski

Eastern Washington

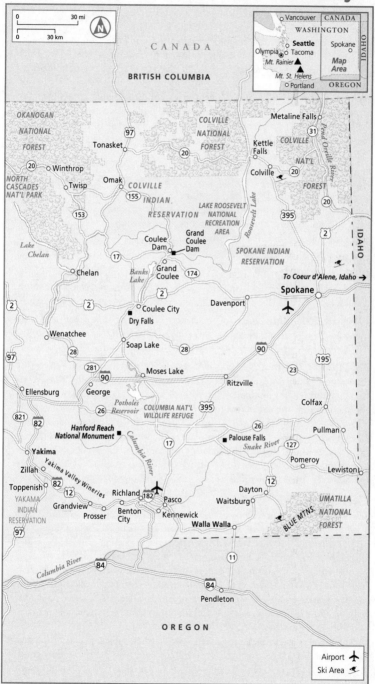

area at Snoqualmie Pass make it a good base for summer hiking or winter skiing. Although the town isn't really a destination per se, its proximity to Seattle and its sunny climate make it a quick escape from the Puget Sound rains.

Most of the buildings in the town's downtown historic district, one of the most attractive in the state, date from 1889, the year in which most of the town's commercial buildings were destroyed in a fire on the Fourth of July. Had it not been for this fire, the town would likely have become the state capital (due to its central location). But with only one commercial building remaining, how could the government set up business in Ellensburg? Instead of becoming the capital, the town became the site of the state college that is now Central Washington University.

While the Ellensburg Rodeo is responsible for perpetuating this town's Wild West image, the Clymer Museum, devoted to the works of John Clymer, who illustrated more than 80 *Saturday Evening Post* magazine covers, does its share as well. Adding one last unusual ingredient to the eclectic milieu of Ellensburg is the Chimpanzee and Human Communication Institute, where chimps have been taught to use American Sign Language.

ESSENTIALS

GETTING THERE   Ellensburg is on I-90. Just east of town, I-82 leads southeast to Yakima and the Tri-Cities area (Wash. 821 provides a scenic route south to Yakima). U.S. 97 leads north over Blewett Pass to Leavenworth and Wenatchee.

VISITOR INFORMATION   Contact the **Ellensburg Chamber of Commerce,** 609 N. Main St., Ellensburg, WA 98926 (© **888/925-2204** or 509/925-3137; www.visitellen.com or www.Ellensburg-chamber.com).

FESTIVALS   The third weekend of May each year sees the annual Western Art Association's **Ellensburg National Art Show & Auction** (© **509/962-2934**), which features works by some of the nation's finest Western artists. On the last weekend in July, the city stages its annual **Jazz in the Valley** festival (© **888/925-2204** or 509/925-2002), a 3-day binge of jazz and blues. The annual **Ellensburg Rodeo,** held each year on Labor Day weekend, is the town's biggest event and is one of the top 10 rodeos in the United States. For more information, contact the Ellensburg Rodeo and Kittitas County Fair, 609 N. Main St. (© **800/637-2444** or 509/962-7831; http://ellensburgrodeo.com).

EXPLORING THE TOWN

Ellensburg's most unusual attraction can be experienced at the university's **Chimpanzee and Human Communication Institute,** Nicholson Boulevard and D Street (© **509/963-2244;** www.cwu.edu/~cwuchci), a research facility that stages what it calls **"Chimposiums."** At these programs, visitors learn about the primate communication project and get to observe several chimpanzees that have learned to use American Sign Language (ASL). Among these chimps is the famous Washoe, which was the first chimpanzee to learn ASL. The programs, held on Saturday and Sunday, cost $10 for adults and $7.50 for students; reservations are recommended.

The Western art of Ellensburg native John Clymer is displayed at the **Clymer Museum of Art,** 416 N. Pearl St. (© **509/962-6416;** www.clymermuseum.com). A member of the prestigious Cowboy Artists of America, Clymer is best known for producing more than 80 *Saturday Evening Post* covers. The museum is open Monday through Saturday from 10am to 5pm (until 8pm on the first Fri of each month) and Sunday from noon to 5pm; admission by donation. In this same

The Gorge at George

Although it is roughly 150 miles from Seattle to the community of George, Washington, the town each summer attracts tens of thousands of music fans who drive from Seattle and all over the Northwest to attend concerts (primarily rock) at a natural amphitheater overlooking the Columbia River. **The Gorge Amphitheatre,** 754 Silica Rd. NW, George (www.hob.com/venues/concerts/gorge), is in a spectacular setting that's surrounded by basalt cliffs. Tickets are sold through **Ticketmaster (℃ 296/ 628-0888** in Seattle, 509/735-0500 in eastern Washington, or 509/453-7139 in Yakima; www.ticketmaster.com/venue/122913).

block you'll find Ellensburg's oldest art gallery. **Gallery One,** 408½ N. Pearl St. (℃ **509/925-2670**), features works by regional, national, and international artists. More art can be seen at the **Sarah Spurgeon Gallery,** Randall Hall, 14th Avenue and Nicholson Boulevard (℃ **509/963-2665**), on the campus of Central Washington University. This gallery is open Monday through Friday from 8:30am to 4:30pm and Saturday and Sunday from noon to 3pm; admission is free. For a look at some unique local art, cruise by **Dick & Jane's Spot,** 101 N. Pearl Street. The house and yard here are decorated with hundreds of colorful objects, including thousands of little reflective disks. However, the town's most famous work of art is the *Ellensburg Bull,* a cement statue that sits on a bench in a plaza in the downtown historic district.

Downtown you'll also find the **Kittitas County Museum,** 114 E. Third St. (℃ **509/925-3778**), which has an interesting collection of Native American artifacts, as well as a large rock and mineral collection that focuses on petrified wood. The museum is open Monday through Saturday from 10am to 4pm. Admission is by donation.

If you want to shop for some of the region's rare Ellensburg blue agate, stop by the **Ellensburg Agate & Bead Shop,** 201 S. Main St. (℃ **509/925-4998**). But be forewarned—this pale-blue semiprecious stone can be quite pricey.

Some 4½ miles southeast of town you'll find **Olmstead Place State Park** (℃ **509/925-1943**), a heritage site that preserves a pioneer homestead of the 1870s. Northwest of Ellensburg at exit 101 off I-90, in the town of Thorp, is the **Thorp Mill (℃ 509/964-9640;** www.thorp.org), an 1880s gristmill that now houses a museum; it's open Saturday and Sunday from 1 to 4pm.

Anyone wanting to cool off on a hot summer day should make for the waters of the nearby Yakima River, which offers lots of easy floating. **Rill Adventures,** 10471 Thorp Hwy. North (℃ **888/281-1561** or 509/964-2520; www.rillsonline. com), rents rafts, with prices ranging from $60 to $90 per day. The section of this river south of town, through Yakima Canyon, is a popular stretch of river with tubers and canoeists, and is a favorite of fly anglers as well.

WHERE TO STAY

The Inn at Goose Creek ⭐   Located just off I-90 on the south side of Ellensburg, this inn is sort of a cross between a highway off-ramp motel and a bed-and-breakfast inn. Though it's in a nondescript building surrounded by gas stations and fast-food restaurants, it keeps all this at bay with the over-the-top modern country decor in the lobby. All of the 10 suites here are also decorated to the max and each has a different theme (Ellensburg Rodeo, Victorian, Sports

Fan, Christmas). There are down comforters on all the beds, and all the rooms have whirlpool tubs.

1720 Canyon Rd., Ellensburg, WA 98926. © **800/533-0822** or 509/962-8030. Fax 509/962-8031. www.innatgoosecreek.com. 10 units. $89–$130 double. Rates include continental breakfast. AE, MC, V. *In room:* A/C, TV, dataport, fridge, coffeemaker, hair dryer, iron.

WHERE TO DINE

If you're in need of some espresso, pull up a saddle at the Cowboy Espresso Bar inside **Jaguar's,** 423 N. Pearl St. (© **509/962-6081**), a Western-clothing store. Alternatively, you can drive up to the window at **D & M Coffee,** 408 S. Main St. (© **509/962-6333**), which is located in a 1920s gas station, or step inside the **D&M Coffee** at Third and Pine streets (© **509/962-9333**), which is in a building that was once a gas station. If you're looking for a place to hang out and have a beer or glass of wine, check out **Pearl's on Pearl,** 311 N. Pearl St. (© **509/ 962-8899;** www.pearlsonpearl.com), a smoke-free bar and restaurant with live jazz, blues, and rock that attracts Ellensburg professionals and professors.

Valley Café ⭐ *Finds* INTERNATIONAL   Behind the shining black glass facade of this easily overlooked vintage cafe, you'll find a classic 1930s diner straight out of an Edward Hopper painting. Take a seat in one of the wooden booths and you'll swear you've stepped back in time. The menu, however, is quite contemporary and features such dishes as roasted rack of lamb with a cabernet-balsamic reduction, seafood coconut curry, and cioppino. At lunch, meals are just as likely to range the globe. Lots of local wines are available.

105 W. Third St. © **509/925-3050.** Main courses $8–$24. DISC, MC, V. Daily 11am–9pm.

The Yellow Church Cafe ⭐ AMERICAN   Though primarily an inexpensive college lunch place, this restaurant is well worth checking out for its setting in a little yellow church that was built back in 1923. Saturday and Sunday breakfasts are among the most popular meals here, and the baked goods are favorite items. Pastas and salads are good, and the dinner menu includes inexpensive steaks and prawn dishes that are usually good bets. There are always interesting specials listed on the blackboard. If you can't find a table on the main floor, check up in the choir loft.

111 S. Pearl St. © **509/933-2233.** www.yellowchurchcafe.com. Main courses $5–$9 lunch, $6.50–$19 dinner. AE, MC, V. Mon–Fri 11am–8pm; Sat–Sun 8am–8pm.

2 Yakima & the Wine Country

150 miles SE of Seattle, 92 miles NW of Richland, 195 miles SW of Spokane

Considering the fact that Washington is notorious for its rainfall, it may seem hard to believe that eastern Washington's Yakima Valley receives only about 8 inches of rain per year. Located only 3 hours from Seattle, Yakima is in another world—the sunny side of the Cascades. Despite the lack of rainfall, the area has become one of Washington's main apple-growing regions. Hops, used in making beer, are another important crop in the Yakima Valley, but it is grapes and the wines produced from those grapes that have been bringing the valley international attention in recent years. On a visit to Yakima, you can sample the area's bounties at fruit stands, wineries, and microbreweries.

The city of Yakima lies at the western end of the Yakima Valley winery region, while at the eastern end is the Tri-Cities area, which is comprised of the cities of Richland, Kennewick, and Pasco. Although the Tri-Cities area has its share of wineries, it is best known as the site of the Hanford Site, the huge military reservation where the first nuclear bomb was developed. Today Hanford is notorious for its many nuclear contamination sites, which luckily are well removed from any towns or vineyards, so there's no need to worry about glow-in-the-dark wine.

All the land around Yakima was once the homeland of the Yakama people. The first white settlers, Catholic missionaries, arrived in 1847 and set up their mission south of present-day Yakima, and by the 1850s growing hostilities between settlers and Native Americans had led to the establishment of Fort Simcoe, 38 miles west of Yakima. In 1880, when residents of Yakima City refused to sell land to the Northern Pacific Railroad, the railroad built North Yakima 4 miles away and proceeded to move 50 buildings from Yakima City to the new town site, which grew into the Yakima of today.

Despite the many wineries up and down the Yakima Valley, the region has never really caught on as a wine-touring destination and there are very few B&Bs or memorable restaurants in the region. This is due to several factors. First, the wineries begin more than 20 miles away from Yakima, and so the city of Yakima isn't exactly an ideal base for exploring this wine country. Also, the small towns scattered along the length of the Yakima Valley are basically farm towns and are certainly not what you would call quaint. In fact Sunnyside has stockyards, the stench of which permeates the town. Vineyards are just part of the picture here, and you'll have to drive through a lot of unattractive scenery to reach the wineries. However, despite these caveats, a visit to the Yakima Valley can be worthwhile if you are looking to familiarize yourself with Washington wine.

ESSENTIALS
GETTING THERE   Yakima is on I-82 at the junction with U.S. 12, which connects to I-5 south of Centralia. You can also get to Yakima on U.S. 97 (from Ellensburg from the north and just east of The Dalles, Oregon, from the south).

The Yakima Municipal Airport, 2300 W. Washington Ave., on the southern outskirts of town, is served by Horizon Airlines.

VISITOR INFORMATION   Contact the **Yakima Valley Visitors & Convention Bureau,** 101 N. Fair St., Yakima, WA 98901 (© **800/221-0751** or 509/575-3010; www.visityakima.com). For information on Toppenish, contact the **Toppenish Chamber of Commerce,** 5 S. Toppenish Ave. (P.O. Box 28), Toppenish, WA 98948 (© **509/865-3262**).

FESTIVALS   **Red Wine and Chocolate,** held each year over the Presidents' Day weekend, marks the start of the wine-tasting season at Yakima Valley wineries. The annual **Spring Barrel Tasting** on the last weekend in April is Yakima's biggest wine festival. During this event, the previous year's vintages are often tasted before being bottled. In late September, there's the **Catch the Crush** event, and then in November, there's **Thanksgiving in Wine Country.** Both of these are big wine-tasting weekends. Each year over the Fourth of July weekend the **Toppenish Pow Wow & Rodeo** brings crowds of people to Toppenish to watch broncobusters and Native American dances. The fourth full weekend in September sees the skies over Prosser fill with hot-air balloons in the **Great Prosser Balloon Rally.**

WINE-COUNTRY TOURING
Located on the same latitude as France's main wine regions, the **Yakima Valley** is Washington's premier wine region. The valley sees sunshine on about 300 days of the year, which, combined with the rich volcanic soil, provides near perfect

grape-growing conditions. The only thing missing here is rain. Central Washington is virtually a desert, but irrigation long ago overcame this minor inconvenience and today the area produces award-winning chardonnay, Riesling, chenin blanc, sauvignon blanc, semillon, gewürztraminer, cabernet sauvignon, merlot, lemberger, and muscat wines. Because of the clear weather here at harvest, and because freezing weather often arrives when there are still grapes on the vines, many wineries in the valley produce limited amounts of sweet and delicious ice wine, which is made from frozen berries. Quite a few wineries here are also now producing port.

The Yakima Valley wine country stretches roughly from Zillah (about 20 miles east of Yakima) to the Tri-Cities area (Richland, Pasco, and Kennewick), although the Tri-Cities area is officially in a Columbia Valley appellation. You can get a guide and map of the wine country from the Yakima Valley Visitors & Convention Bureau (see above) or the **Yakima Valley Winery Association,** P.O. Box 63, Prosser, WA 99350 (© **800/258-7270;** www.yakimavalleywine.com). This map covers the area from Zillah to Benton City's Red Hills region. For a map of Tri-Cities area wineries, contact the **Columbia Valley Winery Association,** P.O. Box 6644, Kennewick, WA 99336 (© **866/360-6611** or 509/628-8082; www.columbiavalleywine.com). However, even without a map, signs throughout the valley point the way to various vineyards and wineries, and you can just follow Yakima Valley Highway/Wine Country Road (U.S. 12) between Zillah and Prosser, dropping in at whichever wineries strike your fancy. There are more than 30 wineries in the valley, and you could easily spend a week here visiting them all. However, most people spend no more than a weekend in the area. We suggest picking no more than four or five to visit during a day of wine tasting. It's also advisable to have a designated driver.

THE ZILLAH AREA

Also, if you want to pick up some fresh Yakima Valley fruit or indulge in a fresh peach sundae (in season, of course), drop by **Donald Fruit & Mercantile,** 2560 Donald-Wapato Rd., Wapato (© **509/877-3115**), which first opened in 1911 and is reached by driving north from exit 44 off I-82. This country store is also the tasting room for Piety Flats Winery.

Bonair Winery ⚑   This small family-run winery just outside Zillah produces a number of semisweet wines (including a couple of different meads) and even some inexpensive red wines. They also do a variety of dry wines, including decent chardonnay. Good values and a good sense of humor make this winery a must if you are *not* a wine snob.

500 S. Bonair Rd., Zillah. © **509/829-6027.** www.bonairwine.com. Apr–Nov daily 10am–5pm; Dec–Mar Fri–Sun 10am–4:30pm. Take exit 50 off I-82, go north to Highland Dr., and then turn right on Bonair Rd.

Claar Cellars   Although the Claar Cellars winery is north of the Tri-Cities area, it has its main tasting room here in Zillah so as to reach more of the people touring the wine country. Claar Cellars produces only wines from estate-grown grapes, and the Rieslings and late-harvest Rieslings here can be quite good.

1001 Vintage Valley Pkwy., Zillah. © **509/829-6810.** www.claarcellars.com. Daily 10am–6pm. Take exit 52 off I-82.

Eaton Hill Winery ⚑   Housed in the old Rinehold Cannery building, this is the best place in the valley to get a quick education in how different wines of one varietal can be depending on how the grapes are grown and the wine is

---

Finds **Texas Tea?**

While in Zillah, don't miss the opportunity to see the **Teapot Dome gas station,** 14691 Yakima Valley Hwy. (© 509/829-5100), a national historic building built in 1922 in the shape of a giant teapot to call attention to a scandal in the administration of President Warren G. Harding. You'll find the teapot on the south side of I-82.

---

made. This winery focuses on cabernet sauvignon and chardonnay, and generally has a wide selection of vintages and varietals available.

530 Gurley Rd., Granger. © 509/854-2220. Feb–Nov Fri–Wed 10am–5pm; Dec–Jan daily noon–4pm. Take exit 58 off I-82; go west on Yakima Valley Hwy. then right on Gurley Rd.

Hyatt Vineyards ★ *Value*   With its wide lawns, valley views, and immaculately tended gardens, it's obvious that this winery does a brisk wedding business and is a good spot for a picnic. Their white wines are often good values, and they also do a wide range of red wines. One of the best reasons to drop by is to try their black muscat dessert wines.

2020 Gilbert Rd., Zillah. © 509/829-6333. www.hyattvineyards.com. Daily 11am–5pm (call for winter hours). Take exit 50 off I-82, go north to Highland Dr., turn left on Bonair Rd., and turn right on Gilbert Rd.

Maison de Padgett Winery ★★   Another of the valley's new wineries, this place does a very wide range of wines, including malbec and sherry. Although you might at first think the odd labels, cute wine names, and unusual bottles are just a way to distract you from mediocre wines, you'd be wrong. Sure there are some odd wines here, but there are also some superb (and pricey) wines.

2231 Roza Dr., Zillah. © 509/829-6412. Mar–Nov Thurs–Mon 11am–5pm; Dec–Feb by appointment. Take exit 52 off I-82, go east on First Ave., turn left on Fifth St., which becomes Roza Dr.

Paradisos del Sol ★★   Barrel-aged dry white wines are one of the hallmarks of winemaker Paul Vandenberg, who has also made wines for Portteus Vineyards (another of our favorite wineries). The wines made here at Paradisos del Sol are full-bodied, complex, and among the most distinctive wines in the state.

3230 Highland Dr., Zillah. © 509/829-9000. www.paradisosdelsol.com. Daily 11am–5pm. Take exit 52 off I-82, go east on First Ave., turn left on Fifth St., which becomes Roza Dr.; at Highland Dr., turn right.

Portteus Vineyards ★★   With excellent views across the valley, this winery produces some of the best red wines in the Yakima Valley. Bold, full-bodied wines are the hallmark here. While most of the wines here are in the $20 to $25 range, the very drinkable Rattlesnake Red weighs in at under $15.

5201 Highland Dr., Zillah. © 509/829-6970. www.portteus.com. Mon–Fri 10am–5pm; Sat 11am–5pm; Sun noon–4:30pm. Take exit 50 off I-82, go north, and then follow Highland east as far as it goes.

Silver Lake Winery ★   This is one of the state's larger wineries and has tasting rooms here and in Woodinville (near Seattle). Producing a wide range of wines, Silver Lake keeps prices reasonable and often has great sales and discounts on its wines. The tasting room is in the hills on the north side of the valley and has good views.

1500 Vintage Rd., Zillah. © 509/829-6235. www.silverlakewinery.com. Apr–Nov daily 10am–5pm; Dec–Mar Thurs–Mon 11am–4pm. Take exit 52 off I-82 and go north over the freeway, turn left on Cheyne Rd., right on Highland Rd., and left on Vintage Rd.

Tefft Cellars ✷ Tefft produces primarily easy drinking, moderately priced wines, including a good red table wine, cabernet sauvignon, and merlot. They also do an unusual cabernet port. Lots of good values are to be had here.

1320 Independence Rd., Outlook. © **888/549-7244** or 509/837-7651. www.tefftcellars.com. Daily 10am–5pm (Jan by appointment). Take exit 63 off I-82; go north on Outlook Rd. and west on Independence Rd.

Windy Point Vineyards This is one of the newer wineries in the Yakima Valley and is perched atop a hill with an outstanding view from the glass-walled tasting room. This family winery produces everything form Riesling to zinfandel.

420 Windy Point Dr., Wapato. © **509/877-4446**. Fri–Sun 10am–5pm. Closed Dec–Presidents' Weekend. Take exit 40 off I-82, go south on Yakima Valley Hwy. for 2 miles and turn left onto Parker Heights Rd., continue ½ mile to Windy Point Dr.

Wineglass Cellars ✷✷✷ *(Finds* This small husband-and-wife winery may be the most underrated and little known winery in the state. Owners/winemakers David and Linda Lowe produce only about 3,500 cases of wine a year, and almost everything they make is deliciously complex and cellar-worthy. Be sure to sample the reserve wines. The cabernet sauvignons and merlots are the highlights here.

260 N. Bonair Rd. © **509/829-3011**. www.wineglasscellars.com. Fri–Mon 10:30am–5pm. Closed Dec–Presidents' Weekend. Take exit 50 off I-82, go north to Highland Dr., turn left on Bonair Rd.

SUNNYSIDE

If you need some cheese to go with your wine, drop by Sunnyside's **Darigold Dairy Fair,** 400 Alexander Rd. (© **509/837-4321**), which is a half-mile south of I-82 at exit 67. A sort of circus atmosphere prevails, and ice cream and sandwiches are available, as well as plenty of cheese. Dairy Fair is open daily 8am to 6pm.

Washington Hills Cellars ✷ Just off the interstate in Sunnyside, you'll find, in a former Carnation building, one of the most versatile of the Yakima Valley wineries. Washington Hills produces wines under three different labels (and in three different price ranges). Most tend to be soft, ready-to-drink wines.

111 E. Lincoln Ave., Sunnyside. © **800/814-7004** or 509/839-9463. www.washingtonhills.com. Daily 9am–5pm. Take exit 67 off I-82, north on Midvale Rd. to Lincoln Ave.

PROSSER

Here in Prosser, at exit 80 off I-82, you can also stop in at **Chukar Cherry Company,** 320 Wine Country Rd. (© **509/786-2055**), and sample dried cherries and lots of other dried fruits and candies. The shop is open Monday through Saturday from 8am to 6pm and on Sunday from 8am to 4pm.

Chinook Wines ✷ Dry wines, both red and white, are the focus at this Prosser winery, which is a husband-and-wife operation. The reds are big and bold and tend to be fairly pricey. There's a pretty garden that's perfect for an afternoon picnic.

Wine Country Rd. at Wittkopf Loop, Prosser. © **509/786-2725**. www.chinookwines.com. May–Oct Sat–Sun noon–5pm. Take exit 82 off I-82 and go east on Wine Country Rd. (away from Prosser).

Columbia Crest ✷ Located roughly 25 miles south of Prosser on 2,500 acres of vineyards overlooking the Columbia River, Columbia Crest is one of the largest wineries in the state. Although it's out of the way, the winery is worth visiting for its dramatic setting and châteaulike facility.

Wash. 221, Paterson. © **888/309-WINE** or 509/875-2061. www.columbia-crest.com. Daily 10am–4:30pm. Take Wash. 221 south from Prosser.

The Hogue Cellars ★★   Located in an industrial park just off the freeway, Hogue is one of Washington's largest and most reliable wineries, which makes this a good place to visit if you're on a budget or just want to sample some decent Washington state wine. This winery produces three levels of wine; hopefully you'll get to sample some of the reserve wines.

2800 Lee Rd., Prosser. © **509/786-4557.** www.hoguecellars.com. Daily 10am–5pm. Take exit 82 off I-82 and go east on Wine Country Rd. (away from Prosser).

Kestrel Vintners ★★★   This winery produces premium cabernet sauvignon, merlot, syrah, and chardonnay, and you should be sure to pay to taste the reserve wines, which can be quite extraordinary. Winemaker Ray Sandidge has developed quite a following for his complex, full-bodied red wines. He's even started his own Sandidge Winery right next door and has done work for Chandler Reach as well.

2890 Lee Rd., Prosser. © **888/343-CORK** or 509/786-2675. Daily 10am–5pm. Take exit 82 off I-82, go east on Wine Country Rd., and turn left on Bennitz Rd. and then right on Lee Rd.

Pontin del Roza ★   This small family-owned winery is one of the oldest in the area and has been producing wines since 1984. They produce a variety of whites and reds, including good chenin blanc and sangiovese.

35502 N. Hinzerling Rd., Prosser. © **509/786-4449.** Daily 10am–5pm. Take exit 80 off I-82 and go north, then go east on Johnson Rd. and north on Hinzerling Rd.

Snoqualmie Vineyards ★   This is another of Washington's large wine producers; you'll find Snoqualmie wines in grocery stores all across the state. Predictably reliable wine at reasonable prices are the specialty. A good place to start if you're new to wine or aren't into spending a lot of money.

660 Frontier Rd., Prosser. © **509/786-2104.** www.snoqualmie.com. Daily 10am–5pm. Take exit 82 off I-82 and drive south on Frontier Rd.

Thurston Wolfe Winery ★   This small, family winery, located in an industrial park outside of Prosser, focuses its attentions on producing exclusively red wines—zinfandel, sangiovese, lemberger, and syrah. They also do a port.

2880 Lee Rd., Suite C. © **509/786-3313.** Thurs–Sun 11am–5pm. Closed Dec–Mar. Take exit 82 off I-82, go east on Wine Country Rd. and continue 300 ft. past Hogue Cellars.

Willow Crest Winery ★★   Set high in the hills north of Prosser, this is one of the Yakima Valley's smallest wineries and does a very limited variety of wines. However, since winemaker David Minick likes to experiment, you'll often find some rather unusual wines here, such as a syrah port and a syrah sparkling wine. Well worth the drive.

135701 Snipes Rd., Prosser. © **509/786-7999.** Sat–Sun 10am–5pm. Closed Dec–Mar. Take exit 80 off I-82, go north on Gap Rd., then right on Snipes Rd.

Yakima River Winery   Founded in 1978 as the third winery in eastern Washington, and located across the river from downtown Prosser, this is another of the old family-owned wineries in the valley. This winery specializes in lemberger and barrel-aged red wines but also does port (including a shiraz port).

143302 W. North River Rd., Prosser. © **509/786-2805.** www.yakimariverwinery.com. Daily 9am–5pm. Take exit 80 off I-82, go south toward Prosser, and turn right on North River Rd.

BENTON CITY

Chandler Reach ★★   This is one of the newest wineries in the valley, and at press time was still working on its new Tuscan villa–style winery and tasting room overlooking the Yakima River. However, they did have their barrel-aging

---

⌒Tips Let's Do Lunch

Because good restaurants are few and far between in the Yakima Valley, you should consider bringing along picnic supplies when you go out wine tasting. Lots of wineries have patios, picnic tables, and great views.

---

caves completed. At press time, Ray Sandidge, one of the region's best wine-makers, was producing the wines for Chandler Reach. Chandler Reach produces exclusively big red wines, with prices in the $20 to $25 range.

9506 W. Chandler Rd., Benton City. ⓒ 509/588-8800. www.chandlerreach.com. Call for current hours. Take exit 93 off I-82 and go north.

Hedges Cellars at Red Mountain 𝆑𝆑   Focusing its attentions on its caber-net sauvignon–merlot blend and an unusual sauvignon blanc–chardonnay blend, this winery, which has tasting rooms both at its Red Mountain vineyards and in the city of Issaquah near Seattle, is one of Washington's more reliable wineries.

53511 N. Sunset Rd., Benton City ⓒ 509/588-3155. www.hedgescellars.com. Apr–Dec Fri–Sun 11am–5pm. Take exit 96 off I-82, go east on Wash. 224, and then turn left on Sunset Rd.

Kiona Vineyards 𝆑   Located down a gravel road in the Red Hills region of the valley, this large winery produces a wide variety of easy-to-drink wines at moderate prices.

44612 N. Sunset Rd., Benton City. ⓒ 509/588-6716. Daily noon–5pm. Take exit 96 off I-82, go east on Wash. 224, and then turn left on Sunset Rd.

Oakwood Cellars   The view of Rattlesnake Mountain makes this boutique winery a good choice for a picnic on a day of tasting wines in the Benton City area. Oakwood Cellars produces a wide range of both red and white wines.

40504 N. DeMoss Rd., Benton City. ⓒ 509/588-5332. Thurs–Sun noon–5pm (winter by appointment). Take exit 96 off I-82; go east on Wash. 224, then left on DeMoss Rd.

Terra Blanca Vintners 𝆑   Despite the name, which translates as "white earth," this winery has its vineyards on the slopes of Red Mountain, which is known for producing outstanding wines. Tannic bordeaux blends, syrah, and chardonnay are the main focus, but they also produce viognier and several dessert wines. This is one of the only wineries in the state with barrel-aging caves.

34715 N. DeMoss Rd., Benton City. ⓒ 509/588-6082. www.terrablanca.com. Daily 11am–6pm (Dec 25–Feb 14 by appointment). Take exit 96 off I-82; go east on Wash. 224, then left on DeMoss Rd.

THE TRI-CITIES AREA

Barnard Griffin 𝆑   Lots of good white wines, including semillon, fumé blanc, and chardonnay, can usually be had here, and the winery also does a good job with its dessert wines. Prices are quite reasonable.

878 Tulip Lane, Richland. ⓒ 509/627-0266. www.barnardgriffin.com. Daily 10am–6pm. Take exit 3 off I-182 and turn left on Columbia Dr.

Bookwalter Winery 𝆑𝆑   Producing everything from light, drinkable picnic wines to complex, full-bodied cabernet sauvignon and merlot, this winery on the west side of Richland is one of the valley's more reliable operations. No mat-ter what your tastes, you're likely to find something here that you'll like.

894 Tulip Lane, Richland. ⓒ 877/667-8300 or 509/627-5000. www.bookwalterwines.com. Daily 10am–6pm. Take exit 3 off I-182 and turn left on Columbia Dr.

Gordon Brothers Cellars ★   This winery tasting room is located on the edge of the suburbs, and though the setting is none too impressive, the wines are generally quite good. Prices are generally in the $10 to $20 range.

5960 Burden Blvd., Pasco. © 509/547-6331. www.gordonwines.com. Daily 10am–6pm. Take exit 9 off I-182; go north on Rd. 68 and then east on Burden Blvd.

TOPPENISH & ITS MURALS

Before or after visiting wineries around Zillah, you might want to drive into the town of **Toppenish,** which was just a quiet little cow town until someone got the great idea of enlivening a few town walls with historical murals. Today, there are more than 60 **murals** depicting aspects of Toppenish history. You'll see these murals on walls all over town, and if you stop in at almost any store in town you can pick up a map to the murals. Though some murals have taken as much as a month to paint, each year on the first Saturday in June, crowds descend on the town to watch a new mural being created in just 1 day. One of the best ways to see the murals is on a horse-drawn trolley tour with **Toppenish Mural Tours** (© **509/697-8995**). Tours last 1½ hours and cost $12 for adults, $10 for seniors, and $4 for children 12 and under.

Toppenish is within the boundaries of the Yakama Indian Reservation, which operates the **Cultural Heritage Center** on U.S. 97 (© **509/865-2800**), just outside town. This large building, designed to resemble a traditional Yakama winter lodge, contains a museum, library, gift shop, and restaurant (see p. 340 for restaurant details). Exhibits in the museum present the history and culture of the Yakama people. The Yakama are well known for their beadwork and you'll find pieces for sale in the gift shop. The center is open daily from 8am to 5pm; admission is $4 for adults, $2 for seniors and students, $1 for children ages 7 to 10, 75¢ for children 6 and under.

Several other attractions in town provide glimpses into the area's history. The most entertaining of these is the **Northern Pacific Railway Museum,** 10 S. Asotin Ave. (© **509/865-1911;** www.nprymuseum.org; May–Oct Mon–Sat 10am–5pm, Sun noon–4pm; closed Nov–Apr; $2 adults, $1 seniors and children 17 and under accompanied by a parent), which has its museum in the town's 1911 railway depot and also operates, a few times a year, 22-mile scenic railway excursions on the Toppenish, Simcoe & Western Railroad. Excursions are $10 for adults and $5 for children ages 4 to 17. The Yakima Valley is one of the world's top hops-growing regions, and it is here that you will find the **American Hop Museum,** 22 S. B St. (© **509/865-HOPS**), where you can learn all about this crucial beer ingredient. The museum is open May through September daily from 11am to 4pm; admission is by donation.

Fort Simcoe, 27 miles west of Toppenish in the Cascade foothills, was established in the late 1850s because of conflicts between Indians and settlers. Today, the fort is preserved as **Fort Simcoe State Park Heritage Site** (© **509/874-2372**) and is the site of surprisingly elegant quarters that were used for only a few years before becoming the Indian Agency headquarters and school. The park's buildings are open April through September Wednesday through Sunday from 9:30am to 4:30pm. However, the grounds are open daily.

ATTRACTIONS & ACTIVITIES IN THE YAKIMA AREA

Local history is chronicled at the **Yakima Valley Museum** ★★, 2105 Tieton Dr. (© **509/248-0747;** www.yakimavalleymuseum.org), where a collection of restored horse-drawn vehicles is on display. There are also displays on the

---

Of Apples & Birdies

Golfers take note. Here in Yakima, you'll find a golf course with the world's only green on an apple-shaped island. The **Apple Tree Golf Course,** 8804 Occidental Ave. (© **509/966-5877;** www.appletreegolf.com), on the west side of town is rated among the best golf courses in the state but is most noteworthy for its unusual apple island. Greens fees are $22 to $55.

Yakama tribe and on former Supreme Court justice and environmentalist William O. Douglas, who was a Yakima resident. Perhaps the museum's most enjoyable exhibit is a functioning replica of a 1930s soda fountain. The museum is open Tuesday through Sunday from 11am to 5pm; admission is $3 for adults, $1.50 for seniors and students. The museum also operates the **H. M. Gilbert Homeplace,** an 1898 Victorian farmhouse, at 2109 W. Yakima Ave. This historic home is open by appointment, and admission is $3 for adults and $1.50 for seniors and students.

If you're interested in learning more about the other fruits of this region (apples, pears, cherries), drop by the **Washington's Fruit Place Visitor Center,** 105 S. 18th St. (© **509/576-3090;** www.fruitplace.com), which is located east of downtown off Yakima Avenue. Hours vary with the seasons, so call ahead.

Extending between Union Gap and Selah Gap, the **Yakima Greenway** follows the banks of the **Yakima River,** with 10 miles of paved pathways within the greenway. The easiest place to access the path is at Sherman Park on Nob Hill Boulevard. In summer, **kayaking, rafting, and tubing** are popular on this section of the river, and the **bird-watching** is good year-round.

If you'd like to see another scenic stretch of the river, head north to Selah and then take Wash. 821 north through the **Yakima River Canyon.** The river has been around for longer than the surrounding hills, which have risen concurrent with the river slicing through them.

ATTRACTIONS & ACTIVITIES IN THE TRI-CITIES AREA

If you're interested in learning more about the history (including the nuclear history), science, and technology of this region, pay a visit to the **Columbia River Exhibition of History, Science & Technology,** 95 Lee Blvd., Richland (© **509/ 943-9000;** www.crehst.org), which is located adjacent to the attractive Howard Amon Park in downtown Richland. Be sure to ask to watch the video on the great floods that scoured this landscape during the last ice age. The museum is open Monday through Saturday from 10am to 5pm and Sunday from noon to 5pm. Admission is $3.50 for adults, $2.75 for seniors, and $2.50 for students.

Up river from the Tri-Cities area are both the Hanford Site (where the plutonium for the first nuclear bombs was made) and the Hanford Reach National Monument, which preserves the last free-flowing stretch of the Columbia River in the United States. Although there are some remote areas of the monument that are accessible by vehicle, the best way to see this national monument is on the jet boat tours offered by **Columbia River Journeys** (© **888/486-9119** or 509/734-9941; www.columbiariverjourneys.com). The 4-hour tours cost $45 for adults and $35 for children. Along the way you'll see not only the wild shores of the Columbia River but also the nuclear reactors of the Hanford Site.

WHERE TO STAY

For a list of bed-and-breakfast inns in the wine country, contact the **Yakima Valley Winery Association,** P.O. Box 63, Prosser, WA 99350 (© **800/258-7270;** www.yakimavalleywine.com).

IN YAKIMA

Birchfield Manor ★★   Located 2½ miles east of Yakima, Birchfield Manor is surrounded by pastures and is well known for its elegant dinners (see below for restaurant review). Both upstairs from the dining room in the 1910 Victorian farmhouse and in a new building constructed to resemble a vintage home, you'll find antiques-filled guest rooms, most of which have good views out over the countryside. Several of these rooms have fireplaces, whirlpool tubs, and decks to take in the view. Breakfasts here are nearly as legendary as the dinners and are a great start for a day of wine-country touring. Note that the rooms in the new building have TVs and phones.

2018 Birchfield Rd., Yakima, WA 98901. © 800/375-3420 or 509/452-1960. www.birchfieldmanor.com. 11 units. $119–$219 double. Rates include full breakfast. Children 8 and older welcome. AE, DC, DISC, MC, V. **Amenities:** Restaurant (Continental); outdoor pool; limited room service. *In room:* A/C, coffeemaker, hair dryer, iron, no phone.

Oxford Inn ★   Located east of I-82 on the banks of the Yakima River, these are Yakima's most pleasant and popular budget accommodations. As such it regularly books up on weekends. The rooms are spacious, and many have balconies overlooking the river. Most also have refrigerators. Walkers and joggers will be pleased to find a 10-mile riverside walking/biking path running past the motel. Right next door you'll find the affiliated Oxford Suites, which offers larger rooms and complimentary buffet breakfasts.

1603 Terrace Heights Dr., Yakima, WA 98901. © 800/521-3050 or 509/457-4444. Fax 509/453-7593. www. oxfordsuites.com. 92 units. $69–$95 double. Rates include continental breakfast. AE, DC, DISC, MC, V. Pets accepted ($15 nonrefundable deposit). **Amenities:** Outdoor pool; exercise room; Jacuzzi; coin-op laundry; dry cleaning. *In room:* A/C, TV, fridge, coffeemaker.

IN THE TRI-CITIES AREA

Hampton Inn Richland/Tri-Cities ★★ *Kids*   Located right on the banks of the Columbia River adjacent to Richland's Howard Amon Park, this newer hotel claims the best location of any hotel in the Tri-Cities area. Not only do you have the walking paths and green lawns of the park right next door, but there are good restaurants within a short walk. Rooms are well designed and comfortable and many have balconies overlooking the river. With the indoor pool, complimentary breakfast, and park next door, this is a good bet for families.

486 Bradley Blvd., Richland, WA 99352. © 800/HAMPTON or 509/943-4400. Fax 509/943-1797. www. hamptoninn.com. 130 units. $83–$99 double; $225 suite. Rates include continental breakfast. Children under 18 stay free in parent's room. AE, DC, DISC, MC, V. **Amenities:** Indoor swimming pool; exercise room; Jacuzzi; airport courtesy shuttle; business center; coin-op laundry; laundry service; dry cleaning. *In room:* A/C, TV, dataport, fridge, coffeemaker, hair dryer, free local calls.

WHERE TO DINE

IN YAKIMA

If you're looking for someplace to hoist a pint of microbrew ale, **Grant's Brewery Pub** ★★, 32 N. Front St. (© **509/575-2922;** www.grants.com), housed in Yakima's restored train station, is the place. This is the oldest brewpub in the country.

Barrel House ⭐ NORTHWEST   Located in downtown Yakima, this casual wine bar and restaurant is a great place to end a day of wine tasting if you aren't in the mood to get dressed up and go someplace formal. You can get a gourmet burger or steak sandwich, but you can also get good grilled prawns and salmon with a Chinese-style hoisin glaze. There are lots of Washington wines available by the glass, and wine-tasting flights are available also. You'll find this restaurant on the same block as the Greystone Inn and Café Mélange (around the corner).

22 N. First St. ⓒ 509/453-3769. www.barrelhouse.net. Reservations recommended. Main courses $8–$19. AE, MC, V. Mon–Thurs 11:30am–11pm; Fri–Sat 11:30am–midnight; Sun 4–10pm.

Birchfield Manor Country Inn ⭐⭐ CONTINENTAL   Birchfield Manor, a grand old farmhouse on the eastern outskirts of Yakima, doubles as both Yakima's best B&B (see above) and its best restaurant. The dining room looks as if a wealthy family had cleared out the regular furniture and brought in a few extra tables for a holiday dinner. The menu changes with the season and includes a choice of five or six entrees, and while the house specialty is salmon in puff pastry with a chardonnay sauce, other offerings can be very tempting as well. The filet mignon with cabernet sauce and steak Diane with a brandy-cream sauce are two other standout dishes here. The dinner includes fresh-baked bread, an appetizer, and salad.

2018 Birchfield Rd. ⓒ 509/452-1960. www.birchfieldmanor.com. Reservations required. 5-course dinner $29–$39. AE, DC, DISC, MC, V. Seatings Thurs–Fri 7pm, Sat 6 and 8:45pm.

Café Mélange ⭐ ITALIAN   It's small and inconspicuous, but this restaurant has long been one of Yakima's best and most popular restaurants. Pastas were long the specialty, but you can now get more substantial meals as well. Try the duck with huckleberry-port sauce, which is available both as an appetizer and as an entree. Keep an eye out for the delicious smoked-salmon ravioli with basil-cream sauce. A good wine list includes lots of local wines.

7 N. Front St. ⓒ 509/453-0571. Reservations recommended. Complete meals $8.50–$23. AE, MC, V. Mon–Thurs 5–8:30pm; Fri–Sat 5–9:30pm.

Greystone Restaurant ⭐⭐ NEW AMERICAN   Housed in, you guessed it, a gray stone building, this restaurant has for more than 20 years now been Yakima's favorite upscale downtown dining establishment. With its historic character, lively little bar, and convivial atmosphere, this is an excellent place to end a day of wine tasting. Gravlax salmon, pan-fried oysters, and spicy south-of-the-border-style crab cakes all make good starters here, before moving on to spicy prawns in Tabasco-cream sauce or salmon with a sun-dried tomato sauce. Desserts are pure comfort foods—brownies, ice cream, cheesecake. Of course, there's a long list of regional wines.

5 N. Front St. ⓒ 509/248-9801. www.greystonerestaurant.com. Reservations recommended. Main courses $14–$35. AE, DISC, MC, V. Tues–Sat 6–10pm (bar opens at 4:30pm).

IN ZILLAH & TOPPENISH

Heritage Inn Restaurant ⭐ *Finds* AMERICAN/NATIVE AMERICAN Located on the grounds of the Yakama Nation Cultural Heritage Center, this casual restaurant is noteworthy for its Native American dishes, including a traditional Yakama salmon stew and fry bread. In fact, even the salad bar comes with fry bread. There are also buffalo burgers, buffalo steaks, and buffalo stew. For dessert, don't pass up the huckleberry pie.

Yakama Nation Cultural Heritage Center, 280 Buster Rd., Toppenish. ⓒ 509/865-2551. Main courses $4–$19. MC, V. Mon–Sat 7:30am–3pm.

IN SUNNYSIDE

Snipes Mountain Microbrewery & Restaurant ☆ PUB FARE   While it might at first seem treasonous to dine at a brewpub in the heart of wine country, keep in mind that the Yakima Valley is also one of the nation's main hops-growing regions. While most of the food here is fairly basic (burgers, sandwiches, pizza), you can also get seafood satay and hazelnut-crusted rack of lamb. The beers are decent, and local wines are also available. Basically, this is one of the only decent places to eat between Yakima and the Tri-Cities area.

905 Yakima Valley Hwy. ✆ **509/837-2739.** Main courses $6–$22. AE, DISC, MC, V. Sun–Thurs 10am–10pm; Fri–Sat 11am–11pm.

IN GRANDVIEW

Dykstra House Restaurant ☆ ITALIAN/CONTINENTAL   This eclectic eatery, housed in a historic building that dates from 1914, is primarily a lunch spot, but on Friday and Saturday nights, dinners are also served. Friday is Italian night and usually features familiar standards. Saturday night is a bit more eclectic, and there might be salmon in puff pastry, chicken Mediterranean, or pork loin. Lunches are equally unpredictable—you never know what might show up on the menu, which makes a meal here all the more fun. There's a good selection of local wines to accompany meals.

114 Birch Ave. ✆ **509/882-2082.** Reservations required for dinner. Main courses $7 lunch, $12–$22 dinner. AE, DISC, MC, V. Tues–Thurs 10am–4pm; Fri 10am–4pm and 6–9pm; Sat 11am–2pm and 6–9pm.

IN THE TRI-CITIES AREA

If you're just in the mood for some pub food and a microbrew, head to **Atomic Ale Brewpub & Eatery,** 1015 Lee Blvd., Richland (✆ **509/946-5465**), which is just a block off Richland's George Washington Way in downtown Richland.

Aioli's ☆☆ (Finds) MEDITERRANEAN   Half a block from Richland's riverfront Howard Amon Park, you'll find one of the most enjoyable little restaurants in central Washington. With only a handful of tables and a tiny wine bar, Aioli's is a cozy place with a suitably Mediterranean decor that is surprisingly chic. The best way to eat here is to assemble an assortment of tapas, and then, if you're still hungry, order some more. Keep an eye out for the chicken made with cumin, coriander, and cinnamon. Plenty of wines by the glass and by the bottle make this restaurant a must if you're in the area on a wine-tasting trip.

94 Lee Blvd., Richland. ✆ **509/942-1914.** Tapas $3.75–$7.75; main courses $6.75–$16. AE, DISC, MC, V. Tues–Thurs 11am–8pm; Fri–Sat 11am–9pm.

Sundance Grill ☆☆ CONTINENTAL/NORTHWEST   The Sundance Grill is the Tri-Cities' most contemporary restaurant, and it's the closest you'll come in this area to a dash of urban chic. The menu mixes traditional with contemporary. You might start your meal with escargot or crab cakes accompanied by Thai dipping sauce and then move on to broiled or seared salmon topped with strawberry-mango salsa or perhaps prime rib with apple-horseradish sauce. Before ordering a big meal, you might want to first take a look at the dessert tray.

450 Columbia Point Dr., Richland. ✆ **509/942-7120.** Reservations recommended. Main courses $7–$13 at lunch, $18–$30 at dinner. AE, DISC, MC, V. Daily 11am–4pm and 5–9:30pm.

3 Walla Walla

50 miles E of Richland/Pasco/Kennewick, 155 miles S of Spokane, 39 miles NE of Pendleton

Although Walla Walla is perhaps best known as the home of the Walla Walla sweet onion, in recent years the town has become the epicenter of a burgeonir wine industry. New wineries have been popping up as fast as champagne corks on New Year's Eve, making this town the single best locale in the state for a few days of wine touring. The explosion of wineries has also brought on something of a downtown renaissance that includes a restored historic hotel, new restaurants, and a few wine bars.

Before there was wine, it was onions that made Walla Walla famous (well, maybe not exactly famous). The Walla Walla onion is a big sweet variety, similar to the Vidalia onion of Georgia, and owes its sweetness not to sugar but to a high water content and a low sulfur content. These onions, which can weigh as much as 2 pounds, are legendary around the Northwest as the very best onions for putting on burgers at summer barbecues. Between June and August each year, produce stands all over the area sell big bags of these sweet onions. There's even a Walla Walla Sweet Onion Festival here in early July.

This is also a college town with three schools of higher learning: Walla Walla College, Whitman College, and Walla Walla Community College. Due in large part to these colleges, the town wears a rather cultured air. The town's residential streets, lined with stately old homes and large shade trees, add yet another layer to Walla Walla's character. A stroll or drive through the town's old neighborhoods conjures up times past when the pace of life was slower.

Walla Walla is also one of the oldest communities in the Northwest and was the site of both an early mission and one of the region's first forts. Before white settlers arrived, the area was home to several Indian tribes, and it is from these tribes that the town's name, which means "many waters" or "small, rapid streams" has come.

ESSENTIALS

GETTING THERE   Walla Walla is on U.S. 12, 45 miles east of I-82/I-182 in the Tri-Cities area. From I-82 west of Richland, take I-182 to Pasco and continue south and then west on U.S. 12. From Pendleton, Oregon, and I-84, take Ore. 11 north. From Spokane, take U.S. 195 south to Colfax, continuing south on Wash. 26 and then Wash. 127. In Dodge, you pick up U.S. 12 and continue south to Walla Walla.

Walla Walla Regional Airport (© **509/525-3100**) is served by Horizon Airlines.

VISITOR INFORMATION   Contact the **Walla Walla Area Chamber of Commerce,** 29 E. Sumach St. (P.O. Box 644), Walla Walla, WA 99362 (© **877/ WWVISIT;** www.wallawalla.org).

GETTING AROUND   Rental cars are available in Walla Walla through Hertz and Budget.

FESTIVALS   In early May there's the **Walla Walla Balloon Stampede,** and in mid-July there's the **Walla Walla Sweet Onion Festival.** Area wine festivals include the **Spring Barrel Tasting** over the first two weekends in May and the **Holiday Barrel Tasting** on the first weekend in December.

EXPLORING THE TOWN

The **Whitman Mission National Historic Site** (© **509/522-6360;** www. nps.gov/whmi), 7 miles west of Walla Walla just off U.S. 12, is dedicated to a tragic page in Northwest history. Missionaries Marcus and Narcissa Whitman were some of the very first settlers to travel overland to the Northwest and arrived in this area in 1836. Although the Whitmans had come here to convert

Indians, Marcus Whitman was also a doctor and often treated the local Cayuse people. During the mid-1840s a wagon train brought a measles epidemic to the area, and the Cayuse, who had no resistance to the disease, began dying. Though Whitman was able to save his own family, most of the Cayuse who contracted the disease died from it. Legend has it that the Cayuse had a tradition of killing medicine men who could not cure an illness, and on November 29, 1847, several Cayuse attacked and killed the Whitmans and 11 other residents of the mission. The massacre at the Whitman mission prompted a war on the Cayuse and a demand for territorial status for what was at that time the Oregon country. In 1848, in response to pleas brought about by the Whitman massacre, Oregon (which at that time included present-day Washington state) became the first territory west of the Rocky Mountains.

Today nothing remains of the mission, but a trail leads through the mission site and the locations of buildings are outlined with concrete. An interpretive center provides historical background on the mission and includes numerous artifacts from the days when the Whitmans worked with the Cayuse. The site is open daily (except Thanksgiving, Christmas, and New Year's Day) until dusk; the museum is open from 8am to 6pm in summer and from 8am to 4:30pm in other months. Admission is $3 per person or $5 per family.

In town, you'll find the **Fort Walla Walla Museum Complex,** 755 Myra Rd. (② **509/525-7703;** www.fortwallawallamuseum.org). The museum is a collection of pioneer-era buildings, including log cabins, a one-room schoolhouse, an old railway station, and several other buildings. It's open April through October, daily from 10am to 5pm. Admission is $6 for adults, $5 for seniors and students, and $2 for children ages 6 to 12, free for children under 6. In addition to the displays on pioneer life, there's a large collection of horse-era farming equipment, including an old combine pulled by 33 life-size fiberglass mules.

WINE TOURING

Although Washington's main winery region lies to the west of the Tri-Cities area, the Walla Walla area has seen a proliferation of wineries recently and has become the state's hottest new wine region. The climate and soils are perfect for growing wine grapes, and the emphasis is now on syrah grapes. In fact, because Walla Walla is such an attractive town, this is a far more appealing wine-touring region than the Yakima Valley. In addition to the area wineries listed below, which are open to the public on a regular basis, there are some that are generally only open by appointment or on a couple of weekends a year.

IN WALLA WALLA

Amavi Cellars ★★   This is one of the newer wineries in Walla Walla and is a sister winery to the celebrated Pepper Bridge Winery. Although Amavi doesn't produce very many varietals, what they do make tends to be complex and delicious. You'll find the tasting room, which incorporates an 1890s log cabin, next door to Canoe Ridge Vineyard.

635 N. 13th Ave. ② 509/525-3541. www.amavicellars.com. Tues–Sat 11am–5pm. From U.S. 12, go south on W. Pine St. and then right on 13th Ave.

Canoe Ridge Vineyard ★   Taking its name from a nearby vineyard region, this winery is in an old streetcar engine house on the outskirts of Walla Walla. The emphasis is on cabernet sauvignon and merlot, which tend to be very tannic, but for our money, the white wines are better and are also better values.

1102 W. Cherry St. ℭ **509/527-0885.** www.canoeridgevineyard.com. May–Sept daily 11am–5pm; Oct–Apr daily 11am–4pm. From U.S. 12, go south on W. Pine St. and then right on 13th Ave.

Cayuse Vineyards ★★ Located just down the street from the Waterbrook tasting room, this winery, under the direction of French winemaker Christophe Baron, produces superb Rhone- and bordeaux-style wines, with the focus on deliciously smooth and oaky syrah and viognier.

17 E. Main St. ℭ **509/526-0686.** www.cayusevineyards.com. Hours vary throughout the year, call ahead. From U.S. 12, take Second Ave. to Main St.

Patrick M. Paul Vineyards ★ In business since 1988, this is one of the smaller wineries in the area and produces only about 350 cases of wine per year. They are best known for their cabernet franc, but also produce cabernet sauvignon and merlot.

1554 School Ave. ℭ **509/526-0676.** Sat–Sun 1–4pm. From U.S. 12, take Wilbur Ave. south to Alder St., turn left, and continue to School Ave.

Seven Hills Winery ★ Housed in the same renovated woodworking-mill building that also houses the Whitehouse-Crawford Restaurant, this winery produces some excellent red wines, including merlot and syrah. Most wines are in the $20 to $30 range.

212 N. Third Ave. ℭ **877/777-7870** or 509/529-7198. www.sevenhillswinery.com. May–Sept Tues–Sat 11am–4pm; Oct–Apr Thurs–Sat noon–4pm.

Waterbrook Winery ★ Although Waterbrook Winery itself is located in nearby Lowden, the winery's tasting room is in downtown Walla Walla. The focus here is on cabernet sauvignon and merlot in the $15 to $25 range. Whites include chardonnay, sauvignon blanc, and the less familiar viognier, all of which can be both quite drinkable and very reasonably priced. There are some good values to be had here.

31 E. Main St. ℭ **509/522-1262.** www.waterbrook.com. Daily 10:30am–4:30pm.

WEST OF WALLA WALLA

L'Ecole No. 41 ★ Housed in a former elementary school and using children's art on its labels, this is one of the oldest wineries in this region. This winery started with semillon and merlot, and the semillon is still one of their best wines, though the chardonnays and cabernet merlots are good also. The semillon tends to be in the $15 to $20 range.

41 Lowden School Rd., Lowden. ℭ **509/525-0940.** www.lecole.com. Daily 11am–4pm (call for winter hours). On U.S. 12, 12 miles west of Walla Walla.

Three Rivers Winery This large winery may be the wave of the future for the Walla Walla wine business. Housed in a large building in the middle of the Walla Walla farm country, Three Rivers produces a wide range of wines from robust syrahs and sangioveses to late-harvest gewürztraminer. Red wines tend to be high in tannins and high in price.

5641 W. Hwy. 12 ℭ **509/526-9463.** www.threeriverswinery.com. Daily 10am–6pm. Located 8 miles west of Walla Walla on U.S. 12.

Woodward Canyon Winery ★★ This winery is well known in the Northwest for its full-bodied red wines and vineyard-designate chardonnays and is one of Washington's best wineries. The winery's Nelms Road red wines usually come in at under $20 and are a particularly good value. The tasting room is in a renovated old farmhouse adjacent to the winery.

11920 W. Hwy. 12, Lowden. © **509/525-4129**. www.woodwardcanyon.com. Spring and summer Mon–Sat 10am–5pm, Sun noon–5pm. On U.S. 12, 12 miles west of Walla Walla.

EAST OF WALLA WALLA

At the Walla Walla Airport, you'll find several small wineries. These include **Reininger,** 720 C St. (© **509/522-1994;** www.reiningerwinery.com; open by appointment), **Russell Creek Winery,** C Street and Aeronica Avenue (© **509/386-4401;** www.russellcreek-winery.com; open daily 10am–5pm), **Tamarack Cellars,** 700 C St. (© **509/526-3533;** www.tamarackcellars.com; open Sat 10am–4pm or by appointment), and **Buty,** 535 E. Cessna Ave. (© **509/527-0901;** www.butywinery.com; open daily 11am–4pm).

Dunham Cellars Located adjacent to the Walla Walla airport, this winery produces an exceptional red blend called trutina, the composition of which varies from year to year. The wines made here are for the most part big, long-keeping reds.

150 E. Boeing Ave. © **509/529-4685**. www.dunhamcellars.com. Daily 11am–4pm. Take the airport exit off U.S. 12 east of downtown.

Walla Walla Vintners 🅐 This small winery does only red wines and in the past has produced some excellent cabernet sauvignon and merlot. They also make sangiovese, cabernet franc, and a red cuvee.

225 Vineyard Lane. © **509/525-4724**. www.wallawallavintners.com. Mar–Dec Sat 10:30am–4:30pm; Jan–Feb Sat 1–4:30pm. Located east of town off Mill Creek Rd.

SOUTH OF WALLA WALLA

Glen Fiona 🅐 Although it focuses almost exclusively on syrah, this winery still manages to produce a range of distinctively different wines. Prices range from $15 to $45, so there's usually something for almost any budget.

1249 Lyday Lane. © **509/522-2566**. www.glenfiona.com. Sat 11am–4pm. Drive south on Wash. 125, turn left on Old Milton Hwy., turn right on Braden Rd., and right on Lyday Lane.

Pepper Bridge Winery 🅐🅐 Crafting ultra-premium wines from estate-grown grapes, Pepper Bridge is one of the state's premier producers of bordeaux-style wines, with the emphasis on cabernet sauvignon. A state-of-the-art gravity-flow winery ensures as little handling of the grapes as possible, which produces smoother, more cellar-worthy wines.

1704 J.B. George Rd. © **509/525-6502**. www.pepperbridge.com. Mon–Sat 10am–4pm. Drive south on Wash. 125, turn left on Old Milton Hwy, turn right on Pepper Bridge Rd., and then left on J.B. George Rd.

Rulo Winery 🅐🅐 *(Finds* This small, family-run winery on the south side of town produces outstanding and reasonably priced syrah and viognier. This latter is a delicious, food-friendly white wine with a wonderful nose. Don't miss this winery. They also produce some outstanding chardonnays.

2525 Pranger Rd. © **509/525-7856**. www.rulowinery.com. Open by appointment. Drive south on Wash. 125, turn left on Old Milton Hwy., and then right on Pranger Rd.

SPORTS & OUTDOOR ACTIVITIES

Though the land immediately surrounding Walla Walla is rolling farm country, less than 20 miles to the east the **Blue Mountains** rise to more than 6,000 feet. Hiking, mountain biking, fishing, and hunting are all popular in these little-visited mountains. For more information, contact the **Walla Walla Ranger District,** 1415 W. Rose St., Walla Walla, WA 99362 (© **509/522-6290;** www.fs.fed.us/r6/uma).

WHERE TO STAY

Green Gables Inn ⭐   Located on a quiet, shady street, this large 1909 home, with its three large front gables, is only a block from the Whitman College campus, which makes it a good choice if you are here on college business or to visit your kids. Two sitting rooms downstairs are furnished with antiques and have fireplaces at each end that make it quite cozy on a chilly evening. Guest room names are from the book *Anne of Green Gables.* Dryad's Bubble is filled with Maxfield Parrish prints and has a claw-foot tub, while in the master suite, you'll find a fireplace, whirlpool tub, deck, and mahogany furniture. The carriage house easily sleeps four and has 1½ bathrooms and a kitchen.

922 Bonsella St., Walla Walla, WA 99362. © 888/525-5501 or 509/525-5501. www.greengablesinn.com. 5 units, 1 carriage house. $115–$145 double; $145 carriage house for 2, $35 each additional guest. Rates include full breakfast. AE, DISC, MC, V. Children over age 12 welcome in main house; younger children welcome in carriage house. *In room:* A/C, TV/VCR, fridge, hair dryer, no phone.

Inn at Abeja ⭐⭐ *Finds*   Set on a classically picturesque farm a few miles outside of town, this inn is surrounded by green lawns and big shade trees. The main house's wide veranda, hammocks under the trees, and colorful perennial gardens all add up to the quintessential farm getaway everyone imagines when they think of running away to their own green acres. Guest rooms are in a collection of converted outbuildings, including an old summer kitchen, a bunkhouse, and even the old chicken coop (which now has vaulted ceilings and its own kitchen). An on-site winery makes this an ideal place to use as a base for a wine tour of the Walla Walla area.

2014 Mill Creek Rd., Walla Walla, WA 99362. © 509/522-1234. www.abeja.net. 5 units. $185–$245 double. Rates include full breakfast. MC, V. Pets accepted ($15). *In room:* A/C, TV, kitchen, fridge, coffeemaker, hair dryer, iron.

Marcus Whitman Hotel ⭐⭐   Originally opened in 1928, this historic highrise hotel in downtown Walla Walla underwent a complete restoration a few years ago and is now the finest hotel in this corner of the state; it makes an excellent base for a Walla Walla wine tour. Not only is there an excellent restaurant and wine bar on the premises, but several others are within a few blocks of the hotel. Guest rooms were designed with a classic elegance to match that of the lobby, which is filled with dark wood paneling, ornate plasterwork, and lots of original details. Most of the guest rooms are in a modern addition, so if you absolutely must stay in the original tower, you'll have to spring for one of the luxurious suites. Other than the suites, the best rooms are the king executives, which are spacious and well designed.

6 W. Rose St., Walla Walla, WA 99362. © 866/826-9422 or 509/525-2200. Fax 509/524-1747. www.marcus whitmanhotel.com. 91 units. $75–$139 double; $149–$279 suite. Rates include continental breakfast. AE, DC, DISC, MC, V. **Amenities:** Restaurant (Northwest); lounge; exercise room; concierge; business center; laundry service; dry cleaning. *In room:* A/C, TV, dataport, coffeemaker, hair dryer, iron.

WHERE TO DINE

For breakfast, lunch, or snacks, **Merchants Ltd.,** 21 E. Main St. (© **509/525-0900**), has long been Walla Walla's favorite downtown establishment. Basically a huge, glorified deli, it even has live music some evenings. When it's coffee time, try **Coffee Perk,** 4 S. First Ave. (© **509/526-0636**), a favorite downtown espresso place. If it's pub food and microbrews you're after, then head to **Mill Creek Brew Pub,** 11 S. Palouse St. (© **509/522-2440**).

Creek Town Cafe ⭐⭐ NORTHWEST   You'll find this popular little restaurant 10 blocks south of downtown in a new building that has loads of modern wine-country character. Start your meal with the spinach salad or the oysters dusted with *panko* breading (Japanese-style bread crumbs). Entrees include lots of intriguing dishes with sauces made from cream and a variety of wines and liquors. The hoisin-ginger-glazed pork loin and the salmon baked in Riesling-lime sauce are two good bets. In summer, try to get a table on the patio. Lots of local wines are available by the glass.

1129 S. Second St. ✆ 509/522-4777. Reservations recommended both lunch and dinner. Main courses $6–$10 lunch, $14–$20 dinner. AE, DISC, MC, V. Tues–Sat 11am–2:30pm and 5–9pm.

Grapefields ★★ FRENCH   Riding the Walla Walla wine wave, this casual bistro, wine bar, and wine shop is the ideal spot in town for a light meal. The menu is thoroughly Gallic, with lots of small dishes that are perfect for accompanying a glass of wine. Be sure to get an order of the olive cake, a sort of sponge cake embedded with olives and served with aioli. If you're looking for something to accompany a robust red wine try the flank steak with blue cheese–thyme butter. The daily specials menu sometimes strays from French (for example, coconut-curry soup) and there's also a daily pizza special. Oh, by the way, the wine list here has lots of wines from outside the immediate vicinity, in case you want to expand your horizons.

4 E. Main St. ✆ **509/522-3993.** Main courses $6–$12. AE, MC, V. Tues–Thurs 11am–9pm; Fri–Sat 11am–10pm; Sun noon–6pm.

Paisano ★ (Value) ITALIAN   At this casual Italian restaurant in downtown Walla Walla, small-town sophistication prevails. The menu includes well-prepared Italian classics, but you'll also find non-Italian fare, including chicken or vegetarian curry and maple-glazed meatloaf. We like to start a meal here with the black-olive pâté, which you can spread over grilled bread. If the pesto ravioli shows up as the ravioli of the day, be sure to order it. It's creamy yet not too rich. Out front, there's a sidewalk cafe area complete with a low fence topped with flower boxes. The wine list features plenty of local wines. At press time, there were plans to add a wine-tasting room.

26 E. Main St. ✆ **509/527-3511.** Reservations recommended. Main courses $16–$23. MC, V. Mon–Sat 11am–2pm and 5:30–8 or 8:30pm.

Whitehouse-Crawford Restaurant ★★ NORTHWEST   Housed in what was once a woodworking mill, this stylish restaurant has brought a touch of urban sophistication to remote Walla Walla. The menu is as creative as you'll find anywhere east or west of the Cascades and changes daily. Start out with the warm spinach salad, which here comes with smoked trout and grilled onions. You can count on reliable preparations of grilled beef tenderloin as well as smoked pork tenderloin. Anything with the brick-oven flatbread is another good bet, as are, of course, any dishes with Walla Walla sweet onions. There are plenty of excellent wines available and many can be ordered by the glass. If you don't have the deep pockets necessary to eat in the main dining room, you can dine in the wine bar.

55 W. Cherry St. ✆ **509/525-2222.** Reservations highly recommended. Main courses $12–$28. AE, DISC, MC, V. Wed–Sun 5–9pm.

4 The Palouse: A Slice of Small-Town Rural Washington

Dayton: 33 miles NE of Walla Walla, 62 miles E of Tri-Cities, 129 miles SW of Spokane

Between Walla Walla and Spokane lie the rolling Palouse Hills, which are among the most productive wheat lands in the nation. Before the settlement of the region by whites, Native American peoples had discovered that the Palouse, as it's known, offered ideal horse-grazing land. Horses had reached the Northwest sometime after the Spanish conquered the southern regions of North America, and by the time Lewis and Clark passed through the Palouse, the tribes of the region had become well known for their horses, which they bred for stamina and sure-footedness. On the site of present-day Dayton, there was even a Native American horse-racing track. Today these native-bred horses are known as Appaloosas for the Palouse Hills from which they came.

Although the Lewis and Clark expedition passed through this area in 1806, it was not until the 1850s that the first pioneers began settling in the area. By the 1880s, the region was booming as a major wheat- and barley-growing region. Throughout the Palouse, small towns that have long been out of the mainstream of Northwest development are nestled along creek banks below rolling hills. Several of these towns are classic examples of small-town America, with attractive Victorian homes lining their shady streets. Between the towns, the roads wind up hill and down, through a distinctive zebra-striped landscape that is created by farming practices developed to reduce erosion on the steep hills.

ESSENTIALS

GETTING THERE   U.S. 12, which runs from Walla Walla to Clarkston, is the main route through the southern part of the Palouse. From Lewiston, Idaho, across the Snake River from Clarkston, U.S. 195 runs north through the heart of the Palouse to Spokane.

VISITOR INFORMATION   For more information on the Dayton area, contact the **Dayton Chamber of Commerce,** 166 E. Main St., Dayton, WA 99328 (© **800/882-6299** or 509/382-4825; www.historicdayton.com). For more information on the Pullman area, contact the **Pullman Chamber of Commerce,** 415 N. Grand Ave., Pullman, WA 99163 (© **800/365-6948** or 509/334-3565; www.pullmanchamber.com).

EXPLORING THE PALOUSE

Among the many little towns along the route from Walla Walla to Spokane, **Dayton** is by far the prettiest. Its old-fashioned small-town American feel is as genuine as it gets. Dayton was once one of the most important towns in this region and is still the county seat of Columbia County. Its 1887 **Columbia County Courthouse** is the oldest county courthouse still in use as such in the state of Washington. It's open Monday through Friday from 8:30am to 4:30pm. Here you'll also find the **Dayton Historic Depot,** 222 E. Commercial Street (© 509/382-2026; www.daytondepot.org), the oldest railway depot in the state (built 1881), which is open for tours Tuesday through Saturday from 11am to 4pm. Admission is by $3 suggested donation. All in all, Dayton has 90 buildings on the National Historic Register. On the second Sunday in October each year there is a historic homes tour. In nearby Waitsburg, where there are more Victorian homes, you can also tour the 1883 **Bruce Memorial Museum** (© **509/ 337-6582**), which is open Friday and Saturday from 1 to 4pm and is filled with Victorian-era furnishings.

About 44 miles northwest of Dayton, you'll find **Palouse Falls State Park.** The spectacular falls here cascade 198 feet into a rock-walled canyon. South of town 21 miles, you'll find **Ski Bluewood** (© **509/382-4725;** www.bluewood. com), a small ski area in the Blue Mountains.

Pullman is the largest town in the region and is the home of Washington State University. The university's **Museum of Art,** Fine Arts Center, Stadium Way (© **509/335-1910**), is worth a visit. It's open Monday through Wednesday

---

Fun Fact **Go, Team, Go!**

In **Colfax** you can take a look at the **Codger Pole,** the largest chain-saw sculpture in the world. The pole depicts the members of two football teams that got together in 1988 to replay their 1938 game. You'll find the Codger Pole on John Crawford Boulevard just off Main Street.

---

and Friday from 10am to 4pm, Thursday from 10am to 7pm, and Saturday and Sunday from 1 to 5pm; admission is free. Also on the WSU campus, you'll find the **Museum of Anthropology,** College Hall, Room 110 (© **509/335-3441**), which has exhibits on human evolution. The museum is open Monday through Friday from 9am to 4pm (closed June 16–Aug 15); admission is free.

Some 18 miles north of Colfax, **Kamiak Butte County Park** provides the ideal vantage point for surveying the vast Palouse. Nearby is **Steptoe Butte State Park,** which also offers good views of the surrounding landscape.

A trip to the Palouse can also include an exploration of **Hell's Canyon,** which was carved by the Snake River and is the deepest gorge in North America. **Beamer's Hells Canyon Tours** (© **800/522-6966;** www.hellscanyontours.com), which operates out of Clarkston, Washington, offers a variety of day and overnight jet-boat trips up the Snake River. Prices range from $52 for a half-day tour to $98 for a full-day tour. Overnight trips are $260.

WHERE TO STAY

The Purple House ✦   Well, it isn't quite purple, more a tasteful plum, but this 1882 Queen Anne Victorian home certainly does stand out from the other houses in the neighborhood. With its backyard pool and antiques-filled rooms, these are the most distinctive accommodations in the Palouse. German hostess Christine Williscroft takes great pride in her cooking and is sometimes willing to prepare dinners as well as breakfast. The inn is located a block off Dayton's main street.

415 E. Clay St., Dayton, WA 99328. © **800/486-2574** or 509/382-3159. 4 units, 2 with private bathroom. $85–$125 double. Rates include full breakfast. MC, V. Pets accepted ($20). **Amenities:** Outdoor pool. *In room:* A/C.

The Weinhard Hotel ✦   Constructed in 1889 to house a saloon operated by Jacob Weinhard, the nephew of Portland, Oregon, brewer Henry Weinhard, this brick building is now a comfortable and generally inexpensive Victorian inn. In the large lobby, you'll find a grand piano and, off in one corner, board games and magazines. Guest rooms have high ceilings with overhead fans and in each room there is at least one piece of antique furniture. The best room in the house has a whirlpool tub in the bathroom. Up on the roof, you'll find a terrace garden where you can enjoy a cup of espresso.

235 E. Main St., Dayton, WA 99328. © **509/382-4032.** Fax 509/382-2640. www.weinhard.com. 15 units. $75–$150 double. Rates include continental breakfast. DISC, MC, V. Pets accepted ($20). **Amenities:** Restaurant (American); concierge. *In room:* A/C, TV/VCR, dataport.

WHERE TO DINE
IN DAYTON

Patit Creek Restaurant ✦✦ FRENCH   This restaurant, located in a little green cottage beside the road on the north side of Dayton, is worth the trip to this small Palouse town. Don't let the proximity to the highway worry you;

stained-glass windows hide the passing traffic from diners and allow guests to focus on their food. Though lunches include everything from a smoked turkey sandwich to top sirloin steak bordelaise (and all at reasonable prices), dinners are on a very different level. You might start a meal with chevre cheese–stuffed dates or a delicious smoked salmon cheesecake. The entree menu includes such dishes as filet mignon *poivre verte* with green peppercorns, cognac, and cream; and sautéed duck breast with red wine, currant, and port demi-glace.

725 Dayton Ave. ℂ 509/382-2625. Reservations recommended. Main courses $9–$15 lunch, $19–$29 dinner. MC, V. Wed–Fri 11:30am–1:30 or 2pm and 4:30–8 or 9pm; Sat 4:30–8 or 9pm.

5 Spokane

284 miles E of Seattle, 195 miles NE of Yakima, 155 miles N of Walla Walla

Until the 1974 World's Fair focused the eyes of the nation on Spokane and its renovated waterfront and downtown area, this city was little more than a forgotten railroad town deep in the inland Northwest. Today, however, Spokane is the second-largest city in Washington, the largest city between Seattle and Minneapolis, and a center for both commercial and cultural pursuits. Although Spokane isn't really a tourist destination, its proximity to Lake Coeur d'Alene and several Idaho ski areas makes it something of a jumping-off point for explorations of the northern Idaho Rocky Mountains.

For thousands of years Native Americans lived along the Spokane River, and it was at Spokane Falls that the Spokan-ee tribe congregated each year to catch salmon. When the first explorers and fur traders arrived in 1807, it was near these falls that they chose to establish a trading post where they could barter with the Native Americans for beaver pelts. Spokan House (the original spelling had no letter *e*), established in 1810 down-river from Spokane Falls, became the first settlement in the area, but it was not until 1872 that a settlement was established at the falls themselves. When the Northern Pacific Railroad arrived in 1881, the town of Spokan Falls became the most important town in the region. However, in the summer of 1889 the city's downtown commercial district was destroyed by fire. Within 2 years the city had fully recovered from the fire and also changed the spelling of its name.

Today, the Spokane River is still this city's greatest asset. Along the river you'll find numerous parks and a paved hiking/biking trail. The falls themselves are an impressive sight, despite being hemmed in by industrial buildings, and only a few miles from downtown, the Spokane River still looks wild and untamed.

ESSENTIALS

GETTING THERE   Spokane is on I-90, Washington's east-west interstate. U.S. 2 is an alternative route from western Washington. U.S. 395 is the main route from Canada south to Spokane. U.S. 195 connects to Lewiston, Idaho.

Spokane International Airport, 9000 W. Airport Dr. (ℂ **509/455-6455;** www.spokaneairports.net) is located 10 miles west of downtown and is served by Air Canada, Alaska Airlines, America West, Big Sky Airlines, Delta, Horizon, Northwest, Southwest, and United.

Amtrak passenger trains provide service to Spokane. The station is at 221 W. First Ave. (ℂ **509/624-5144**).

VISITOR INFORMATION   Contact the **Spokane Area Visitor Information Center,** 201 W. Main Ave., Spokane, WA 99201 (ℂ **888/SPOKANE** or 509/747-3230; www.visitspokane.com).

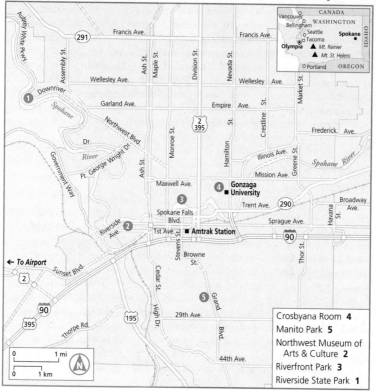

Crosbyana Room **4**

Manito Park **5**

Northwest Museum of Arts & Culture **2**

Riverfront Park **3**

Riverside State Park **1**

GETTING AROUND **Rental cars** are available from Avis, Budget, Dollar, Enterprise, Hertz, National, and Thrifty. If you need a taxi, contact **Spokane Cab** (© 509/568-8000). Public bus service is provided by the **Spokane Transit Authority** (© 509/328-7433; www.spokanetransit.com); the fare is $1.

FESTIVALS Spokane's nickname is the Lilac City, and the city's biggest annual event is the **Lilac Festival,** which is held each year in mid-May. On the first Sunday in May, the city holds its annual **Lilac Bloomsday Run,** one of the largest timed races in the world (more than 50,000 runners participate).

WHAT TO SEE & DO

Spokane has made it very easy for visitors to get a sense of what the city is all about by mapping out a Spokane City Drive that takes in all the city's highlights. The well-marked route meanders through Spokane and passes by all the city attractions listed below. The drive also takes in some great vistas from the hills to the south of the city.

RIVERFRONT PARK

Created for the 1974 World's Fair Expo and set on an island in the middle of the Spokane River, 100-acre **Riverfront Park** ✿ (© 509/456-4-FUN; www.spokaneriverfrontpark.com) is the city's pride and joy. The land on which the park stands was once a maze of railroad tracks and depots, and the polluted river was nearly inaccessible to the public. The creation of the park helped rejuvenate downtown Spokane, and today crowds flock here to enjoy everything from summertime concerts to ice-skating in the winter. Activities for both adults and children abound. The restored 1909 **Looff Carrousel** ✦✦, with its hand-carved horses, is one of the most beautiful in the country. More contemporary entertainment is offered at the **IMAX Theatre** (© **509/625-6686**), where 70mm films are shown on screens five stories high. A family-fun center includes kiddie rides, miniature golf, and arcade games. Throughout the summer there are many special events.

Serving as a spectacular backdrop for the park is the Spokane River, which here cascades over Spokane Falls. The best view of the falls is from the Gondola Skyride that swings out over the falls. However, due to bridge construction in the area, the gondola is out of service until late 2004 or early 2005.

MANITO PARK

Manito Park ✦✦ (© **509/625-6622**), Spokane's other major green space, is a far more traditional place than Riverfront Park and is located south of downtown beginning at the corner of Division Street and 18th Avenue. Here at Manito, which is located among rocks and pine forest, you'll find several of the most beautiful public gardens in the Northwest. Foremost of these is the classically proportioned **Duncan Garden,** a formal garden patterned after those of 17th-century Europe. Adjacent to this garden is the **Gaiser Conservatory,** which brims with exotic tropical plants. The perennial garden and rose garden are at their exuberant peaks in June and should not be missed. The lilac garden is also well worth a visit during the May flowering season. There is also the **Nishinomiya Japanese Garden,** a strolling pond garden that is a tranquil spot for contemplation. This garden is open from April through October daily from 8am to dusk. Within this expansive park, you'll also find a picnic area, duck pond, and playground.

MORE ATTRACTIONS

Crosbyana Room ✦   Bing Crosby got his start here in Spokane, where he spent most of his youth. When young Bing's aspirations soared beyond the bounds of Spokane and he made his name in Los Angeles, the members of his band who chose to stay safely at home must have long regretted their decision. All of Crosby's gold records, his Oscar, and plenty of other memorabilia (including a Bing-endorsed mousetrap and a Bing Crosby Ice Cream box) are on view. You can also take a look at Crosby's boyhood home, which is now home to the Gonzaga Alumni Association, 508 E. Sharp St.

Crosby Student Center, Gonzaga University, 502 E. Boone Ave. © **509/328-4220**, ext. 4297. Free admission. Mon–Fri 7:30am–midnight; Sat–Sun 11am–midnight. Closed holidays.

Northwest Museum of Arts & Culture ✦✦   From the dramatic architecture and landscaping to the eclectic collections and exhibits, this museum makes a very big impression. One of the most unusual exhibits is a celebration of small-town life that will run through June 2004. In this exhibit life in America's small towns is put on display as a historical and artistic museum piece. In one section of the exhibit, visitors get to sit in lawn chairs and watch a video playing in the back of an old camper. You can also sit in the cab of a combine and see what it's like to harvest wheat. There's also an extensive Plateau Indians exhibit. Other galleries are used to mount temporary art exhibits. Next door to the museum is the historic Campbell House; a tour of this old mansion is included in the museum admission price. With its well-balanced blend of history, art, and culture, this is one of the finest museums in the Northwest and should not be missed on a visit to Spokane.

2316 W. First Ave. ℃ **509/456-3931.** www.northwestmuseum.org. Admission $7 adults, $5 seniors and students, free for children 5 and under; open by donation 1st Fri of each month. Tues–Sun 11am–5pm.

WINE TOURING

While the Spokane area is far too cold to produce much in the way of wine grapes, there are a handful of wineries in the area that produce wines from Yakima and Columbia Valley grapes.

Arbor Crest Wine Cellars ⭐ Located northeast of downtown Spokane in the historic Cliff House atop a 450-foot-high bluff overlooking the Spokane River, this winery boasts one of the most spectacular settings of any winery in the state. The views more than the wines are the reason to visit. Prices are generally reasonable, though the wines are not very memorable. In summer there are concerts here.

4705 N. Fruithill Rd. ℃ **509/927-9463.** www.arborcrest.com. Daily noon–5pm. Take exit 287 off I-90, go north on Argonne Rd., turn right on Upriver Dr. and then left on Fruithill Rd.

Caterina ⭐⭐ Located downtown in the historic Broadview Dairy Building, Caterina is one of the most consistent wineries in the state. Prices are moderate ($10–$20). The merlot and chardonnay both tend to be quite good.

905 N. Washington St. ℃ **509/328-5069.** www.caterina.com. Daily noon–5pm. Take exit 281 off I-90, go north on Division St. and then left on N. River Dr.

Knipprath Cellars ⭐ Housed in an old school building in a residential neighborhood on Spokane's east side, this small winery is most noteworthy for its port wines, one of which is flavored with chocolate and is absolutely delicious.

5634 E. Commerce Ave. ℃ **509/534-5121.** www.knipprath-cellars.com. Thurs–Sun noon–5pm. Take exit 287, go north on Argonne Rd., turn left on Trent Ave., then turn right on Fancher Rd.

Latah Creek Wine Cellars Housed in a Spanish mission–style building amid industrial complexes that back I-90, this winery seems more interested in its extensive gift shop offerings than its wines. Although it's known for its merlot, we've found the reds to have very odd flavors. A May wine is a specialty here.

13030 E. Indiana Ave. ℃ **509/926-0164.** www.latahcreek.com. Daily 9am–5pm. Take exit 289, go north on Pines Rd. and then turn right on Indiana Ave.

Townshend Cellar ⭐⭐ *(Finds)* This may be the most out-of-the-way winery in the Spokane area, but it is well worth searching out for its delicious port wines, including some made exclusively with huckleberries and some made with grapes and huckleberries. This winery also does good chardonnay and syrah, and a fun huckleberry blush that's made with viognier.

16112 Greenbluff Rd. ℃ **509/238-1400.** www.townshendcellar.com. May–Nov Fri–Sat noon–6pm; Dec–Apr Sat–Sun noon–5pm. From I-90, take exit 287, go north on Argonne Rd., which becomes Bruce Rd., turn left at the "T" intersection onto Day-Mt. Spokane Rd., go ½ mile and turn right on Greenbluff Rd.

SPORTS & OUTDOOR ACTIVITIES

Walkers, joggers, and cyclists will want to get in some exercise on the **Spokane River Centennial Trail.** The paved trail starts at Nine Mile Falls west of the city and parallels the river for 37 miles to the Idaho state line, where it connects to the Idaho Centennial Trail for a final leg into Coeur d'Alene (for a total of 65 miles of pathway). Bicycle rentals are available at Riverfront Park.

Kids **Cat Tales**

Fifteen miles north of Spokane is a wildlife park unlike any other in the state. **Cat Tales Zoological Park,** 17020 N. Newport Hwy., Mead (© 509/238-4126; www.cattales.org), lets visitors get up close to tigers and other big cats from around the world. There's also a petting zoo where you might be able to pet a baby tiger. Treat bags can also be purchased, if you want to help feed the big cats.

Riverside State Park ★★ (© 509/469-5064), which lies along the banks of the meandering Spokane River on the west edge of the city, has 32 miles of hiking trails, picnic areas, campgrounds, and access to the Spokane River Centennial Trail. Despite its proximity to the city, the park has a surprisingly wild feel, and the river, as it flows through the park, is one of the prettiest stretches of river in the state. The Bowl and Pitcher Overlook, near the park headquarters, provides a vista of huge basalt boulders on the banks of the river. Adjacent to the park is the Spokane House Interpretive Site, which tells the story of the early fur trade in this area and is open from Memorial Day to Labor Day, Thursday through Monday from 10am to 6pm. To find the park, drive north from downtown on Maple Street, turn left on Northwest Boulevard, left on Menach Drive, and right on Downriver Drive. Park admission is $5.

For a great view of the region, head northwest 30 miles to **Mount Spokane State Park** (© 509/238-4258), where you can drive to the top of the mountain. Hiking trails wander for miles through the forest here. Park admission is $5.

SHOPPING

Three renovated downtown buildings provide some interesting shopping opportunities in Spokane. The **Flour Mill,** 621 W. Mallon Ave. (just across Riverfront Park from downtown), is housed in an old mill that was built beside Spokane Falls and has, in addition to its many interesting shops and restaurants, displays on the mill and Spokane history. **Steam Plant Square,** 159 S. Lincoln St., is the city's most unusual recycling of a downtown industrial building. In this case, the steam plant that once produced heat for all of downtown Spokane has been turned into a fashionable space that preserved as much of the original workings as possible. Old boilers and pipes when juxtaposed against the modern restaurant and shopping facilities here give the entire space the feel of some strange post-apocalyptic sci-fi setting. Don't miss the smokestack room! The **Bennet Block,** on the corner of Main Avenue and Stevens Street, also houses specialty shops and restaurants.

WHERE TO STAY

The Davenport Hotel ★★★   Far and away the state's finest hotel east of Seattle, this recently restored and reopened grand dame is an absolute work of art. Originally opened in 1914 and reopened in 2002, the Davenport has an astonishingly ornate Spanish Renaissance lobby that is way over the top and gives the hotel the feel of a European palace. The many ballrooms, each of which draws on different European periods and countries for styling, continue the palatial feel of the hotel. However, the highlight is the Hall of the Doges, which you should be sure to sneak a peek in while you're here. Guest rooms are as classically elegant as the lobby, with hand-carved furniture imported from

Indonesia. This should be anyone's first choice of hotel in Spokane if cost is no object. In fact, the Davenport is reason enough to visit Spokane. Oh, and if you fall in love with the hotel's soft peanut butter brittle, you can stock up at the candy shop.

10 S. Post St., Spokane, WA 99201. ℂ 800/899-1482 or 509/455-8888. Fax 509/624-4455. www.the davenporthotel.com. 284 units. $169–$249 double; $249–$1,950 suite. Pets accepted. AE, DC, DISC, MC, V. Self parking $10, valet parking $15. **Amenities:** 2 restaurants (Continental, American); 2 lounges; indoor pool; exercise room; full-service spa; Jacuzzi; concierge; business center; shopping arcade; limited room service; massage; laundry service; dry cleaning. *In room:* A/C, TV, dataport, hair dryer, iron, safe.

The Fotheringham House ★★   Located in the historic Browne's Addition neighborhood, this pretty Queen Anne Victorian home, built in 1891 by the first mayor of Spokane, is set behind a white picket fence and is surrounded by a colorful perennial garden. Inside you'll find an abundance of ornate woodwork and antique furniture. Most of the furnishings are period antiques, and in the large shared bathroom you'll find the original claw-foot bathtub. Across the street is a shady park and historic mansions line the streets of the neighborhood.

2128 W. Second Ave., Spokane, WA 99204. ℂ 509/838-1891. Fax 509/838-1807. www.fotheringham.net. 4 units, 1 with private bathroom. $95–$115 double. Rates include full breakfast. AE, DISC, MC, V. Children over age 12 welcome. *In room:* A/C, hair dryer, no phone.

Hotel Lusso ★★   Until the recent reopening of the Davenport Hotel, across the street, this was the most luxurious hotel in Spokane. Although far less ostentatious than the Davenport, the Lusso is nearly as luxurious. Affecting a sort of contemporary Italianate styling, this boutique hotel has a very posh European feel. Because the hotel was created from two existing buildings, the rooms here are all a little bit different. Some of the standard rooms can be a bit small, but upgrades are possible in $20 increments. We'd suggest opting to upgrade one or two levels. Most of the rooms have 12- to 14-foot ceilings that make even the smallest rooms feel big. For a splurge, there are the penthouse suites, which have deluxe bathrooms with double whirlpool tubs surrounded by walls of glass. The hotel's Fugazzi restaurant (see below) is one of Spokane's hippest and best restaurants. There's also a separate lounge and a complimentary reception each afternoon.

1 N. Post St., Spokane, WA 99201. ℂ 509/747-9750. Fax 509/747-9751. www.hotellusso.com. 60 units. $165–$185 double; $205–$305 suite. Rates include continental breakfast. AE, DC, DISC, MC, V. Parking $9. **Amenities:** Restaurant (Northwest); lounge; access to nearby health club; concierge; courtesy airport and downtown shuttle service; limited room service; massage; dry cleaning. *In room:* A/C, TV, dataport, minibar, hair dryer, iron.

Red Lion Hotel at the Park ★★ *Kids*   Although this is primarily a convention hotel, its location adjacent to downtown Spokane's Riverfront Park makes this the most conveniently located hotel in the city if you're here on a family vacation. In addition to the fun that can be had in Riverfront Park, the hotel offers a resortlike, lagoon-style pool complete with water slide that kids love. A wide variety of rooms accommodate all types of travelers, even those without kids in tow, and anyone wishing a bit of extra luxury may want to opt for the executive rooms, which come with balconies overlooking the pool or the river.

303 W. North River Dr., Spokane, WA 99201. ℂ 800/RED-LION or 509/326-8000. Fax 509/325-7329. www. westcoasthotels.com. 400 units. $79–$119 double; $195–$950 suite. AE, DC, DISC, MC, V. Pets accepted. **Amenities:** Restaurant (Continental, American); lounge; 2 swimming pools (indoor/outdoor); exercise room; Jacuzzi; concierge; limited room service; laundry service; dry cleaning. *In room:* A/C, TV, dataport, coffeemaker, hair dryer, iron.

WHERE TO DINE

For espresso and muffins, we like **Cabin Coffee,** 141 S. Cannon St. (© **509/ 747-3088**), which is located just a few blocks from the new Northwest Museum of Arts & Culture. **The Milk Bottle,** 802 W. Garland Ave. (© **509/325-1772**), located a few miles north of downtown, is a unique Spokane landmark. It's an old-time ice-cream parlor fronted by a three-story cement milk bottle. The Milk Bottle is open Monday through Saturday from 11am to 4pm.

Catacombs Pub ⁕ INTERNATIONAL   Located down in the basement of an old building in downtown Spokane and only about a block away from the historic Davenport Hotel, this casual place comes pretty close to living up to its name. Stone walls and heavy ceiling beams set the tone; the only things missing are the old bones that catacombs are supposed to have. Designer pizzas are the specialty here, but there are also good salads. For dessert, don't miss the chocolate calzone.

110 S. Monroe St. © **509/838-4610**. Main courses $9–$18. AE, DISC, MC, V. Mon–Thurs 11am–midnight; Fri 11am–1am; Sat 4pm–1am; Sun 4–11pm.

The Elk ⁕ *Value* INTERNATIONAL   The Elk has been around since the early 1900s when it was the Elk Drug Company, supplying medicines and soda fountain treats to neighborhood residents. Today it has been restored and turned into a chic little pub serving the best of Northwest microbrews along with such unusual pub fare as grilled lamb sandwiches and seared ahi sandwiches. The excellent and unusual chicken Caesar soft tacos are our favorite light lunch in Spokane. During the warmer months, try to get a table out front on the sidewalk patio. This is one of Spokane's best bets for cheap eats.

1931 W. Pacific Ave. © **509/363-1973**. Main courses $6.75–$9.50. MC, V. Sun–Thurs 11am–10pm; Fri–Sat 11am–11pm.

Fugazzi ⁕⁕ INTERNATIONAL   With its blend of contemporary styling and earthy materials (brick walls and wood floor), this restaurant feels both hip and cozy, historical yet stylish. It also happens to serve some of the best food in town. Using the freshest seasonal ingredients, Fugazzi assembles menus that cater to the city's adventuresome palates. How about spicy Asian-style calamari to start things out? The menu often has a decided slant toward seafood, which is usually well prepared, and Asian flavors show up frequently.

1 N. Post St. © **509/624-1133**. Reservations recommended. Main courses $7–$9 lunch, $15–$28 dinner. AE, DC, DISC, MC, V. Tues–Thurs 11:30am–2:30pm and 5–9pm; Fri 11:30am–2:30pm and 5–10pm; Sat 5–10pm.

Herbal Essence Café ⁕ INTERNATIONAL   Popular both as a casual lunch spot for downtown office workers and as a hip spot for dinner, this restaurant serves deliciously creative food. At lunch try the south Philly smashed sub or the crab-and-artichoke sub. At dinner, the Jamaican chicken satay with mango barbecue sauce makes a zesty starter. For an entree, the top sirloin with huckleberry sauce, the salmon with Moroccan spices, and the wild-mushroom ravioli with smoked chicken are all good bets. This place is just a couple of blocks from Riverfront Park.

115 N. Washington St. © **509/838-4600**. Reservations recommended. Main courses $6–$9 lunch, $14–$24 dinner. MC, V. Mon–Tues 10am–3:30pm; Thurs–Sat 10am–3:30pm and 5:30–9:30pm.

Steam Plant Grill ⁕ *Finds* INTERNATIONAL   Housed in a renovated former steam-generating plant that is now a historic landmark, the Steam Plant Grill is the most unusual restaurant in Spokane. Although utterly contemporary in design, the restaurant is surrounded by the girders, pipes, and boilers that once served to pump steam heat to the buildings of downtown Spokane. At lunch, burgers, sandwiches, and wraps comprise most of the menu, but there are also more substantial entrees such as grilled salmon and steaks. At dinner, there's much more creativity, including a good almond-crusted pork and a variety of pastas dishes. The restaurant also serves the microbrews of the Coeur d'Alene Brewing Company.

159 S. Lincoln St. ✆ 509/777-3900. Reservations recommended. Main courses $8–$13 lunch, $8.50–$32 dinner. AE, DISC, MC, V. Sun–Thurs 11:30am–9:30pm; Fri–Sat 11:30am–11pm.

SPOKANE AFTER DARK

As one of the largest cities in Washington, Spokane has a lively cultural and nightlife scene. To find out what's going on around Spokane, pick up a copy of *The Pacific Northwest Inlander*, a free weekly arts-and-entertainment newspaper. You'll find copies in restaurants, record stores, and bookstores. Also check with the **Spokane Arts Commission** (✆ **509/625-6050;** www.spokanearts.org). Particularly noteworthy are the concerts held throughout the year at the **Cathedral of St. John the Evangelist,** 127 E. 12th Ave. (✆ **509/838-4277**), a Gothic cathedral with a 5,000-pipe organ.

6 The Grand Coulee Dam Area

85 miles W of Spokane, 92 miles NE of Wenatchee

Grand Coulee, formerly a wide, dry valley, is a geologic anomaly left over from the last Ice Age. At that time, a glacier dammed an upstream tributary of the Columbia River and formed a huge lake in what is today Montana. When this prehistoric lake burst through its ice dam, massive floods poured down from the Rocky Mountains. So great was the volume of water that the Columbia River overflowed its normal channel and, as these flood waters flowed southward, they carved deep valleys into the basalt landscape of central Washington. As the floodwaters reached the Cascade Range, they were forced together into one great torrent that was so powerful it scoured out the Columbia Gorge, carving cliffs and leaving us with today's beautiful waterfalls. With the end of the Ice Age, however, the Columbia returned to its original channel and the temporary flood channels were left high and dry. Early French explorers called these dry channels *coulées,* and the largest of them all was Grand Coulee, which is 50 miles long, between 2 miles and 5 miles wide, and 1,000 feet deep.

Located at the northern end of the Grand Coulee, Grand Coulee Dam is considered one of the greatest engineering marvels of the 20th century. Constructed during the Great Depression, it was the largest man-made structure on earth at the time of its completion in 1941 and is still the largest concrete dam in North America. The dam is 550 feet tall, 5,223 feet wide (almost a mile), and impounds the waters of the Columbia River, forming 130-mile-long Roosevelt Lake. Despite the name, the Grand Coulee Dam did not, however, fill the Grand Coulee with water. That did not happen until the 1950s when Dry Falls Dam was built at the south end of the coulee and waters from Roosevelt Lake were used to fill the Grand Coulee and form 31-mile-long Banks Lake. The waters of both Roosevelt Lake and Banks Lake have been used to irrigate the arid lands of eastern Washington, turning this region into productive farmlands. The Grand Coulee Dam is also a major producer of hydroelectric power.

ESSENTIALS

GETTING THERE   The towns of Grand Coulee, Coulee Dam, and Electric City are at the junction of Wash. 155, which runs south to Coulee City and north to Omak, and Wash. 174, which runs west to Wash. 17 and east to U.S. 2.

VISITOR INFORMATION   Contact the **Grand Coulee Dam Area Chamber of Commerce,** 306 Midway, Wash. 155, Grand Coulee, WA 99133-0760 (© **800/268-5332** or 509/633-3074; www.grandcouleedam.org).

WHAT TO SEE & DO

You can learn the history of the dam by stopping in at the **Grand Coulee Dam Visitor Arrival Center** (© **509/633-9265**), which is open daily. This center is also where you can arrange for a free guided tour of the dam (tours are held daily on the hour 10am–5pm). Every night between the end of May and the end of September, the **world's largest laser-light show** is projected onto the face of the dam. The accompanying narration is broadcast over the radio at 90.1 FM and tells the history of Grand Coulee and the dam. There is also a self-guided walking tour through historic Coulee Dam, the government town built to house workers during the construction of the dam.

Lake Roosevelt, with its 660 miles of shoreline, provides ample opportunities for watersports and fishing and comprises the **Lake Roosevelt National Recreation Area,** 1008 Crest Dr., Coulee Dam, WA 99116 (© **509/738-6266** or 509/725-2715; www.nps.gov/laro). Along the shores of the lake are 17 car or walk-in campgrounds and 10 boat-in campgrounds. About 21 miles north of Davenport, at the confluence of the Spokane and Columbia rivers, stands **Fort Spokane,** which was built in 1880. Four of the original buildings are still standing. An 1892 brick guardhouse here now serves as a visitor center, though the recreation area's main visitor center is the Grand Coulee Dam Visitor Arrival Center right at the dam.

Much of the land bordering Roosevelt Lake lies within the Colville Indian Reservation. In the town of Coulee Dam, you can visit the **Colville Confederated Tribes Museum,** 512 Mead Way (© **509/633-0751**), a small museum with interesting displays of baskets and tribal regalia, as well as historical photos. The museum is open April through December, Monday through Saturday from 10am to 6pm. Admission is by donation. The Colville tribes also operate the adjacent **Coulee Dam Casino,** 515 Birch St. (© **800/556-7492;** www. colvillecasinos.com).

Some 30 miles down the Grand Coulee, just south of Coulee City on Wash. 17, you can have a look at a natural wonder that's as impressive as the dam. **Dry Falls** are the remains of a massive waterfall created by the same flood waters that scoured out the Grand Coulee. At their peak flow, the waters cascading 400 feet over these falls stretched 3½ miles wide (in comparison, Niagara Falls are only 1 mile wide and 165 ft. tall). Between mid-May and the end of September, you can learn more about the falls and floods at the **Dry Falls Visitor Center** (© **509/632-5214**), which is located at the Dry Falls Overlook on Wash. 17. If you're interested in going to the base of the falls, continue south 2 miles to **Sun Lakes State Park,** which has a road leading back to the falls. Within this park you'll also find a campground and lakes for swimming, boating, and fishing. Park admission is $5.

For a glimpse of another unusual waterfall, head 10 miles south of Coulee City on Pinto Ridge Road. Here you'll find **Summer Falls,** an impressive manmade waterfall that only flows in, you guessed it, summer. The falls are formed by the runoff water from the Grand Coulee's Banks Lake. The 165-foot-tall falls pour over a basalt cliff and into Billy Clapp Lake.

Ten miles south of Sun Lakes State Park, you'll find **Lake Lenore Caves.** These caves were created by the same floodwaters that carved Dry Falls. In this case, the waters tore off chunks of basalt as they flowed past the cliffs above today's Lake Lenore. The caves were later used by wandering bands of prehistoric Indians. There are seven caves accessible along an established trail.

Continuing south will bring you to **Soap Lake,** an alkaline lake named for the soapsuds that gather on its shores. For centuries the lake has attracted people who believe the waters have medicinal properties. Once a busy health spa, Soap Lake today is a quiet little town. However, it does have a couple of good lodges where you can soak in the lake's waters. A public town beach also provides access to the lake.

About 25 miles south of Soap Lake lies **Moses Lake,** which is popular with water-skiers. South of Moses Lake lies the **Potholes Reservoir** and **Columbia National Wildlife Refuge.** This area is a stark contrast of desert and water, with lots of basalt outcroppings adding drama to the landscape. To explore this region, drive south from Moses Lake on Wash. 17, west on Wash. 262, south on K2 SE Road (which becomes Morgan Lake Rd.), and west on Wash. 26.

WHERE TO STAY
IN COULEE DAM

Columbia River Inn ⋆   Located right across the street from Grand Coulee Dam Visitor Center, this remodeled motel is convenient for viewing the laser light show (just cross the street to the park). Guest rooms have attractive pine furnishings and small balconies with partial dam views, and some have their own whirlpool tubs.

10 Lincoln St., Coulee Dam, WA 99116. ⓒ 800/633-6421 or 509/633-2100. www.columbiariverinn.com. 34 units. $75–$85 double; $95–$190 suite. AE, DISC, MC, V. **Amenities:** Outdoor pool; Jacuzzi; coin-op laundry. *In room:* A/C, TV, dataport, coffeemaker.

Four Winds Guest House ⋆   Located in the picture-perfect company town that was built to house engineers and laborers working on the dam, this inn is in a former engineers dorm where Pres. Franklin D. Roosevelt once held a meeting during his visit to the dam site. The guest rooms are simply furnished in a traditional style that evokes the 1930s, when the dam was built.

301 Lincoln St., Coulee Dam, WA 99116. ⓒ 800/786-3146 or 509/633-3146. Fax 509/633-2454. www.four windsbandb.com. 10 units, 1 with private bathroom. $68 double with shared bathroom; $90 double with private bathroom. Rates include continental breakfast. AE, DISC, MC, V. Children over age 8 welcome. *In room:* No phone.

Index

Great Trips Like Great Days Begin with a Plan

FranklinCovey and Frommer's Bring You *Frommer's Favorite Places*® Planner

22 THURSDAY · JANUARY · 2004

PRIORITIZED DAILY TASK LIST

- ✓ A1 REVIEW PRESENTATION BOARDS
- ✓ B1 PICK UP BOOK ORDERED AT B & N
- ✓ B2 CHECK W/ LUCY RE: PRODUCTION SCHEDULE
- ✓ C2 DROP OFF SHIRTS @ CLEANERS
- C1 CALL TRAVEL AGENT RE: BOOK FLIGHT TO IRELAND - VACATION
- → A2 CALL BRETT SET UP MEETING FOR NEXT WEEK

APPOINTMENT SCHEDULE

- 6:00AM WORKOUT
- 7:00 CAR SERVICE PICKUP
- 8:00
- 8:00 JFK FLIGHT #9619
- 10:00
- 11:00 MERCHANDISE REVIEW MEETING
- 12:00
- 1:00
- 2:00
- 3:00
- 4:00
- 5:00
- 6:00 SLC FLIGHT #2300
- 7:00
- 8:00 BOOK CLUB

Frommer's

MERCHANDISE REVIEW MEETING
EMAIL ERIC MERCHANDISE
PRODUCT MANAGERS

CALL PHOTOGRAPHER ABOUT
PRODUCT PHOTOS
- NEED TO SCHEDULE
ON LOCATION

BOOK TRAVEL FOR VACATION
LEAVING FOR ONE WE
SECOND WEEK STA
- SCHEDU
PACKAGE

BRUGES, BELGIUM
CRUISING THE CANALS AND
STROLLING THE BACE STREETS

Classic Size Planning Pages $39

The planning experts at FranklinCovey have teamed up with the travel experts at Frommer's. The result is a full-year travel-themed planner filled with rich images and travel tips covering fifty-two of Frommer's Favorite Places.

- Each week will make you an expert about an intriguing corner of the world
- New facts and tips every day
- Beautiful, full-color photos of some of the most beautiful places on earth
- Proven planning tools from FranklinCovey for keeping track of tasks, appointments, notes, address/phone numbers, and more

Save 15%

when you purchase Frommer's Favor Places travel-themed planner and a binder.

Order today before yo next big trip.

www.franklincovey.com/frommers
Enter promo code 12252 at checkout for discount. Offer expires June 1, 200!

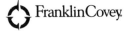

FranklinCovey

Frommer's is a trademark of Arthur Frommer.

Booked aisle seat.

Reserved room with a view.

With a queen – no, make that a king-size bed.

th Travelocity, you can book your flights and hotels together, so
u can get even better deals than if you booked them separately.
u'll save time and money without compromising the quality of your
p. Choose your airline seat, search for alternate airports, pick your
tel room type, even choose the neighborhood you'd like to stay in.

Travelocity

**Visit www.travelocity.com
or call 1-888-TRAVELOCITY**